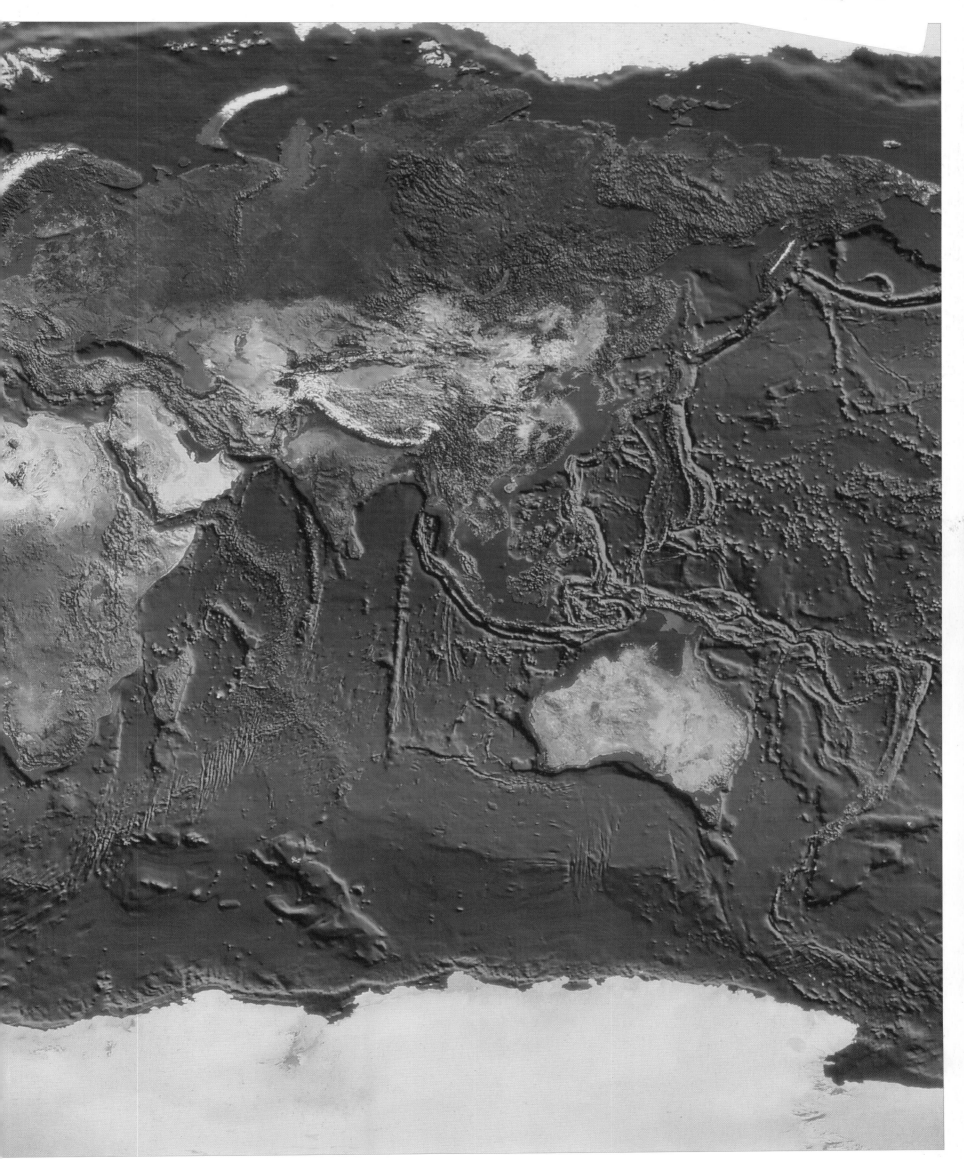

TWO-IN-ONE
WORLD
ATLAS

The Two-in-One World Atlas
English Language Edition

Published by AND Cartographic Publishers Ltd.,
Alberto House, Hogwood Lane,
Finchampstead, Berks, RG40 4RF,
United Kingdom

www: http://www.and.com

First edition 1999
1999 © AND Cartographic Publishers Ltd.,
Finchampstead, UK
1999 © WorldSat International Inc.,
Ontario, Canada
1998 © SPOT Image, Toulouse, France

ISBN 1-84178-003-0
HRR
987654321

Cover and preliminary section design:
Phil Jacobs

Cartographic production, design and layout:
AND Cartographic Publishers Ltd., Finchampstead, UK

Consultants: Simon Butler, Nigel Bradley
Editorial: Craig Asquith, Veronica Beattie, John Watkins
Cartography: Ben Brown, Ross Clode, Dave Edwards
Rachel Hopper, Adam Meara, Lee Rowe, Glyn Rozier, James Smith
DTP: Richard Fox
Production Coordinator: Caroline Beckley

Production of satellite imagery:
Robert Stacey, WorldSat International Inc.,
Ontario, Canada; Jim Knighton
Satellite data: NOAA
Ocean floor bathymetry by NOAA courtesy of USGS
Images on pages 26, 36, 38, 40 based on the
Resurs satellite imagery, provided by SSC/Satellitbild of
Kiruna, Sweden

Colour separations by AND Cartographic Publishers Ltd.
Printed in China

TWO-IN-ONE
WORLD
ATLAS

TWO STUNNING VIEWS OF OUR WORLD

Contents

How to Use This Atlas

This section enables you to check the page locations and scale of each map, and provides a key to the symbols used throughout.

How to Use This Book   6 – 7
Index to Map Pages   8 – 9

Earth watch

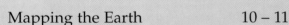

This section provides an overview of the complex processes by which satellite images are created.

Mapping the Earth   10 – 11

Satellite Images of the World

Eight pages of large-scale satellite images, featuring major cities and contrasting habitats. These highly detailed images provide a fascinating perspective on both the natural and man-made world.

Satellite images of the World   12 – 21

Maps of the World

The maps in this section are arranged by continent beginning with Europe. Each section starts with a double-page spread featuring the continent as a whole, followed by larger scale maps of individual countries and regions.

Each map has been created using the following:

Satellite images that enable mapping on the same scale and projection.

Highly accurate, one kilometre resolution satellite cartography.

Up-to-date satellite elevation data creating an enhanced three-dimensional effect.

The latest digital technology, enabling increased levels of clarity.

Maps of the World   22 – 112

Europe

Europe *1:22,700,000*   24 – 25

Belgium &
the Netherlands *1:2,600,000*   26 – 27

Scandinavia *1:6,500,000*   28 – 29
   Iceland *1:6,500,000*

European Russia *1:11,700,000*   30 – 31

Poland, Czech Rep, Slovakia,
& Hungary *1:3,900,000*   32 – 33

Germany *1:2,900,000*   34 – 35

British Isles *1:3,900,000*   36 – 37

France *1:3,900,000*   38 – 39

Spain & Portugal *1:3,900,000*   40 – 41

The Alps *1:2,900,000*   42 – 43

Italy *1:3,900,000*   44 – 45

The Balkans *1:3,900,000*   46 – 47

Greece & West Turkey *1:3,900,000*   48 – 49

Turkey *1:6,500,000*   50 – 51

Middle East

The Middle East *1:14,300,000*   52 – 53

Israel, Jordan &
Lebanon *1:3,200,000*   54

The Gulf States *1:6,500,000*   55

Africa

Africa *1:33,700,000*   56 – 57

Northwest Africa *1:13,000,000*   58 – 59
   Azores *1:13,000,000*

Northeast Africa *1:13,000,000*   60 – 61

West Africa *1:13,000,000*   62 – 63
   Cape Verde *1:13,000,000*

Central Africa *1:13,000,000*   64 – 65

Southern Africa *1:13,000,000*   66 – 67
   Mauritius *1:13,000,000*
   Seychelles *1:13,000,000*

Asia

Asia *1:37,000,000*   68 – 69

Northwest Asia *1:15,500,000*   70 – 71

Northeast Asia *1:15,500,000*   72 – 73

Southern Asia *1:13,000,000*   74 – 75

Southeast Asia *1:13,000,000*   76 – 77

China *1:13,000,000*   78 – 79

Japan & Korea *1:6,500,000*   80 – 81

Malaysia & Indonesia *1:13,000,000*   82 – 83

Oceania

Oceania *1:45,500,000*   84 – 85

Australia *1:15,500,000*   86 – 87

New Zealand *1:5,200,000*   88 – 89
   Pacific Islands *1:5,200,000*

North America

North America *1:39,000,000*   90 – 91

Canada *1:15,500,000*   92 – 93

United States *1:17,400,000*   94 – 95

Northwest United States *1:8,100,000*   96 – 97

Northeast United States *1:8,100,000*   98 – 99

Southwest United States *1:8,100,000*   100 – 101
   Hawaii *1:8,100,000*
   Alaska *1:8,100,000*
    Aleutian Islands *1:22,200,000*
Southeast United States *1:8,100,000*   102 – 103

Middle America *1:18,100,000*   104 – 105

South America

South America *1:31,500,000*   106 – 107

Northern S America *1:18,100,000*   108 – 109
   Galapagos Islands *1:18,100,000*

Southern S America *1:18,100,000*   110 – 111

Polar Regions

Arctic *1:57,000,000*   112

Antarctica *1:57,000,000*   112

Index

How to use the index   113

Glossary   114

Index to names   115 – 176

Endpapers

World Physical   Front Endpaper
World Political   Back Endpaper

How to Use This Book

T HE ILLUSTRATION shows the different items of
information presented in this atlas. Below it is
the key to all the symbols used on the maps and
satellite pictures.

Scale

Scale is the ratio between distance on the map and
distance on the Earth's surface. A scale of 1:12,000,000
means that the distance on the map is 12 million times
smaller than the actual distance measured on the
Earth's surface. For example, one centimetre on the
map represents 12,000,000 centimetres, or 120
kilometres, in reality.

Place location

The grid of lines on maps - the graticule - represent
longitude (measured east or west of the Greenwich
meridian) and latitude (measured north or south of
the equator). These lines are used by cartographers to
accurately pinpoint locations. A similar network
system has been used in this atlas, though here the
longitudinal and latitudinal references have been
replaced with letters and figures respectively. The grid
reference A2, for example, signifies that the feature
you are looking for lies in the 'square' made by the
intersection of Column A with row 2.

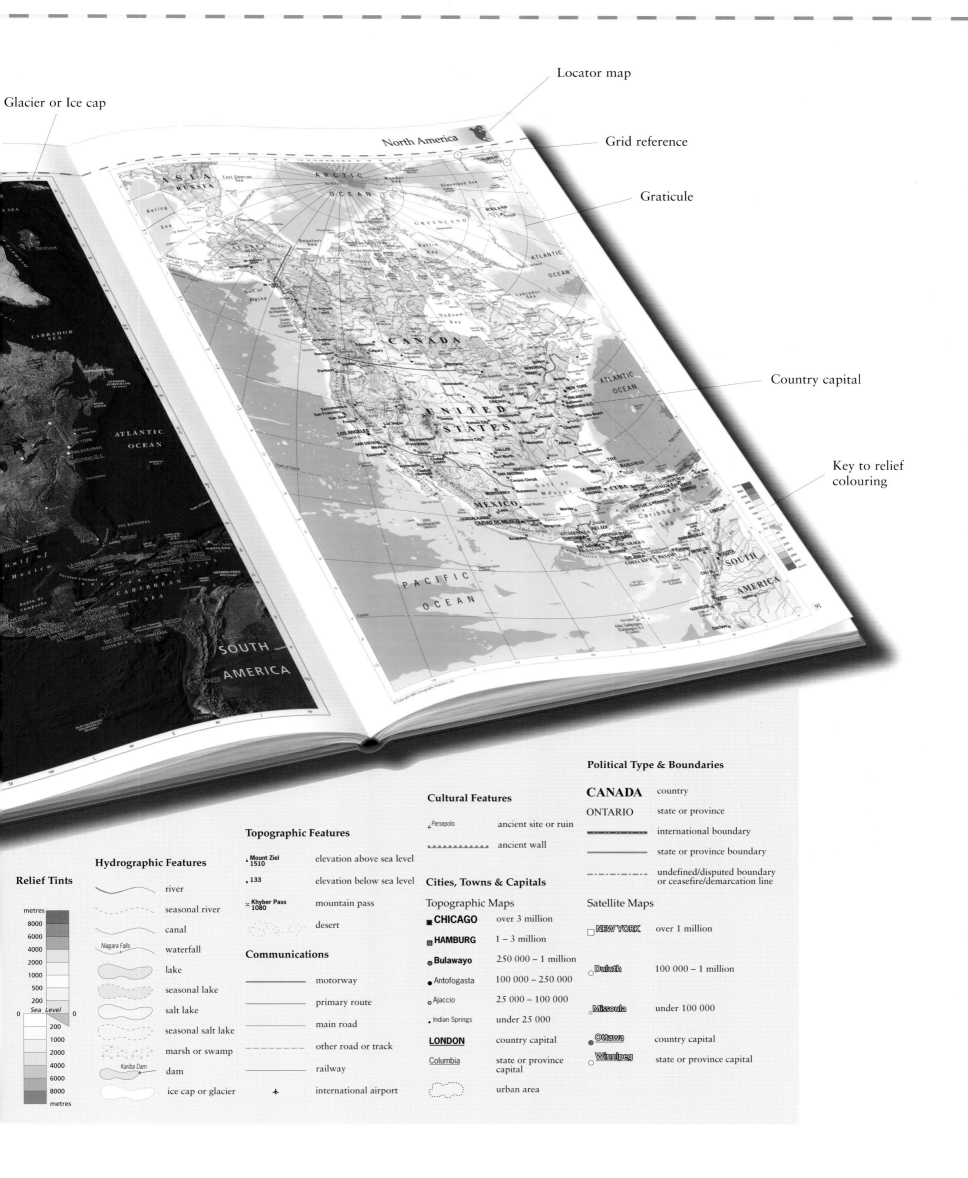

Glacier or Ice cap

Locator map

North America

Grid reference

Graticule

Country capital

Key to relief colouring

Relief Tints

metres	
8000	
6000	
4000	
2000	
1000	
500	
200	
0	Sea Level 0
200	
1000	
2000	
4000	
6000	
8000	
metres	

Hydrographic Features

	river
	seasonal river
	canal
Niagara Falls	waterfall
	lake
	seasonal lake
	salt lake
	seasonal salt lake
	marsh or swamp
Kariba Dam	dam
	ice cap or glacier

Topographic Features

Mount Ziel 1510	elevation above sea level
133	elevation below sea level
Khyber Pass 1080	mountain pass
	desert

Communications

	motorway
	primary route
	main road
	other road or track
	railway
✈	international airport

Cultural Features

Persepolis	ancient site or ruin
	ancient wall

Cities, Towns & Capitals

Topographic Maps

■ CHICAGO	over 3 million
■ HAMBURG	1 – 3 million
● Bulawayo	250 000 – 1 million
● Antofagasta	100 000 – 250 000
○ Ajaccio	25 000 – 100 000
∙ Indian Springs	under 25 000
LONDON	country capital
Columbia	state or province capital
	urban area

Political Type & Boundaries

CANADA	country
ONTARIO	state or province
	international boundary
	state or province boundary
	undefined/disputed boundary or ceasefire/demarcation line

Satellite Maps

□ NEW YORK	over 1 million
○ Duluth	100 000 – 1 million
○ Missoula	under 100 000
○ Ottawa	country capital
○ Winnipeg	state or province capital

7

Index
to
Map
Pages

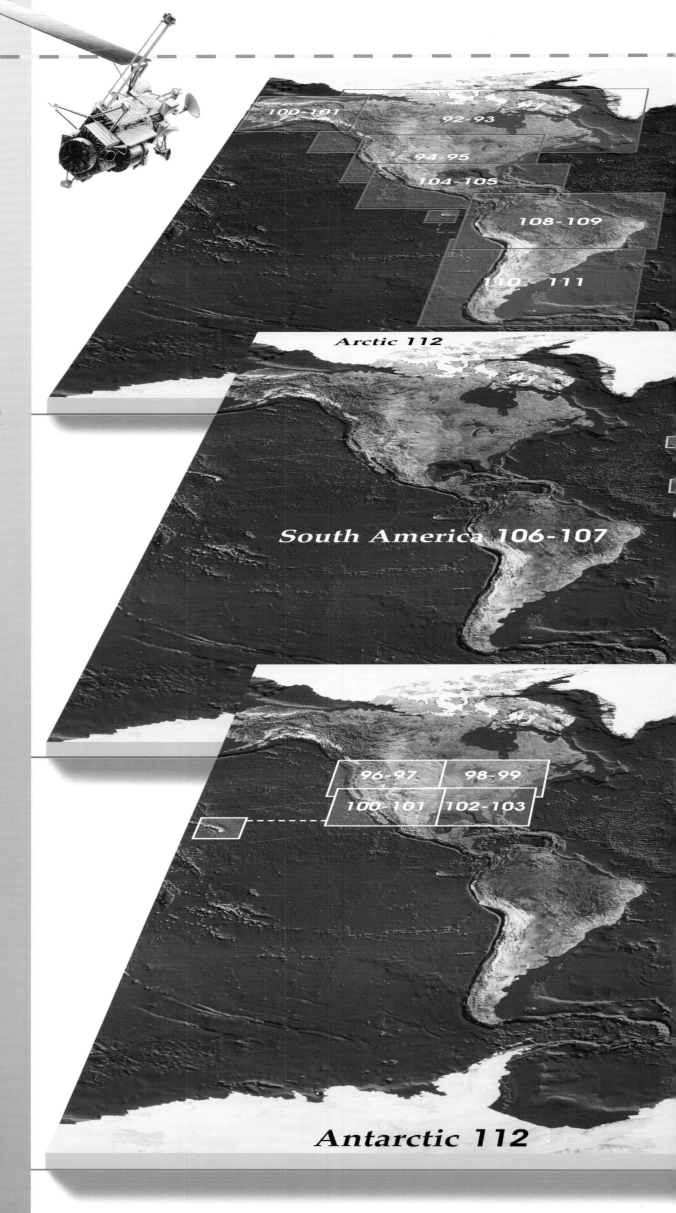

100-101

92-93

94-95

104-105

108-109

110 - 111

Arctic 112

Scale 1:14 300 000 - 1:22 200 000

South America 106-107

Scale 1:11 700 000 - 1:13 000 000

96-97   98-99

100-101   102-103

Antarctic 112

Scale 1:2 600 000 - 1:8 100 000

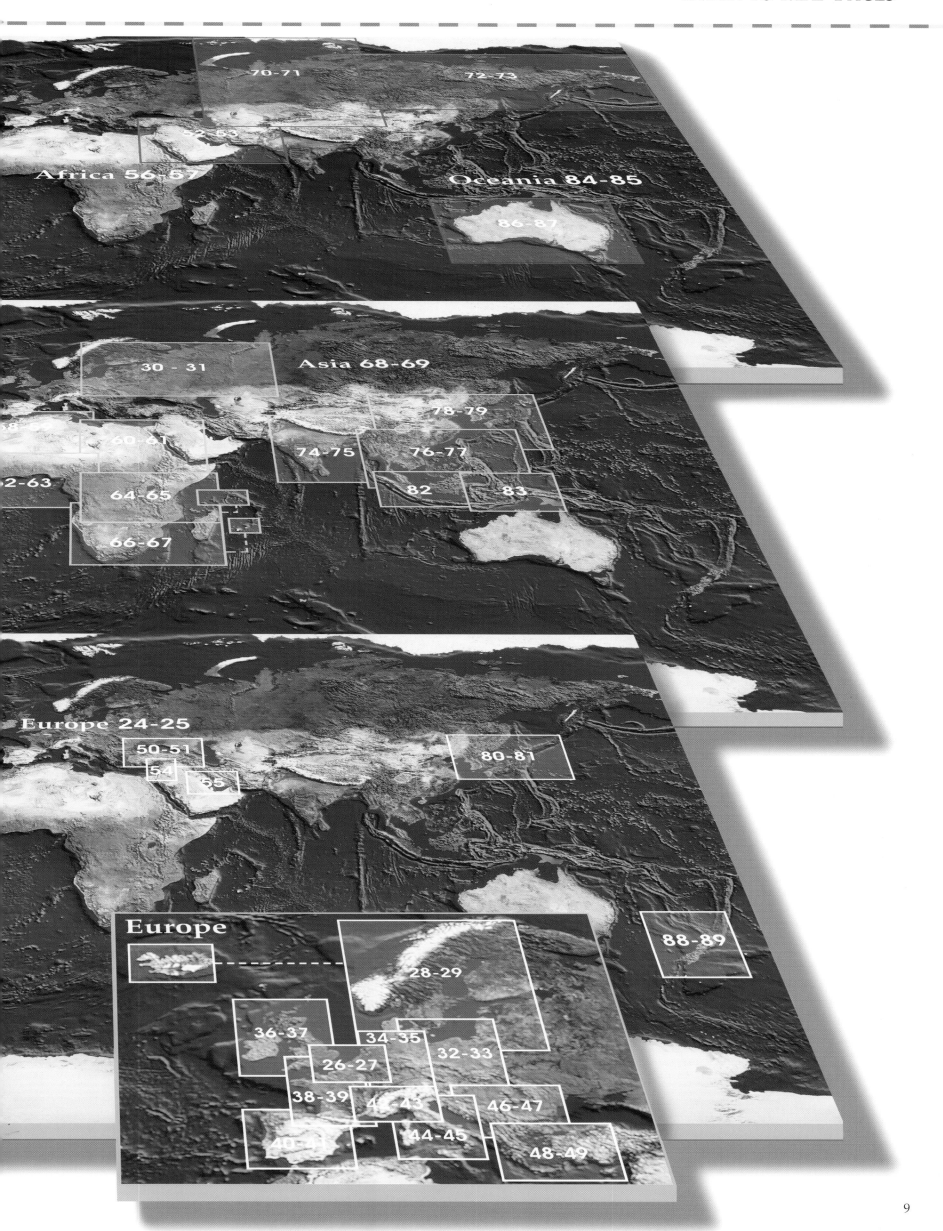

Mapping the Earth

THERE ARE MANY HUNDREDS of man-made satellites orbiting the Earth. The majority are communication satellites, receiving and sending signals for radio, television and telecommunications. But a significant minority of satellites are used solely for observation. Not only do these retrieve information for espionage, weather forecasting and studying the universe, they provide mapmakers with vital data about the surface of our planet.

There are two main ways in which mapping satellites study the Earth. Some use optical scanners. These, while often extremely accurate, are limited by factors such as low light levels, cloud cover and atmospheric blurring. Moreover, they collect only visible light – just one part of what is known as the electromagnetic spectrum. The electromagnetic spectrum comprises waves which vary in size and have different properties. Yet while these are invisible to the naked eye, they can be detected and converted into images by electronic scanners. A scanner using microwaves, for example, can penetrate clouds and 'see in the

dark' – a distinct advantage over optical scanners. The result is that an electronic scanner can extract geological and geographical information such as changes in elevation, differences in land cover and variations in temperature.

But whatever the comparative virtues of optical and electronic scanners, the combination of both methods results in maps that are both informative and extremely useful.

ELECTROMAGNETIC RADIATION

All wavelengths collected by a satellite, whether they are visible light or belong to the invisible part of the electromagnetic radiation spectrum, 'bounce' off the surface or object being viewed. Electromagnetic radiation used in mapping can come from a number of sources such as visible and infrared light from the sun, and thermal infrared (heat) from the Earth. The way an electromagnetic radiation wave bounces off an object is called its 'spectral signature', because it gives a characteristic reading when detected. This enables technicians to process data for creating maps.

| Ultra-violet | Infrared | Thermal infrared | Microwaves |

'Polar orbiting' satellites such as Landsat and Spot observe a different strip or 'track' of the Earth after every rotation of the planet. this way a complete picture of the surface can be compiled.

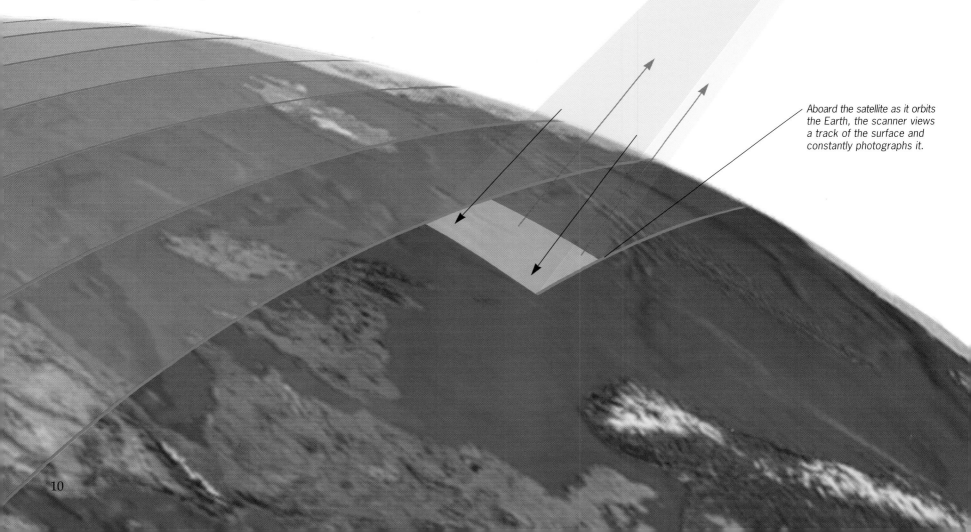

Aboard the satellite as it orbits the Earth, the scanner views a track of the surface and constantly photographs it.

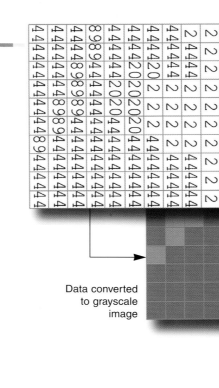

Coded raw data

Data converted to grayscale image

Colour coded data

The European Space Agency Satellite ERS–2, which generates its own microwaves. The radiation 'bounced' off the Earth's surface is converted into the data needed to produce a computer-generated map.

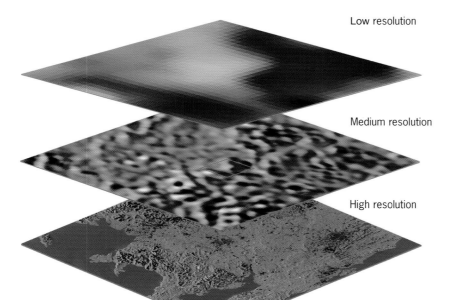

Low resolution

Medium resolution

High resolution

IMAGE ENHANCEMENT

The data collected by the satellite's scanner is processed by computers into binary code – a series of ones and zeros. This code is translated to supply the pixels (dots which form an electronic picture) with separate digital numbers, each of which represents a tonal value. Such information is used initially to generate grey scale images with 256 possible tones. Computer processing can be used to group pixels with similar spectral signatures in order to make maps of environmental phenomena such as landuse or geology.

A CLEAR VIEW

Electronic images derived from scanners vary in detail and clarity depending on their spatial resolution. Just like a picture on a TV screen, electronic images are made up of rows and columns of dots that are assigned different colours or shades of grey. These dots are known as pixels. The spatial resolution of the image is the area that the pixel represents on the Earth's surface. For mapping and monitoring the entire globe, spatial resolutions of $1km^2$ are commonly used; however, for detailed mapping of the Earth's resources, spatial resolutions of between 5 and 30 metres are more appropriate. In the near future, satellite imagery with a spatial resolution of 1 metre or less will become available and this will revolutionize large-scale mapping.

False colour image

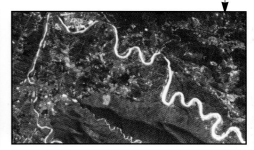

True-colour image

THE FINAL STEPS

Raw data has to be processed before being used to generate images. Atmospheric disturbances, faults with scanning sensors and flaws in transmission are among the possible causes of distorted or incomplete data. Overlap of scanned tracks and the problem of converting data about a curved surface into a flat format also have to be overcome. By comparing two or more similar scans, however, accurate images can soon be created.

The accentuation of certain parts of the pictures with artificial colours results in 'false colour' images. These can be used for specialized applications such as monitoring the depletion of rainforests or aiding geological prospecting. A further, intriguing development has been their use in identifying archaeological sites.

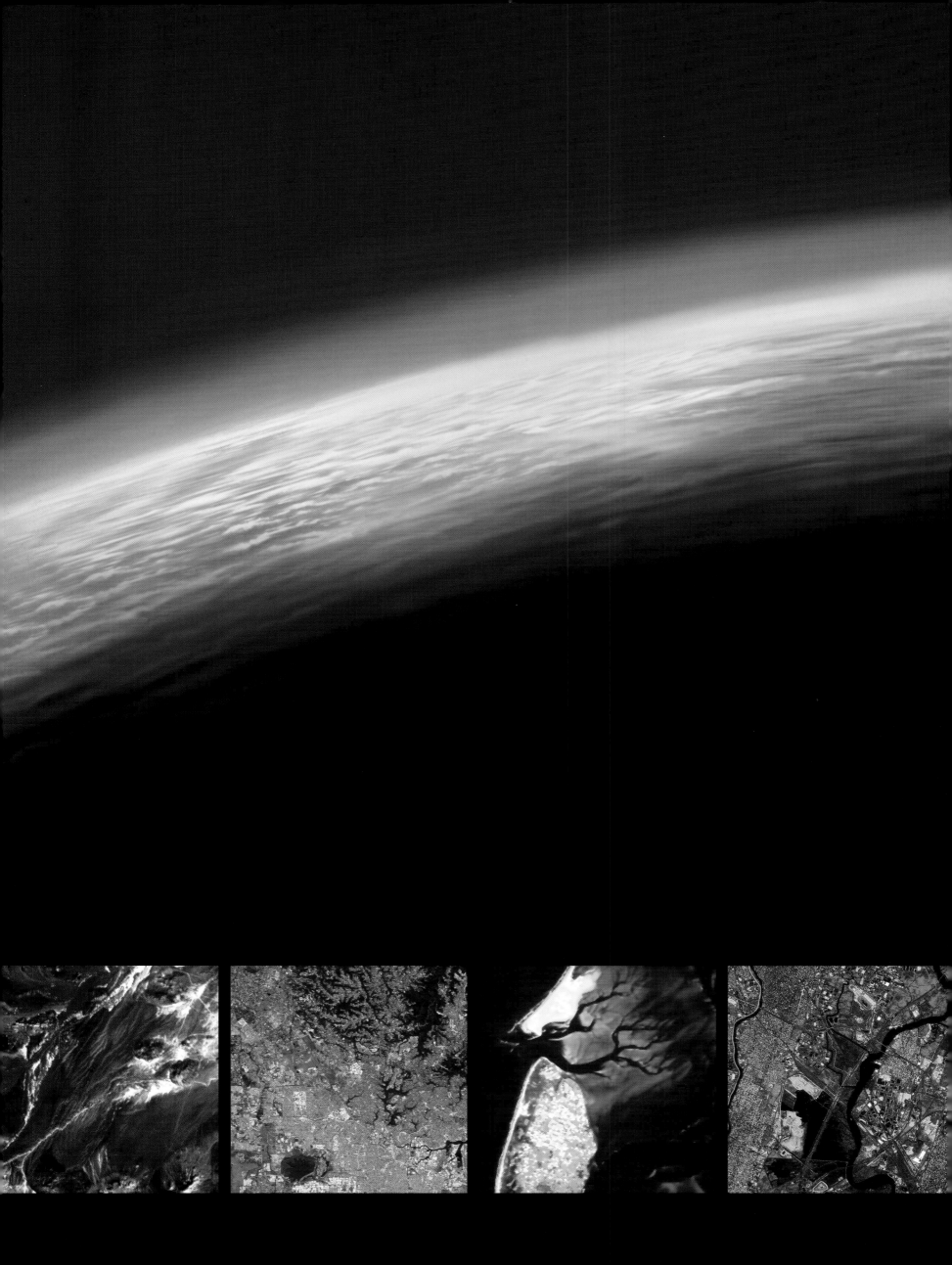

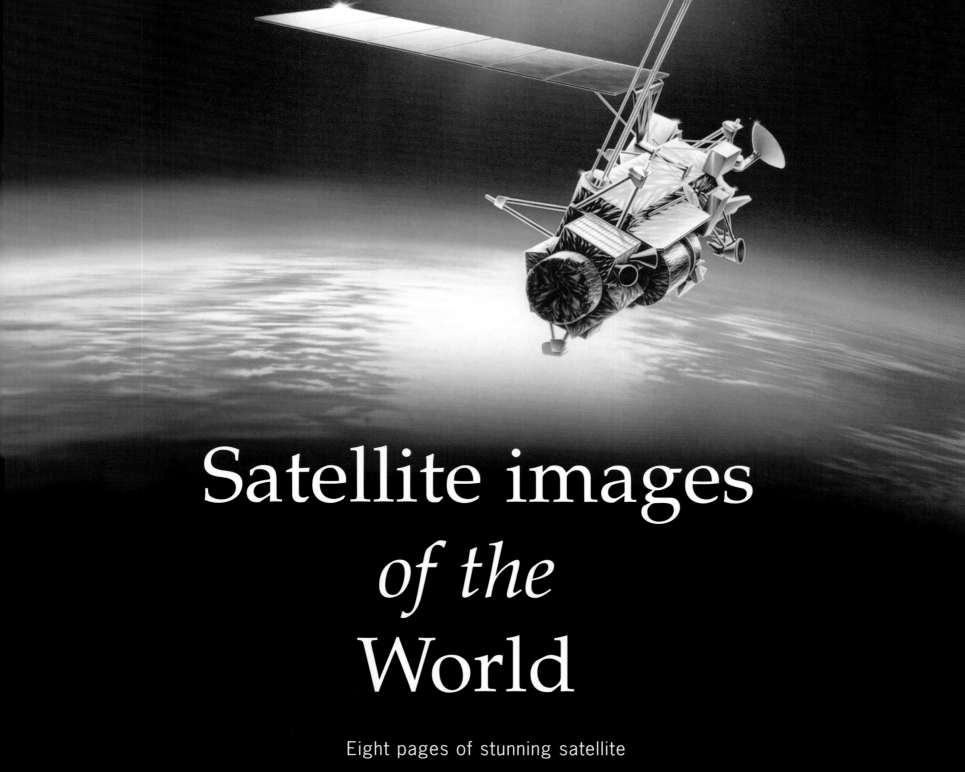

Satellite images
of the
World

Eight pages of stunning satellite
images featuring major cities and contrasting
geographical habitats from around the world.
These breathtaking images of our Earth show the
natural and man-made world from
a new perspective.

CLEARLY SPOTTED. An extremely detailed infrared image of New York, taken by the French Spot I satellite. The image resolution is so high that roads, stadiums, bridges and even boats and jetties are all visible. The very small oval island (lower right of centre) is Liberty Island, and the white speck at its eastern end is the Statue of Liberty.

CROWDED CAPITAL. This infrared image offers an excellent view of one of the world's largest cities, Beijing. Over five million people live in the city's central area - registered here as a slaty blue-grey. In the middle of the image lie the palaces and lakes of the Forbidden City, while to the south lies the vast space of Tiananmen Square.

LONDON TOWN. An infrared image of Great Britain's capital, taken by the French Spot II satellite. The River Thames winds its way through the city to Docklands, clearly visible in the centre of the image. The black spaces (top) represent the reservoirs that provide some of London's drinking water. Areas of open land - such as Hyde Park, Regent's Park and Buckingham Palace grounds - all show up as red and are visible to the north of the river (left).

SHOWING ITS TRUE COLOURS. A near-true colour image taken by the French Spot I satellite of Sydney and its environs. The city's Parramatta River is crossed by the Sydney Harbour Bridge at the point where it flows into Port Jackson. On the white promontory just east of the bridge stands the Sydney Opera House. South of the city is Botany Bay, with Sydney Airport extending from its northern shore.

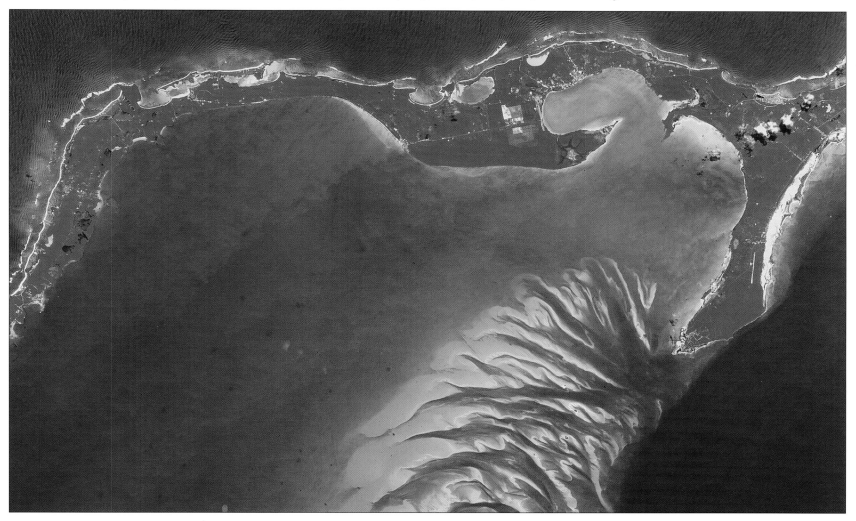

CARIBBEAN ISLAND. An infra-red image of Eleuthera in the Bahamas. Off the east coast (top), parallel rows of waves can be seen approaching the shore, blown by winds across the Atlantic. This is in marked contrast to their total absence in the very shallow, sheltered water to the west. Wave action on the western tip of the island's southern end has caused the offshore deposition of a spectacular series of sandbanks.

BETWEEN EAST AND WEST. Istanbul sits astride the Bosporus Strait, the narrow waterway separating Europe (left) from Asia (right) and connecting the Black Sea (top) and the Aegean Sea (bottom). Founded as Byzantium in 667BC, the city's name was changed to Constantinople in 330AD and became Istanbul following its conquest by the Turks in 1453.

DESERT LANDS. This false-colour image of the Arabian Desert provides a vivid record of the desertification process. Two distinct kinds of terrain are shown. The pink area is an arid, windswept plateau, while the coppery green one is a great plain scored with dried-up watercourses, or wadis. If every wadi was once a river running off the plateau, this desert must once have been a truly rich, fertile land.

RIBBONS OF WATER. An infra-red image of the Mahakam River delta on the island of Borneo, with water represented in blue. As the river entered the sea, it slowed down so much that it gradually deposited most of its sediment load, forming a fan-shaped delta of swampland (shown as dark red). As the delta developed, so the river also branched off into many meandering distributaries in order to cross it, each following its own path to the sea.

VOLCANIC LANDSCAPE. Part of the Atacama region in Chile is shown in this near true-colour image. Several lava flows from past eruptions are visible, notably at the top right. Two snow-covered peaks show evidence of gullies gouged out as meltwater or rainfall flowed down them to join the river (top) flowing from right to left along the valley floor. A salt lake is also clearly visible at the bottom of the picture.

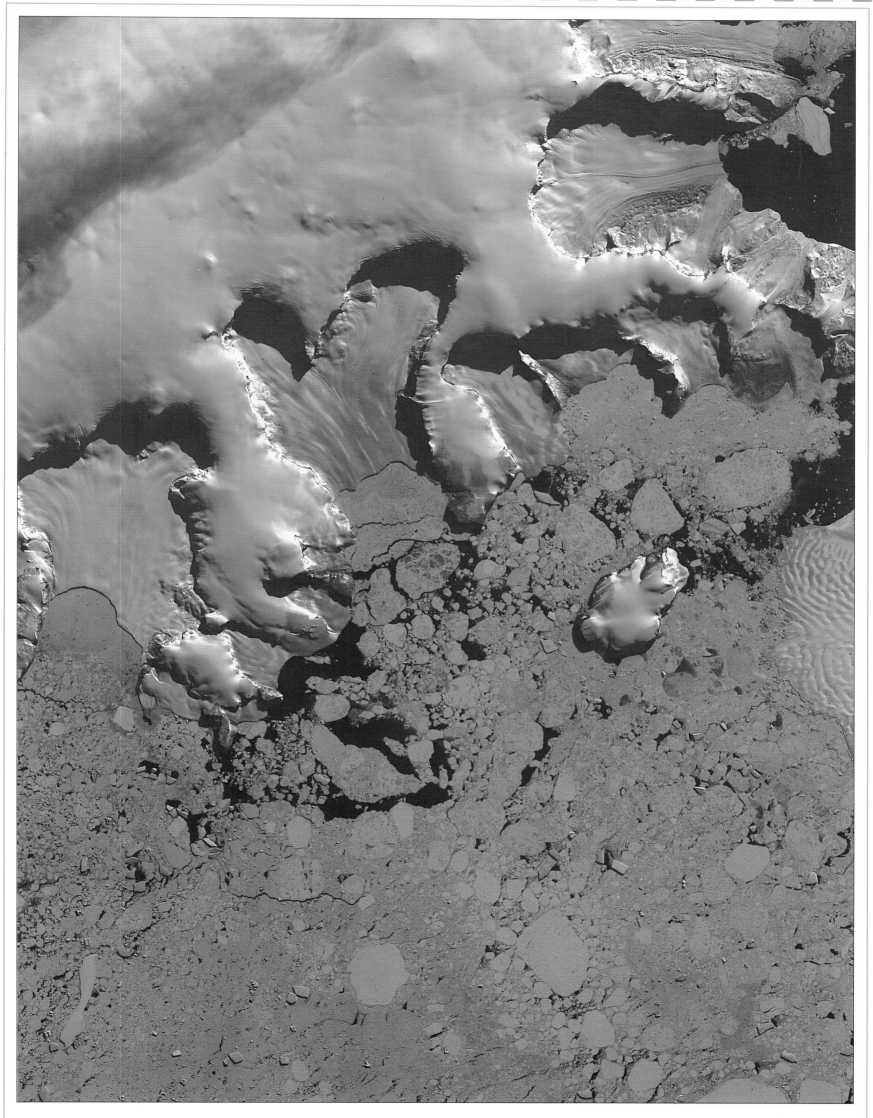

POLAR VISION. A crystal-clear view of Antarctica, demonstrating yet another aspect of satellite technology. Images such as this enable scientists to monitor long-term changes in ice landscapes, such as the movements of iceberg fields and the retreat of glaciers. In this way, forecasts can be made of the possible climatic effects of global warming.

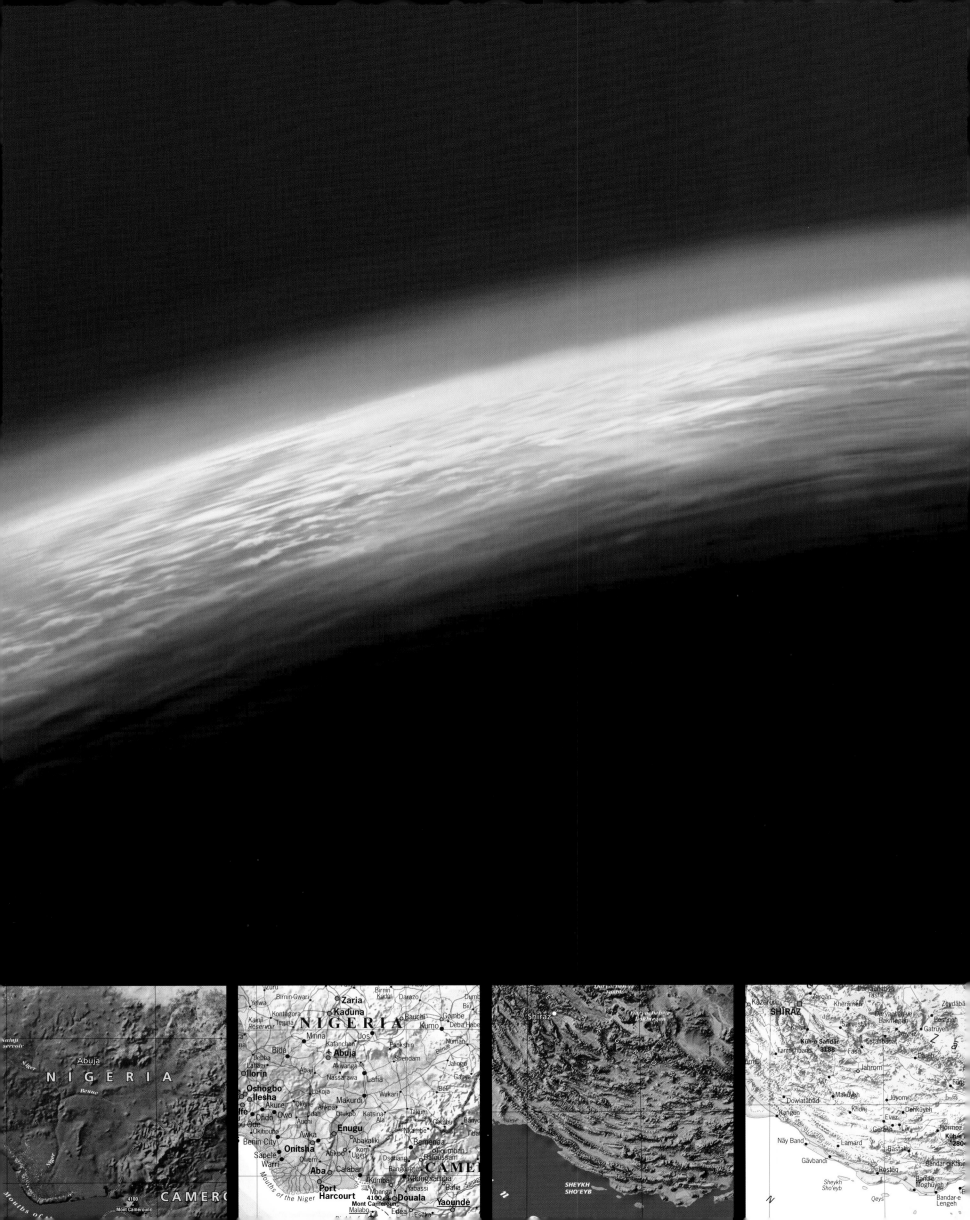

Maps
of the
World

Forty-eight pairs of full colour satellite images and maps covering
the world. Each pair created to the same projection for easy comparison.
Each satellite image enhanced with elevation data, plus a layer of
cartographic information related directly to the detail on the map.
The following pages provide a unique view of our Earth – lines and
symbols of traditional maps seen for the first time alongside images
of the world as seen from space.

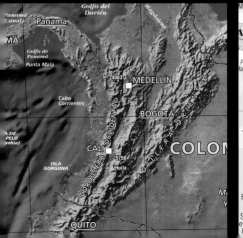

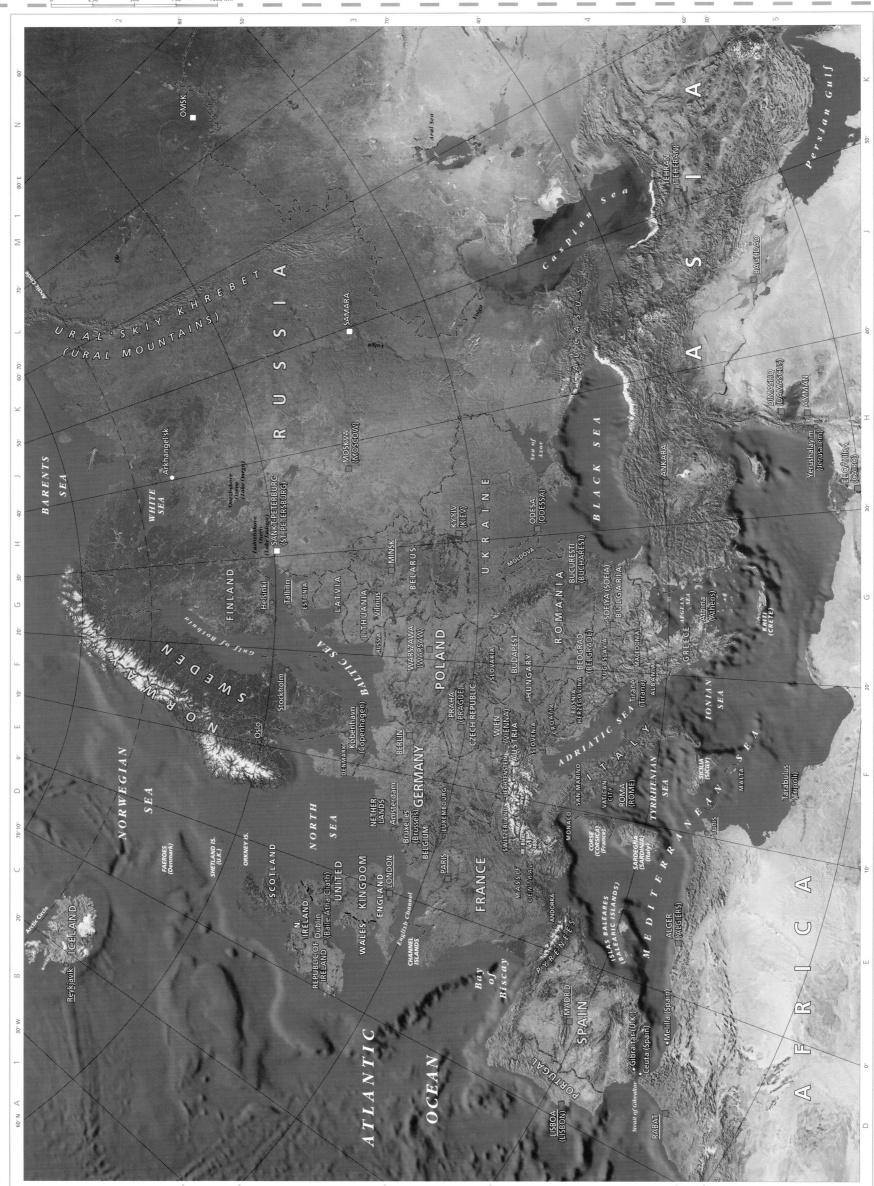

Scale 1 : 22 700 000

0   250   500   750   1000 km

ATLANTIC

OCEAN

NORWEGIAN

SEA

NORTH

SEA

BARENTS

SEA

WHITE
SEA

ICELAND

Reykjavik

FAEROES
(Denmark)

SHETLAND IS.
(U.K.)

ORKNEY IS.

SCOTLAND

N.
IRELAND

REPUBLIC OF
IRELAND
(Baile Átha Cliath)
Dublin

UNITED
KINGDOM

WALES
ENGLAND
LONDON

English Channel

CHANNEL
ISLANDS

Bay
of
Biscay

PORTUGAL

LISBOA
(LISBON)

RABAT

SPAIN

MADRID

Strait of Gibraltar

Gibraltar (U.K.)
Ceuta (Spain)
Melilla (Spain)

ANDORRA

PYRENEES

FRANCE

PARIS

MASSIF
CENTRAL

BELGIUM

Bruxelles
(Brussels)

LUXEMBOURG

NETHER-
LANDS

Amsterdam

GERMANY

DENMARK

København
(Copenhagen)

BERLIN

NORWAY

Oslo

SWEDEN

Stockholm

FINLAND

Helsinki

Gulf of Bothnia

BALTIC SEA

ESTONIA

Tallinn

LATVIA

LITHUANIA

Vilnius

Rīga

BELARUS

MINSK

POLAND

WARSZAWA
(WARSAW)

PRAHA
(PRAGUE)

CZECH REPUBLIC

SLOVAKIA

WIEN
(VIENNA)

AUSTRIA

SWITZERLAND
LIECHTENSTEIN

MONACO

MT. BLANC
4807

SLOVENIA

CROATIA

BUDAPEST

HUNGARY

ROMANIA

BUCUREŞTI
(BUCHAREST)

MOLDOVA

UKRAINE

KYIV
(KIEV)

ODESA
(ODESSA)

Sea of
Azov

BLACK SEA

MOSKVA
(MOSCOW)

RUSSIA

SANKT-PETERBURG
(ST. PETERSBURG)

Ladozhskoye
Ozero
(Lake Ladoga)

Onezhskoye
Ozero
(Lake Onega)

Arkhangel'sk

URAL'SKIY KHREBET
(URAL MOUNTAINS)

Arctic Circle

OMSK

Volga

SAMARA

Aral Sea

Caspian Sea

CAUCASUS

TEHRĀN
(TEHERAN)

Persian Gulf

BAGHDĀD

DIMASHQ
(DAMASCUS)

AMMĀN

Yerushalayim
(Jerusalem)

EL QĀHIRA
(CAIRO)

ANKARA

A S I A

AFRICA

MEDITERRANEAN SEA

ALGER
(ALGIERS)

ISLAS BALEARES
(BALEARIC ISLANDS)

CORSE
(CORSICA)
(France)

SARDEGNA
(SARDINIA)
(Italy)

ITALY

SAN MARINO

ROMA
(ROME)

VATICAN
CITY

TYRRHENIAN
SEA

SICILIA
(SICILY)

MALTA

Tunis

Tarābulus
(Tripoli)

ADRIATIC SEA

BOSNIA
HERZEGOVINA

YUGOSLAVIA

BEOGRAD
(BELGRADE)

MACEDONIA

Tiranë
(Tirana)

ALBANIA

GREECE

Athína
(Athens)

IONIAN
SEA

AEGEAN
SEA

KRITI
(CRETE)

BULGARIA

SOFIYA
(SOFIA)

24

© Copyright

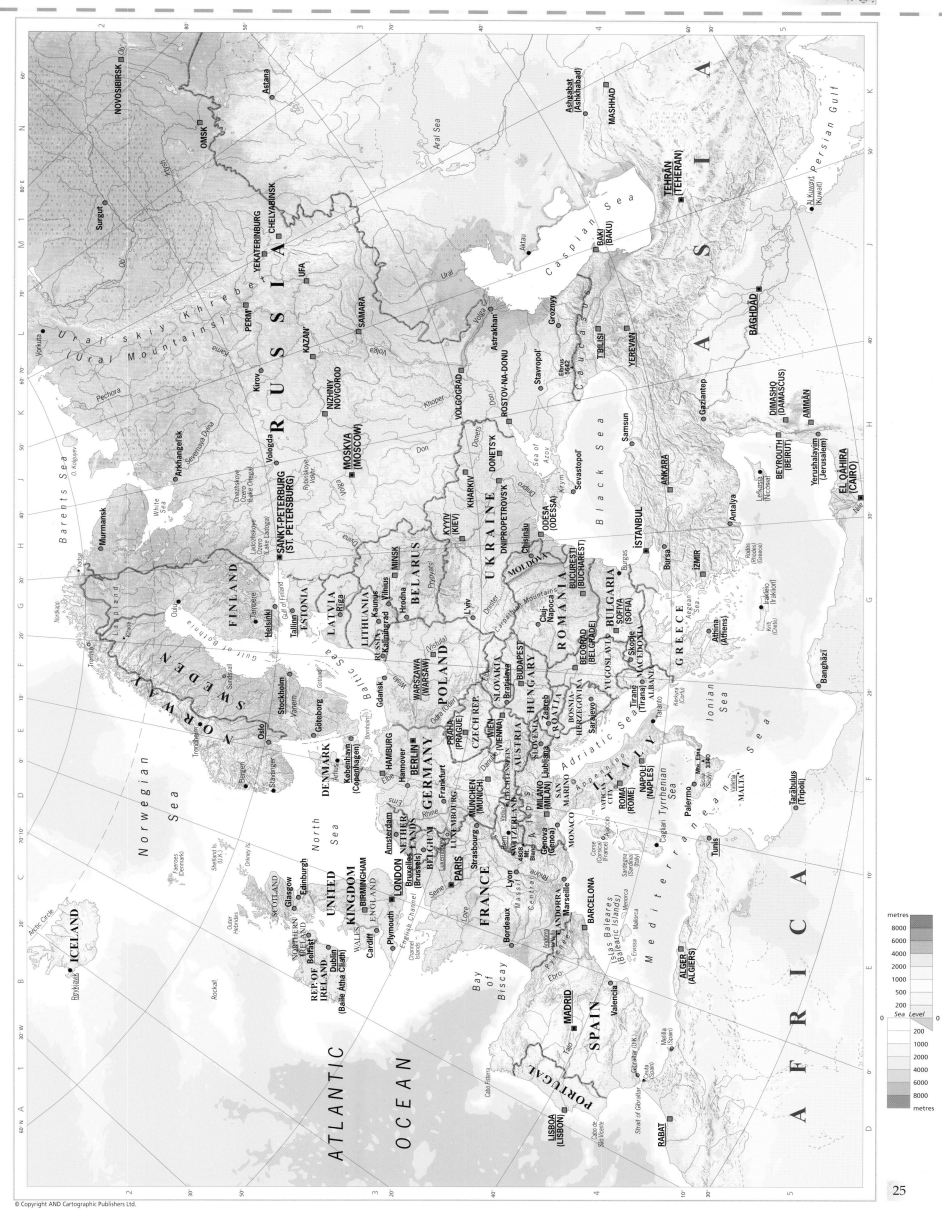

Scale 1 : 2 600 000

0   50   100 km

NORTH SEA

UNITED KINGDOM

England

South Downs

The Wash

Nottingham
Leicester
BIRMINGHAM
Norwich
Ipswich
Luton
Oxford
LONDON
Southampton
Portsmouth
ISLE OF WIGHT

Thames

North Foreland
Dover
Dungeness
Beachy Head
Calais
Cap Gris-Nez
Strait of Dover

English Channel

NETHERLANDS

Groningen
BORKUM
SCHIERMONNIKOOG
AMELAND
TERSCHELLING
VLIELAND
TEXEL
WADDENZEE
W A D D E N   E I L A N D E N
EMS

Amsterdam
'S-Gravenhage
Rotterdam
Enschede
Ijsselmeer
Ijssel

GERMANY

Bremen
Bielefeld
Essen
Düsseldorf
Köln
Bonn
Wiesbaden
Frankfurt
TAUNUS
Rhine (Rhein)
Rhine (Rhein)
Waal
Maas

BELGIUM

Antwerpen (Antwerp)
Bruxelles (Brussel)
Brugge
Lille
Maastricht
Liège
Hasselt
Oosterschelde
Westerschelde
Schelde
A R D E N N E S

LUXEMBOURG

Luxembourg
Metz
Nancy
Moselle

FRANCE

Amiens
Somme
Somme
Lille
Reims
Rouen
PARIS
Seine
Seine
Le Havre
Cap d'Antifer
Caen
Baie de la Seine
Karlsruhe

26

© Copyright

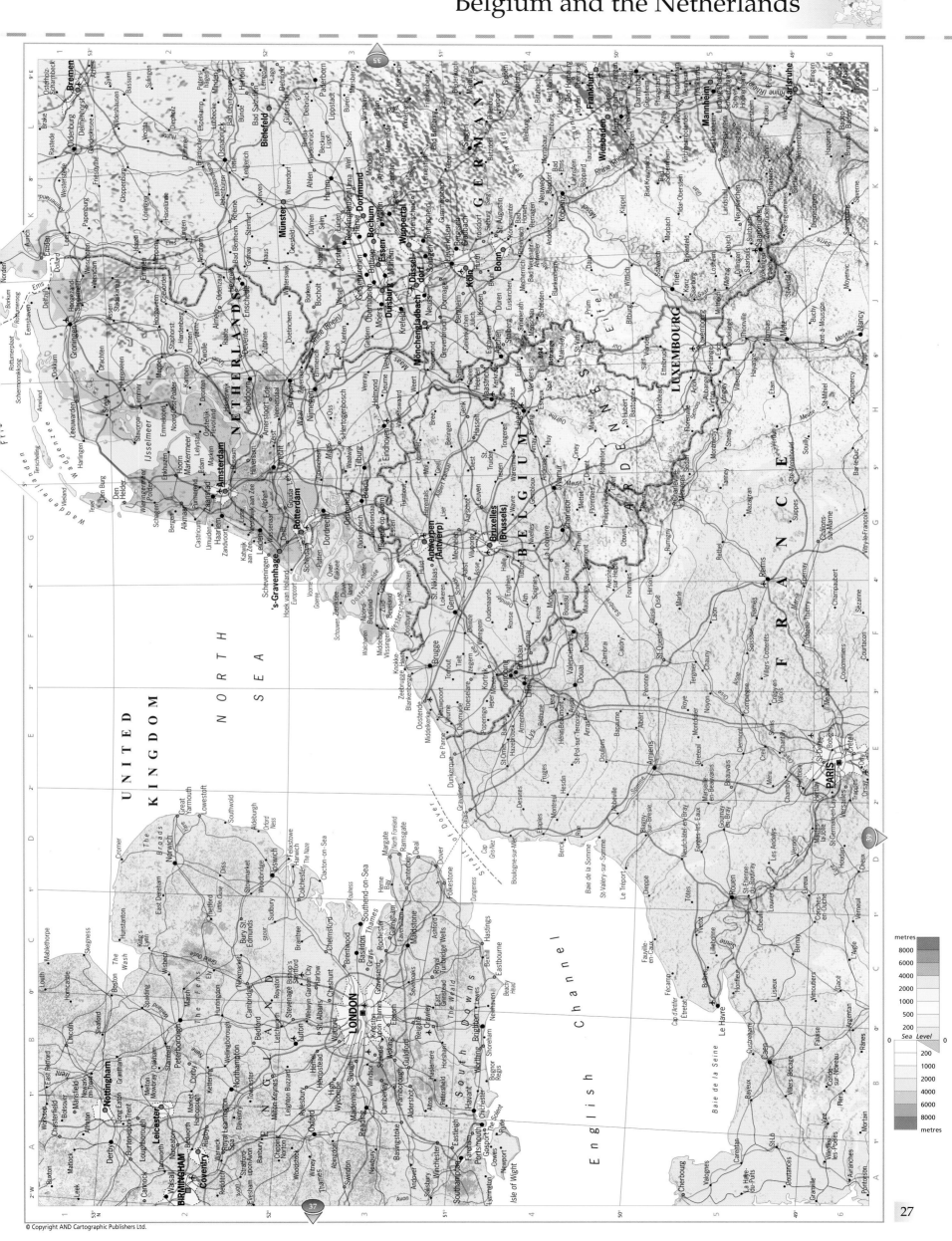

Scale 1 : 6 500 000

0   100   200   300 km

© Copyright

ICELAND

GREENLAND SEA

Arctic Circle

GRÍMSEY

Fontur

Húnaflói

VATNAJÖKULL

Faxaflói

Reykjavík

ATLANTIC OCEAN

HEIMAEY

Hvannadalshnúkur 2119

NORWEGIAN

SEA

NORTH SEA

BARENTS SEA

Nordkapp

MAGERØYA

SØRØYA

ARNØYA

RINGVASSØYA

SENJA

VESTERÅLEN

LANGØYA

LOFOTEN

VESTVÅGØY

Kebnekaise 2123

Murmansk

RUSSIA

LAPPLAND

FINLAND

KARELIYA

Arctic Circle

N O R W A Y

S W E D E N

Trondheim

VIKNA

FRØYA

HITRA

SMØLA

Bergen

HARDANGER-VIDDA

Oslo

Lindesnes

Skagerrak

Kattegat

Göteborg

LÆSØ

Ålborg

Ålborg Bugt

JYLLAND

Århus

Helsingborg

DENMARK

Odense

FYN

SJÆLLAND

København (Copenhagen)

Malmö

Hanøbukten

MØN

LOLLAND FALSTER

BORNHOLM

RÜGEN

Kiel

Rostock

Szczecin

FANØ

SYLT

HELGOLAND

OSTFRIESISCHE INSELN

WADDENEILANDEN

Groningen

HAMBURG

GERMANY

Bremen

NETHERLANDS

HAILUOTO

Oulu

Tampere

Gulf of Bothnia

ÅLAND

Uppsala

Stockholm

Vänern

HIIUMAA

SAAREMAA

Vättern

Norrköping

Linköping

Jönköping

GOTLAND

ÖLAND

BALTIC SEA

SANKT-PETERBURG

Turku

Helsinki

Gulf of Finland

Tallinn

ESTONIA

Lake Peipus

Tartu

Pskov

RUSSIA

Gulf of Riga

Riga

LATVIA

Daugavpils

Liepāja

Klaipėda

LITHUANIA

Kaliningrad

RUSSIA

Gulf of Gdansk

Gdansk

Koszalin

Ladozhskoye Ozero (Lake Ladoga)

Nemunas

Kaunas

Vilnius

Hrodna

BELARUS

Olsztyn

Białystok

Bydgoszcz

POLAND

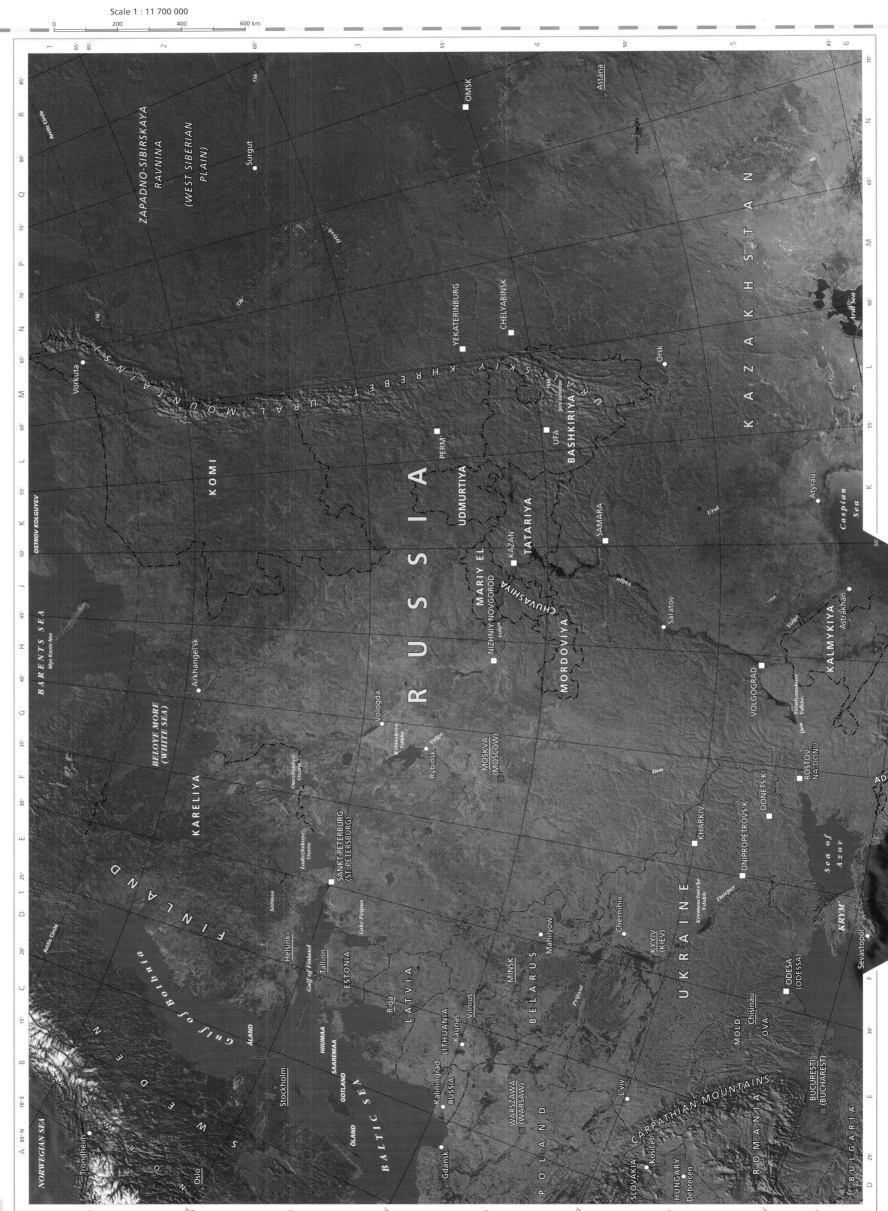

Scale 1 : 11 700 000

0   200   400   600 km

© Copyright

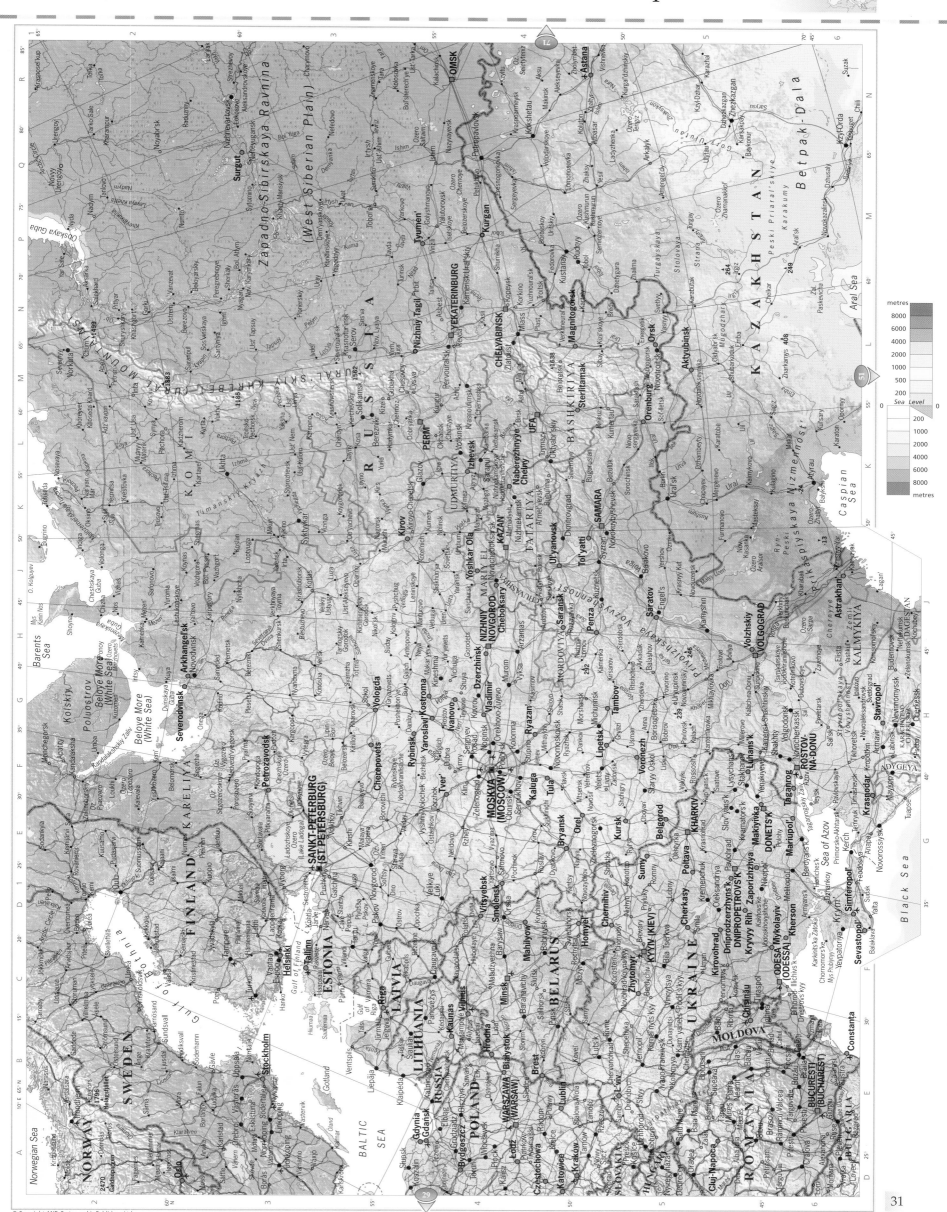

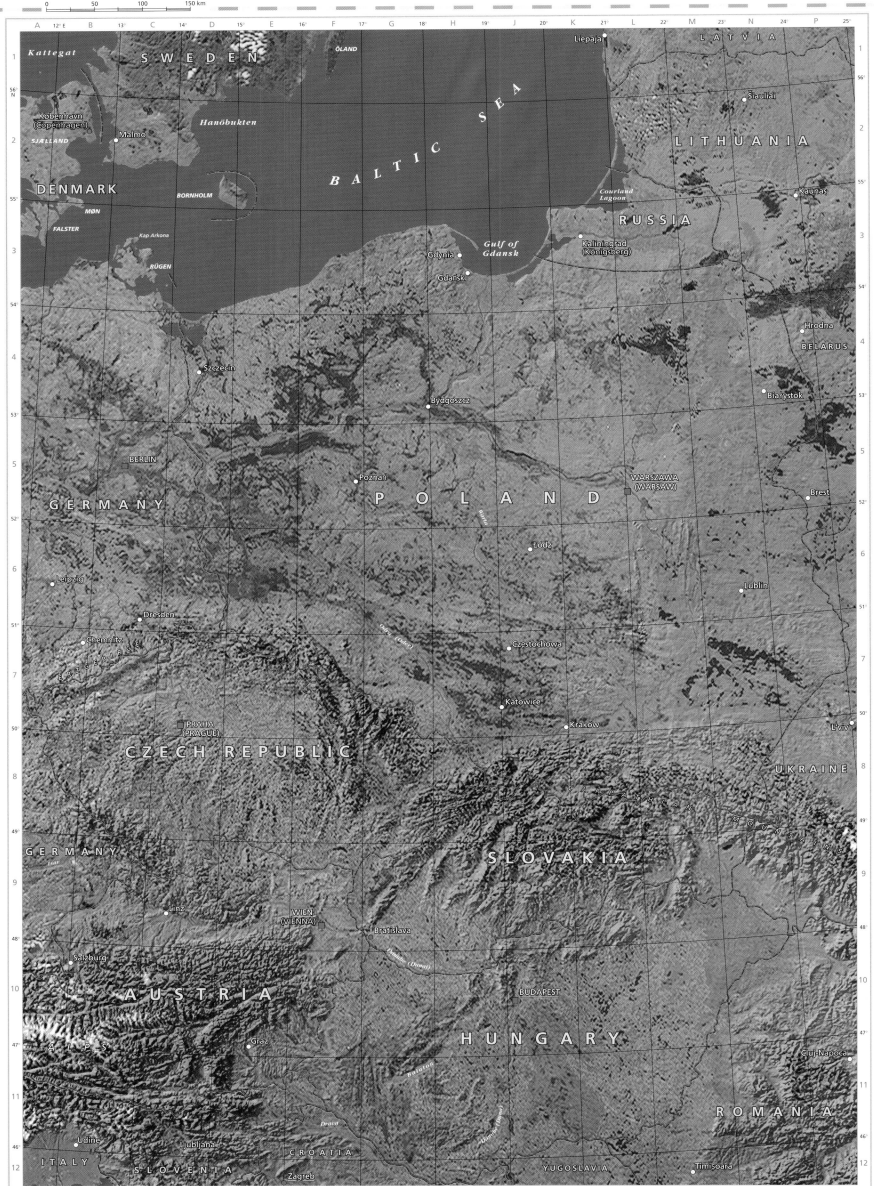

Scale 1 : 3 900 000

0   50   100   150 km

© Copyright

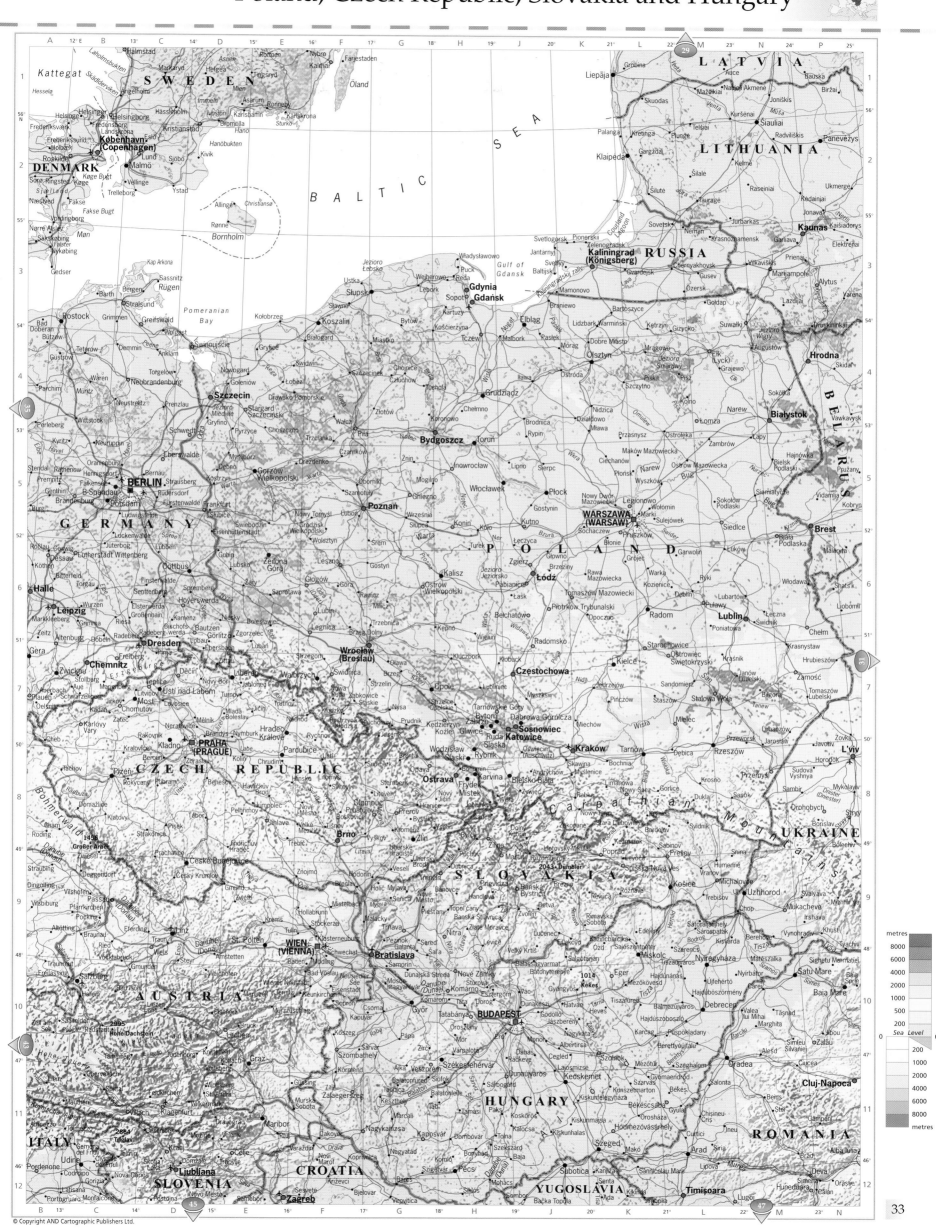

0   50   100   150 km

A   6° E   B   7°   C   8°   D   9°   E   10°   F   11°   G   12°   H   13°   J   14°   K

SWEDEN   BORNHOLM

Odense   FYN   SJÆLLAND

D E N M A R K   Store Bælt   BALTIC

1

55°
N   ALS   MØN   SEA

ÆRØ   LANGELAND   LOLLAND   FALSTER   Kap Arkona

SYLT   HIDDENSEE

N O R T H   S E A   Föhr   FEHMARN   RÜGEN

Kiel   Mecklenburger   Greifswalder
Bucht   Bodden

NORDFRIESISCHE INSELN   2

HELGOLAND   Rostock

54°   Helgoländer
Bucht   Szczecin

WADDENEILANDEN   OSTFRIESISCHE INSELN   Müritz

TERSCHELLING   SCHIERMONNIKOOG   NORDERNEY   LANGEOOG   WANGEROOG   HAMBURG   3

AMELAND   BORKUM   Groningen

WADDENZEE   Bremen
Weser   53°

Ems

IJssel-   BERLIN
meer   Hannover   4

NETHERLANDS   Braunschweig   Magdeburg   POL

Enschede   Cottbus

52°   Arnhem   Bielefeld

Münster   Ems

G E R M A N Y   Halle

Dortmund   Leipzig   5

Essen   Dresden

Krefeld   Düsseldorf

51°   Köln   ERZGEBIRGE

Maastricht   THÜRINGER WALD

Liège   Bonn

Rhine
(Rhein)   6

BELGIUM   CZECH REPUBLIC

Frankfurt

Wiesbaden   Main   50°

LUXEMBOURG

Luxembourg

Nürnberg   K

Mannheim   7

Heidelberg   Neckar

Karlsruhe   49°

Stuttgart

Rhine (Rhein)   Danube (Donau)   8

Strasbourg   Inn

F R A N C E   SCHWÄBISCHE ALB

SCHWARZWALD

48°   MÜNCHEN
(MUNICH)   AUSTRIA

1424   Salzburg   9
Grand Ballon

Lake
Constance

A   6°   B   7°   C   Basel   D   8°   E   10°   F   G   12°   H   13°   J

SWITZERLAND   A U S T R I A

Zürich

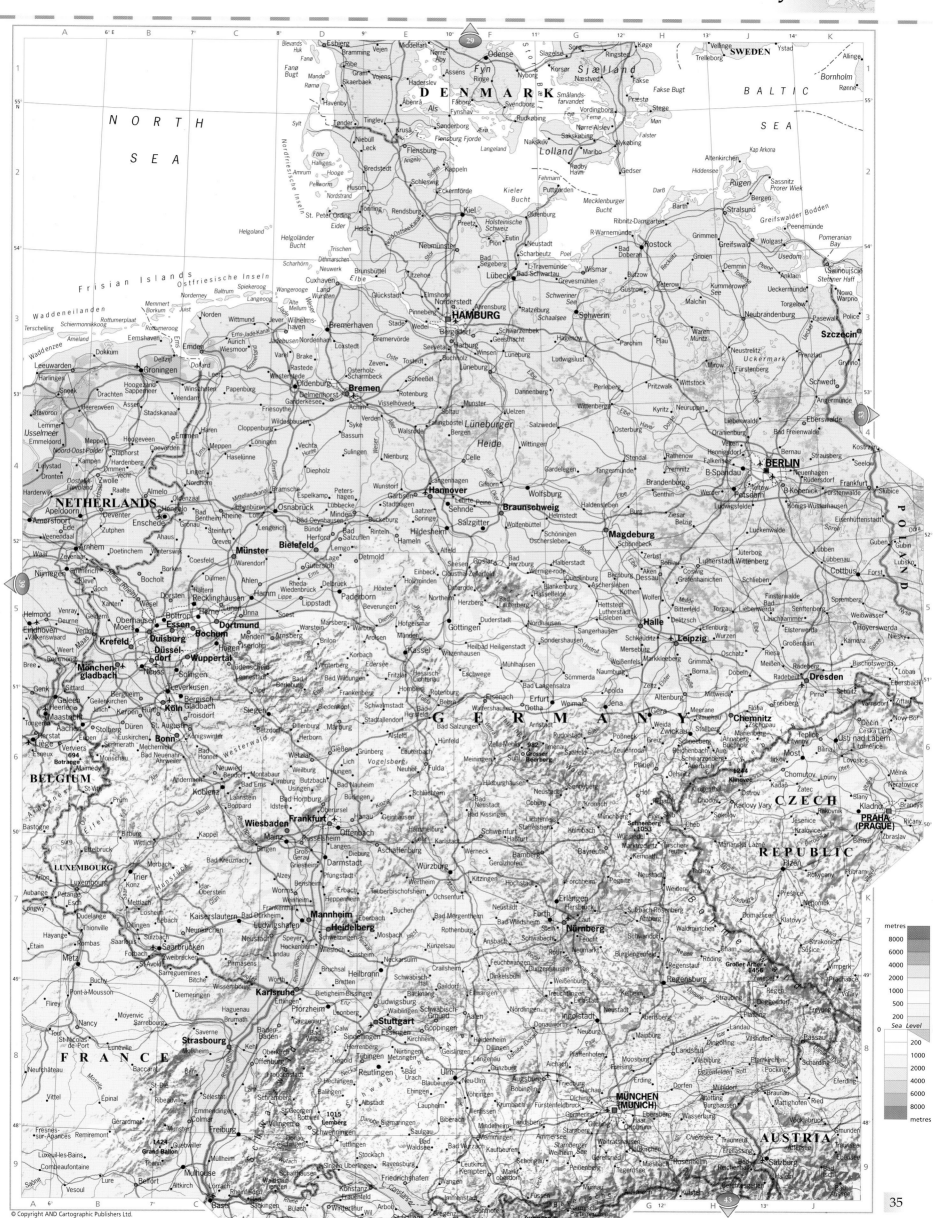

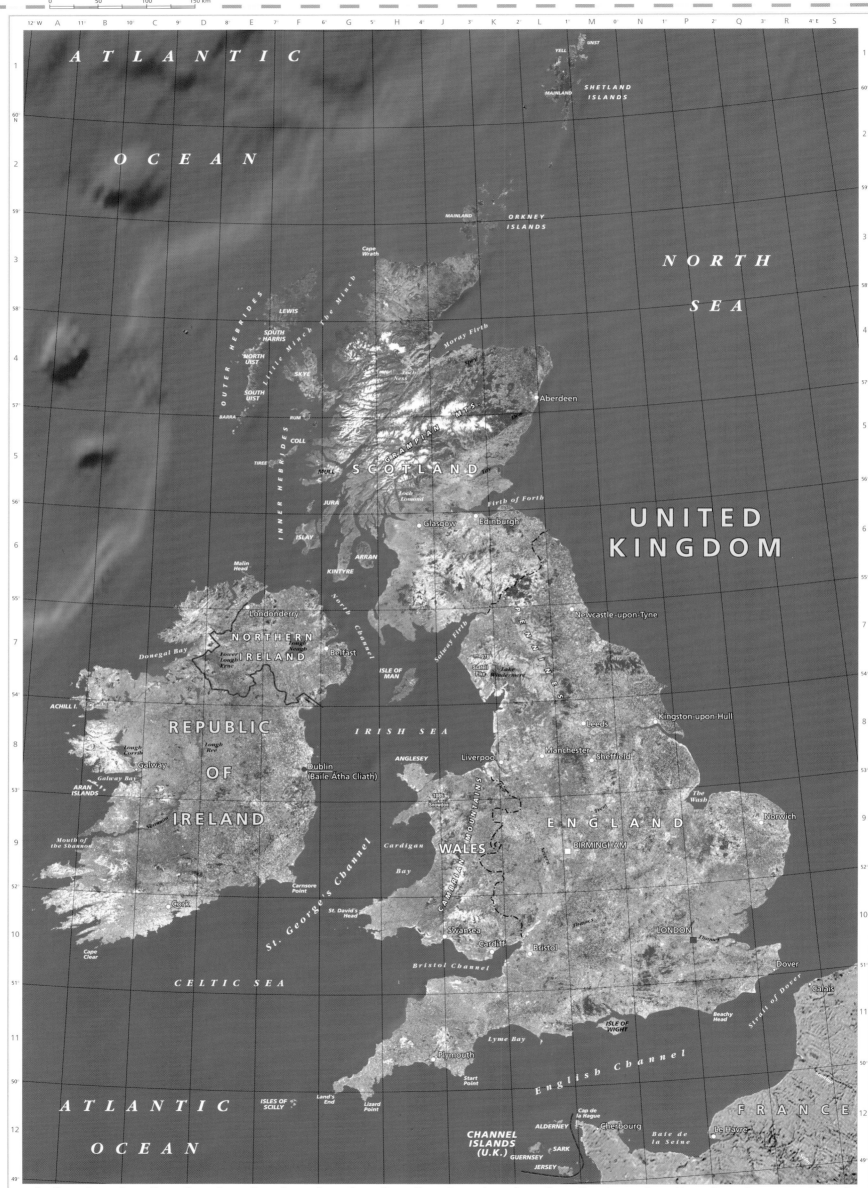

Scale 1 : 3 900 000

0   50   100   150 km

ATLANTIC

OCEAN

YELL
UNST

MAINLAND

*SHETLAND
ISLANDS*

NORTH

SEA

MAINLAND

*ORKNEY
ISLANDS*

Cape
Wrath

Moray Firth

Spy

OUTER HEBRIDES

LEWIS

*SOUTH
HARRIS*

*NORTH
UIST*

SKYE

*Loch
Ness*

The Minch

Little Minch

Aberdeen

*SOUTH
UIST*

BARRA

RUM

GRAMPIAN MTS.

COLL

TIREE

Tay

MULL

SCOTLAND

Toy

INNER HEBRIDES

JURA

*Loch
Lomond*

Firth of Forth

ISLAY

Glasgow   Edinburgh

**UNITED
KINGDOM**

ARRAN

Malin
Head

KINTYRE

*North
Channel*

PENNINES

Newcastle-upon-Tyne

Londonderry

**NORTHERN
IRELAND**

*Lough
Neagh*

*Lower
Lough
Erne*

Belfast

*ISLE OF
MAN*

Solway Firth

*978
Scafell
Pike*   *Lake
Windermere*

Donegal Bay

ACHILL I.

REPUBLIC

IRISH SEA

Leeds

Kingston-upon-Hull

*Lough
Corrib*

*Lough
Ree*

Galway

OF

Liverpool   Manchester   Sheffield

ANGLESEY

Galway Bay

*ARAN
ISLANDS*

IRELAND

Dublin
(Baile Átha Cliath)

*1085
Snowdon*

WALES

CAMBRIAN MOUNTAINS

Trent

*The
Wash*

E N G L A N D

Norwich

Shannon

*Cardigan
Bay*

BIRMINGHAM

Severn

Mouth of
the Shannon

Carnsore
Point

St. George's Channel

St. David's
Head

Thames

LONDON

Thames

Cork

Swansea

Cardiff

Bristol

Dover

Cape
Clear

CELTIC SEA

Bristol Channel

Calais

Lyme Bay

*ISLE OF
WIGHT*

*Beachy
Head*

Strait of Dover

ATLANTIC

*ISLES OF
SCILLY*

Land's
End

Lizard
Point

Plymouth

Start
Point

English Channel

FRANCE

OCEAN

*Cap de
la Hague*

**CHANNEL
ISLANDS
(U.K.)**

ALDERNEY

Cherbourg

*Baie de
la Seine*

Le Hávre

SARK

GUERNSEY

JERSEY

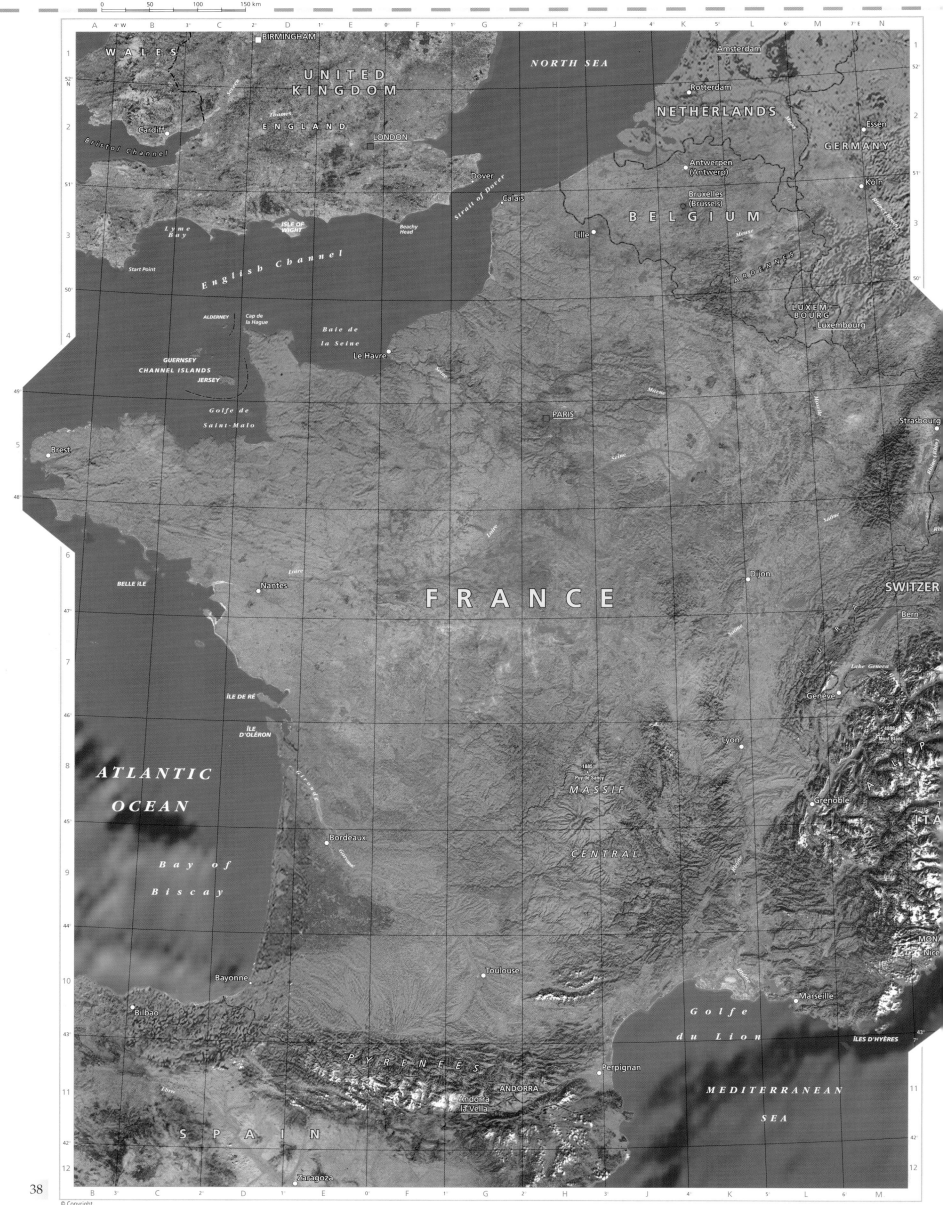

Scale 1 : 3 900 000

0   50   100   150 km

© Copyright

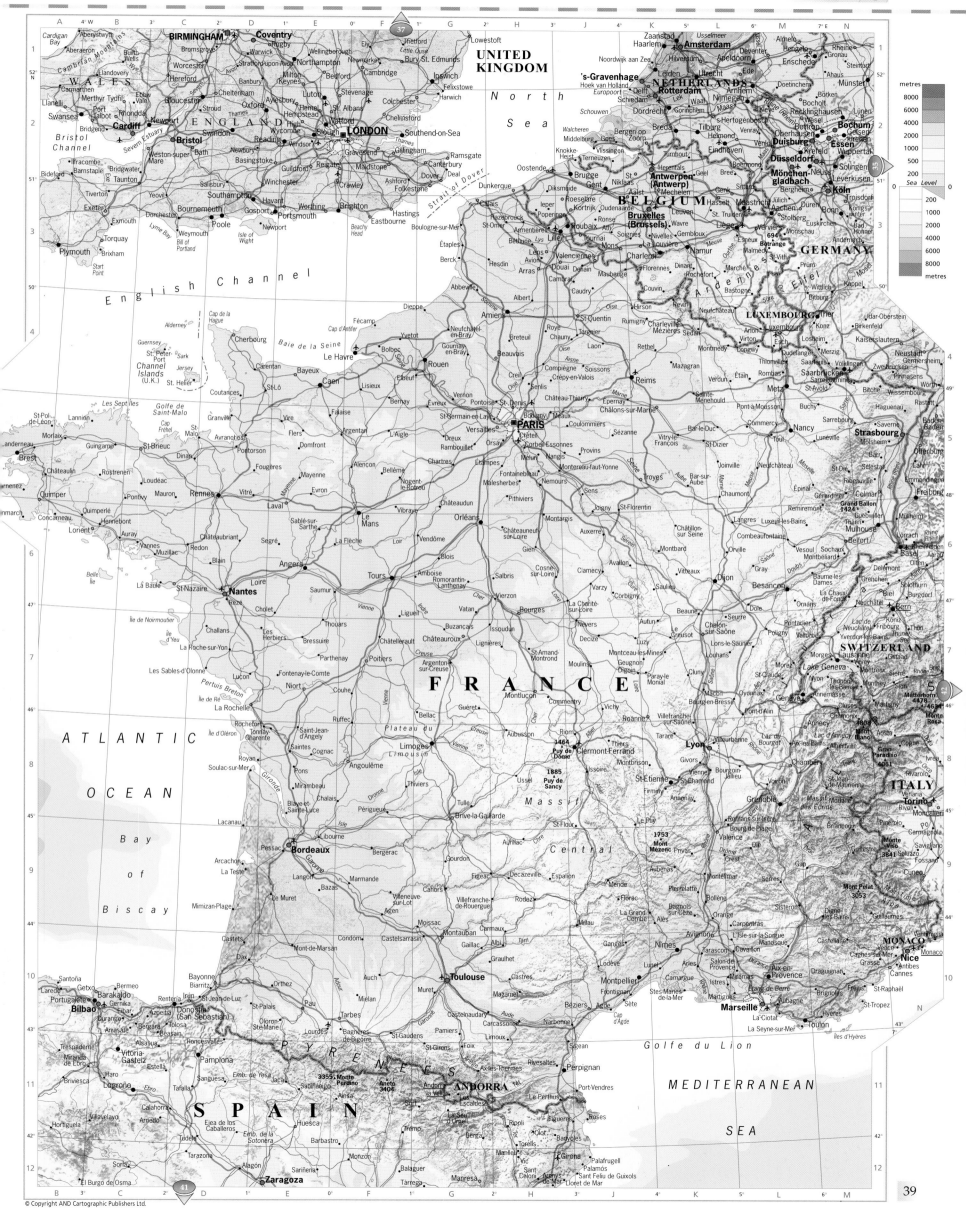

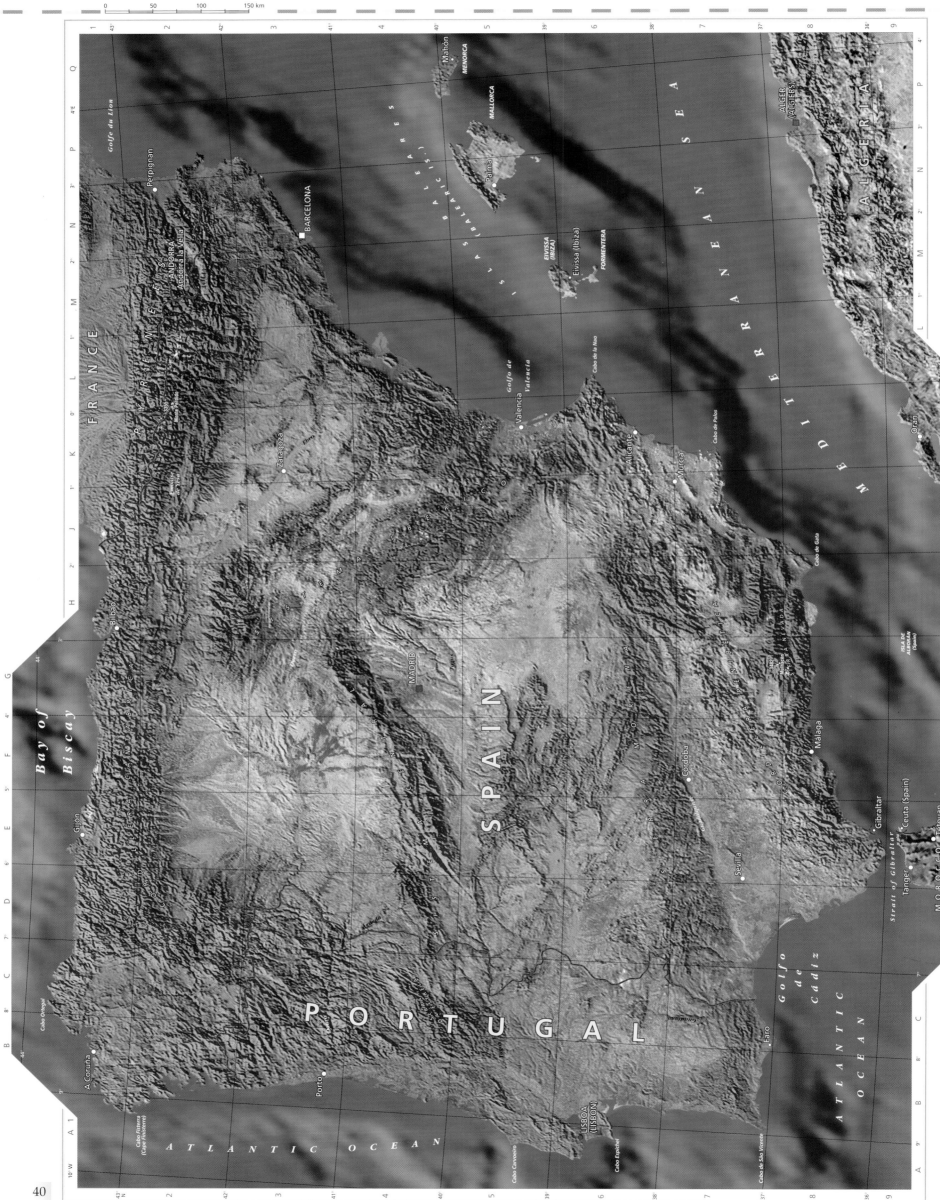

Scale 1 : 3 900 000

0   50   100   150 km

Map labels:

Bay of Biscay

ATLANTIC OCEAN

FRANCE

PYRENEES

ANDORRA
Andorra la Vella

Perpignan

BARCELONA

Golfe du Lion

MENORCA
Mahón

MALLORCA
Palma

ISLAS (BALEARIC IS.)

EIVISSA (IBIZA)
Eivissa (Ibiza)
FORMENTERA

BALEARIC SEA

MEDITERRANEAN SEA

ALGERIA

ALGER (ALGIERS)

Oran

ISLA DE
ALBORAN
(Spain)

A Coruña
Cabo Ortegal
Cabo Prior

Gijón
Oviedo

Bilbao

Zaragoza
Ebro

MADRID

Valencia
Golfo de Valencia

Cabo de la Nao

Alicante

Murcia
Cabo de Palos

Cabo de Gata

Córdoba

Sevilla

Málaga

Gibraltar
Ceuta (Spain)
Strait of Gibraltar
Tánger
Tetuán
MOROCCO

SPAIN

PORTUGAL

Porto

LISBOA (LISBON)
Cabo Espichel

Faro
Cabo de São Vicente
Cabo Carvoeiro

Golfo de Cádiz

ATLANTIC OCEAN

SIERRA MORENA

SIERRA NEVADA

SISTEMA IBERICO

SISTEMA CENTRAL

CORDILLERA CANTABRICA

CORDILLERA BÉTICA

Cabo Finisterre
(Cape Finisterre)

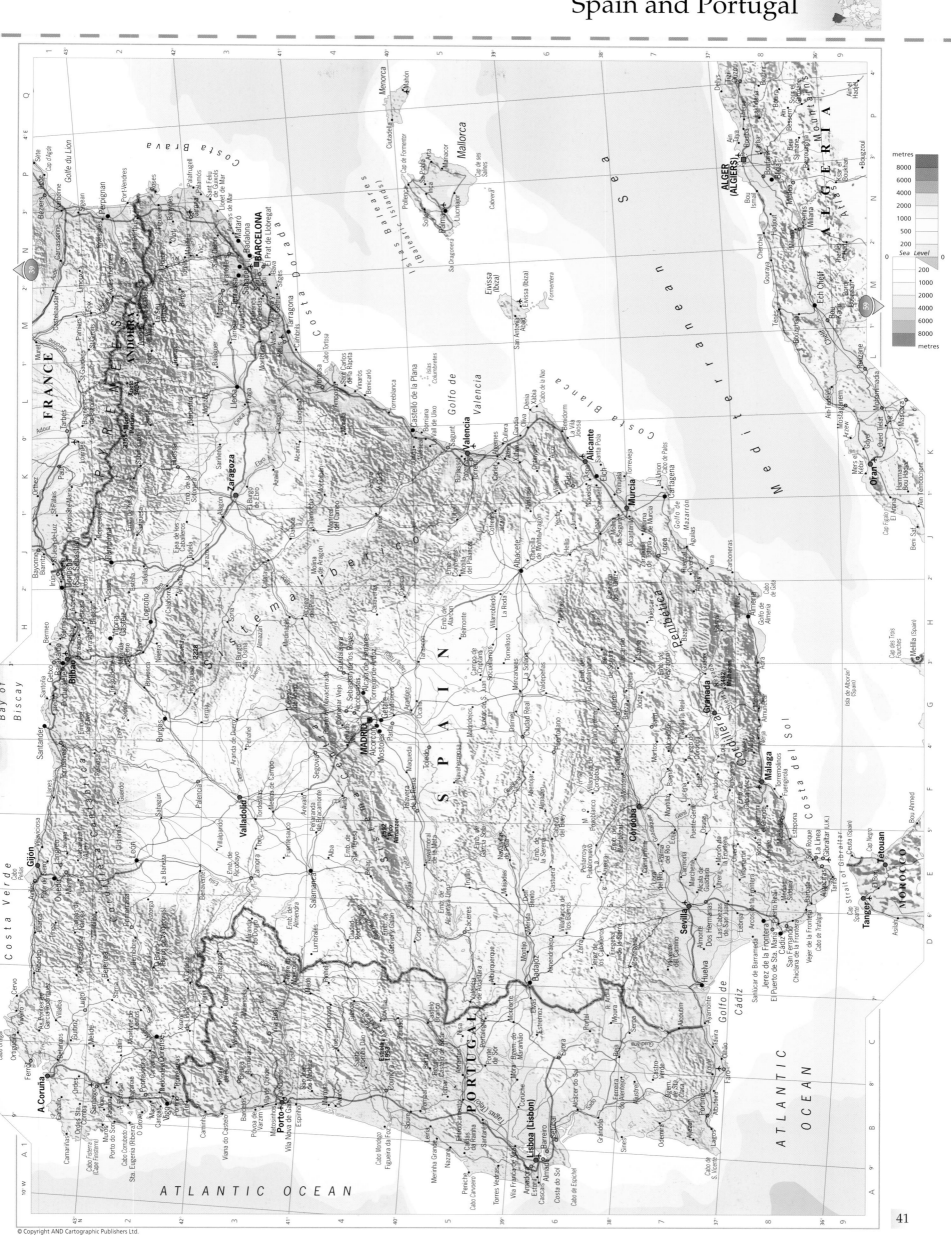

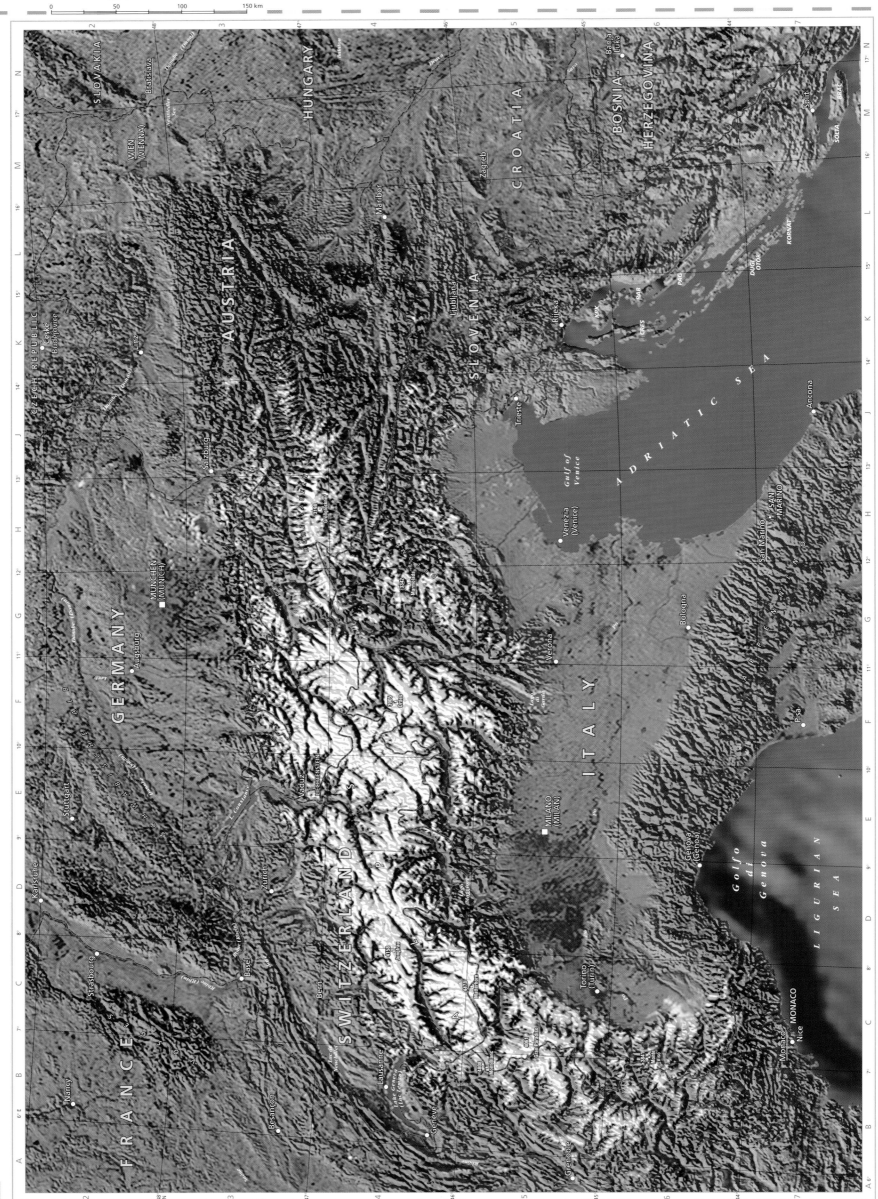

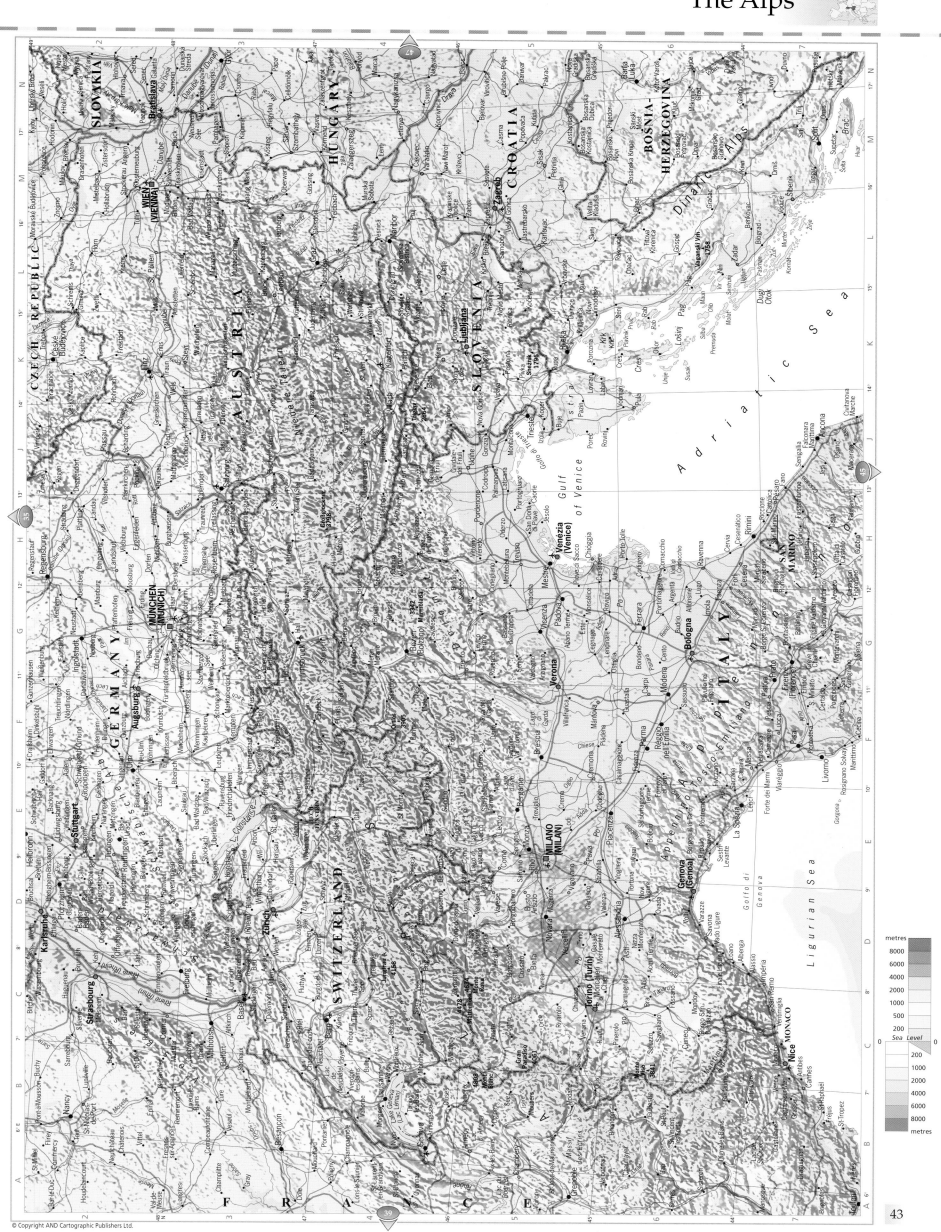

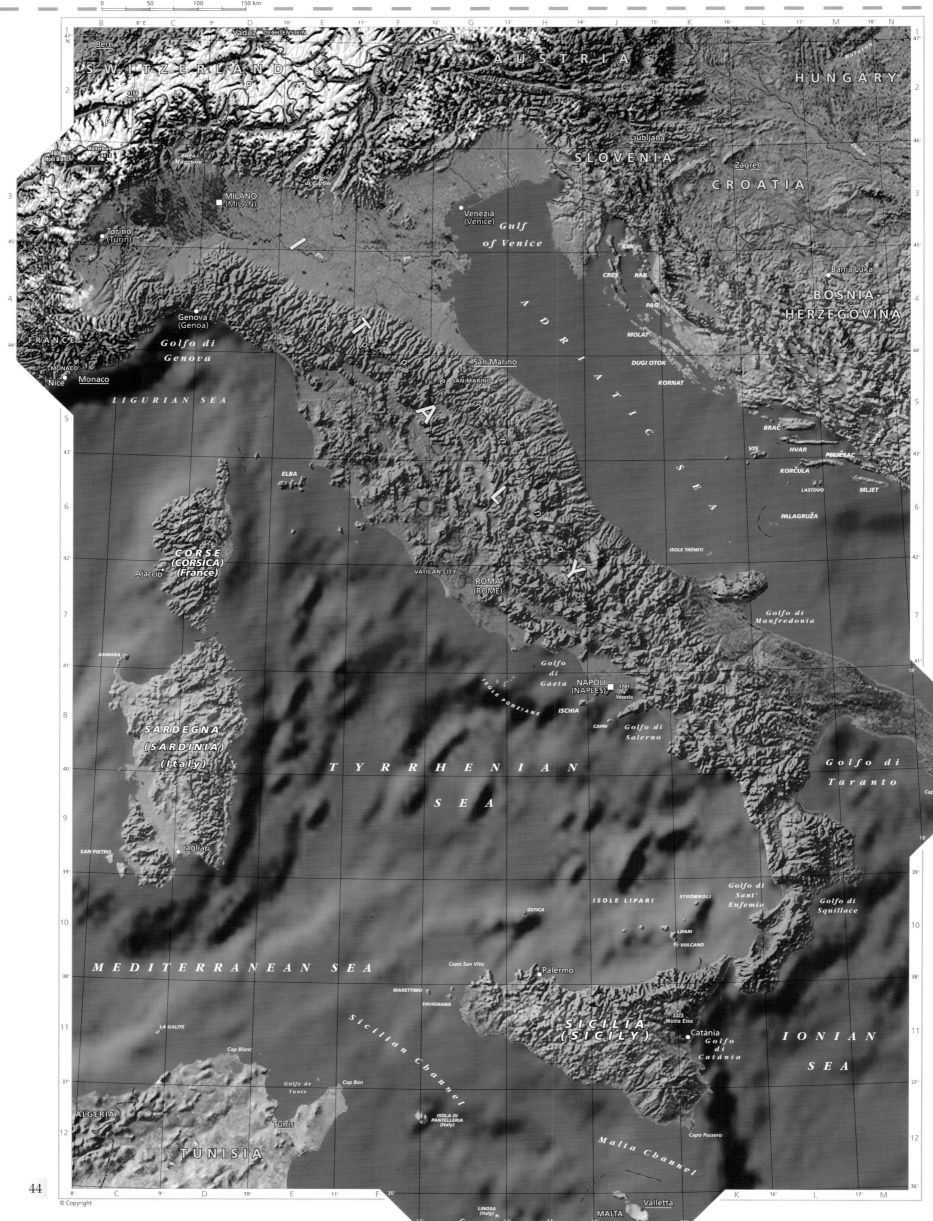

Scale 1 : 3 900 000

0   50   100   150 km

© Copyright

0 50 100 150 km

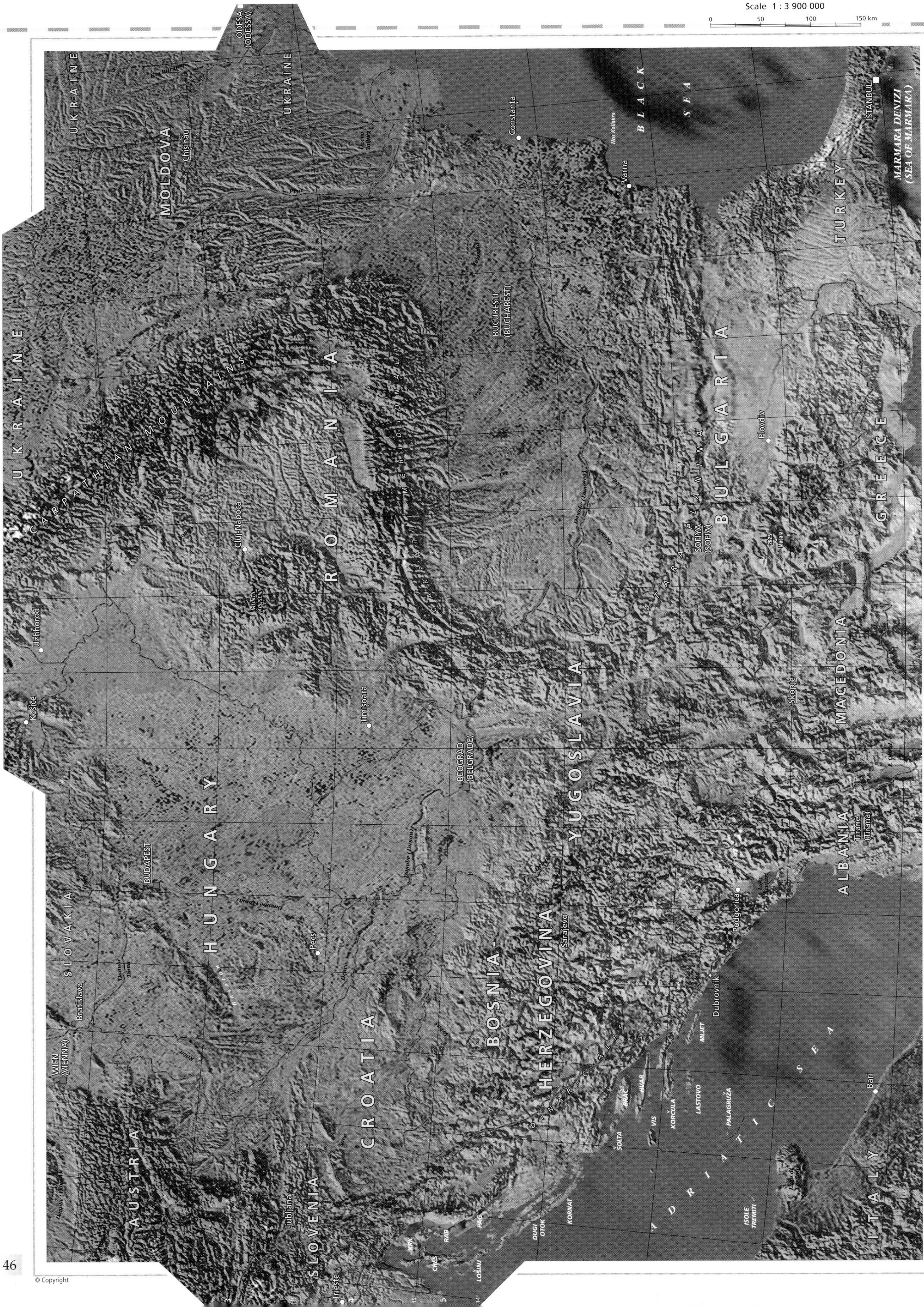

UKRAINE

MOLDOVA

Chişinău

UKRAINE

ODESA
(ODESSA)

B L A C K   S E A

Nos Kaliakra

Constanţa

Varna

R O M A N I A

C A R P A T H I A N   M O U N T A I N S

MUNTII
APUSENI

Cluj-Napoca

BUCUREŞTI
(BUCHAREST)

Argeş

MERIDIONALI

CARPATI

Dunărea (Danube)

B U L G A R I A

Plovdiv

S T A R A   P L A N I N A

SOFIYA
(SOFIA)

T U R K E Y

ISTANBUL

MARMARA DENIZI
(SEA OF MARMARA)

G R E E C E

Uzhhorod

Košice

Timişoara

BEOGRAD
(BELGRADE)

Y U G O S L A V I A

Skopje

M A C E D O N I A

A U S T R I A

S L O V A K I A

Bratislava

WIEN
(VIENNA)

H U N G A R Y

BUDAPEST

Pécs

Danube (Dunărea)

B O S N I A -
H E R Z E G O V I N A

Sarajevo

Podgorica

Tiranë
(Tirana)

A L B A N I A

S L O V E N I A

C R O A T I A

Ljubljana

Trieste

D I N A R I C   A L P S

Dubrovnik

MLJET

LASTOVO

PALAGRUŽA

KORČULA

VIS

HVAR

BRAČ

ŠOLTA

Bari

I T A L Y

ISOLE
TREMITI

A D R I A T I C   S E A

DUGI
OTOK

KORNAT

PAG

RAB

CRES

LOŠINJ

46

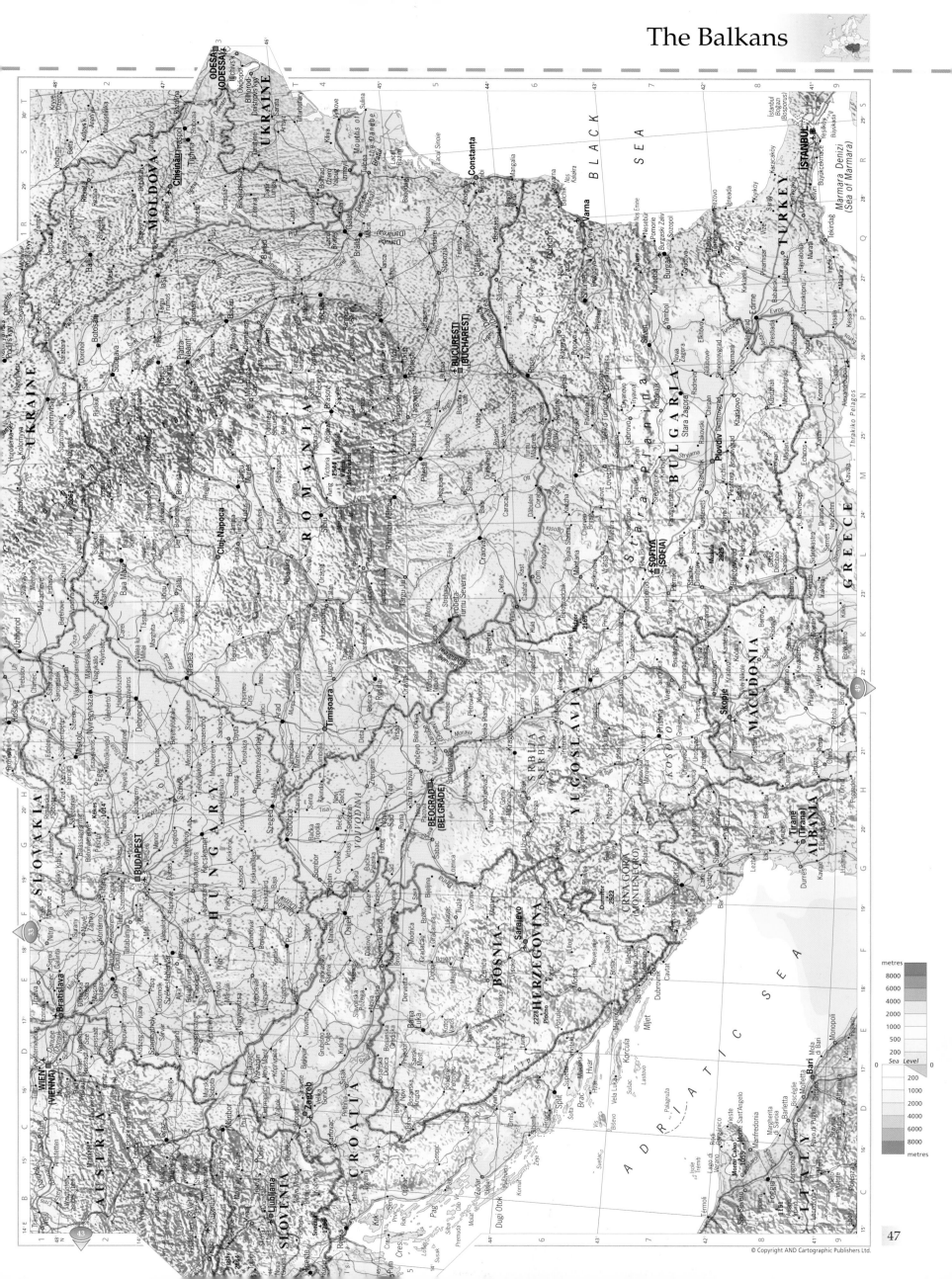

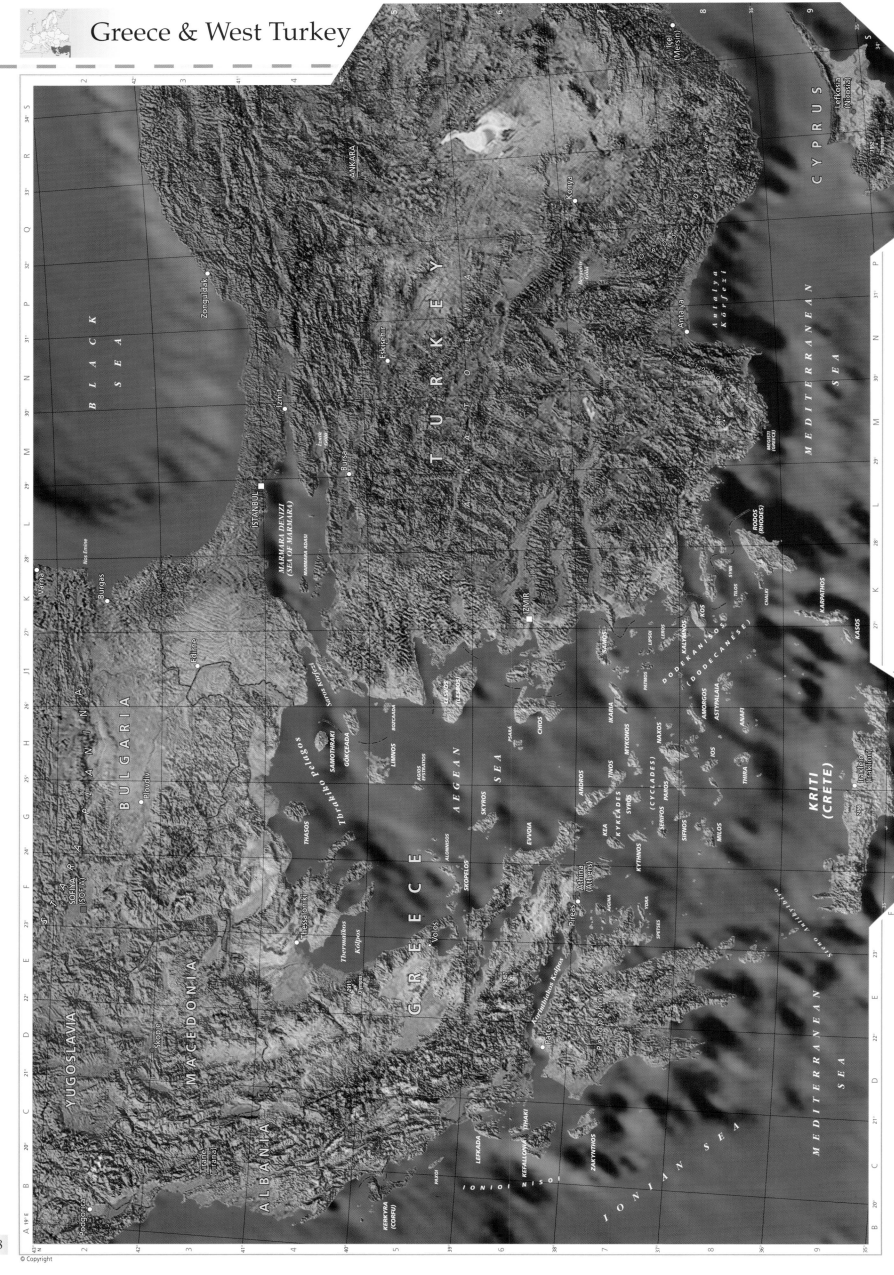

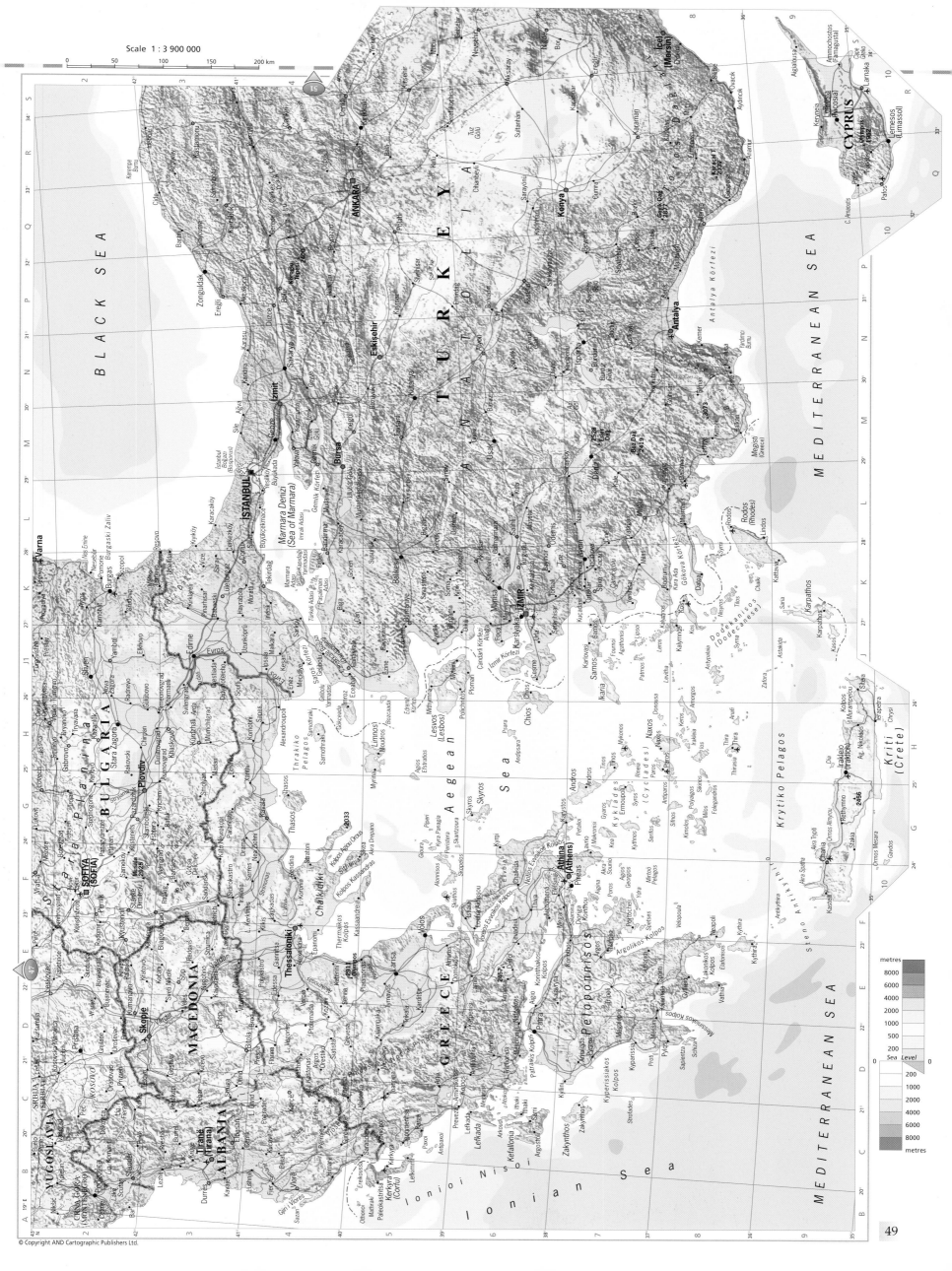

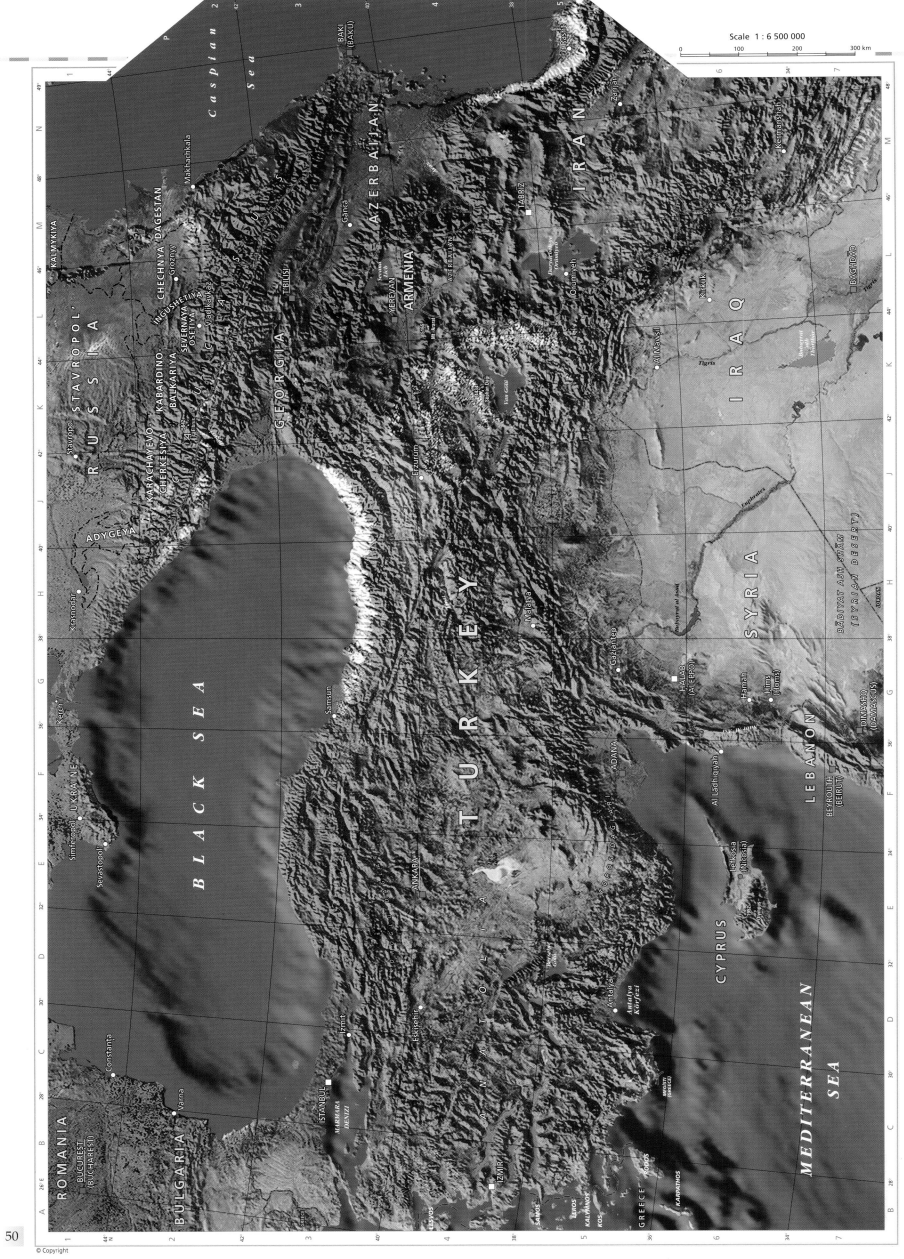

Scale 1 : 6 500 000

0   100   200   300 km

© Copyright

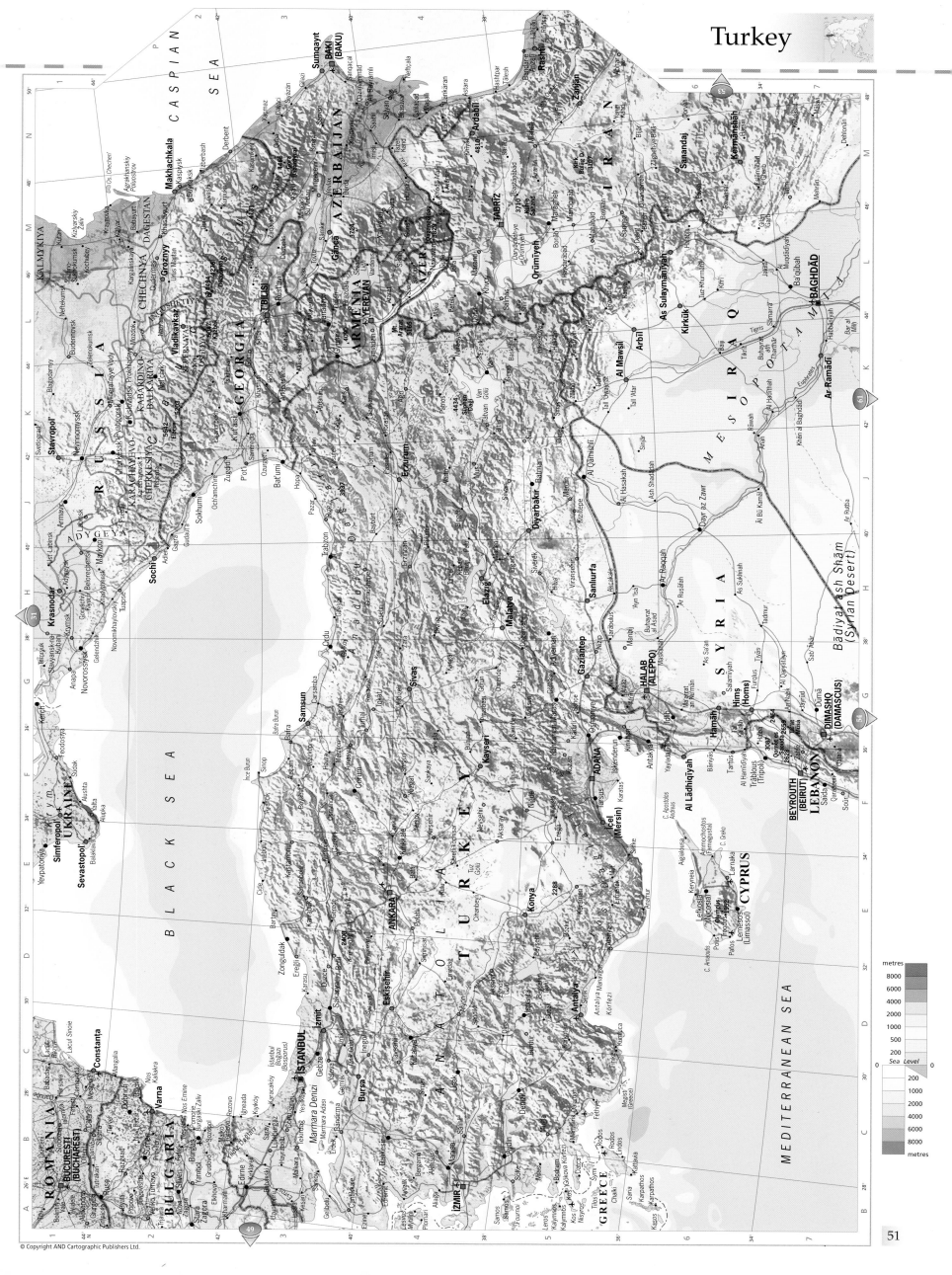

Turkey

51

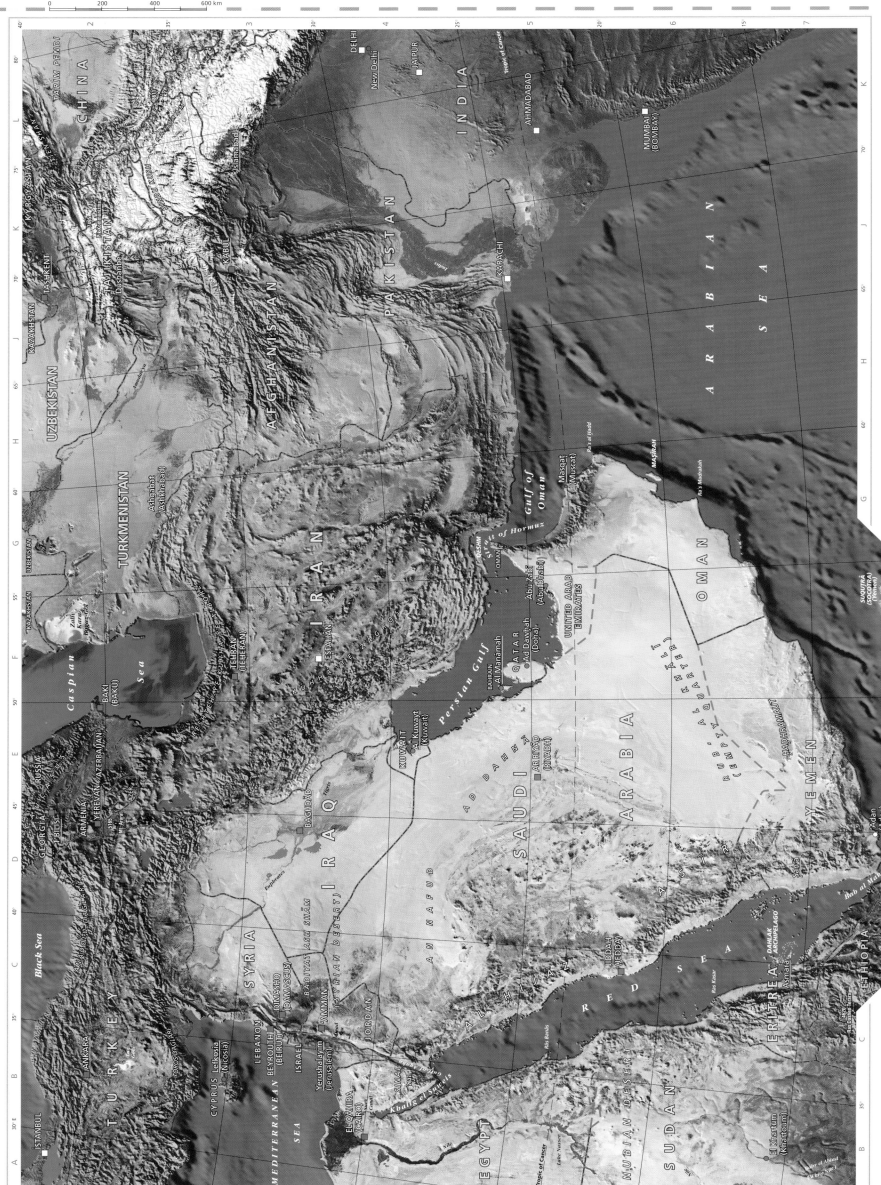

Scale 1 : 14 300 000

0   200   400   600 km

Black Sea

ISTANBUL

ANKARA

TURKEY

TOROS DAĞLARI

CYPRUS Lefkosia
        (Nicosia)

LEBANON
BEYROUTH
(BEIRUT)
DIMASHQ
(DAMASCUS)
ISRAEL
Yerushalayim
(Jerusalem)

*MEDITERRANEAN
SEA*

EL QÂHIRA
(CAIRO)

Suez Canal

SINAI

Khalig el Suweis

EGYPT

El Khartûm
(Khartoum)

Lake Nasser

NUBIAN DESERT

SUDAN

SYRIA

AMMAN

JORDAN

BADIYAT ASH SHÂM
(SYRIAN DESERT)

AL HIJAZ

AN NAFUD

Euphrates

Tigris

BAGHDÂD

IRAQ

AL KUWAYT
(Kuwait)

KUWAIT

AD DAHNÂ

AR RIYÂD
(RIYADH)

SAUDI ARABIA

RUB' AL KHÂLI
(EMPTY QUARTER)

Persian Gulf

BAHRAIN
Al Manâmah

QATAR
Ad Dawhah
(Doha)

Abu Zabî
(Abu Dhabi)

UNITED ARAB
EMIRATES

OMAN

AL HAJAR

HADHRAMAUT

YEMEN

'Adan
(Aden)

Bab al Mandeb

RED SEA

JIDDAH
(JEDDA)

Ras Kasar

Ras Banâs

RED SEA

DAHLAK
ARCHIPELAGO

Asmara

ERITREA

ETHIOPIA

Strait of Hormuz

QESHM
Oman

Masqat
(Muscat)

Ra's al Hadd

*Gulf of
Oman*

Ra's Madrakah

MASIRAH

SUQUTRÁ
(SOCOTRA)
(Yemen)

*A   R   A   B   I   A   N

S   E   A*

KARACHI

Indus

PAKISTAN

INDIA

New Delhi

DELHI

JAIPUR

AHMADABAD

MUMBAI
(BOMBAY)

Tropic of Cancer

AFGHANISTAN

KÂBUL

Islamabad

HINDU KUSH

TAJIKISTAN

Dushanbe

TASHKENT

UZBEKISTAN

KYRGYZSTAN

TIEN SHAN

TARIM PENDI

CHINA

KAZAKHSTAN

TURKMENISTAN

Aşgabat
(Ashkhabad)

IRAN

TEHRÂN
(TEHERAN)

ESFAHAN

ZAGROS

KÛH-E

*Caspian

Sea*

BAKÎ
(BAKU)

AZERBAIJAN

ARMENIA
YEREVAN

GEORGIA
TBILISI

RUSSIA

BÜYÜK AĞRI DAĞI

Zaliv
Kara-Bogaz-Gol

Tropic of Cancer

52
© Copyright

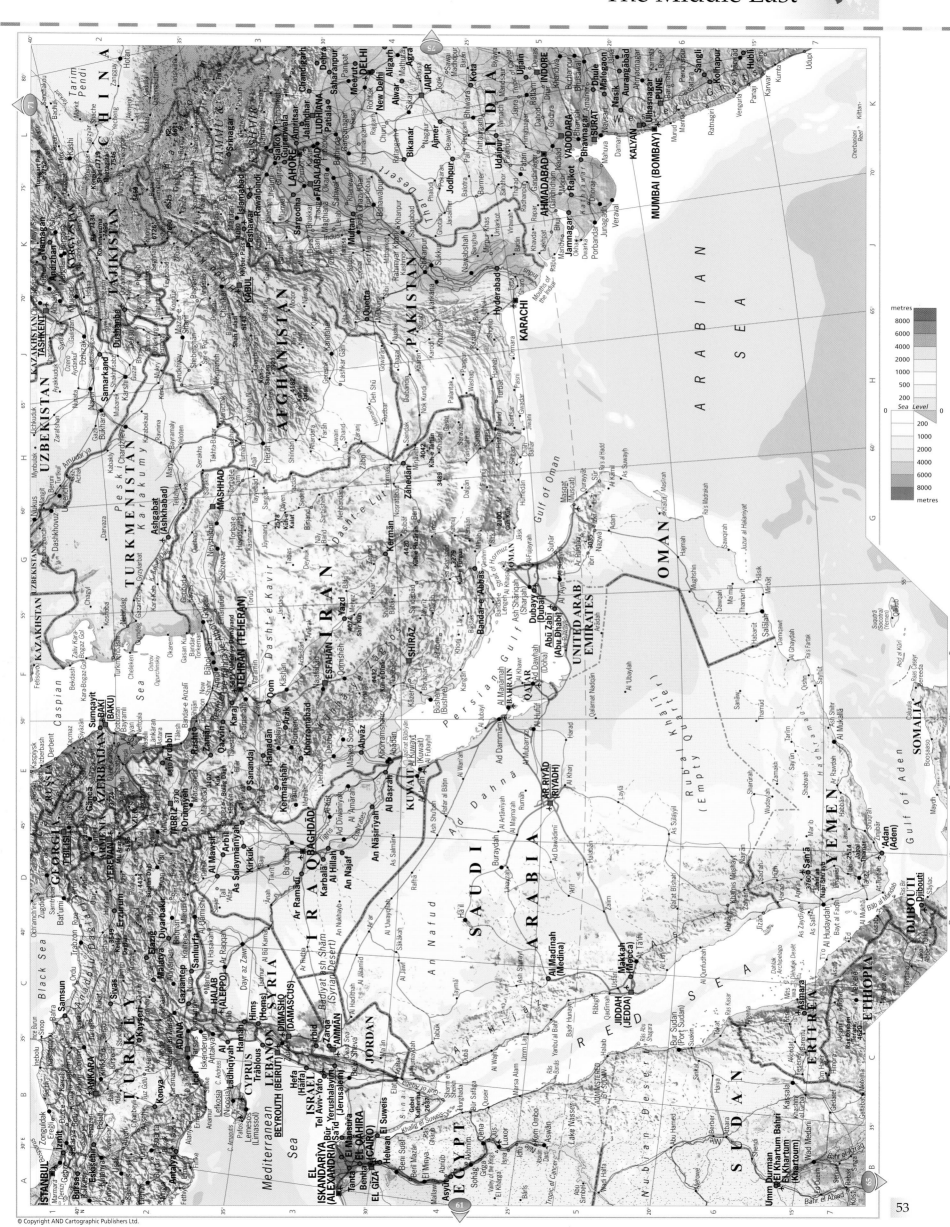

Scale 1 : 3 200 000

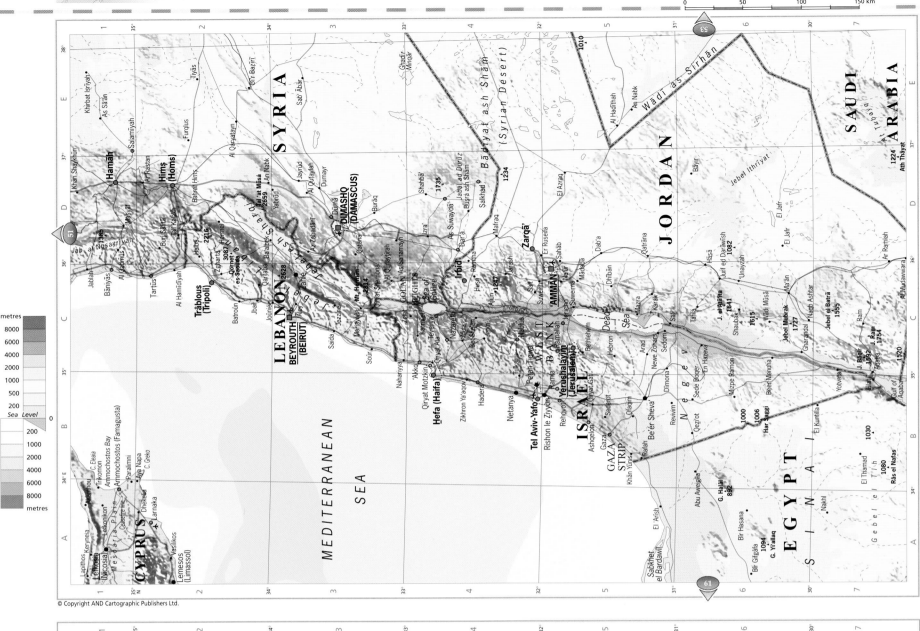

Scale 1 : 6 500 000

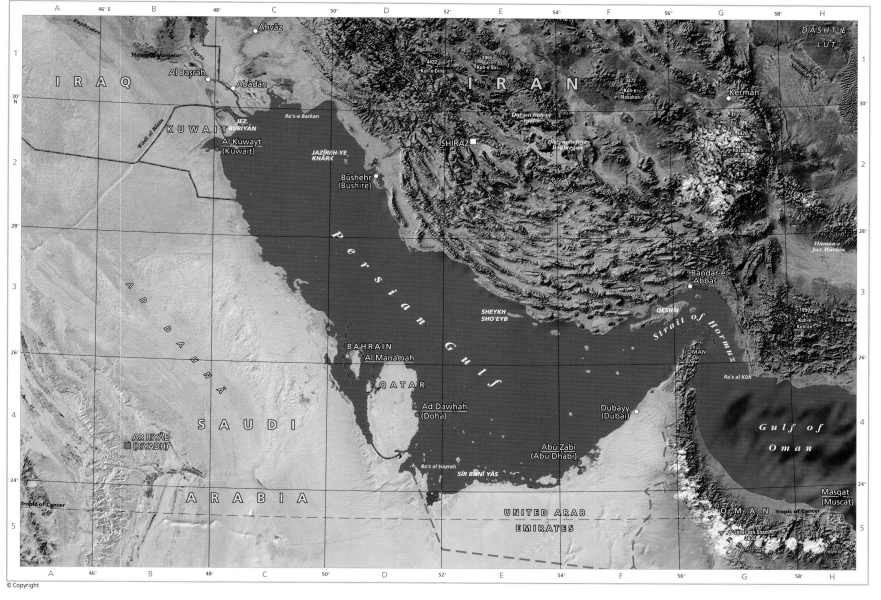

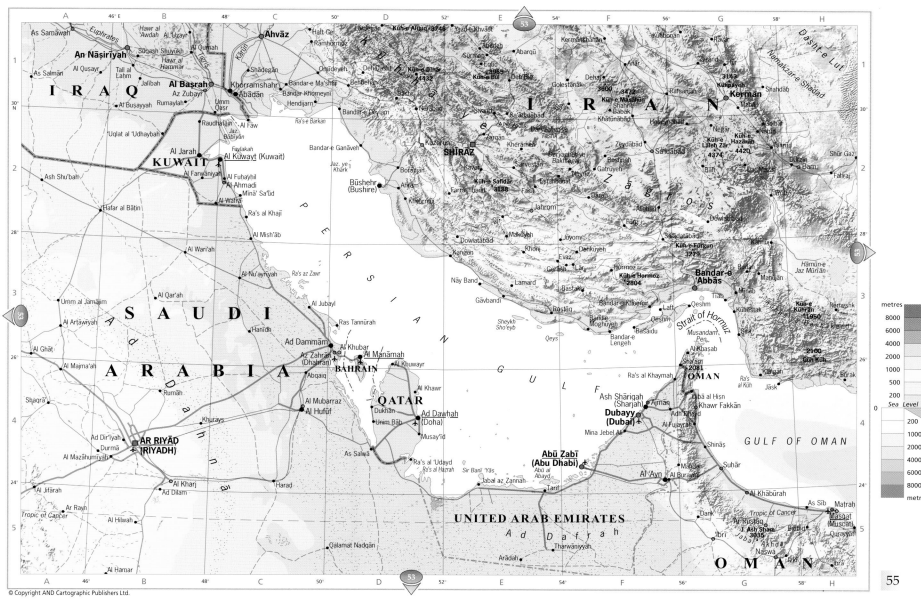

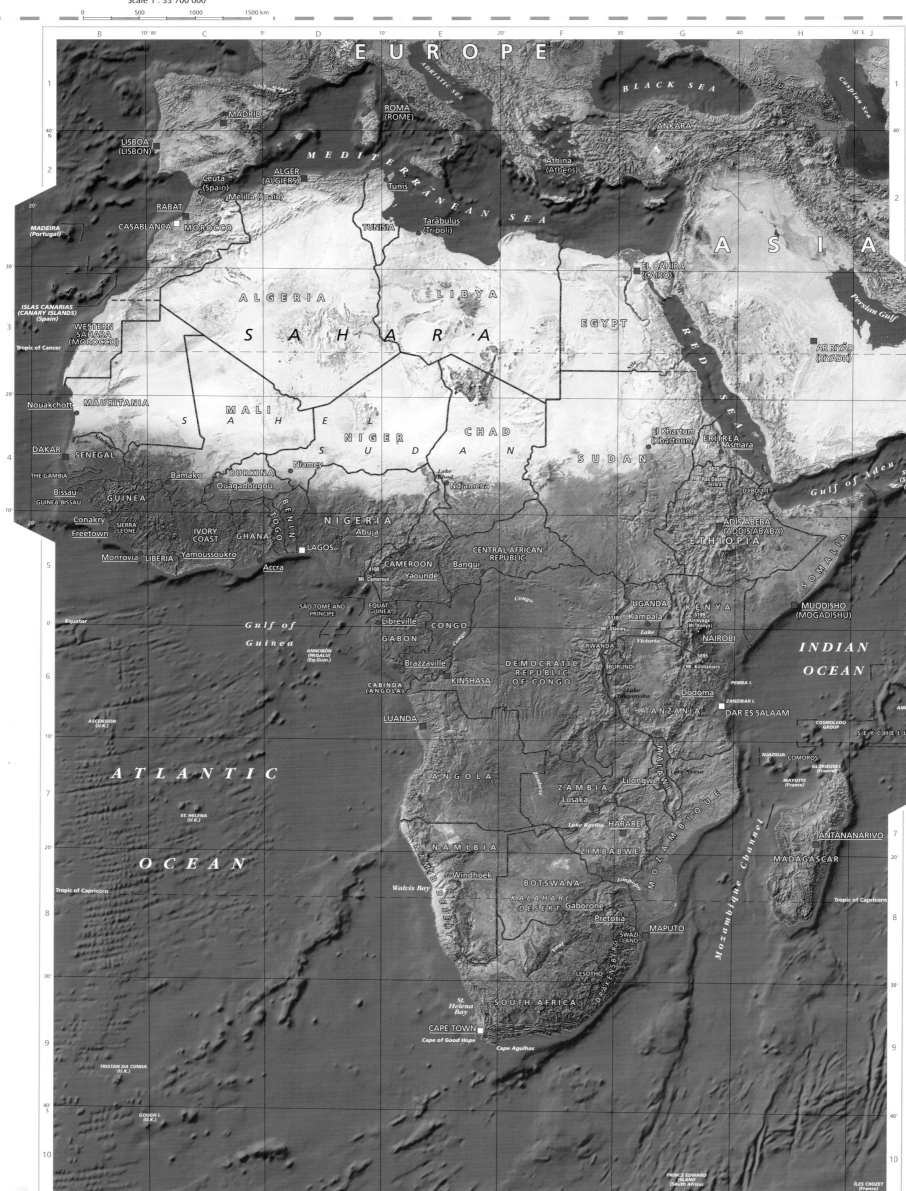

Scale 1 : 33 700 000

EUROPE

ASIA

Map labels:

BLACK SEA
CAUCASUS
Caspian Sea
ANKARA
ADRIATIC SEA
Athina (Athens)
MADRID
ROMA (ROME)
MEDITERRANEAN SEA
LISBOA (LISBON)
Tunis
ALGER (ALGIERS)
Ceuta (Spain)
Melilla (Spain)
RABAT
Tarãbulus (Tripoli)
EL QÃHIRA (CAIRO)
MADEIRA (Portugal)
CASABLANCA
MOROCCO
TUNISIA
Persian Gulf
ISLAS CANARIAS (CANARY ISLANDS) (Spain)
ALGERIA
LIBYA
EGYPT
RED SEA
AR RIYÄD (RIYADH)
WESTERN SAHARA (MOROCCO)
SAHARA
Tropic of Cancer
Nile
Nouakchott
MAURITANIA
MALI
NIGER
CHAD
El Khartum (Khartoum)
ERITREA
DAKAR
SENEGAL
SAHEL
SUDAN
SUDAN
Asmara
Gulf of Aden
THE GAMBIA
Bamako
Niamey
BURKINA
Lake Chad
Ndjamena
4620 Ras Dashen Terara
DJIBOUTI
SUQU (SOCO (Yeme
Bissau
Ouagadougou
GUINEA BISSAU
GUINEA
NIGERIA
ADIS ABEBA (ADDIS ABABA)
Conakry
SIERRA LEONE
IVORY COAST
GHANA
BENIN
TOGO
Abuja
CENTRAL AFRICAN REPUBLIC
ETHIOPIA
Freetown
Monrovia
LIBERIA
Yamoussoukro
Accra
LAGOS
CAMEROON
Bangui
SOMALIA
4100 Mt. Cameroun
Yaoundé
SÃO TOMÉ AND PRÍNCIPE
EQUAT. GUINEA
UGANDA
5199 Kirinyaga (Mt. Kenya)
KENYA
MUQDISHO (MOGADISHU)
Equator
Congo
5110 Mt. Stanley
Kampala
NAIROBI
INDIAN OCEAN
Gulf of Guinea
Libreville
CONGO
GABON
RWANDA
Lake Victoria
ANNOBÓN (PAGALU) (Eq.Guin.)
Brazzaville
DEMOCRATIC REPUBLIC OF CONGO
BURUNDI
5895 Mt. Kilimanjaro
PEMBA I.
CABINDA (ANGOLA)
KINSHASA
Congo
Lake Tanganyika
Dodoma
ZANZIBAR I.
SEYC
ASCENSION (U.K.)
LUANDA
TANZANIA
DAR ES SALAAM
COSMOLEDO GROUP
AMIRANTE
ATLANTIC
ANGOLA
MALAWI
Lake Nyasa
NJAZIDJA
COMOROS
SEYCHELLES
Zambezi
ZAMBIA
Lilongwe
GLORIEUSES (France)
ST. HELENA (U.K.)
Lusaka
MAYOTTE (France)
Lake Kariba
HARARE
MOZAMBIQUE
OCEAN
NAMIBIA
ZIMBABWE
ANTANANARIVO
ZAMBEZI DESERT
Windhoek
BOTSWANA
Limpopo
Mozambique Channel
MADAGASCAR
Tropic of Capricorn
Walvis Bay
KALAHARI DESERT
Gaborone
Tropic of Capricorn
Pretoria
SWAZI LAND
MAPUTO
Orange
SOUTH AFRICA
DRAKENSBERG
LESOTHO
Vaal
TRISTAN DA CUNHA (U.K.)
St. Helena Bay
SOUTH AFRICA
CAPE TOWN
Cape of Good Hope
Cape Aguilhas
GOUGH I. (U.K.)
PRINCE EDWARD ISLAND (South Africa)
ÎLES CROZET (France)

56

© Copyright

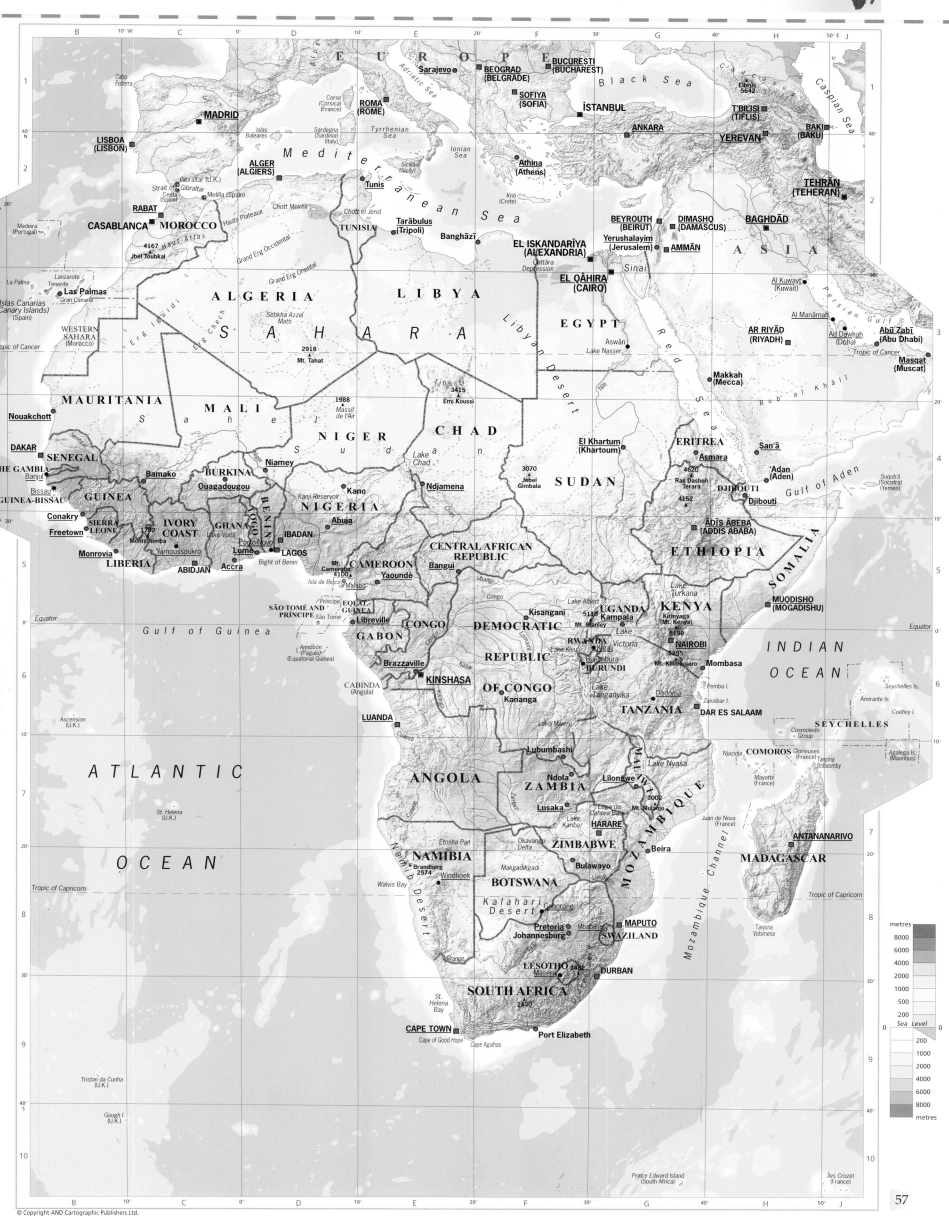

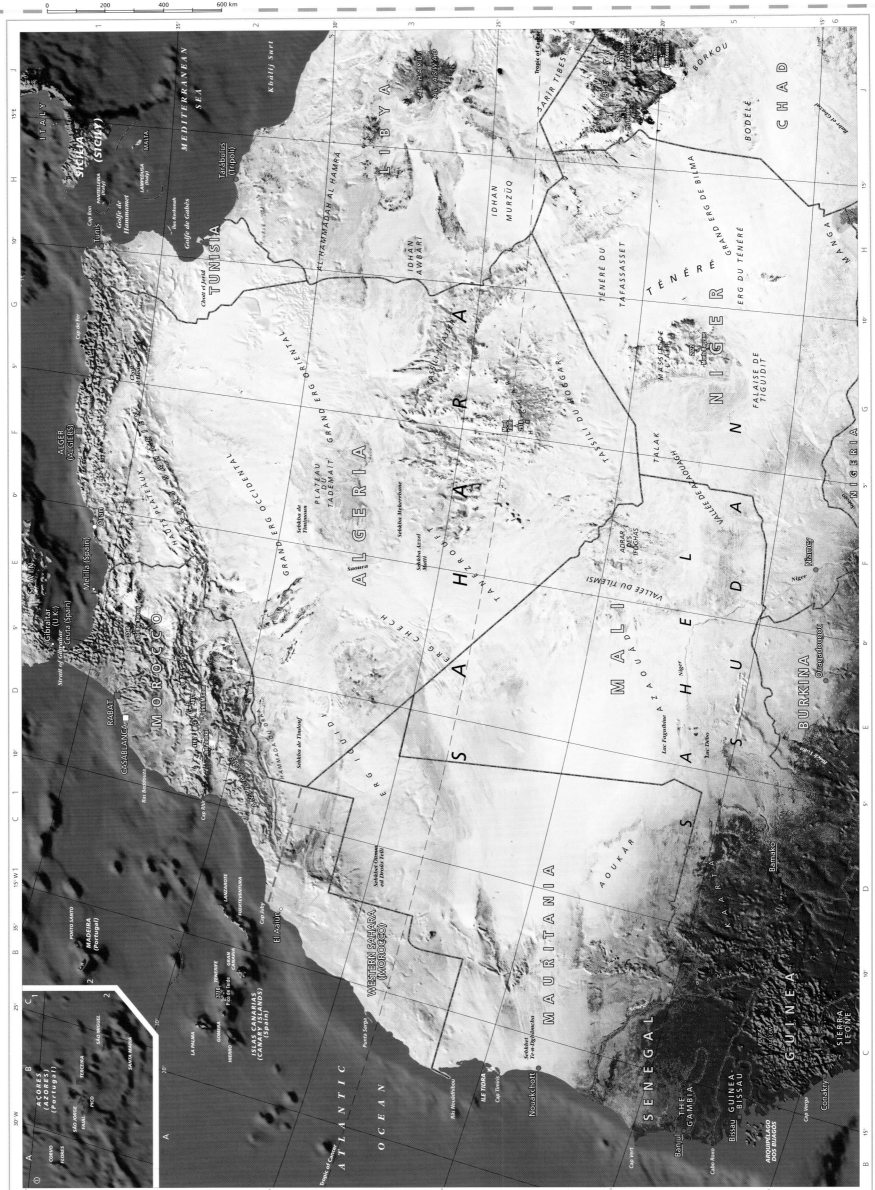

Scale 1 : 13 000 000

0   200   400   600 km

58

© Copyright

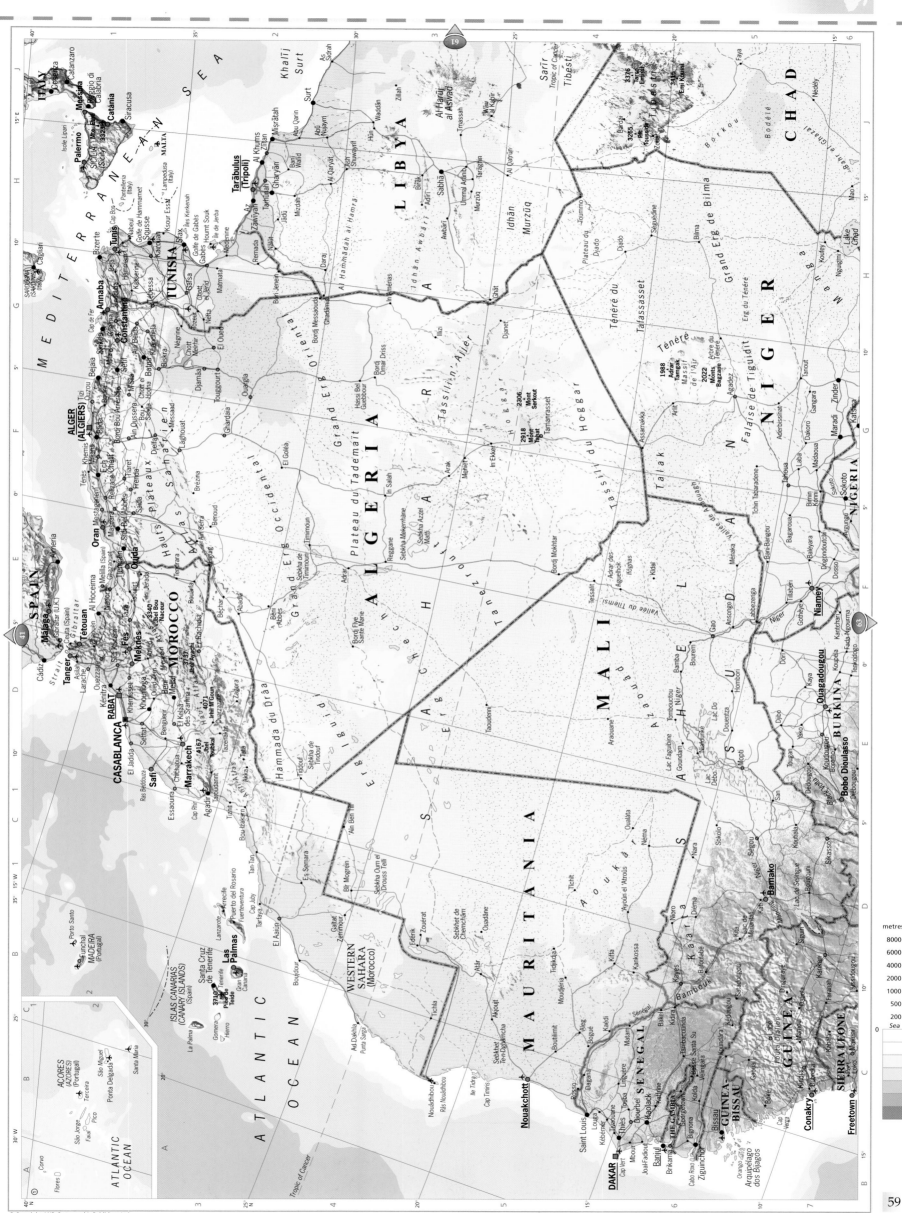

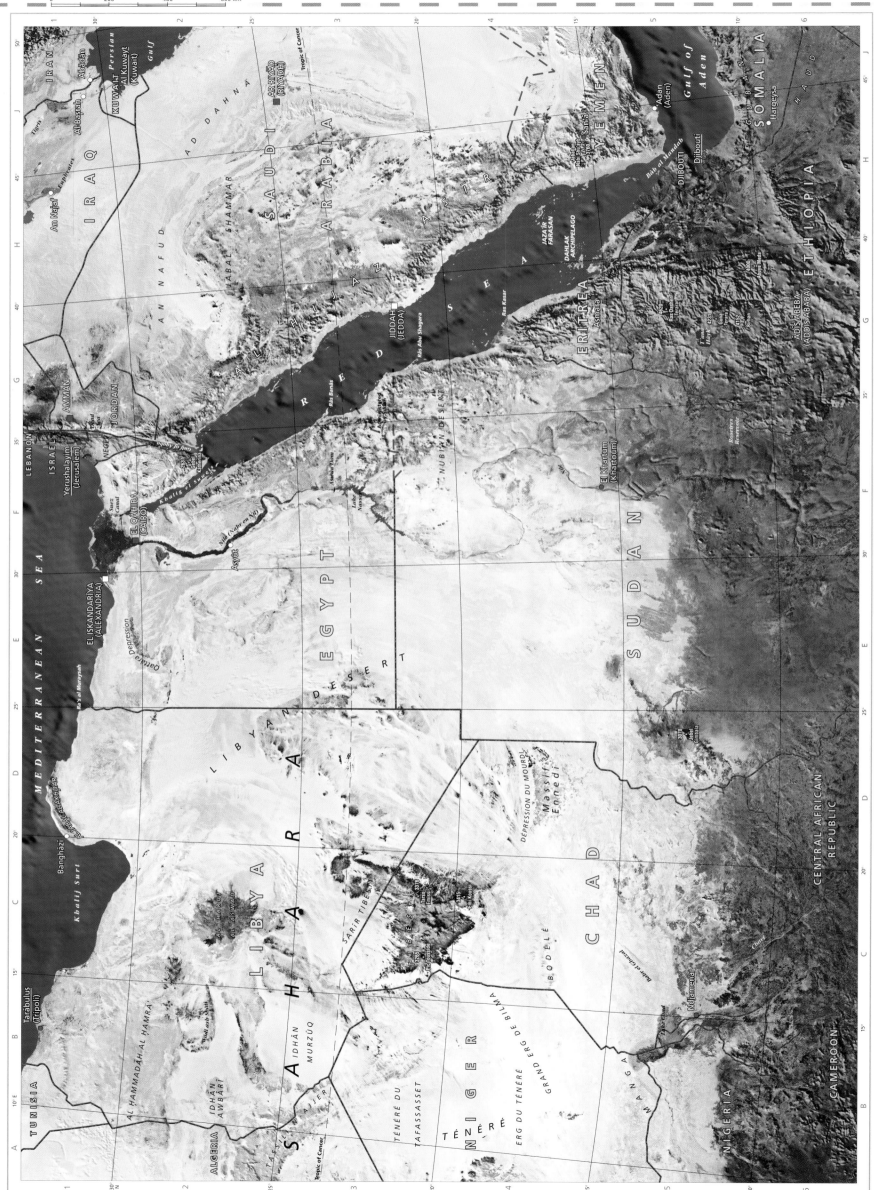

Scale 1 : 13 000 000

0   200   400   600 km

MEDITERRANEAN SEA

TUNISIA

ALGERIA

LIBYA

Tarābulus
(Tripoli)

Banghāzī

Khalīj Surt

AL 'AQĀBAT AL KHAQRA'

AL HAMMĀDAH AL HAMRA'

Wādī ash Shāṭī

IDHĀN AWBĀRĪ

IDHĀN MURZŪQ

SAHARA

AL 'AQĀBĀR

AL ASWAD

SARĪR TIBESTĪ

T I B E S T I

3300
Emi Koussi

S A H A R A

TÉNÉRÉ DU TAFASSASSET

TÉNÉRÉ

ERG DU TÉNÉRÉ

GRAND ERG DE BILMA

NIGER

CHAD

B O D É L É

Bahr el Ghazal

DÉPRESSION DU MOURDI

Massif Ennedi

LIBYAN DESERT

EGYPT

El Iskandarīya
(Alexandria)

Qattara Depression

Ra's al Murays̄ah

El Qāhira
(Cairo)

Suez Canal

Asyūṭ

Nile (Nahr en Nīl)

Lake Nasser

Yerushalayim
(Jerusalem)

ISRAEL

LEBANON

JORDAN

AMMAN

Dead Sea

NEGEV

Gulf of Suez

Khalīj el Suweis

Jabal Katrina
2637

Gulf of Aqaba

SINAI

JORDAN

IRAQ

An Najaf

Euphrates

Al Başrah

KUWAIT

Al Kuwayt
(Kuwait)

Persian Gulf

Abādān

IRAN

ARRIYĀḌ
(RIYADH)

S A U D I   A R A B I A

AD DAHNĀ'

AN NAFUD

JABAL SHAMMAR

A L   H I J Ā Z

A S Ī R

JIDDAH
(JEDDA)

Rās Bânâs

RED SEA

Administered by Sudan

NUBIAN DESERT

SUDAN

El Khartum
(Khartoum)

Roseires Reservoir

JAZĀ'IR FARASAN

Rās Kasar

DAHLAK ARCHIPELAGO

ERITREA

Asmara

YEMEN

San'ā'

Bab al Mandab

DJIBOUTI

Djibouti

'Adan
(Aden)

Gulf of Aden

GULF

SOMALIA

Hargeysa

HAUD

ETHIOPIA

ADĪS ABĒBA
(ADDIS ABABA)

Tropic of Cancer

Tropic of Cancer

NIGERIA

Ndjamena

MANGA

Tyo Canal

CAMEROON

CENTRAL AFRICAN REPUBLIC

60

© Copyright

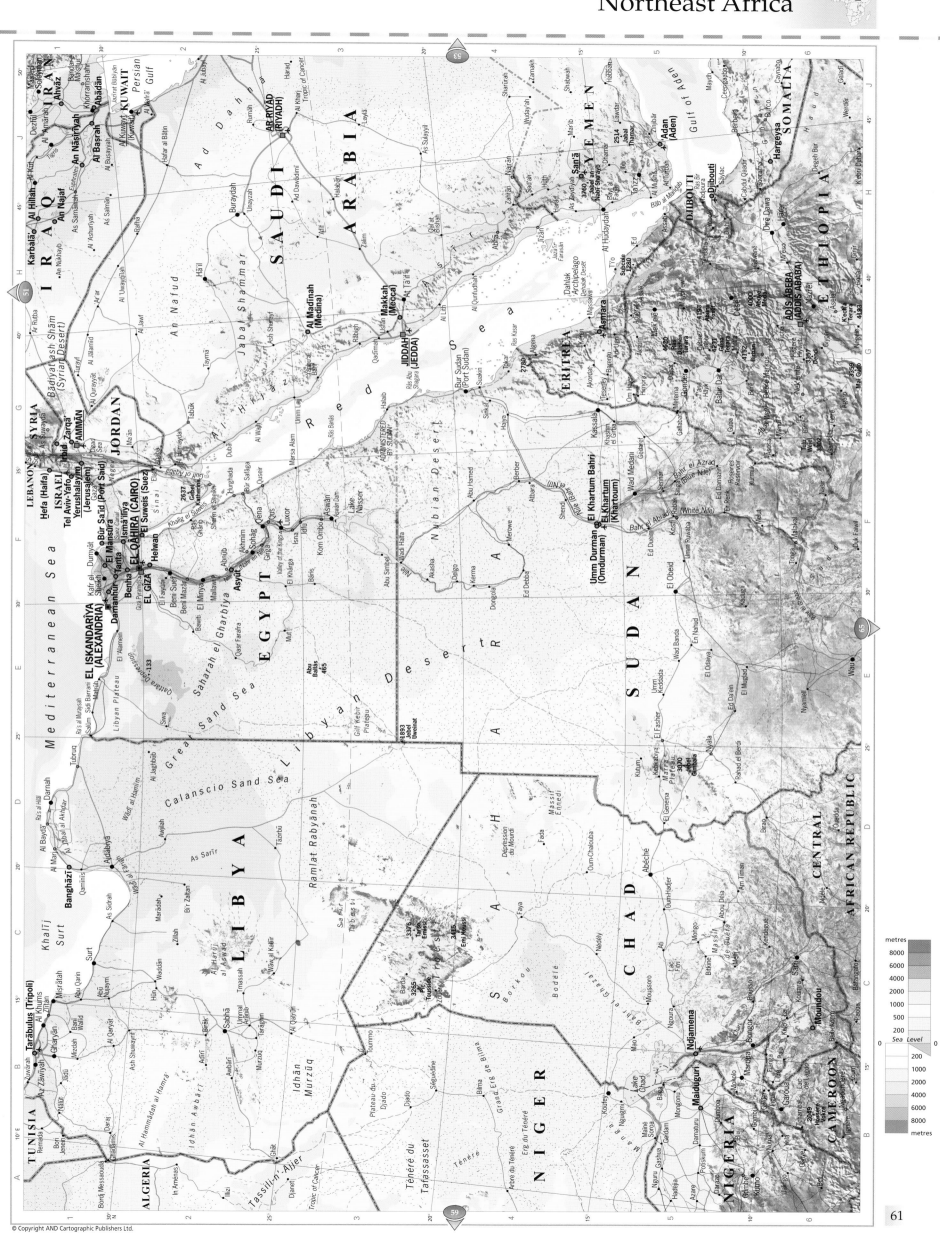

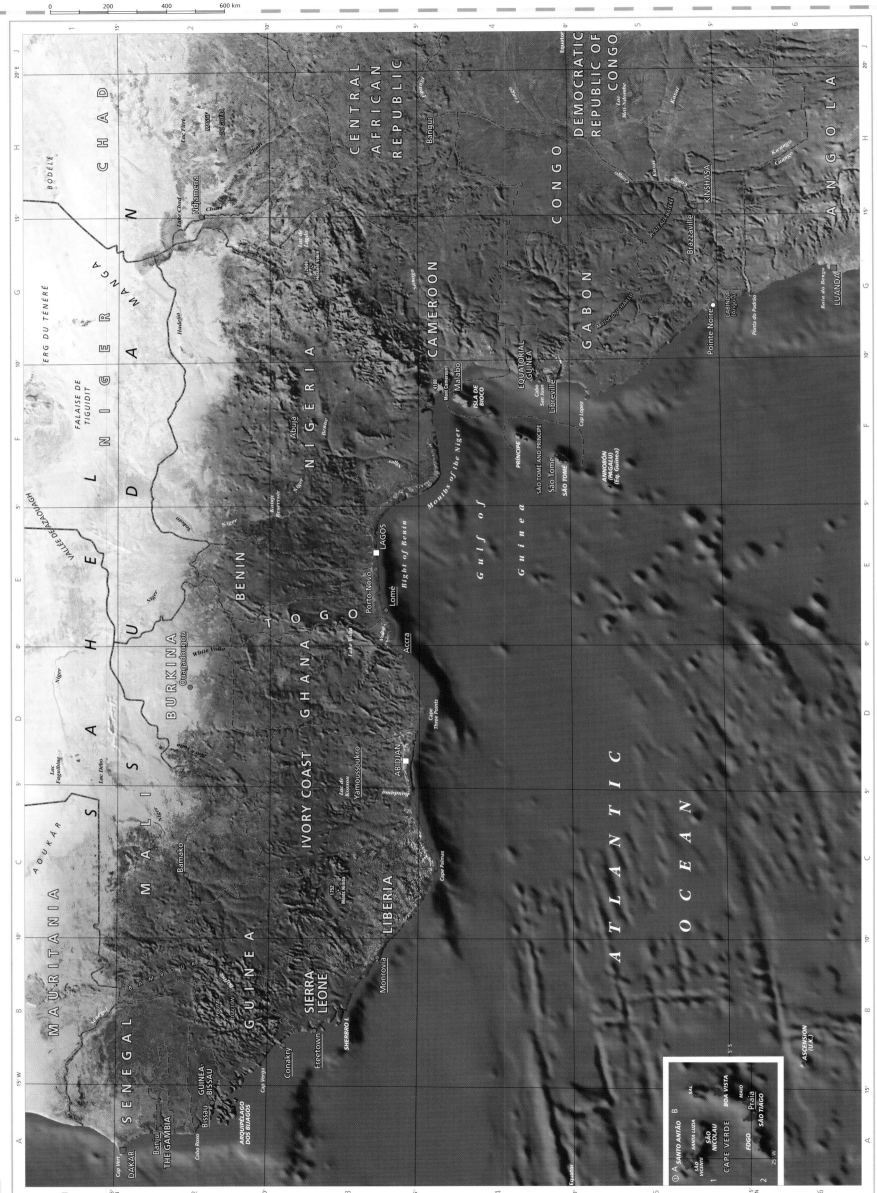

Scale 1 : 13 000 000

0   200   400   600 km

© Copyright

MAURITANIA

SENEGAL

DAKAR
Cap Vert
Banjul
THE GAMBIA
Cabo Roxo
GUINEA-BISSAU
Bissau
ARQUIPÉLAGO DOS BIJAGÓS
Cap Verga

AOUKAR

MALI

Bamako

GUINEA

FOUTA
DJALLON

SIERRA LEONE
Freetown
Conakry
SHERBRO I.

Montserrado
Monrovia
LIBERIA

1752
Monts Nimba

Cape Palmas

BURKINA
Ouagadougou

IVORY COAST
Yamoussoukro
ABIDJAN

GHANA
Lac de Kossou

Lac Volta
White Volta

TOGO
Accra
Lomé

BENIN
Porto-Novo

NIGERIA
Abuja
LAGOS
Bight of Benin
Cape Three Points

Kainji Reservoir

Niger

SAHEL

A D R A R D E S I F O R A S

MANGA

CHAD
Ndjamena
Lake Chad
Chari

BODÉLÉ
ERG DU TÉNÉRÉ

FALAISE DE TIGUIDIT

NIGER

Lac Fitri
Lac Iro

2046
Massif de Hossélé Viano

Chari

CENTRAL AFRICAN REPUBLIC
Bangui

CAMEROON
Mont Cameroun 4100
Malabo
ISLA DE BIOCO
Mouths of the Niger

EQUATORIAL GUINEA
Cabo San Juan
Libreville
Cap Lopez

SÃO TOMÉ AND PRÍNCIPE
PRÍNCIPE
São Tomé
SÃO TOMÉ

ANNOBON (PAGALU)
(Eq. Guinea)

Gulf of Guinea

GABON

CONGO
Brazzaville

DEMOCRATIC REPUBLIC OF CONGO
KINSHASA

ANGOLA
CABINDA (Angola)
Pointe Noire
LUANDA
Baía do Bengo
Ponta do Padrão

Equator

ATLANTIC OCEAN

ASCENSION (U.K.)

SANTO ANTÃO
SANTA LUZIA
SÃO NICOLAU
SÃO VICENTE
SAL
BOA VISTA
MAIO
FOGO
Praia
SÃO TIAGO
CAPE VERDE

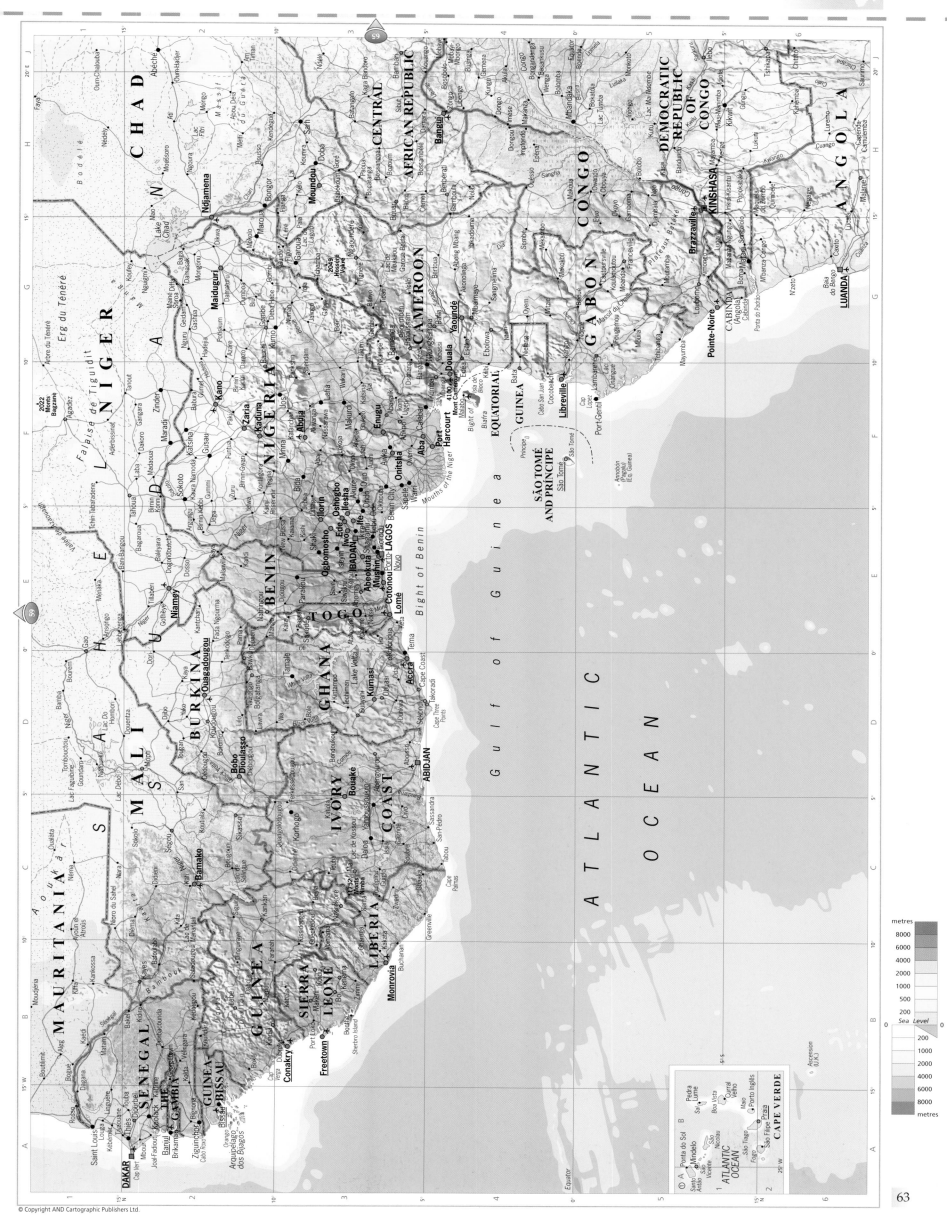

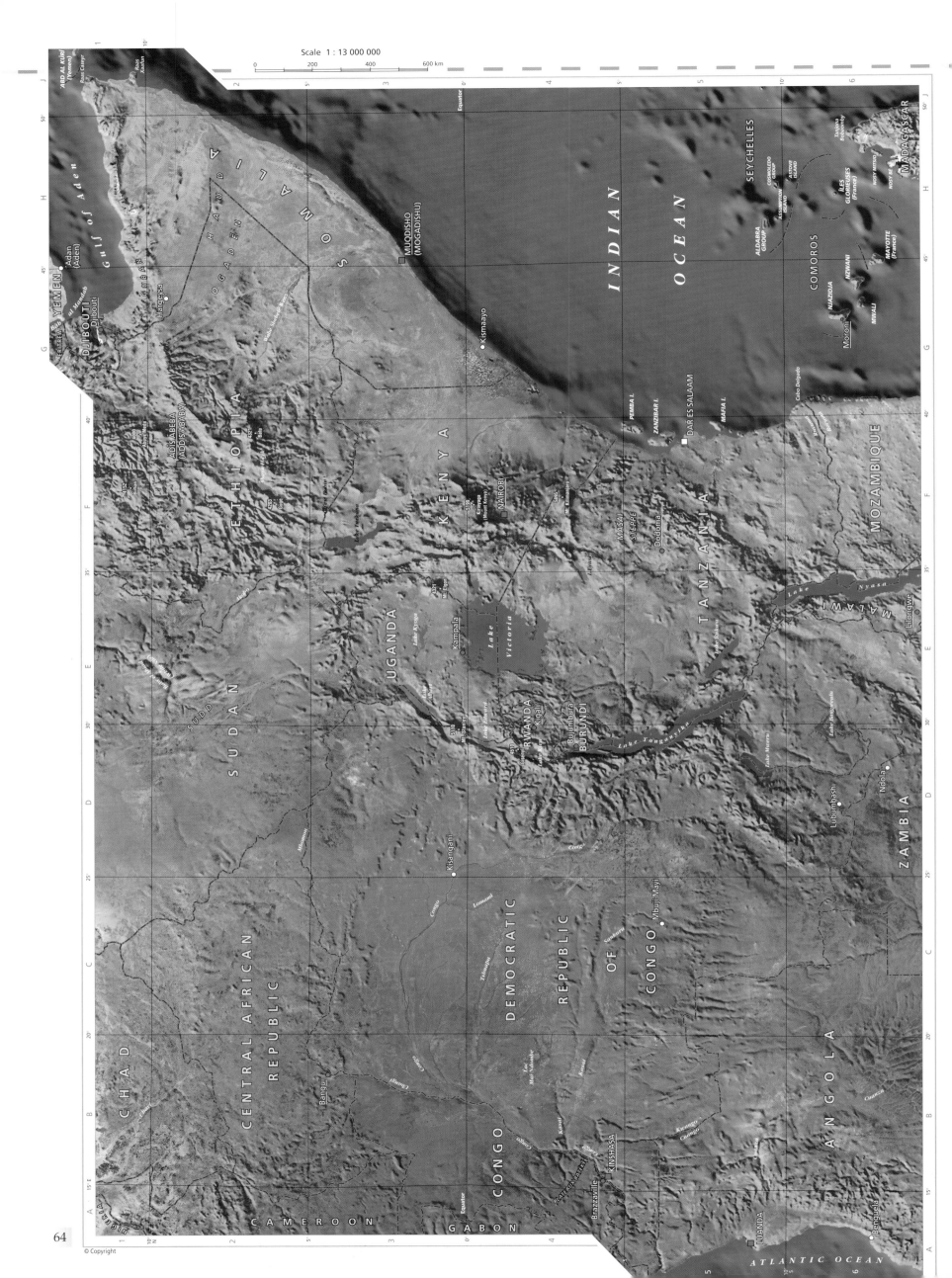

Scale 1 : 13 000 000

0   200   400   600 km

INDIAN OCEAN

SEYCHELLES

COSMOLEDO GROUP
ALDABRA GROUP
ASSUMPTION ISLAND
ASTOVE ISLAND
ÎLES GLORIEUSES (France)
NOSY MITSIO
NOSY BE
Tanjona Bobaomby

COMOROS
NZWANI
NJAZIDJA
MWALI
Moroni

MAYOTTE (France)

MADAGASCAR

ABD AL KURI (Yemen)
Raas Caseyr
Raas Xaafun

Gulf of Aden

YEMEN
Adan (Aden)
ERITREA
Bāb al Mandab
DJIBOUTI
Djibouti
Hargeysa

SOMALIA

GUBAN

HAUD

OGADEN

ETHIOPIA
ĀDĪS ĀBEBA (ADDIS ABABA)

SUDAN

SUDD

MUQDISHO (MOGADISHU)

Equator

Kismaayo

KENYA
NAIROBI
Kirinyaga (Mount Kenya)
Mt. Kilimanjaro
MASAI STEPPE

PEMBA I.
ZANZIBAR I.
DAR ES SALAAM
MAFIA I.

Lake Turkana

UGANDA
Lake Kyoga
Kampala
Lake Albert
Lake Edward
Mt. Stanley
Lake Kivu

RWANDA
Kigali
BURUNDI
Bujumbura

Lake Victoria

TANZANIA
Dodoma

Lake Tanganyika

MOZAMBIQUE

Cabo Delgado

Lake Nyasa

MALAWI
Lilongwe

CENTRAL AFRICAN REPUBLIC

CHAD

NIGERIA

Bangui

CAMEROON

CONGO

Brazzaville
KINSHASA
PLATEAUX BATÉKÉ

GABON

DEMOCRATIC REPUBLIC OF CONGO

Kisangani

Congo

Mbuji-Mayi

Lubumbashi

ZAMBIA

Ndola

ANGOLA

LUANDA

Benguela

ATLANTIC OCEAN

Equator

64

© Copyright

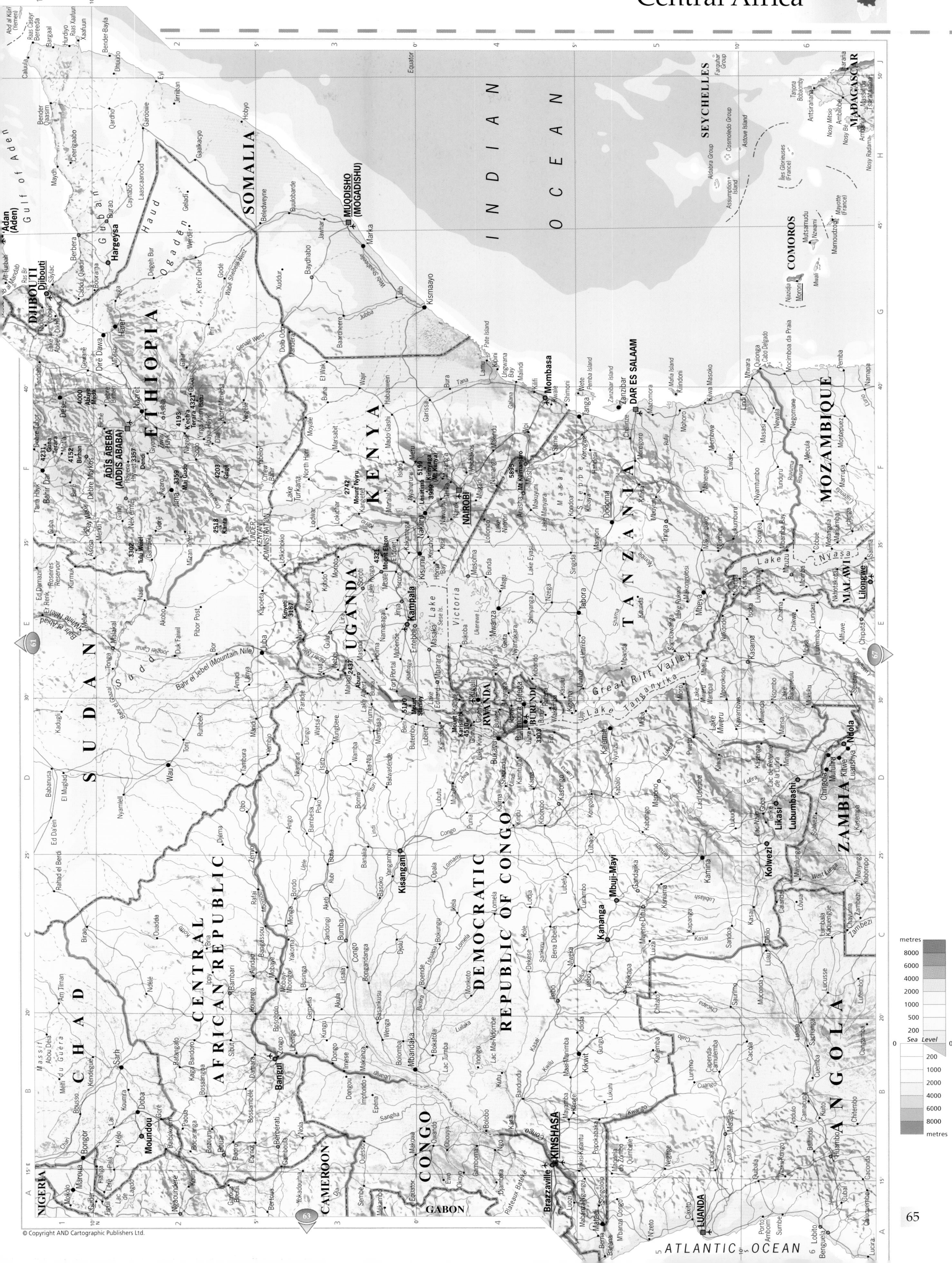

NIGERIA
CHAD
CENTRAL AFRICAN REPUBLIC
CAMEROON
CONGO
GABON
SUDAN
ETHIOPIA
DJIBOUTI
SOMALIA
KENYA
UGANDA
RWANDA
BURUNDI
DEMOCRATIC REPUBLIC OF CONGO
TANZANIA
ANGOLA
ZAMBIA
MALAWI
MOZAMBIQUE
MADAGASCAR
SEYCHELLES
COMOROS

Gulf of Aden
'Adan (Aden)
INDIAN OCEAN
ATLANTIC OCEAN
Lake Victoria
Lake Tanganyika
Lake Nyasa
Great Rift Valley

ĀDĪS ĀBEBA (ADDIS ABABA)
MUQDISHO (MOGADISHU)
NAIROBI
KAMPALA
DAR ES SALAAM
KINSHASA
Brazzaville
Bangui
Moundou
LUANDA
LILONGWE
Lubumbashi
Kananga
Mbuji-Mayi
Kisangani
Mombasa
DODOMA
Kolwezi
Likasi
Ndola
Kitwe
Mufulira
Chingola

Equator

© Copyright AND Cartographic Publishers Ltd.

65

Scale 1 : 13 000 000

0   200   400   600 km

SEYCHELLES

COSMOLEDO GROUP
ASTOVE ISLAND
ALDABRA GROUP
ASSUMPTION ISLAND
ILES GLORIEUSES (France)

NOSY BE
NOSY MITSIO

Tanjona Bobaomby
Tanjona Masoala
NOSY BORAHA

2876

COMOROS
NJAZIDJA
Moroni
NZWANI
MWALI
MAYOTTE (France)

ANTANANARIVO

2643
Maizitoana

MADAGASCAR

Tanjona Vilanandro

JUAN DE NOVA (France)

Tanjona Vohimena

ILE EUROPA (France)

BASSAS DA INDIA (France)

Mozambique Channel

INDIAN

OCEAN

TANZANIA

Cabo Delgado

MOZAMBIQUE

Lake
Nyasa
MALAWI
Blantyre
Lilongwe

2419
Monte Namuli

DEMOCRATIC
REPUBLIC
OF CONGO

Lubumbashi
Ndola

Lake
Mweru
Lake
Bangweulu

ZAMBIA

Lusaka
Zambezi

Kafue

Lake Kariba

Victoria Falls

Zambezi

HARARE

ZIMBABWE

Bulawayo

Limpopo

MAPUTO

Mbabane
SWAZI LAND

DURBAN
KWAZULU NATAL

Pretoria
MPUMALANGA
GAUTENG
Johannesburg
NORTH WEST

NORTHERN PROVINCE

Gaborone

BOTSWANA

KALAHARI
DESERT

Maseru
LESOTHO

FREE STATE
Bloemfontein

SOUTH AFRICA

NORTHERN
CAPE

EASTERN CAPE

Port Elizabeth
Cape St. Francis

GREAT
KAROO

ANGOLA

Benguela
Lubango

NAMIBIA

Windhoek

Etosha Pan

Cunene

Cuito

Cubango

Okavango
Delta

Cuando

Molopo

Orange

WESTERN
CAPE

CAPE TOWN
Cape of Good Hope
Cape Agulhas

St.
Helena
Bay
Cape Columbine

ATLANTIC

OCEAN

Tropic of Capricorn

SEYCHELLES IS
PRASLIN I.
SILHOUETTE I.
MAHÉ (VICTORIA ISLAND)
Victoria

AMIRANTE IS.

S E Y C H E L L E S

SAINT PIERRE I.
PROVIDENCE I.

FARQUHAR GROUP

COSMOLEDO GROUP
ALDABRA GROUP
ASSUMPTION ISLAND
ASTOVE ISLAND

COETIVY I.

AGALEGA IS. (Mauritius)

Port Louis

MAURITIUS

RÉUNION (Fr.)

INDIAN

OCEAN

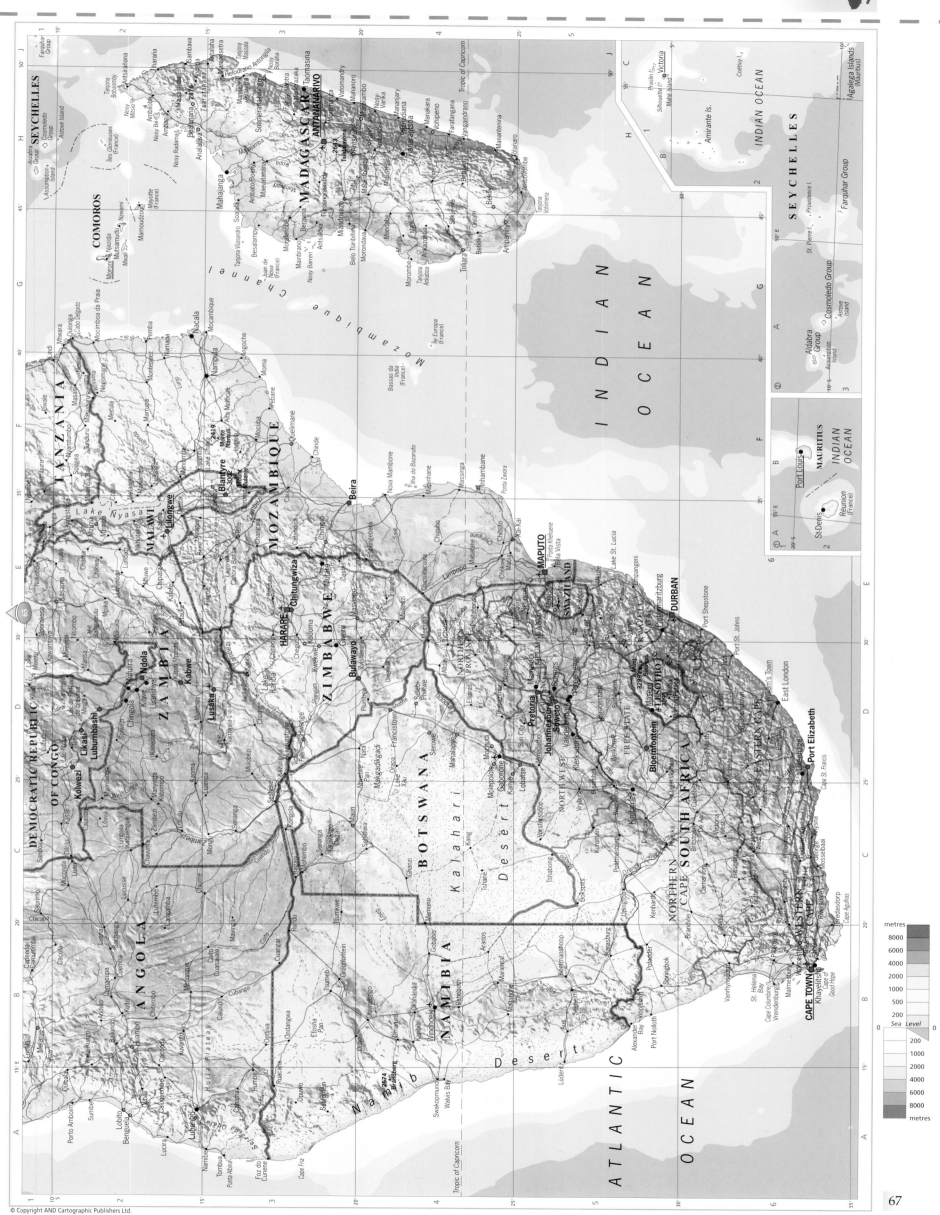

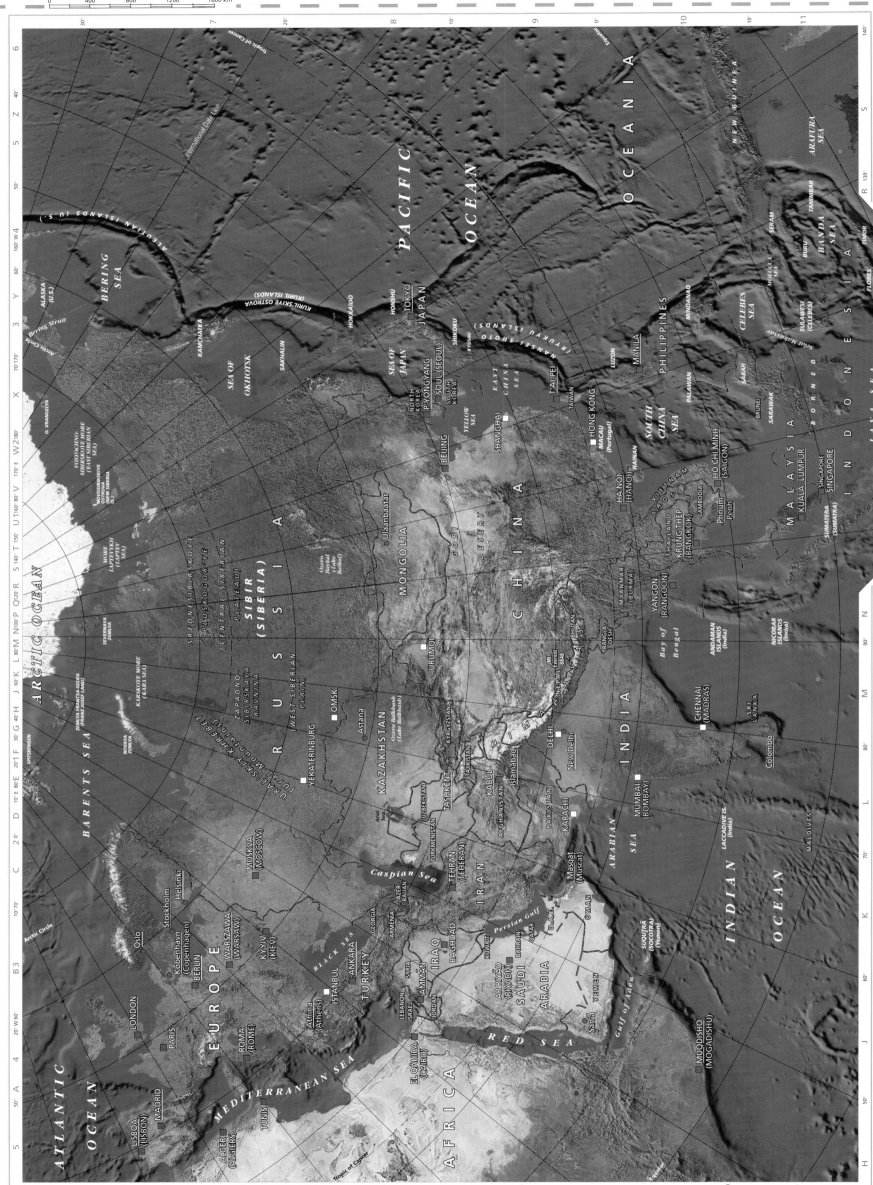

Scale 1 : 37 000 000

0   400   800   1200   1600 km

ATLANTIC OCEAN

ARCTIC OCEAN

PACIFIC OCEAN

OCEANIA

INDIAN OCEAN

EUROPE

AFRICA

ASIA

RUSSIA

SIBIR (SIBERIA)

CHINA

INDIA

BERING SEA

BARENTS SEA

SEA OF OKHOTSK

KAZAKHSTAN

MONGOLIA

GOBI DESERT

MEDITERRANEAN SEA

RED SEA

ARABIAN SEA

BAY of Bengal

SOUTH CHINA SEA

ARAFURA SEA

JAVA SEA

LONDON
PARIS
MADRID
LISBOA (LISBON)
ALGER (ALGIERS)
TUNIS
ROMA (ROME)
BERLIN
København (Copenhagen)
WARSZAWA (WARSAW)
Stockholm
Oslo
Helsinki
MOSKVA (MOSCOW)
KYIV (KIEV)
Athina (Athens)
ISTANBUL
ANKARA
TURKEY
GEORGIA
ARMENIA
AZERBAIJAN
SYRIA
LEBANON
ISRAEL
JORDAN
AMMAN
BAGHDAD
IRAQ
IRAN
TEHRAN (TEHERAN)
KUWAIT
BAHRAIN
QATAR
AR RIYĀD (RIYADH)
SAUDI ARABIA
YEMEN
Sana
EL QAHIRA (CAIRO)
MUQDISHO (MOGADISHU)
OMAN
Masqat (Muscat)
U.A.E.
SUQUTRĀ (SOCOTRA) (Yemen)
Gulf of Aden
Persian Gulf
Caspian Sea
BLACK SEA

YEKATERINBURG
OMSK
Astana
URUMQI
TURKMENISTAN
UZBEKISTAN
TASHKENT
TAJIKISTAN
KYRGYZSTAN
AFGHANISTAN
KABUL
Islamabad
PAKISTAN
KARACHI
New Delhi
DELHI
NEPAL
Kathmandu
BHUTAN
BANGLA DESH
HIMALAYA
Mt. Everest 8848
MUMBAI (BOMBAY)
CHENNAI (MADRAS)
Colombo
SRI LANKA
MALDIVES
LACCADIVE IS. (India)

Ulaanbaatar
BEIJING
SHANGHAI
HONG KONG
MACAU (Portugal)
HAINAN
T'AI-PEI
TAIWAN
SEOUL (SEOUL)
SOUTH KOREA
NORTH KOREA
P'YONGYANG
TOKYO
JAPAN
HONSHŪ
HOKKAIDO
SHIKOKU
KYŪSHŪ
SEA OF JAPAN
EAST CHINA SEA
YELLOW SEA
NANSEI SHOTO (RYUKYU ISLANDS)

MYANMAR (BURMA)
YANGON (RANGOON)
LAOS
THAILAND
KRUNG THEP (BANGKOK)
CAMBODIA
Phnum Penh
VIETNAM
HANOI (HANOI)
HO CHI MINH (SAIGON)
ANDAMAN ISLANDS (India)
NICOBAR ISLANDS (India)
MALAYSIA
KUALA LUMPUR
SINGAPORE
SUMATERA (SUMATRA)
INDONESIA
BORNEO
SARAWAK
BRUNEI
SABAH
PHILIPPINES
MANILA
LUZON
MINDANAO
PALAWAN
CELEBES SEA
MOLUCCA SEA
SULAWESI (CELEBES)
SERAM
BURU
BANDA SEA
TANIMBAR
TIMOR
FLORES
NEW GUINEA

ALASKA (U.S.)
Bering Strait
KAMCHATKA
KURIL'SKIYE OSTROVA (KURIL ISLANDS)
SAKHALIN
ALEUTIAN ISLANDS (U.S.)
VOSTOCHNO-SIBIRSKOYE MORE (EAST SIBERIAN SEA)
NOVOSIBIRSKIYE OSTROVA (NEW SIBERIAN IS.)
MORE LAPTEVYKH (LAPTEV SEA)
SEVERNAYA ZEMLYA
KARSKOYE MORE (KARA SEA)
ZEMLYA FRANTSA-IOSIFA (FRANZ JOSEF LAND)
NOVAYA ZEMLYA
SPITSBERGEN
O. VRANGELYA
Arctic Circle
Tropic of Cancer
Tropic of Cancer
Equator
International Date Line
Arctic Circle

SREDNESIBIRSKOYE PLOSKOGOR'YE (CENTRAL SIBERIAN PLATEAU)
ZAPADNO-SIBIRSKAYA RAVNINA (WEST SIBERIAN PLAIN)
URAL'SKIY KHREBET (URAL MOUNTAINS)
Ozero Baykal (Lake Baikal)
Ozero Balhash (Lake Balkhash)
Aral Sea

© Copyright

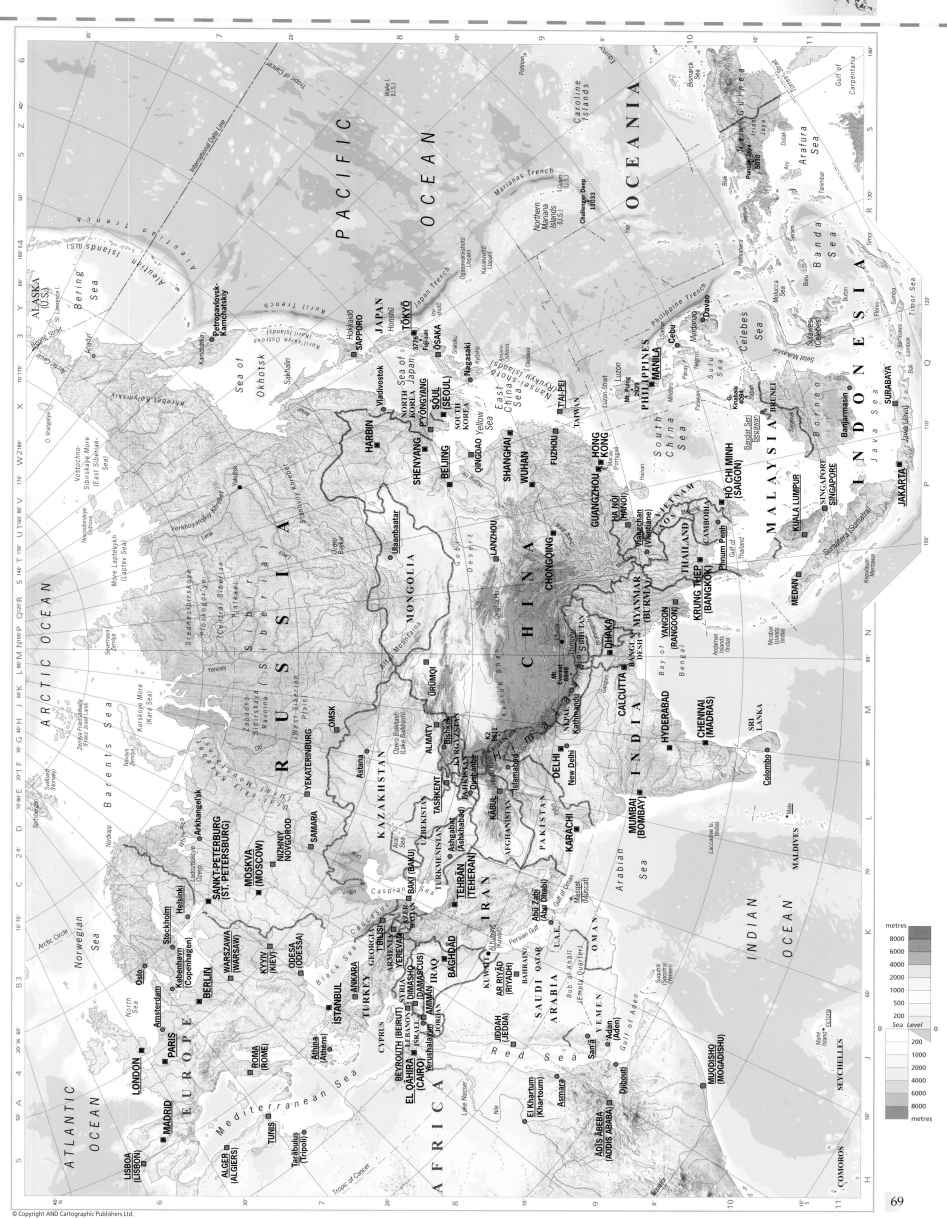

Scale 1 : 15 500 000

0   200   400   600 km

BARENTS SEA

NORWAY

Murmansk

Arctic Circle

ZEMLYA FRANTSA-IOSIFA
(FRANZ JOSEF LAND)

NOVAYA ZEMLYA

KARSKOYE MORE
(KARA SEA)

OSTROV BELYY

SEVERNAYA ZEMLYA

MORE LAPTEVYKH
(LAPTEV SEA)

OSTROV
BOL'SHOY
BEGICHEV

SAKHA

Arkhangel'sk

BELOYE MORE
(WHITE SEA)

Mys Kanin Nos

OSTROV
KOLGUYEV

Pechorskoye
More

OSTROV
VAYGACH

Vorkuta

Ob'

KOMI

Noril'sk

Yenisey

Ozero
Taymyr

SREDNE SIBIRSKOYE

PLOSKOGOR'YE

Arctic Circle

ZAPADNO-SIBIRSKAYA

RAVNINA

(WEST SIBERIAN

PLAIN)

Surgut

Ob'

RUSSIA

Bratsk

MARIY EL

UDMURTIYA

PERM

CHUVASHIYA

KAZAN

TATARIYA

YEKATERINBURG

Tyumen'

Ob'

URAL'SKIY KHREBET
(URAL MOUNTAINS)

Krasnoyarsk

UFA

CHELYABINSK

BASHKIRIYA

SAMARA

Irtysh

OMSK

NOVOSIBIRSK

KHAKASIYA

Yenisey

TYVA

Barnaul

Orsk

Aktyubinsk

ALTAY

Ozero
Us Nuur

Ozero Tengiz

Astana

Semipalatinsk

PRIKASPIYSKAYA NIZMENNOST'

KAZAKHSTAN

Karaganda

ALTAI MOUNTAINS

MONGOLIA

Altay

Caspian
Sea

Aktau

Ozero Zaysan

KHR. TARBAGATAY

Aral Sea

Ozero Balkhash

Ozero
Alakol

4925
Karlik Shan

URÜMQI

Kara
Bogaz Gol

UZBEKISTAN

Syrdarya

Shihezi

CHINA

TURKMENISTAN
Peski Karakumy

TASHKENT

Zhambyl

ALMATY

Bishkek

Ysyk-Köl

7439
Pik Pobedy

TIEN SHAN

Korla

Aksu

Ashgabat
(Ashkhabad)

Samarkand

Andizhan

KYRGYZSTAN

Kashi

TARIM PENDI

Qatman He

Dushanbe

7495
Pik Kommunizma

IRAN MASHHAD

7546
Muztagata

TAJIKISTAN

Mazar-e Sharif

AFGHANISTAN

PAKISTAN

KUN LUN SHAN

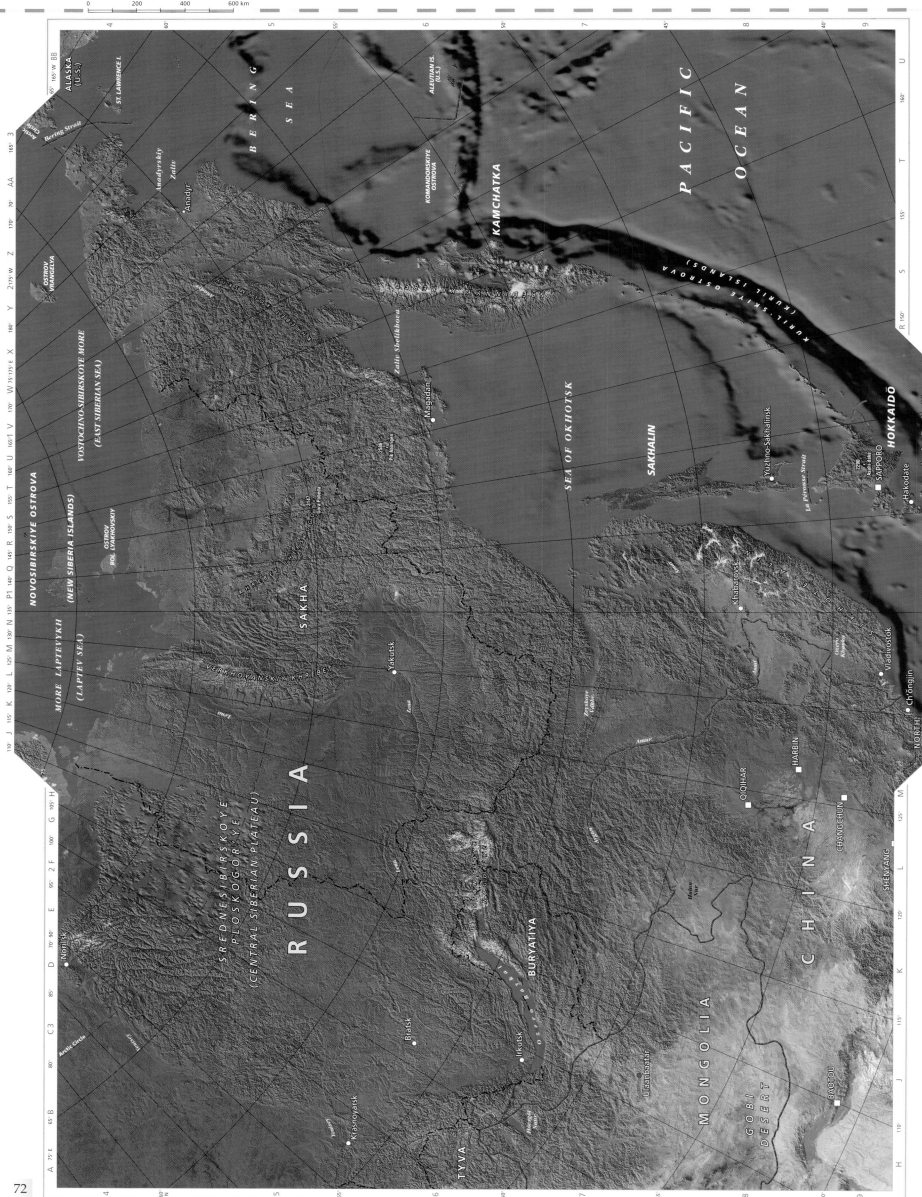

Scale 1 : 15 500 000

0   200   400   600 km

© Copyright

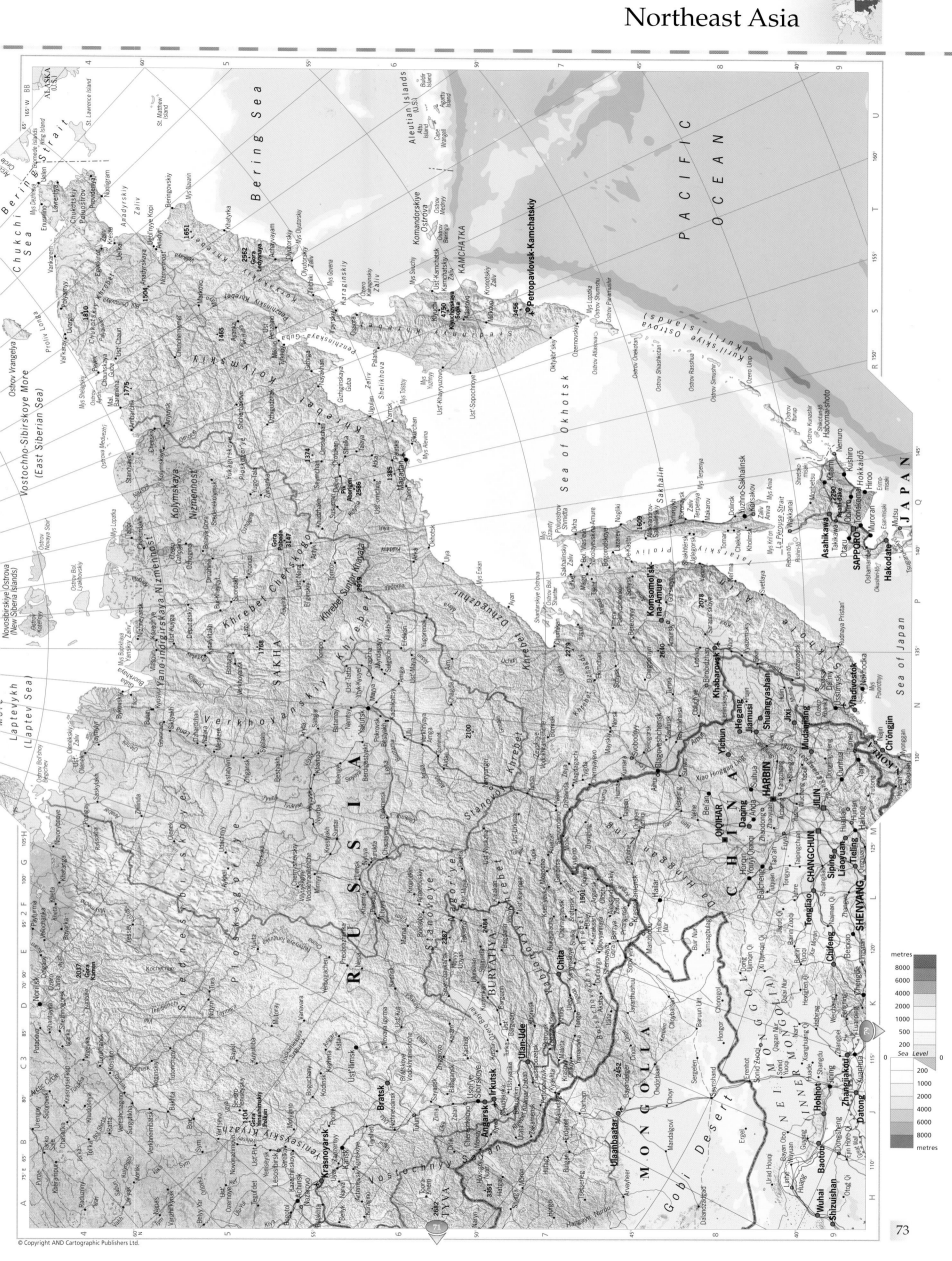

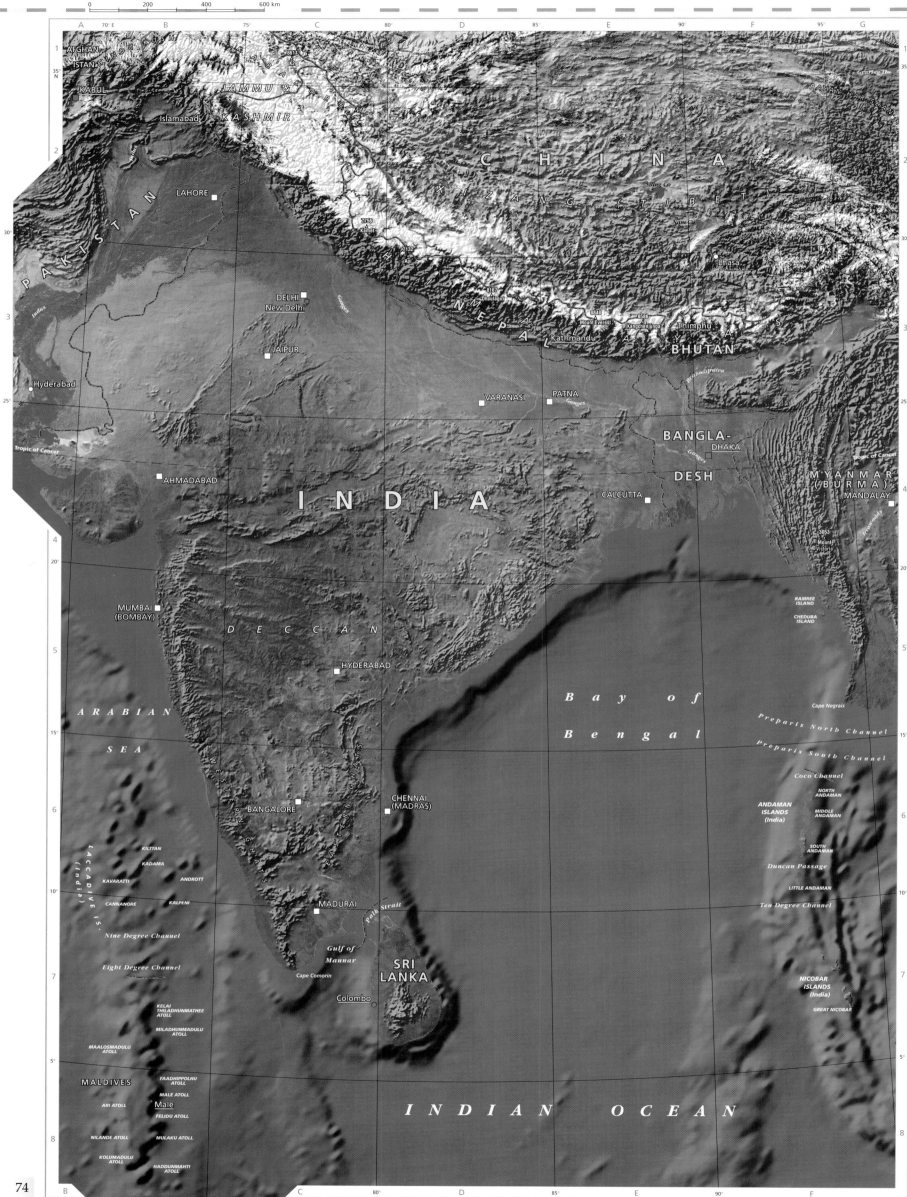

Scale 1 : 13 000 000

0   200   400   600 km

© Copyright

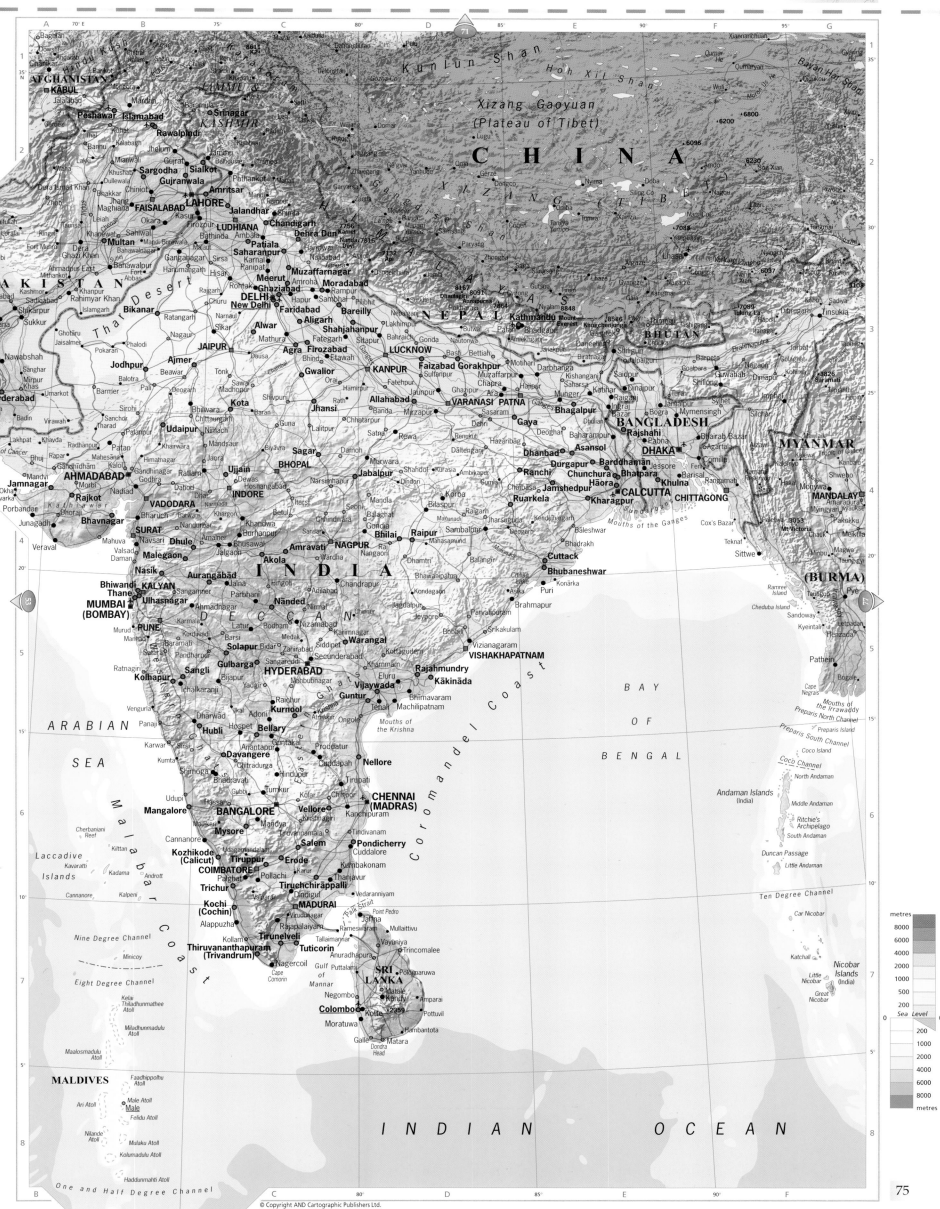

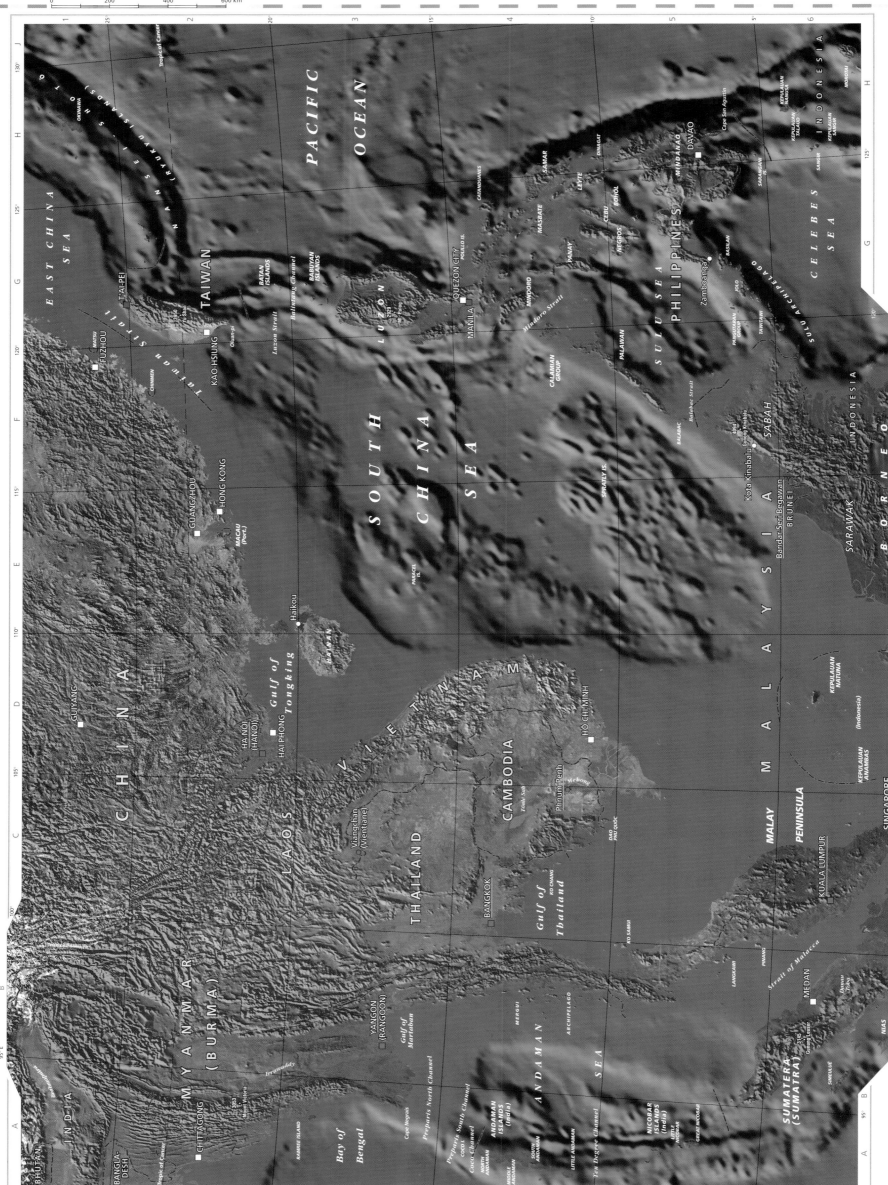

Scale 1 : 13 000 000

0   200   400   600 km

PACIFIC

OCEAN

EAST CHINA SEA

TAIWAN

T'AI-PEI

FUZHOU
MATSU

CHINMEN

KAO-HSIUNG

BATAN ISLANDS

BABUYAN ISLANDS

Balintang Channel

Luzon Strait

Olzan-pi

LUZON

Mt Pulog

QUEZON CITY
POLILLO IS.

MANILA

CATANDUANES

SAMAR

MASBATE

PANAY

LEYTE

CEBU

BOHOL

DINAGAT

PHILIPPINES

NEGROS

MINDANAO

DAVAO

Cape San Agustin

KEPULAUAN SANGIR

KEPULAUAN TALAUD

MORATAI

INDONESIA

CELEBES SEA

SANGIR

SARANGANI IS.

BASILAN

JOLO

Zamboanga

TAWITAWI

PANGUTARAN GROUP

SULU SEA

PALAWAN

CALAMIAN GROUP

Mindoro Strait

MINDORO

SOUTH

CHINA

SEA

SPRATLY IS.

Balabac Strait

BALABAC

Kota Kinabalu
Gunung Kinabalu

SABAH

Bandar Seri Begawan
BRUNEI

SARAWAK

B O R N E O

INDONESIA

KEPULAUAN NATUNA
(Indonesia)

KEPULAUAN ANAMBAS
(Indonesia)

KEPULAUAN SANGIR

GUANGZHOU

HONG KONG

MACAU
(Port.)

PARACEL IS.

Haikou

HAINAN

Gulf of Tongking

HA NOI
(HANOI)

HAI PHONG

V I E T N A M

GUIYANG

C H I N A

I N D I A

BHUTAN

BANGLA-DESH

CHITTAGONG

RAMREE ISLAND

Cape Negrais

Preparis North Channel

Preparis South Channel
COCO Channel
Coco Channel

NORTH ANDAMAN
MIDDLE ANDAMAN
SOUTH ANDAMAN

ANDAMAN ISLANDS
(India)

LITTLE ANDAMAN

Ten Degree Channel

NICOBAR ISLANDS
(India)

LITTLE NICOBAR
GREAT NICOBAR

Bay of Bengal

Mount Victoria
3053

MYANMAR
(BURMA)

YANGON
(RANGOON)

Gulf of Martaban

Irrawaddy

MERGUI

ARCHIPELAGO

A N D A M A N

S E A

L A O S

Viangchan
(Vientiane)

T H A I L A N D

BANGKOK

KO CHANG

Gulf of Thailand

KO SAMUI

CAMBODIA

Tonle Sab

Phnum Penh

Mekong

DAO PHU QUOC

HO CHI MINH

M A L A Y S I A

MALAY
PENINSULA

KUALA LUMPUR

SINGAPORE

PINANG

LANGKAWI

Strait of Malacca

MEDAN

Danau Toba

SUMATERA
(SUMATRA)

Gunung Leuser
3145

NIAS

SIMEULUE

INDONESIA

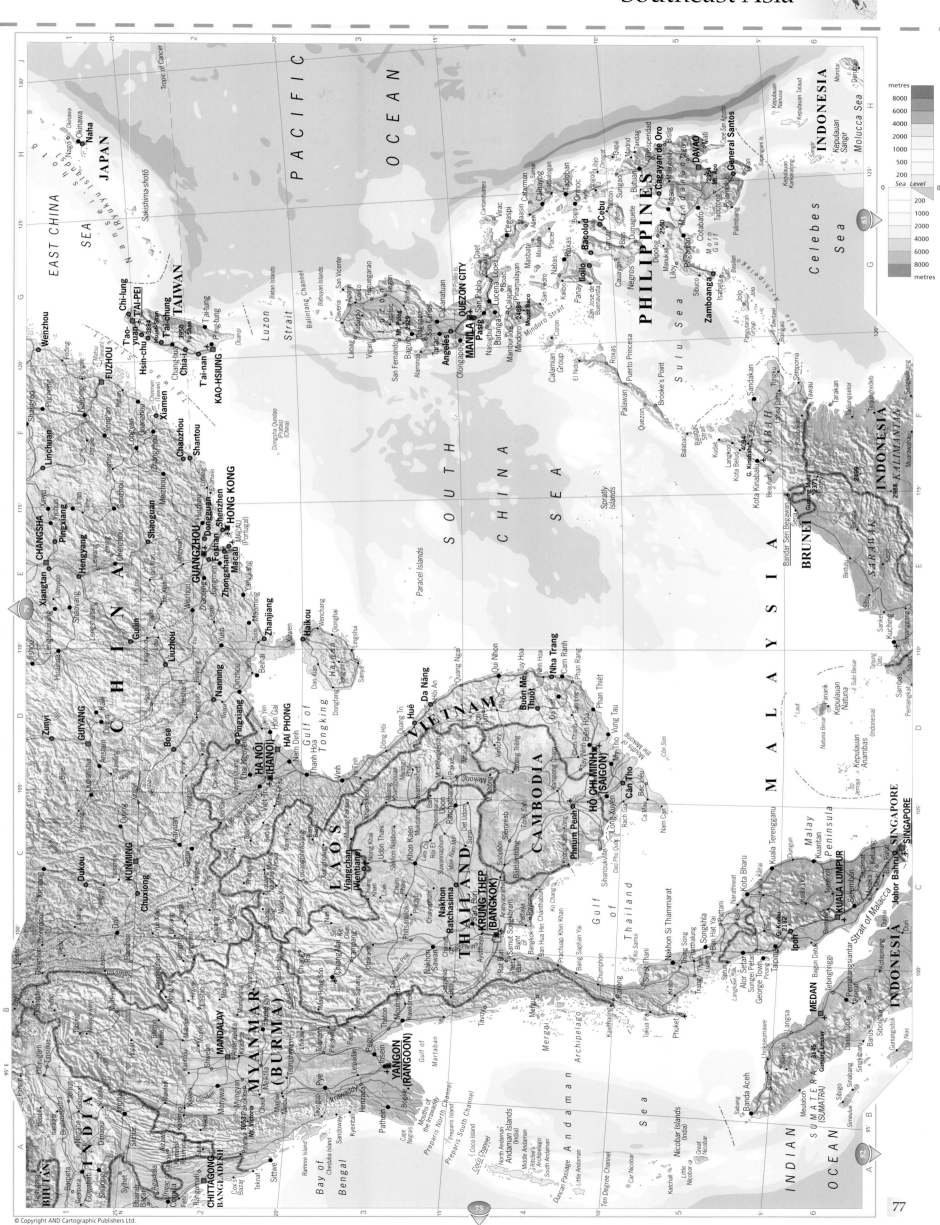

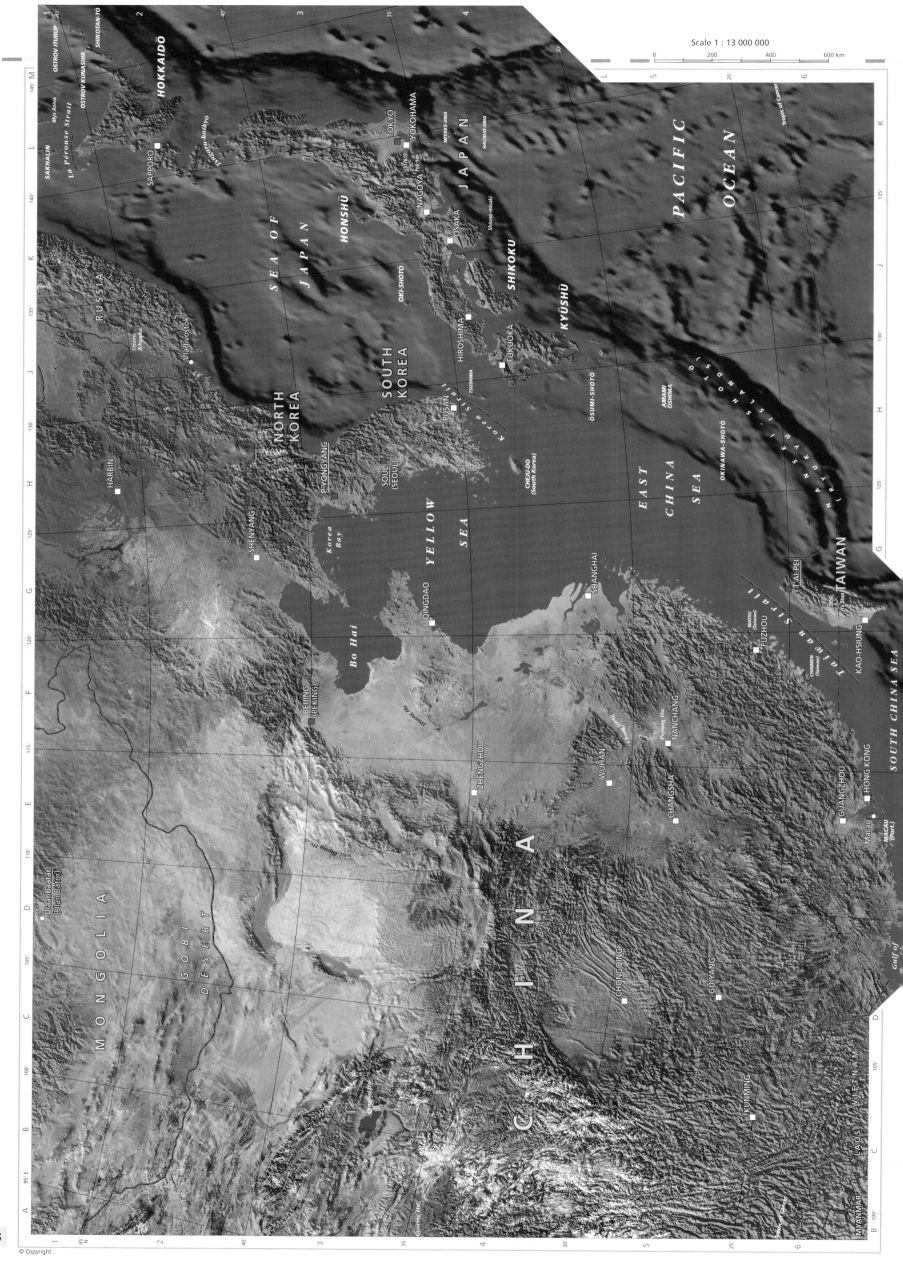

Scale 1 : 13 000 000

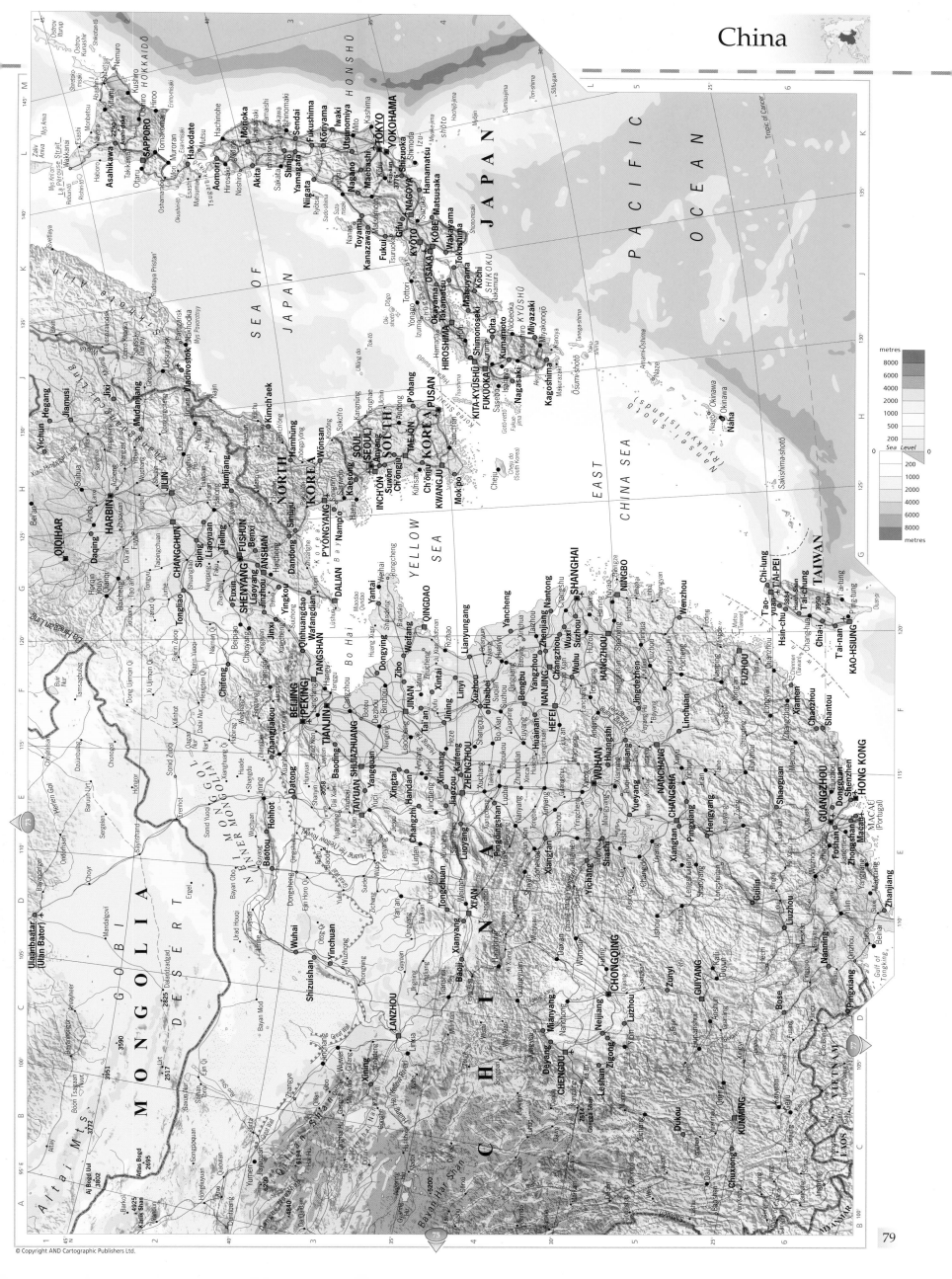

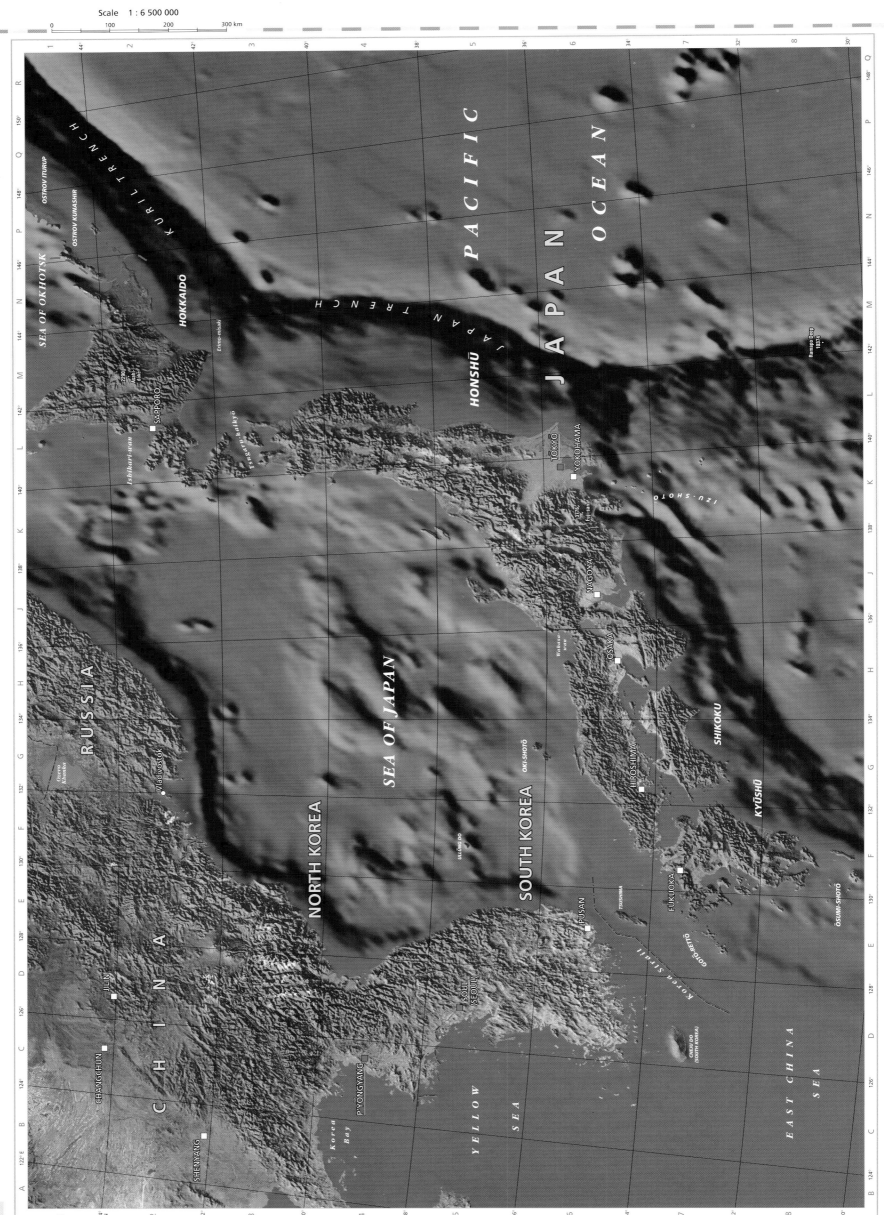

Scale 1 : 6 500 000

0   100   200   300 km

SEA OF OKHOTSK

KURIL TRENCH

OSTROV ITURUP

OSTROV KUNASHIR

HOKKAIDŌ

Erimo-misaki

2290
Asahi-dake

SAPPORO

Ishikari-wan

Tsugaru-kaikyō

PACIFIC

JAPAN OCEAN

JAPAN TRENCH

HONSHŪ

Ramapo Deep
10374

IZU-SHOTŌ

TŌKYŌ
YOKOHAMA

3776
Fuji-san

NAGOYA

Wakasa-wan

OSAKA

SHIKOKU

HIROSHIMA

KYŪSHŪ

FUKUOKA

ŌSUMI-SHOTŌ

GOTŌ-RETTŌ

TSUSHIMA

Korea Strait

PUSAN

OKI-SHOTŌ

SEA OF JAPAN

SOUTH KOREA

NORTH KOREA

RUSSIA

Ozero
Khanka

Vladivostok

ULLŬNG-DO

CHINA

JILIN

CHANGCHUN

SHENYANG

P'YŎNGYANG

SŎUL
(SEOUL)

Korea
Bay

YELLOW

SEA

CHEJU DO
(SOUTH KOREA)

EAST CHINA

SEA

© Copyright

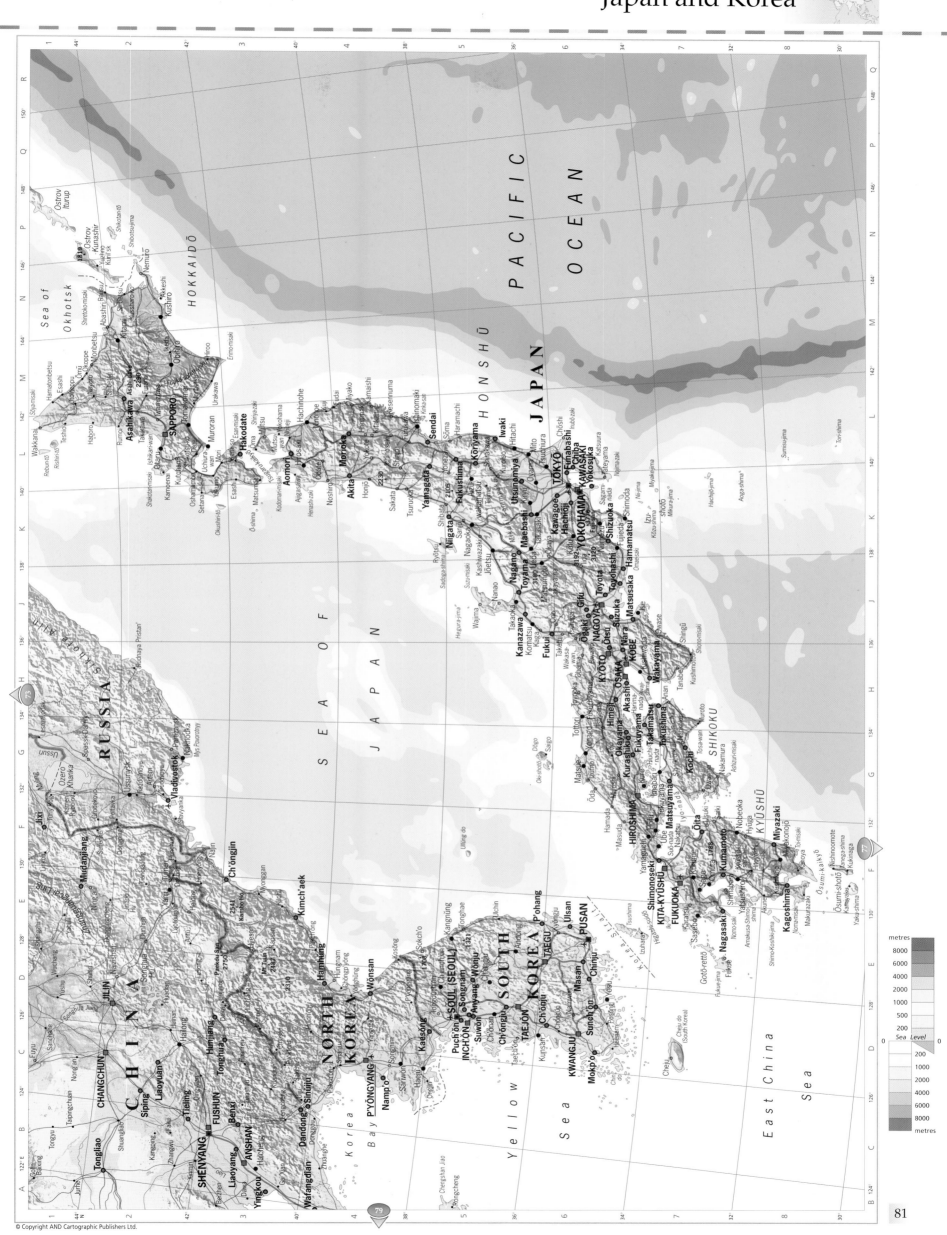

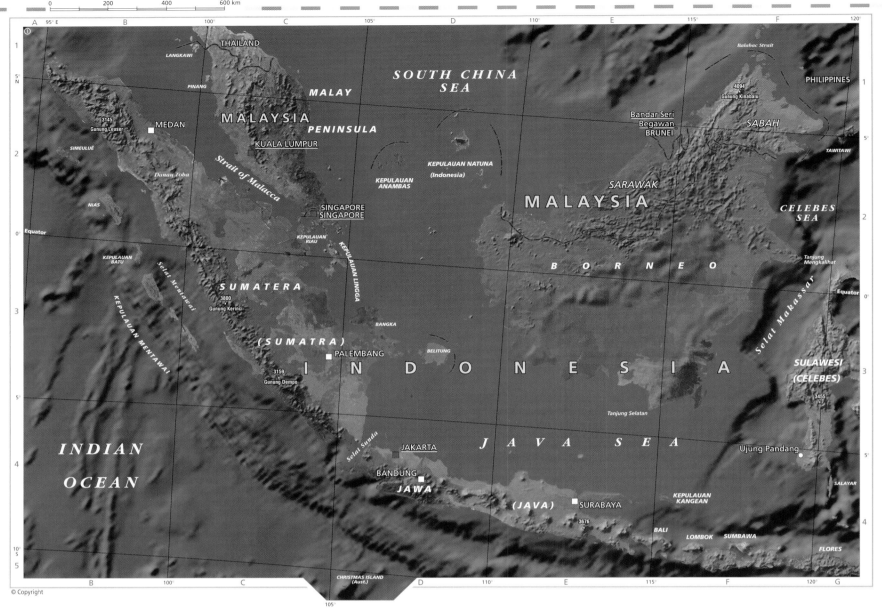

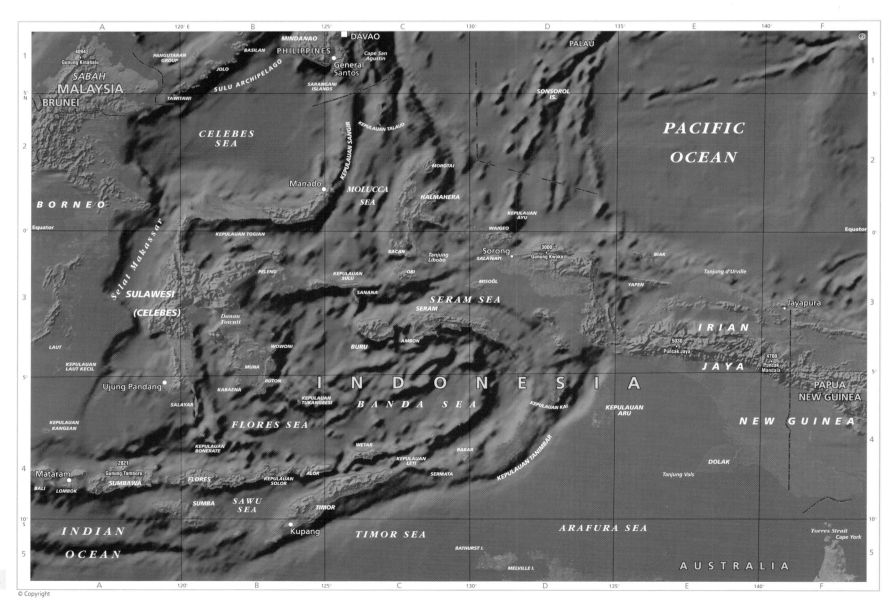

© Copyright

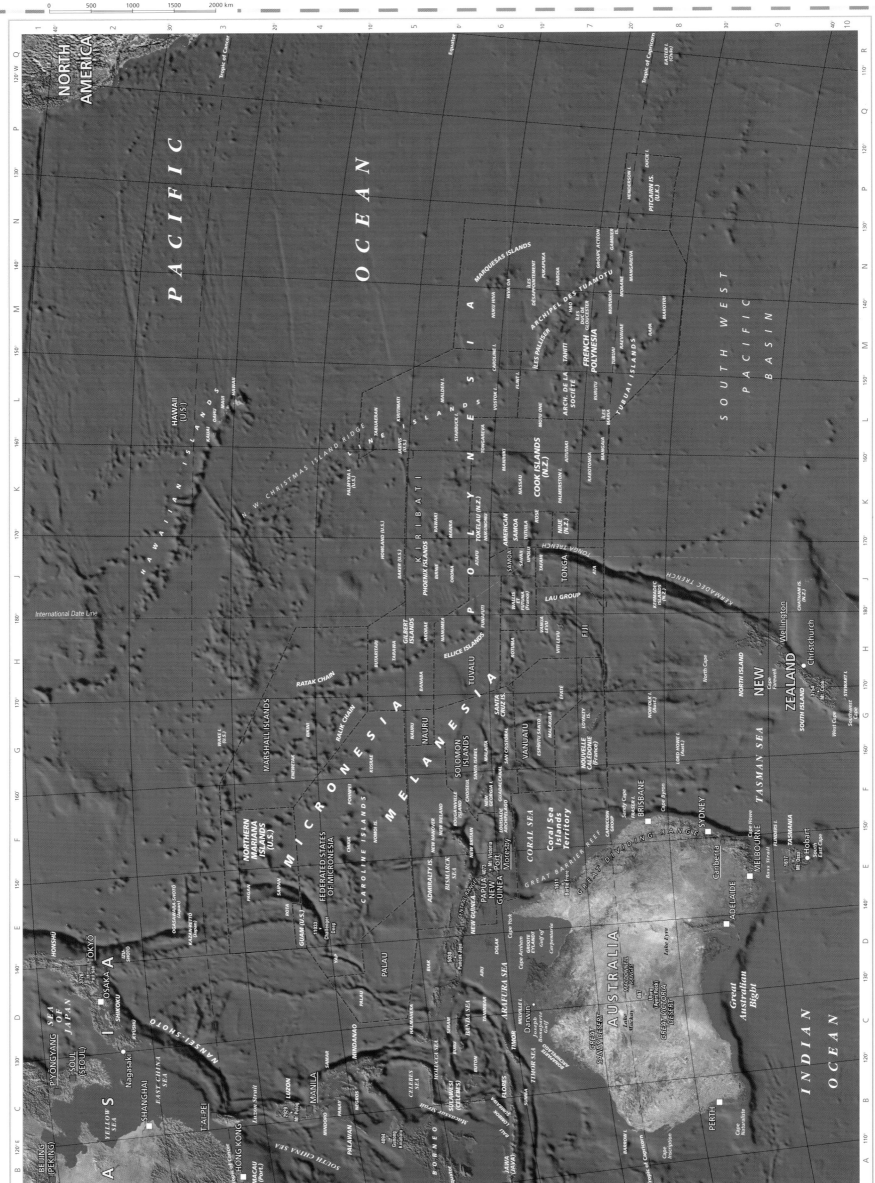

Scale 1 : 45 500 000

0   500   1000   1500   2000 km

NORTH AMERICA

120° W

Tropic of Cancer

PACIFIC

OCEAN

Equator

Tropic of Capricorn

SOUTH WEST

PACIFIC

BASIN

International Date Line

HAWAIIAN ISLANDS

HAWAII (U.S.)
KAUAI   OAHU
MAUI
HAWAII

N.W. CHRISTMAS ISLAND RIDGE

LINE   TABUAERAN

KIRITIMATI

I S L A N D S

MARQUESAS ISLANDS
NUKU HIVA
HIVA OA

ÎLES
DÉSAPPOINTEMENT
PUKAPUKA
RAROIA
HAO
ÎLES DU GLOUCESTER
GROUPE ACTEON
GAMBIER IS.

HENDERSON I.
DUCIE I.

PITCAIRN IS. (U.K.)

CAROLINE I.

ÎLES PALLISER
ARCH. DE LA SOCIÉTÉ
TAHITI

FRENCH POLYNESIA

ÎLES MARIA
RURUTU
TUBUAI
TUBUAI ISLANDS
MURUROA
MANGAREVA
RAPA
MAROTIRI
RAIVAVAE

EASTER I. (Chile)

VOSTOK I.
STARBUCK I.
MALDEN I.
JARVIS (U.S.)

FLINT I.

MOTU ONE

RAROTONGA
MANGAIA
AITUTAKI
PALMERSTON I.

COOK ISLANDS
(N.Z.)

RAKAHANGA
MANIHIKI
NASSAU

SUWARROW

P   O   L   Y   N   E   S   I   A

PHOENIX ISLANDS
BIRNIE
ORONA
MANRA

HOWLAND (U.S.)
BAKER (U.S.)

KIRIBATI

BUTARITARI
TARAWA
MARAKEI
ABAIANG
MAIANA
ABEMAMA
KURIA
ARORAE

BANABA

GILBERT ISLANDS

ELLICE ISLANDS

TUVALU

FUNAFUTI

NAURU

ROTUMA

TOKELAU (N.Z.)
NUKUNONU

SAMOA
SAVAI'I
UPOLU

AMERICAN SAMOA
TUTUILA
ROSE

NIUE (N.Z.)

WALLIS ET FUTUNA (France)

TAFAHI
TARAWA

TONGA
ATA

LAU GROUP

VANUA LEVU
VITI LEVU

FIJI

TONGA TRENCH

KERMADEC TRENCH

KERMADEC IS. (N.Z.)

M   I   C   R   O   N   E   S   I   A

MARSHALL ISLANDS
RATAK CHAIN
RALIK CHAIN

WAKE I. (U.S.)

ENEWETAK
BIKINI

KOSRAE

NORTHERN MARIANA ISLANDS (U.S.)
PAGAN
SAIPAN
ROTA

GUAM (U.S.)

OGASAWARA-SHOTŌ (Japan)

KAZAN-RETTŌ (Japan)

YAP
PALAU

FEDERATED STATES OF MICRONESIA

CAROLINE ISLANDS
CHUUK
POHNPEI
NOMOI IS.

PALAU

M   E   L   A   N   E   S   I   A

ADMIRALTY IS.
NEW HANOVER
NEW IRELAND
BISMARCK SEA
NEW BRITAIN

BOUGAINVILLE
SOLOMON ISLANDS
CHOISEUL
SANTA ISABEL
MALAITA
GUADALCANAL
SAN CRISTOBAL

SANTA CRUZ IS.

ESPÍRITU SANTO
MALAKULA
VANUATU
EFATE

LOYALTY IS.

NOUVELLE CALÉDONIE (France)

NORFOLK I. (Aust.)

LORD HOWE I. (Aust.)

NEW GUINEA
PAPUA NEW GUINEA
4073 Mt Victoria
CENTRAL RANGE
Port Moresby
LOUISIADE ARCHIPELAGO

BIAK

CELEBES SEA

BANDA SEA

SERAM

BURU

MOLUCCA SEA

HALMAHERA

MINDANAO

SAMAR
LEYTE
NEGROS
MINDORO
PANAY
MANILA
LUZON

2929 Mt Pulog

PALAWAN

SOUTH CHINA SEA

4101 Gunung Kinabalu

BORNEO

SABAH
SARAWAK

Macassar Strait

SULAWESI (CELEBES)

SUMBAWA
FLORES
SUMBA
LOMBOK
BALI
JAWA (JAVA)

BUTON

TIMOR SEA

TIMOR

ARAFURA SEA

ARU

DOLAK

MELVILLE I.

Darwin
Joseph Bonaparte Gulf

Cape Arnhem

GROOTE EYLANDT
Gulf of Carpentaria

WESSEL ISLANDS

Cape York

AUSTRALIA

GREAT SANDY DESERT

GREAT VICTORIA DESERT

Lake Mackay

MACDONNELL RANGES
1531 Mt Zeil

Lake Eyre

Great Australian Bight

PERTH

Cape Naturaliste
BARROW I.
Cape Inscription

FLINDERS RANGES

ADELAIDE

1611 Mt Dora

MELBOURNE
Bass Strait
TASMANIA
1617
Mt Ossa

Canberra

SYDNEY
Cape Byron

Sandy Cape
FRASER I.
BRISBANE

CAPRICORN GROUP

Coral Sea Islands Territory

CORAL SEA

GREAT BARRIER REEF

GREAT DIVIDING RANGE

Cape Howe

TASMAN SEA

Cape Farewell
North Cape

NORTH ISLAND

NEW ZEALAND

Wellington
CHATHAM IS. (N.Z.)

Christchurch

SOUTH ISLAND
3764 Mt Cook

STEWART I.
West Cape
Southwest Cape

INDIAN OCEAN

BEIJING (PEKING)

PYONGYANG

SOUL (SEOUL)

SEA OF JAPAN

HONSHŪ
TOKYO
3776 Fuji-san
OSAKA
SHIKOKU
KYŪSHŪ
Nagasaki

EAST CHINA SEA
NANSEI-SHOTŌ

YELLOW SEA

SHANGHAI

T'AI-PEI

HONG KONG

MACAU (Port.)

Tropic of Cancer

A   S   I   A

84

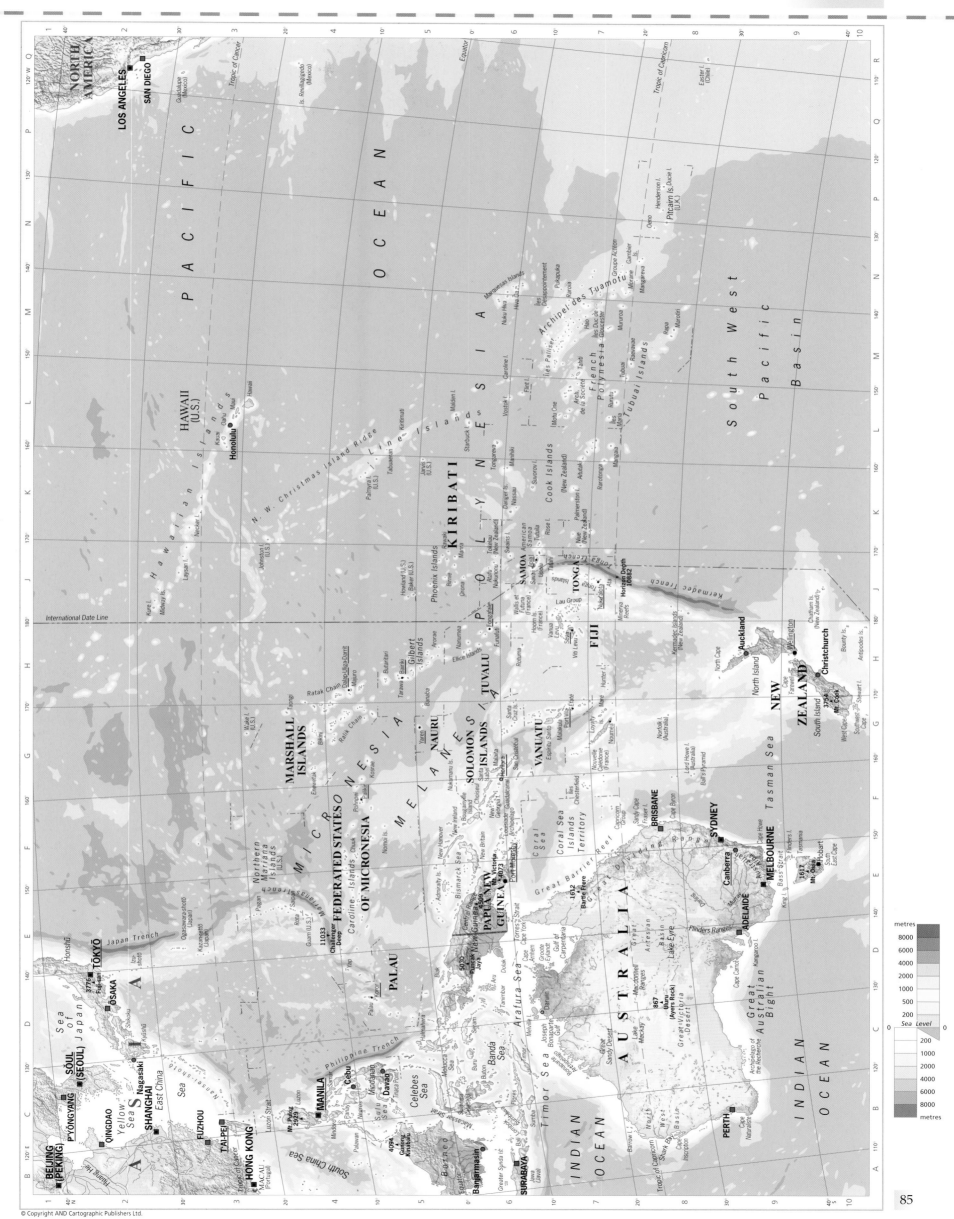

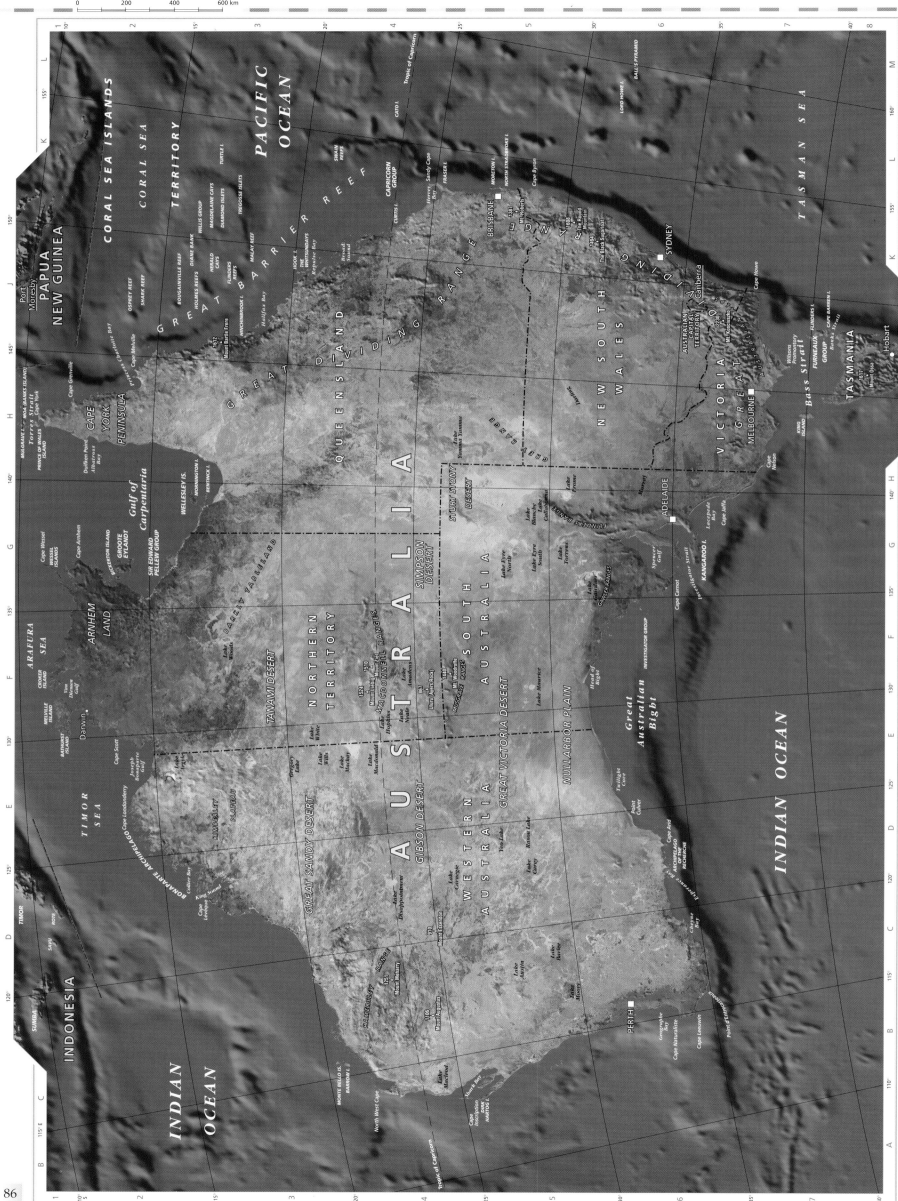

Scale 1 : 15 500 000

0   200   400   600 km

INDIAN
OCEAN

PACIFIC
OCEAN

INDONESIA

PAPUA
NEW GUINEA

Port
Moresby

CORAL SEA ISLANDS

CORAL SEA

TERRITORY

ARAFURA
SEA

TIMOR
SEA

SUMBA
SAVU
ROTE
TIMOR

Gulf of
Carpentaria

CAPE
YORK
PENINSULA

ARNHEM
LAND

Darwin

NORTHERN
TERRITORY

TANAMI DESERT

BARKLY TABLELAND

QUEENSLAND

GREAT BARRIER REEF

GREAT DIVIDING RANGE

Brisbane

WESTERN
AUSTRALIA

GREAT SANDY DESERT

GIBSON DESERT

GREAT VICTORIA DESERT

SOUTH
AUSTRALIA

SIMPSON
DESERT

STURT STONY
DESERT

AUSTRALIA

NULLARBOR PLAIN

Great
Australian
Bight

ADELAIDE

NEW SOUTH
WALES

SYDNEY

Canberra
AUSTRALIAN
CAPITAL
TERRITORY

VICTORIA

MELBOURNE

INDIAN OCEAN

PERTH

GREAT AUSTRALIAN BIGHT

TASMAN SEA

BASS STRAIT

TASMANIA

Hobart

© Copyright

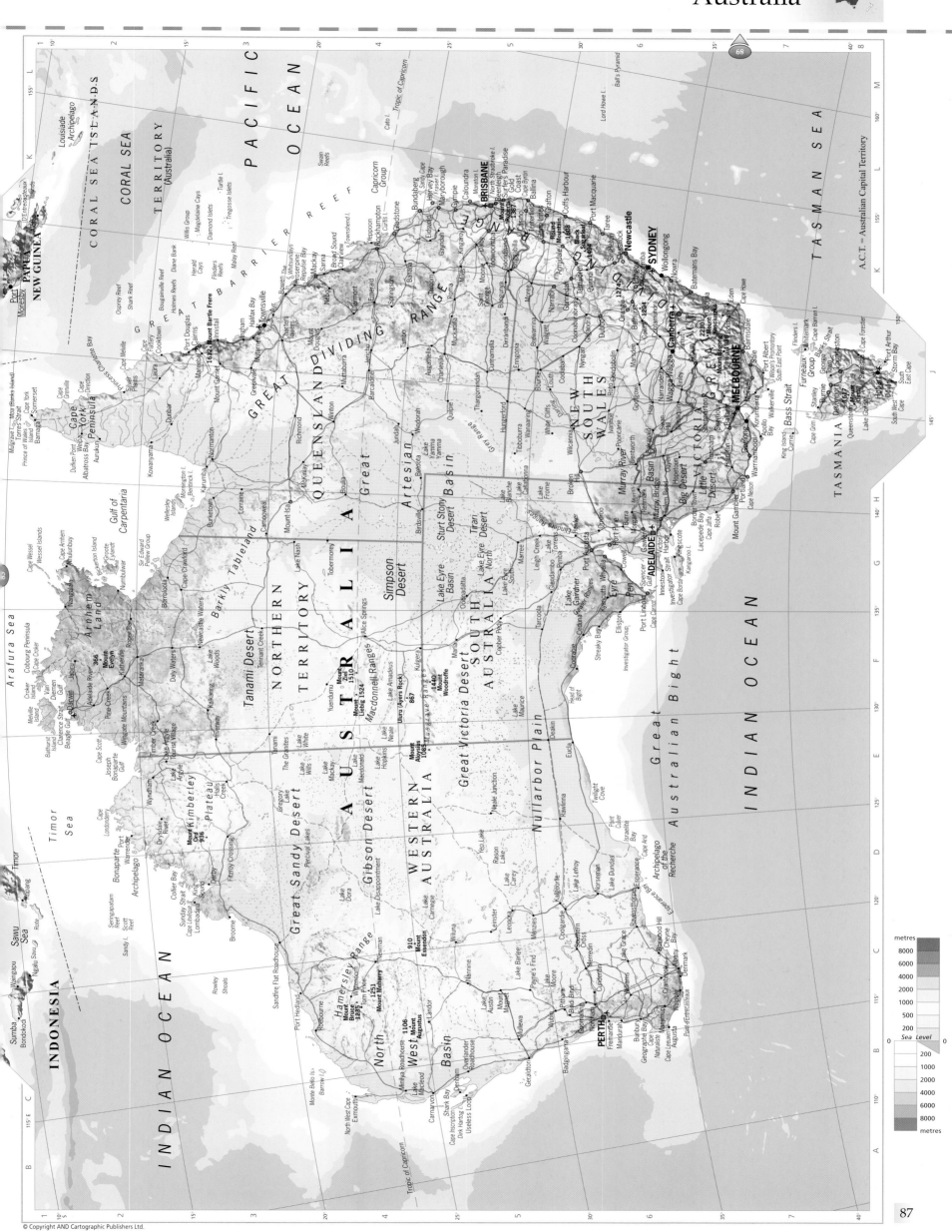

A.C.T. = Australian Capital Territory

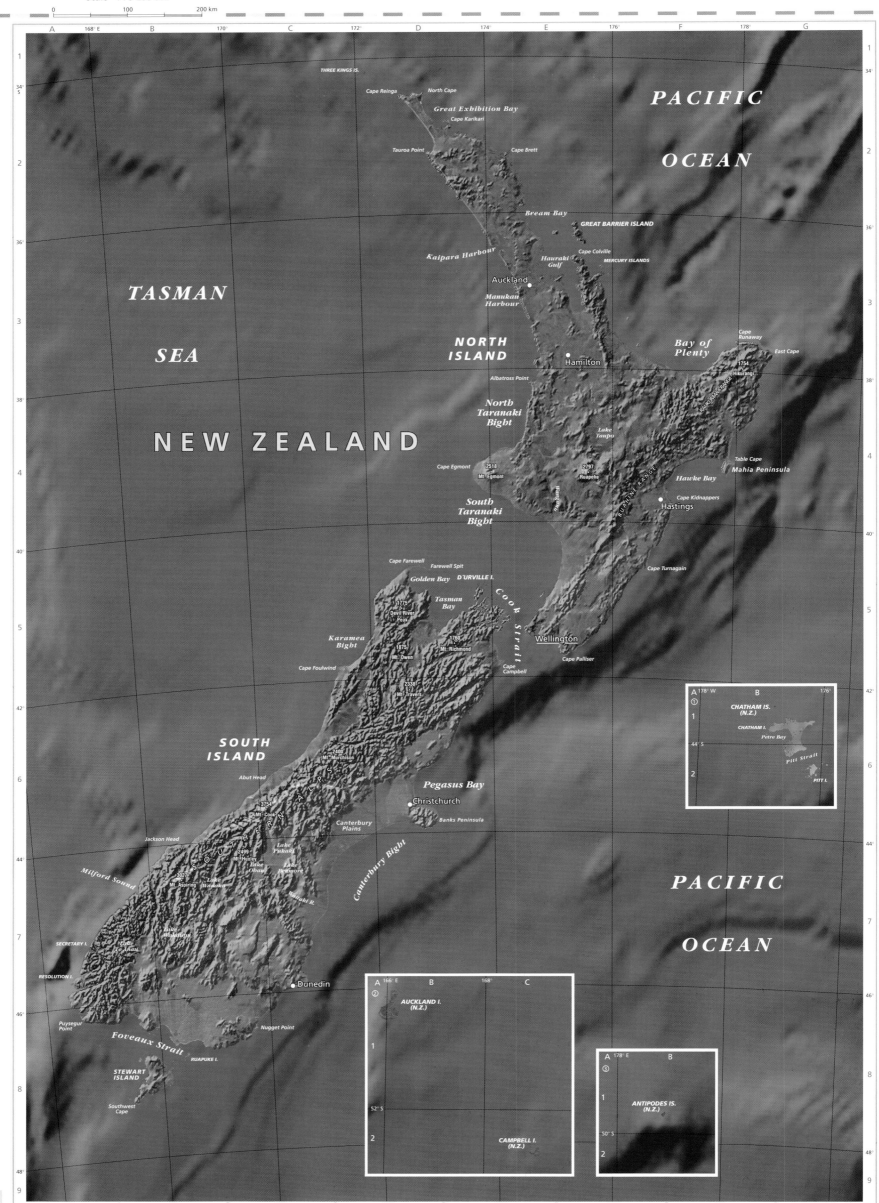

Scale 1 : 5 200 000

0   100   200 km

PACIFIC

OCEAN

THREE KINGS IS.

Cape Reinga   North Cape
Great Exhibition Bay
Cape Karikari

Tauroa Point   Cape Brett

Bream Bay
GREAT BARRIER ISLAND

TASMAN   Kaipara Harbour   Cape Colville
Hauraki   MERCURY ISLANDS
Gulf

SEA   Auckland

Manukau
Harbour

Cape Runaway
Bay of   1754   East Cape
Plenty   Hikurangi

NORTH   Hamilton
ISLAND

NEW ZEALAND   Albatross Point

North
Taranaki   Lake
Bight   Taupo

Table Cape
Cape Egmont   2518   2797   Mahia Peninsula
Mt. Egmont   Ruapehu   Hawke Bay

South   Cape Kidnappers
Taranaki   Hastings
Bight

Cape Turnagain

Cape Farewell   Farewell Spit
D'URVILLE I.
Golden Bay
1775   Tasman
Devil River   Bay
Peak

Karamea   1875   1760
Bight   Mt. Owen   Mt. Richmond   Wellington

Cape Foulwind   Cape Palliser
2338   Cape
Mt. Travers   Campbell

CHATHAM IS.
(N.Z.)

CHATHAM I.

Petre Bay

SOUTH   2400
ISLAND   Mt. Murchison
Pitt Strait

Abut Head   PITT I.

Pegasus Bay
3754   Christchurch
Mt. Cook
Banks Peninsula
Jackson Head   Canterbury
2499   Lake   Plains
Mt. Huxley   Pukaki
3027   Lake   Canterbury Bight
Mt. Aspiring   Wanaka   Lake
Benmore
Lake
Wakatipu   Waitaki R.   PACIFIC

SECRETARY I.   Lake
Te Anau   OCEAN

RESOLUTION I.   Dunedin

Puysegur   Nugget Point   AUCKLAND I.
Point   (N.Z.)
Foveaux Strait
ANTIPODES IS.
STEWART   (N.Z.)
ISLAND

Southwest   RUAPUKE I.
Cape   CAMPBELL I.
(N.Z.)

88

© Copyright

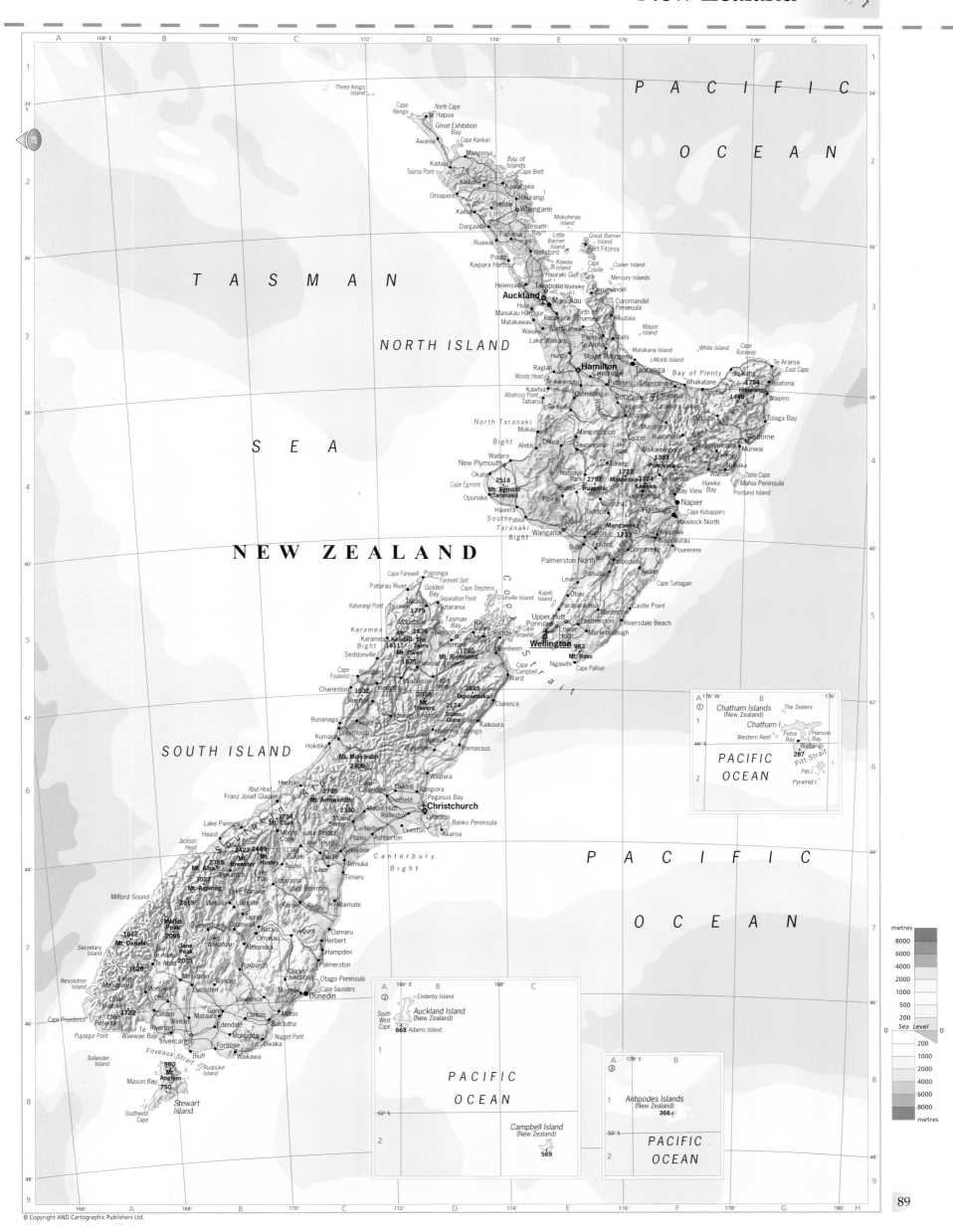

© Copyright AND Cartographic Publishers Ltd.

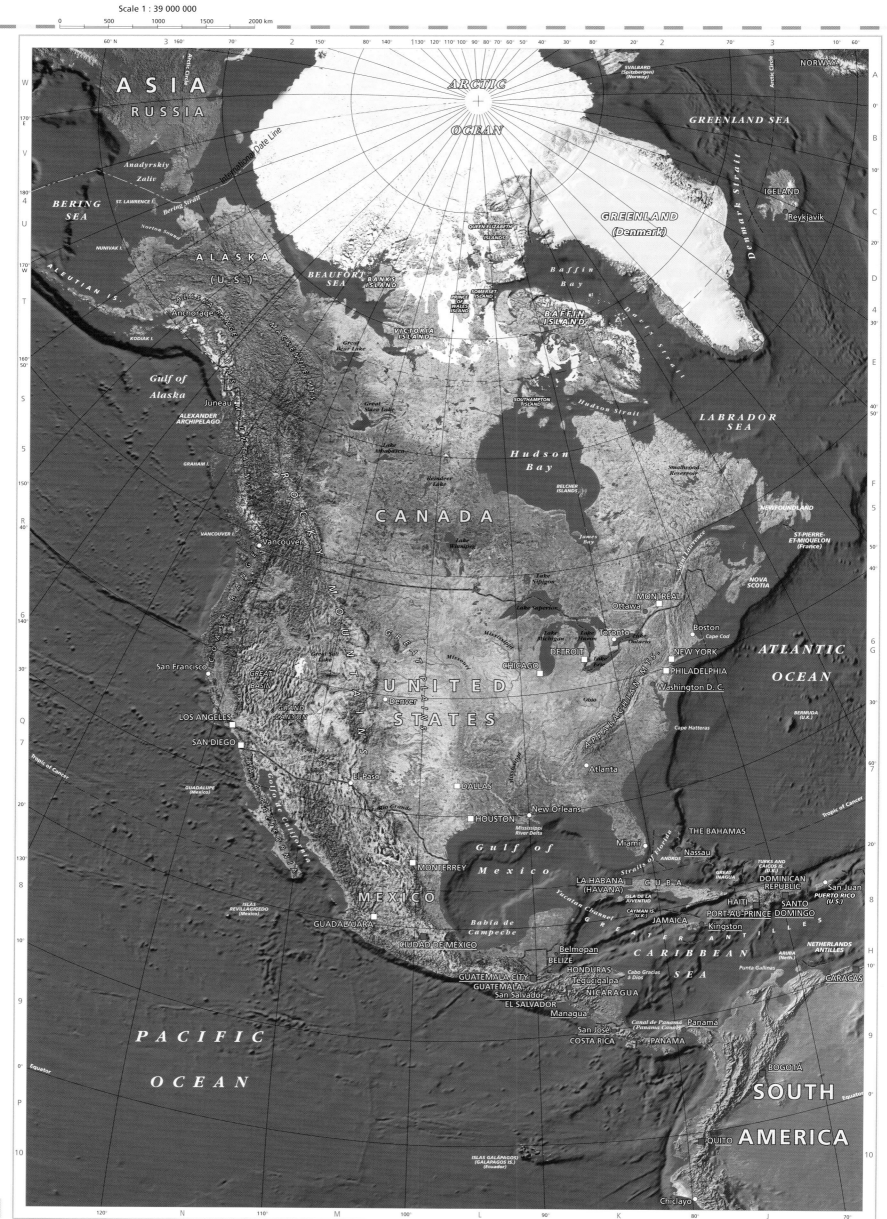

Scale 1 : 39 000 000

0   500   1000   1500   2000 km

60° N   3   160°   70°   2   150°   80°   140°   130°   120° 110° 100° 90° 80° 70° 60°   50°   40°   30°   80°   20°   2   70°   3   10°   60°

W

170°
E

A
0°
B
0°
C
10°
20°
D
30°
4
40°
E
50°
F
5
6
G
30°
60°
7
20°
8
10°
9
0°
P
10

ASIA
RUSSIA

ARCTIC
OCEAN

SVALBARD
(Spitsbergen)
(Norway)

NORWAY

GREENLAND SEA

Anadyrskiy
Zaliv

International Date Line

ST. LAWRENCE I.

Bering Strait

BERING
SEA

Norton Sound

NUNIVAK I.

ALASKA
(U.S.)

BEAUFORT
SEA

BANKS
ISLAND

VICTORIA
ISLAND

QUEEN ELIZABETH
ISLANDS

SOMERSET
ISLAND
PRINCE
OF
WALES
ISLAND

Baffin
Bay

GREENLAND
(Denmark)

Denmark Strait

Arctic Circle

ICELAND

Reykjavik

Davis Strait

BAFFIN
ISLAND

ALASKA RANGE

Anchorage

KODIAK I.

Gulf of
Alaska

ALEUTIAN IS.

MACKENZIE MTS.

Great
Bear Lake

SOUTHAMPTON
ISLAND

Hudson Strait

LABRADOR
SEA

Juneau

Great
Slave Lake

Smallwood
Reservoir

ALEXANDER
ARCHIPELAGO

GRAHAM I.

Lake
Athabasca

Reindeer
Lake

Hudson
Bay

NEWFOUNDLAND

CANADA

James
Bay

ST-PIERRE-
ET-MIQUELON
(France)

VANCOUVER I.

Lake
Winnipeg

Lake
Nipigon

Saint Lawrence

NOVA
SCOTIA

Vancouver

Lake Superior

MONTRÉAL

Ottawa

Lake
Michigan
Lake
Huron
Toronto

Boston
Cape Cod

ATLANTIC

DETROIT
CHICAGO

Lake
Ontario
Lake
Erie

NEW YORK

OCEAN

San Francisco

GREAT
BASIN

Great Salt
Lake

Missouri

Mississippi

Denver

UNITED
STATES

Ohio

PHILADELPHIA
Washington D. C.

APPALACHIAN MTS.

BERMUDA
(U.K.)

COAST RANGE

ROCKY MOUNTAINS

GREAT PLAINS

LOS ANGELES

GRAND
CANYON

Cape Hatteras

SAN DIEGO

Tropic of Cancer

El Paso

Mississippi

Atlanta

DALLAS

GUADALUPE
(Mexico)

Rio Grande

BAJA CALIFORNIA

Golfo de California

HOUSTON

New Orleans

Mississippi
River Delta

Tropic of Cancer

ISLAS
REVILLAGIGEDO
(Mexico)

MONTERREY

Gulf of
Mexico

Miami

THE BAHAMAS

Nassau

Straits of Florida

ANDROS

CUBA

GREAT
INAGUA

TURKS AND
CAICOS IS.
(U.K.)

DOMINICAN
REPUBLIC

San Juan
PUERTO RICO
(U.S.)

MEXICO

LA HABANA
(HAVANA)

ISLA DE LA
JUVENTUD

CAYMAN IS.
(U.K.)

JAMAICA

HAITI
PORT-AU-PRINCE

SANTO
DOMINGO

GUADALAJARA

Bahía de
Campeche

GREATER ANTILLES

Kingston

NETHERLANDS
ANTILLES

PACIFIC

CIUDAD DE MÉXICO

Yucatán Channel

Belmopan
BELIZE

HONDURAS
Tegucigalpa

Cabo Gracias
a Dios

ARUBA
(Neth.)

Punta Gallinas

CARACAS

CARIBBEAN

SEA

GUATEMALA CITY
GUATEMALA
San Salvador
EL SALVADOR
Managua

NICARAGUA

OCEAN

San José
COSTA RICA

Canal de Panamá
(Panama Canal)

Panamá

PANAMA

Equator

BOGOTÁ

QUITO

SOUTH

AMERICA

ISLAS GALÁPAGOS
(GALAPAGOS IS.)
(Ecuador)

Chiclayo

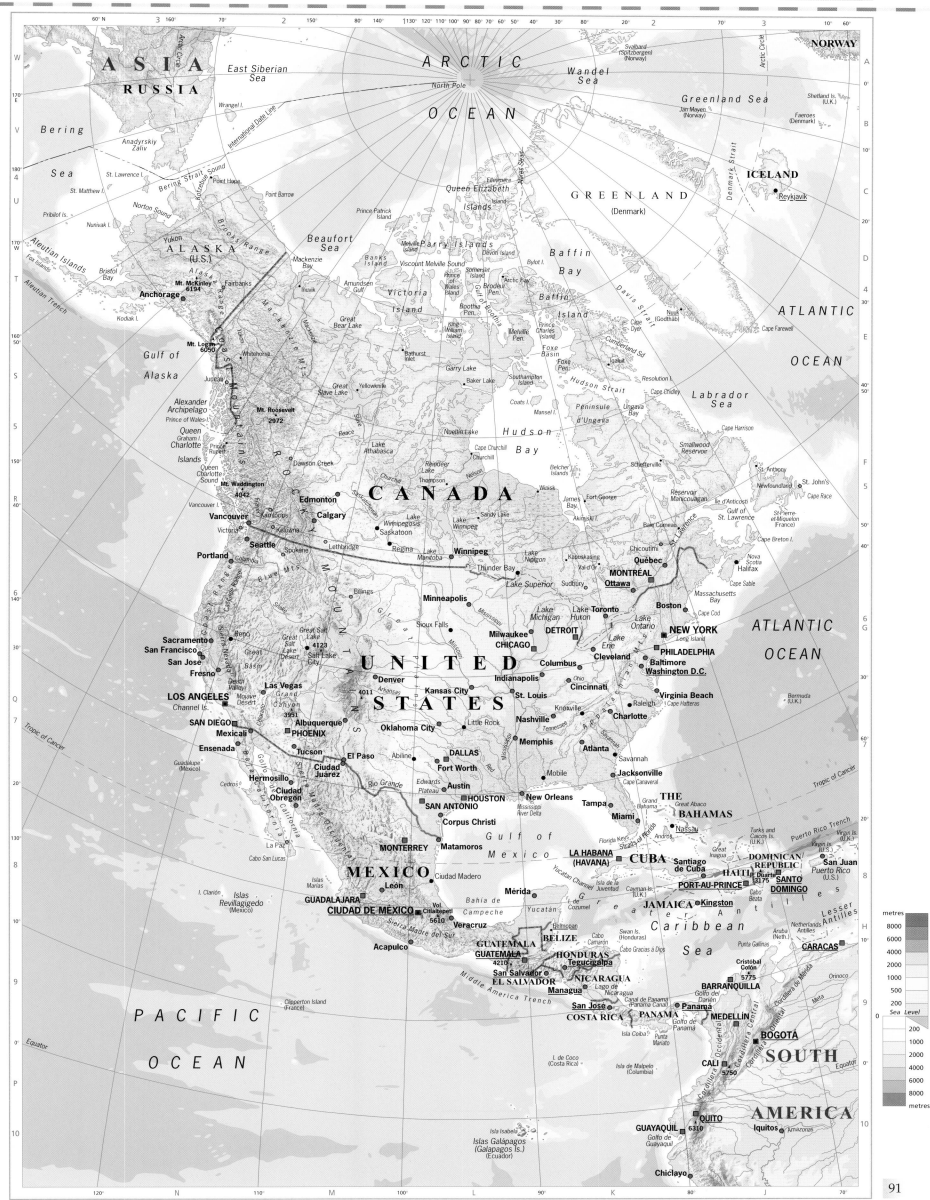

Scale 1 : 15 500 000

200   400   600 km

© Copyright

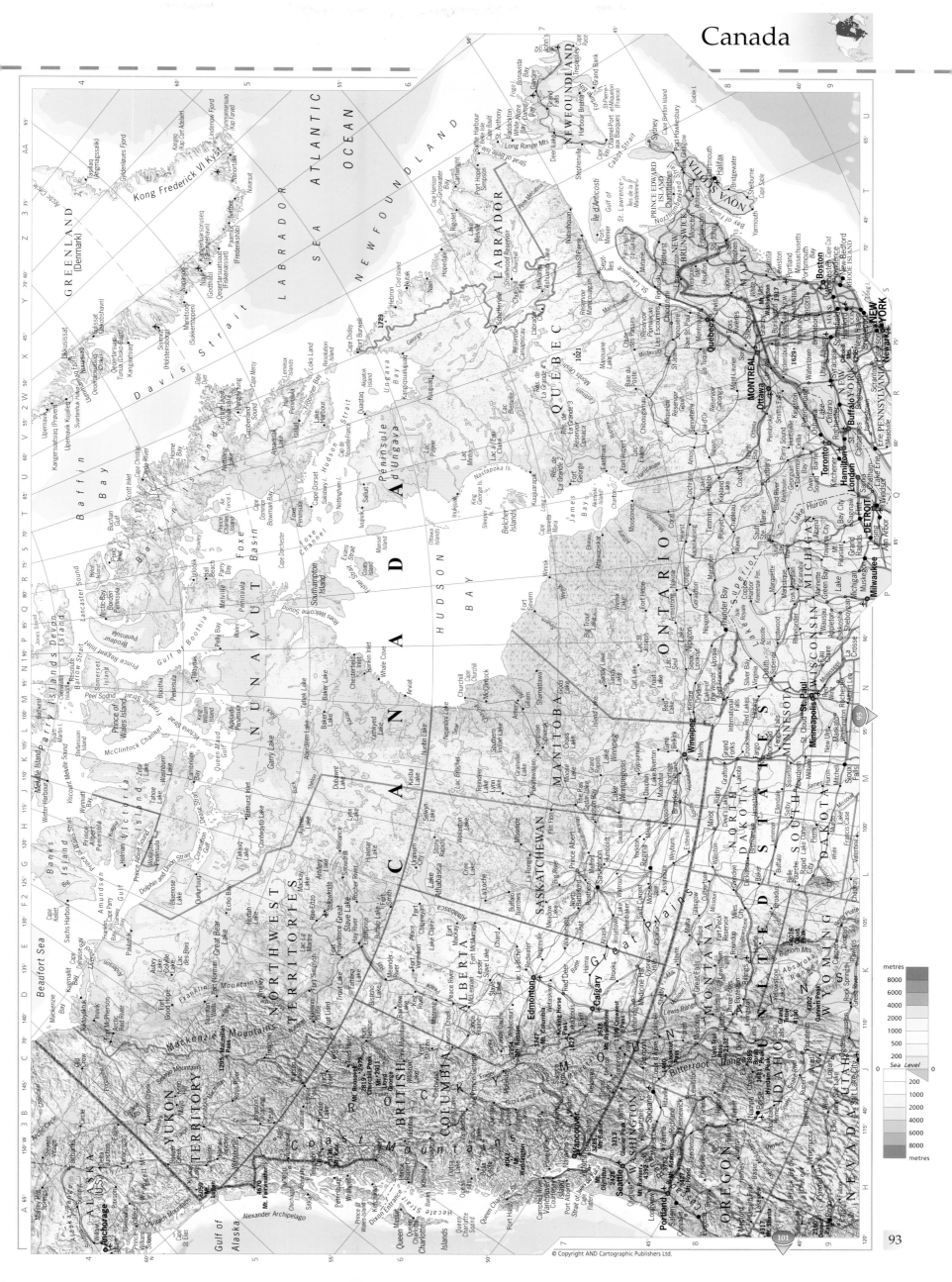

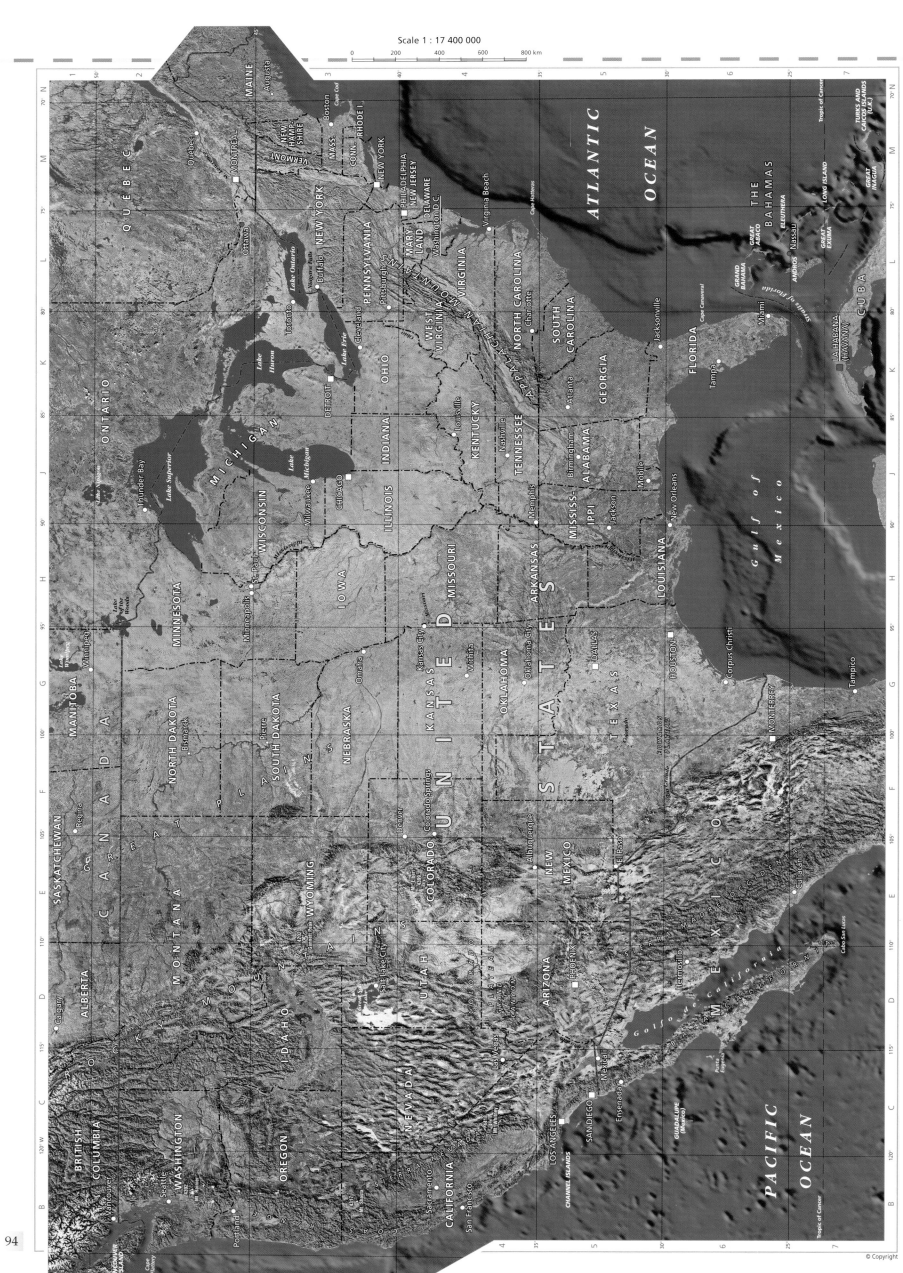

0   200   400   600   800 km

94

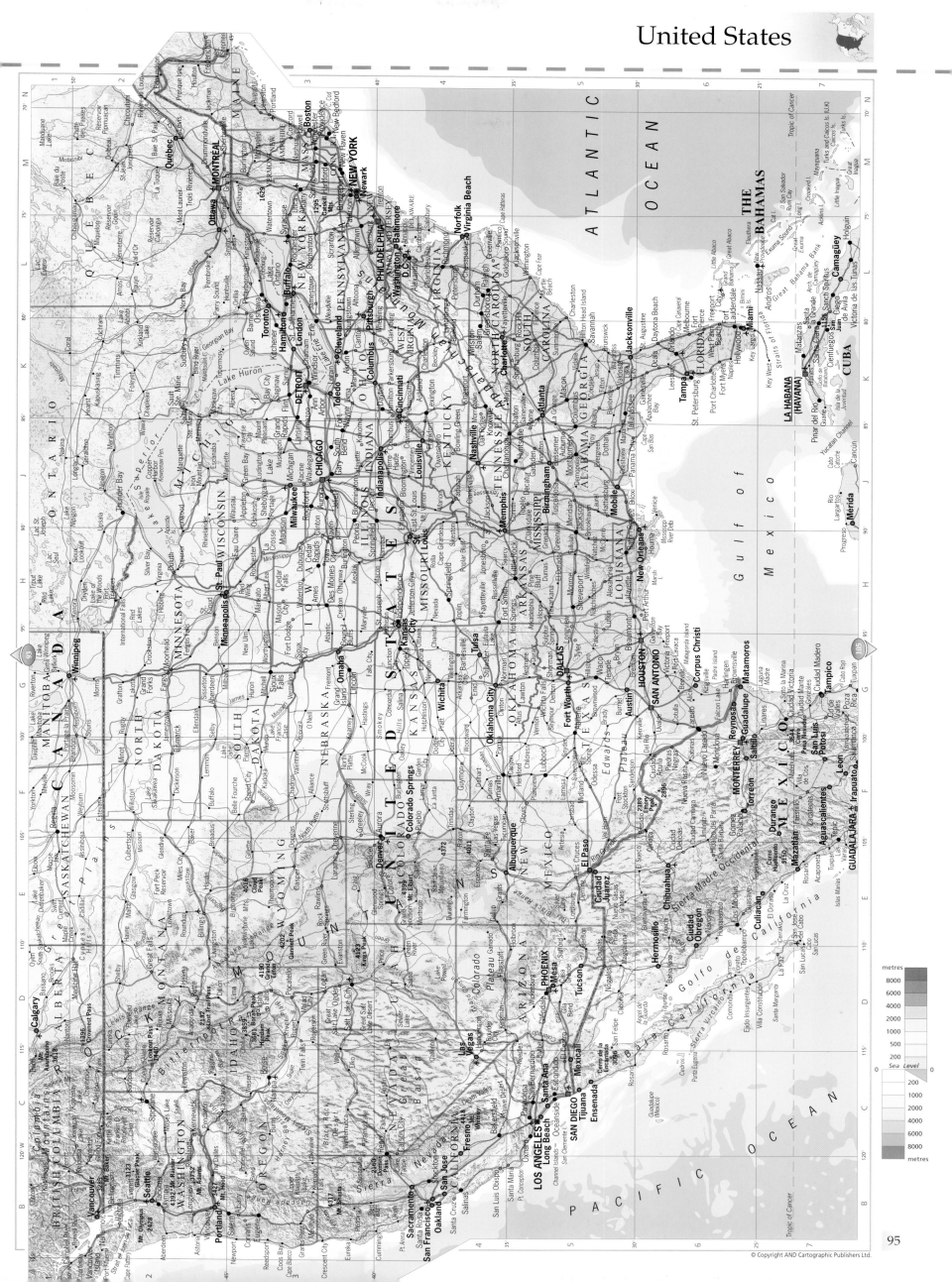

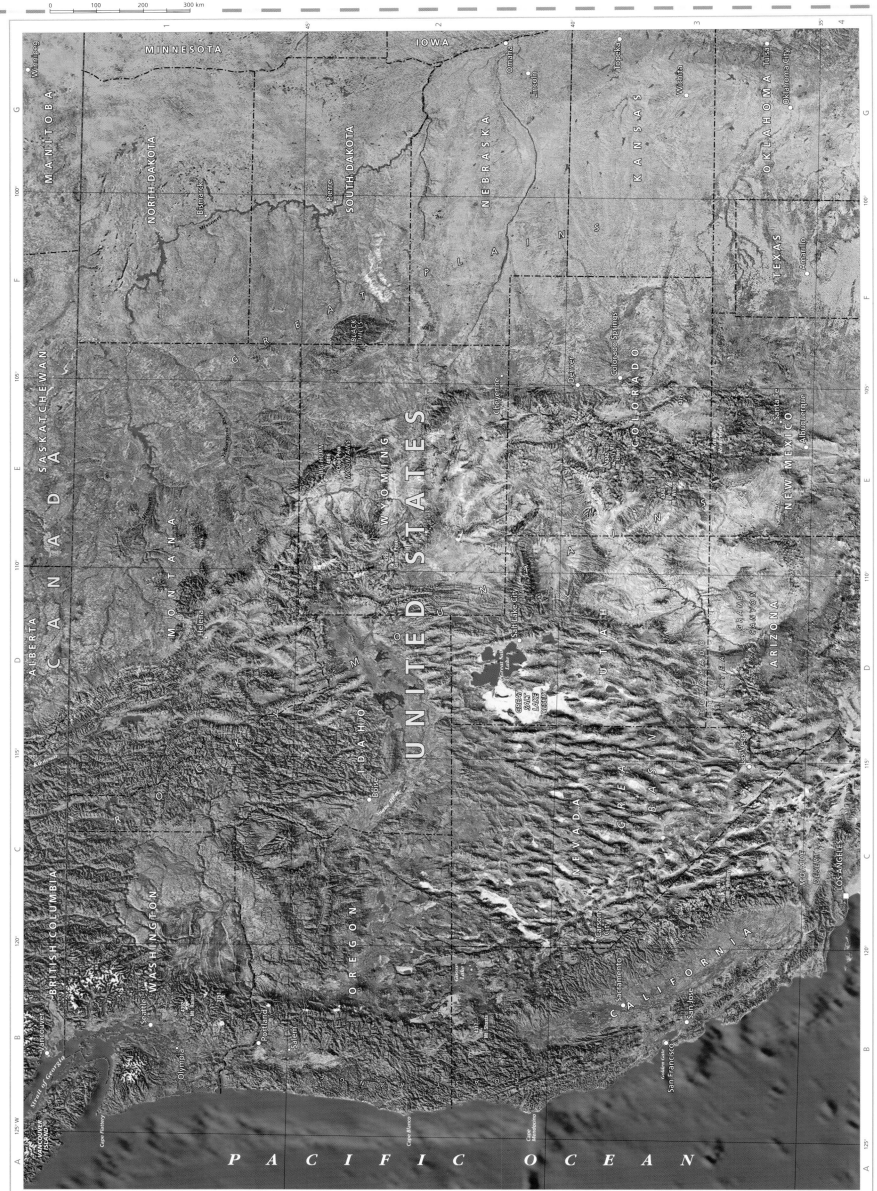

Scale 1 : 8 100 000

0   100   200   300 km

MANITOBA
SASKATCHEWAN
ALBERTA
CANADA
BRITISH COLUMBIA

VANCOUVER ISLAND
Vancouver
Cape Flattery

MINNESOTA
NORTH DAKOTA
Bismarck
SOUTH DAKOTA
Pierre
BLACK HILLS

IOWA
Omaha
Lincoln
NEBRASKA
GREAT
PLAINS

KANSAS
Topeka
Wichita

OKLAHOMA
Tulsa
Oklahoma City

TEXAS
Amarillo

COLORADO
Denver
Colorado Springs
Cheyenne

NEW MEXICO
Santa Fe
Albuquerque

WYOMING
BIG HORN
MOUNTAINS

MONTANA
Helena

IDAHO
Boise

UNITED STATES

ROCKY MOUNTAINS

UTAH
Salt Lake City
GREAT SALT LAKE
GREAT SALT LAKE DESERT

ARIZONA
GRAND CANYON
COLORADO PLATEAU

NEVADA
GREAT BASIN
Las Vegas
Carson City

CALIFORNIA
Sacramento
San Jose
San Francisco
Golden Gate
LOS ANGELES
MOJAVE DESERT

WASHINGTON
Seattle
Olympia
Mt. Rainier

OREGON
Portland
Salem
Mt. Shasta

PACIFIC OCEAN

96

© Copyright

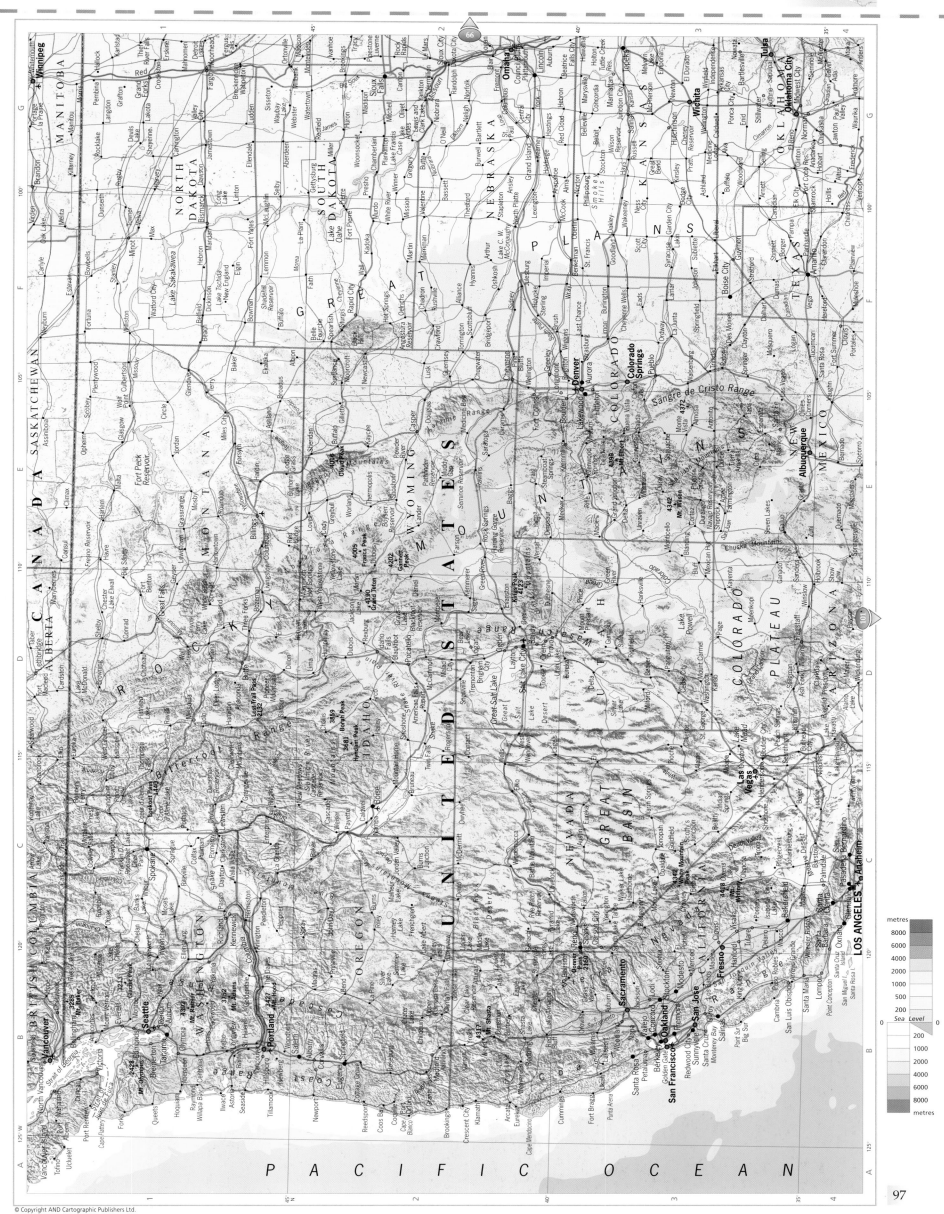

Scale 1 : 8 100 000

0   100   200   300 km

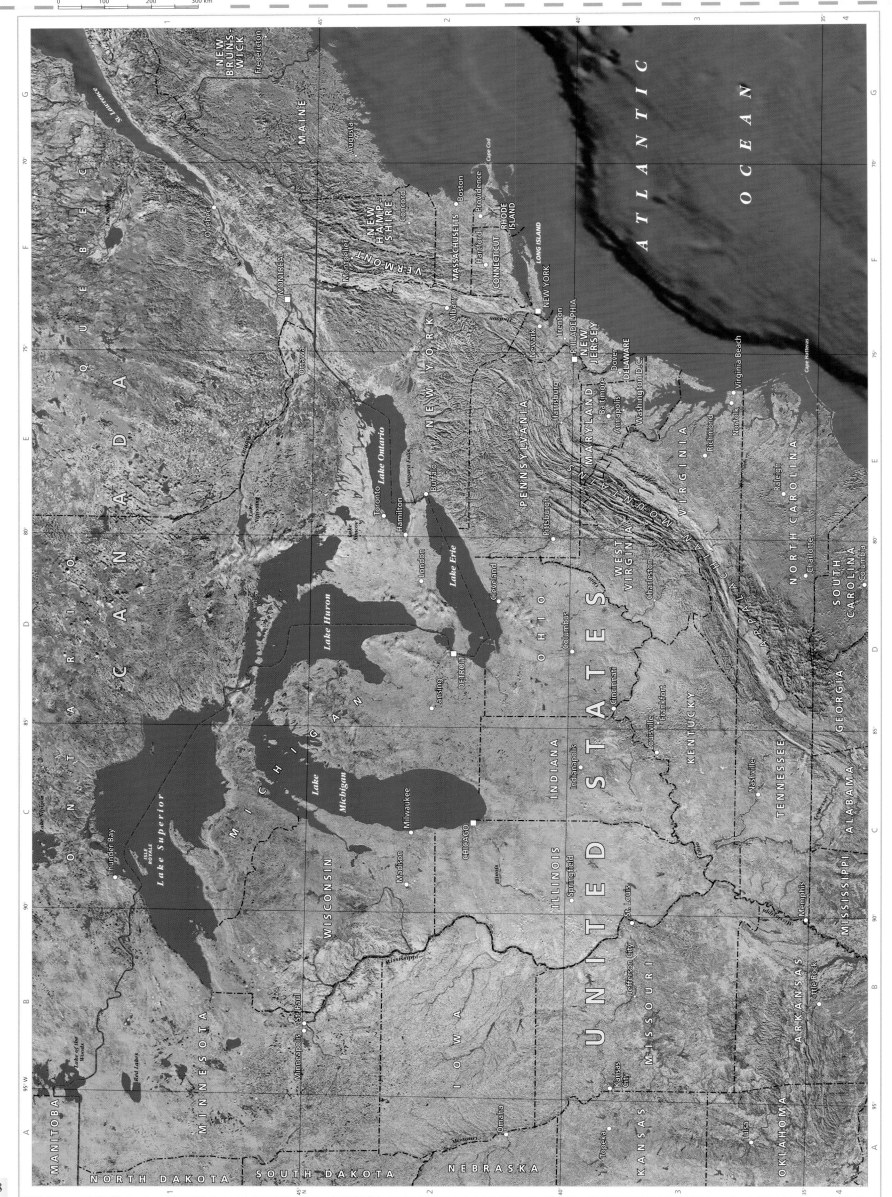

98

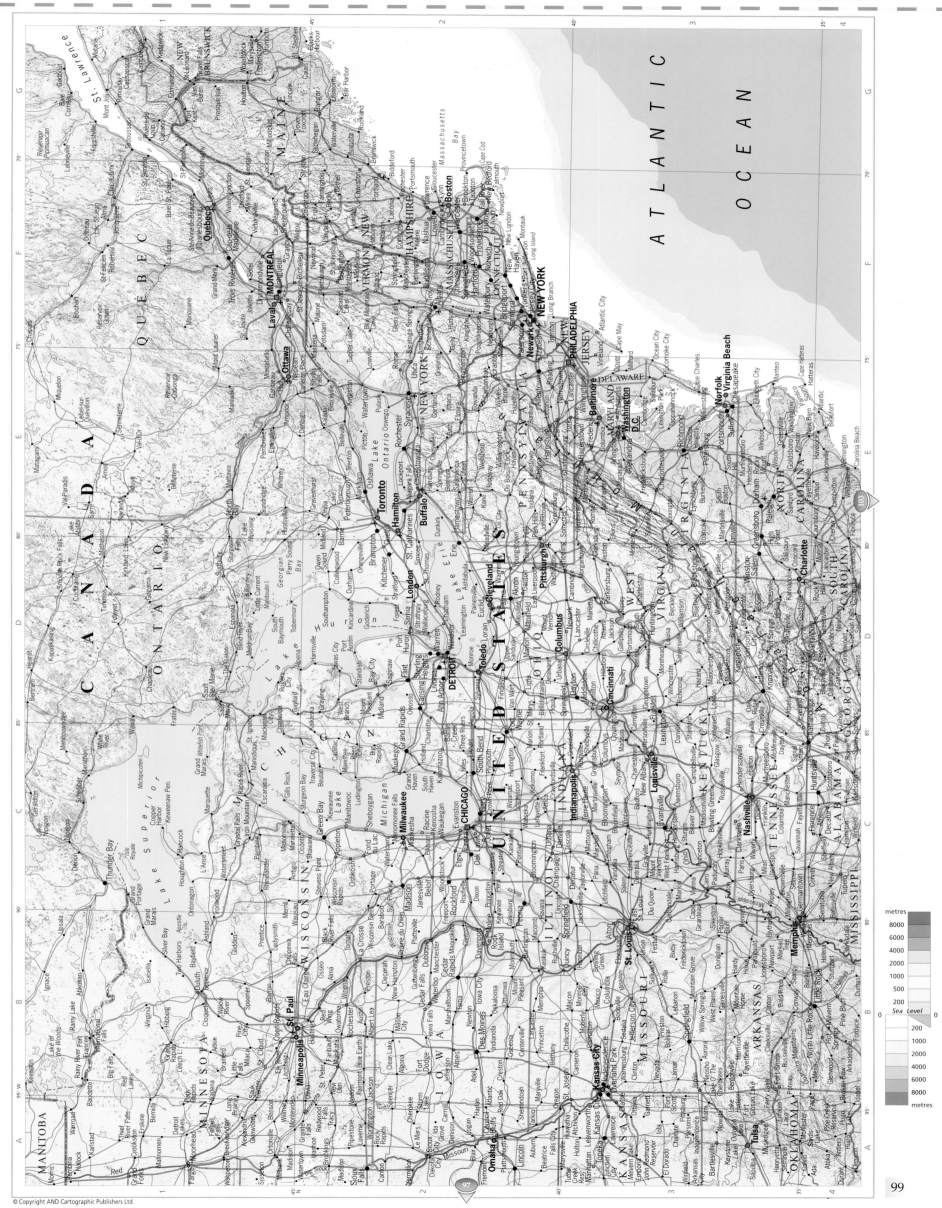

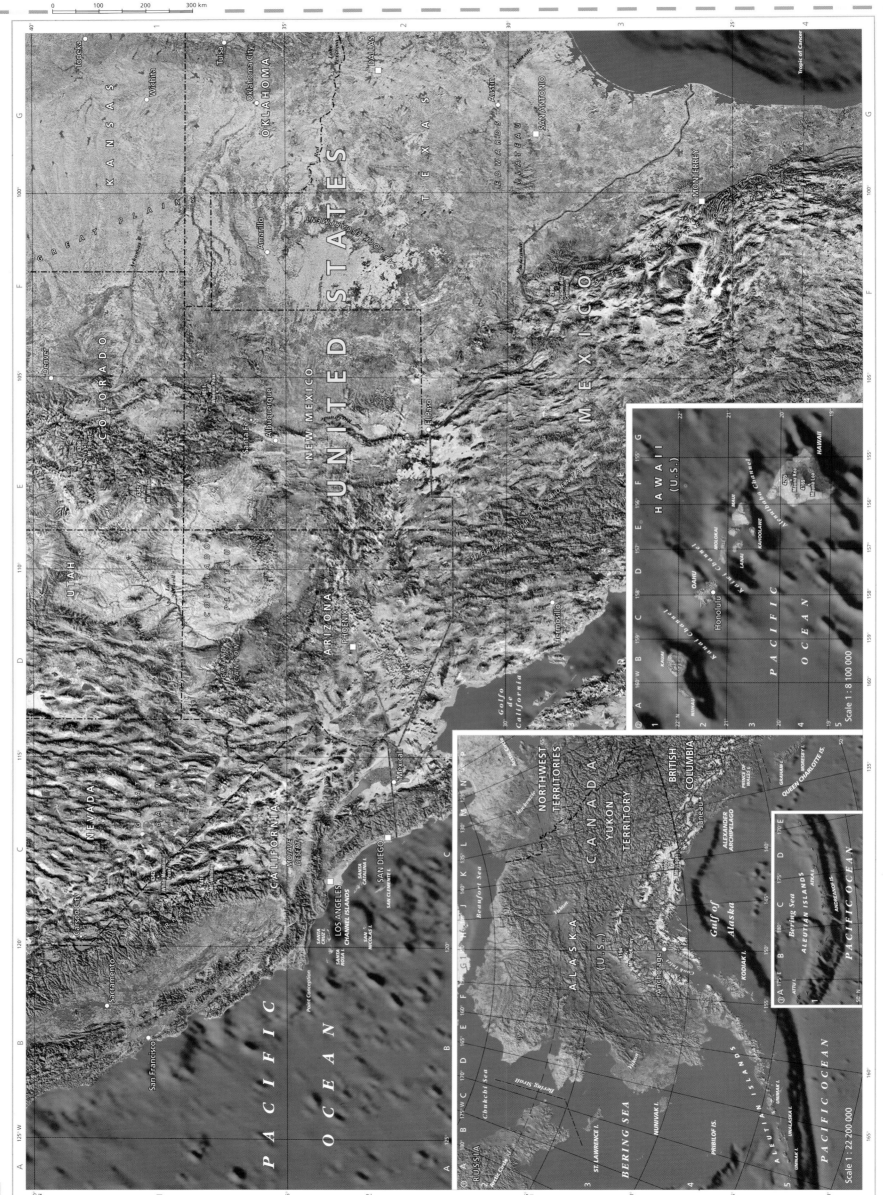

Scale 1 : 8 100 000

0   100   200   300 km

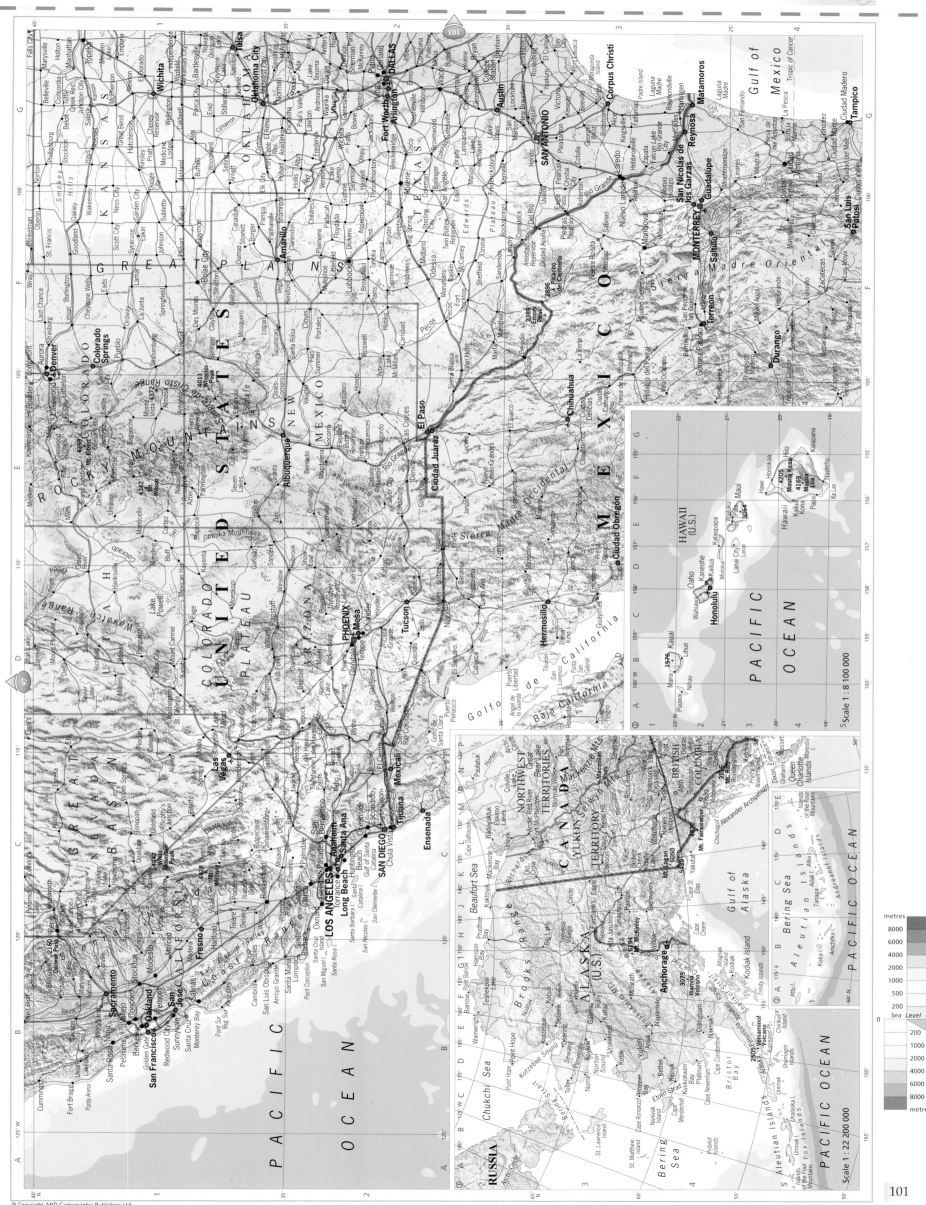

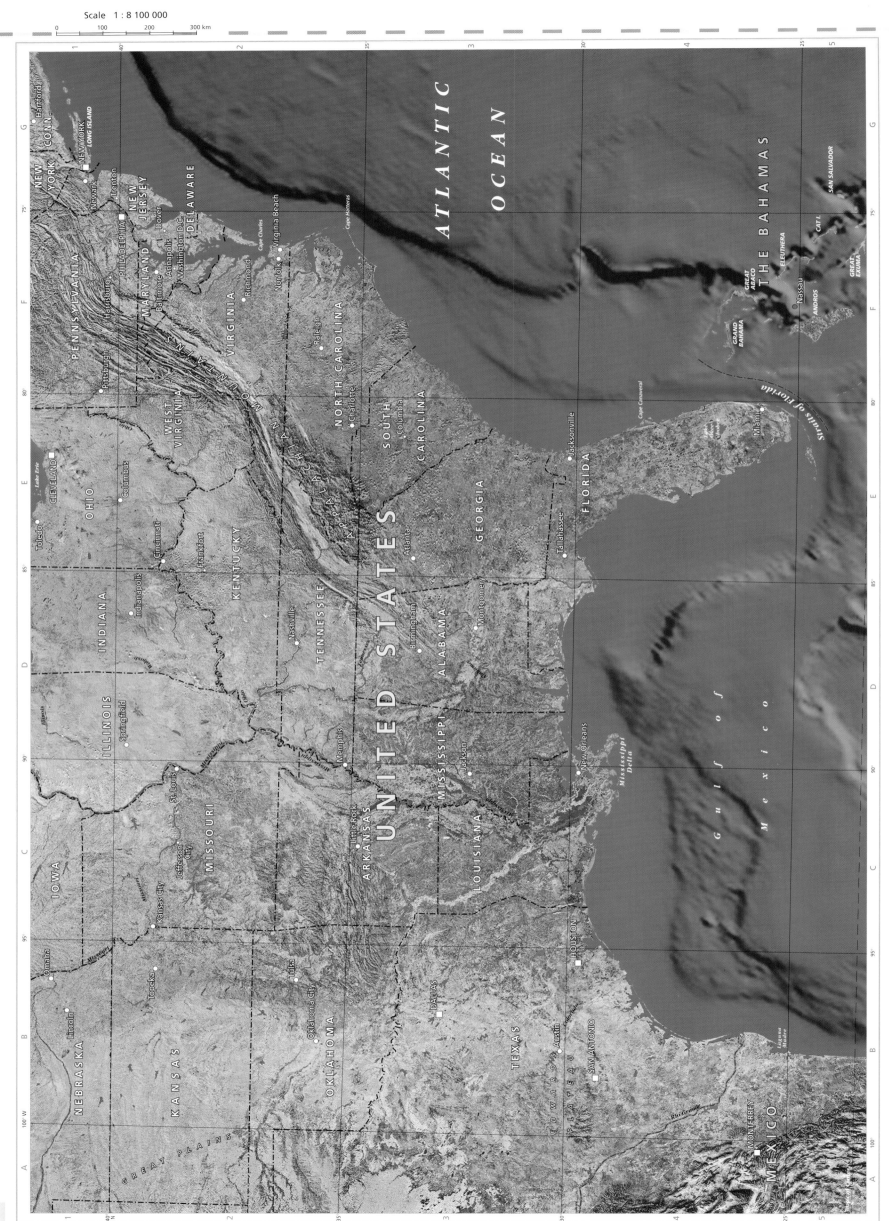

Scale 1 : 8 100 000

0   100   200   300 km

ATLANTIC

OCEAN

THE BAHAMAS

GRAND BAHAMA
GREAT ABACO
ELEUTHERA
CAT I.
SAN SALVADOR
Nassau
ANDROS
GREAT EXUMA

Straits of Florida

Cape Canaveral

Miami

FLORIDA

Jacksonville

Tallahassee

GEORGIA

Atlanta

ALABAMA

Montgomery

Birmingham

MISSISSIPPI

Jackson

LOUISIANA

New Orleans

Mississippi Delta

Gulf of

Mexico

UNITED STATES

Memphis

TENNESSEE

Nashville

KENTUCKY

Frankfort

ARKANSAS

Little Rock

MISSOURI

Jefferson City

St. Louis

SOUTH

CAROLINA

Columbia

NORTH CAROLINA

Charlotte

Raleigh

Cape Hatteras

VIRGINIA

Richmond

Norfolk   Virginia Beach

Cape Charles

APPALACHIAN MOUNTAINS

WEST VIRGINIA

MARYLAND

Washington D.C.

Annapolis

Baltimore

DELAWARE

Dover

NEW JERSEY

Philadelphia

Trenton

Newark

NEW YORK

NEW YORK

LONG ISLAND

Hartford   **CONN.**

PENNSYLVANIA

Harrisburg

Pittsburgh

OHIO

Columbus

Cincinnati

Frankfort

Toledo

CLEVELAND

Lake Erie

Ohio

INDIANA

Indianapolis

ILLINOIS

Springfield

IOWA

Omaha

Lincoln

NEBRASKA

Kansas City

Topeka

KANSAS

Tulsa

Oklahoma City

OKLAHOMA

GREAT PLAINS

TEXAS

DALLAS

SAN ANTONIO

Austin

HOUSTON

EDWARDS PLATEAU

Rio Grande

Laguna Madre

MONTERREY

MEXICO

102

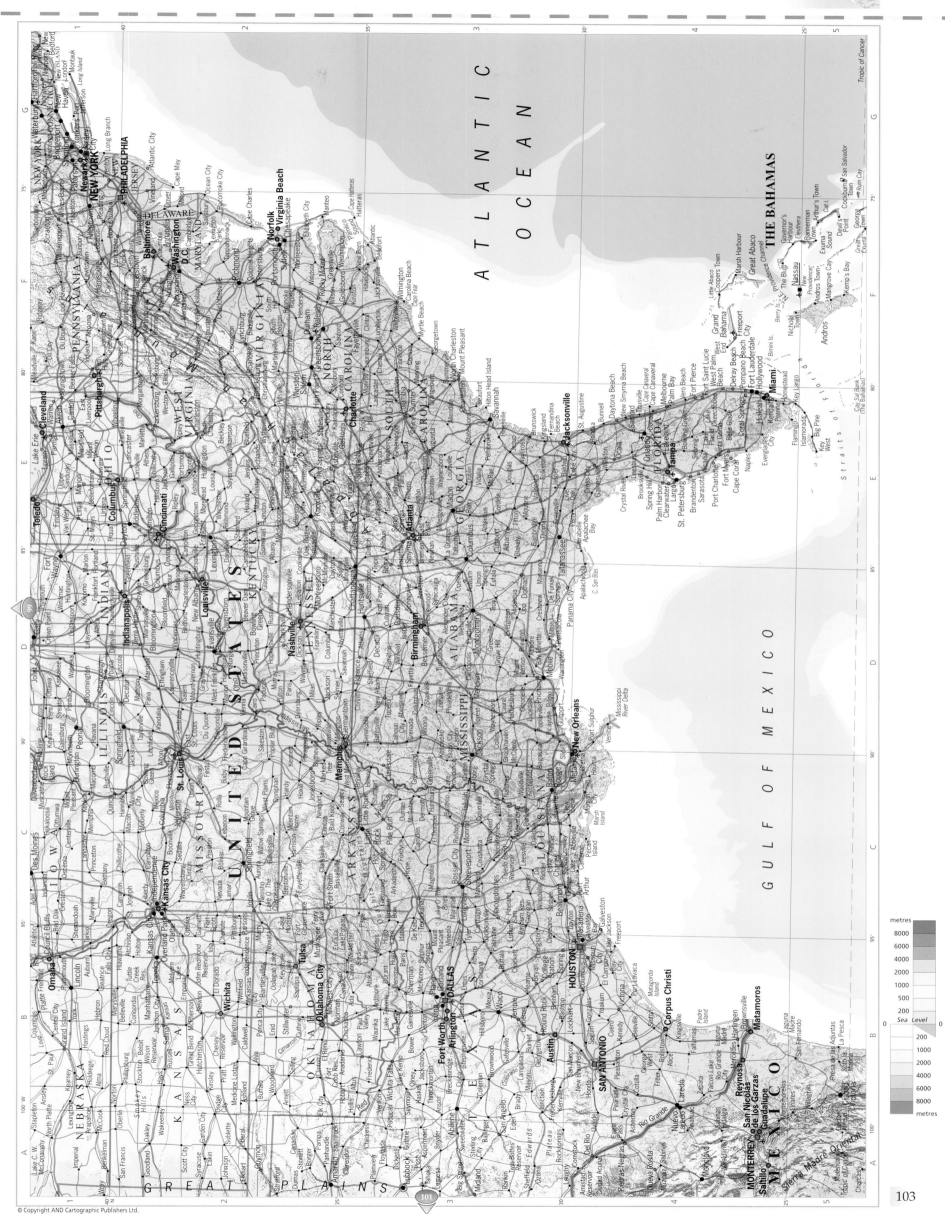

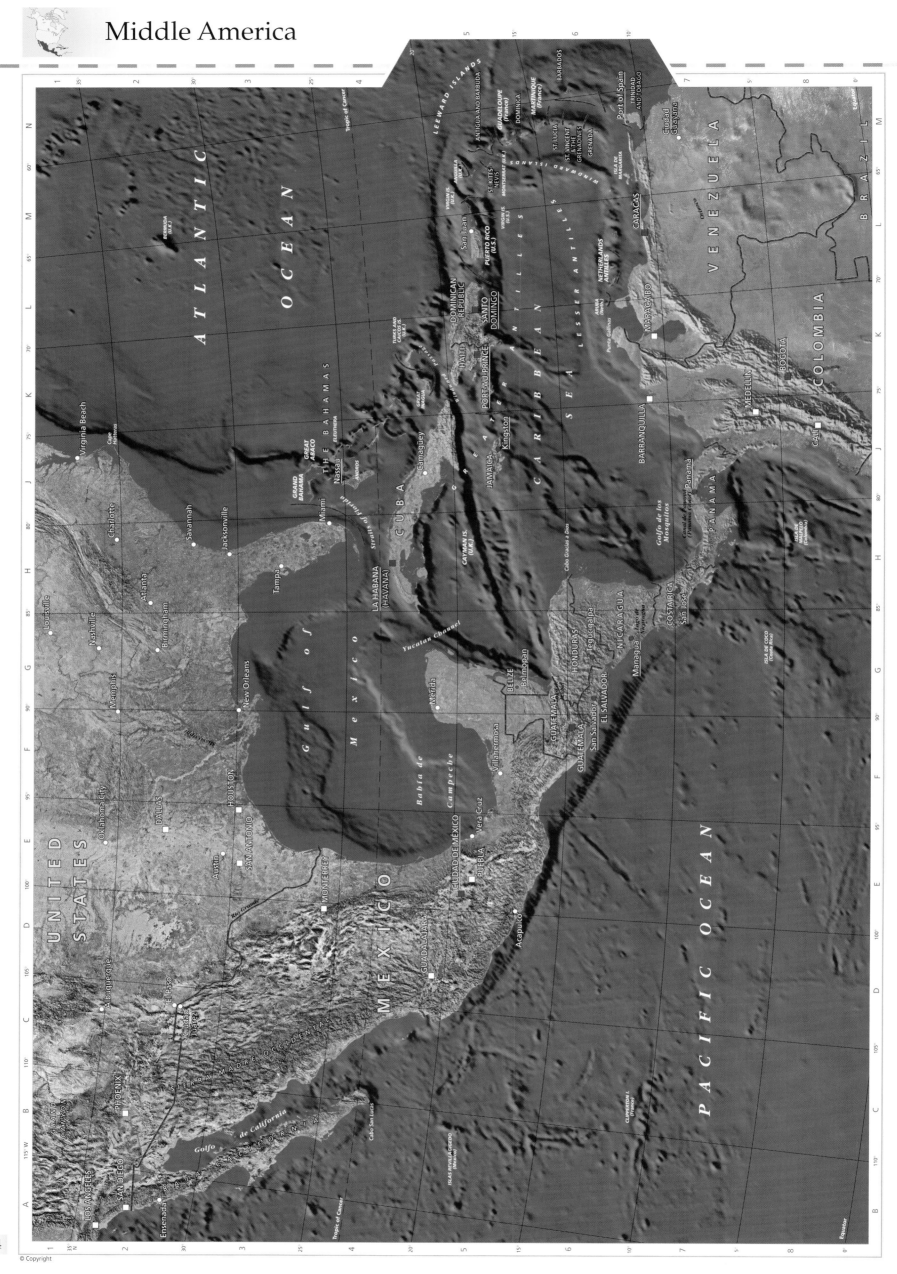

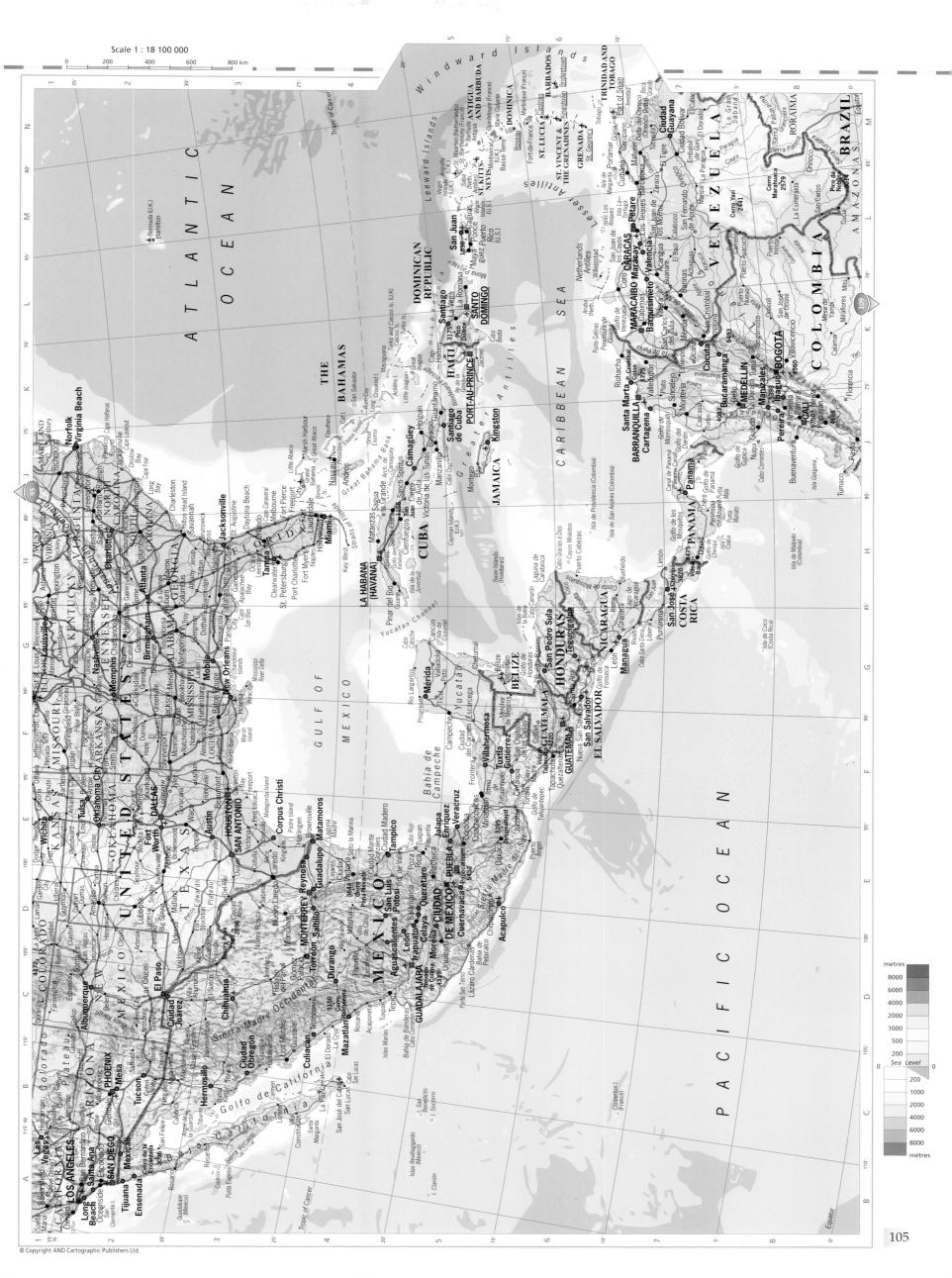

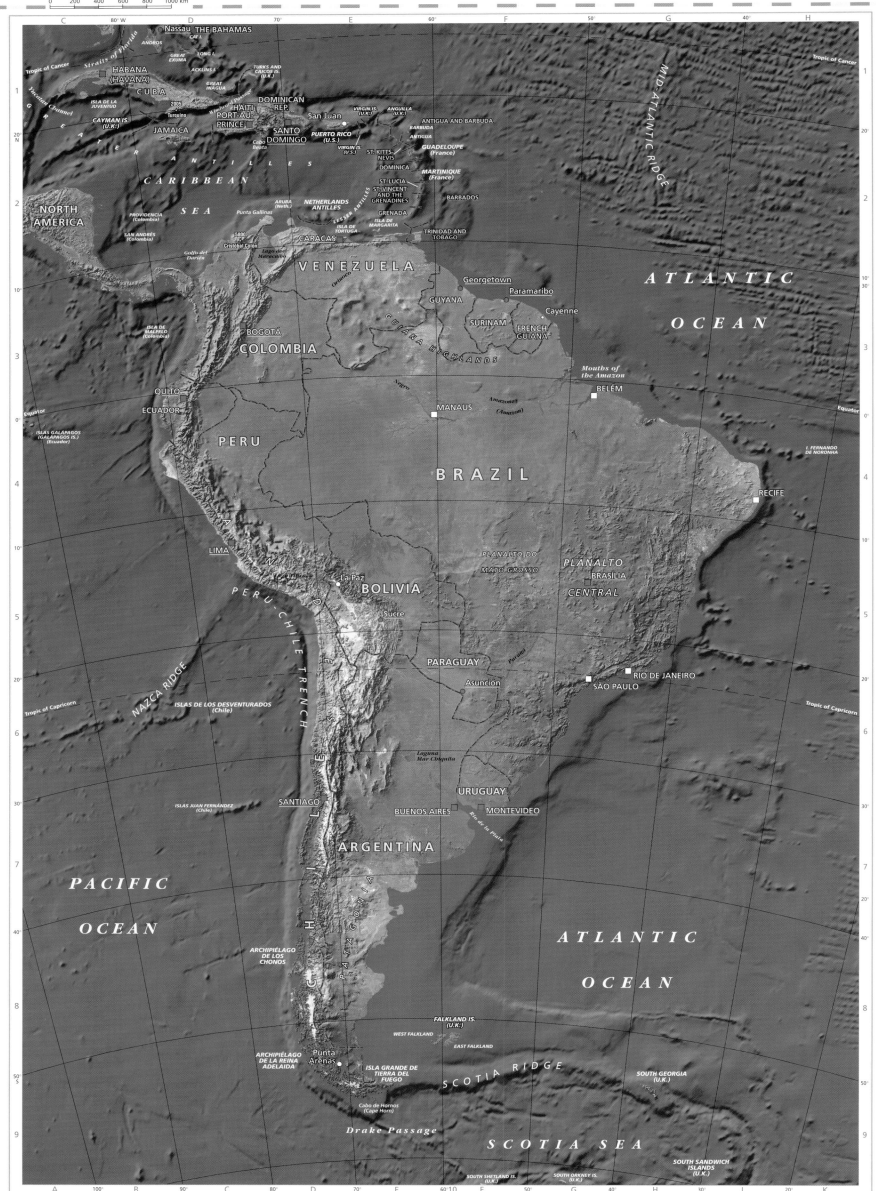

Scale 1 : 31 500 000

0   200   400   600   800   1000 km

© Copyright

NORTH AMERICA

Tropic of Cancer

THE BAHAMAS
Nassau
ANDROS
GREAT
EXUMA
LONG I.
CAT I.
ACKLINS I.
TURKS AND CAICOS I. (U.K.)

Straits of Florida

Yucatan Channel

HABANA (HAVANA)
CUBA
ISLA DE LA JUVENTUD
2005
Turquino

GREAT INAGUA

Windward Passage

HAITI
PORT-AU-PRINCE
DOMINICAN REP.
SANTO DOMINGO

San Juan
PUERTO RICO (U.S.)
VIRGIN IS. (U.S.)
VIRGIN IS. (U.K.)
ANGUILLA (U.K.)
ANTIGUA AND BARBUDA
BARBUDA
ANTIGUA
ST. KITTS NEVIS
GUADELOUPE (France)
DOMINICA
MARTINIQUE (France)
ST. LUCIA
ST. VINCENT AND THE GRENADINES
BARBADOS
GRENADA

CAYMAN IS. (U.K.)
JAMAICA

Cabo Beata

CARIBBEAN SEA

GREATER ANTILLES

LESSER ANTILLES

PROVIDENCIA (Colombia)

SAN ANDRÉS (Colombia)

Punta Gallinas
ARUBA (Neth.)
NETHERLANDS ANTILLES
ISLA DE MARGARITA
ISLA DE TORTUGA
TRINIDAD AND TOBAGO

Golfo del Darién

5800
Cristóbal Colón

Lago de Maracaibo

CARACAS

Orinoco

VENEZUELA

Georgetown
Paramaribo
Cayenne

GUYANA
SURINAM
FRENCH GUIANA

GUIANA HIGHLANDS

ATLANTIC OCEAN

ISLA DE MALPELO (Colombia)

BOGOTÁ
COLOMBIA

QUITO
ECUADOR

Equator

ISLAS GALAPAGOS (GALAPAGOS IS.) (Ecuador)

PERU

Negro

MANAUS

Amazonas (Amazon)

Mouths of the Amazon

BELÉM

BRAZIL

I. FERNANDO DE NORONHA

RECIFE

LIMA

PERU-CHILE TRENCH

La Paz
BOLIVIA
Sucre

Titicaca

PLANALTO DO MATO GROSSO

PLANALTO CENTRAL
BRASÍLIA

PARAGUAY

Paraná

Asunción

Laguna Mar Chiquita

RIO DE JANEIRO
SÃO PAULO

NAZCA RIDGE

ISLAS DE LOS DESVENTURADOS (Chile)

Tropic of Capricorn

PACIFIC OCEAN

ISLAS JUAN FERNÁNDEZ (Chile)

SANTIAGO

A N D E S

URUGUAY
MONTEVIDEO
BUENOS AIRES

Río de la Plata

ARGENTINA

P A T A G O N I A

C H I L E

ARCHIPIÉLAGO DE LOS CHONOS

ATLANTIC OCEAN

ARCHIPIÉLAGO DE LA REINA ADELAIDA

Punta Arenas

ISLA GRANDE DE TIERRA DEL FUEGO

FALKLAND IS. (U.K.)
WEST FALKLAND
EAST FALKLAND

SCOTIA RIDGE

SOUTH GEORGIA (U.K.)

Cabo de Hornos (Cape Horn)

Drake Passage

SCOTIA SEA

SOUTH SHETLAND IS. (U.K.)
SOUTH ORKNEY IS. (U.K.)

SOUTH SANDWICH ISLANDS (U.K.)

MID-ATLANTIC RIDGE

Tropic of Cancer

Equator

Tropic of Capricorn

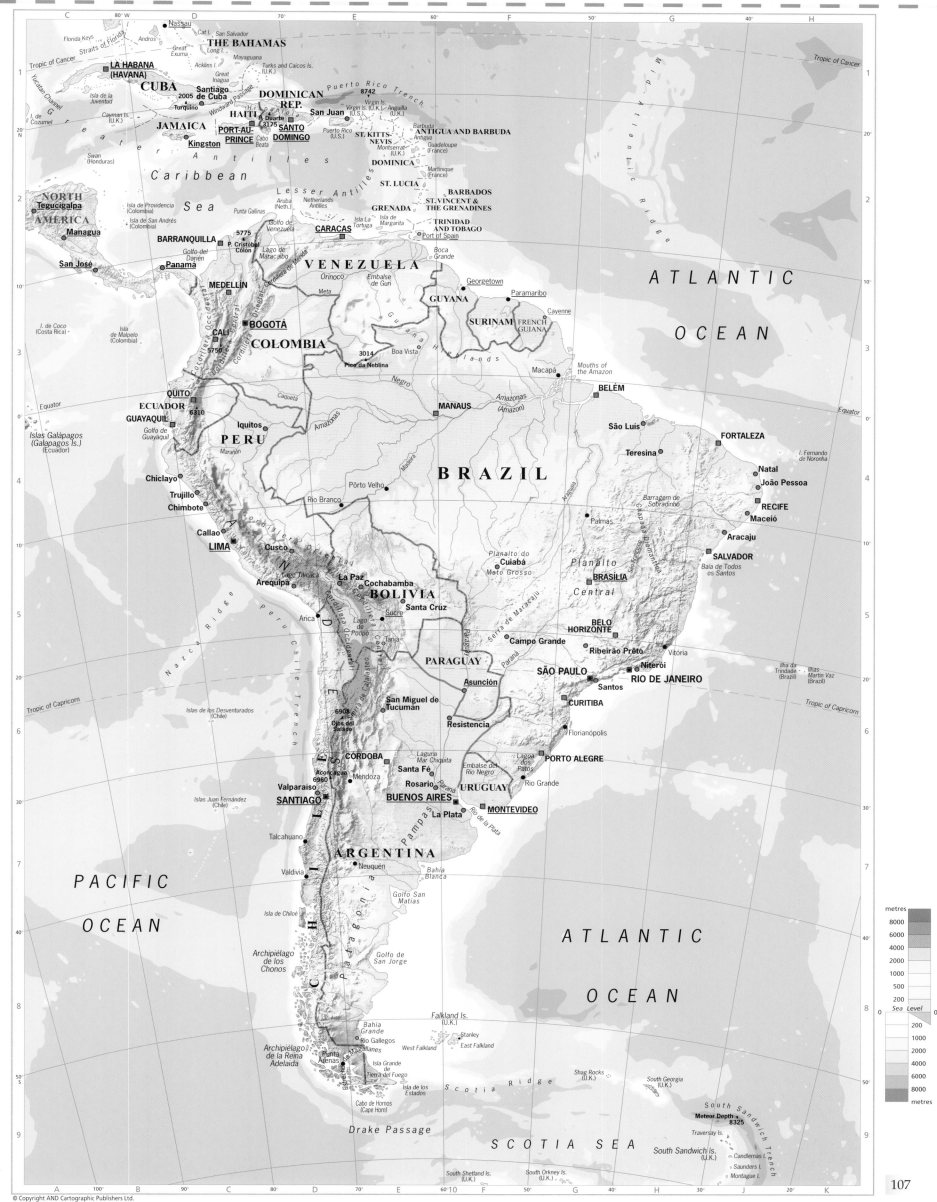

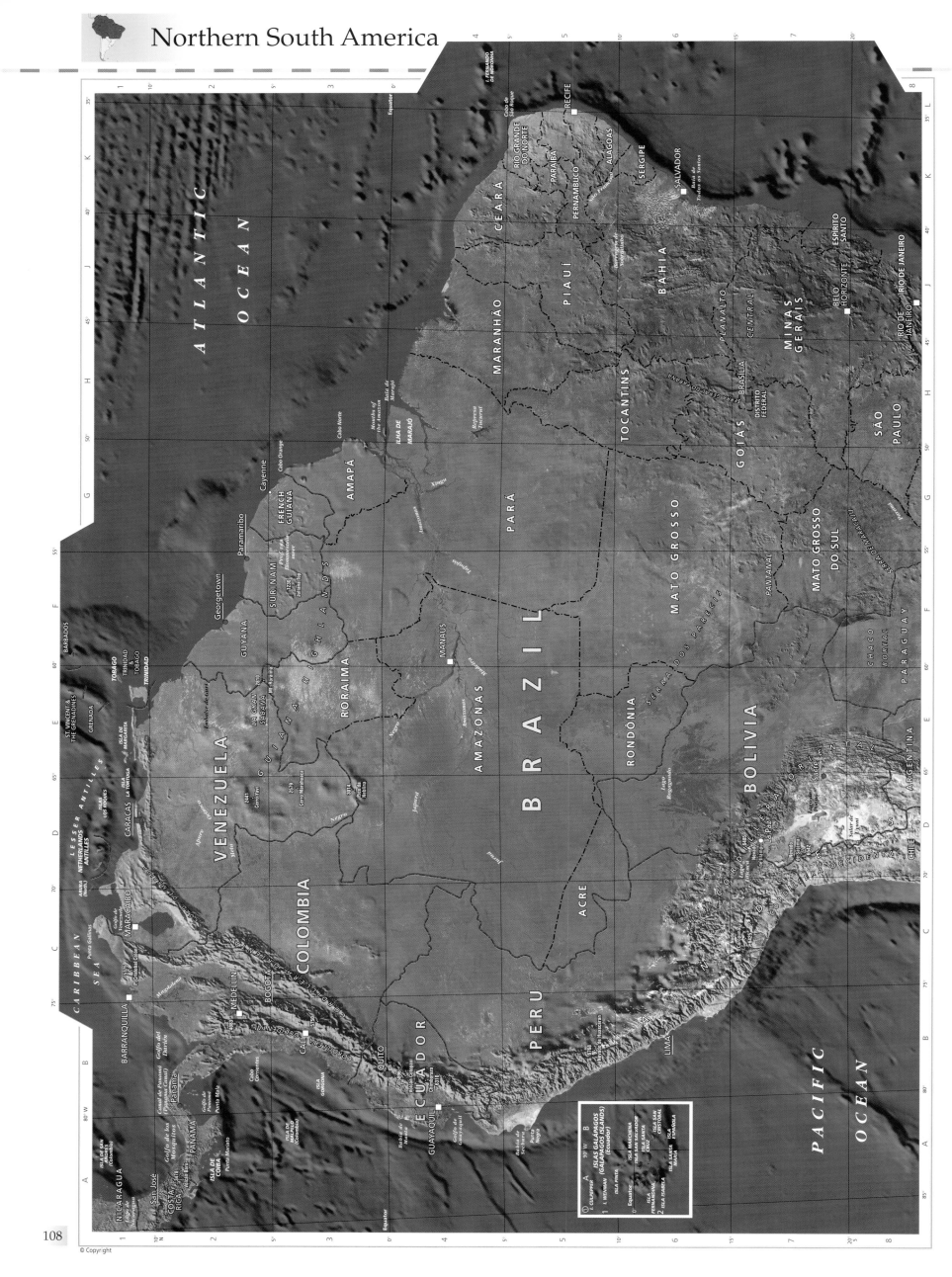

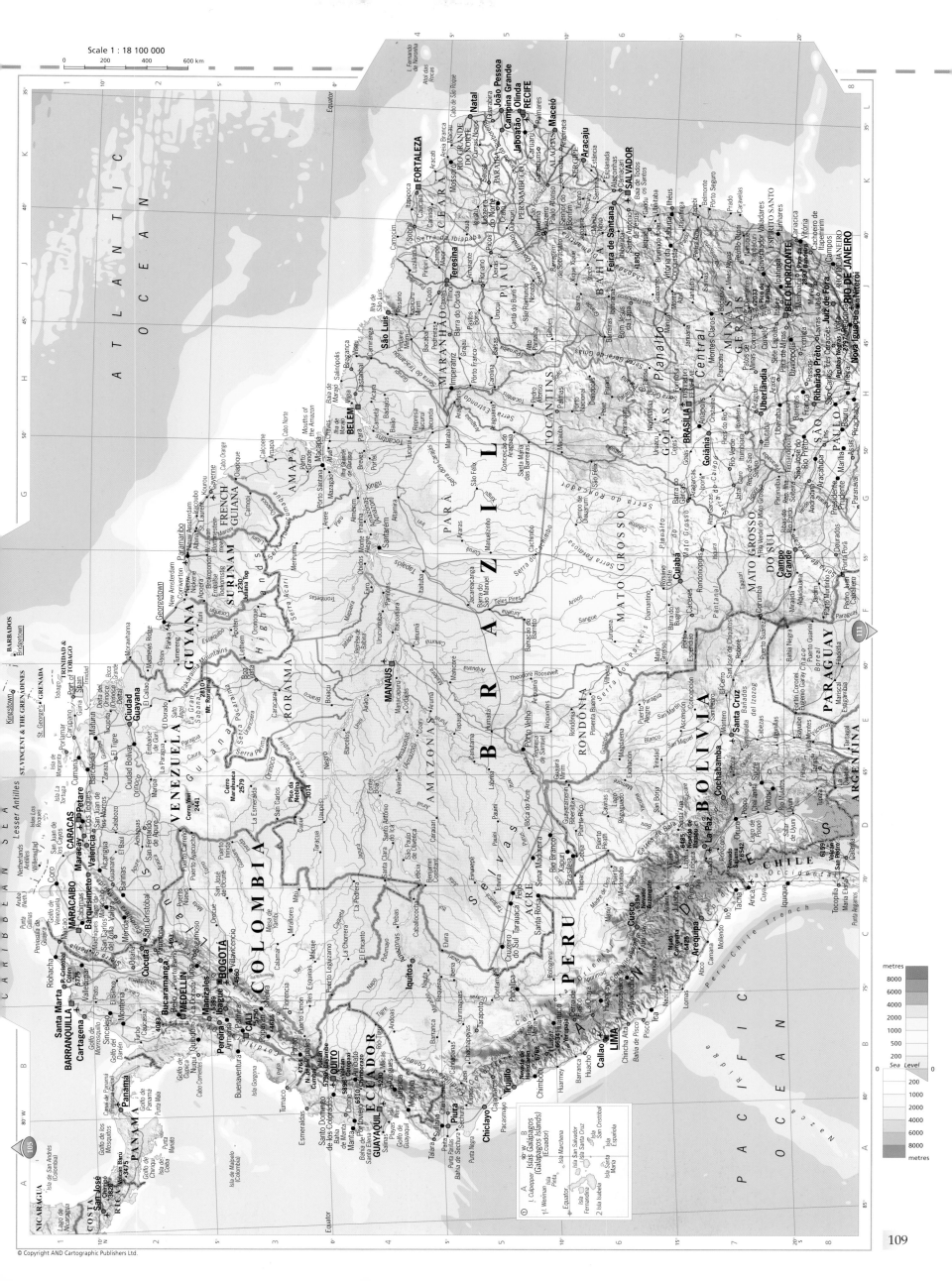

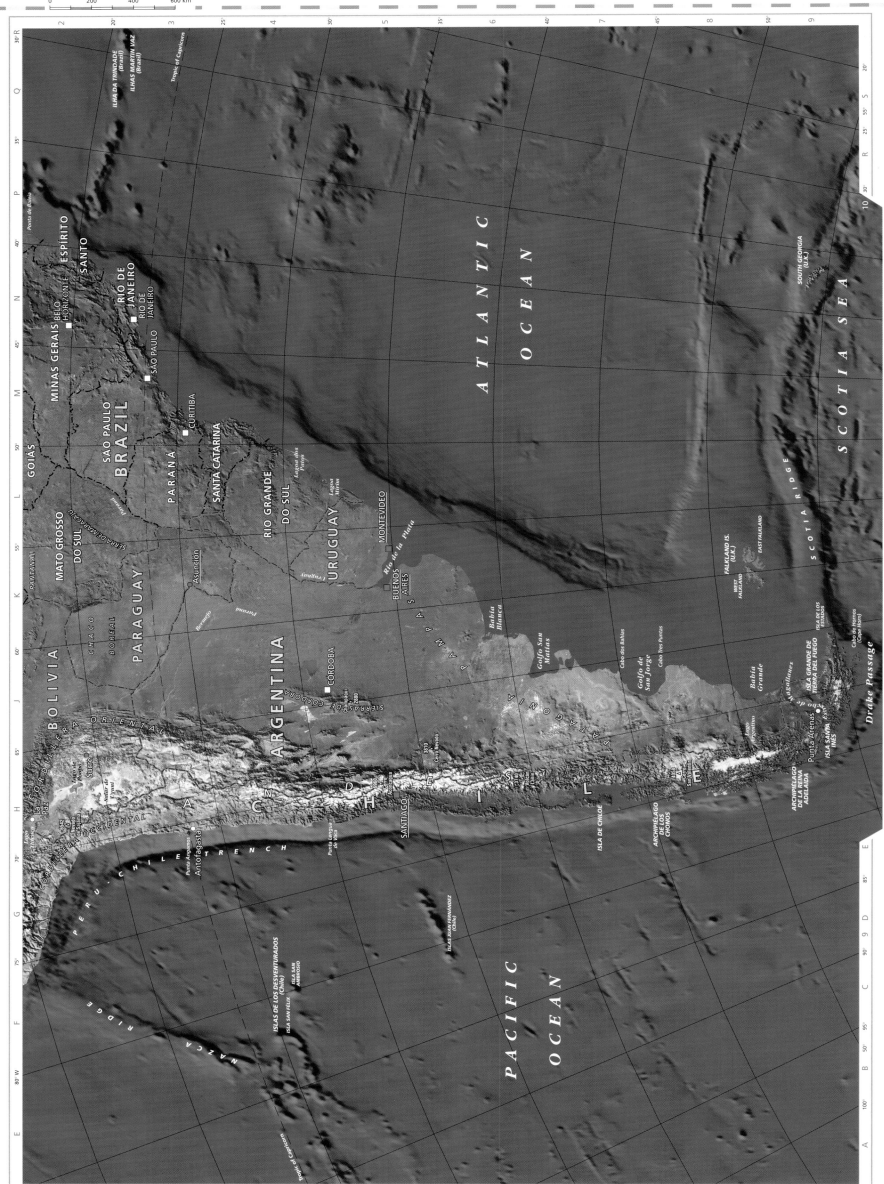

Scale 1 : 18 100 000

0   200   400   600 km

ATLANTIC

OCEAN

PACIFIC

OCEAN

SCOTIA SEA

Drake Passage

BRAZIL

BOLIVIA

PARAGUAY

ARGENTINA

CHILE

URUGUAY

MINAS GERAIS

ESPÍRITO SANTO

SÃO PAULO

GOIÁS

MATO GROSSO DO SUL

PARANÁ

SANTA CATARINA

RIO GRANDE DO SUL

ILHA DA TRINDADE (Brazil)

ILHAS MARTIN VAZ (Brazil)

Tropic of Capricorn

BELO HORIZONTE

RIO DE JANEIRO

RIO DE JANEIRO

SÃO PAULO

CURITIBA

MONTEVIDEO

Río de la Plata

BUENOS AIRES

CÓRDOBA

SANTIAGO

Asunción

Sucre

La Paz

Antofagasta

Punta Arenas

SOUTH GEORGIA (U.K.)

SCOTIA RIDGE

FALKLAND IS. (U.K.)

WEST FALKLAND

EAST FALKLAND

Bahía Blanca

Golfo San Matías

Golfo de San Jorge

Bahía Grande

Cabo dos Bahías

Cabo Tres Puntas

ISLA GRANDE DE TIERRA DEL FUEGO

ISLA DE LOS ESTADOS

Cabo de Hornos (Cape Horn)

ISLA SANTA INÉS

ARCHIPIÉLAGO DE LA REINA ADELAIDA

ARCHIPIÉLAGO DE LOS CHONOS

ISLA DE CHILOÉ

ISLAS JUAN FERNÁNDEZ (Chile)

ISLAS DE LOS DESVENTURADOS (Chile)

ISLA SAN FÉLIX

ISLA SAN AMBROSIO

NAZCA RIDGE

PERU-CHILE TRENCH

CORDILLERA OCCIDENTAL

CORDILLERA ORIENTAL

SIERRAS DE CÓRDOBA

PAMPAS

PATAGONIA

CHACO BOREAL

PANTANAL

SERRA DE MARACAJU

Laguna dos Patos

Laguna Mirim

Paraná

Paraguay

Paraná

Uruguay

Bermejo

Tropic of Capricorn

Punta de Bahía

Punta Angamos

Punta Lengua de Vaca

80° W

Tropic of Capricorn

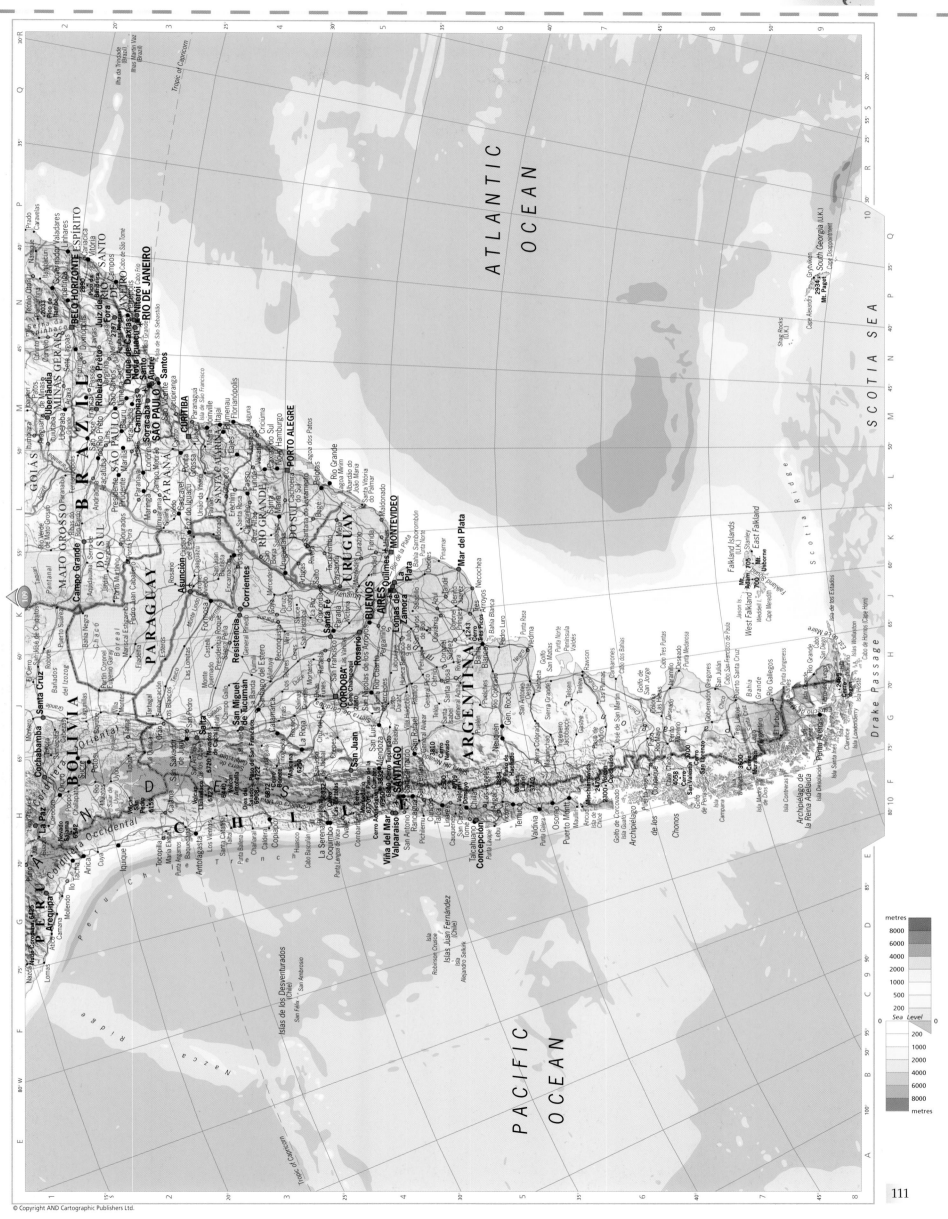

Scale 1 : 57 000 000

0   500   1000   1500   2000 km

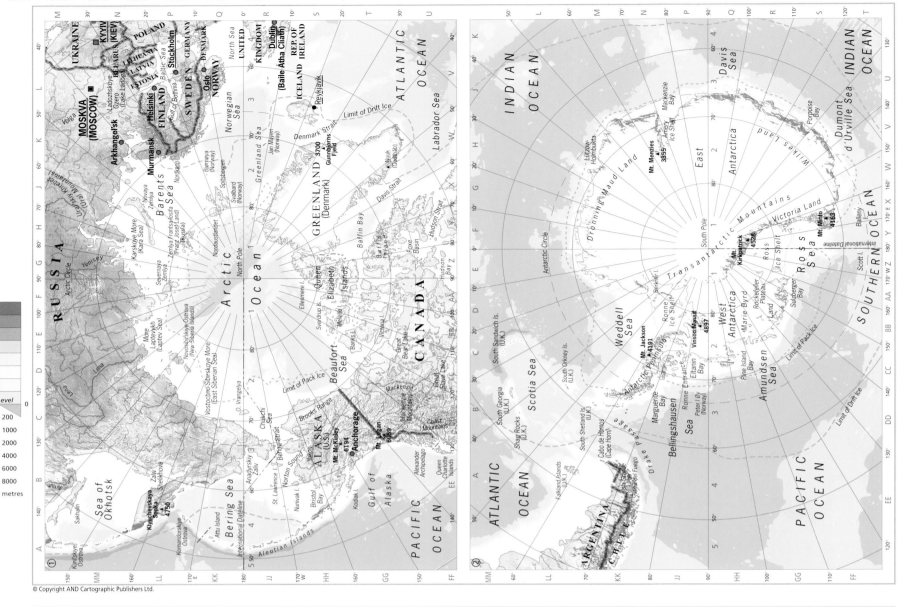

metres
8000
6000
4000
2000
1000
500
200
0   Sea Level   0
200
1000
2000
4000
6000
8000
metres

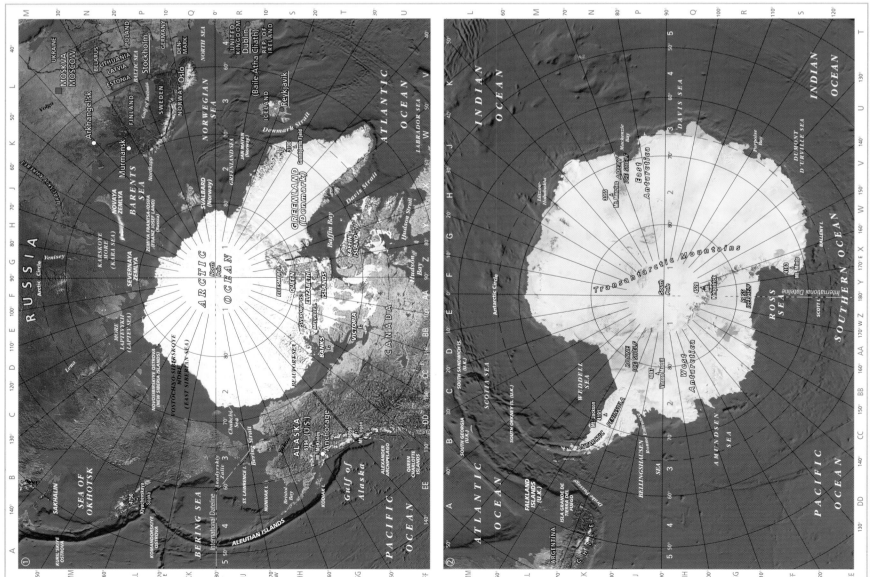

Index

How to use the index

This is an alphabetically arranged index of the places and features that can be found on the maps in this atlas. Each name is generally indexed to the largest scale map on which it appears.

Names composed of two or more words are alphabetised as if they were one word.

All names appear in full in the index, except for 'St.' and 'Ste.', which although abbreviated, are indexed as though spelled in full.

Where two or more places have the same name, they can be distinguished from each other by the country or province name which immediately follows the entry. These names are indexed in the

alphabetical order of the country or province.

Alternative names, such as English translations, can also be found in the index and are cross-referenced to the map form by the '=' sign. In these cases the names also appear in brackets on the maps.

Settlements are indexed to the position of the symbol, all other features are indexed to the position of the name on the map.

Abbreviations used in this index are explained in the list on page 115.

Finding a name on the map

Each index entry contains the name, followed by a symbol indicating the feature type (see below), a page reference and a grid reference:

Name —————— Owosso .... ▣ 99 D2
Owyhee .... ▣ 97 C2
Owyhee .... ⧄ 97 C2
Symbol —————— Oxford, *New Zealand* .... ▣ 89 D6
Oxford, *United Kingdom* .... ▣ 27 A3
Oxnard .... ▣ 101 C2
Page reference —————— Oyama .... ▣ 81 K5
Oyapock .... ⧄ 109 G3
Oyem .... ▣ 63 G4
Grid reference —————— Oyen .... ▣ 95 D1

The grid reference locates a place or feature within a rectangle formed by the network of lines of longitude and latitude. A name can be found by referring to the red letters and numbers placed around the maps. First find the letter, which appears along the top and bottom of the map, and then the number, down the sides. The name will be found within the rectangle uniquely defined by that letter and number.

A number in brackets preceding the grid reference indicates that the name is to be found within an inset map.

Symbols

☒	Continent name
Ⓐ	Country name
ⓐ	State or province name
■	Country capital
▣	State or province capital
▣	Settlement

▲	Mountain, volcano, peak
▙	Mountain range
⬨	Physical region or feature
⧄	River, canal
⬗	Lake, salt lake
◣	Gulf, strait, bay

▱	Sea, ocean
▷	Cape, point
⬚	Island or island group, rocky or coral reef
✳	Place of interest
ℋ	Historical or cultural region

Glossary

This is an alphabetically arranged glossary of the geographical terms used on the maps and in this index. The first column shows the map form, the second the language of origin and the third the English translation.

A

açude	Portuguese	reservoir
adası	Turkish	island
akra	Greek	peninsula
alpen	German	mountains
alpes	French	mountains
alpi	Italian	mountains
älven	Swedish	river
archipiélago	Spanish	archipelago
arquipélago	Portuguese	archipelago

B

bab	Arabic	strait
bahía	Spanish	bay
bahir, bahr	Arabic	bay, lake, river
baía	Portuguese	bay
baie	French	bay
baja	Spanish	lower
bandar	Arabic, Somalian, Malay, Persian	harbour, port
baraji	Turkish	dam
barragem	Portuguese	reservoir
ben	Gaelic	mountain
Berg(e)	German	mountain(s)
boğazı	Turkish	strait
Bucht	German	bay
buḥayrat	Arabic	lake
burnu, burun	Turkish	cape

C

cabo	Spanish	cape
canal	French, Spanish	canal, channel
canale	Italian	canal, channel
cerro	Spanish	mountain
chott	Arabic	marsh, salt lake
co	Tibetan	lake
collines	French	hills
cordillera	Spanish	range

D

dağ(ı)	Turkish	mountain
dağlar(ı)	Turkish	mountains
danau	Indonesian	lake
daryacheh	Persian	lake
dasht	Persian	desert
djebel	Arabic	mountain(s)
-do	Korean	island

E

embalse	Spanish	reservoir
erg	Arabic	sandy desert
estrecho	Spanish	strait

F

feng	Chinese	mountain
-fjördur	Icelandic	fjord
-flói	Icelandic	bay

G

Gebirge	German	range
golfe	French	bay, gulf
golfo	Italian, Portuguese, Spanish	bay, gulf
göl, gölü	Turkish	lake
gora	Russian	mountain
gory	Russian	mountains
gunong	Malay	mountain
gunung	Indonesian	mountain

H

hai	Chinese	lake, sea
hāmūn	Persian	lake, marsh
hawr	Arabic	lake
hu	Chinese	lake, reservoir

I

île(s)	French	island(s)
ilha(s)	Portuguese	island(s)
isla(s)	Spanish	island(s)

J

jabal	Arabic	mountain(s)
-järvi	Finnish	lake
jaza'īr	Arabic	islands
jazīrat	Arabic	island
jbel	Arabic	mountain
jebel	Arabic	mountain
jezero	Serbo-Croatian	lake
jezioro	Polish	lake
jiang	Chinese	river
-jima	Japanese	island
-joki	Finnish	river
-jökull	Icelandic	glacier

K

kepulauan	Indonesian	islands
khrebet	Russian	mountain range
-ko	Japanese	lake
kolpos	Greek	bay, gulf
körfezi	Turkish	bay, gulf
kryazh	Russian	ridge
küh(ha)	Persian	mountain(s)

L

lac	French	lake
lacul	Romanian	lake
lago	Italian, Portuguese, Spanish	lake
lagoa	Portuguese	lagoon
laguna	Spanish	lagoon, lake
limni	Greek	lake
ling	Chinese	mountain(s), peak
liqeni	Albanian	lake
loch, lough	Gaelic	lake

M

massif	French	mountains
-meer	Dutch	lake, sea
mont	French	mount
monte	Italian, Portuguese, Spanish	mount
montes	Portuguese, Spanish	mountains
monts	French	mountains
muntii	Romanian	mountains
mys	Russian	cape

N

| nafud | Arabic | desert |

O

| ostrov(a) | Russian | island(s) |
| ozero | Russian | lake |

P

pegunungan	Indonesian	mountains
pelagos	Greek	sea
pendi	Chinese	basin
pesky	Russian	sandy desert
pic	French	peak
pico	Portuguese, Spanish	peak
planalto	Portuguese	plateau
planina	Bulgarian	mountains
poluostrov	Russian	peninsula
puerto	Spanish	harbour, port
puncak	Indonesian	peak
punta	Italian, Spanish	point
puy	French	peak

Q

| qundao | Chinese | archipelago |

R

ras, râs, ra's	Arabic	cape
represa	Portuguese	dam, reservoir
-rettō	Japanese	archipelago
rio	Portuguese	river
río	Spanish	river

S

sahra	Arabic	desert
salar	Spanish	salt flat
-san	Japanese, Korean	mountain
-sanmaek	Korean	mountains
sebkha	Arabic	salt flat
sebkhet	Arabic	salt marsh
See	German	lake
serra	Portuguese	range
severnaya, severo-	Russian	northern
shan	Chinese	mountain(s)
-shima	Japanese	island
-shotō	Japanese	islands
sierra	Spanish	range

T

tanjona	Malagasy	cape
tanjung	Indonesian	cape
teluk	Indonesian	bay, gulf
ténéré	Berber	desert
-tō	Japanese	island

V

vârful	Romanian	mountain
-vesi	Finnish	lake
vodokhranilishche	Russian	reservoir
volcán	Spanish	volcano

W

| wādī | Arabic | watercourse |
| Wald | German | forest |

Z

| -zaki | Japanese | cape |
| zaliv | Russian | bay, gulf |

N (continued)

nevado	Spanish	snow-capped mountain
nuruu	Mongolian	mountains
nuur	Mongolian	lake

Abbreviations

Ak.	Alaska
Al.	Alabama
Ariz.	Arizona
Ark.	Arkansas
B.C.	British Columbia
Calif.	California
Colo.	Colorado
Conn.	Connecticut
Del.	Delaware
Dem. Rep. of Congo	Democratic Republic of Congo
Eng.	England
Fla.	Florida
Ga.	Georgia
Ia.	Iowa
Id.	Idaho
Ill.	Illinois
Ind.	Indiana
Kans.	Kansas
Ky.	Kentucky
La.	Louisiana
Man.	Manitoba
Mass.	Massachusetts
Md.	Maryland
Me.	Maine
M.G.	Mato Grosso
Mich.	Michigan
Minn.	Minnesota
Miss.	Mississippi
Mo.	Missouri
Mont.	Montana
N.B.	New Brunswick
N.C.	North Carolina
N.D.	North Dakota
Nebr.	Nebraska
Nev.	Nevada
Nfld.	Newfoundland
N.H.	New Hampshire
N. Ire.	Northern Ireland
N.J.	New Jersey
N. Mex.	New Mexico
N.W.T.	Northwest Territories
N.Y.	New York
Oh.	Ohio
Okla.	Oklahoma
Ont.	Ontario
Oreg.	Oregon
Orkney Is.	Orkney Islands
Pa.	Pennsylvania
R.G.S.	Rio Grande do Sul
R.I.	Rhode Island
S.C.	South Carolina
Scot.	Scotland
S.D.	South Dakota
Shetland Is.	Shetland Islands
Tenn.	Tennessee
Tex.	Texas
Ut.	Utah
Va.	Virginia
Vt.	Vermont
Wash.	Washington
Wis.	Wisconsin
W. Va.	West Virginia
Wyo.	Wyoming
Y.T.	Yukon Territory

A

Name		Page	Grid
Aachen	●	27	J4
Aalen	●	35	F8
Aalst	●	27	G4
Aarau	●	43	D3
Aare	◪	43	C3
Aarschot	●	27	G4
Aba	●	63	F3
Ābādān	●	55	C1
Ābādeh	●	55	E1
Abadla	●	59	E2
Abaji	●	63	F3
Abakaliki	●	63	F3
Abakan	◨	71	S7
Abancay	●	109	C6
Abano Terme	●	43	G5
Abarqū	●	55	E1
Abashiri	●	81	N1
Abava	◪	29	M8
Ābaya Häyk'	●	65	F2
Abay Wenz	◪	61	G5
Abbeville, France	●	27	D4
Abbeville, United States	●	103	C4
Abd al Kūrī	⊠	53	F7
Abéché	●	61	D5
Abengourou	●	63	D3
Abenójar	●	41	F6
Åbenrå	●	35	E1
Abensberg	●	35	G8
Abeokuta	●	63	E3
Aberaeron	●	37	H9
Aberdeen, South Africa	●	67	C6
Aberdeen, United Kingdom	●	37	K4
Aberdeen, Miss., United States	●	103	D3
Aberdeen, S.D., United States	●	97	G1
Aberdeen, Wash., United States	●	97	B1
Aberdeen Lake	◪	93	M4
Aberystwyth	●	37	H9
Abez'	●	31	M1
Abhā	●	61	H4
Abhar	●	51	N5
Abidjan	●	63	D3
Abilene	◉	101	G2
Abiline	●	91	M6
Abingdon, United Kingdom	●	27	A3
Abingdon, United States	●	103	E2
Abnûb	●	61	F2
Aboisso	●	63	D3
Abomey	●	63	E3
Abong Mbang	●	63	G4
Abou Déia	●	61	C5
Abqaiq	●	55	C4
Abrantes	●	41	B5
Absaroka Range	◣	97	E1
Abū al Abayḍ	⊠	55	E4
Abu Aweigîla	●	54	B6
Abu Ballâs	◣	61	E3
Abu Dhabi = Abū Ẓabī	◼	55	F4
Abu Hamed	●	61	F4
Abuja	◉	63	F3
Ābune Yosëf	◣	61	G5
Abū Nujaym	●	61	C1
Abu Qarin	●	61	C1
Aburo	◣	65	E3
Abu Simbel	●	61	F3
Abut Head	▷	89	B6
Abuye Meda	◣	65	F1
Abū Ẓabī	◼	55	F4
Abv Nujaym	●	59	J2
Acaponeta	●	95	E7
Acapulco	●	105	E5
Acará	●	109	H4
Acarigua	●	109	D2
Accra	◼	63	D3
Achaguas	●	105	L7
Achayvayam	●	73	W4
Acheng	●	79	H1
Achenkirch	●	43	G3
Achen See	◪	43	G3
Achill Island	⊠	37	B8
Achim	●	35	E3
Achinsk	●	71	S6
Achit	●	31	L3
Aci Göl	◪	49	M7
A Cihanbeyli	●	49	Q6
Acireale	●	45	K11
Acklins Island	⊠	105	K4
Aconcagua	◣	107	D7
Açores	⊠	59	(1)B2
A Coruña	●	41	B1
Acqui Terme	●	43	D6
Acre	●	109	C5
Acri	●	45	L9
Ada	●	33	K12
Ada	●	103	B3
Adak Island	⊠	101	(3)C1
Adam	●	53	G5
Adams Island	⊠	89	(2)B1
'Adan	●	53	E7
Adana	●	51	F5
Adda	◪	43	E5
Ad Dafrah	⊗	55	E5
Ad Dahnā	⊗	55	B3
Ad Dakhla	●	59	B4
Ad Dammām	●	55	D3
Ad Dawādimī	●	53	D5
Ad Dawḩah	◼	55	D4
Ad Dilam	●	55	B5
Ad Dir'īyah	●	55	B4
Addis Ababa = Ādīs Ābeba	◼	65	F2
Ad Dīwānīyah	●	53	D3
Adel	●	99	B2
Adelaide	◻	87	G6
Adelaide Peninsula	⊘	93	M3
Adelaide River	●	87	F2
Aden = Adan	●	53	E7
Aderbissinat	●	63	F1
Adh Dhayd	●	55	F4
Adi	⊠	83	(2)D3
Adige	◪	43	G5
Adīgrat	●	61	G5
Adilabad	●	75	C5
Adin	●	97	B2
Adīrī	●	61	B2
Ādīs Ābeba	◼	65	F2
Adi Ugri	●	61	G5
Adıyaman	●	53	C2
Adjud	●	47	Q3
Adler	●	51	H2
Admiralty Island	⊠	93	E5
Admiralty Islands	⊠	85	E6
Adoni	●	75	C5
Adour	◪	39	F10
Adra	●	41	H8
Adrano	●	45	J11
Adrar	●	59	E3
Adrar des Ifôghas	⊘	59	F5
Adrar Tamgak	◣	59	G5
Adria	●	43	H5
Adriatic Sea	◛	45	H4
Adycha	◪	73	P3
Adygeya	ⓐ	51	J1
Adygeysk	●	51	H1
Adz'vavom	●	31	L1
Aegean Sea	◛	49	H5
A Estrada	●	41	B2
Afghanistan	Ⓐ	53	H3
'Afīf	●	61	H3
Afikpo	●	63	F3
Afognak Island	⊠	101	(1)G4
A Fonsagrada	●	41	C1
Afragóla	●	45	J8
'Afrīn	●	51	G5
Afuá	●	109	G4
'Afula	●	54	C4
Afyon	●	49	N6
Agadez	●	59	G5
Agadir	●	59	D2
Agadyr'	●	71	N8
Agalega Islands	⊠	57	J7
Agan	◪	73	B4
Āgaro	●	65	F2
Agartala	●	75	F4
Agathonisi	⊠	49	J7
Agattu Island	⊠	73	W6
Agde	●	39	J10
Agen	●	39	F9
Ağin	●	51	H4
Aginskoye	●	71	S6
Agios Efstratios	⊠	49	H5
Agios Georgios	⊠	49	F7
Agios Nikolaos	●	49	H9
Agnita	●	47	M4
Agra	●	75	C3
Agrakhanskiy Poluostrov	⊘	51	M2
Agri	◪	45	L8
Ağri	●	51	K4
Agrigento	●	45	H11
Agrinio	●	49	D6
Agrópoli	●	45	K8
Agryz	●	31	K3
Agua Prieta	●	101	E2
Aguascalientes	●	105	D4
A Gudiña	●	41	C2
Aguelhok	●	59	F5
Águilas	●	41	J7
Agulhas Negras	◣	109	H8
Ağva	●	49	M3
Ahar	●	51	M4
Ahaura	●	89	C6
Ahaus	●	27	K2
Ahititi	●	89	E4
Ahlen	●	27	K3
Ahmadabad	●	75	B4
Ahmadnagar	●	75	B5
Ahmadpur East	●	75	B3
Ahr	◪	35	B6
Ahram	●	55	D2
Ahrensburg	●	35	F3
Ahvāz	●	53	E3
Aichach	●	35	G8
Aigialousa	●	51	F6
Aigina	⊠	49	F7
Aigio	●	49	E6
Aigosthena	●	49	F6
Aihui	●	73	M6
Aim	●	73	N5
Ain	◪	39	L7
Aïn Beïda	●	59	G1
'Aïn Ben Tili	●	59	D3
Aïn Bessem	●	41	P8
Aïn el Hadjel	●	41	P9
Ain Oussera	●	59	F1
Ainsa	●	41	L2
Aïn Sefra	●	59	E2
Ain Taya	●	41	P8
Aïn-Tédélès	●	41	L8

Name	Page	Grid
Aïn Témouchent	41	J9
Airão	109	E4
Aire	37	L8
Air Force Island	93	S3
Airolo	43	D4
Airpanas	83	(2)C4
Aisne	27	F5
Aitape	83	(2)F3
Aitkin	99	B1
Aitutaki	85	K7
Aiud	47	L3
Aix-en-Provence	39	L10
Aix-les-Bains	39	L8
Aizawl	75	F4
Aizkraukle	29	N8
Aizpute	29	L8
Aizu-wakamatsu	81	K5
Ajaccio	45	C7
Aj Bogd Uul	79	B2
Ajdābiyā	61	D1
Ajigasawa	81	L3
Ajka	33	G10
Ajlun	54	C4
Ajmān	55	F4
Ajmer	75	B3
Ajo	101	D2
Akanthou	54	A1
Akaroa	89	D6
Akasha	61	F3
Akashi	81	H6
Akbalyk	71	P8
Akçakale	51	H5
Akçakoca	49	P3
Aken	35	H5
Aketi	65	C3
Akhalk'alak'i	51	K3
Akhisar	49	K6
Akhmîm	61	F2
Akhty	51	M3
Akimiski Island	93	Q6
Akita	81	L4
Akjoujt	59	C5
Akka	59	D3
Akkajaure	29	J3
Akkeshi	81	N2
'Akko	54	C4
Akmeqit	53	L2
Aknanes	29	(1)B2
Akobo	65	E2
Akola	75	C4
Akonolinga	63	G4
Akordat	61	G4
Akpatok Island	93	T4
Akqi	71	P9
Akra Drepano	49	G5
Akra Sounio	49	F7
Akra Spatha	49	F9
Akra Trypiti	49	G9
Åkrehamn	29	C7
Akron	99	D2
Aksaray	51	E4
Aksarka	71	M4
Akşehir	49	P6
Akseki	49	P7
Aksha	73	J6
Akshiy	71	P9
Aksu	71	Q9
Aksuat	71	Q8
Āksum	61	G5
Aktau, Kazakhstan	25	K3
Aktau, Kazakhstan	71	N7
Aktogay	71	N8
Aktuma	71	M8
Aktyubinsk	31	L4
Akula	65	C3
Akune	81	F8
Akure	63	F4
Akureyri	29	(1)E2
Akwanga	63	F3
Alabama	103	D3
Alaçam	51	F3
Alagoas	109	K5
Alagoinhas	109	K6
Alagón	41	J3
Al Ahmadi	55	C2
Al 'Amārah	53	E3
Alaminos	77	F3
Alamo	97	C3
Alamogordo	101	E2
Alamo Lake	101	D2
Åland	29	K6
Alanya	51	E5
Alappuzha	75	C7
Al Arṭāwīyah	53	E4
Alaşehir	49	L6
Al 'Ashurīyah	61	H1
Alaska	101	(1)F2
Alaska Peninsula	101	(1)E4
Alaska Range	101	(1)G3
Alassio	43	D6
Alatri	45	H7
Alatyr'	31	J4
Alaverdı	51	L3
Alavus	29	M5
Alaykuu	71	N9
Al 'Ayn	55	F4
Alazeya	73	S2
Alba, Italy	43	D6
Alba, Spain	41	E4
Albacete	41	J5
Alba Iulia	47	L3
Albania	49	B3
Albany	93	Q6
Albany, Australia	87	C6
Albany, Ga., United States	103	E3
Albany, Ky., United States	103	E2
Albany, N.Y., United States	99	F2
Albany, Oreg., United States	97	B2
Albardão do João Maria	111	L4
Al Başrah	53	E3
Albatross Bay	87	H2
Albatross Point	89	E4
Al Baydā'	61	D1
Albenga	43	D6
Albert	27	E4
Alberta	93	H6
Albertirsa	33	J10
Albert Kanaal	27	G3
Albert Lea	99	B2
Albert Nile	65	E3
Albertville	39	M8
Albi	39	H10
Albina	109	G2
Albino	43	E5
Albion	97	F1
Ålborg	29	E8
Ålborg Bugt	29	F8
Albox	41	H7
Albstadt	35	E8
Albufeira	41	B7
Albuquerque	101	E1
Al Buraymī	53	G5
Alburquerque	41	D5
Albury	87	J7
Al Buşayyah	55	B1
Alcácer do Sal	41	B6
Alcala de Guadaira	41	E7
Alcala de Henares	41	G4
Alcalá la Real	41	G7
Alcamo	45	G11
Alcañiz	41	K3
Alcantarilla	41	J7
Alcaraz	41	H6
Alcaudete	41	F7
Alcazar de San Juan	41	G5
Alcobendas	41	G4
Alcoi	41	K6
Alcolea del Pinar	41	H3
Alcorcón	41	G4
Alcoutim	41	C7
Aldabra Group	67	(2)A2
Aldan	73	M5
Aldan	73	N5
Aldeburgh	27	D2
Alderney	39	C4
Aldershot	27	B3
Aleg	59	C5
Aleksandrov-Sakhalinskiy	73	Q6
Aleksandrovskiy Zavod	73	K6
Aleksandrovskoye	31	Q2
Alekseyevka	71	N7
Aleksinac	47	J6
Alençon	39	F5
Aleppo = Ḥalab	51	G5
Aléria	45	D6
Alès	39	K9
Aleşd	33	M10
Alessándria	43	D6
Ålesund	29	D5
Aleutian Islands	101	(3)B1
Aleutian Range	101	(1)F4
Aleutian Trench	69	W5
Alexander Archipelago	101	(1)K4
Alexander Bay	67	B5
Alexander City	103	D3
Alexandra	89	B7
Alexandreia	49	E4
Alexandria = El Iskandarîya, Egypt	61	E1
Alexandria, Romania	47	N6
Alexandria, La., United States	103	C3
Alexandria, Minn., United States	99	A1
Alexandria, Va., United States	99	E3
Alexandroupoli	49	H4
Alexis Creek	93	G6
'Āley	54	C3
Aley	71	Q7
Aleysk	71	Q7
Al Farwāniyah	55	B2
Al Fāw	55	C2
Alfeld	35	E5
Alföld	47	H2
Alfonsine	43	H6
Alfreton	27	A1
Al Fuḥayḥil	55	C2
Al-Fujayrah	55	G4
Algeciras	41	E8
Algemes	41	K5
Algena	61	G4
Alger	59	F1
Algeria	59	E3
Al Ghāṭ	55	A3
Al Ghaydah	53	F6
Alghero	45	C8
Algiers = Alger	59	F1
Algona	99	B2
Al Hadīthah	54	E5
Alhama de Murcia	41	J7
Al Ḥamar	55	B5
Al Ḥamīdīyah	54	C2
Al Ḥammādah al Ḥamrā'	59	G3
Al Harūj al Aswad	61	C2
Al Ḥasakah	51	J5
Alhaurmín el Grande	41	F8
Al Ḥijāz	61	G2
Al Ḥillah	53	D3
Al Ḥilwah	55	B5
Al Hoceima	59	E1
Al Ḥudaydah	61	H5
Al Hufūf	55	C4
Al Ḥumaydah	53	C4
Aliabad	55	F2
Aliağa	49	J6
Aliakmonas	49	E4
Äli Bayramlı	51	N4
Alicante	41	K6
Alice	103	B4
Alice Springs	87	F4
Alicudi	45	J10
Aligarh	75	C3
Alindao	65	C2
Alingås	29	G8
Alisos	101	D2
Aliwal North	67	D6
Al Jabal al Akhḍar	61	D1
Al Jaghbūb	61	D2
Al Jālamīd	61	G1
Al Jarah	55	B2
Al Jawf	61	G2
Aljezur	41	B7
Al Jifārah	55	A5
Al Jubayl	55	C3
Aljustrel	41	B7
Al Kāmil	53	G5
Al Khābūrah	55	G5
Al Kharj	55	B4
Al Khaşab	55	G3
Al Khawr	55	D4
Al Khubar	55	D3
Al Khums	59	H2
Al Khuwayr	55	D3
Alkmaar	27	G2
Al Küt	53	E3
Al Kuwayt	55	C2
Al Lādhiqīyah	51	F6
Allahabad	75	D3
Allakh-Yun'	73	P4
Alldays	67	D4
Allen	77	D4
Allendale	103	E3
Allentown	99	E2
Aller	35	E4
Aller = Cabañquinta	41	E1
Alliance	97	F2
Allier	39	J8
Allinge	33	D2
Al Lith	61	H3
Alma, Canada	99	F1
Alma, Nebr., United States	97	G2
Alma, Wis., United States	99	B2
Almada	41	A6
Almadén	41	F6
Al Madīnah	61	G3
Al Majma'ah	53	E4
Almalyk	71	M9
Al Manāmah	55	D3
Almansa	41	J6
Al Marj	61	D1
Almaty	71	P9
Al Mawşil	51	K5
Al Mazāhumīyah	55	B4
Almazán	41	H3
Almeirim	109	G4
Almelo	27	J2
Almendralejo	41	D6
Almería	41	H8
Al'met'yevsk	71	J7
Almiros	49	E5
Al Mish'āb	55	C2
Almonte	41	D7
Almora	75	C3
Almosa	97	E3
Al Mubarraz	55	C4
Al Mudawwara	54	D7
Al Mukallā	53	E7
Al Mukhā	61	H5
Almuñécar	41	G8
Al Muqdādīyah	51	L7
Al Nu'ayrīyah	55	C3
Alnwick	37	L6
Alonnisos	49	F5
Alor	83	(2)B4
Alor Setar	77	C5
Alotau	87	K2
Alpena	99	D1
Alphen	27	G2
Alpi Lepontine	43	D4
Alpine	101	E2
Alpi Orobie	43	E4
Alps	43	B5
Al Qadmūs	54	D1
Al Qāmishlī	51	J5
Al Qar'ah	55	B3
Al Qaryāt	61	B1
Al Qaryatayn	54	E2
Al Qaţrūn	61	B3
Al Qunayţirah	54	C3
Al Qunfudhah	61	H4
Al Qurayyāt	61	G1
Al Qurnah	55	B1
Al Quşayr	55	A1
Al Quţayfah	54	D3
Als	35	E1
Alsask	93	K6
Alsasua	41	H2
Alsfeld	35	E6
Altaelva	29	M2
Altai Mountains	79	A1
Altamira	109	G4
Altamura	45	L8
Altanbulag	73	H6
Altay	71	R7
Altay, China	71	R8
Altay, Mongolia	79	B1
Altdorf	43	D4
Alte Mellum	35	D3
Altenburg	35	H6

Name	Page	Grid
Altenkirchen	35	J2
Altkirch	43	C3
Alto Garças	109	G7
Alto Molócuè	67	F3
Alton, *United Kingdom*	27	B3
Alton, *United States*	99	B3
Altoona	99	E2
Alto Parnaíba	109	H5
Altötting	43	H2
Altun Shan	71	S10
Alturas	97	B2
Altus	103	B3
Al 'Ubaylah	53	F5
Alūksne	29	P8
Alupka	51	E1
Alushta	51	F1
Al 'Uwayqīlah	61	H1
Al 'Uzayr	55	B1
Alva	103	B2
Alvarães	109	E4
Älvdalen	29	H6
Älvsbyn	29	L4
Al Wafrā'	55	B2
Al Wajh	61	G2
Alwar	75	C3
Al Wari'ah	55	B3
Alytus	33	P3
Alzey	35	D7
Alzira	41	K5
Amadi	65	E2
Amādīyah	51	K5
Amadjuak Lake	93	S4
Amadora	41	A6
Amahai	83	(2)C3
Amakusa-Shimo-shima	81	E7
Amaliada	49	D7
Amalner	75	C4
Amamapare	83	(2)E3
Amami-Ōshima	69	S7
Amanab	83	(2)F3
Amándola	45	H6
Amantéa	45	L9
Amapá	109	G3
Amapá	109	G3
Amarante	109	J5
Amarapura	77	B2
Amarillo	101	F1
Amasya	51	F3
Amay	27	H4
Amazar	73	L6
Amazon = Amazonas	107	F4
Amazonas	109	D4
Amazonas	109	E4
Ambala	75	C2
Ambanjä	67	H2
Ambarchik	73	U3
Ambato	109	B4
Ambato Boeny	67	H3
Ambatondrazaka	67	H3
Amberg	35	G7
Ambikapur	75	D4
Ambilobe	67	H2
Amboise	39	G6
Ambon	83	(2)C3
Ambositra	67	H4
Ambovombe	67	H5
Amchitka Island	101	(3)B1
Amderma	71	L4
Amdo	75	F2
Ameland	27	H1
Amengel'dy	71	M7
American Falls	97	D2
American Samoa	85	J7
Americus	103	E3
Amersfoort	27	H2
Amery	93	N5
Amery Ice Shelf	112	(2)M2
Ames	99	B2
Amfilochia	49	D6
Amfissa	49	E6
Amga	73	L5
Amga	73	N4
Amgun'	73	P6
Amherst	93	U7
Amiens	27	E5
Amirante Islands	67	(2)B2
Amistad Reservoir	101	F3
Amlekhganj	75	D3
Åmli	29	E7
'Ammān	54	C5
Ammerland	27	K1
Ammersee	43	F2
Ammochostos	51	E6
Ammochostos Bay	54	A1
Amo	77	C2
Amol	53	F2
Amorgos	49	H8
Amos	99	E1
Ampana	83	(2)B3
Ampanihy	67	G4
Amparai	75	D7
Ampezzo	43	H4
Amposta	41	L4
Amrān	53	D6
Amravati	75	C4
Amritsar	75	B2
Amroha	75	C3
Amrum	35	D2
Amsterdam, *Netherlands*	27	G2
Amsterdam, *United States*	99	F2
Amstetten	43	K2
Am Timan	61	D5
Amudar'ya	71	L9
Amundsen Gulf	93	G2
Amundsen Sea	112	(2)GG3
Amungen	29	H6
Amuntai	83	(1)F3
Amur	73	P6
Amursk	73	P6
Amvrakikos Kolpos	49	C6
Anabar	73	J2
Anaconda	97	D1
Anacortes	97	B1
Anadarko	97	G3
Anadolu Dağları	51	H3
Anadyr'	73	X4
Anadyrskaya Nizmennost'	73	X3
Anadyrskiy Zaliv	73	Y3
Anafi	49	H8
'Ānah	51	J6
Anaheim	101	C2
Anáhuac	101	F3
Analalava	67	H2
Anamur	51	E5
Anan	81	H7
Anantapur	75	C6
Anan'yiv	47	T2
Anapa	51	G1
Anápolis	109	H7
Anār	55	F1
Anārak	53	F3
Anardara	53	H3
Anatolia	49	M6
Añatuya	111	J4
Anchorage	101	(1)H3
Ancona	45	H5
Ancud	111	G7
Anda	79	H1
Andalgalá	111	H4
Åndalsnes	29	D5
Andalusia	103	D3
Andaman Islands	77	A4
Andaman Sea	77	A4
Andapa	67	H2
Andarāb	53	J2
Andenne	27	H4
Andernach	27	K4
Anderson	93	F3
Anderson	103	D2
Andes	107	D5
Andfjorden	29	J2
Andipsara	49	H6
Andizhan	71	N9
Andkhvoy	53	J2
Andoas	109	B4
Andong	81	E5
Andorra	41	L2
Andorra la Vella	41	M2
Andover	27	A3
Andøya	29	H2
Andradina	111	L3
Andreanof Islands	101	(3)C1
Andrews	101	F2
Andria	45	L7
Andros	49	G7
Andros, *Greece*	49	G7
Andros, *The Bahamas*	103	F5
Andrott	75	B6
Andrychów	33	J8
Andūjar	41	F6
Andulo	67	B2
Aneto	41	L2
Angara	73	G5
Angarsk	73	G6
Änge	29	H5
Angel de la Guarda	101	D3
Angeles	77	G3
Ängelholm	29	G8
Angeln	35	E2
Angermünde	35	K4
Angern	43	M2
Angers	39	E6
Anglesey	37	H8
Angmagssalik = Tasiilaq	93	Z3
Ango	65	D3
Angoche	67	F3
Angol	111	G6
Angola	57	E7
Angola	99	D2
Angostura Reservoir	97	F2
Angoulême	39	F8
Angren	71	M9
Anguilla	105	M5
Aniak	101	(1)F3
Anina	47	J4
Anıyaman	51	H5
Ankang	79	D4
Ankara	51	E4
Ankazoabo	67	G4
Anklam	35	J3
Ankpa	63	F3
Ånn	29	G5
Anna	31	H4
Annaba	59	G1
Annaberg-Buchholz	35	H6
An Nabk, *Saudi Arabia*	54	E5
An Nabk, *Syria*	54	D2
An Nafud	61	G2
An Nāīrīyah	53	E3
An Najaf	53	D3
Annapolis	99	E3
Annapurna	75	D3
Ann Arbor	99	D2
An Nāşirīyah	61	J1
Annecy	43	B5
Annemasse	43	B4
Anniston	103	D3
Annobón	63	F5
Annonay	39	K8
An Nukhayb	53	D3
Anqing	79	F4
Ansbach	35	F7
Anshan	81	B3
Anshun	79	D5
Ansley	97	G2
Anson	103	B3
Ansongo	59	F5
Antakya	51	G5
Antalaha	67	J2
Antalya	49	N8
Antalya Körfezi	49	N8
Antananarivo	67	H3
Antarctic Peninsula	112	(2)LL3
Antequera	41	F7
Anti-Atlas	59	D3
Antibes	43	C7
Antigo	99	C1
Antigua	105	M5
Antigua and Barbuda	105	M5
Antikythira	49	F9
Antiparos	49	G7
Antipaxoi	49	C5
Antipayuta	71	P4
Antipodes Islands	89	(3)A1
Antlers	103	B3
Antofagasta	111	G3
Antonito	97	E3
Antropovo	31	H3
Antsalova	67	G3
Antsirabe	67	H3
Antsirañana	67	H2
Antu	81	E2
Antwerp = Antwerpen	27	G3
Antwerpen	27	G3
Anuradhapura	75	D7
Anxi	79	B2
Anyang, *China*	79	E3
Anyang, *South Korea*	81	D5
Anyuysk	73	U3
Anzhero-Sudzhensk	71	R6
Anzio	45	G7
Aoga-shima	81	K7
Aomori	81	L3
Aosta	43	C5
Aoukâr	59	C5
Aoukoukar	63	C1
Apalachee Bay	103	E4
Apalachicola	103	D4
Aparri	77	G3
Apatin	47	F4
Apatity	31	F1
Ape	29	P8
Apeldoorn	27	H2
Api	75	D2
Apia	85	J7
Apoera	109	F2
Apolda	35	G5
Apollo Bay	87	H7
Aporé	109	G7
Apostle Islands	99	B1
Apoteri	109	F3
Appalachian Mountains	103	E3
Appennino	45	G5
Appennino Abruzzese	45	H6
Appennino Calabro	45	K10
Appennino Lucano	45	K8
Appennino Tosco-Emiliano	43	E6
Appennino Umbro-Marchigiano	45	H6
Appleton	99	C2
Aprília	45	G7
Apure	109	D2
Apurimac	109	C6
Āqā	53	H3
'Aqaba	54	C7
Aquidauana	109	F8
Ara	75	D3
Arabian Sea	53	H6
Aracaju	109	K6
Aracati	109	K4
Araçatuba	109	G8
Aracuca	105	L7
Arad	47	J3
Arādah	53	F5
Arafura Sea	83	(2)D5
Aragarças	109	G7
Araguaia	107	F4
Araguaína	109	H5
Araguari	109	H7
Araguatins	109	H5
Arāk	53	E3
Arak	59	F3
Aral Sea	71	K8
Aral'sk	31	M5
Aranda de Duero	41	G3
Aranđelovac	47	H5
Aran Island	37	D6
Aran Islands	37	B8
Aranjuez	41	G4
Aranos	67	B4
Aranyaprathet	77	C4
Araouane	59	E5
Arapahoe	97	G2
Arapiraca	109	K5
'Ar'ar	53	D3
Araras	109	G5
Ararat	51	L4
Arauca	109	D2
Arauca	109	D2
Araxá	109	H7
Araz	51	L4
Arbīl	51	K5
Arbon	43	E3
Arbre du Ténéré	59	G5
Arbroath	37	K5
Arcachon	39	D9
Arcadia	103	E4
Arcata	97	B2

Name	Page	Grid
Archidona	41	F7
Archipelago of the Recherche	87	D6
Archipel de la Société	85	L7
Archipel des Tuamotu	85	M7
Archipiélago de Camagüey	105	J4
Archipiélago de la Reina Adelaida	111	F9
Archipiélago de los Chonos	111	F7
Arco	97	D2
Arcos de la Frontera	41	E8
Arctic Bay	93	P2
Arctic Ocean	112	(1)A1
Arctic Red River	93	E3
Arda	49	H3
Ardabīl	51	N4
Ardahan	51	K3
Årdalstangen	29	D6
Ardas	49	J3
Ardatov	31	J4
Ardennes	27	G4
Ardestān	53	F3
Ardila	41	C6
Ardmore	95	G5
Aredo	83	(2)D3
Areia Branca	109	K5
Arendal	29	E7
Arenys de Mar	41	N3
Arequipa	109	C7
Arere	109	G4
Arévalo	41	F3
Arezzo	45	F5
Argan	71	R9
Argenta	43	G6
Argentan	27	B6
Argentina	111	H6
Argenton-sur-Creuse	39	G7
Argeş	47	N5
Argolikos Kolpos	49	E7
Argos	49	E7
Argos Orestiko	49	D4
Argostoli	49	C6
Argun'	73	K6
Argungu	63	E2
Argunsk	73	L6
Argyll	37	G5
Århus	29	F8
Ariano Irpino	45	K7
Ari Atoll	75	B8
Arica	109	C7
Ariège	39	G11
Arihge	41	M2
Arinos	109	F6
Aripuanã	109	E5
Aripuanã	109	E5
Ariquemes	109	E5
Arizona	101	D2
Arjäng	29	G7
Arka	73	Q5
Arkadak	31	H4
Arkadelphia	103	C3
Arkalyk	71	M7
Arkansas	103	C3
Arkansas	103	C3
Arkansas City	103	B2
Arkhalts'ikhe	51	K3
Arkhangel'sk	31	H2
Arkhipelag Nordenshel'da	71	R2
Arklow	37	F9
Arkoudi	49	C6
Arles	39	K10
Arlington, Oreg., United States	97	B1
Arlington, Tex., United States	103	B3
Arlington, Va., United States	99	E3
Arlit	59	G5
Arlon	27	H4
Armagh	37	F7
Armavir	51	J1
Armenia	51	K3
Armenia	109	B3
Armentières	27	E4
Armidale	87	K6
Armstrong	93	P6
Armyans'k	31	F5
Arnedo	41	H2
Arnett	103	B2
Arnhem	27	H3
Arnhem Land	87	F2
Arno	43	F7
Arnøy	29	G3
Arnøya	29	L1
Arnprior	99	E1
Arnsberg	27	L3
Arnstadt	35	F6
Arolsen	35	E5
Arorae	85	H6
Arquipélago dos Bijagós	63	A2
Ar Ramādī	53	D3
Ar Ramlah	54	C7
Arran	37	G6
Ar Raqqah	51	H6
Arras	27	E4
Ar Rastan	54	D2
Ar Rawḍah	53	E7
Ar Rayn	55	A5
Arrecife	59	C3
Ar Riyāḍ	53	E5
Arrow Lake	97	C1
Arroyo Grande	101	B1
Ar Ruṣāfah	51	H6
Ar Rustāq	53	G5
Ar Ruṭba	53	D3
Ar Ruways	53	F5
Årsandøy	29	G4
Arsiè	43	G5
Arta, Greece	49	C5
Arta, Mallorca	41	P5
Artem	81	G2
Artemovsk	71	S7
Artemovskiy	73	K5
Artesia	101	F2
Arthur	97	F2
Arthur's Town	103	F5
Artigas	111	K5
Artillery Lake	93	J4
Artsyz	47	S4
Artux	71	P10
Artvin	51	J3
Artyk	73	Q4
Aru	85	D6
Arua	65	E3
Aruba	105	K6
Arumã	109	E4
Arusha	65	F4
Arvayheer	79	C1
Arviat	93	N4
Arvidsjaur	29	K4
Arvika	29	G7
Ary	71	Y3
Aryta	73	M4
Arzamas	31	H3
Arzew	41	K9
Arzignano	43	G5
Asahi-dake	81	M2
Asahikawa	81	M2
Åsalē	61	G5
Asansol	75	E4
Asarum	33	D1
Asbest	31	M3
Ascension	57	B6
Ascensión	109	E7
Aschaffenburg	35	E7
Aschersleben	35	G5
Áscoli Piceno	45	H6
Åsela	65	F2
Åsele	29	J4
Asenovgrad	49	G3
Asha	31	L3
Ashburton	89	C6
Asherton	103	B4
Asheville	99	D3
Ashford	27	C3
Ash Fork	101	D1
Ashgabat	53	G2
Ashington	37	L6
Ashizuri-misaki	81	G7
Ashkhabad = Ashgabat	53	G2
Ashland, Kans., United States	97	G3
Ashland, Ky., United States	99	D3
Ashland, Mont., United States	97	E1
Ashland, Oreg., United States	97	B2
Ashland, Wis., United States	99	B1
Ashqelon	54	B5
Ash Shadādah	51	J5
Ash Shāriqah	55	F4
Ash Shiḥr	53	E7
Ash Shu'bah	55	A2
Ash Shurayf	61	G2
Ash Shuwayrif	59	H3
Ashtabula	99	D2
Ashuanipi	93	T6
Ashuanipi Lake	93	T6
Asia	85	D5
Āsika	75	D5
Asilah	59	D1
Asinara	45	C7
Asino	71	R6
Asīr	61	H3
Aşkale	51	J4
Askim	29	F7
Askot	75	D3
Asmara	61	G4
Åsnen	29	H8
Aso	43	J7
Āsosa	65	E1
Aspang Markt	43	M3
Aspe	41	K6
Aspermont	101	F2
As Pontes de García Rodríguez	41	C1
As Sa'an	54	E1
Assab	61	H5
As Şalīf	53	D6
As Salmān	53	E3
As Salwā	55	B2
Assamakka	59	G5
As Samāwah	61	J1
Aş Şanamayn	54	D3
As Sarīr	61	D2
Asse	27	G4
Assen	27	J2
Assens	35	E1
As Sīb	55	H5
As Sidrah	61	C1
Assiniboia	93	K7
Assiniboine	93	M7
Assis	111	L3
Assisi	45	G5
As Sukhnah	51	H6
As Sulaymānīyah	51	L6
As Sulayyil	53	E5
Assumption Island	65	H5
As Suwaydā'	54	D4
As Suwayh	53	G5
Astakida	49	J9
Astana	71	N7
Astara	53	E2
Asti	43	D6
Astorga	41	D2
Astoria	97	B1
Astove Island	65	H6
Astrakhan'	31	J5
Astypalaia	49	J8
Asunción	111	K4
Aswān	61	F3
Aswān Dam	61	F3
Asyût	61	F2
As Zaydīyah	61	H4
Ata	85	J8
Atafu	85	J6
Atakpamé	63	E3
Atâr	59	C4
Atasu	71	N8
Atbara	61	F4
Atbasar	31	N4
Atchison	103	B2
Aternus	45	H6
Ath	27	F4
Athabasca	93	J5
Athens = Athina	49	F7
Athens, Al., United States	103	D3
Athens, Ga., United States	103	E3
Athens, Oh., United States	103	E2
Athens, Tenn., United States	103	E2
Athens, Tex., United States	103	B3
Athina	49	F7
Athlone	37	E8
Ath Thāyat	54	D7
Athy	37	F8
Ati	61	C5
Atiamuri	89	F4
Atico	109	C7
Atikokan	99	B1
Atka	73	S4
Atka Island	101	(3)C1
Atlanta	103	E3
Atlantic, Ia., United States	103	B1
Atlantic, N.C., United States	103	F3
Atlantic City	99	F3
Atlantic Ocean	37	C2
Atlantic Ocean	57	C7
Atlas Bogd	79	B2
Atlas Mountains	41	N9
Atlasovo	73	T5
Atlas Saharien	59	E2
Atlin	93	E5
Atmakur	75	C5
Atmore	103	D3
Atoka	103	B3
Atokos	49	C6
Atol das Rocas	109	L4
Aṭ Ṭā'if	53	D5
Attapu	77	D4
Attawapiskat	93	Q6
Attersee	43	J3
Attica	99	C2
Attu Island	101	(3)A1
Attu Island	112	(1)KK4
At Turbah	61	H5
Atyrau	31	K5
Aubagne	39	L10
Aubange	27	H5
Aube	39	K5
Aubenas	39	K9
Aubry Lake	93	F3
Aubusson	39	H8
Auce	33	M1
Auch	39	F10
Auchi	63	F3
Auckland	89	E3
Auckland Island	89	(2)B1
Aude	39	H10
Aue	35	H6
Auerbach	35	H6
Augathella	87	J5
Augsburg	43	F2
Augusta, Australia	87	C6
Augusta, Italy	45	K11
Augusta, Ga., United States	103	E3
Augusta, Me., United States	99	G2
Augustów	33	M4
Aulla	43	E6
Aurangābād	75	C5
Auray	39	C6
Aurich	27	K1
Aurillac	39	H9
Aurora, Colo., United States	97	F3
Aurora, Ill., United States	99	C2
Aurora, Mo., United States	103	C2
Aurukun	87	H2
Aus	67	B5
Auschwitz = Oświęcim	33	J7
Austin, Minn., United States	99	B2
Austin, Nev., United States	97	C3
Austin, Tex., United States	103	B3
Australia	87	E4
Australian Alps	85	E9
Australian Capital Territory	87	J7
Austria	43	J3
Autun	39	K7
Auxerre	39	J6
Avallon	39	J6
Avam	73	E2
Ävärsin	51	M4
Aveiro	41	B4
Avellino	45	J8
Averøya	29	D5
Avesnes-sur-Helpe	27	F4
Avesta	29	J6
Avezzano	45	H6
Aviemore	37	J4
Avignon	39	K10
Ávila	41	F4
Avilés	41	E1
Avion	27	E4

Name	Page	Grid
Avola	45	K12
Avon, *United Kingdom*	27	A2
Avon, *United Kingdom*	27	A3
Avranches	39	D5
Avrig	47	M4
Awaji-shima	81	H6
Awanui	89	D2
Awat	71	Q9
Awatere	89	D5
Awbārī	61	B2
Awjilah	61	D2
Awka	63	F3
Ax-les-Thermes	39	G11
Ayacucho	109	C6
Ayaguz	71	Q8
Ayakkuduk	71	M9
Ayamonte	41	C7
Ayan	73	E3
Ayan	73	P5
Aya Napa	54	A2
Ayancık	51	F3
Ayanka	73	V4
Ayaviri	109	C6
Aydin	51	B5
Aydıncık	49	R8
Ayers Rock = Uluru	87	F5
Aykhal	73	J3
Aykino	71	H5
Aylesbury	27	B3
Aylmer Lake	93	K4
Ayní	53	J2
Ayní	71	M10
Ayn 'Isá	51	H5
Ayoûn el 'Atroûs	59	D5
Ayr, *Australia*	87	J3
Ayr, *United Kingdom*	37	H6
Aytos	47	Q7
Ayutthaya	77	C4
Ayvalik	49	J5
Azaila	41	K3
Azaouâd	59	E5
Āzārān	51	M5
Azare	63	G2
A'zāz	51	G5
Azdavay	49	R3
Azerbaijan	51	M3
Azogues	109	B4
Azores = Açores	59	(1)B2
Azov	31	G5
Azpeitia	41	H1
Azrou	59	D2
Aztec	97	E3
Azuaga	41	E6
Azul	111	K6
Az Zabadānī	54	D3
Az Zahrān	55	D3
Az Zāwīyah	61	B1
Az Zubayr	55	B1

B

Name	Page	Grid
Ba'albek	54	D2
Baardheere	65	G3
Babadag	47	R5
Babaeski	49	K3
Bāb al Mandab	53	D7
Babanusa	65	D1
Babar	83	(2)C4
Babayevo	31	G3
Babayurt	51	M2
Babo	83	(2)D3
Bābol	53	F2
Babruysk	31	E4
Babura	63	F2
Babushkin	73	H6
Babuyan Islands	77	G3
Bacabal	109	J4
Bacan	83	(2)C3
Bacău	47	P3
Baccarat	43	B2
Bachu	53	L2
Back	93	M3
Bačka Palanka	47	G4
Bačka Topola	47	G4
Backnang	43	E2
Bac Liêu	77	D5

Name	Page	Grid
Bacolod	77	G4
Badajós	109	H4
Badajoz	41	D6
Bad al Milḥ	51	K7
Badalona	41	N3
Bad Ausee	43	J3
Bad Bentheim	27	K2
Bad Berleburg	35	D5
Bad Doberan	35	G2
Bad Dürkheim	35	D7
Bad Ems	27	K4
Baden	33	F9
Baden-Baden	43	D2
Bad Freienwalde	35	K4
Badgastein	43	J3
Badgingarra	87	C6
Bad Harzburg	35	F5
Bad Hersfeld	35	E6
Bad Homburg	35	D6
Bad Honnef	27	K4
Badin	75	A4
Bad Ischl	43	J3
Bādiyat ash Shām	54	D4
Bad Kissingen	35	F6
Bad Kreuznach	27	K5
Bad Langensalza	35	F5
Bad Lauterberg	35	F5
Bad Liebenwerda	35	J5
Bad Mergentheim	35	E7
Bad Nauheim	35	D6
Bad Neuenahr-Ahrweiler	27	K4
Bad Neustadt	35	F6
Bad Oeynhausen	35	D4
Badong	79	E4
Bad Reichenhall	43	H3
Bad Säckingen	35	C9
Bad Salzuflen	35	D4
Bad Salzungen	35	F6
Bad Schwartau	35	F3
Bad Segeberg	35	F3
Bad Sobernheim	27	K5
Bad Urach	43	E2
Bad Vöslau	47	D2
Bad Waldsee	43	E3
Bad Wilbad	43	D2
Bad Wildungen	35	E5
Bad Windsheim	35	F7
Bad Wurzach	43	E3
Baena	41	F7
Bærum	29	F7
Baeza	41	G6
Baffin Bay	91	J2
Baffin Island	93	R2
Bafia	63	G4
Bafoulabé	63	B2
Bafoussam	63	G3
Bāfq	53	G3
Bafra	51	F3
Bafra Burun	51	G3
Bāft	55	G2
Bafwasende	65	D3
Baga	61	B5
Bagani	67	C3
Bagaroua	63	E2
Bagdad	101	D2
Bagdarin	73	J6
Bagé	111	L5
Baggs	97	E2
Baghdād	53	D3
Bagheria	45	H10
Baghlān	53	J2
Bagnères-de-Bigorre	39	F10
Bagno di Romagna	43	G7
Bagnols-sur-Cèze	39	K9
Baguio	77	G3
Bagun Datuk	83	(1)C2
Baharampur	75	E4
Bahawalnagar	75	B3
Bahawalpur	75	B3
Bahçe	51	G5
Bahia	109	J6
Bahía Blanca	111	J6
Bahía Blanca	111	J6
Bahía de Banderas	105	C4
Bahía de Campeche	105	F4
Bahía de Manta	109	A4
Bahía de Petacalco	105	D5

Name	Page	Grid
Bahía de Pisco	109	B6
Bahía de Santa Elena	109	A4
Bahía de Sechura	109	A5
Bahía Grande	111	H9
Bahia Kino	95	D6
Bahía Kino	105	B3
Bahía Negra	111	K3
Bahía Samborombón	111	K6
Bahir Dar	61	G5
Bahraich	75	D3
Bahrain	55	D4
Bahrat Ḥimş	54	D2
Bahr el Abiad	61	F5
Bahr el Azraq	61	F5
Bahr el Ghazal	61	C5
Bahr el Ghazal	65	D2
Bahr el Jebe	65	E2
Bahr el Nîl = Nile	61	F4
Baía de Marajó	109	H4
Baía de Todos os Santos	109	K6
Baía do Bengo	63	G6
Baia Mare	47	L2
Baião	109	H4
Baia Sprie	47	L2
Baïbokoum	65	B2
Baicheng, *China*	71	Q9
Baicheng, *China*	79	G1
Baie Comeau	99	G1
Baie de la Seine	27	B5
Baie de la Somme	27	D4
Baie du Poste	93	S6
Baie St. Paul	99	F1
Baiji	51	K6
Baile Átha Cliath = Dublin	37	F8
Bailén	41	G6
Bailleul	27	E4
Bailundo	67	B2
Bainbridge	103	E3
Bairiki	85	H5
Bairin Yuoqi	79	F2
Bairin Zuoqi	79	F2
Bairnsdale	87	J7
Bais	77	G5
Baja	47	F3
Baja California	95	C5
Bakchar	71	Q6
Bakel	63	B2
Baker	85	J5
Baker, *Calif., United States*	97	C3
Baker, *Mont., United States*	97	F1
Baker, *Oreg., United States*	97	C2
Baker Lake	93	M4
Baker Lake	93	N4
Bakersfield	101	C1
Bakhta	73	D4
Baki	53	E1
Bakkafjörđur	29	(1)F1
Bakkaflói	29	(1)F1
Baku = Baki	53	E1
Balā	51	E4
Balabac	77	F5
Balabac Strait	77	F5
Balagansk	73	G6
Balaghat	75	D4
Balaguer	41	L3
Balakhta	71	S6
Balaklava	51	E1
Balakovo	31	J4
Bālā Morghāb	71	L10
Balan	47	N3
Balāngīr	75	D4
Balashov	31	H4
Balassagyarmat	47	G1
Balaton	47	E3
Balatonfüred	47	E3
Balatonlelle	47	E3
Balchik	51	C2
Balclutha	89	B8
Bald Knob	99	B3
Baldwin	103	E3
Balearic Islands = Islas Baleares	41	N5
Bāleshwar	75	E4
Baley	73	K6
Baléyara	63	E2
Balguntay	71	R9
Bali	83	(1)F4
Balige	83	(1)B2

Name	Page	Grid
Balıkesir	49	K5
Balikpapan	83	(1)F3
Balimo	83	(2)F4
Balingen	43	D2
Balintang Channel	77	G3
Balkhash	71	N8
Ballarat	87	H7
Balleny Island	112	(2)Y3
Ballina, *Australia*	87	K5
Ballina, *Republic of Ireland*	37	C7
Ballinasloe	37	D8
Ballinger	101	G2
Ball's Pyramid	87	L6
Ballymena	37	F7
Balmazújváros	47	J2
Balotra	75	B3
Balranald	87	H6
Balş	47	M5
Balsas	105	D5
Balsas	109	H5
Balta	47	S2
Bălţi	47	Q2
Baltic Sea	29	J8
Baltijsk	33	J3
Baltimore	99	E3
Baltrum	35	C3
Balvi	29	P8
Balykchy	71	P9
Balykshi	31	K5
Bam	53	G4
Bamaga	87	H2
Bamako	63	C2
Bamba	59	E5
Bambari	65	C2
Bamberg	35	F7
Bambesa	65	D3
Bambouk	59	C6
Bambouk Kaarta	63	B2
Bamda	79	B4
Bamenda	63	G3
Bāmiān	53	J3
Banaba	85	G6
Bañados del Izozog	109	E7
Banalia	65	D3
Banana, *Australia*	87	K4
Banana, *Dem. Rep. of Congo*	65	A5
Banaz	49	M6
Ban Ban	77	C3
Banbury	37	L9
Banda	75	D3
Banda Aceh	77	B5
Bandama	63	C3
Bandar-e 'Abbās	55	G3
Bandar-e Anzalī	53	E2
Bandar-e Deylam	55	D1
Bandar-e Ganāveh	55	D2
Bandar-e Khoemir	55	F3
Bandar-e Lengeh	55	F3
Bandar-e Ma'shur	55	C1
Bandar-e Torkeman	53	F2
Bandar Khomeynī	55	C1
Bandar Seri Begawan	83	(1)E2
Banda Sea	83	(2)C3
Band-e Moghüyeh	55	F3
Bandirma	49	K4
Bandundu	65	B4
Bandung	83	(1)D4
Băneasa	47	Q5
Bāneh	51	L6
Banff, *Canada*	93	H6
Banff, *United Kingdom*	37	K4
Bangalore	75	C6
Bangangté	63	G3
Bangassou	65	C3
Bangbong	83	(2)B3
Banggi	83	(1)F1
Banghāzī	61	D1
Bangka	83	(1)D3
Bangkok = Krung Thep	77	C4
Bangladesh	75	E4
Bangor, *N.Ire., United Kingdom*	37	G7
Bangor, *Wales, United Kingdom*	37	H8
Bangor, *United States*	99	G2
Bang Saphan Yai	77	B4
Bangui	65	B3
Ban Hat Yai	77	C5
Ban Hua Hin	77	B4

Name	Page	Ref
Bani-Bangou	63	E1
Banī Walīd	59	H2
Bāniyās	51	F6
Banja Luka	47	E5
Banjarmasin	83	(1)E3
Banjul	63	A2
Ban Khemmarat	77	D3
Banks Island = Moa, *Australia*	87	H2
Banks Island, *B.C., Canada*	93	E6
Banks Island, *N.W.T., Canada*	93	G2
Banks Lake	97	C1
Banks Peninsula	89	D6
Banks Strait	87	J8
Bannerman Town	103	F5
Bannu	75	B2
Bánovce	33	H9
Banská	33	J9
Banská Štiavnica	33	H9
Bansko	49	F3
Bantry	37	C10
Banyo	63	G3
Banyoles	41	N2
Banyuwangi	83	(1)E4
Baode	79	E3
Baoding	79	F3
Baoji	79	D4
Bao Lôc	77	D4
Baoro	65	B2
Baoshan	77	B1
Baotou	79	E2
Baoying	79	F4
Bapaume	27	E4
Ba'qūbah	53	D3
Baquedano	111	H3
Bar	47	G7
Barabai	83	(1)F3
Baraboo	99	C2
Barakaldo	41	H1
Baramati	75	B5
Baramula	75	B2
Baran	75	C3
Baranavichy	31	E4
Baraolt	47	N3
Barbados	109	F1
Barbastro	41	L2
Barbate	41	E8
Barbuda	105	M5
Barcaldine	87	J4
Barcău	47	K2
Barcellona Pozzo di Gotto	45	K10
Barcelona, *Spain*	41	N3
Barcelona, *Venezuela*	105	M6
Barcelos, *Brazil*	109	E4
Barcelos, *Spain*	41	B3
Barco de Valdeorras = O Barco	41	D2
Barcs	47	E4
Bärdä	51	M3
Bardai	61	C3
Barddhamān	75	E4
Bardejov	33	L8
Bareilly	75	C3
Barents Sea	71	E3
Barentu	61	G4
Bareo	83	(1)F2
Barga	75	D2
Bargaal	65	J1
Barguzin	73	H6
Bar Harbor	99	G2
Bari	45	L7
Barikot	75	B1
Barinas	109	C2
Bârîs	61	F3
Barisal	75	F4
Barito	83	(2)A3
Barkam	79	C4
Barkava	29	P8
Barkly Tableland	87	F3
Barkol	71	S9
Bârlad	47	Q3
Bârlad	47	Q3
Bar-le-Duc	27	H6
Barletta	45	L7
Barmer	75	B3
Barmouth Bay	37	H9
Barnaul	71	Q7
Barnsley	37	L8
Barnstaple	37	H10
Barnstaple Bay	37	H10
Barpeta	75	F3
Barquisimeto	109	D1
Barr	43	C2
Barra, *Brazil*	109	J6
Barra, *United Kingdom*	37	E4
Barracão do Barreto	109	G5
Barra do Bugres	109	F7
Barra do Corda	109	H5
Barra do Garças	109	G7
Barra do São Manuel	109	G5
Barragem de Santa Clara	41	B7
Barragem de Sobradinho	109	J5
Barragem do Castelo de Bode	41	B5
Barragem do Maranhão	41	C6
Barranca, *Peru*	109	B4
Barranca, *Peru*	109	B6
Barranquilla	105	K6
Barreiras	109	H6
Barreiro	41	A6
Barretos	109	H8
Barrie	99	E2
Barron	99	B1
Barrow	101	(1)F1
Barrow-in-Furness	37	J7
Barrow Island	87	B4
Barrow Strait	93	N2
Barshatas	71	P8
Barsi	75	C5
Barstow	101	C2
Bar-sur-Aube	39	K5
Barth	35	H2
Bartın	51	E3
Bartle Frere	85	E7
Bartlesville	103	B2
Bartlett	97	G2
Bartoszyce	33	K3
Barus	83	(1)B2
Baruun Urt	79	E1
Barwani	75	B4
Barysaw	31	E4
Basaidu	55	F3
Basankusu	65	B3
Basarabeasca	47	R3
Basarabi	47	R5
Basca	45	C2
Basel	43	C3
Bashkiriya	31	K4
Bāsht	55	D1
Basilan	83	(2)B1
Basildon	27	C3
Basiluzzo	45	K10
Basingstoke	37	L10
Başkale	51	K4
Basoko	65	C3
Bassano	95	D1
Bassano del Grappa	43	G5
Bassar	63	E3
Bassas da India	67	F4
Basse Santa Su	59	C6
Basse Terre	105	M5
Bassett	97	G2
Bass Strait	87	H7
Bassum	35	D4
Bastak	55	F3
Bastānābād	51	M5
Basti	75	D3
Bastia	45	D6
Bastogne	27	H4
Bastrop, *La., United States*	103	C3
Bastrop, *Tex., United States*	103	B3
Bata	63	F4
Batagay	73	N3
Batak	49	G3
Batamay	73	M4
Batangas	77	G4
Batan Islands	77	G2
Batanta	83	(2)C3
Batemans Bay	87	K7
Batesville	103	D3
Bath, *United Kingdom*	37	K10
Bath, *United States*	99	E2
Bathinda	75	B2
Bathurst, *Australia*	87	J6
Bathurst, *Canada*	93	T7
Bathurst Inlet	93	K3
Bathurst Island, *Australia*	87	E2
Bathurst Island, *Canada*	93	M1
Batman	53	D2
Batna	59	G1
Baton Rouge	103	C3
Bátonyterenye	47	G2
Batroûn	54	C2
Battipaglia	45	J8
Battle	93	J6
Battle Creek	99	C2
Battle Harbour	93	V6
Battle Mountain	97	C2
Batu	65	F2
Batui	83	(2)B3
Bat'umi	51	J3
Batu Pahat	83	(1)C2
Baturino	71	R6
Baubau	83	(2)B4
Bauchi	63	F2
Baudette	99	B1
Baukau	83	(2)C4
Baume-les-Dames	39	M6
Bauru	111	M3
Bauska	29	N8
Bautzen	33	D6
Bawean	83	(1)E4
Bawiti	61	E2
Bawku	63	D2
Bayamo	105	J4
Bayanaul	71	P7
Bayandelger	73	H7
Bayan Har Shan	79	B4
Bayanhongor	79	C1
Bayan Mod	79	C2
Bayan Obo	79	D2
Bayansumküre	71	Q9
Bayburt	51	J3
Bay City, *Mich., United States*	99	D2
Bay City, *Tex., United States*	103	B4
Baydhabo	65	G3
Bayerische Alpen	43	G3
Bayeux	27	B5
Bayfield	99	B1
Bayindir	49	K6
Bāyir	54	D6
Baykit	71	T5
Baykonur	71	M8
Bay Minette	103	D3
Bay of Bengal	75	E5
Bay of Biscay	39	C9
Bay of Fundy	93	T8
Bay of Islands	89	E2
Bay of Plenty	89	F3
Bayonne	39	D10
Bayramaly	53	H2
Bayramiç	49	J5
Bayreuth	35	G7
Baysun	53	J2
Bayt al Faqīh	61	H5
Bay View	89	F4
Baza	41	H7
Bazas	39	E9
Bazdar	53	J4
Beach	97	F1
Beachy Head	27	C4
Beagle Gulf	87	E2
Bealanana	67	H2
Bear Island	37	B10
Bear Island = Bjørnøya	71	B3
Bear Lake	97	D2
Beasain	41	H1
Beas de Segura	41	H6
Beatrice	103	B1
Beatty	101	C1
Beaufort, *Malaysia*	83	(1)F1
Beaufort, *N.C., United States*	103	F3
Beaufort, *S.C., United States*	103	E3
Beaufort Sea	91	Q2
Beaufort West	67	C6
Beaumont	103	C3
Beaune	39	K6
Beauvais	27	E5
Beaver	97	D3
Beaver Creek	101	(1)J3
Beaver Dam	99	C3
Beaver Falls	99	D2
Beawar	75	B3
Beazley	111	H5
Bebra	35	E6
Bečej	47	H4
Béchar	59	E2
Beckley	103	E2
Becks	89	B7
Beckum	27	L3
Beclean	47	M2
Bedford, *United Kingdom*	37	M9
Bedford, *United States*	103	D2
Bedworth	27	A2
Beenleigh	87	K5
Beer Menuha	54	C6
Be'ér Sheva'	54	B5
Beeville	103	B4
Behbehān	55	D1
Bei'an	73	M7
Beihai	77	D2
Beijing	79	F3
Beipan	79	D5
Beipiao	79	G2
Beira	67	E3
Beirut = Beyrouth	54	C3
Beiuş	47	K3
Beizhen	81	A3
Béja	59	G1
Bejaïa	59	G1
Béjar	41	E4
Bekdash	53	F1
Békés	33	L11
Békéscsaba	47	J3
Bekily	67	H4
Bela	53	J4
Bela Crkva	47	J5
Belaga	83	(1)E2
Belarus	25	G2
Bela Vista	67	E5
Belaya	31	K3
Belaya Gora	73	R3
Bełchatów	33	J6
Belcher Islands	93	Q5
Beledweyne	65	H3
Belém	109	H4
Belen	105	C2
Belfast	37	G7
Belfield	97	F1
Belfort	43	B3
Belgazyn	71	T7
Belgium	27	G4
Belgorod	31	G4
Belgrade = Beograd	47	H5
Beli	63	G3
Belice	45	H11
Beli Manastir	47	F4
Belinyu	83	(1)D3
Belitung	83	(1)D3
Belize	105	G5
Belize	105	G5
Bellac	39	G7
Bella Coola	93	F6
Bellary	75	C5
Bellefontaine	99	D2
Belle Fourche	97	F2
Belle Glade	103	E4
Belle Île	39	B6
Belle Isle	93	V6
Bellême	39	F5
Belleterre	99	E1
Belleville, *Canada*	99	E2
Belleville, *United States*	103	B2
Bellingham	97	B1
Bellingshausen Sea	112	(2)JJ4
Bellinzona	43	E4
Bello	109	B2
Belluno	43	H4
Bellyk	73	E6
Belmont	99	E2
Belmonte, *Brazil*	109	K7
Belmonte, *Spain*	41	H5
Belmopan	105	G5
Belmullet	37	B7
Belogorsk	73	M6
Belogradchik	47	K6
Belo Horizonte	109	J7
Beloit, *Kans., United States*	103	B2
Beloit, *Wis., United States*	99	C2
Belomorsk	31	F2
Belorechensk	51	H1

Name	Page	Ref
Beloretsk	31	L4
Belo Tsiribihina	67	G3
Belovo	71	R7
Beloyarskiy	71	M5
Beloye More	31	G1
Belozersk	31	G2
Belozerskoye	31	N3
Belye Vody	71	M9
Belyy Yar	71	Q6
Belzig	35	H4
Bembibre	41	D2
Bemidji	99	A1
Bena Dibele	65	C4
Benavente	41	E3
Benbecula	37	E4
Bend	97	B2
Bender-Bayla	65	J2
Bender Qaasim	65	H1
Bendorf	27	K4
Bene	67	E3
Benešov	33	D8
Benevento	45	J7
Bengbu	79	F4
Bengkulu	83	(1)C3
Benguela	67	A2
Benguerir	59	D2
Benha	61	F1
Beni	65	D3
Beni	109	D6
Beni Abbès	59	E2
Benicarló	41	L4
Benidorm	41	K6
Benî Mazâr	61	F2
Beni Mellal	59	D2
Benin	63	E2
Benin City	63	F3
Beni Saf	41	J9
Beni Slimane	41	P8
Beni Suef	61	F2
Benito Juaréz	111	K6
Benjamin Constant	109	D4
Benkelman	97	F2
Benkovac	43	L6
Ben More Assynt	37	H3
Ben Nevis	37	H5
Bennington	99	F2
Benoud	59	F2
Bensheim	35	D7
Benson, Ariz., United States	101	D2
Benson, Minn., United States	95	G2
Benteng	83	(2)B4
Bentinck Island	87	G3
Bentonville	103	C2
Bentung	83	(1)C2
Benue	63	G3
Benxi	79	G2
Beograd	47	H5
Bepazarı	51	D3
Berat	49	B4
Beravina	67	H3
Berber	61	F4
Berbera	61	H5
Berbérati	65	B3
Berchtesgaden	43	J3
Berck	27	D4
Berdigestyakh	73	M4
Berdyans'k	31	G5
Berdychiv	31	E5
Bereeda	65	J1
Berehove	47	K1
Bererreá	41	C2
Berettyóújfalu	47	J2
Berettys	33	L10
Bereznik	31	H2
Berezniki	31	L3
Berezovo	31	N2
Berezovyy	73	P6
Berga	41	M2
Bergama	49	K5
Bérgamo	43	E5
Bergara	41	H1
Bergedorf	35	F3
Bergen, Netherlands	27	G2
Bergen, Norway	29	C6
Bergen, Germany	35	J2
Bergen, Germany	35	E4
Bergen op Zoom	27	G3
Bergerac	39	F9
Bergheim	27	J4
Bergisch Gladbach	35	C6
Bergsfjordhalvøya	29	L1
Beringen	27	H3
Beringovskiy	73	X4
Bering Sea	101	(1)C4
Bering Strait	101	(1)C2
Berkeley	101	B1
Berkner Island	112	(2)A2
Berkovitsa	47	L6
Berlin, Germany	35	J4
Berlin, United States	99	F2
Bermejillo	101	F3
Bermejo	111	K4
Bermeo	41	H1
Bermuda	91	H6
Bern	43	C4
Bernado	101	E2
Bernau	35	J4
Bernay	27	C5
Bernburg	35	G5
Berner Alpen	43	C4
Beroun	33	D8
Berounka	35	J7
Berovo	49	E3
Berrouaghia	41	N8
Berry Islands	103	F4
Bertoua	63	G4
Bertram	99	D1
Beruni	71	L9
Berwick-upon-Tweed	37	L6
Besalampy	67	G3
Besançon	39	M6
Beshneh	55	F2
Bessemer	103	D3
Bestamak	71	P8
Bestuzhevo	31	H2
Bestyakh, Russia	73	L3
Bestyakh, Russia	73	M4
Betanzos	41	B1
Bĕtdâmbâng	77	C4
Bethany	99	B2
Bethel, Ak., United States	101	(1)E3
Bethel, Pa., United States	99	F2
Bethlehem, Israel	54	C5
Bethlehem, South Africa	67	D5
Béthune	27	E4
Betioky	67	G4
Betoota	87	H5
Bet-She'an	54	C4
Bettiah	75	D3
Betul	75	C4
Betzdorf	35	C6
Beulah	99	C2
Beverley	37	M8
Beverungen	35	E5
Bexhill	27	C4
Bey Dağları	49	M8
Beyla	63	C3
Beyneu	71	J8
Beypazarı	49	P4
Beyrouth	54	C3
Beyşehir	49	M4
Beyşehir Gölü	49	P7
Bezhetsk	31	G3
Béziers	39	J10
Bhadgaon	75	E3
Bhadrakh	75	E4
Bhadravati	75	C6
Bhagalpur	75	E3
Bhairab Bazar	75	F4
Bhakkar	75	B2
Bhamo	77	B2
Bharuch	75	B4
Bhatpara	75	E4
Bhavnagar	75	B4
Bhawanipatna	75	D5
Bhilai	75	D4
Bhilwara	75	B3
Bhīmavaram	75	D5
Bhind	75	C3
Bhiwandi	75	B5
Bhopal	75	C4
Bhubaneshwar	75	E4
Bhuj	75	A4
Bhusawal	75	C4
Bhutan	75	E3
Biak	83	(2)E3
Biak	83	(2)E3
Biała	33	K8
Biała Podlaska	33	N5
Białogard	33	F3
Białystok	33	N4
Biarritz	39	D10
Biasca	43	D4
Bibbiena	43	G7
Biberach	43	E2
Bicaz	47	P3
Bickerton Island	87	G2
Bicske	47	F2
Bida	63	F3
Bidar	75	C5
Bidbid	55	H5
Biddeford	99	F2
Bideford	37	H10
Biedenkopf	35	D6
Biel	43	C3
Bielefeld	35	D4
Biella	43	D5
Bielsko-Biała	33	J8
Bielsk Podlaski	33	N5
Biên Hoa	77	D4
Bietigheim-Bissingen	43	E2
Big	93	G2
Biga	49	K4
Bigadiç	49	L5
Big Desert	87	H7
Big Falls	99	B1
Bighorn	95	E2
Bighorn Lake	97	E1
Bighorn Mountains	97	E2
Bight of Bangkok	77	C4
Bight of Benin	63	E3
Bight of Biafra	63	F4
Big Lake	101	(1)H2
Bignona	59	B6
Big Pine	103	E5
Big Rapids	99	C2
Big River	93	K6
Big Sandy	97	D1
Big Sioux	97	G2
Big Spring	101	F2
Big Sur	101	B1
Big Trout Lake	93	P6
Bihać	43	L6
Bijapur	75	C5
Bījār	51	M6
Bijeljina	47	G5
Bijelo Polje	47	G6
Bijie	79	D5
Bikanar	75	B3
Bikin	73	N7
Bikini	85	G4
Bilaspur	75	D4
Biläsuvar	51	N4
Bila Tserkva	31	F5
Bilbao	41	H1
Bileća	47	F7
Bilecik	49	M4
Bilečko Jezero	47	F7
Biled	47	H4
Biłgoraj	33	M7
Bilhorod-Dnistrovs'kyy	31	F5
Bílina	35	J6
Billings	97	D1
Bill of Portland	37	K11
Bilma	61	B4
Biloxi	103	D3
Bimini Islands	103	F4
Binche	27	G4
Bindi Bindi	87	C6
Bindura	67	E3
Bingen	35	C7
Binghamton	99	E2
Bingöl	51	J4
Binongko	83	(2)B4
Bintulu	83	(1)E2
Bintuni	83	(2)D3
Binyang	77	D2
Binzhou	79	F3
Biograd	43	L7
Birāk	59	H3
Birao	61	D5
Biratnagar	75	E3
Bi'r Bażīrī	54	E2
Birdsville	87	G5
Bireun	83	(1)B1
Bîr Gifgâfa	54	A6
Birhan	61	G5
Bîr Hasana	54	A6
Bīrjand	53	G3
Birkenfeld	27	K5
Birmingham, United Kingdom	37	L9
Birmingham, United States	103	D3
Bîr Mogreïn	59	C3
Birnie	85	J6
Birnin-Gwari	63	F2
Birnin Kebbi	63	E2
Birnin Konni	63	F2
Birnin Kudu	63	F2
Birobidzhan	73	N7
Birsk	31	L3
Biržai	33	P1
Bi'r Zalṭan	61	C2
Bisbee	101	E2
Biscéglie	45	L7
Bischofshofen	43	J3
Bischofswerda	33	D6
Biševo	45	L6
Bishkek	71	N9
Bishop	97	C3
Bishop Auckland	37	L7
Bishop's Stortford	27	C3
Biskra	59	G2
Bislig	77	H5
Bismarck	95	F2
Bismarck Sea	85	E6
Bissau	59	B6
Bistcho Lake	93	H5
Bistriţa	47	M2
Bistriţa	47	P3
Bitburg	27	J5
Bitche	35	C7
Bitkine	61	C5
Bitlis	51	K4
Bitola	49	D3
Bitonto	45	L7
Bitterfeld	35	H5
Bitterroot Range	97	C1
Bitti	45	D8
Bitung	83	(2)C2
Biu	63	G2
Biwa-ko	81	H6
Bixby	99	B3
Biyāvra	75	C4
Biysk	71	R7
Bizerte	59	G1
Bjelovar	47	D4
Bjørnøya	71	B3
B-Köpenick	35	J4
Blackburn	37	K8
Blackfoot	97	D2
Blackfoot Reservoir	97	D2
Black Hills	97	F2
Blackpool	37	J8
Black Range	101	E2
Black River Falls	99	B2
Black Rock Desert	97	C2
Blacksburg	99	D3
Black Sea	51	D2
Blacks Harbour	99	G1
Black Sugarloaf	87	K6
Black Volta	63	D3
Blackwater	37	D9
Blagny-sur-Bresle	27	D5
Blagodarnyy	51	K1
Blagoevgrad	49	F3
Blagoveshchenka	71	P7
Blagoveshchensk	73	M6
Blain	39	D6
Blair	99	G2
Blairsden	97	B3
Blairsville	103	E3
Blaj	47	L3
Blakely	103	E3
Blanco	109	E6
Blanding	101	E1
Blankenberge	27	F3

Place	Pg	Grid
Blankenburg	35	F5
Blankenheim	27	J4
Blantyre	67	F3
Blasket Islands	37	B9
Blaubeuren	43	E2
Blaye-et-Sainte-Luce	39	E8
Bled	43	K4
Blenheim	89	D5
Blevands Huk	35	D1
Blida	59	F1
Blind River	95	K2
Bloemfontein	67	D5
Bloemhof	67	D5
Blois	39	G6
Blönduós	29	(1)C2
Błonie	33	K5
Bloomfield	103	D2
Bloomington, Ill., United States	99	C2
Bloomington, Ind., United States	99	C3
Bludenz	43	E3
Blue Earth	99	B2
Bluefield	99	D3
Bluefields	105	H6
Blue Mountain Lake	99	F2
Blue Mountains	97	C2
Blue Nile = Bahr el Azraq	61	F5
Bluenose Lake	93	H3
Bluff, New Zealand	89	B8
Bluff, United States	101	E1
Blumenau	111	M4
Blythe	101	D2
Blytheville	103	D2
Bo	63	B3
Boac	77	G4
Boa Vista, Brazil	109	E3
Boa Vista, Cape Verde Islands	63	(1)B1
Bobbili	75	D5
Bóbbio	43	E6
Bobigny	27	E6
Bobingen	43	F2
Boblingen	43	E2
Bobo Dioulasso	63	D2
Bobr	33	E6
Bobrov	31	H4
Bôca do Acre	109	D5
Boca Grande	105	M7
Boca Grande	107	E3
Bocaiúva	109	J7
Bocaranga	65	B2
Bochart	99	F1
Bochnia	33	K8
Bocholt	35	B5
Bochum	35	C5
Bodaybo	73	J5
Bode	35	G4
Bodélé	61	C4
Boden	29	L4
Bodham	75	C5
Bodmin	37	H11
Bodø	29	H3
Bodrog	33	L9
Bodrum	49	K7
Boe	97	D2
Boende	65	C4
Bogale	77	B3
Bogalusa	103	D3
Boggabilla	87	K5
Boghni	41	P8
Bognor Regis	27	B4
Bogo	77	G4
Bogor	83	(1)D4
Bogorodskoye	73	Q6
Bogotá	109	C3
Bogotol	71	R6
Bogra	75	E4
Boguchany	73	F5
Bogué	59	C5
Bo Hai	79	F3
Bohmerwald	35	H7
Bohol	77	G5
Bohumin	33	H8
Boiaçu	109	E4
Boise	97	C2
Boise City	101	F1
Bojnürd	71	K10
Bokatola	65	B4
Boké	63	B2
Bokspits	67	C5
Bokungu	65	C4
Bolbec	27	C5
Bole, China	71	Q9
Bole, Ghana	63	D3
Bolechiv	33	N8
Bolesławiec	33	E6
Bolgatanga	63	D2
Bolhrad	47	R4
Bolintin-Vale	47	N5
Bolivar	99	B3
Bolivia	109	D7
Bollène	39	K9
Bollnäs	29	J6
Bolmen	29	G8
Bolnisi	51	L3
Bolobo	63	H5
Bolotnoye	71	Q6
Bol'shaya Pyssa	31	J2
Bol'sherech'ye	31	P3
Bol'shezemel'skaya Tundra	71	J4
Bol Shirta	73	C4
Bolshoy Atlym	31	N2
Bol'shoy Osinovaya	73	W3
Bol'shoy Vlas'evo	31	P2
Bolshoy Yuga	31	P2
Bolsover	27	A1
Bolton	37	K8
Bolu	51	D3
Bolvadin	49	P6
Bolzano = Bozen	43	G4
Boma	63	G6
Bombala	87	J7
Bombay = Mumbai	75	B5
Bomili	65	D3
Bom Jesus da Lapa	109	J6
Bømlo	29	C7
Bomnak	73	M6
Bonáb	51	M5
Bonaparte Archipelago	87	B2
Bonavista Bay	93	W7
Bondeno	43	G6
Bondo	65	C3
Bondokodi	87	C1
Bondoukou	63	D3
Bondowoso	83	(1)E4
Bongao	83	(2)A1
Bongor	63	H2
Bonifacio	45	D7
Bonn	35	C6
Bonners Ferry	97	C1
Bonorva	45	C8
Bonthe	63	B3
Bontoc	77	G3
Bonyhád	47	F3
Boone	99	D3
Boonville	103	C2
Boorama	65	G2
Boosaaso	53	E7
Boothia Peninsula	93	M2
Booué	63	G5
Boppard	35	C6
Bor, Russia	73	D4
Bor, Sudan	65	E2
Bor, Turkey	49	S7
Bor, Yugoslavia	47	K5
Borah Peak	97	C3
Borås	29	G8
Borāzjān	55	D2
Bordeaux	39	E9
Borden Peninsula	93	Q2
Border Town	87	H7
Bordj Bou Arréridj	59	F1
Bordj Bounaam	41	M9
Bordj Flye Sante Marie	59	E3
Bordj Messauda	59	G2
Bordj Mokhtar	59	F4
Bordj Omar Driss	59	G3
Borgarnes	29	(1)C2
Borger	101	F1
Borgomanero	43	D5
Borgo San Dalmazzo	43	C6
Borgo San Lorenzo	43	G7
Borgosésia	43	D5
Borgo Val di Taro	43	E6
Bori Jenein	59	H2
Borislav	33	N8
Borisoglebsk	31	H4
Borjomi	51	K3
Borken	27	J3
Borkou	61	C4
Borkum	27	J1
Borlänge	29	H6
Bórmida	43	D6
Bormio	43	F4
Borna	35	H5
Borneo	83	(1)E3
Bornholm	29	H9
Borodino	71	R5
Borodinskoye	29	Q6
Boromo	63	D2
Borovichi	31	F3
Borovskoy	31	M4
Borriana	41	K5
Borroloola	87	G3
Borşa	47	M2
Borshchiv	47	P1
Borshchovochnyy Khrebet	73	J7
Borđeyri	29	(1)C2
Borüjerd	53	E3
Borzya	73	K6
Bosa	45	C8
Bosanska Dubica	47	D4
Bosanska Gradiška	47	E4
Bosanska Kostajnica	43	M5
Bosanska Krupa	47	D5
Bosanski Brod	47	F4
Bosanski Novi	47	D4
Bosanski Petrovac	47	D5
Bosansko Grahovo	43	M6
Boşca	47	J4
Bose	77	D2
Bosilegrad	47	K7
Boskovice	33	F8
Bosna	47	F5
Bosnia-Herzegovina	47	E5
Bosobolo	65	B3
Bosporus = İstanbul Boğazı	49	M3
Bosporus	53	A1
Bossámbélé	65	B2
Bossangoa	65	B2
Bossier City	103	C3
Bosten Hu	71	R9
Boston, United Kingdom	37	M9
Boston, United States	99	F2
Botevgrad	47	L7
Botlikh	53	E1
Botna	47	R3
Botoşani	47	P2
Botou	79	F3
Botrange	27	J4
Botswana	67	C4
Bottrop	27	J3
Bou Ahmed	41	F9
Bouaké	63	C3
Bouar	65	B2
Bouârfa	59	E2
Boufarik	41	N8
Bougainville Island	85	F6
Bougainville Reef	87	J3
Bougouni	63	C2
Bougzoul	41	N9
Bouira	59	F1
Bou Ismaïl	41	N8
Bou Izakarn	59	D3
Boujdour	59	C3
Bou Kadir	41	M8
Boulder	97	E2
Boulder City	101	D1
Boulia	87	G4
Boulogne-sur-Mer	27	D4
Bounty Islands	85	H10
Bourem	59	E5
Bourg-de-Piage	39	L9
Bourg-en-Bresse	39	L7
Bourges	39	H6
Bourgoin-Jallieu	39	L8
Bourke	87	J6
Bournemouth	37	L11
Bou Saâda	59	F1
Bousso	61	C5
Boussu	27	F4
Boutilimit	59	C5
Bouzghaïa	41	M8
Bowbells	97	F1
Bowen	87	J4
Bowie, Ariz., United States	101	E2
Bowie, Tex., United States	101	G2
Bowkan	51	M5
Bowling Green, Fla., United States	103	E4
Bowling Green, Ky., United States	103	D2
Bowling Green, Mo., United States	103	C2
Bowman	97	F1
Bowman Bay	93	R3
Bo Xian	79	F4
Boxwood Hill	87	C6
Boyabat	51	F3
Boyang	79	F5
Boyarka	73	F2
Boysen Reservoir	97	E2
Boyuibe	111	J3
Bozcaada	49	H5
Boz Dağ	49	M7
Bozeman	97	D1
Bozkir	43	G4
Bozoum	65	B2
Bozüyük	49	N5
Bra	43	C6
Brač	47	D6
Bracciano	45	G6
Bräcke	29	H5
Brad	47	K3
Brádano	45	L8
Bradford	37	L8
Brady	103	B3
Braga	41	B3
Bragança, Brazil	109	H4
Bragança, Portugal	41	D3
Brahmapur	75	D5
Brahmaputra	75	F3
Brăila	47	Q4
Brainerd	99	B1
Braintree	27	C3
Brake	35	D3
Bramming	35	D1
Brampton	99	E2
Bramsche	35	D4
Branco	109	E3
Brandberg	67	A4
Brandenburg	35	H4
Brandenton	103	E4
Brandon	93	M7
Brandvlei	67	C5
Brandýs	33	D7
Braniewo	33	J3
Brasileia	109	D6
Brasília	109	H7
Braslaw	29	P9
Braşov	47	N4
Bratislava	33	G9
Bratsk	73	G5
Bratskoye Vodokhranilishche	73	G5
Brattleboro	99	F2
Braţul	47	R4
Braunau	43	J2
Braunschweig	35	F4
Brawley	101	C2
Bray	37	F8
Brazil	107	F4
Brazzaville	65	B4
Brčko	47	F5
Brda	33	G4
Bream Bay	89	E2
Breckenridge	101	G2
Břeclav	33	F9
Breda	27	G3
Bredasdorp	67	C6
Bredstedt	35	E2
Bredy	31	M4
Bree	27	H3
Bree	39	L2
Bregenz	43	E3

Name	Page	Grid
Breiðafjörður	29	(1)A2
Bremangerlandet	29	B6
Bremen, *Germany*	35	D3
Bremen, *United States*	103	D3
Bremerhaven	35	D3
Bremerton	97	B1
Bremervörde	35	E3
Brenham	103	B3
Brennero	43	G4
Breno	43	F5
Brentwood	27	C3
Bréscia	43	F5
Breslau = Wrocław	33	G6
Bressanone = Brixen	45	F2
Bressay	37	M1
Bressuire	39	E7
Brest, *Belarus*	31	D4
Brest, *France*	39	A5
Breteuil	27	E5
Bretten	35	D7
Breves	109	G4
Brewarrina	87	J5
Brewton	103	D3
Brežice	47	C4
Brézina	59	F2
Brezno	33	J9
Bria	65	C2
Briançon	43	B6
Briceni	47	Q1
Bridgend	37	J10
Bridgeport, *Calif., United States*	101	C1
Bridgeport, *Conn., United States*	99	F2
Bridgeport, *Nebr., United States*	97	F2
Bridgetown	109	F1
Bridgewater	93	U8
Bridgwater	37	J10
Bridlington	37	M7
Brienzer See	43	D4
Brig	43	C4
Brigham City	97	D2
Brighton, *United Kingdom*	27	B4
Brighton, *United States*	97	F3
Brignoles	43	B7
Brikama	63	A2
Brilon	35	D5
Bríndisi	45	M8
Brinkley	103	C3
Brisbane	87	K5
Bristol, *United Kingdom*	37	K10
Bristol, *United States*	103	E2
Bristol Bay	101	(1)E4
Bristol Channel	37	H10
British Columbia	93	F5
Britstown	67	C6
Brive-la-Gaillarde	39	G8
Briviesca	41	G2
Brixen	43	G4
Brixham	37	J11
Brlik	71	N9
Brno	33	F8
Broad Sound	87	J4
Broadus	97	E1
Brockton	99	F2
Brockville	99	E2
Brod	47	J9
Brodeur Peninsula	93	P2
Brodick	37	G6
Brodnica	33	J4
Broken Arrow	105	E1
Broken Bow	103	C3
Broken Hill	87	H6
Brokopondo	109	F2
Bromölla	33	D1
Bromsgrove	37	K9
Brønderslev	29	E8
Brooke's Point	77	H6
Brookhaven	95	H5
Brookhaven	103	C3
Brookhaven	105	F2
Brookings, *Oreg., United States*	97	B2
Brookings, *S.D., United States*	97	F2
Brooks	93	J6
Brooks Range	101	(1)F2
Brooksville	103	E4
Broome	87	D3
Brösarp	29	H9
Brovary	31	F4
Brownfield	101	F2
Browning	97	D1
Brownsville, *Tenn., United States*	103	D2
Brownsville, *Tex., United States*	103	B4
Brownwood	103	B3
Bruchsal	35	D7
Bruck, *Austria*	43	L3
Bruck, *Austria*	43	M2
Bruck an der Mur	47	C2
Brugge	27	F3
Brühl	27	J4
Bruint	75	G3
Brumado	109	J6
Brumath	43	C2
Bruneau	97	C2
Bruneck	43	G4
Brunei	83	(1)E2
Brunflo	29	H5
Brunico = Bruneck	45	F2
Brunsbüttel	35	E3
Brunswick, *Ga., United States*	103	E3
Brunswick, *Me., United States*	99	G2
Bruntal	33	G8
Brush	97	F2
Brussels = Bruxelles	27	G4
Bruxelles	27	G4
Bryan	103	B3
Bryanka	71	S6
Bryansk	31	F4
Brzeg	33	G7
Brzeg Dolny	33	F6
Brzeziny	33	J6
B-Spandau	33	C5
Bubi	67	E4
Bucak	51	D5
Bucaramanga	109	C2
Buchanan	63	B3
Buchan Gulf	93	S2
Bucharest = București	47	P5
Buchen	35	E7
Buchholz	35	E3
Buchy	39	M5
Bückeburg	35	E4
București	47	P5
Budapest	47	G2
Budennovsk	51	L1
Büdingen	35	E6
Budrio	43	G6
Buenaventura, *Colombia*	109	B3
Buenaventura, *Mexico*	101	E3
Buena Vista	97	E3
Buenos Aires	111	K5
Buffalo, *Okla., United States*	103	B2
Buffalo, *N.Y., United States*	99	E2
Buffalo, *S.D., United States*	97	F1
Buffalo, *Tex., United States*	103	B3
Buffalo, *Wyo., United States*	97	E2
Buffalo Lake	93	J4
Buffalo Narrows	93	K5
Buftea	47	N5
Bug	33	L5
Bugojno	47	E5
Bugrino	71	H4
Bugul'ma	31	K4
Buguruslan	31	K4
Buhayrat al Asad	51	H5
Buhayrat ath Tharthar	51	K6
Buhuşi	47	P3
Builth Wells	37	J9
Buinsk	31	J3
Buir Nuur	79	F1
Bujanovac	47	J7
Buje	43	J5
Bujumbura	65	D4
Bukachacha	73	K6
Bukavu	65	D4
Bukhara	53	H2
Bukkittinggi	83	(1)C3
Bukoba	65	E4
Bula, *Indonesia*	83	(2)D3
Bula, *Papua New Guinea*	83	(2)F4
Bülach	43	D3
Bulawayo	67	D4
Buldir Island	73	X6
Bulgan	73	G7
Bulgaria	47	M7
Buli	83	(2)C2
Bulle	43	C4
Bullhead City	101	D1
Bulls	89	E5
Bulukumba	83	(2)B4
Bulun	73	M2
Bumba	65	C3
Bumbeşti Jiu	47	L4
Buna	65	F3
Bunbury	87	C6
Buncrana	37	E6
Bunda	65	E4
Bundaberg	87	K4
Bünde	35	D4
Bungunya	87	J5
Bunia	65	E3
Bunkie	103	C3
Bunnell	103	E4
Bünyan	51	F4
Buôn Mê Thuôt	77	D4
Buotama	73	M4
Bura	65	F4
Buran	71	R8
Buranj	75	D2
Burao	65	H2
Burāq	54	D3
Buraydah	53	D4
Burco	61	J6
Burdur	51	D5
Burdur Gölü	49	N7
Burē	61	G5
Büren	27	L3
Burg	35	G4
Burgas	47	Q7
Burgaski Zaliv	47	Q7
Burgdorf	43	C3
Burghausen	43	H2
Burglengenfeld	35	H7
Burgos	41	G2
Burgsvik	29	K8
Burhaniye	49	K5
Burhanpur	75	C4
Burjassot	41	K5
Burj Sāfītā	54	D2
Burketown	87	G3
Burkeville	99	E3
Bur-Khaybyt	73	P3
Burkina	63	D2
Burlin	31	K4
Burlington, *Colo., United States*	101	F1
Burlington, *Ia., United States*	99	B2
Burlington, *Vt., United States*	99	F2
Burma = Myanmar	77	B2
Burnet	103	B3
Burney	97	B2
Burnie	87	J8
Burns	97	C2
Burns Junction	97	C2
Burns Lake	93	F6
Burqin	71	R8
Burra	87	G6
Burrel	49	C3
Bursa	49	M4
Bûr Safâga	61	F2
Bûr Sa'îd	61	F1
Bur Sudan	61	G4
Burtnieks	29	N8
Burton-upon-Trent	37	L9
Buru	83	(2)C3
Burundi	65	D4
Bururi	65	D4
Burwell	97	G2
Buryatiya	73	J6
Bury St. Edmunds	27	C2
Bûshehr	55	D2
Bushire = Bûshehr	55	D2
Businga	65	C3
Busira	65	C4
Buşrá ash Shām	54	D4
Bussum	27	H2
Busto Arsizio	43	D5
Buta	65	C3
Butare	65	D4
Butaritari	85	H5
Bute	37	G6
Butembo	65	D3
Buđardalur	29	(1)C2
Buton	83	(2)B3
Butte, *Mont., United States*	97	D1
Butte, *Nebr., United States*	97	G2
Butuan	77	H5
Butwal	75	D3
Butzbach	35	D6
Bützow	35	G3
Buulobarde	65	H3
Buxton	27	A1
Buy	31	H3
Buynaksk	51	M2
Büyükada	49	L4
Büyükçekmece	49	L4
Buzai Gumbad	53	K2
Buzançais	39	G7
Buzău	47	P4
Buzău	47	Q4
Buzuluk	31	K4
Byala	47	N6
Byala Slatina	47	L6
Byam Martin Island	93	L2
Byaroza	29	N10
Bydgoszcz	33	H4
Bygdin	29	D6
Bygland	29	D7
Bykovskiy	73	M2
Bylot Island	93	R2
Byskeälven	29	L4
Bystřice	33	G8
Bystrzyca Kłodzka	33	F7
Bytatay	73	N3
Bytča	33	H8
Bytom	33	H7
Bytów	33	G3
Bzura	33	J5

C

Name	Page	Grid
Caaguazú	111	K4
Caballococha	109	C5
Caballo Reservoir	101	E2
Cabanatuan	77	G3
Cabano	99	G1
Cabañaquinta	41	E1
Cabdul Qaadir	61	H5
Cabeza del Buey	41	E6
Cabezas	109	E7
Cabimas	109	C1
Cabinda	63	G6
Cabinda	63	G6
Cabo Bascuñán	111	G4
Cabo Beata	105	K5
Cabo Camarón	105	G5
Cabo Carvoeiro	41	A5
Cabo Catoche	105	G4
Cabo Corrientes, *Colombia*	109	B2
Cabo Corrientes, *Mexico*	105	C4
Cabo Corrubedo	41	A2
Cabo Cruz	105	J5
Cabo de Espichel	41	A6
Cabo de Gata	41	H8
Cabo de Hornos	111	H10
Cabo de la Nao	41	L6
Cabo Delgado	67	G2
Cabo de Palos	41	K7
Cabo de São Roque	109	K5
Cabo de Sao Tomé	111	N3
Cabo de São Vicente	41	A7
Cabo de Trafalgar	41	D8
Cabo dos Bahías	111	H8
Cabo Fisterra	41	A2
Cabo Frio	111	N3
Cabo Gracias á Dios	105	H6
Cabo Mondego	41	A4
Cabo Norte	109	H3
Cabo Orange	109	G3
Cabo Ortegal	41	B1
Cabo Peñas	41	E1
Caborca	101	D2
Cabo Rojo	105	C4
Cabo Roxo	63	A2
Cabo San Diego	111	H9
Cabo San Francisco de Paula	111	H8
Cabo San Juan	63	F4
Cabo San Lucas	95	D7
Cabo Santa Elena	105	J7

Name	Page	Grid
Cabo Tortosa	41	L4
Cabo Tres Puntas	111	H8
Cabot Strait	93	U7
Cabrera	41	N5
Čačak	47	H6
Cáceres, *Brazil*	109	F7
Cáceres, *Spain*	41	D5
Cachimbo	109	G5
Cachoeira do Sul	111	L4
Cachoeiro de Itapemirim	109	J8
Cacola	67	B2
Caconda	67	B2
Čadca	33	H8
Cadillac, *Mich., United States*	99	C2
Cadillac, *Mont., United States*	95	E2
Cádiz	41	D8
Caen	27	B5
Caernarfon	37	H8
Cagayan de Oro	77	G5
Cagli	43	H7
Cagliari	45	D9
Cagnes-sur-Mer	43	C7
Caguas	105	L5
Cahama	67	A3
Cahors	39	G9
Cahuapanas	109	B5
Cahul	47	R4
Caia	67	F3
Caianda	67	C2
Caicos Islands	105	K4
Cairns	87	J3
Cairo = El Qâhira	61	F1
Cairo	103	D2
Caiundo	67	B3
Cajamarca	109	B5
Čakovec	47	D3
Calabar	63	F3
Calabozo	109	D2
Calafat	47	K6
Calahorra	41	J2
Calais	27	D4
Calama	111	H3
Calamar	109	C3
Calamian Group	77	F4
Calamocha	41	J4
Călan	47	L4
Calanscio Sand Sea	61	D2
Calapan	77	G4
Călăraşi, *Moldova*	47	R2
Călăraşi, *Romania*	47	Q5
Calatafim	45	G11
Calatayud	41	J3
Calauag	77	G4
Calbayog	77	G4
Calçoene	109	G3
Calcutta	75	E4
Caldas da Rainha	41	A5
Caldera	111	G4
Caldwell, *Id., United States*	97	C2
Caldwell, *Kans., United States*	103	B2
Calf of Man	37	H7
Calgary	93	J6
Calhoun	103	E3
Calhoun City	103	D3
Calhoun Falls	103	E3
Cali	109	B3
Calicut = Kozhikode	75	C6
Caliente	97	D3
California	95	B4
Calilabad	51	N4
Callao	109	B6
Caloundra	87	K5
Caltagirone	45	J11
Caltanissetta	45	J11
Caluquembe	67	A2
Caluula	65	J1
Calvi	45	C6
Calvin	103	B3
Calvinia	67	B6
Calw	43	D2
Camaçari	109	K6
Camacupa	67	B2
Camagüey	105	J4
Camaiore	43	F7
Camana	109	C7
Camargue	39	K10
Camariñas	41	A1
Camarones	111	H7
Ca Mau	77	D5
Camberley	37	M10
Cambodia	77	C4
Cambrai	27	F4
Cambria	97	B3
Cambrian Mountains	37	H10
Cambridge, *New Zealand*	89	E3
Cambridge, *United Kingdom*	37	N9
Cambridge, *Md., United States*	99	E3
Cambridge, *Mass., United States*	99	F2
Cambridge, *Oh., United States*	99	D3
Cambridge Bay	93	K3
Cambrils	41	M3
Camden, *Ark., United States*	103	C3
Camden, *S.C., United States*	103	E3
Cameron, *La., United States*	103	C4
Cameron, *Mo., United States*	103	C2
Cameron, *Tex., United States*	103	B3
Cameroon	63	G3
Cametá	109	H4
Çamiçigölü	49	K7
Caminha	41	B3
Camiranga	109	H4
Camocim	109	J4
Camooweal	87	G3
Camopi	109	G3
Campbell Island	89	(2)C2
Campbell River	93	F7
Campbellsville	99	C3
Campbellton	99	G1
Campbeltown	37	G6
Campeche	105	F5
Câmpeni	47	L3
Câmpia Turzii	47	L3
Câmpina	47	N4
Campina Grande	109	L5
Campinas	111	M3
Campobasso	45	J7
Campo de Criptana	41	G5
Campo de Diauarum	109	G6
Campo Gallo	111	J4
Campo Grande	111	L3
Campo Maior	109	J4
Campo Mourão	111	L3
Campos	111	N3
Câmpulung	47	N4
Câmpulung Moldovenesc	47	N2
Cam Ranh	77	D4
Çan	49	K4
Canada	91	M4
Canadian	101	F1
Canadian	101	F1
Çanakkale	49	J4
Çanakkale Boğazı	49	J4
Canal de Panamá	105	J7
Cananea	101	D2
Canary Islands = Islas Canarias	57	A3
Canary Islands = Islas Canarias	59	B3
Cañaveras	41	H4
Canberra	87	J7
Cancún	105	G4
Çandarli Körfezi	49	J6
Candelaro	47	C8
Candlemas Island	107	J9
Cangamba	67	B2
Cangas	41	B2
Cangas de Narcea	41	D1
Cangyuan	77	B2
Cangzhou	79	F3
Canicattì	45	J11
Canindé	109	K4
Çankiri	51	E3
Canna	37	F4
Cannanore	75	B6
Cannanore	75	C6
Cannes	43	C7
Cannock	27	A2
Canon City	101	E1
Cantanduanes	77	G4
Canterbury	27	D3
Canterbury Bight	89	C7
Canterbury Plains	89	C6
Cân Tho	77	D5
Canto do Buriti	109	J5
Canton, *Miss., United States*	103	D3
Canton, *Oh., United States*	103	E1
Canton, *S.D., United States*	97	G2
Canumã	109	F4
Canumã	109	F5
Canutama	109	E5
Canyon	101	F1
Canyon Ferry Lake	97	D1
Cao Băng	77	D2
Caorle	43	H5
Cap Blanc	45	D11
Cap Bon	59	H1
Cap Corse	45	D5
Cap d'Agde	39	J10
Cap d'Antifer	27	C5
Cap de Fer	59	G1
Cap de Formentor	41	P5
Cap de la Hague	39	D4
Cap-de-la-Madeleine	99	F1
Cap de Nouvelle-France	93	S4
Cap de ses Salines	41	P5
Cap des Trois Fourches	41	H9
Cape Agulhas	67	C6
Cape Alexandra	111	P9
Cape Andreas	53	B2
Cape Apostolos Andreas	51	F6
Cape Arid	87	D6
Cape Arnaoutis	51	D6
Cape Arnhem	87	G2
Cape Barren Island	87	J8
Cape Bauld	93	V6
Cape Blanco	97	B2
Cape Borda	87	G7
Cape Breton Island	93	U7
Cape Brett	89	E2
Cape Byron	87	K5
Cape Campbell	89	E5
Cape Canaveral	103	E4
Cape Canaveral	103	E4
Cape Carnot	87	F6
Cape Charles	99	E3
Cape Chidley	93	U4
Cape Christian	93	T2
Cape Churchill	93	N5
Cape Clear	37	C10
Cape Cleare	101	(1)H4
Cape Coast	63	D3
Cape Cod	99	G2
Cape Columbine	67	B6
Cape Colville	89	E3
Cape Comorin	75	C7
Cape Constantine	101	(1)E4
Cape Coral	103	E4
Cape Crawford	87	G3
Cape Croker	87	F2
Cape Dalhousie	101	(1)L1
Cape Direction	87	H2
Cape Disappointment	111	P9
Cape Dominion	93	R3
Cape Dorchester	93	Q3
Cape Dorset	93	R4
Cape Dyer	93	U3
Cape Egmont	89	D4
Cape Eleaia	54	B1
Cape Farewell, *Greenland*	91	F4
Cape Farewell, *New Zealand*	89	D5
Cape Fear	103	F3
Cape Finisterre = Cabo Fisterra	41	A2
Cape Flattery, *Australia*	87	J2
Cape Flattery, *United States*	97	A1
Cape Forestier	87	J8
Cape Foulwind	89	C5
Cape Fria	67	A3
Cape Girardeau	99	C3
Cape Greko	51	F6
Cape Grenville	87	H2
Cape Grim	87	H8
Cape Harrison	93	V6
Cape Hatteras	103	F2
Cape Henrietta Maria	93	Q5
Cape Horn = Cabo de Hornos	111	H10
Cape Howe	87	K7
Cape Inscription	87	B5
Cape Jaffa	87	G7
Cape Karikari	89	D2
Cape Kellett	93	F2
Cape Kidnappers	89	F4
Cape Leeuwin	87	B6
Cape Lévêque	87	D3
Cape Londonderry	87	E2
Cape Lookout	105	J2
Cape May	99	F3
Cape Melville	87	H2
Cape Mendenhall	101	(1)D4
Cape Mendocino	97	A2
Cape Mercy	93	U4
Cape Meredith	111	J9
Cape Naturaliste	87	B6
Capenda-Camulemba	67	B1
Cape Negrais	77	A3
Cape Nelson	87	H7
Cape Newenham	101	(1)E4
Cape of Good Hope	67	B6
Cape Palliser	89	E5
Cape Palmas	63	C4
Cape Parry	93	G2
Cape Providence	89	A8
Cape Race	91	G5
Cape Ray	93	V7
Cape Reinga	89	D2
Cape Romanzof	101	(1)D3
Cape Runaway	89	G3
Cape Sable	93	T8
Cape St. Elias	101	(1)J4
Cape St. Francis	67	C6
Cape San Agustin	77	H5
Cape San Blas	103	D4
Cape Saunders	89	C7
Cape Scott	87	E1
Cape Stephens	89	D5
Cape Terawhiti	89	E5
Cape Three Points	63	D4
Cape Town	67	B6
Cape Turnagain	89	F5
Cape Verde	63	(1)B2
Cape Wessel	87	G2
Cape Wrangell	73	W6
Cape Wrath	37	G3
Cape York	87	H2
Cape York Peninsula	87	H2
Cap Figalo	41	J9
Cap Fréhel	39	C5
Cap Gris-Nez	27	D4
Cap-Haïtien	105	K5
Cap Juby	59	C3
Cap Lopez	63	F5
Cap Negro	41	E9
Capo Carbonara	45	D10
Capo Colonna	45	M9
Capo Gallo	45	H10
Capo Granitola	45	G11
Capo Murro di Porco	45	K11
Capo Palinuro	45	J8
Capo Passero	45	K12
Capo Santa Maria di Leuca	45	N9
Capo San Vito	45	G10
Capo Spartivento	45	C10
Capo Vaticano	45	K10
Capraia	45	D5
Cap Rhir	59	C2
Capri	45	J8
Capricorn Group	87	K4
Cap Rosa	45	C11
Cap Serrat	45	D11
Cap Spartel	41	E9
Cap Timiris	59	B5
Capua	45	J7
Cap Verga	63	B2
Cap Vert	63	A2
Caquetá	109	C4
Caracal	47	M5
Caracarai	109	E3
Caracas	109	D1
Caransebeş	47	K4
Carauari	109	D4
Caravaca de la Cruz	41	J6
Caravelas	109	K7
Carazinho	111	L4
Carballiño	41	B2
Carballo	41	B1
Carbondale, *Ill., United States*	103	D2
Carbondale, *Pa., United States*	103	F1
Carboneras	41	J7
Carbónia	45	C9
Carcar	77	G4

Name	Page	Grid
Carcassonne	39	H10
Cardiff	37	J10
Cardigan Bay	37	H9
Cardston	97	D1
Carei	47	K2
Carentan	39	D4
Cariacica	111	N3
Cariati	45	L9
Caribbean Sea	105	J6
Carlet	41	K5
Carleton Place	99	E1
Carlisle, *United Kingdom*	37	K7
Carlisle, *United States*	99	E2
Carlow	37	F9
Carlsbad	101	F2
Carlyle	97	F1
Carmacks	93	D4
Carmagnola	43	C6
Carmarthen	37	H10
Carmarthen Bay	37	G10
Carmaux	39	H9
Carmen	105	B3
Carmona	41	E7
Carnarvon, *Australia*	87	B4
Carnarvon, *South Africa*	67	C6
Car Nicobar	75	F7
Carnot	65	B2
Carnsore Point	37	F9
Carolina	109	H5
Carolina Beach	103	F3
Caroline Island	85	L6
Caroline Islands	85	E5
Carpathian Mountains	33	J8
Carpatii Meridionali	47	K4
Carpentras	39	L9
Carpi	43	F6
Carrabelle	103	E4
Carrara	43	F6
Carrickfergus	37	G7
Carrick-on-Suir	37	E9
Carrington	97	G1
Carrizozo	101	E2
Carroll	99	B2
Carrollton, *Ky., United States*	99	D3
Carrollton, *Mo., United States*	103	C1
Çarşamba	51	G3
Carson City	97	C3
Cartagena, *Colombia*	109	B1
Cartagena, *Spain*	41	K7
Carthage	103	C3
Cartwright	93	V6
Caruarú	109	K5
Carúpano	109	E1
Casablanca	59	D2
Casa Grande	101	D2
Casale Monferrato	43	D5
Casalmaggiore	43	F6
Casarano	45	N9
Cascade, *Id., United States*	97	C2
Cascade, *Mont., United States*	97	C1
Cascade Range	97	B2
Cascade Reservoir	97	C2
Cascais	41	A6
Cascavel	111	L3
Caserta	45	J7
Cashel	67	E4
Casino	87	K5
Ćasma	43	M5
Caspe	41	K3
Casper	97	E2
Caspian Sea	25	J3
Cassiar	93	F5
Cassino	45	H7
Castanhal	109	H4
Castelbuono	45	J11
Castel di Sangro	45	J7
Castellamare del Golio	45	G10
Castellane	43	B7
Castellaneta	45	L8
Castelli	111	J4
Castelló de la Plana	41	K5
Castelnaudary	39	G10
Castelsarrasin	39	G10
Castelvetrano	45	G11
Castets	39	D10
Castiglion Fiorentino	43	G7
Castlebar	37	C8
Castleford	37	L8
Castle Point	89	F5
Castres	39	H10
Castricum	27	G2
Castries	105	M6
Castro	111	M3
Castro Verde	41	B7
Castrovillari	45	L9
Castuera	41	E6
Catamarca	111	H4
Catandica	67	E3
Catánia	45	K11
Catanzaro	45	L10
Catanzaro Marina	45	L10
Catarman	77	G4
Catbalogan	77	H4
Cat Island	103	F5
Cat Lake	93	N6
Cato Island	87	L4
Catriló	111	J6
Catskill Mountains	95	M3
Cattólica	43	H7
Cauayan	77	G5
Cauca	109	C2
Caucaia	109	K4
Caucasia	109	B2
Caucasus	51	K2
Caudry	27	F4
Cauquenes	111	G6
Caura	109	E2
Causapscal	99	G1
Căuşeni	47	S3
Cavaillon	39	L10
Cavalese	43	G4
Cavan	37	E8
Cavárzere	43	H5
Cave	89	C7
Cavinas	109	D6
Cavtat	47	F7
Caxias	109	J4
Caxias do Sul	111	L4
Caxito	63	G6
Çay	49	P6
Cayce	103	E3
Çaycuma	49	Q3
Cayenne	109	G3
Cayman Islands	105	H5
Caynabo	65	H2
Cayos Miskitos	105	H6
Cay Sal Bank	103	E5
Cazorla	41	H7
Ceanannus Mor	37	F8
Ceará	109	J4
Cebu	77	G4
Cebu	77	G4
Cécina	43	F7
Cedar City	97	D3
Cedar Falls	99	B2
Cedar Lake	93	L6
Cedar Rapids	99	B2
Cedros	95	C6
Ceduna	87	F6
Ceerigaabo	65	H1
Cefalù	45	J10
Cegléd	47	G2
Celaya	105	D4
Celebes = Sulawesi	83	(2)A3
Celebes Sea	83	(2)B2
Celje	47	C3
Celldömölk	47	E2
Celle	35	F4
Celtic Sea	37	E10
Centerville	99	B2
Cento	43	G6
Central African Republic	65	C2
Central City	97	G2
Centralia, *Ill., United States*	99	C3
Centralia, *Wash., United States*	97	B1
Central Range	83	(2)F3
Central Siberian Plateau = Srednesibirskoye Ploskogor'ye	69	N2
Cenxi	77	E2
Ceres, *Argentina*	111	J4
Ceres, *Brazil*	109	H7
Cerezo de Abajo	41	G3
Cerignola	45	K7
Çerikli	51	E4
Çerkes	49	Q4
Çerkezköy	49	K3
Cernavodă	47	R5
Cero Champaqui	111	J5
Cerralvo	95	E7
Cërrik	49	C3
Cerritos	101	F4
Cerro Aconcagua	111	G5
Cerro Bonete	111	H4
Cerro de la Encantada	95	C5
Cerro de Pasco	109	B6
Cerro Huehuento	105	C4
Cerro Las Tórtolas	111	H5
Cerro Marahuaca	109	D3
Cerro Mercedario	111	G5
Cerro Murallón	111	G8
Cerro Nevado	111	H6
Cerro Pena Nevade	105	D4
Cerro San Lorenzo	111	G8
Cerro San Valentín	111	G8
Cerros de Bala	109	D6
Cerro Tres Picos	111	J6
Cerro Tupungato	111	H5
Cerro Yaví	109	D2
Cerro Yogan	111	H9
Certaldo	43	G7
Cervaro	45	K7
Cervia	43	H6
Cervionne	45	D6
Cervo	41	C1
Cesena	43	H6
Cesenático	43	H6
Cēsis	29	N8
Česká Lípa	35	K6
České Budějovice	43	K2
Český Krumlov	43	K2
Çeşme	49	J6
Česna	43	M5
Cessano	43	J7
Cessnock	87	K6
Cetate	47	L5
Cetinje	47	F7
Cetraro	45	K9
Ceuta	59	D1
Cevizli	49	P7
Chachapoyas	109	B5
Chaco Boreal	111	K3
Chad	61	C5
Chadan	71	S7
Chadron	97	F2
Chagai	53	H4
Chagda	73	N5
Chaghcharān	53	J3
Chagyl	53	G1
Chāh Bahār	53	H4
Chāībāsa	75	E4
Chainat	77	C3
Chaiyaphum	77	C3
Chalais	39	F8
Chalhuanca	109	C6
Chalinze	65	F5
Chalki	49	K8
Chalkida	49	F6
Chalkidiki	49	F4
Challans	39	D7
Challapata	109	D7
Challenger Deep	85	E4
Challis	97	D2
Châlons-sur-Marne	27	G6
Chalon-sur-Saône	39	K7
Cham	35	H7
Chama	67	E2
Chamba	75	C2
Chambal	75	C3
Chamberlain	97	G2
Chambersburg	99	E3
Chambéry	43	A5
Chambly	27	E5
Chamonix	43	B5
Champagnole	43	A4
Champaign	99	C2
Champaubert	27	F6
Champlitte	43	A3
Chañaral	111	G4
Chandalar	93	B3
Chandeleur Islands	105	G3
Chandigarh	75	C2
Chandler	101	D2
Chandrapur	75	C5
Changane	67	E4
Changara	67	E3
Changchun	81	C2
Changde	79	E5
Chang-hua	79	G6
Chang Jiang	79	D4
Changsha	79	E5
Changshu	79	G4
Changting	79	F5
Changzhi	79	E3
Changzhou	79	F4
Chania	49	G9
Channel Islands, *United Kingdom*	37	K12
Channel Islands, *United States*	95	C5
Channel-Port aux Basques	93	V7
Chanthaburi	77	C4
Chantilly	27	E5
Chanute	103	B2
Chao Phraya	77	C4
Chaouèn	59	D1
Chao Xian	79	F4
Chaoyang	79	G2
Chaozhou	79	F6
Chapada Diamantina	109	J6
Chapais	99	F1
Chapayev	31	K4
Chapayevo	73	K4
Chapayevskoye	71	N7
Chapecó	111	L4
Chapleau	99	D1
Chapra	75	D3
Chara	73	K5
Charcas	101	F4
Chard	93	J5
Chardara	53	J1
Chardzhev	53	H2
Chari	61	C5
Chārīkār	53	J2
Charleroi	27	G4
Charlesbourg	99	F1
Charleston, *New Zealand*	89	C5
Charleston, *S.C., United States*	103	F3
Charleston, *W.Va., United States*	103	E2
Charlestown	103	D2
Charleville	87	J5
Charleville-Mézières	27	G5
Charlevoix	99	C1
Charlotte, *Mich., United States*	99	D2
Charlotte, *N.C., United States*	103	E2
Charlottesville	103	E2
Charlottetown	93	U7
Charlton Island	93	Q6
Charsk	71	Q8
Charters Towers	87	J4
Chartres	39	G5
Charymovo	31	Q3
Chasel'ka	73	C3
Chastyye	31	K3
Châteaguay	99	F1
Châteaubriant	39	D6
Châteaudun	39	G5
Châteaulin	39	A5
Châteauneuf-sur-Loire	39	H6
Châteauroux	39	G7
Château-Thierry	27	F5
Châtellerault	39	F7
Châtenois	43	A2
Chatham	99	D2
Chatham Island	89	(1)B1
Chatham Islands	89	(1)B1
Châtillon-sur-Seine	39	K6
Chattanooga	95	J4
Chauffayer	43	B6
Chauk	75	F4
Chaumont	39	L5
Chaunskaya Guba	73	V3
Chauny	27	F5
Chaves, *Brazil*	109	G4
Chaves, *Portugal*	41	C3
Chavuma	67	C2
Cheb	35	H6
Cheboksary	31	J3

Name	Page	Grid	Name	Page	Grid
Chechnya	51	L2	Chicopee	99	F2
Cheduba Island	75	F5	Chicoutimi	93	S7
Cheektowaga	99	E2	Chicualacuala	67	E4
Chegdomyn	73	N6	Chiemsee	43	H3
Chegutu	67	E3	Chieri	43	C5
Chehalis	97	B1	Chiese	43	F5
Cheju	81	D7	Chieti	45	J6
Cheju do	81	D7	Chifeng	79	F2
Chekhov	73	Q7	Chiganak	71	N8
Chelan	97	C1	Chigubo	67	E4
Cheleken	53	F2	Chihuahua	101	E3
Chélif	41	L8	Chiili	71	M9
Chelkar	71	K8	Chikwa	67	E2
Chełm	33	N6	Chilas	75	B1
Chełmno	33	H4	Childress	101	F2
Chelmsford	27	C3	Chile	107	D8
Cheltenham	37	L10	Chile Chico	111	G8
Chelyabinsk	31	M3	Chilik	71	P9
Chelyuskin	71	U2	Chilika Lake	75	D4
Chemnitz	35	H6	Chillán	111	G6
Chenab	75	B2	Chillicothe, Mo., United States	99	B3
Cheney Reservoir	103	B2	Chillicothe, Oh., United States	99	D3
Chengde	79	F2	Chilliwack	97	B1
Chengdu	79	C4	Chiloquin	97	B2
Chengshan Jiao	81	B5	Chilpancingo	105	E5
Chennai	75	D6	Chi-lung	79	G5
Chenzhou	79	E5	Chimbay	71	K9
Chepes	111	H5	Chimborazo	109	B4
Cher	39	G6	Chimbote	109	B5
Cheraw	103	F3	Chimchememel'	73	V3
Cherbaniani Reef	75	B6	Chimec	47	J1
Cherbourg	39	D4	Chimoio	67	E3
Cherchell	41	N8	China	69	N6
Cherdyn	31	L2	Chincha Alta	109	B6
Cheremkhovo	73	G6	Chincilla de Monte-Aragón	41	J6
Cherepovets	31	G3	Chinde	67	F3
Cherkasy	31	F5	Chin do	81	C6
Cherkessk	51	K1	Chindwin	77	A2
Chermoz	31	L3	Chingola	67	D2
Cherniv	31	F4	Chinhoyi	67	E3
Chernivtsi	31	E5	Chiniot	75	B2
Chernushka	31	L3	Chinju	81	E6
Chernyakhovsk	33	L3	Chinmen	77	F2
Chernyayevo	73	M6	Chinnur	75	C5
Chernyshevsk	73	K6	Chióggia	43	H5
Chernyshevskiy	73	J4	Chios	49	H6
Chernyye Zemli	31	J5	Chios	49	J6
Cherokee	99	A2	Chipata	67	E2
Cherskiy	73	U3	Chippewa Falls	99	B2
Cherven Bryag	47	M6	Chipping Norton	27	A3
Červonohrad	31	D4	Chirchik	71	M9
Chesapeake	103	F2	Chirikof Island	101	(1)F5
Cheshskaya Guba	31	J1	Chiromo	67	F3
Cheshunt	27	C3	Chirpan	49	H2
Chester, United Kingdom	37	K8	Chirripo	105	H7
Chester, Calif., United States	97	B2	Chişinău	47	R2
Chester, Mont., United States	97	D1	Chişineu-Criş	47	J3
Chesterfield	37	L8	Chita	73	J6
Chesterfield Inlet	93	N4	Chitato	65	C5
Chetumal	105	G5	Chitembo	67	B2
Chetwynd	93	G5	Chitipa	65	E5
Ch'ew Bahir	65	F3	Chitradurga	75	C6
Cheyenne	97	F2	Chitral	75	B1
Cheyenne	97	F2	Chitré	105	H7
Cheyenne Wells	101	F1	Chittagong	75	F4
Cheyne Bay	87	C6	Chittaurgarh	75	B4
Chhatarpur	75	C4	Chittoor	75	C6
Chhindwara	75	C4	Chitungwiza	67	E3
Chhuka	75	E3	Chiume	67	C3
Chia-i	79	G6	Chivasso	43	C5
Chiang Khan	77	C3	Chizha	31	H1
Chiang-Mai	77	B3	Chodov	35	H6
Chiang Rai	77	B3	Chojnice	33	G4
Chiavari	43	E6	Chokurdakh	73	R2
Chiavenna	43	E4	Chókwé	67	E4
Chiba	81	L6	Cholet	39	E6
Chibougamau	93	S6	Choma	67	D3
Chibuto	67	E4	Chomutov	33	C7
Chicago	99	C2	Chona	73	H4
Chicapa	65	C5	Chonan	81	D5
Chichagof Island	101	(1)K4	Chone	109	A4
Chichaoua	59	D2	Ch'ŏngjin	81	E3
Chichester	27	B4	Ch'ŏngju	81	D6
Chickasha	103	B3	Chŏngp'yŏng	81	D4
Chiclana de la Frontera	41	D8	Chongqing	69	P7
Chiclayo	109	B5	Chŏngŭp	81	D6
Chico	111	H8			

Name	Page	Grid	Name	Page	Grid
Ch'ŏnju	81	D5	Ciudad Camargo	101	E3
Chonogol	79	F1	Ciudad del Carmen	105	F5
Chon Thanh	77	D4	Ciudad del Este	111	L4
Chop	33	M9	Ciudad Delicias	101	E3
Chornobyl'	31	F4	Ciudad del Maíz	101	G4
Chornomors'ke	31	F5	Ciudad de México	105	E5
Ch'osan	81	C3	Ciudad de Valles	105	E4
Chōshi	81	L6	Ciudad Guayana	109	E2
Choszczno	33	E4	Ciudad Juárez	101	E2
Choteau	97	D1	Ciudad Madero	101	G4
Chott el Hodna	59	F1	Ciudad Mante	105	E4
Chott el Jerid	59	G2	Ciudad Obregón	105	C3
Chott Melrhir	59	G2	Ciudad Real	41	G6
Choybalsan	73	J7	Ciudad-Rodrigo	41	D4
Choyr	79	D1	Ciudad Valles	101	G4
Chre	39	H9	Ciudad Victoria	95	G7
Christchurch	89	D6	Ciutadella	41	P4
Christiansburg	99	D3	Cividale del Friuli	43	J4
Christiansø	33	E2	Cívita Castellana	45	G6
Christmas Island	83	(1)D5	Civitanova Marche	45	H5
Chrudim	33	E8	Civitavécchia	45	F6
Chrysi	49	H10	Cizre	51	K5
Chu	71	N9	Clacton-on-Sea	27	D3
Chubut	111	H7	Clair Engle Lake	97	B2
Chugach Mountains	93	B4	Clairview	87	J4
Chūgoku-sanchi	79	J3	Clamecy	39	J6
Chugwater	97	F2	Clare Island	37	B8
Chukchi Sea	101	(1)C2	Clarence	89	D6
Chukotskiy Khrebet	73	W3	Clarence Strait	87	E2
Chukotskiy Poluostrov	73	Z3	Clarendon	101	F2
Chula Vista	101	C2	Clarkdale	101	D2
Chulucanas	109	A5	Clarksburg	103	E2
Chulym	71	R6	Clarksdale	103	C3
Chum	31	M1	Clarks Junction	89	C7
Chumikan	73	P6	Clarkston	97	C1
Chum Phae	77	C3	Clarksville, Ark., United States	103	C2
Chumphon	77	B4	Clarksville, Tenn., United States	103	D2
Ch'unch'ŏn	81	D5	Claro	109	G7
Chunchura	75	E4	Clausthal-Zellerfeld	35	F5
Chundzha	71	P9	Claveria	77	G3
Ch'ungju	81	D5	Clayton	101	F1
Chur	43	E4	Clear Island	37	C10
Churapcha	73	N4	Clear Lake	99	B2
Churchill, Man., Canada	93	N5	Clear Lake Reservoir	97	B2
Churchill, Nfld., Canada	93	U6	Clearwater	97	C1
Churchill Falls	93	U6	Clearwater	103	E4
Churchill Peak	93	F5	Clearwater Mountains	97	C1
Churu	75	B3	Cleburne	103	B3
Chuska Mountains	101	E1	Clermont, Australia	87	J4
Chusovoy	31	L3	Clermont, France	27	E5
Chute des Passes	93	S7	Clermont-Ferrand	39	J8
Chuuk	85	F5	Cles	43	F4
Chuvashiya	31	J3	Cleveland, Oh., United States	99	D2
Chuxiong	77	C2	Cleveland, Tenn., United States	103	E2
Chuya	73	J5	Cleveland, Tex., United States	103	B3
Ciadîr-Lunga	47	R3	Clifden	89	A7
Cide	51	E3	Clifton	101	E2
Ciechanów	33	K5	Climax	97	E1
Ciego de Avila	105	J4	Clines Corners	101	E2
Cienfuegos	105	H4	Clinton, Canada	93	G6
Cieza	41	J6	Clinton, New Zealand	89	B8
Cihanbeyli	51	E4	Clinton, Ark., United States	99	B3
Cijulang	83	(1)D4	Clinton, Ia., United States	95	H3
Cilacap	83	(1)D4	Clinton, Miss., United States	103	C3
Cili	79	E5	Clinton, Mo., United States	99	B3
Cimarron	103	B2	Clinton, N.C., United States	103	F3
Cimişlia	47	R3	Clinton, Okla., United States	103	B2
Cîmpeni	33	N11	Clipperton Island	105	C6
Cinca	41	L3	Clonmel	37	E9
Cincinnati	99	D3	Cloppenburg	35	D4
Çine	49	L7	Cloquet	99	B1
Ciney	27	H4	Cloud Peak	97	E2
Cintalapa	105	F5	Clovis, Calif., United States	97	C3
Circle, Ak., United States	101	(1)J2	Clovis, N.Mex., United States	101	F2
Circle, Mont., United States	97	E1	Cluj-Napoca	47	L3
Circleville	99	D3	Cluny	39	K7
Cirebon	83	(1)D4	Cluses	43	B4
Cirò Marina	45	M9	Clyde	37	H6
Cisco	103	B3	Clyde River	93	T2
Cistierna	41	E2	Coaldale	97	C3
Citronelle	103	D3	Coalville	97	C2
Cittadella	43	G5	Coari	109	E4
Città di Castello	43	H7	Coast Mountains	93	E5
Ciucea	47	K3	Coast Range	97	B3
Ciudad Acuña	101	F3	Coatbridge	37	J6
Ciudad Bolívar	109	E2	Coats Island	93	Q4
			Coatzacoalcos	105	F5

Name	Page	Grid
Cobalt	93	R7
Cobán	105	F5
Cobija	109	D6
Cobourg	95	L3
Cobourg Peninsula	87	F2
Cóbuè	67	E2
Coburg	35	F6
Cochabamba	109	D7
Cochin = Kochi	75	C7
Cochrane	99	D1
Cockburn Town	103	G5
Coco	105	H6
Cocoa	103	E4
Cocobeach	63	F4
Coco Channel	77	A4
Coco Island	77	A4
Codajás	109	E4
Codigoro	43	H6
Cod Island	93	U5
Codlea	47	N4
Codó	109	J4
Codogno	43	E5
Codroipo	43	J5
Cody	97	E2
Coesfeld	35	C5
Coëtivy Island	57	J6
Coeur d'Alene	97	C1
Coeur d'Alene Lake	97	C1
Coevorden	27	J2
Coffs Harbour	87	K6
Cofrents	41	J5
Cognac	39	E8
Cogne	43	C5
Coiba	107	C3
Coihaique	111	G8
Coimbatore	75	C6
Coimbra	41	B4
Colchester	27	C3
Colebrook	99	F1
Coleman	103	B3
Coleraine	37	F6
Colesberg	67	D6
Colfax	97	C1
Colibaşi	47	M5
Colico	43	E4
Coll	37	F5
Collado-Villalba	41	F4
College Station	103	B3
Collier Bay	87	D3
Collingwood	99	E2
Collins	103	D3
Colmar	43	C2
Colmenar Viejo	41	G4
Colombia	109	C3
Colombo	75	C7
Colonia Las Heras	111	H8
Colonial Heights	99	E3
Colonsay	37	F5
Colorado	97	E3
Colorado, Colo., United States	101	E1
Colorado, Tex., United States	101	G2
Colorado Plateau	101	D1
Colorado Springs	97	F3
Columbia	97	C1
Columbia, La., United States	103	C3
Columbia, Md., United States	103	F2
Columbia, Mo., United States	103	C2
Columbia, S.C., United States	103	E3
Columbia, Tenn., United States	103	D2
Columbia Mountains	93	G6
Columbus, Ga., United States	103	E3
Columbus, Ind., United States	103	D2
Columbus, Miss., United States	103	D3
Columbus, Mont., United States	97	E1
Columbus, Nebr., United States	97	G2
Columbus, N.Mex., United States	101	E2
Columbus, Oh., United States	103	E1
Columbus, Tex., United States	103	B4
Colville	101	(1)G2
Colville Lake	101	(1)M2
Comacchio	43	H6
Comăneşti	47	P3
Comarnic	47	N4
Combarbalá	111	G5
Combeaufontaine	39	M6
Comilla	77	A2
Comino = Kemmuna	45	J12
Commentry	39	H7
Commercy	27	H6
Como	43	E5
Comoé	63	D3
Comondú	95	D6
Comoros	67	G2
Compiègne	27	E5
Comrat	47	R3
Comstock	101	F3
Conakry	63	B3
Concarneau	39	B6
Conceição do Araguaia	109	H5
Concepción, Bolivia	109	E7
Concepción, Chile	111	G6
Conches-en-Ouche	27	C6
Conchos	105	C3
Concord, Calif., United States	101	B1
Concord, N.H., United States	99	F2
Concord, N.C., United States	103	E2
Concordia, Argentina	111	K5
Concordia, United States	103	B2
Condé-sur-Noireau	27	B6
Condobolin	87	J6
Condom	39	F10
Condon	97	D1
Conegliano	43	H5
Conggar	75	F3
Congo	57	E6
Congo	63	G5
Connecticut	99	F2
Connemara	37	C8
Conrad	97	D1
Côn Son	77	D5
Constanţa	51	C1
Constantina	41	E7
Constantine	59	G1
Consul	97	E1
Contact	97	D2
Contamana	109	B5
Contwoyto Lake	93	J3
Convay	103	F3
Conway	103	C2
Conwy	37	J8
Conwy Bay	37	H8
Coober Pedy	87	F5
Cookeville	99	C3
Cook Inlet	101	(1)G4
Cook Islands	85	K7
Cook Strait	89	E5
Cooktown	87	J3
Coolabah	87	J6
Coolgardie	87	D6
Cooma	87	J7
Coonabarabran	87	J6
Coon Rapids	99	B1
Coopers Town	103	F4
Coorabie	87	F6
Coos Bay	97	B2
Cootamundra	87	J6
Copenhagen = København	29	G9
Copiapó	111	G4
Copper Harbor	99	C1
Coquille	97	B2
Coquimbo	111	G4
Corabia	47	M6
Coral	95	K1
Coral Sea	87	K2
Coral Sea Islands Territory	85	F7
Coral Sea Islands Territory	87	J2
Coral Springs	103	E4
Corantijn	109	F3
Corbeil-Essonnes	39	H5
Corbigny	39	J6
Corby	27	B2
Cordele	103	E3
Cordillera Cantábrica	41	D2
Cordillera Central	107	E5
Cordillera del Condor	109	B5
Cordillera de Mérida	107	D3
Cordillera de Oliva	111	G4
Cordillera Isabella	105	G6
Cordillera Occidental	107	E5
Cordillera Oriental	107	D5
Cordillera Penibética	41	F8
Cordillera Vilcabamba	109	C6
Córdoba, Argentina	111	J5
Córdoba, Spain	41	F7
Corfu = Kerkyra	49	B5
Coria	41	D5
Corigliano	45	L9
Corinth	103	D3
Corinto	109	H7
Cork	37	D10
Cork Harbour	37	D10
Corleone	45	H11
Çorlu	49	K3
Corn Islands	107	C2
Cornwall	95	M2
Cornwallis Island	93	M2
Coro	109	D1
Corocoro	109	D7
Coromandel	89	E3
Coromandel Coast	75	D6
Coromandel Peninsula	89	E3
Coron	77	G4
Coronation Gulf	93	J3
Coronel Oviedo	111	K4
Coronel Pringles	111	J6
Coronel Suárez	111	J6
Corpus Christi	103	B4
Corrientes	111	K4
Corrigan	103	C3
Corriverton	109	F2
Corse	45	D6
Corsica = Corse	45	D6
Corsicana	103	B3
Corte	45	D6
Cortegana	41	D7
Cortez	101	E1
Cortina d'Ampezzo	43	H4
Cortland	99	E2
Cortona	45	F5
Coruche	41	B6
Çorum	51	F3
Corumbá	109	F7
Corvallis	97	B2
Corvo	59	(1)A2
Cosenza	45	L9
Cosmoledo Group	67	(2)A2
Cosne-sur-Loire	39	H6
Cossato	43	D5
Costa Blanca	41	K7
Costa Brava	41	P3
Costa del Sol	41	F8
Costa de Mosquitos	105	H6
Costa Dorada	41	M4
Costa do Sol	41	A6
Costa Rica	105	G7
Costa Smeralda	45	D7
Costa Verde	41	D1
Costeşti	47	M5
Coswig	35	H5
Cotabato	77	G5
Cotonou	63	E3
Cottage Grove	97	B2
Cottbus	33	D6
Cotulla	103	B4
Couhe	39	F7
Coulommiers	27	F6
Council Bluffs	97	F2
Courland Lagoon	33	L2
Courtacon	27	F6
Courtenay	95	B2
Coushatta	103	C3
Coutances	39	D4
Couvin	27	G4
Covasna	47	P4
Coventry	37	L9
Covilhã	41	C4
Covington, Ga., United States	103	E3
Covington, Ky., United States	103	E2
Covington, Va., United States	99	D3
Cowell	87	G6
Cowes	27	A4
Cowra	87	J6
Cox's Bazar	75	F4
Cradock	67	D6
Craig	97	E2
Crailsheim	35	F7
Craiova	47	L5
Cranbrook, Australia	87	C6
Cranbrook, United States	95	C2
Crater Lake	97	B2
Crato	109	K5
Crawford	97	F2
Crawfordsville	99	C2
Crawley	27	B3
Cree Lake	93	K5
Creil	27	E5
Crema	43	E5
Cremona	43	F5
Crépy-en-Valois	27	E5
Cres	43	K6
Cres	43	K6
Crescent City	97	B2
Crest	39	L9
Creston	99	B2
Crestview	95	J5
Crestview	105	G2
Crete = Kriti	49	H10
Créteil	27	E6
Creuse	39	G7
Crevillent	41	K6
Crewe	37	K8
Crianlarich	37	H5
Criciúma	111	M4
Cristalina	109	H7
Cristóbal Colón	91	J8
Crna Gora	47	F7
Croatia	47	C4
Crockett	103	B3
Croker Island	87	F2
Cromer	37	P9
Cromwell	89	B7
Crooked Island	105	K4
Crookston	95	G2
Cross City	103	E3
Cross Lake	93	M6
Crossville	99	C3
Crotone	45	M9
Crowley	103	C3
Crownest Pass	95	D2
Crown Point	99	C2
Cruz Alta	111	L4
Cruz del Eje	111	J5
Cruzeiro do Sul	109	C5
Crvenka	47	G4
Crystal City	103	B4
Crystal Falls	99	C1
Crystal River	103	E4
Crystal Springs	103	C3
Csorna	47	E2
Csurgó	43	N4
Cuamba	67	F2
Cuando	67	C3
Cuangar	67	B3
Cuango	65	B5
Cuanza	65	B5
Cuatro Ciénegas	101	F3
Cuauhtémoc	101	E3
Cuba	97	E3
Cuba	105	H4
Cubal	65	A6
Cubali	67	A2
Cubango	67	B3
Çubuk	49	R4
Cucuí	109	D3
Cúcuta	109	C2
Cuddalore	75	C6
Cuddapah	75	C6
Cuemba	67	B2
Cuenca, Ecuador	109	B4
Cuenca, Spain	41	H4
Cuernavaca	105	E5
Cuero	103	B4
Cuiabá	109	F7
Cuilo	65	B5
Cuito	67	B3
Cuito Cuanavale	67	B3
Culbertson	97	E1
Culfa	51	L4
Culiacán	105	C4
Cullera	41	K5
Cullman	103	D3
Culpepper	109	(1)A1
Culuene	109	G6
Culverden	89	D6
Cumaná	109	E1
Cumberland	99	E3

Name	Page	Ref
Cumberland Peninsula	93	T3
Cumberland Sound	93	T3
Cummings	97	B3
Cumpas	101	E2
Çumra	49	Q7
Cunderdin	87	C6
Cunene	67	A3
Cuneo	43	C6
Cunnamulla	87	J5
Čuprija	47	J6
Cure	39	J6
Curicó	111	G5
Curitiba	111	M4
Currais Novos	109	K5
Curral Velho	63	(1)B1
Currie	87	H7
Curtea de Argeş	47	M4
Curtici	47	J3
Curtis Island	87	K4
Curuá	109	G5
Curup	83	(1)C3
Curuzú Cuatiá	111	K4
Curvelo	109	J7
Cusco	109	C6
Cuthbert	103	E3
Cutro	45	L9
Cuttack	75	E4
Cuvier Island	89	E3
Cuxhaven	35	D3
Cuya	109	C7
Cuyuni	109	F2
Cwmbran	37	J10
Cyclades = Kyklades	49	G7
Cypress Hills	95	D2
Cyprus	51	E6
Czarnków	33	F5
Czech Republic	33	C8
Częstochowa	33	J7
Człuchów	33	G4

D

Name	Page	Ref
Da'an	79	G1
Daaquam	99	F1
Dab'a	54	D5
Dabas	47	G2
Dabat	61	G5
Dabola	63	B2
Dąbrowa Górnicza	33	J7
Dăbuleni	47	M6
Dachau	43	G2
Daet	77	G4
Dagana	59	B5
Dagestan	51	M2
Dagupan	77	G3
Da Hinggan Ling	79	G1
Dahlak Archipelago	61	H4
Dahlonega	103	E3
Dahn	27	K5
Dahod	75	B4
Dahongliutan	53	L2
Dahūk	51	K5
Daimiel	41	G5
Dai Xian	79	E3
Dakar	63	A2
Dakoro	63	F2
Dakota City	97	G2
Dakovica	47	H7
Dakovo	47	F4
Dalai Nur	79	F2
Dalälven	29	H6
Dalaman	51	C5
Dalandzadgad	79	C2
Dalap-Uliga-Darrit	85	H5
Da Lat	77	D4
Dalbandin	53	H4
Dalby	87	K5
Dalgān	53	G4
Dalhart	101	F1
Dalhousie	75	C2
Dali	77	C1
Dalian	79	G3
Dalizi	81	D3
Dallas	103	B3
Daloa	63	C3
Dalry	37	H6

Name	Page	Ref
Dāltenganj	75	D4
Dalton	103	E3
Dalvík	29	(1)D2
Daly Waters	87	F3
Daman	75	B4
Damanhûr	61	F1
Damar	83	(2)C4
Damara	63	H3
Damasak	63	G2
Damascus = Dimashq	54	D3
Damaturu	63	G2
Damoh	75	C4
Damqawt	53	F6
Danau Poso	83	(2)A3
Danau Toba	83	(1)B2
Danau Towuti	83	(2)B3
Danba	79	C4
Dandeldhura	75	D3
Dandong	81	C3
Da Nĕng	77	D3
Dangara	53	J2
Danger Islands	85	K7
Danghe Nanshan	79	B3
Daniel	97	D1
Danilov	31	H3
Dank	55	G5
Dankov	31	G4
Dannenberg	35	G3
Dannevirke	89	F5
Dansville	99	E2
Danube	25	F3
Danville, Ill., United States	103	D1
Danville, Ky., United States	103	E2
Danville, Va., United States	103	F2
Dan Xian	77	D3
Dao Phu Quôc	77	C4
Dapa	77	H5
Dapaong	63	E2
Da Qaidam	79	B3
Daqing	73	M7
Dar'ā	54	D4
Dārāb	55	F2
Darabani	47	P1
Daraj	61	B1
Darazo	63	G2
Darbhanga	75	E3
Dardanelles = Çanakkale Boğazı	49	J4
Darende	51	G4
Dar es Salaam	65	F5
Darfo	43	F5
Dargaville	89	D2
Darham	73	H7
Darjeeling	75	E3
Darling	87	H6
Darlington	37	L7
Darłowo	29	J9
Dărmăneşti	47	P3
Dar Mazār	55	G2
Darmstadt	35	D7
Darnah	61	D1
Darnley Bay	93	G3
Daroca	41	J3
Darß	35	H2
Dartmouth	93	U8
Daru	83	(2)F4
Daruba	83	(2)C2
Daruvar	43	N5
Darvaza	71	K9
Darwin	87	F2
Daryacheh-ye Bakhtegan	55	E2
Daryācheh-ye Orūmīyeh	51	L5
Daryācheh-ye Tashk	55	E2
Dārzīn	55	H2
Dashkhovuz	71	K9
Dasht-e Kavir	53	F3
Dasht-e Lut	55	H1
Datça	49	K8
Datça	51	B5
Date	81	L2
Datong	79	C3
Datong	79	E2
Daugava	31	E3
Daugavpils	31	E3
Daun	27	J4
Dauphin	93	M6
Dausa	75	C3

Name	Page	Ref
Däväci	51	N3
Davangere	75	C6
Davao	77	H5
Davenport	99	B2
Daventry	27	A2
David	105	H7
Davis Sea	112	(2)Q3
Davis Strait	93	V3
Davlekanovo	71	J7
Davos	43	E4
Dawa	79	G2
Dawqah	53	F6
Dawson	101	(1)K3
Dawson Creek, B.C., Canada	93	G5
Dawson Creek, Y.T., Canada	93	D4
Dawu	79	C4
Dax	39	D10
Daxian	79	D4
Dayong	79	E5
Dayr az Zawr	51	J6
Dayton, Oh., United States	99	D3
Dayton, Tenn., United States	99	C3
Dayton, Tex., United States	103	C4
Dayton, Wash., United States	97	C1
Daytona Beach	103	E4
De Aar	67	C6
Deakin	87	E6
Deal	27	D3
De'an	79	F5
Deán Funes	111	J5
Dease Lake	101	(1)M4
Dease Strait	93	J3
Death Valley	97	C3
Deba Habe	63	G2
Debar	49	C3
Dębica	33	L7
Debin	73	S4
Dęblin	33	L6
Dębno	33	D5
Debre Birhan	65	F2
Debrecen	47	J2
Debre Markos	61	G5
Debre Tabor	61	G5
Decatur, Al., United States	99	C4
Decatur, Ill., United States	99	C3
Decazeville	39	H9
Deccan	75	C5
Děčín	33	D7
Decize	39	J7
Decorah	99	B2
Dedoplis	51	M3
Dédougou	63	D2
Dedza	67	E2
Dee, Scot., United Kingdom	37	K4
Dee, Wales, United Kingdom	37	J9
Deering	101	(1)E2
Deer Lake	93	V7
Deer Lodge	97	D1
Deer Park	97	C1
De Funiak Springs	103	D3
Degeh Bur	65	G2
Deggendorf	43	J2
Dehaj	55	F1
Dehalak Desēt	53	D6
Deh Bid	55	E1
Deh-Dasht	55	D1
Dehküyeh	55	F3
Dehlonān	53	E3
Dehra	53	L3
Dehra Dun	75	C2
Dehri	75	D4
Deh Shū	53	H3
Deinze	27	F4
Dej	47	L2
De Kalb	103	C3
De-Kastri	73	Q6
Dekese	65	C4
Delano	101	C1
Delaware	99	D2
Delaware	103	F2
Delbrück	35	D5
Delémont	43	C3
Delfoi	49	E6
Delft	27	G2
Delfzijl	27	J1
Delgo	61	F3

Name	Page	Ref
Delhi, India	75	C3
Delhi, United States	99	F2
Delitzsch	35	H5
Dellys	41	P8
Delmenhorst	35	D3
Delnice	43	K5
Delray Beach	103	E4
Del Rio	101	F3
Delta, Colo., United States	97	E3
Delta, Ut., United States	97	D3
Delta del Orinoco	109	E2
Delta Junction	101	(1)H3
Deming	101	E2
Demirci	49	L5
Demmin	35	J3
Democratic Republic of Congo	65	C4
Demopolis	103	D3
Demyanka	31	P3
Dem'yanskoye	31	N3
Denain	27	F4
Denau	53	J2
Denbigh	99	E1
Den Burg	27	G1
Dender	27	F4
Dendi	65	F2
Denham	87	B5
Den Helder	27	G2
Dénia	41	L6
Deniliquin	87	H7
Denio	97	C2
Denison, Ia., United States	99	A2
Denison, Tex., United States	103	B3
Denizli	51	C5
Denmark	25	E2
Denmark	87	C6
Denmark Strait	91	D3
Denpasar	83	(1)E4
Denton	101	G2
D'Entrecasteaux Islands	87	K1
Denver	97	F3
Deogarh, India	75	B3
Deogarh, India	75	D4
Deoghar	75	E4
De Panne	27	E3
Depok	83	(1)D4
Dépression du Mourdi	61	D4
Deputatskiy	73	P3
Dêqên	77	B1
Dera Ghazi Khan	53	K3
Dera Ismail Khan	53	K3
Derbent	51	E1
Derby, Australia	87	D3
Derby, United Kingdom	37	L9
De Ridder	103	C3
Dermott	103	C3
Derventa	47	E5
Desē	61	G5
Deseado	111	H8
Deseado	111	H8
Desert Center	101	C2
Des Moines, Ia., United States	95	H3
Des Moines, N.Mex., United States	101	F1
Desna	31	F4
Dessau	35	H5
Desvres	27	D4
Deta	47	J4
Detmold	35	D5
Detroit	95	K3
Detroit Lakes	99	A1
Det Udom	77	C4
Detva	33	J9
Deurne	27	H3
Deva	47	K4
Deventer	27	J2
Devil's Lake	93	L7
Devils Lake	97	G1
Devil's Point	103	F5
Devnya	47	Q6
Devon Island	93	P1
Devonport	87	J8
Dewas	75	C4
Deyang	79	C4
Deyhuk	53	G3
Dezfūl	53	E3
Dezhou	79	F3
Dhahran = Az̧ Zahrān	55	D3

Name	Page	Grid
Dhaka	75	F4
Dhamār	61	H5
Dhamtri	75	D4
Dhanbad	75	E4
Dhar	75	C4
Dhārwād	75	B5
Dhaulagiri	75	D3
Dhekelia	54	A2
Dhībān	54	C5
Dhoraji	75	B4
Dhule	75	B4
Dhulian	75	E4
Dhuudo	65	J2
Dia	49	H9
Diamantina	109	H7
Diamantino	109	F6
Diamond Islets	87	K3
Diane Bank	87	J3
Dianópolis	109	H6
Dibā al Ḥiṣn	55	G4
Dibbiena	45	F5
Dibrugarh	75	F3
Dickens	101	F2
Dickinson	97	F1
Dickson	103	D2
Didiéni	63	C2
Didymoteicho	49	J3
Die	39	L9
Diébougou	63	D2
Dieburg	35	D7
Diéma	63	C2
Diemel	35	E5
Diemeringen	35	C8
Diepholz	35	D4
Dieppe	27	D5
Diest	27	H4
Diffa	63	G2
Digne-les-Bains	43	B6
Digoin	39	J7
Dijon	39	L6
Dikhil	61	H5
Dikili	49	J5
Diklosmta	51	L2
Diksmuide	27	E3
Dikson	71	Q3
Dikwa	63	G2
Dīla	65	F2
Dili	83	(2)C4
Dilijan	51	L3
Dillenburg	35	D6
Dillingen, Germany	35	F8
Dillingen, Germany	35	B7
Dillingham	101	(1)F4
Dillon	95	D2
Dillon	97	D1
Dillon Cone	89	D6
Dilolo	67	C2
Dimapur	75	F3
Dimashq	54	D3
Dimitrovgrad, Bulgaria	47	N7
Dimitrovgrad, Russia	31	J4
Dimitrovgrad, Yugoslavia	47	K7
Dīmona	54	C5
Dinagat	77	H4
Dinajpur	75	E3
Dinan	39	C5
Dinant	27	G4
Dinar	51	D4
Dinaric Alps	43	L6
Dindigul	75	C6
Dindori	75	D4
Dingle Bay	37	B9
Dingolfing	43	H2
Dinguiraye	63	B2
Dingwall	37	H4
Dinkelsbühl	35	F7
Dinosaur	97	E2
Diomede Islands	73	AA3
Dioriga Kointhou	49	F7
Diourbel	59	B6
Dipolog	77	G5
Dir	75	B1
Dirē Dawa	65	G2
Dirk Hartog Island	87	B5
Dirranbandi	87	J5
Disko = Qeqertarsuaq	93	V2
Disko Bugt = Qeqertarsuup Tunua	93	V3
Diss	27	D2
Distrito Federal	109	H7
Dithmarschen	35	D2
Dīvāndarreh	51	M6
Divinópolis	111	N3
Divo	63	C3
Divriği	51	H4
Dixon	99	C2
Dixon Entrance	101	(1)L5
Diyarbakır	51	J5
Dja	63	G4
Djado	59	H4
Djamâa	59	G2
Djambala	63	G5
Djanet	59	G4
Djelfa	59	F2
Djéma	65	D2
Djibo	63	D2
Djibouti	61	H5
Djibouti	61	H5
Djolu	65	C3
Djougou	63	E3
Djúpivogur	29	(1)F2
Dnieper	31	F5
Dniester	47	Q1
Dnipro	25	H3
Dniprodzerzhyns'k	31	F5
Dnipropetrovs'k	31	F5
Dnister	25	G3
Dno	31	E3
Doba, Chad	65	B2
Doba, China	75	E2
Döbeln	35	J5
Doboj	47	F5
Dobre Miasto	33	K4
Dobrich	47	Q6
Dobryanka	31	L3
Doctor Arroyo	101	F4
Dodecanese = Dodekanisos	49	J8
Dodge City	97	F3
Dodoma	65	F5
Doetinchem	27	J3
Doğanşehir	51	G4
Dōgo	81	G5
Dogondoutchi	63	E2
Doha = Ad Dawḥah	55	D4
Doka	83	(2)D4
Dokkum	35	B3
Dolak	83	(2)E4
Dolbeau	99	F1
Dole	43	A3
Dolgany	73	E2
Dolinsk	73	Q7
Dollard	35	C3
Dolný Kubrín	33	J8
Dolomiti	43	G4
Dolo Odo	65	G3
Dolores	111	K6
Dolphin and Union Strait	93	H3
Domar	75	D2
Domažlice	35	H7
Dombås	29	E5
Dombóvár	47	F3
Domfront	39	E5
Dominica	107	E2
Dominican Republic	107	D1
Domodóssola	43	D4
Domokos	49	E5
Dompu	83	(2)A4
Domžale	43	K4
Don	25	H2
Donau = Danube	43	H2
Donaueschingen	43	D3
Donauwörth	35	F8
Don Benito	41	E6
Doncaster	37	L8
Dondra Head	75	D7
Donegal	37	D7
Donegal Bay	37	D7
Donets	25	H3
Donets'k	31	G5
Dongco	75	D2
Dongfang	77	D3
Donggala	83	(2)A3
Donggou	81	C4
Dongguan	77	E2
Dōng Hôi	77	D3
Dongjingcheng	81	E1
Donglük	71	R10
Dongning	81	F2
Dongo	63	H4
Dongola	61	F4
Dongou	63	H4
Dongsha Qundao	77	F2
Dongsheng	79	E3
Dong Ujimqin Qi	79	F1
Dongying	79	F3
Doniphan	103	C2
Donji Vakuf	43	N6
Donner Pass	97	B3
Donostia	41	J1
Donousa	49	H7
Dora	43	C5
Dorchester	37	K11
Dordrecht	27	G3
Dorfen	43	H2
Dori	63	D2
Doring	67	B6
Dorion	99	C1
Dormagen	27	J3
Dornbirn	43	E3
Dorog	33	H10
Dorohoi	47	P2
Döröö Nuur	71	S8
Dorsten	27	J3
Dortmund	35	C5
Dos Hermanas	41	E7
Dosse	35	H4
Dosso	63	E2
Dothan	103	D3
Douai	27	F4
Douala	63	F4
Douarnenez	39	A5
Doubs	43	B3
Douentza	63	C2
Douglas, South Africa	67	C5
Douglas, United Kingdom	37	H7
Douglas, Ariz., United States	101	E2
Douglas, Ga., United States	103	E3
Douglas, Wyo., United States	97	E2
Doullens	27	E4
Dourados	111	L3
Douro	41	B3
Dover, United Kingdom	27	D3
Dover, United States	103	F2
Dover, Australia	87	J8
Dover-Foxcroft	99	G1
Dowlatābād, Iran	55	E2
Dowlatābād, Iran	55	G2
Dowshī	53	J2
Drac	43	B6
Drachten	27	J1
Dragan	29	H4
Drăgăneşti-Olt	47	M5
Drăgăşani	47	M5
Draguignan	43	B7
Drakensberg	67	D6
Drake Passage	111	G10
Drama	49	G3
Drammen	29	F7
Drasenhofen	43	M2
Drau	43	J4
Drava	47	E4
Dravograd	45	K2
Drawsko Pomorskie	33	E4
Dresden	35	J5
Dreux	27	D6
Drezdenko	33	E5
Drina	47	G5
Driva	29	E5
Drniš	47	D6
Drobeta-Turnu Severin	47	K5
Drochia	47	Q1
Drogheda	37	F8
Drohobych	33	N8
Drôme	39	K9
Dronning Maud Land	112	(2)F2
Dronten	27	H2
Drummondville	99	F1
Druskininkai	29	M9
Druzhina	73	Q3
Drvar	47	D5
Dryanovo	47	N7
Dryden	95	H2
Drysdale River	87	E3
Dschang	63	G3
Dubā	61	G2
Dubai = Dubayy	55	F4
Dubăsari	47	S2
Dubawnt Lake	93	L4
Dubayy	55	F4
Dubbo	87	J6
Dübendorf	43	D3
Dublin, Republic of Ireland	37	F8
Dublin, United States	103	E3
Dublin Bay	37	F8
Dubna	31	G3
Dubnica	33	H9
Du Bois	99	E2
Dubois, Id., United States	97	D2
Dubois, Wyo., United States	97	E2
Dubovskoye	31	H5
Dubreka	63	B3
Dubrovnik	47	F7
Dubuque	99	B2
Duchesne	97	D2
Ducie Island	85	P8
Dudelange	27	J5
Duderstadt	35	F5
Dudinka	71	R4
Dudley	37	K9
Duero	41	F3
Dugi Otok	47	B6
Duifken Point	87	H2
Duisburg	27	J3
Duiveland	27	F3
Duk Faiwil	65	D4
Dukhān	55	D4
Dukla	33	L8
Dukou	79	C5
Dulan	79	B3
Dulce	101	E1
Dulce	111	J4
Dul'Durga	73	J6
Dullewala	75	B2
Dülmen	35	C5
Dulovo	47	Q6
Duluth	99	B1
Dūmā	54	D3
Dumaguete	77	G5
Dumai	83	(1)C2
Dumas, Ark., United States	103	C3
Dumas, Tex., United States	97	F3
Dumayr	54	D3
Dumbarton	37	H5
Dumbier	33	J9
Dumboa	63	G2
Dumfries	37	J6
Dümmer	35	D4
Dumont d'Urville Sea	112	(2)U3
Dumyât	61	F1
Duna = Danube	47	E2
Dunaj = Danube	33	G10
Dunajská Streda	47	E2
Dunakeszi	47	G2
Dunărea = Danube	47	K5
Dunaújváros	47	F3
Dunav = Danube	47	J5
Dunayivtsi	31	E5
Dunbar, Australia	87	H3
Dunbar, United Kingdom	37	K6
Duncan	97	F3
Duncan Passage	77	A4
Dundaga	29	M8
Dundalk	37	F7
Dundalk Bay	37	F8
Dundee, South Africa	67	E5
Dundee, United Kingdom	37	K5
Dunedin	89	C7
Dunfermline	37	J5
Dungarvan	37	E9
Dungeness	27	C4
Dungu	65	D3
Dungun	77	C6
Dunhua	81	E2
Dunhuang	79	A2
Dunkerque	27	E3
Dunkirk	99	E2
Dunkwa	63	D3

Name	Page	Ref.
Dun Laoghaire	37	F8
Dunnet Head	37	J3
Dunseith	97	G1
Dunsmuir	97	B2
Duque de Caxias	111	N3
Du Quoin	103	D2
Durance	39	L10
Durango, *Mexico*	101	F4
Durango, *Spain*	41	H1
Durango, *United States*	97	E3
Durant	103	B3
Durazno	111	K5
Durban	67	E5
Düren	27	J4
Durgapur	75	E4
Durham, *Canada*	99	D2
Durham, *United Kingdom*	37	L7
Durham, *United States*	103	F2
Duri	83	(1)C2
Durmä	55	B4
Durmanec	47	C3
Durmitor	47	G6
Durrës	49	B3
Dursey	37	B10
Dursunbey	49	L5
D'Urville Island	89	D5
Dushanbe	53	J2
Düsseldorf	27	J3
Duvno	43	N7
Duyun	79	D5
Düzce	49	P4
Dvina	25	H2
Dvinskaya Guba	31	G1
Dwarka	75	A4
Dworshak Reservoir	97	C1
Dyat'kovo	31	F4
Dyersburg	103	D2
Dyje	43	M2
Dzavhan	71	S8
Dzerzhinsk	31	H3
Dzhalinda	73	L6
Dzhambeyty	31	K4
Dzhankoy	31	F5
Dzhardzhan	73	L3
Dzharkurgan	53	J2
Dzhetygara	31	M4
Dzhezkazgan	31	N5
Dzhigudzhak	73	T4
Dzhizak	71	M9
Dzhusaly	31	M5
Działdowo	33	K4
Dzüünbulag	79	F1

E

Name	Page	Ref.
Eads	97	F3
Eagle	101	(1)J3
Eagle Lake	97	B2
Eagle Pass	101	F3
East Antarctica	112	(2)P2
Eastbourne	27	C4
East Cape	89	G3
East China Sea	79	H4
East Dereham	27	C2
Easter Island	85	Q8
Eastern Cape	67	D6
Eastern Ghats	75	C6
Easter Ross	37	H4
East Falkland	111	K9
East Grinstead	27	C3
East Kilbride	37	H6
Eastleigh	27	A4
East Liverpool	103	E1
East London	67	D6
Eastmain	93	R6
Eastmain	93	S6
East Point	103	E3
East Retford	27	B1
East St. Louis	99	B3
East Siberian Sea = Vostochno-Sibirskoye More	73	U2
Eatonton	103	E3
Eau Claire	99	B2
Ebbw Vale	37	J10
Ebensee	43	J3
Eberbach	35	D7
Ebersbach	33	D6
Ebersberg	43	G2
Eberswalde	35	J4
Ebinur Hu	71	Q9
Éboli	45	K8
Ebolowa	63	G4
Ebro	41	K3
Eceabat	49	J4
Ech Chélif	59	F1
Echinos	49	G3
Echo Bay	93	H3
Écija	41	E7
Eckernförde	35	E2
Ecuador	109	B4
Ed	61	H5
Edam	27	H2
Eday	37	K2
Ed Da'ein	61	E5
Ed Damazin	61	F5
Ed Debba	61	F4
Ed Dueim	61	F5
Ede, *Netherlands*	27	H2
Ede, *Nigeria*	63	E3
Edéa	63	G4
Edelény	33	K9
Eden, *Australia*	87	J7
Eden, *United States*	101	G2
Edendale	89	B8
Eder	35	D5
Edersee	35	E5
Edessa	49	E4
Edgecumbe	89	F3
Edinburgh	37	J6
Edineţ	47	Q1
Edirne	49	J3
Edmonds	97	B1
Edmonton	93	J6
Edmundson	95	N2
Edmundston	99	G1
Edolo	43	F4
Edremit	49	J5
Edremit Körfezi	49	H5
Edwards	101	C2
Edwards Plateau	101	F2
Eemshaven	27	J1
Éfaté	85	G7
Eferding	33	D9
Effingham	103	D2
Eganville	99	E1
Eger	35	G6
Eger	47	H2
Egersund	29	D7
Eggenfelden	43	H2
Egilsstaðir	29	(1)F2
Eğridir	49	N7
Eğridir Gölü	49	N6
Egvekinot	73	Y3
Egypt	61	E2
Ehingen	43	E2
Eibar	41	H1
Eichstätt	43	G2
Eider	35	D2
Eidsvold	87	K5
Eidsvoll	29	F6
Eifel	27	J4
Eigg	37	F5
Eight Degree Channel	75	B7
Eilenburg	35	H5
Einbeck	35	E5
Eindhoven	27	H3
Eirunepé	109	D5
Eiseb	67	C4
Eisenach	35	F6
Eisenerz	43	K3
Eisenhüttenstadt	33	D5
Eisenstadt	43	M3
Eisleben	35	G5
Eivissa	41	M5
Eivissa	41	M6
Ejea de los Caballeros	41	J2
Ejido Insurgentes	95	D6
Ejin Horo Qi	79	D3
Ejin Qi	79	C2
Ejmiadzin	51	L3
Ekalaka	97	F1
Ekenäs	29	M7
Ekibastuz	71	P7
Ekimchan	73	N6
Ekonda	71	V4
Eksjo	29	H8
Ekwan	93	Q6
El Aaiún	59	C3
Elafonisos	49	E8
El 'Alamein	61	E1
El Amria	41	J9
El 'Arîsh	54	A5
Elat	54	B7
Elazığ	51	H4
El Azraq	54	D5
Elba	45	E6
El Banco	109	C2
Elbasan	49	C3
El Baúl	109	D2
Elbe	35	F3
Elbeuf	27	D5
Elbistan	51	G4
Elblag	33	J3
El Borj	41	E9
Elbow	95	E1
Elbrus	51	K2
El Burgo de Ebro	41	K3
El Burgo de Osma	41	G3
El Cajon	101	C2
El Callao	109	E2
El Campo	103	B4
El Centro	101	C2
El Cerro	109	E7
Elch	41	K6
Elda	41	K6
El'dikan	73	P4
Eldorado	111	L4
El Dorado, *Mexico*	95	E7
El Dorado, *Ark., United States*	103	C3
El Dorado, *Kans., United States*	103	B2
El Dorado, *Venezuela*	109	E2
Eldoret	65	F3
Elefsína	49	F6
Elektrénai	33	P3
El Encanto	109	C4
Elephant Butte Reservoir	101	E2
Eleuthera	95	L6
El Fahs	45	D12
El Faiyûm	61	F2
El Fasher	61	E5
El Geneina	61	D5
Elgin, *United Kingdom*	37	J4
Elgin, *Ill., United States*	99	C2
Elgin, *N.D., United States*	97	F1
El'ginskiy	73	Q4
El Gîza	61	F1
El Goléa	59	F2
El Iskandarîya	61	E1
Elista	31	H5
Elizabeth	99	F2
Elizabeth City	103	F2
Elizabethton	103	E2
El Jadida	59	D2
El Jafr	54	D6
El Jafr	54	D6
Ełk	33	M4
Ełk	33	M4
El Kala	45	C12
Elk City	101	G1
El Kef	45	C12
El Kelaâ des Srarhna	59	D2
El Khârga	61	F2
Elkhart, *Ind., United States*	99	C2
Elkhart, *Kans., United States*	103	A2
El Khartum	61	F4
El Khartum Bahri	61	F4
Elkhorn	97	G2
Elkhorn	99	C2
Elkhovo	49	E3
Elkins	99	E3
Elko, *Canada*	97	C1
Elko, *United States*	97	C2
Elk River	99	B1
El Kuntilla	54	B7
Ellendale	95	D6
Ellensburg	97	B1
Ellesmere Island	91	K1
Ellice Islands	85	H6
Elliot	67	D6
Ellis	93	J8
Ellisras	67	D4
Elliston	87	F6
Ellsworth	99	G2
Ellwangen	43	F2
Elmadağ	49	R5
Elmali	49	M8
El Mansûra	61	F1
El Minya	61	F2
Elmira	99	E2
Elmshorn	35	E4
El Muglad	61	E5
El Nido	77	F4
El Obeid	61	F5
El Odaiya	61	E5
El Oued	59	G2
El Paso	101	E2
El Portal	101	C1
El Potosi	101	F4
El Prat de Llobregat	41	N3
El Puerto de Santa María	41	D8
El Qâhira	61	F1
El Reno	103	B2
El Sahuaro	101	D2
El Salvador	105	F6
Elster	35	H5
Elsterwerda	35	J5
El Sueco	101	E3
El Suweis	61	F2
Eltanin Bay	112	(2)JJ2
El Tarf	45	C12
El Thamad	54	B7
El Tigre	109	E2
El Turbio	111	G9
Eluru	75	D5
Elvas	41	C6
Elverum	29	F6
Elvira	109	C5
El Wak	65	G3
Ely, *United Kingdom*	37	N9
Ely, *United States*	97	D3
Emajõgi	29	P7
Emämrüd	53	F2
Emba	31	L5
Emba	31	L5
Embalse de Alarcon	41	H5
Embalse de Alcántara Uno	41	D5
Embalse de Almendra	41	D3
Embalse de Contreras	41	J5
Embalse de Gabriel y Galán	41	D4
Embalse de Garcia Sola	41	E5
Embalse de Guadalhorce	41	F8
Embalse de Guadalmena	41	G6
Embalse de Guri	109	E2
Embalse de la Serena	41	E6
Embalse de la Sotonera	41	K2
Embalse del Bembézar	41	E6
Embalse del Ebro	41	G1
Embalse del Río Negro	107	F7
Embalse de Negratmn	41	G7
Embalse de Ricobayo	41	E3
Embalse de Santa Teresa	41	E4
Embalse de Yesa	41	J2
Embalse Toekomstig	109	F3
Embarcación	111	J3
Emden	35	C3
Emerald	87	J4
Emi Koussi	61	C4
Emin	71	Q8
Emirdağ	49	P5
Emmeloord	27	H2
Emmen	27	J2
Emmendingen	43	C2
Emmerich	27	J3
Emory Peak	101	F3
Empalme	101	D3
Empangeni	67	E5
Empoli	43	F7
Emporia	103	B2
Empty Quarter = Rub' al Khālī	53	E6
Ems	27	J1
Ems-Jade-Kanal	35	C3
Enafors	31	B2
Encarnación	111	K4
Encs	47	J1
Ende	83	(2)B4
Enderby Island	89	(2)B1
Energetik	31	L4

Name	Page	Grid
Enewetak	85	F4
Enez	49	J4
Enfida	45	E12
Engel's	31	J4
Enggano	83	(1)C4
Enghien	27	G4
England	37	L9
English Channel	37	J12
Engozero	29	S4
'En Hazeva	54	C6
Enid	103	B2
Enkhuizen	27	H2
Enköping	29	J7
Enna	45	J11
En Nahud	61	E5
Enngonia	87	J5
Ennis, Republic of Ireland	37	D9
Ennis, United States	97	D1
Enniscorthy	37	F9
Enniskillen	37	E7
Enns	43	K2
Enns	43	K3
Enschede	27	J2
Ensenada	101	C2
Enshi	79	D4
Entebbe	65	E3
Enterprise	97	C1
Entrevaux	43	B7
Entroncamento	41	B5
Enugu	63	F3
Enurmino	73	Z3
Envira	109	C5
Enz	43	D2
Enza	43	F6
Epanomi	49	E4
Epéna	65	B3
Épernay	39	J4
Épinal	43	B2
Epsom	27	B3
Eqlīd	55	E1
Equatorial Guinea	63	F4
Erbach	35	D7
Erçek	51	K4
Erciş	51	K4
Ercolano	45	J8
Érd	47	F2
Erdek	49	K4
Erdemli	49	S8
Erdenet	73	G7
Erding	43	G2
Erechim	111	L4
Ereğli, Turkey	51	D3
Ereğli, Turkey	51	F5
Ereikoussa	49	B5
Erenhot	79	E2
Erfurt	35	G6
Ergani	51	H4
Erg Chech	59	D4
Erg du Ténéré	59	H5
Ergel	79	D2
Erg Iguidi	59	D3
Erie	99	D2
Erimo-misaki	81	M3
Eriskay	37	E4
Eritrea	61	G4
Erlangen	35	G7
Ermenek	51	E5
Ermoupoli	49	G7
Erode	75	C6
Er Rachidia	59	E2
Er Renk	65	E1
Errol	99	F2
Er Ruseifa	54	D4
Ersekë	49	C4
Erskine	99	A1
Ertai	71	S8
Ertix	71	R8
Erzgebirge	35	H6
Erzin	71	S7
Erzincan	51	H4
Erzurum	51	J4
Esan-misaki	81	L3
Esashi, Japan	81	L3
Esashi, Japan	81	M1
Esbjerg	29	E9
Escanaba	99	C1
Escárcega	105	F5
Esch	27	J5
Eschwege	35	F5
Eschweiler	27	J4
Escondido	101	C2
Eséka	63	G4
Eşfahān	53	F3
Eskifjörður	29	(1)G2
Eskilstuna	29	J7
Eskimo Lakes	101	(1)L2
Eskişehir	51	D4
Esla	41	E3
Eslämäbäd e Gharb	51	M6
Eslamshahr	53	F2
Esler Dağ	33	M7
Eslöv	33	C2
Esmeraldas	109	B3
Esneux	27	H4
Espalion	39	H9
Espanola, Canada	99	D1
Espanola, United States	97	E3
Espelkamp	35	D4
Esperance	87	D6
Esperance Bay	87	D6
Espinho	41	B4
Espírito Santo	109	J7
Espíritu Santo	85	G7
Esplanada	109	K6
Espoo	29	N6
Espungebera	67	E4
Essaouira	59	D2
Es Semara	59	C3
Essen, Belgium	27	G3
Essen, Germany	27	K3
Essequibo	109	F2
Esslingen	43	E2
Eşţahbānāt	55	F2
Este	43	G5
Estella	41	H2
Estepona	41	E8
Esteros	111	J3
Estevan	95	F2
Estonia	29	M7
Estoril	41	A6
Estrecho de Le Maire	111	H10
Estrecho de Magallanes	111	G9
Estrela	41	C4
Estremoz	41	C6
Estuário do Rio Amazonaz	109	H3
Esztergom	47	F2
Étain	27	H5
Étampes	39	H5
Étang de Berre	39	L10
Étaples	27	D4
Etawah	75	C3
Ethiopia	57	G5
Etolin Strait	101	(1)D3
Etosha Pan	67	B3
Étretat	27	C5
Ettelbruck	35	B7
Ettlingen	35	D8
Eucla	87	E6
Euclid	99	D2
Eufala	103	D3
Eufaula Lake	103	B2
Eugene	97	B2
Eupen	35	B6
Euphrates = Fırat	51	H4
Euphrates	53	D3
Eure	27	D6
Eureka, Calif., United States	97	B2
Eureka, Mont., United States	97	C1
Eureka, Nev., United States	101	C1
Eureka, Ut., United States	97	D3
Europoort	27	F3
Euskirchen	35	B6
Eutin	35	F2
Eutsuk Lake	93	F6
Evans Strait	93	Q4
Evanston, Ill., United States	99	C2
Evanston, Wyo., United States	97	D2
Evansville	103	D2
Evaz	55	F3
Everett	97	B1
Everglades City	103	E4
Evergreen	103	D3
Evesham	27	A2
Évora	41	C6
Évreux	27	D5
Evron	39	E5
Evron	49	J3
Evvoia	49	F6
Ewo	63	G5
Exaltación	109	D6
Exe	37	J11
Exeter	37	J11
Exmouth, Australia	87	B4
Exmouth, United Kingdom	37	J11
Exuma Sound	95	L7
Eyl	65	H2
Eyre Peninsula	87	G2
Ezine	49	J5

F

Name	Page	Grid
Faadippolu Atoll	75	B8
Fåborg	35	F1
Fabriano	43	H7
Fada	61	D4
Fada Ngourma	63	E2
Faenza	43	G6
Færingehavn = Kangerluarsoruseq	93	W4
Faeroes	25	D1
Făgăraş	47	M4
Fagernes	29	E6
Fagersta	29	H6
Fagurhólsmýri	29	(1)E3
Fahraj	55	H2
Faial	59	(1)B2
Fairbanks	101	(1)H3
Fair Isle	37	L2
Fairlie	89	C7
Fairmont	99	B2
Faisalabad	75	B2
Faith	97	F1
Faizabad	75	D3
Fakfak	83	(2)D3
Fakse	35	H1
Fakse Bugt	29	G9
Faku	79	G2
Falaise	27	B6
Falaise de Tiguidit	59	G5
Falconara Maríttima	43	J7
Falcon Lake	103	B4
Fălești	47	Q2
Falfurrias	103	B4
Falkenberg	29	G8
Falkensee	35	J4
Falkland Islands	111	K9
Falkland Sound	111	J9
Falköping	29	G7
Fallingbostel	35	E4
Fallon	97	C3
Fall River	99	F2
Falls City	95	G3
Falmouth, United Kingdom	37	G11
Falmouth, United States	99	F2
Falster	35	H2
Fălticeni	47	P2
Falun	29	H6
Famagusta = Ammochostos	54	A1
Fanchang	79	F4
Fandriana	67	H4
Fangzheng	79	H1
Fannūj	53	G4
Fanø	35	D1
Fano	43	J7
Fanø Bugt	35	D1
Faradje	65	D3
Farafangana	67	H4
Farāh	53	H3
Farah Rud	53	H3
Faranah	63	B2
Fareham	27	A4
Farewell Spit	89	D5
Fargo	95	G2
Faribault	99	B2
Faridabad	75	C3
Farihy Alaotra	67	H3
Färjestaden	33	F1
Farmington, Me., United States	99	F2
Farmington, N.Mex., United States	101	E1
Farnborough	27	B3
Farne Islands	37	L6
Fårö	29	K8
Faro, Brazil	109	F4
Faro, Portugal	41	C7
Farquhar Group	67	(2)B3
Farrāshband	55	E2
Farson	97	E2
Fasā	55	E2
Fasano	45	M8
Fategarh	75	C3
Fatehpur	75	D3
Făurei	47	Q4
Fauske	29	H3
Fauville-en-Caux	27	C5
Favara	45	H11
Faversham	27	C3
Favignana	45	G11
Faxaflói	29	(1)B2
Faya	61	C4
Fayette	103	D3
Fayetteville, Ark., United States	103	C2
Fayetteville, N.C., United States	99	E3
Fayetteville, Tenn., United States	103	D2
Faylakah	55	C4
Fdérik	59	C4
Featherston	89	E5
Fécamp	27	C5
Federated States of Micronesia	85	B5
Fedorovka	31	M4
Fehmarn	35	G2
Feijó	109	C5
Feilding	89	E5
Feira de Santana	109	K6
Feistritz	43	L3
Fejø	35	G2
Feldbach	43	L4
Feldkirch	43	E3
Feldkirchen	43	K4
Felidu Atoll	75	B8
Felixstowe	27	D3
Feltre	43	G4
Femø	35	G2
Femund	29	F5
Fengcheng	81	C3
Fenghua	79	G5
Fengning	79	F2
Feng Xian	79	D4
Feni	75	F4
Fenyang	79	E3
Feodosiya	51	F1
Fergana	53	K1
Fergus Falls	95	G2
Ferkessédougou	63	C3
Ferlach	43	K4
Fermo	45	H5
Fernandina Beach	103	E3
Fernandópolis	111	L3
Ferrara	43	G6
Ferreira do Alentejo	41	B7
Ferrol	41	B1
Ferry Lake	103	C2
Fès	59	E2
Festus	99	B3
Feteşti	47	Q5
Fethiye	49	M8
Fetisovo	53	F1
Fetlar	37	M1
Feucht	35	G7
Feuchtwangen	35	F7
Feyzābād	53	K2
Fianarantsoa	67	H4
Fianga	65	B2
Fichē	65	F2
Fidenza	43	G6
Fieni	47	N4
Fier	49	B4
Figeac	39	G9
Figline Valdarno	43	G7
Figueira da Foz	41	B1
Figueres	41	N2
Figuig	59	E2
Figuil	63	G3
Fiji	85	H8
Filadélfia	111	J3
Fil'akovo	33	J9
Filiaşi	47	L5

Name	Page	Grid
Filicudi	45	J10
Finale Ligure	43	D6
Findlay	99	D2
Fingoè	67	E3
Finike	49	N8
Finland	29	P3
Finlay	93	F5
Finley	87	J7
Finnsnes	29	K2
Finsterwalde	35	J5
Firat	51	H4
Firenze	43	G7
Firminy	39	K8
Firozabad	75	C3
Firozpur	75	B2
Firth of Clyde	37	G6
Firth of Forth	37	K5
Firth of Lorn	37	G5
Firth of Thames	89	E3
Fish	67	B5
Fisher Strait	93	Q4
Fishguard	37	H9
Fiskenæsset = Qeqertarsuatsiaat	93	W4
Fismes	27	F5
Fitzroy Crossing	87	E3
Fivizzano	43	F6
Fizi	65	D4
Flaming Gorge Reservoir	97	E2
Flamingo	103	E4
Flannan Islands	37	E3
Flåsjön	29	H4
Flateyri	29	(1)B1
Flathead Lake	97	D1
Flensburg	35	E2
Flensburg Fjorde	35	E2
Flers	27	B6
Flinders Island	87	J7
Flinders Ranges	87	G6
Flinders Reefs	87	J3
Flin Flon	93	L6
Flint	99	D2
Flint Island	85	L7
Flirey	43	A2
Flöha	35	J6
Florac	39	J9
Florence = Firenze, Italy	43	G7
Florence, Al., United States	103	D3
Florence, S.C., United States	103	F3
Florencia	109	B3
Florennes	27	G4
Florenville	27	H5
Flores, Azores	59	(1)A2
Flores, Indonesia	83	(2)B4
Flores Sea	83	(2)A4
Floreşti	47	R2
Floriano	109	J5
Florianópolis	111	M4
Florida	103	E4
Florida	111	K5
Florida Keys	91	K7
Florina	49	D4
Florissant	99	B3
Florø	29	C6
Floydada	101	F2
Flumendosa	45	D9
Fly	83	(2)F4
Foča	47	F6
Foça	49	J6
Focşani	47	Q4
Fóggia	45	K7
Fogo	63	(1)B1
Fogo Island	93	W7
Fohnsdorf	43	K3
Föhr	35	D2
Foix	39	G11
Folegandros	49	G8
Foleyet	99	D1
Foligno	45	G6
Folkestone	27	D3
Folkston	103	E3
Follónica	45	E6
Fond du Lac	99	C2
Fondi	45	H7
Fongafale	85	H6
Fontainebleau	39	H5
Fonte Boa	109	D4
Fontenay-le-Comte	39	E7
Fontur	29	(1)F1
Fonyód	45	M2
Forbach, France	27	J5
Forbach, Germany	27	L6
Forchheim	35	G7
Førde	29	C6
Fordyce	103	C3
Forest, Canada	99	D2
Forest, United States	103	D3
Forestville	99	G1
Forfar	37	K5
Forges-les-Eaux	27	D5
Forks	97	B1
Forli	43	H6
Formazza	43	D4
Formentera	41	M6
Fórmia	45	H7
Formiga	111	M3
Formosa, Brazil	109	H7
Formosa, Paraguay	111	K4
Fornovo di Taro	43	F6
Forssa	29	M6
Forst	35	K5
Forsyth	97	E1
Fort Abbas	75	B3
Fortaleza	109	K4
Fort Bayne	99	C4
Fort Beaufort	67	D6
Fort Benton	97	D1
Fort Bragg	101	B1
Fort Chipewyan	93	J5
Fort Cobb Reservoir	103	B2
Fort Collins	97	E2
Fort-de-France	105	M6
Fort Dodge	99	B2
Forte dei Marmi	43	F7
Fort Frances	99	B1
Fort George	93	R6
Fort Gibson Lake	103	B2
Fort Good Hope	93	F3
Forth	37	H5
Fort Hope	93	P6
Fortín Coronel Eugenio Garay	111	J3
Fort Kent	99	G1
Fort Lauderdale	103	E4
Fort Liard	93	G4
Fort Mackay	93	J5
Fort Macleod	97	D1
Fort McMurray	93	J5
Fort McPherson	101	(1)L2
Fort Munro	53	J4
Fort Myers	103	E4
Fort Nelson	93	G5
Fort Norman	101	(1)M3
Fort Payne	103	D3
Fort Peck Reservoir	97	E1
Fort Pierce	103	E4
Fort Pierre	97	F2
Fort Portal	65	E3
Fort Providence	93	H4
Fort Rupert	93	R6
Fort St. John	93	G5
Fort Saint Lucie	103	E4
Fort Scott	103	C2
Fort Severn	93	P5
Fort Shevchenko	71	J9
Fort Simpson	93	G4
Fort Smith, Canada	93	J4
Fort Smith, United States	103	C2
Fort Stockton	101	F2
Fort Summer	101	F2
Fortuna	97	F1
Fortune Bay	93	V7
Fort Vermilion	93	H5
Fort Wayne	103	D1
Fort William	37	G5
Fort Worth	103	B3
Fort Yates	97	F1
Foshan	77	E2
Fossano	43	C6
Fossombrone	43	H7
Fougamou	63	G5
Fougères	39	D5
Foula	37	K1
Foulness	27	C3
Foumban	63	G3
Fourmies	27	G4
Fournoi	49	J7
Fouta Djallon	63	B2
Foveaux Strait	89	A8
Foxe Basin	93	R3
Foxe Channel	93	R4
Foxe Peninsula	93	R4
Fox Islands	101	(1)D5
Foz do Cunene	67	A3
Foz do Iguaçu	111	L4
Fraga	41	L3
Franca	111	M3
Francavilla	45	M8
Francavilla al Mare	45	J6
France	39	G7
Franceville	63	G5
Francisco I. Madero	101	F4
Francistown	67	D4
Francs Peak	97	E2
Frankenberg	35	D5
Frankenthal	35	D7
Frankfort, Ind., United States	103	D1
Frankfort, Ky., United States	103	E2
Frankfurt, Germany	35	K4
Frankfurt, Germany	35	D6
Franklin, N.C., United States	99	D3
Franklin, Tenn., United States	99	C3
Franklin Bay	93	F2
Franklin D. Roosevelt Lake	97	C1
Franklin Mountains	93	F3
Franklin Strait	93	M2
Franz Josef Glacier	89	C6
Franz Josef Land = Zemlya Frantsa-Iosifa	71	J2
Fraser	93	G6
Fraserburg	67	C6
Fraserburgh	37	L4
Fraser Island	87	K5
Frater	99	D1
Frauenfeld	43	D3
Fredensborg	33	B2
Frederick, Md., United States	99	E3
Frederick, Okla., United States	103	B3
Fredericksburg, Tex., United States	103	B3
Fredericksburg, Va., United States	99	E3
Fredericktown	99	B3
Fredericton	93	T7
Frederikshåb = Paamiut	93	X4
Frederikshavn	29	F8
Frederikssund	33	B2
Frederiksværk	29	G9
Fredrikstad	29	F7
Freeport, Ill., United States	99	C2
Freeport, Tex., United States	103	B4
Freeport City	103	F4
Freer	103	B4
Free State	67	D5
Freetown	63	B3
Fregenal de la Sierre	41	D6
Freiberg	35	J6
Freiburg	43	C3
Freilassing	43	H3
Freising	43	G2
Freistadt	43	K2
Fréjus	39	M10
Fremantle	87	C6
Fremont, Calif., United States	101	B1
Fremont, Nebr., United States	95	G3
Frenchglen	97	C2
French Guiana	109	G3
French Polynesia	85	L7
Frenda	59	F1
Fresnes-sur-Apances	43	A3
Fresnillo	105	D4
Fresno	101	C1
Fresno Reservoir	97	E1
Freudenstadt	43	D2
Freyung	35	J8
Frias	111	H4
Fribourg	43	C4
Friedburg	43	G2
Friedrichshafen	43	E3
Friesach	43	K4
Friesoythe	35	C3
Frisian Islands	27	H1
Fritzlar	35	E5
Frobisher Bay	93	T4
Frolovo	31	H5
Frome	37	K10
Frontera	105	F5
Frontignan	39	J10
Frosinone	45	H7
Frøya	29	D5
Fruges	27	E4
Frýdek Místek	33	H8
Fudai	81	L4
Fuding	79	G5
Fuengirola	41	F8
Fuentesauco	41	E3
Fuerteventura	59	C3
Fugu	79	E3
Fuhai	71	R8
Fujieda	81	K6
Fujin	73	N7
Fuji-san	81	K6
Fukuchiyama	81	H6
Fukue	81	E7
Fukue-jima	81	E7
Fukui	81	J5
Fukuoka	81	F7
Fukushima	81	L5
Fukuyama	81	G6
Fulda	35	E6
Fulda	35	E6
Fuling	79	D5
Fulton	103	D2
Funabashi	81	L6
Funafuti	85	H6
Funchal	59	B2
Fundão	41	C4
Funing	77	D2
Funtua	63	F2
Furano	81	M2
Fürg	55	F2
Furmanovka	71	N9
Furmanovo	31	J5
Furneaux Group	87	J8
Furqlus	54	E2
Fürstenberg	35	J3
Fürstenfeldbruck	43	G2
Fürstenwalde	35	K4
Fürth	35	F7
Furukawa	81	L4
Fushun	81	B3
Fusong	81	D2
Füssen	43	F3
Futog	47	G4
Fuxhou	79	F5
Fu Xian	79	D3
Fuxin	79	G2
Fuyang	79	F4
Fuyu	79	G1
Fuyun	71	R8
Fuzhou	77	F1
Fyn	35	F1
Fynshav	35	F2

G

Name	Page	Grid
Gaalkacyo	65	H2
Gabès	59	H2
Gabon	63	G5
Gaborone	67	D4
Gabrovo	47	N7
Gacé	27	C6
Gacko	47	F6
Gäddede	29	H4
Gadsden	103	D3
Găeşti	47	N5
Gaeta	45	H7
Gafsa	59	G2
Gaggenau	43	D2
Gagnoa	63	C3
Gagra	51	J2
Gaildorf	43	E2
Gaillac	39	G10
Gainesville, Fla., United States	103	E4
Gainesville, Ga., United States	103	E3
Gainesville, Mo., United States	103	C2
Gainesville, Tex., United States	103	B3

Name	Page	Grid
Gai Xian	81	B3
Gala	75	E3
Galana	65	F4
Galanta	43	N2
Galapagos Islands = Islas Galápagos	109	(1)B1
Galashiels	37	K6
Galați	47	R4
Galdhøpiggen	29	D6
Galena	101	(1)F3
Galesburg	99	B2
Galich	31	H3
Gallabat	61	G5
Galle	75	D7
Gallípoli	45	N8
Gallipolis	103	E2
Gällivare	29	L3
Gallup	101	E1
Galtat Zemmour	59	C3
Galveston Bay	95	G6
Galway	37	C8
Galway Bay	37	C8
Gambëla	65	E2
Gambier Islands	85	N8
Gamboma	65	B4
Gamboula	65	B3
Gan	73	L7
Ganado	101	E1
Gäncä	51	M3
Gandajika	65	C5
Gander	93	W7
Ganderkesee	35	D3
Gandesa	41	L3
Gāndhīdhām	75	B4
Gandhinagar	75	B4
Gandia	41	K6
Gandu	109	K6
Ganganagar	75	B3
Gangara	63	F2
Gangdise Shan	75	D2
Ganges	39	J10
Ganges	75	E3
Gangi	45	J11
Gangtok	75	E3
Gannett Peak	97	E2
Ganta	63	C3
Ganye	63	G3
Ganzhou	79	E5
Gao	59	E5
Gaoual	59	C6
Gap	43	B6
Garanhuns	109	K5
Garbsen	35	E4
Gardelegen	35	G4
Garden City	97	F3
Gardēz	53	J3
Gardone Val Trómpia	43	F5
Gargždai	33	L2
Gariau	83	(2)D3
Garissa	65	F4
Garland	103	B3
Garlasco	43	D5
Garliava	33	N3
Garmisch-Partenkirchen	43	G3
Garnett	103	B2
Garonne	39	E9
Garoowe	65	H2
Garoua	63	G3
Garoua Boulaï	63	G3
Garry Lake	93	L3
Garut	83	(1)D4
Garwolin	33	L6
Gary	95	J3
Garyarsa	75	D2
Garzê	79	B4
Gasan Kuli	53	F2
Gasht	53	H4
Gashua	63	G2
Gastonia	103	E2
Gastre	111	H7
Gatchina	31	F3
Gateshead	37	L7
Gatesville	103	B3
Gatineau	99	E1
Gatrüyeh	55	F2
Gauja	29	N8
Gaula	29	F5
Gauteng	67	D5
Gava	41	N3
Gâvbandï	55	E3
Gavdos	49	G10
Gävle	29	J6
Gawler	87	G6
Gawler Ranges	87	G6
Gaxun Nur	79	C2
Gaya, India	75	E4
Gaya, Niger	63	E2
Gaylord	99	D1
Gayndah	87	K5
Gayny	31	K2
Gaza	54	B5
Gaz-Achak	71	L9
Gazandzhyk	71	K10
Gaza Strip	54	B5
Gaziantep	51	G5
Gazipaşa	49	Q8
Gazli	71	L9
Gbaaka	63	C3
Gbarnga	63	C3
Gdańsk	33	H3
Gdov	29	P7
Gdyel	41	K9
Gdynia	33	H3
Gebel el Tîh	54	A7
Gebel Halâl	54	A6
Gebel Katherina	61	F2
Gebel Yi'allaq	54	A6
Gebze	49	M4
Gedaref	61	G5
Gediz	49	K6
Gediz	49	M6
Gedser	35	G2
Geel	27	H3
Geelong	87	H7
Geesthacht	35	F3
Gê'gyai	75	D2
Geidam	63	G2
Geilenkirchen	27	J4
Geilo	29	E6
Geinhausen	35	E6
Geislingen	43	E2
Geita	65	E4
Gejiu	77	C2
Gela	45	J11
Geladï	65	H2
Geldern	27	J3
Geleen	27	H4
Gelendzhik	51	H1
Gelibolu	49	J4
Gelibolu Yarimadasi	49	J4
Gelsenkirchen	27	K3
Gembloux	27	G4
Gembu	63	G3
Gemena	65	B3
Gemlik	49	M4
Gemlik Körfezi	49	L4
Gemona del Friuli	43	J4
Genalë Wenz	65	G2
General Acha	111	J6
General Alvear	111	H6
General Pico	111	J6
General Pinedo	111	J4
General Roca	111	H6
General Santos	77	H5
Geneva	99	E2
Genève	43	B4
Gengma	77	B2
Genil	41	F7
Genk	27	H4
Genoa = Genova	43	D6
Genova	43	D6
Gent	27	F3
Genteng	83	(1)D4
Genthin	35	H4
Geographe Bay	87	B6
George	67	C6
George	93	T5
George Town, Australia	87	J8
George Town, Malaysia	83	(1)C1
George Town, United States	103	F5
Georgetown, Gambia	63	B2
Georgetown, Guyana	109	F2
Georgetown, Ky., United States	103	E2
Georgetown, S.C., United States	103	F3
Georgetown, Tex., United States	103	B3
George West	103	B4
Georgia	51	K2
Georgia	103	E3
Georgian Bay	99	D1
Gera	35	H6
Geraldine	89	C7
Geraldton, Australia	87	B5
Geraldton, Canada	95	J2
Gérardmer	43	B2
Gerâsh	55	F3
Gerede	51	E3
Gerefsried	43	G3
Gereshk	53	H3
Gérgal	41	H7
Gerik	77	C5
Gerlach	97	C2
Germantown	99	C3
Germany	35	E6
Germencik	49	K7
Germering	43	G2
Germersheim	27	L5
Gernika	41	H1
Gerolzhofen	35	F7
Gêrzê	75	D2
Geser	83	(2)D3
Getafe	41	G4
Gettysburg	97	F2
Getxo	41	H1
Geugnon	39	K7
Gevaş	51	K4
Gevgelija	49	E3
Gewanë	61	H5
Geyik Dağ	49	Q8
Geyser	97	D1
Geyve	49	N4
Ghadāmis	59	G2
Ghadîr Minqâr	54	E3
Ghana	63	D3
Ghanzi	67	C4
Gharandal	54	C6
Ghardaïa	59	F2
Gharo	53	J5
Gharyān	59	H2
Ghât	61	B2
Ghazaouet	59	E1
Ghaziabad	75	C3
Ghazipur	75	D3
Ghazn	53	J3
Gheorgheni	47	N3
Gherla	47	L2
Ghizar	75	B1
Ghotâru	75	B3
Giannitsa	49	E4
Giannutri	45	F6
Giarre	45	K11
Gibraltar	41	E8
Gibson Desert	87	D4
Gideån	29	K5
Gien	39	H6
Gießen	35	D6
Gifhorn	35	F4
Gifu	81	J6
Giglio	45	E6
Gijón	41	E1
Gila	101	E2
Gila Bend	101	D2
Gilan Garb	51	L6
Gilazi	51	N3
Gilbert Islands	85	H5
Gilbués	109	H5
Gilching	43	G2
Gilf Kebir Plateau	61	E3
Gilgandra	87	J6
Gilgit	53	K2
Gilgit	75	B1
Gillam	93	N5
Gillette	97	E2
Gillingham	27	C3
Gills Rock	99	C1
Gilroy	97	B3
Gîmbï	65	F2
Gimli	93	M6
Gimol'skoe Ozero	29	R5
Gīnīr	65	G2
Gîôia del Colle	45	L8
Gióia Tauro	45	K10
Gioura	49	F5
Giresun	51	H3
Girga	61	F2
Girona	41	N3
Gironde	39	E8
Girvan	37	H6
Gisborne	89	G4
Gisenyi	65	D4
Gitega	65	D4
Giurgiu	47	N6
Givet	27	G4
Givors	39	K8
Giyon	65	F2
Gizhiga	73	U4
Gizhiginskaya Guba	73	T4
Giżycko	33	L3
Gjiri i Vlorës	49	B4
Gjirokaster	49	C4
Gjøvik	29	F6
Glacier Peak	97	B1
Gladstone	87	K4
Glamoč	47	D5
Glan	35	C7
Glan	83	(2)C1
Glarner Alpen	43	D4
Glasgow, United Kingdom	37	H6
Glasgow, Ky., United States	99	C3
Glasgow, Mont., United States	97	E1
Glauchau	35	H6
Glazov	71	J6
Gleisdorf	43	L3
Glendale, Ariz., United States	101	D2
Glendale, Calif., United States	101	C2
Glendambo	87	G6
Glendive	97	F1
Glennallen	101	(1)H3
Glenn Innes	87	K5
Glenrothes	37	J5
Glens Falls	99	F2
Glenwood, Ark., United States	99	B4
Glenwood, Minn., United States	99	A1
Glenwood, N.Mex., United States	101	E2
Glenwood Springs	97	E3
Glidden	99	B3
Glina	43	M5
Gliwice	33	H7
Głogów	33	F6
Glomfjord	29	H3
Glomma	29	F5
Glorieuses	57	H7
Gloucester, United Kingdom	37	K10
Gloucester, United States	99	F2
Głowno	33	J6
Głuchołazy	33	G7
Glückstadt	35	E3
Gmünd, Austria	43	J4
Gmünd, Austria	43	L2
Gmunden	43	J3
Gniezno	33	G5
Gnjilane	49	D2
Gnoien	35	H3
Goalpara	75	F3
Goba	65	F2
Gobabis	67	B4
Gobernador Gregores	111	G8
Gobi Desert	79	C2
Gobustan	53	E1
Goch	27	J3
Godbout	99	G1
Godé	65	G2
Goderich	99	D2
Godhra	75	B4
Gödöllő	47	G2
Gods Lake	93	N6
Godthâb = Nuuk	93	W4
Goeree	27	F3
Goes	27	F3
Gogama	99	D1
Goiânia	109	H7
Goiás	109	G6
Goiás	109	G7
Gökçeada	49	H4
Gökova Körfezi	49	K8
Göksun	51	G5
Golaghat	75	F3

Name	Page	Grid
Golan Heights	54	C3
Golbäf	55	G2
Gölbasi	51	G5
Gol'chikha	71	Q3
Gölcük	49	K5
Gołdap	33	M3
Gold Coast	87	K5
Golden Bay	89	D5
Goldendale	97	B1
Golden Gate	101	B1
Goldfield	97	C3
Goldsboro	99	E3
Göle	51	K3
Goleniów	33	D4
Golestänak	55	F1
Golfe d'Ajaccio	45	C7
Golfe de Gabès	59	H2
Golfe de Hammamet	59	H1
Golfe de Porto	45	C6
Golfe de Sagone	45	C6
Golfe de Saint-Malo	39	C5
Golfe de Tunis	45	E11
Golfe de Valinco	45	C7
Golfe du Lion	39	J10
Golfo de Almería	41	H8
Golfo de Batabanó	105	H4
Golfo de Cádiz	41	C7
Golfo de California	105	B3
Golfo de Chiriquí	105	H7
Golfo de Corcovado	111	F7
Golfo de Cupica	109	B2
Golfo de Fonseca	105	G6
Golfo de Guayaquil	109	A4
Golfo de Honduras	105	G5
Golfo del Darién	109	B2
Golfo dell' Asinara	45	C7
Golfo de los Mosquitos	109	A2
Golfo de Mazarrón	41	J7
Golfo de Morrosquillo	109	B1
Golfo de Panamá	105	J7
Golfo de Penas	111	F8
Golfo de San Jorge	111	H8
Golfo de Santa Clara	101	D2
Golfo de Tehuantepec	105	E5
Golfo de València	41	L5
Golfo de Venezuela	109	C1
Golfo di Augusta	45	K11
Golfo di Catánia	45	K11
Golfo di Gaeta	45	H7
Golfo di Gela	45	J11
Golfo di Genova	45	C4
Golfo di Manfredonia	45	L7
Golfo di Ólbia	45	D8
Golfo di Oristano	45	C9
Golfo di Orosei	45	D8
Golfo di Palmas	45	C10
Golfo di Policastro	45	K9
Golfo di Salerno	45	J8
Golfo di Sant'Eufemia	45	K10
Golfo di Squillace	45	L10
Golfo di Taranto	45	L8
Golfo di Trieste	43	J5
Golfo San Matías	111	J6
Gölhisar	49	M8
Golin Baixing	81	A1
Gölköy	51	G3
Gölmarmara	49	K6
Golyshmanovo	71	M6
Goma	65	D4
Gombe	63	G2
Gombi	63	G2
Gomera	59	B3
Gómez Palacio	101	F3
Gonam	73	M5
Gonbad-e Kavus	53	G2
Gonda	75	D3
Gonder	61	G5
Gondia	75	D4
Gondomar	41	B3
Gönen	49	K4
Gongga Shan	79	C5
Gonghe	79	C3
Gongliu	71	Q9
Gongpoquan	79	B2
Gongshan	77	B1
Gonzáles	95	G7
Gonzales	103	B4
González	101	G4
Goodland	97	F3
Goolgowi	87	J6
Goomalling	87	C6
Goondiwindi	87	K5
Goose Lake	97	B2
Göppingen	43	E2
Góra	33	F6
Gora Bazardyuzi	51	M3
Gora Kamen	71	S4
Gorakhpur	75	D3
Gora Ledyanaya	73	W4
Gora Pobeda	73	R4
Gora Yenashimskiy Polkan	71	S6
Goražde	47	F6
Gorbitsa	73	K6
Goré	63	H3
Gorē	65	F2
Gore	89	B8
Gorgän	53	F2
Gorgona	43	E7
Gori	51	L2
Gorinchem	27	H3
Goris	51	M4
Gorizia	43	J5
Gorki	31	N1
Gorlice	33	L8
Görlitz	33	D6
Gorna Oryakhovitsa	47	N6
Gornji Milanovac	47	H5
Gorno-Altaysk	71	R7
Gorno Oryakhovitsa	49	H1
Gorodets	31	H3
Gorontalo	83	(2)B2
Goryachiy Klyuch	51	H1
Gory Belukha	71	R8
Gory Ulutau	31	N5
Gorzów Wielkopolski	33	E5
Goslar	35	F5
Gospić	45	K4
Gosport	39	D3
Gostivar	49	C3
Gostyń	33	G6
Gostynin	33	J5
Göteborg	29	F8
Gotha	35	F6
Gothèye	63	E2
Gotland	29	K8
Gotō-rettō	81	E7
Gotse Delchev	49	F3
Gotska Sandön	29	K7
Göttingen	35	E5
Gouda	27	G2
Gough Island	57	B10
Goundam	59	E5
Gouraya	41	M8
Gourdon	39	G9
Gournay-en-Bray	27	D5
Governador Valadares	109	J7
Governor's Harbour	103	F4
Govorovo	73	M3
Gowärän	53	J4
Goya	111	K4
Gozha Co	75	D1
Gozo = Gwardex	45	J12
Graaff-Reinet	67	C6
Grabovica	47	K5
Gračac	43	L6
Gračanica	47	F5
Gradačac	47	F5
Gräfenhainichen	35	H5
Grafton, Australia	87	K5
Grafton, United States	97	G1
Graham Island	101	(1)L5
Grajaú	109	H5
Grajewo	33	M4
Gram	35	E1
Grampian Mountains	37	H5
Granada, Nicaragua	105	G6
Granada, Spain	41	G7
Granby	99	F1
Gran Canaria	59	B3
Grand Bahama	103	F4
Grand Ballon	39	N6
Grand Bank	93	V7
Grand Canyon	97	D3
Grande, Bolivia	109	E7
Grande, Brazil	109	J6
Grande Cache	93	H6
Grande Prairie	93	H5
Grand Erg de Bilma	59	H5
Grand Erg Occidental	59	E3
Grand Erg Oriental	59	F3
Grand Falls, N.B., Canada	99	G1
Grand Falls, Nfld., Canada	93	V7
Grand Forks, Canada	95	C2
Grand Forks, United States	97	G1
Grand Haven	99	C2
Grand Island	97	G2
Grand Junction	97	E3
Grand Marais, Mich.,United States	99	C1
Grand Marais, Minn.,United States	99	B1
Grand-Mère	99	F1
Grândola	41	B6
Grand Portage	99	C1
Grand Rapids, Canada	93	M6
Grand Rapids, Mich.,United States	99	C2
Grand Rapids, Minn.,United States	99	B1
Grand Teton	97	D2
Grangeville	97	C1
Granite Falls	99	A2
Granollers	41	N3
Gran Paradiso	43	C5
Grantham	37	M9
Grants	101	E1
Grants Pass	97	B2
Granville	39	D5
Granville Lake	93	M5
Gräsö	29	K6
Grasse	43	B7
Grassrange	97	E1
Grass Valley	97	B3
Graulhet	39	G10
Gravelines	27	E3
Gravenhurst	99	E2
Gravesend	27	C3
Gravina in Puglia	45	L8
Gray	39	L6
Grayling	99	D2
Grays	27	C3
Grays Lake	97	D2
Grayville	99	C3
Graz	43	L3
Great Abaco	103	F4
Great Artesian Basin	87	H4
Great Australian Bight	87	E6
Great Bahama Bank	105	J4
Great Barrier Island	89	E3
Great Barrier Reef	87	J2
Great Basin	97	C3
Great Bear Lake	101	(1)M2
Great Bend	101	G1
Great Dividing Range	87	J4
Greater Antilles	105	J5
Greater Sunda Islands	85	B6
Great Exhibition Bay	89	D2
Great Exuma	95	L7
Great Falls	97	D1
Great Inagua	105	K4
Great Karoo	67	C6
Great Malvern	37	K9
Great Nicobar	75	F7
Great Ouse	37	N9
Great Plains	97	F2
Great Rift Valley	65	E5
Great Salt Lake	97	D2
Great Salt Lake Desert	97	D2
Great Sand Sea	61	D2
Great Sandy Desert	87	D4
Great Slave Lake	91	N3
Great Victoria Desert	87	E5
Great Wall	79	C3
Great Yarmouth	37	P9
Greece	49	D5
Greeley	97	F2
Green	97	D3
Green Bay	99	C2
Greenfield	103	D2
Greenland	91	G2
Greenland Sea	91	B2
Greenock	37	H6
Green River, Wyo., United States	97	E2
Green River, Ut., United States	97	D3
Greensboro	103	F2
Greensburg, Ind., United States	103	D2
Greensburg, Pa., United States	99	E2
Greenvale	87	J3
Green Valley	105	B2
Greenville, Liberia	63	C3
Greenville, Al., United States	103	D3
Greenville, Fla., United States	103	E3
Greenville, Miss., United States	103	C3
Greenville, N.C., United States	99	E3
Greenville, S.C., United States	103	E3
Greenwood, Miss.,United States	103	C3
Greenwood, S.C., United States	103	E3
Gregory	97	G2
Gregory Lake	87	E4
Greifswald	35	J2
Greifswalder Bodden	35	J2
Greiz	35	H6
Grenada	95	J5
Grenada	109	E1
Grenchen	43	C3
Grenoble	39	L8
Gretna	103	C4
Greve in Chianti	43	G7
Greven	27	K2
Grevena	49	D4
Grevenbroich	27	J3
Grevesmühlen	35	G3
Greybull	97	E2
Greymouth	89	C6
Grey Range	87	H5
Griesheim	35	D7
Grieskirchen	43	J2
Grigoriopol	47	S2
Grimma	35	H5
Grimmen	35	J2
Grimsby	37	M8
Grimsey	29	(1)D1
Grimsstaðir	29	(1)E2
Grímsvötn	29	(1)E2
Grindsted	29	E9
Grobina	33	L1
Gröbming	43	J3
Grodekovo	79	J2
Grodzisk Wielkopolski	33	F5
Grójec	33	K6
Gronau	35	C4
Groningen	35	B3
Groote Eylandt	87	G2
Grootfontein	67	B3
Großenhain	35	J5
Großer Arber	35	J7
Grosser Beerberg	35	F6
Grosseto	45	F6
Groß-Gerau	35	D7
Großglockner	43	H3
Groswater Bay	93	V6
Grottaglie	45	M8
Groupe Actéon	85	N8
Grove Hill	103	D3
Groznyy	51	L2
Grubišno Polje	47	E4
Grudovo	49	K2
Grudziądz	33	H4
Grünberg	35	D6
Gryazi	31	G4
Gryazovets	31	H3
Gryfice	33	E4
Gryfino	35	K3
Grytøya	29	J2
Grytviken	111	P9
Gstaad	43	C4
Guadalajara, Mexico	105	D4
Guadalajara, Spain	41	G4
Guadalcanal	85	F7
Guadalquivir	41	E7
Guadalupe	105	A3
Guadalupe	105	E3
Guadeloupe	107	C4
Guadiana	41	C7
Guadix	41	G7
Guaíra	111	L3
Guajará Mirim	109	D6
Guam	85	E4
Guanambi	109	J6
Guanare	109	D2
Guane	105	H4
Guangshui	79	E4

Name	Page	Grid
Guangyuan	79	D4
Guangzhou	77	E2
Guanipa	109	E2
Guanling	79	D5
Guantánamo	105	J4
Guanyun	79	F4
Guaporé	109	E6
Guaqui	109	D7
Guarabira	109	K5
Guarda	41	C4
Guardo	41	F2
Guasave	95	E6
Guastalla	43	F6
Guatemala	105	F5
Guatemala	105	F6
Guaviare	109	D3
Guayaquil	109	B4
Guayaramerín	109	D6
Guaymas	101	D3
Guba, *Democratic Republic of Congo*	65	D6
Guba, *Ethiopia*	61	G5
Guba Buorkhaya	73	N2
Gubakha	31	L3
Guban	65	G2
Gubbi	75	C6
Gúbbio	43	H7
Guben	35	K5
Gubin	33	D6
Gudaut'a	51	J2
Gudbransdalen	29	E6
Gudermes	51	M2
Gudvangen	29	D6
Guebwiller	35	C9
Guéckédou	63	B3
Guelma	59	G1
Guelph	99	D2
Guéret	39	B7
Guernsey	39	C4
Guernsey	97	F2
Guerrero Negro	101	D3
Gugê	65	F2
Gûh Kûh	53	G4
Guiana	105	L7
Guiana Highlands	109	G3
Guider	63	G3
Guiglo	63	C3
Guildford	37	M10
Guilianova	45	H6
Guilin	77	E1
Guillaumes	43	B6
Guillestre	43	B6
Guimarães	41	B3
Guinea	63	B2
Guinea-Bissau	63	A2
Güines	105	H4
Guingamp	39	B5
Güiria	109	E1
Guise	27	F5
Guitiriz	41	C1
Guiyang	79	D5
Gujranwala	75	B2
Gujrat	75	B2
Gulang	79	C3
Gulbarga	75	C5
Gulbene	29	P8
Gulf of Aden	53	E7
Gulf of Alaska	101	(1)H4
Gulf of Aqaba	53	B4
Gulf of Boothia	93	N2
Gulf of Bothnia	29	K6
Gulf of Carpentaria	87	G2
Gulf of Finland	29	M7
Gulf of Gdansk	33	J3
Gulf of Guinea	63	D4
Gulf of Mannar	75	C7
Gulf of Martaban	77	B3
Gulf of Mexico	105	F3
Gulf of Oman	55	G4
Gulf of Riga	29	M8
Gulf of St. Lawrence	93	U7
Gulf of Santa Catalina	101	C2
Gulf of Thailand	77	C4
Gulf of Tongking	77	D3
Gulf of Venice	43	H5
Gulfport	103	D3
Gulistan	71	M9
Gülşehir	49	S6
Gulu	65	E3
Gülübovo	49	H2
Gumdag	53	F2
Gumel	63	F2
Gumla	75	D4
Gummersbach	27	K3
Gummi	63	F2
Gümüşhane	51	H3
Guna	75	C4
Guna Terara	61	G5
Gungu	65	B5
Gunib	51	M2
Gunnbjørns Fjeld	112	(1)U2
Gunnedah	87	K6
Gunnison, *Colo., United States*	97	E3
Gunnison, *Ut., United States*	97	D3
Gunong Kinabalu	83	(1)F1
Guntakal	75	C5
Guntur	75	D5
Gunung Kerinci	83	(1)C3
Gunung Korbu	83	(1)C2
Gunung Kwoka	83	(2)D3
Gunung Leuser	83	(1)B2
Gunung Mekongga	83	(2)B3
Gunung Mulu	83	(1)E2
Gunung Pangrango	83	(1)D4
Gunungsitoli	83	(1)B2
Gunung Togwomeri	83	(2)D3
Günzburg	43	F2
Gunzenhausen	35	F7
Guoyang	79	F4
Gura Humorului	47	N2
Gurk	43	K4
Gurskoye	73	P6
Gürün	51	G4
Gurupi	109	H4
Gusau	63	F2
Gusev	33	M3
Gushgy	53	H2
Gusinoozersk	73	H6
Gúspini	45	C9
Güssing	43	M3
Güstrow	33	B4
Gütersloh	35	D5
Guthrie, *Okla., United States*	97	G3
Guthrie, *Tex., United States*	101	F2
Gutsuo	75	E3
Guttenberg	99	B2
Guwahati	75	F3
Guyana	109	F2
Guyang	79	E2
Guymon	101	F1
Guyuan	79	D3
Guzar	53	J2
Gvardejsk	33	L3
Gwadar	53	H4
Gwalior	75	C3
Gwanda	67	D4
Gwardex	45	J12
Gwda	33	F4
Gweebarra Bay	37	C7
Gweru	67	D3
Gyangzê	75	E3
Gyaring Hu	79	B4
Gyaros	49	G7
Gyda	71	P3
Gydanskiy Poluostrov	71	P3
Gyirong	75	E3
Gyldenløues Fjord	93	Y4
Gympie	87	K5
Gyomaendrőd	47	H3
Gyöngyös	47	G2
Győr	47	E2
Gypsumville	93	M6
Gytheio	49	E8
Gyula	47	J3
Gyumri	51	K3
Gyzylarbat	53	G2

H

Name	Page	Grid
Haapajärvi	29	N5
Haapsalu	29	M7
Haar	43	G2
Haarlem	27	G2
Haast	89	B6
Habahe	71	R8
Habarût	53	F6
Habaswein	65	F3
Habbân	53	E7
Habbânîyah	51	K7
Habirag	79	F2
Habomai-Shoto	73	R8
Haboro	81	L1
Hachijō-jima	81	K7
Hachinohe	81	L3
Hachiōji	81	K6
Hadadong	71	Q9
Haddunmahti Atoll	75	B8
Hadejia	63	F2
Hadejia	63	G2
Hadera	54	B4
Haderslev	35	E1
Haḍhramaut	53	E6
Hadilik	71	R10
Hadjout	41	N8
Haeju	81	C4
Haenam	81	D6
Hafar al Bāṭin	55	A2
Hafnarfjördur	29	(1)C2
Haft Gel	55	C1
Hagen	27	K3
Hagenow	35	G3
Hägere Hiywet	65	F2
Hagerstown	99	E3
Haguenau	27	K6
Haicheng	81	B3
Haifa = Hefa	54	B4
Haikou	77	E3
Hā'il	53	D4
Hailar	73	K7
Hailey	97	D2
Hailong	81	C2
Hailuoto	29	N4
Haines Junction	101	(1)K3
Haining	79	G4
Hai Phong	77	D2
Haiti	105	K5
Haiya	61	G4
Hajdúböszörmény	47	J2
Hajdúhadház	33	L10
Hajdúnánás	33	L10
Hajdúszoboszló	33	L10
Hajipur	75	E3
Hajmah	53	G6
Hajnówka	33	N5
Haka	75	F4
Hakkâri	51	K5
Hakodate	81	L3
Ḥalab	51	G5
Ḥalabān	61	H3
Ḥalabja	51	L6
Halaib	61	G3
Halba	54	D2
Halberstadt	35	G5
Halden	29	F7
Haldensleben	35	G4
Halifax	93	U8
Halifax Bay	87	J3
Hall	43	G3
Hall Beach	93	Q3
Halle	27	G4
Hallein	43	J3
Halligen	35	D2
Hallock	97	G1
Hall Peninsula	93	T4
Halls Creek	87	E3
Halmahera	83	(2)C2
Halmahera Sea	83	(2)C3
Halmstad	33	B1
Haltern	27	K3
Hamada	81	G6
Hamadān	53	E3
Hamāh	51	G6
Hamamatsu	81	J6
Hamar	29	F6
Hamarøy	29	H2
Hamatonbetsu	81	M1
Hambantota	75	D7
Hamburg, *Germany*	35	E3
Hamburg, *Ark., United States*	103	C3
Hamburg, *N.Y., United States*	99	E2
Hämeenlinna	29	N6
Hameln	35	E4
Hamersley Range	87	C4
Hamhŭng	81	D3
Hami	71	S9
Hamilton, *Australia*	87	H7
Hamilton, *Bermuda*	105	M2
Hamilton, *Canada*	99	E2
Hamilton, *New Zealand*	89	E3
Hamilton, *Al., United States*	103	D3
Hamilton, *Mont., United States*	97	D1
Hamilton, *Oh., United States*	99	D3
Hamina	29	P6
Hamirpur	75	D3
Hamm	35	C5
Hammada du Drâa	59	D3
Hammam Bou Hadjar	41	K9
Hammamet	45	E12
Hammam Lif	59	H1
Hammelburg	35	E6
Hammerfest	29	M1
Hammer Springs	89	D6
Hampden	89	C7
Hāmūn-e Jaz Mūrīān	55	H3
Hanamaki	81	L4
Hanau	35	D6
Hânceşti	47	R3
Hancheng	79	E3
Hancock	99	C1
Handan	79	E3
Handeni	65	F5
Handerslev	29	E9
Handlová	33	H9
Hanford	101	C1
Hangayn Nuruu	71	T8
Hangu	79	F3
Hangzhou	79	F4
Hanīdh	55	C3
Hanko	29	M7
Hanksville	97	D3
Hanna	93	K6
Hannibal	103	C2
Hannover	35	E4
Hanö	33	D2
Hanöbukten	33	D2
Ha Nôi	77	D2
Hanoi = Ha Nôi	77	D2
Hanover	99	F2
Han Shui	79	D4
Hanson Bay	89	(1)B1
Hanumangarh	75	B3
Hanzhong	79	D4
Hao	85	M7
Haora	75	E4
Haparanda	29	N4
Hāpoli	75	F3
Hapur	75	C3
Ḥaraḍ, *Saudi Arabia*	53	E5
Ḥaraḍ, *Yemen*	61	H4
Haramachi	81	L5
Harare	67	E3
Harbin	79	H1
Harbour Breton	93	V7
Harburg	35	F3
Hardangerfjorden	29	C7
Hardangervidda	29	D6
Hardenberg	27	J2
Harderwijk	27	H2
Hardin	97	E1
Hardy	103	C2
Haren	27	K2
Härer	65	G2
Hargeysa	65	G2
Har Hu	79	B3
Haridwar	75	C3
Harihari	89	C6
Harima-nada	81	H6
Hari Rud	53	H3
Harlan	99	A2
Hārlău	47	P2
Harlem	97	E1
Harlingen, *Netherlands*	27	H1
Harlingen, *United States*	103	B4
Harlow	37	N10
Harlowtown	97	E1
Harney Basin	95	B3

Name	Page	Grid
Harney Lake	97	C2
Härnösand	29	J5
Har Nuur	71	S8
Haro	41	H2
Harricanaw	93	R6
Harrisburg, *Ill., United States*	99	C3
Harrisburg, *Pa., United States*	103	F1
Harrison	99	B3
Harrison Bay	101	(1)G1
Harrisville	99	D2
Harrogate	37	L8
Har Saggi	54	B6
Harsin	51	M6
Hârşova	47	Q5
Harstad	29	J2
Hartberg	43	L3
Hartford	99	F2
Hartland Point	37	H10
Hartlepool	37	L7
Har Us Nuur	71	S8
Harvey	97	G1
Harwich	27	D3
Harz	35	F5
Häsä	54	C6
Haselünne	35	C4
Hashtpar	51	N5
Häsik	53	G6
Haskell	103	B3
Haslemere	27	B3
Hassan	75	C6
Hasselfelde	35	F5
Hasselt	27	H4
Haßfurt	35	F6
Hassi Bel Guebbour	59	G3
Hässleholm	29	G8
Hastings, *New Zealand*	89	F4
Hastings, *United Kingdom*	27	C4
Hastings, *Minn., United States*	99	B2
Hastings, *Nebr., United States*	97	G2
Haţeg	47	K4
Hatgal	73	G6
Ha Tinh	77	D3
Hatteras	103	F2
Hattiesburg	103	D3
Hatvan	47	G2
Haud	61	H6
Haud Ogadēn	65	G2/H2
Haugesund	29	C7
Hauraki Gulf	89	E3
Haut Atlas	59	D2
Hauts Plateaux	59	E2
Havana	103	C1
Havana = La Habana	105	H4
Havant	37	M11
Havel	33	C5
Havelock, *New Zealand*	89	D5
Havelock, *United States*	103	F3
Havelock North	89	F4
Havenby	35	D1
Haverfordwest	37	H10
Havlíčkův Brod	33	E8
Havre	97	E1
Havre-St-Pierre	93	U6
Havrylivtsi	47	P1
Havza	51	F3
Hawaii	101	(2)E2
Hawaii	101	(2)E4
Hawaiian Islands	85	J3
Hawera	89	E4
Hawi	101	(2)F3
Hawick	37	K6
Hawke Bay	89	F4
Hawker	87	G6
Hawr al'Awdah	55	B1
Hawr al Ḥammar	55	B1
Hawthorne	97	C3
Hay	93	H6
Hay	93	H5
Hayange	27	J5
Haydarābād	51	L5
Hayden	101	D2
Hayrabolu	49	K3
Hay River	93	H4
Hays	103	B2
Hazard	99	D3
Hazāribāg	75	E4
Hazebrouck	27	E4
Hazelton, *Canada*	93	F5
Hazelton, *United States*	99	E2
Head of Bight	87	F6
Hearne	103	B3
Hearst	99	D1
Hebbronville	101	G3
Hebgen Lake	97	D2
Hebi	79	E3
Hebron, *Canada*	93	U5
Hebron, *Israel*	54	C5
Hebron, *Nebr., United States*	97	G2
Hebron, *N.D., United States*	97	F1
Hecate Strait	93	E6
Hechi	77	D2
Hechingen	43	D2
Hede	29	G5
Heerenveen	27	H2
Heerlen	27	J4
Hefa	54	B4
Hefei	79	F4
Hegang	79	J1
Hegura-jima	81	J5
Hegyfalu	43	M3
Heide	35	E2
Heidelberg	35	D7
Heidenheim	43	F2
Heilbad Heiligenstadt	35	F5
Heilbronn	35	E7
Heimaey	29	(1)C3
Heinola	29	N6
Hejing	71	R9
Hekla	29	(1)D3
Helagsfjället	29	G5
Helena, *Ark., United States*	103	C3
Helena, *Mont., United States*	97	D1
Helen Reef	83	(2)D2
Helensville	89	E3
Helgea	33	D1
Helgoland	35	C2
Helgoländer Bucht	35	D2
Hellín	41	J6
Helmand	53	H3
Helmond	27	H3
Helmsdale	37	J3
Helmstedt	35	G4
Helodrano Antongila	67	H3
Helong	81	E2
Helsingborg	29	G8
Helsinge	33	B1
Helsingør	29	G8
Helsinki	29	N6
Helston	37	G11
Helwan	61	F2
Hemel Hempstead	37	M10
Henashi-zaki	81	K3
Henderson, *Ky., United States*	99	C3
Henderson, *Nev., United States*	97	D3
Henderson, *N.C. United States*	103	F2
Henderson Island	85	P8
Hendersonville	99	C3
Hendijarn	55	C1
Hengelo	27	J2
Hengyang	79	E5
Henichesk	31	F5
Hénin-Beaumont	27	E4
Hennebont	39	B6
Hennigsdorf	35	J4
Henryetta	99	A3
Henzada	77	B3
Heppenheim	35	D7
Heppner	97	C1
Hepu	77	D2
Héradsflói	29	(1)F2
Herald Cays	87	J3
Herāt	53	H3
Herbert	89	C7
Herborn	35	D6
Herceg-Novi	47	F7
Hereford, *United Kingdom*	37	K9
Hereford, *United States*	105	D2
Herentals	27	G3
Herford	35	D4
Herisau	43	E3
Herlen Gol	79	E1
Hermagor	43	J4
Herma Ness	37	M1
Hermel	54	D2
Hermiston	97	C1
Hermosillo	95	D6
Hernád	33	L9
Herne	35	C5
Herne Bay	27	D3
Herning	29	E8
Herrenberg	43	D2
Hersbruck	35	G7
Herstat	27	H4
Hertlay	27	E6
Hervey Bay	87	K5
Herzberg	35	F5
Hesdin	27	E4
Heshan	77	D2
Hesselø	33	A1
Hessisch-Lichtenau	35	E5
Hettstedt Lutherstadt	35	G5
Heves	33	K10
He Xian	77	E2
Hexigten Qi	79	F2
Heze	79	F3
Hialeah	103	E4
Hiawatha	103	B2
Hibbing	99	B1
Hickory	99	D3
Hidaka-sammyaku	81	M2
Hidalgo del Parral	105	C3
Hiddensee	35	H2
Hierro	59	B3
Higashi-suidō	81	E7
High Point	99	E3
High Wycombe	27	B3
Hiiumaa	29	M7
Hikurangi	89	E2
Hikurangi	89	G3
Hikutaia	89	E3
Hildburghausen	35	F6
Hildesheim	35	E4
Hillsboro, *Oh., United States*	103	E2
Hillsboro, *Oreg., United States*	97	B1
Hillsboro, *Tex., United States*	101	G2
Hillsville	99	D3
Hillswick	37	L1
Hilo	101	(2)F4
Hilton Head Island	103	E3
Hilva	51	H5
Hilversum	27	H2
Himalayas	69	L6
Himarë	49	B4
Himatnagar	75	B4
Himeji	81	H6
Himora	61	G5
Ḩimş	54	D2
Hindu Kush	75	A1
Hindupur	75	C6
Hinesville	103	E3
Hingoli	75	C5
Hinnøya	29	H2
Hiroo	81	M2
Hirosaki	81	L3
Hiroshima	81	G6
Hirson	27	G5
Hirtshals	29	E8
Hisar	75	C3
Hisdal	29	C6
Hispaniola	107	(2)J3
Hitachi	81	L5
Hitoyoshi	81	F7
Hitra	29	D5
Hiuchi-nada	81	G6
Hiva Oa	85	M6
Hjälmaren	29	H7
Hjalmar Lake	93	K4
Hjelmsøya	29	M1
Hlinsko	33	E8
Hlohovec	43	N2
Hlyboka	47	N1
Hlybokaye	31	E3
Ho	63	E3
Hobart, *Australia*	87	J8
Hobart, *United States*	101	G1
Hobbs	101	E2
Hobro	29	E8
Hobyo	65	H3
Hô Chi Minh	77	D4
Höchstadt	35	F7
Hockenheim	35	D7
Hódmezóvásárhely	47	H3
Hodonin	33	G9
Hoek van Holland	27	G3
Hoeryŏng	81	E2
Hof	35	G6
Hofgeismar	35	E5
Höfn	29	(1)F2
Hofsjökull	29	(1)D2
Höfu	81	F6
Hohe	43	H3
Hohe Dachstein	33	C10
Hohe Tauern	45	G1
Hohhot	79	E2
Hoh Xil Shan	75	E1
Hôi An	77	D3
Hoima	65	E3
Hokitika	89	C6
Hokkaidō	81	N2
Holbæk	33	A2
Holbrook	101	D2
Holdrege	97	G2
Holguín	105	J4
Holíč	43	N2
Hollabrunn	43	M2
Holland	99	C2
Hollis	101	G2
Hollywood	103	E4
Holman	93	H2
Hólmavík	29	(1)C2
Holmes Reefs	87	J3
Holstebro	29	E8
Holsteinische Schweiz	35	F2
Holsteinsborg = Sisimiut	93	W3
Holton	103	B2
Holyhead	37	H8
Holy Island, *Eng., United Kingdom*	37	L6
Holy Island, *Wales, United Kingdom*	37	H8
Holyoke	97	F2
Holzkirchen	43	G3
Holzminden	35	E5
Homa Bay	65	E4
Homberg	35	E5
Hombori	59	E5
Home Bay	93	T3
Homestead	103	E4
Homewood	103	D3
Homs = Ḩimş	54	D2
Homyel'	31	F4
Hondo, *N.Mex., United States*	101	E2
Hondo, *Tex., United States*	101	G3
Honduras	105	G6
Hønefoss	29	F6
Honey Lake	97	B2
Honfleur	27	C5
Hon Gai	77	D2
Hong Kong	77	E2
Hongliuyuan	79	B2
Hongor	79	E1
Honiara	85	F6
Honjō	81	K4
Honokaa	101	(2)F3
Honolulu	101	(2)D2
Honshū	81	L5
Hooge	35	D2
Hoogeveen	27	J2
Hoogezand-Sappemeer	27	J1
Hooper Bay	101	(1)D3
Hoorn	27	H2
Hoorn Islands	85	H7
Hopa	51	J3
Hope, *Canada*	97	B1
Hope, *Ak., United States*	93	B4
Hope, *Ark., United States*	103	C3
Hopedale	93	U5
Hopetoun	87	H7
Hopin	75	G4
Hopkinsville	99	C3
Hoquiam	97	B1
Horadiz	51	M4
Horasan	51	K3
Horgo	73	F7
Horizon Depth	85	D8
Hormak	53	H4
Hormoz	55	F3
Horn	43	L2
Hornavan	29	J3
Horncastle	27	B1

Name	Page	Ref.
Horodenka	47	N1
Horodok	33	N8
Horqin Youyi Qianqi	73	L7
Horsens	29	E9
Horsham, *Australia*	87	H7
Horsham, *United Kingdom*	27	B3
Horten	29	F7
Hortiguela	41	G2
Horton	101	(1)N2
Ḩoseynābād	55	G2
Hoshab	53	H4
Hoshangabad	75	C4
Hospet	75	C5
Hosséré Vokre	63	G3
Hotan	71	Q10
Hotan	71	Q10
Hot Springs, *Ark., United States*	99	B4
Hot Springs, *N.C., United States*	99	D3
Hottah Lake	93	H3
Houdan	27	D6
Houdelaincourt	43	A2
Houghton	99	C1
Houlton	99	G1
Houma, *China*	79	E3
Houma, *United States*	95	H6
Houmt Souk	59	H2
Houston	95	G6
Hovd	71	S8
Hövsgöl Nuur	73	F6
Howard Junction	89	D5
Howland	85	J5
Hoxie	103	C2
Höxter	35	E5
Hoxud	71	R9
Hoy	37	J3
Høyanger	29	D6
Hoyerswerda	35	K5
Hradeç Králové	33	E7
Hranice	33	G8
Hrazdan	51	L3
Hrodna	33	N4
Hron	33	H9
Hrubieszów	33	N7
Hsin-chu	77	G2
Hsueh-Shan	77	G2
Hsweni	77	B2
Huacho	109	B6
Huade	79	E2
Huadian	81	D2
Huaibei	79	F4
Huaibin	79	F4
Huaihua	79	D5
Huainan	79	F4
Huaiyin	79	F4
Huaki	83	(2)C4
Huallaga	109	B5
Huambo	67	B2
Huancayelica	109	B6
Huancayo	109	B6
Huangchuan	79	F4
Huang	79	F3
Huangshan	79	F5
Huangshi	79	F4
Huang Xian	79	G3
Huangyan	79	G5
Huanren	81	C3
Huanuco	109	B5
Huaráz	109	B5
Huarmey	109	B6
Huasco	111	G4
Huashixia	79	B3
Huatabampo	95	E6
Hubli	75	C5
Huch'ang	81	D3
Huddersfield	37	L8
Huddinge	29	K7
Hudiksvall	29	J6
Hudson	99	F2
Hudson	99	F2
Hudson Bay	93	L6
Hudson Bay	93	P5
Hudson Strait	93	S4
Huê	77	D3
Huelva	41	D7
Huercal Overa	41	J7
Huesca	41	K2
Huéscar	41	H7
Huftaroy	29	C6
Hugo	103	B3
Hugo Lake	103	B3
Huia	89	E3
Huich'ön	81	D3
Huila Plateau	67	A3
Huinan	81	C2
Huinca Renancó	111	J5
Huizhou	77	E2
Hulin	73	N7
Hull	99	E1
Hulst	27	G3
Hulun Nur	73	K7
Huma	73	M6
Huma	73	M6
Humaitá	109	E5
Humbe	67	A3
Humboldt	93	L6
Humboldt	97	C2
Hümedän	53	G4
Humenné	33	L9
Humphrey	97	D2
Humpolec	33	E8
Hün	61	C2
Húnaflói	29	(1)C2
Hunchun	81	F2
Hunedoara	47	K4
Hünfeld	35	E6
Hungary	47	F3
Hungen	35	D6
Hungerford	87	H5
Hüngnam	81	D4
Hunjiang	81	D3
Hunsrück	35	B7
Hunstanton	27	C2
Hunte	35	D4
Hunter Island	85	H8
Huntingburg	103	D2
Huntingdon, *United Kingdom*	27	B2
Huntingdon, *United States*	103	E2
Huntington	103	D1
Huntington Beach	101	C2
Huntly	89	E3
Huntsville, *Canada*	99	E1
Huntsville, *Al., United States*	103	D3
Huntsville, *Tex., United States*	105	E2
Hunyuan	79	E3
Ḩūr	55	G1
Hurdiyo	55	J1
Hurghada	61	F2
Huron	97	G2
Hürth	27	J4
Húsavík	29	(1)E1
Huşi	47	R3
Huslia	101	(1)F2
Husn	54	C4
Husum	35	E2
Hutag	73	G7
Hutanopan	83	(1)B2
Hutchinson	101	G1
Ḩūth	61	H4
Huttwil	43	C3
Huvadu Atoll	75	B8
Huy	27	H4
Huzou	79	G4
Hvannadalshnúkur	29	(1)E2
Hvar	47	D6
Hvar	47	D6
Hvolsvöllur	29	(1)C3
Hwange	67	D3
Hyak	97	B1
Hyannis	97	F2
Hyderabad, *India*	75	C5
Hyderabad, *Pakistan*	53	J4
Hyères	39	M10
Hyesan	81	E3
Hyndam Peak	97	D2
Hyūga	81	F7
Hyvinkää	29	N6

I

Name	Page	Ref.
Iaco	109	D6
Ialomiţa	47	P5
Ianca	47	Q4
Iaşi	47	Q2
Ibadan	63	E3
Ibagué	109	B3
Ibar	47	H6
Ibb	61	H5
Ibbenbüren	35	C4
Iberia	109	C5
Ibiza = Eivissa	41	M5
Ibiza = Eivissa	41	M6
Ibotirama	109	J6
Ibrä'	53	G5
'Ibrī	55	G5
Ica	109	B6
İçel	51	F5
Iceland	25	C1
Ichalkaranji	75	B5
Ichinoseki	81	L4
Idabel	103	C3
Ida Grove	99	A2
Idah	63	F3
Idaho	97	D2
Idaho Falls	97	D2
Idar-Oberstein	35	C7
Idfu	61	F3
Idhān Awbārī	59	H3
Idhan Murzūq	59	H4
Idiofa	65	C4
Idlib	51	G6
Idstein	35	D6
Ieper	27	E4
Ierapetra	49	H9
Ifanadiana	67	H4
Ife	63	E3
Igarka	71	R4
Iggesund	29	J6
Igizyar	53	L2
Iglésias	45	C9
Igloolik	93	Q3
Ignace	99	B1
İğneada	49	K3
Igoumenitsa	49	C5
Igra	31	K3
Igrim	31	M2
Igualada	41	M3
Iguatu	109	K5
Ilharaña	67	H2
Ihosy	67	H4
Ihtiman	49	F2
Iida	81	J6
Iim	43	G2
Iisalmi	29	P5
Iiulissat	93	W3
Ijebu Ode	63	E3
IJmuiden	27	G2
IJssel	27	J2
IJsselmeer	27	H2
Ikaria	49	J7
Ikeda	81	M2
Ikela	65	C4
Ikhtiman	47	L7
Iki	81	E7
Ikire	63	E3
Ikom	63	F3
Ikopa	67	H3
Ikorodu	63	E3
Ilagan	77	G3
Īlām	53	E3
Iława	33	J4
Ilbenge	73	L4
Ilebo	65	C4
Île d'Anticosti	93	U7
Île de Jerba	59	H2
Île de la Gonâve	105	K5
Île de Noirmoutier	39	C7
Île de Ré	39	D7
Île d'Oléron	39	D8
Île d'Yeu	39	C7
Île Europa	67	G4
Ilek	31	K4
Ilek	31	K4
Île Plane	45	E11
Îles Cani	45	D11
Îles Chesterfield	85	F7
Îles Crozet	57	J10
Îles de la Madeleine	93	U7
Îles Désappointement	85	M7
Îles d'Hyères	39	M11
Îles Duc de Gloucester	85	M7
Îles Glorieuses	67	H2
Ilesha	63	E3
Îles Kerkenah	59	H2
Îles Maria	85	L8
Îles Palliser	85	M7
Île Tidra	59	B5
Île Zembra	45	E11
Ilfracombe	37	H10
Ilha da Trindade	107	H6
Ilha de Marajó	109	H4
Ilha de São Luís	109	J4
Ilha do Bazaruto	67	F4
Ilha Fernando de Noronha	109	L4
Ilha Grande de Gurupa	109	G4
Ilhas Martin Vaz	111	Q3
Ilhéus	109	K6
Iliamna Volcano	101	(1)G4
Iligan	77	G5
Ilkal	75	C5
Iller	43	F3
Illertissen	43	F2
Illichivs'k	47	T3
Illinois	95	H3
Illinois	99	C2
Illizi	59	G3
Ilmenau	35	F6
Ilo	109	C7
Iloilo	77	G4
Ilorin	63	E3
Ilovlya	31	H5
Il'pyrskiy	73	U4
Ilwaco	97	B1
Ilych	31	L2
Imabari	81	G6
Imatra	29	Q6
Imeni-Babushkina	71	G6
Imeni Polinyosipenko	73	P6
Imese	65	B3
Imī	65	G2
İmişli	51	N4
Immeln	33	D1
Immenstadt	43	F3
Ímola	43	G6
Imotski	47	E6
Imperatriz	109	H5
Impéria	43	D7
Imperial	97	F2
Impfondo	65	B3
Imphal	75	F4
Imrali Adasi	49	L4
Imroz	49	H4
Inambari	109	C6
In Aménas	59	G3
Inangahua	89	C5
Inanwatan	83	(2)D3
Iñapari	109	D6
Inarijärvi	29	P2
Inca	41	N5
İnce Burun	51	F2
Inch'ön	81	D5
Incirliova	49	K7
Indalsälven	29	H5
Independence, *Kans., United States*	103	B2
Independence, *Mo., United States*	99	B3
India	75	C4
Indiana	95	J3
Indiana	99	E2
Indianapolis	103	D2
Indian Ocean	75	D8
Indianola	99	B2
Indian Springs	97	C3
Indiga	31	J1
Indio	101	C2
Indonesia	83	(1)D3
Indore	75	C4
Indramayu	83	(1)D4
Indre	39	G6
Indre Sula	29	C6
Indus	53	K3
İnebolu	51	E3
İnecik	49	K4
İnegöl	51	C3
In Ekker	59	G4
Ineu	47	J3

Name	Page	Grid
Ingelheim	27	L5
Ingeniero Jacobacci	111	H7
Ingham	87	J3
Ingoda	73	J6
Ingolstadt	43	G2
Ingräj Bāzār	75	E3
Ingushetiya	51	L2
Inhambane	67	F4
Inírida	109	D3
Inishmore	37	B8
Inkisi-Kisantu	63	H6
Inn	43	H2
Inner Hebrides	37	F5
Inner Mongolia = Nei Monggol	79	E2
Inneston	87	G7
Innisfail	87	J3
Innsbruck	43	G3
Inongo	65	B4
Inowrocław	33	H5
In Salah	59	F3
Insein	77	B3
Inta	71	K4
Interlaken	43	C4
International Falls	99	B1
Intsy	31	H1
Inubō-zaki	81	L6
Inukjuak	93	R5
Inuvik	101	(1)L2
Invercargill	89	B8
Inverness	37	H4
Inverway	87	E3
Investigator Group	87	F6
Investigator Strait	87	G7
Inya	71	R7
Inya	73	R4
Ioannina	49	C5
Iokanga	71	F4
Iola	103	B2
Iona	37	F5
Ionian Sea	49	B6
Ionioi Nisoi	49	B5
Ios	49	H8
Iowa	95	H3
Iowa City	99	B2
Iowa Falls	99	B2
Ipameri	109	H7
Ipatinga	111	N2
Ipatovo	31	H5
Ipiales	109	B3
Ipiaú	109	K6
Ipoh	83	(1)C2
Iporá	109	G7
Ippy	65	C2
İpsala	49	J4
Ipswich	37	P9
Iqaluit	93	T4
Iquique	111	G3
Iquitos	109	C4
Iracoubo	109	G2
Irakleia	49	F3
Irakleia	49	H8
Irakleio	49	H9
Iraklion = Irakleio	25	G4
Iran	53	F3
Irānshahr	53	H4
Irapuato	105	D4
Iraq	53	D3
Irbid	54	C4
Irbit	31	M3
Irecê	109	J6
Irgiz	31	M5
Irgiz	31	M5
Irhil M'Goun	59	D2
Irian Jaya	83	(2)E3
Iringa	65	F5
Iriri	109	G4
Irish Sea	37	G8
Irkutsk	73	G6
Iron Mountain	99	C1
Ironton	103	E2
Ironwood	99	B1
Irrawaddy	75	F5
Irshava	47	L1
Irta	31	J2
Irtysh	31	P3
Irtyshsk	71	P7
Irumu	65	D3
Irún	41	J1
Irvine	37	H6
Irving	101	G2
Isabela	83	(2)B1
Isabella	99	B1
Isabella Lake	101	C1
Ísafjarðardjúp	29	(1)A1
Ísafjörður	29	(1)B1
Isahaya	79	J4
Isar	43	G3
Ischia	45	H8
Ise	81	J6
Isel	43	H4
Isère	43	B5
Iserlohn	27	K3
Isérnia	45	J7
Isetskoye	31	N3
Iseyin	63	E3
Isfana	53	J2
Ishikari-wan	81	L2
Ishim	31	N3
Ishim	31	N4
Ishinomaki	81	L4
Ishkoshim	53	K2
Isiolo	65	F3
Isiro	65	D3
Iskăr	47	M6
İskenderun	51	G5
Iskitim	71	Q7
Isla Alejandro Selkirk	111	E5
Isla Campana	111	F8
Isla Clarence	111	G9
Isla Clarión	105	B5
Isla Coiba	105	H7
Isla Contreras	111	F9
Isla de Alborán	41	G9
Isla de Bioco	63	F4
Isla de Chiloé	111	G7
Isla de Coco	105	G7
Isla de Cozumel	105	G4
Isla de la Juventud	105	H5
Isla de los Estados	111	J9
Isla de Malpelo	109	A3
Isla de Margarita	109	E1
Isla de Providencia	105	H6
Isla de San Andrés	105	H6
Isla de São Francisco	111	M4
Isla de São Sebastião	111	M3
Isla Desolación	111	F9
Isla Española	109	(1)B2
Isla Fernandina	109	(1)A2
Isla Gorgona	109	B3
Isla Grande	111	N3
Isla Grande de Tierra del Fuego	111	H9
Isla Guafo	111	F7
Isla Hoste	111	G10
Isla Isabela	109	(1)A2
Isla La Tortuga	109	D1
Isla Londonderry	111	G9
Islamabad	75	B2
Isla Madre de Dios	111	F8/9
Isla Marchena	109	(1)A1
Islamgarh	75	B3
Islamorada	103	E5
Isla Navarino	111	H10
Island Lake	93	M6
Islands of the Four Mountains	101	(1)C5
Isla Pinta	109	(1)A1
Isla Puná	109	A4
Isla Riesco	111	G9
Isla Robinson Crusoe	111	E5
Isla San Benedicto	105	B5
Isla San Cristóbal	109	(1)B2
Isla San Salvador	109	(1)A2
Isla Santa Cruz	109	(1)A2
Isla Santa Inés	111	F9
Isla Santa María	109	(1)A2
Islas Baleares	41	N5
Islas Canarias	57	A3
Islas Canarias	59	B3
Islas Columbretes	41	L5
Islas de la Bahía	105	G5
Islas de los Desventurados	111	E4
Islas Galápagos	109	(1)B1
Islas Juan Fernández	111	E5
Islas Los Roques	109	D1
Islas Marías	105	C4
Isla Socorro	105	B5
Islas Revillagigedo	105	B5
Islas Wollaston	111	H10
Isla Wellington	111	F8
Islay	37	F6
Isle	39	F8
Isle of Man	37	H7
Isle of Wight	37	L11
Isle Royale	99	C1
Isles of Scilly	37	F12
Ismâ'ilîya	61	F1
İsmayıllı	51	N3
Isna	61	F2
Isoka	67	E2
Isola delle Correnti	45	J12
Isola di Capo Rizzuto	45	M10
Isola di Pantelleria	45	G12
Isole Égadi	45	F11
Isole Lipari	45	J10
Isole Ponziane	45	H8
Isole Trémiti	45	K6
Iso-Vietonen	29	N3
Isparta	49	N7
İspica	45	J12
Israel	54	B5
Israelite Bay	87	D6
Issia	63	C3
Issimu	83	(2)B2
Issoire	39	J8
Issoudun	39	H7
İstanbul	51	C3
İstanbul Boğazı	51	C3
Istiaia	49	F6
Istmo de Tehauntepec	105	F5
Istra	43	J5
Istres	39	K10
Itaberaba	109	J6
Itabira	109	J7
Itabuna	109	K6
Itacoatiara	109	F4
Itaituba	109	F4
Itajaí	111	M4
Italy	45	E4
Itambacuri	109	J7
Itanagar	75	F3
Itapebi	109	K7
Itapetinga	109	J7
Itapicuru	109	K6
Itapicuru Mirim	109	J4
Itapipoca	109	K4
Itarsi	75	C4
Ithaca	99	E2
Ithaki	49	C6
Ithaki	49	C6
Itiquira	109	F/G7
Ituí	109	C5
Ituiutaba	109	H7
Itumbiara	109	H7
Ituni	109	F2
Ituri	65	D3
Ituxi	109	D5
Itzehoe	35	E3
Ivalo	29	P2
Ivanava	29	N10
Ivangrad	47	G7
Ivanhoe, Australia	87	H6
Ivanhoe, United States	99	A2
Ivano-Frankivs'k	31	D5
Ivanovo	31	H3
Ivatsevichy	29	N10
Ivdel'	31	M2
Ivittuut	93	X4
Ivory Coast	63	C3
Ivosjön	33	D1
Ivrea	43	C5
Ivujivik	93	R4
Iwaki	81	L5
Iwamizawa	81	L2
Iwo	63	E3
Iyo-nada	81	G7
Izberbash	51	M2
Izegem	27	F4
Izhevsk	31	K3
Izhma	31	K1
Izhma	31	K2
Izk	53	G5
Izkī	55	G5
Izmayil	47	R4
İzmir	51	B4
İzmir Körfezi	49	J6
İzmit	51	C3
İznik	51	C3
İznik Gölü	51	C3
Izola	43	J5
Izra'	54	D4
Izuhara	81	E6
Izumo	81	G6
Izu-shotō	81	K6

J

Name	Page	Grid
Jabal ad Durūz	54	D4
Jabal Akhḍar	55	G5
Jabal al Nuṣayrīyah	54	D1
Jabal an Nabī Shu'ayb	61	H4
Jabal Ash Sham	55	G5
Jabal aẓ Ẓannah	55	E4
Jabalpur	75	C4
Jabal Shammar	61	G2
Jabal Thamar	61	J5
Jabiru	87	F2
Jablah	54	C1
Jablonec	33	E7
Jablunkov	33	H8
Jaboatão	109	K5
Jaca	41	K2
Jacareacanga	109	G5
Jackman	99	F1
Jacksboro	103	B3
Jackson, Calif., United States	97	B3
Jackson, Minn., United States	99	B2
Jackson, Miss., United States	103	C3
Jackson, Oh., United States	103	E2
Jackson, Tenn., United States	103	D2
Jackson Head	89	B6
Jackson Lake	97	D2
Jacksonville, Fla., United States	103	E3
Jacksonville, Ill., United States	99	B3
Jacksonville, N.C., United States	103	F3
Jacksonville, Tex., United States	103	B3
Jacmel	105	K5
Jacobabad	75	A3
Jacobina	109	J6
Jacunda	109	H4
Jacupiranga	111	M3
Jade	35	D3
Jadebusen	35	D3
Jādū	59	H2
Jaén	41	G7
Jaen	109	B5
Jaffna	75	D7
Jagdalpur	75	D5
Jagersfontein	67	D5
Jaggang	75	C2
Jagst	35	E7
Jahrom	55	E2
Jaipur	75	C3
Jaisalmer	75	B3
Jajce	47	E5
Jakarta	83	(1)D4
Jakobshavn = Iiulissat	93	W3
Jakobstad	29	M5
Jalālābād	75	B2
Jalandhar	75	C2
Jalapa Enriquez	105	E5
Jalgaon	75	C4
Jalībah	55	B1
Jalingo	63	G3
Jalna	75	C5
Jalón	41	J3
Jalpaiguri	75	E2
Jalūlā	51	L6
Jamaica	105	H5
Jamalpur	75	E3
Jambi	83	(1)C3
James	97	G2
James Bay	93	Q6
Jamestown, N.Y., United States	99	E2
Jamestown, N.D., United States	97	G1
Jammerbugten	29	E8
Jammu	75	B2

Name	Page	Ref.
Jammu and Kashmir	75	C2
Jamnagar	75	B4
Jämsä	29	N6
Jamshedpur	75	E4
Janakpur	75	E3
Janaúba	109	J7
Jandaq	53	F3
Jandongi	65	C3
Jane Peak	89	B7
Janesville	99	C2
Jan Mayen	91	C2
Janos	101	E2
Jánossomorja	43	N3
Janów Lubelski	33	M7
Jantarnyj	33	J3
Januária	109	J7
Jaora	75	C4
Japan	81	L5
Japan Trench	85	E2
Japurá	109	D4
Jarābulus	51	H5
Jaramillo	111	H8
Jarash	54	C4
Jardim	111	K3
Jarosław	33	M7
Järpen	29	G5
Jarud Qi	79	G2
Järvenpää	29	N6
Jarvis	85	K6
Jasel'da	29	N10
Jäsk	55	G4
Jason Islands	111	J9
Jasper, Al., United States	103	D3
Jasper, Fla., United States	103	E3
Jasper, Tex., United States	103	C3
Jastrebarsko	43	L5
Jászberény	47	G2
Jataí	109	G7
Jatapu	109	F4
Jaunpur	75	D3
Java = Jawa	83	(1)E4
Javarthushuu	73	J7
Java Sea	83	(1)E4
Javoriv	33	N8
Jawa	83	(1)E4
Jawhar	65	H3
Jayapura	83	(2)F3
Jayrūd	54	D3
Jaza'īr Farasān	61	H4
Jazīrat Būbīyān	55	C2
Jazīrat-ye Khārk	55	D2
Jbail	54	C2
Jbel Ayachi	59	E2
Jbel Bou Naceur	59	E2
Jbel Toubkal	59	D2
Jean	97	C3
Jebba	63	E3
Jebel Bāqir	54	C7
Jebel el Atā'ita	54	C6
Jebel el Batrā	54	C7
Jebel-esh Sharqi	54	C3
Jebel Gimbala	61	D5
Jebel Ithrīyat	54	D6
Jebel Liban	54	C3
Jebel Mubrak	54	C6
Jebel Ram	54	C7
Jebel Uweinat	61	E3
Jedburgh	37	K6
Jedda = Jiddah	53	C5
Jedeida	45	D12
Jędrzejów	33	K7
Jefferson	99	B2
Jefferson City, Mo., United States	99	B3
Jefferson City, Tenn., United States	103	E2
Jeffersonville	99	C3
Jega	63	E2
Jēkabpils	29	N8
Jelgava	29	M8
Jemaja	83	(1)D2
Jena	35	G6
Jendouba	59	G1
Jenin	54	C4
Jenkins	99	D3
Jequié	109	J6
Jequitinhonha	109	J7
Jerada	59	E2
Jeremoabo	109	K6
Jerez	101	F4
Jerez de la Frontera	41	D8
Jerez de los Caballeros	41	D6
Jericho, Australia	87	J4
Jericho, Israel	54	C5
Jersey	39	
Jersey City	103	G1
Jerusalem = Yerushalayim	54	C5
Jesenice	47	B3
Jesenik	33	G7
Jesi	43	J7
Jésolo	43	H5
Jessore	75	E4
Jesup	103	E3
Jezioro	33	D4
Jezioro Gardno	29	J9
Jezioro Jeziorsko	33	H6
Jezioro Łebsko	33	F3
Jezioro Śniardwy	33	L4
Jezioro Wigry	33	N2
Jezzine	54	C3
Jhang Maghiana	75	B2
Jhansi	75	C3
Jharsuguda	75	D4
Jhelum	75	B2
Jialing Jiang	79	D4
Jiamusi	79	J1
Ji'an	79	E5
Jiangle	79	F5
Jiangling	79	E4
Jiangmen	79	E6
Jiangyou	79	C4
Jiaonan	79	F3
Jiaozou	79	E3
Jiaxing	79	G4
Jiayuguan	79	B3
Jibou	47	L2
Jičín	33	E7
Jiddah	53	C5
Jiesjavrre	29	N2
Jiexiu	79	E3
Jihlava	33	E8
Jijia	47	Q2
Jijiga	65	G2
Jilib	65	G3
Jilin	81	D2
Jima	65	F2
Jimbolia	47	H4
Jiménez	101	F3
Jimsar	71	R9
Jinan	79	F3
Jinapo Hu	81	E2
Jinchang	79	C3
Jincheng	79	E3
Jindřichův Hradec	33	E8
Jingdezhen	79	F5
Jinggu	79	C6
Jinghe	71	Q9
Jinghong	79	C6
Jingmen	79	E4
Jingning	79	D3
Jingxi	79	D6
Jinhua	79	F5
Jining, China	79	E2
Jining, China	79	F3
Jinja	65	E3
Jinka	65	F2
Jinsha	79	C5
Jinshi	79	E5
Jinta	79	B2
Jinxi	79	G2
Jinzhou	79	G2
Jirgatol	53	K2
Jirkov	35	J6
Jīroft	55	G2
Jirriiban	65	H2
Jishou	79	D5
Jiu	47	L4
Jiujiang	79	F5
Jiwani	53	H4
Jixi	81	F1
Jīzān	61	H4
Jizera	33	D7
J. J. Castelli	109	D4
Joal-Fadiout	59	B6
João Pessoa	109	L5
Jódar	41	G7
Jodhpur	75	B3
Joensuu	31	E2
Jōetsu	81	K5
Jõgeva	29	P7
Johannesburg, South Africa	67	D5
Johannesburg, United States	101	C1
John Day	97	C2
John o' Groats	37	J3
John Redmond Reservoir	103	B2
Johnson	103	A2
Johnson City	99	D3
Johnson's Crossing	101	(1)L3
Johnston Island	85	J4
Johnstown	99	E2
Johor Bahru	83	(1)C2
Joigny	39	J5
Joinville, Brazil	111	M4
Joinville, France	39	L5
Jokkmokk	29	K3
Jökulsá á Fjöllum	29	(1)E1
Jolfa	51	L4
Joliet	95	J3
Joliette	99	F1
Jolo	83	(2)B1
Jolo	83	(2)B1
Jonava	33	P2
Jonesboro	99	B3
Jones Sound	93	P1
Jonesville	103	C3
Jonglei Canal	65	E2
Jongunjärvi	29	P4
Joniškis	33	N1
Jönköping	29	H8
Jonquière	99	F1
Joplin	103	C2
Jordan	54	D5
Jordan	97	E1
Jordan Valley	97	C2
Jorhat	75	F3
Jörn	29	L4
Jos	63	F3
José de San Martin	111	G7
Joseph Bonaparte Gulf	87	E2
Joûnié	54	C2
Juan de Nova	67	G3
Juàzeiro	109	J5
Juàzeiro do Norte	109	K5
Juba	65	E3
Jubba	65	G3
Júcar	41	J5
Juchitán	105	F5
Judenburg	43	K3
Juhre	73	L8
Juist	35	B3
Juiz de Fora	111	N3
Julesburg	97	F2
Juli	109	C7
Juliaca	109	C7
Juliana Top	109	F3
Jülich	27	J4
Jumilla	41	J6
Jumla	75	D3
Junagadh	75	B4
Junction	103	B3
Junction City	103	B2
Jundah	87	H4
Juneau	101	(1)L4
Jungfrau	43	C4
Junggar Pendi	71	R8
Jun Xian	79	E4
Jūra	33	M2
Jura	37	G5
Jura	43	B4
Jurbarkas	33	M2
Jurf ed Darāwīsh	54	C6
Jurhe	79	G2
Jūrmala	29	M8
Jūrmala	31	D3
Juruá	109	D4
Juruena	109	F5
Juruena	109	F6
Justo Daract	111	H5
Jutaí	109	D5
Jüterbog	35	J5
Juwain	53	H3
Ju Xian	79	F3
Jūymand	53	G3
Jūyom	55	F2
Juzur al Halaniyat	53	G6
Jylland	29	E8
Jyvädskylä	31	E2
Jyväskylä	29	N5

K

Name	Page	Ref.
K2	75	C1
Kaakhka	53	G2
Kaamanen	29	P2
Kaaresuvanto	29	M2
Kaarta	59	C6
Kabaena	83	(2)B4
Kabakly	53	H2
Kabala	63	B3
Kabale	65	E4
Kabalo	65	D5
Kabardino-Balkariya	51	K2
Kabompo	67	C2
Kabongo	65	D5
Kabugao	77	G3
Kābul	53	J3
Kabwe	67	D2
Kachikattsy	73	M4
Kachug	73	H6
Kadama	75	B6
Kadaň	33	C7
Kadinhanı	49	Q6
Kadirli	51	G5
Kadoka	97	F2
Kadoma	67	D3
Kadugli	61	E5
Kaduna	63	F2
Kadzherom	31	L2
Kaédi	59	C5
Kaesŏng	81	D5
Kafanchan	63	F3
Kaffrine	63	A2
Kafiau	83	(2)C3
Kåfjord	29	N1
Kafr el Sheikh	61	F1
Kafue	67	D3
Kaga	81	J5
Kaga Bandoro	65	B2
Kagoshima	81	F8
Kahemba	65	B5
Kahnūj	55	G3
Kahraman Maraş	51	G5
Kahurangi Point	89	C5
Kaiama	63	E3
Kai Besar	83	(2)D4
Kaifeng	79	E4
Kaihu	89	D2
Kaihua	79	F5
Kai Kecil	83	(2)D4
Kaikohe	89	D2
Kaikoura	89	D6
Kaili	79	D5
Kailua	101	(2)D2
Kailua Kona	101	(2)E4
Kaimana	83	(2)D3
Käina	29	M7
Kainji Reservoir	63	E2
Kaipara Harbour	89	D3
Kairouan	59	H1
Kaiserslautern	35	C7
Kaišiadorys	33	P3
Kaitaia	89	D2
Kaiyuan	77	C2
Kajaani	29	P4
Kakamega	65	E3
Kakata	63	B3
Kakhovs'ke Vodoskhovyshche	31	F5
Kākināda	75	D5
Kaktovik	101	(1)J1
Kalabagh	75	B2
Kalabahi	83	(2)B4
Kalabakan	83	(1)F2
Kalach	31	H4
Kalachinsk	31	P3

Name	Page	Ref
Kalach-na-Donu	31	H5
Kaladar	99	E2
Ka Lae	101	(2)F5
Kalahari Desert	67	C4
Kalajoki	29	M4
Kalakan	73	K5
Kalam	75	B1
Kalamata	49	E7
Kalamazoo	99	C2
Kalampaka	49	D5
Kalaotoa	83	(2)B4
Kalapana	101	(2)G4
Kalaupapa	101	(2)E2
Kalavryta	49	E6
Kale	49	L7
Kalecik	51	E3
Kaledupa	83	(2)B4
Kalemie	65	D5
Kalemyo	75	F4
Kalevala	29	R4
Kalewa	75	F4
Kalgoorlie	87	D6
Kalianda	83	(1)D4
Kalibo	77	G4
Kalima	65	D4
Kalimantan	83	(1)E2
Kaliningrad	33	K3
Kaliningradskij Zaliv	33	J3
Kalispell	97	D1
Kalisz	33	H6
Kalixälven	29	M3
Kalkan	49	M8
Kalkaring	87	F3
Kalkaska	99	C2
Kallavesi	29	P5
Kallsjön	29	G5
Kalmar	29	J8
Kalmykiya	51	M1
Kalmykovo	31	K5
Kalocsa	47	F3
Kalol	75	B4
Kalpakio	49	C5
Kalpeni	75	B6
Kaltag	101	(1)F3
Kaluga	31	G4
Kalyan	75	B5
Kalymnos	49	J7
Kalymnos	49	J8
Kama	25	K1
Kama	65	D4
Kamaishi	81	L4
Kamande	65	D4
Kamango	71	U6
Kambarka	31	K3
Kambo Ho	81	E3
Kamchatka	73	U6
Kamchatskiy Zaliv	73	U5
Kamenica	49	E2
Kamenka, Russia	31	H1
Kamenka, Russia	31	H4
Kamen'-na-Obi	71	Q7
Kamen'-Rybolov	81	F1
Kamensk-Shakhtinskiy	31	H5
Kamensk-Ural'skiy	31	M3
Kamenz	33	D6
Kamet	75	C2
Kamiiso	81	L3
Kamina	65	C5
Kamituga	65	D4
Kamiyaku	81	F8
Kamloops	93	G6
Kamoenai	81	L2
Kampala	65	E3
Kampen	27	H2
Kampong Cham	77	D4
Kam''yanets'-Podil's'kyy	31	E5
Kamyanyets	29	M10
Kamyshin	31	J4
Kamyzyak	31	J5
Kanab	101	D1
Kananga	65	C5
Kanazawa	81	J5
Kanbalu	75	G4
Kanchipuram	75	C6
Kandahār	53	J3
Kandalaksha	29	S3
Kandalakshskiy Zaliv	31	F1
Kandi	63	E2
Kandira	49	N3
Kandy	75	D7
Kane	99	E2
Kaneohe	101	(2)D2
Kang	67	C4
Kangaatsiaq	93	W3
Kangal	51	G4
Kangān, Iran	55	E3
Kangān, Iran	55	G4
Kangaroo Island	87	G7
Kangchenjunga	75	E3
Kangding	79	C4
Kangeq	93	Y4
Kangerluarsoruseq	93	W4
Kangersuatsiaq	93	W2
Kangetet	65	F3
Kangiqsualujjuaq	93	T5
Kangmar	75	E3
Kangnŭng	81	E5
Kango	63	G4
Kangping	79	G2
Kaniama	65	C5
Kanji Reservoir	57	D4
Kanjiža	47	H3
Kankaanpää	29	M6
Kankakee	99	C2
Kankan	63	C2
Kankossa	59	C5
Kannapolis	103	E2
Kano	63	F2
Kanoya	81	F8
Kanpur	75	D3
Kansas	103	A2
Kansas	103	B2
Kansas City, Kans., United States	103	C2
Kansas City, Mo., United States	103	C2
Kansk	71	T6
Kanta	65	F2
Kantchari	63	E2
Kantemirovka	31	G5
Kanye	67	C4
Kao-Hsiung	79	G6
Kaolack	59	B6
Kaoma	67	C2
Kapanga	65	C5
Kap Arkona	33	C3
Kapchagay	71	P9
Kap Cort Adelaer = Kangeq	93	Y4
Kap Farvel = Uummannarsuaq	93	Y5
Kapfenberg	43	L3
Kapidağı Yarimadası	49	K4
Kapiri Mposhi	67	D2
Kapit	83	(1)E2
Kapiti Island	89	E5
Kaplice	43	K2
Kapoeta	65	E3
Kaposvár	47	E3
Kappel	35	C6
Kappeln	35	E2
Kappl	43	F3
Kapsan	81	E3
Kapuskasing	95	K2
Kapuvár	47	E2
Kara	71	M4
Kara, Russia	71	M4
Kara, Togo	63	E3
Kara Ada	49	K8
Kara-Balta	71	N9
Karabekaul	53	H2
Kara-Bogaz-Gol	53	F1
Karabutak	31	M5
Karacabey	49	L4
Karacaköy	49	L3
Karacal Tepe	49	Q8
Karachayevo-Cherkesiya	51	J2
Karachayevsk	51	J2
Karachi	53	J5
Karaganda	71	N8
Karaj	53	F2
Karak	54	C5
Kara-Kala	53	G2
Kara-Köl	71	N9
Karakol	71	P9
Karakoram	69	L6
Karaksar	73	K6
Karam	73	H5
Karaman	51	E5
Karamay	71	R8
Karamea	89	D5
Karamea Bight	89	C5
Karamürsel	49	M4
Karaoy	71	N8
Karapınar	49	R7
Kara-Say	71	P9
Karasburg	67	B5
Kara Sea = Karskoye More	71	L3
Karasu	51	D3
Karasuk	71	P7
Karasuk	71	P7
Karatal	71	P8
Karataş	51	F5
Karatobe	31	K5
Karaton	31	K5
Karatsu	81	E7
Karazhal	31	P5
Karbalā'	53	D3
Karcag	47	H2
Karditsa	49	D5
Kärdla	29	M7
Kareliya	29	R4
Karepino	31	L2
Karesuando	29	M2
Kargalinskaya	51	M2
Kargasok	71	Q6
Kargat	71	P6
Kargil	75	C2
Kargopol'	31	G2
Kariba	67	D3
Kariba Dam	67	D3
Karibib	67	B4
Karimata	83	(1)D3
Karimnagar	75	C5
Karkaralinsk	71	P8
Karkinits'ka Zatoka	31	F5
Karlik Shan	79	A2
Karlovac	47	C4
Karlovasi	49	J7
Karlovo	49	G2
Karlovy Vary	35	H6
Karlshamn	33	D1
Karlskoga	29	H7
Karlskrona	29	H8
Karlsruhe	35	D8
Karlstad, Norway	29	G7
Karlstad, United States	99	A1
Karlstadt	35	E7
Karmala	75	C5
Karmi'el	54	C4
Karmøy	29	C7
Karnafuli Reservoir	75	F4
Karnal	75	C3
Karnische Alpen	43	H4
Karnobat	49	J2
Karodi	53	J4
Karonga	65	E5
Karpathos	49	K9
Karpathos	49	K9
Karpenisi	49	D6
Karpogory	31	H2
Karrabük	51	E3
Kars	51	K3
Karsakpay	31	N5
Kärsava	29	P8
Karshi	53	J2
Karskoye More	71	L3
Karslyaka	49	K6
Karstula	29	N5
Kartaly	31	M4
Kartayel'	31	K2
Kartuzy	33	H3
Karufa	83	(2)D3
Karumba	87	H3
Karur	75	C6
Karvina	33	H8
Karwar	75	B6
Karystos	49	G6
Kasai	65	B4
Kasaji	67	C2
Kasama	67	E2
Kasansay	71	N9
Kasba Lake	93	L4
Kasempa	67	D2
Kasenga	67	D2
Käshän	53	F3
Kashi	53	L2
Kashima	79	L3
Kashiwazaki	81	K5
Käshmar	53	G2
Kashmor	53	J4
Kasimov	31	H4
Kasli	31	M3
Kasongo	65	D4
Kasos	49	K9
Kaspi	51	L3
Kaspiysk	51	M2
Kassala	61	G4
Kassandreia	49	F4
Kassel	35	E5
Kasserine	59	G1
Kastamonu	51	E3
Kastelli	49	F9
Kastoria	49	D4
Kasulu	65	E4
Kasumkent	51	N3
Kasur	75	B2
Kata	73	G5
Katchall	75	F7
Katerini	49	E4
Katete	67	E2
Katha	75	G4
Katherine	87	F2
Kathiawar	53	K5
Kathmandu	75	E3
Kati	63	C2
Katihar	75	E3
Katiola	63	C3
Kato Nevrokopi	49	F3
Katonga	65	E3
Katoomba	87	K6
Katowice	33	J7
Katrineholm	29	J7
Katsina	63	F2
Katsina-Ala	63	F3
Katsuura	81	L6
Kattakurgan	53	J2
Kattavia	49	K9
Kattegat	29	F8
Katun'	71	R7
Katwijkaan Zee	27	G2
Kauai	101	(2)B1
Kaufbeuren	43	F3
Kauhajoki	29	M5
Kaunas	33	N3
Kauno	33	P3
Kaunus	25	G2
Kaura Namoda	63	F2
Kavadarci	49	D3
Kavajë	49	B3
Kavala	49	G4
Kavār	55	E2
Kavaratti	75	B6
Kavarna	47	R6
Kawagoe	81	K6
Kawakawa	89	E2
Kawambwa	65	D5
Kawasaki	81	K6
Kawau Island	89	E3
Kaweka	89	F4
Kawhia	89	E4
Kawkareik	77	B3
Kawthaung	77	B4
Kaya	63	D2
Kaya	71	U3
Kaycee	97	E2
Kayenta	101	D1
Kayes	63	B2
Kaymaz	49	P5
Kaynar	71	P8
Kayseri	51	E5
Kazachinskoye	73	E5
Kazach'ye	73	P2
Kazakdar'ya	71	K9
Kazakhstan	71	L8
Kazan'	31	J3
Kazan	93	M4
Kazanlŭk	49	H2
Kazan-rettō	85	E3
Kazbek	51	L2

Name	Page	Grid
Kāzerūn	55	D2
Kazincbarcika	47	H1
Kazungula	67	D3
Kea	49	G7
Kearney	95	G3
Keban Barajı	51	H4
Kébémèr	59	B5
Kebkabiya	61	D5
Kebnekajse	29	K3
K'ebrī Dehar	65	G2
K'ech'a Terara	65	F2
Keçiborlu	49	N7
Kecskemet	47	G3
Kėdainiai	33	N2
Kedgwick	99	G1
Kédougou	63	B2
Kędzierzyn-Koźle	33	H7
Keele	101	(1)M3
Keene	99	F2
Keetmanshoop	67	B5
Keewatin	99	B1
Kefallonia	49	C6
Kefamenanu	83	(2)B4
Keflavík	29	(1)B2
Kegen'	71	P9
Keg River	93	H5
Kehl	43	C2
Keila	29	N7
Keitele	29	N5
Kékes	47	H2
Kelai Thiladhunmathee Atoll	75	B7
Kelheim	43	G2
Kelibia	45	F12
Kelkit	51	G3
Kelmë	33	M2
Kélo	63	H3
Kelowna	93	H7
Kelso	97	B1
Keluang	83	(1)C2
Kem'	31	F2
Kemalpaşa	49	K6
Kemasik	83	(1)C2
Kemer, Turkey	49	M8
Kemer, Turkey	49	N8
Kemerovo	71	R6
Kemi	29	N4
Kemijärvi	29	P3
Kemijärvi	29	P3
Kemijoki	29	P3
Kemmerer	97	D3
Kemmuna	45	J12
Kemnath	35	G7
Kemp's Bay	103	F5
Kempten	43	F3
Kendal	37	K7
Kendall	103	E4
Kendari	83	(2)B3
Kendawangan	83	(1)E3
Kendégué	63	H2
Kendujhargarh	75	E4
Kenedy	103	B4
Kenema	63	B3
Keneurgench	53	G1
Kenge	65	B4
Kengtung	77	B2
Kenhardt	67	C5
Kénitra	59	D2
Kenmore	37	C10
Kennett	103	D2
Kennewick	97	C1
Keno Hill	101	(1)K3
Kenora	95	H2
Kenosha	99	C2
Kentau	71	M9
Kentucky	95	J4
Kentwood	103	C3
Kenya	57	G5
Keokuk	99	B2
Kępno	33	H6
Kepulauan Anambas	83	(1)D2
Kepulauan Aru	83	(2)E4
Kepulauan Ayu	83	(2)D2
Kepulauan Balabalangan	83	(1)F3
Kepulauan Banggai	83	(2)B3
Kepulauan Barat Daya	83	(2)C4
Kepulauan Batu	83	(1)B3
Kepulauan Bonerate	83	(2)A4
Kepulauan Kai	83	(2)D4
Kepulauan Kangean	83	(1)F4
Kepulauan Karimunjawa	83	(1)D4
Kepulauan Karkaralong	83	(2)B2
Kepulauan Laut Kecil	83	(2)F3
Kepulauan Leti	83	(2)C4
Kepulauan Lingga	83	(1)C2
Kepulauan Lucipara	83	(2)C4
Kepulauan Mentawai	83	(1)B3
Kepulauan Nanusa	83	(2)C2
Kepulauan Natuna	83	(1)D2
Kepulauan Riau	83	(1)C2
Kepulauan Sabalana	83	(1)F4
Kepulauan Sangir	83	(2)C2
Kepulauan Solor	83	(2)B4
Kepulauan Sula	83	(2)B3
Kepulauan Talaud	83	(2)C2
Kepulauan Tanimbar	83	(2)D4
Kepulauan Tengah	83	(1)F4
Kepulauan Togian	83	(2)B3
Kepulauan Tukangbesi	83	(2)B4
Kepulauan Watubela	83	(2)D3
Kerch	51	G1
Kerchevskiy	31	L3
Kerempe Burnu	49	R2
Keren	61	G4
Kericho	65	F4
Kerio	65	F3
Kerki	53	J2
Kerkrade	27	J4
Kerkyra	49	B5
Kerkyra	49	B5
Kerma	61	F4
Kermadec Islands	85	H8
Kermadec Trench	85	J9
Kermān	55	G1
Kermānshāh	53	E3
Kermānshāhān	55	F1
Keros	49	H8
Kerpen	27	J4
Kerrville	103	B3
Kerulen	73	J7
Keryneia	51	E6
Keşan	49	J4
Kesennuma	81	L4
Keşiş Dağları	53	C2
Keszthely	47	E3
Keta	63	E3
Ketapang	83	(1)D3
Ketchikan	101	(1)L4
Kétou	63	E3
Kętrzyn	33	L3
Kettering	37	M9
Kettle Falls	95	C2
Kewanee	99	C2
Keweenaw Peninsula	99	C1
Key Largo	103	E4
Keystone Lake	103	B2
Key West	103	E5
Kezhma	73	G5
Kežmarok	33	K8
Khabarovsk	73	P7
Khadyzhensk	51	H1
Khakasiya	71	R7
Khairwāra	75	B4
Khampa	73	L4
Khamrà	73	J4
Khān al Baghdād	51	K7
Khandagayty	71	S7
Khandwa	75	C4
Khanewal	75	B2
Khannya	71	X4
Khanpur	75	B3
Khān Shaykhūn	54	D1
Khantau	71	N9
Khantayka	73	D3
Khanty-Mansiysk	31	N2
Khān Yūnis	54	B5
Khapalu	75	C1
Kharabali	31	J5
Kharagpur	75	E4
Kharampur	73	B4
Kharan	53	J4
Khargon	75	C4
Kharkiv	31	G5
Kharlu	29	R6
Kharmanli	49	H3
Kharnmam	75	D5
Kharovsk	31	H3
Khartoum = El Khartum	61	F4
Khasavyurt	51	M2
Khāsh	53	H4
Khashgort	31	N1
Khashm el Girba	61	G4
Khashuri	51	K3
Khaskovo	49	H3
Khatanga	73	G2
Khātūnābād	55	F1
Khatyrka	73	X4
Khavda	53	J5
Khawr Fakkān	55	G4
Khaydarken	53	K2
Khayelitsha	67	B6
Khemis Miliana	59	F1
Khemisset	59	D2
Khenchela	59	G1
Kherāmeh	55	E2
Kherson	31	F5
Kheta	71	T3
Kheta	71	T3
Kheygiyakha	31	P2
Khilok	73	J6
Khirbat Isrīyah	54	E1
Khīyāv	51	M4
Khmel'nyts'kyy	31	E5
Khodā Afarīn	51	M4
Kholmsk	73	Q7
Khonj	55	E3
Khon Kaen	77	C3
Khonuu	73	Q3
Khoper	31	H4
Khor	73	P7
Khor	73	P7
Khoreyver	31	L1
Khorinsk	73	H6
Khorramābād	53	E3
Khorramshahr	55	C1
Khorugh	53	K2
Khoseda Khard	31	L1
Khouribga	59	D2
Khrebet Cherskogo	73	P3
Khrebet Dzhagdy	73	N6
Khrebet Dzhugdzhur	73	N5
Khrebet Khamar Daban	73	G6
Khrebet Kolymskiy	69	U3
Khrebet Kopet Dag	53	G2
Khrebet Suntar Khayata	73	P4
Khrebet Tarbagatay	71	Q8
Khroma	73	Q2
Khudoseya	73	C3
Khudzhakh	73	R4
Khujand	53	J1
Khulna	75	E4
Khurayş	55	B4
Khushab	75	B2
Khust	47	L1
Khuzdar	53	J4
Khvormūj	55	D2
Khvoy	51	L4
Khyber Pass	53	K3
Kibaya	65	F4
Kibombo	65	D4
Kibondo	65	E4
Kibre Mengist	65	F2
Kičevo	49	C3
Kichmengskiy Gorodok	31	J3
Kicking Horse Pass	93	H6
Kidal	59	F5
Kidderminster	37	K9
Kidira	63	B2
Kiel	35	F2
Kielce	33	K7
Kieler Bucht	35	F2
Kiev = Kyyiv	31	F4
Kiffa	59	C5
Kigali	65	E4
Kigoma	65	D4
Kihnu	29	M7
Kıkıköy	49	L3
Kikinda	47	H4
Kikori	83	(2)F4
Kikwit	65	B5
Kilchu	81	E3
Kilifi	65	F4
Kilindoni	65	F5
Kilingi-Nõmme	29	N7
Kilis	51	G5
Kiliya	47	S4
Kilkenny	37	E9
Kilkis	49	E4
Killarney, Canada	99	D1
Killarney, Republic of Ireland	37	C9
Kilmarnock	37	H6
Kil'mez	31	K3
Kilosa	65	F5
Kilrush	37	C9
Kilttan	75	B6
Kilwa	65	D5
Kilwa Masoko	65	F5
Kimberley	67	C5
Kimberley Plateau	87	E3
Kimch'aek	81	E3
Kimolos	49	G8
Kimongo	63	G5
Kimry	31	G3
Kincardine	99	D2
Kinder	103	C3
Kindia	63	B2
Kindu	65	D4
Kineshma	31	H3
Kingaroy	87	K5
King City	97	B3
King George Islands	93	R5
Kingisepp	29	Q7
King Island, Australia	87	H7
King Island, Canada	73	AA3
Kingman	101	D1
Kingri	53	J3
Kingscote	87	G7
Kingsland	103	E3
King's Lynn	37	N9
King Sound	87	D3
Kings Peak	97	D2
Kingsport	103	E2
Kingston, Canada	99	E2
Kingston, Jamaica	105	J5
Kingston, United States	99	F2
Kingston-upon-Hull	37	M8
Kingston upon Thames	27	B3
Kingstown	109	E1
Kingsville	103	B4
Kingville	105	E3
King William Island	93	M3
King William's Town	67	D6
Kinik	49	K5
Kinka-san	81	L4
Kinna	29	G8
Kinsale	37	D10
Kinshasa	65	B4
Kinsley	103	B2
Kinston	99	E3
Kintampo	63	D3
Kintyre	37	G6
Kinyeti	65	E4
Kinzig	35	E6
Kipini	65	G4
Kipnuk	101	(1)E3
Kirchheim	43	E2
Kirchheimbolanden	27	L5
Kircudbright	37	H7
Kirenga	73	H5
Kirensk	73	H5
Kiribati	85	J6
Kırıkhan	51	G5
Kırıkkale	51	E4
Kirillov	31	G3
Kirinyaga	65	F4
Kirishi	31	F3
Kiritimati	85	L5
Kirkağaç	49	K5
Kirk Bulāg Dāgh	53	E2
Kirkcaldy	37	J5
Kirkjubæjarklaustur	29	(1)E3
Kirkland Lake	99	D1
Kırklareli	49	K3
Kirkūk	51	L6

Name	Pg	Ref
Kirkwall	37	K3
Kirov, *Kyrgyzstan*	71	N9
Kirov, *Russia*	31	F4
Kirov, *Russia*	31	J3
Kirovohrad	31	F5
Kiroyo-Chepetsk	31	K3
Kirs	31	K3
Kirsanov	31	H4
Kırşehir	51	F4
Kiruna	29	L3
Kiryū	81	K5
Kisangani	65	D3
Kisbér	47	E2
Kiselevsk	71	R7
Kishanganj	75	E3
Kishi	63	E3
Kishiwada	81	H6
Kishtwar	75	C2
Kisii	65	E4
Kiska Island	101	(3)B1
Kiskőrös	47	G3
Kiskunfélegyháza	47	G3
Kiskunhalas	47	G3
Kiskunmajsa	47	G3
Kislovodsk	51	K2
Kismaayo	65	G4
Kissidougou	63	B3
Kisumu	65	E4
Kisvárda	47	K1
Kita	63	C2
Kitakami	81	L4
Kita-Kyūshū	79	H4
Kita-Kyūshū	81	F7
Kitami	81	M2
Kitchener	99	D2
Kitgum	65	E3
Kitimat	93	F6
Kittilä	29	N3
Kitunda	65	E5
Kitwe	67	D2
Kitzingen	35	F7
Kiuruvesi	29	P5
Kivijärvi	29	N5
Kivik	33	D2
Kiya	73	D5
Kıyıköy	51	C3
Kizel	31	L3
Kizilalan	49	R8
Kızılırmak	51	F3
Kızılkaya	49	N7
Kizil'skoye	31	L4
Kızıltepe	51	J5
Kizlyar	51	M2
Kizlyarskiy Zaliv	51	M1
Kladanj	47	F5
Kladno	33	D7
Klagenfurt	43	K4
Klaipėda	29	L9
Klamath	97	B2
Klamath	97	B2
Klamath Falls	97	B2
Klarälven	29	G6
Klatovy	35	J7
Klaus	43	K3
Klerksdorp	67	D5
Kleve	35	B5
Klin	31	G3
Klingenthal	35	H6
Klínovec	35	H6
Klintsy	31	F4
Ključ	43	M6
Kłobuck	33	H7
Kłodzko	33	F7
Kløfta	29	F6
Klosterneuburg	43	M2
Klosters	43	E4
Kluane	93	D4
Kluane Lake	101	(1)J3
Kluczbork	33	H7
Klyuchevskaya Sopka	73	U5
Klyuchi	73	U5
Knezha	47	M6
Knin	47	D5
Knittelfeld	47	B2
Knjaževac	47	K6
Knokke-Heist	27	F3
Knoxville	99	D3
Knysna	67	C6
Koba	83	(1)D3
Kōbe	81	H6
Kobe	83	(2)C2
København	29	G9
Koblenz	35	C6
Kobo	75	G3
Kobroör	83	(2)E4
Kobryn	33	P5
Kobuk	101	(1)F2
Kobuk	101	(1)F2
Kočani	49	E3
Koçarli	49	K7
Kočevje	47	B4
Ko Chang	77	C4
Kochechum	73	F3
Kochi	75	C7
Kōchi	81	G7
Kochkor	71	P9
Kochki	71	Q7
Kochubey	51	M1
Kodiak	101	(1)G4
Kodiak Island	101	(1)G4
Kodino	31	G2
Kodinsk	73	F5
Kodomari-misaki	81	L3
Kodyma	47	S1
Köflach	47	C2
Kōfu	81	K6
Køge	33	B2
Køge Bugt	33	B2
Kohat	75	B2
Kohima	75	F3
Koh-i-Qaisir	53	H3
Koh-i-Sangan	53	J3
Kohtla-Järve	29	P7
Koidu	63	B3
Koitere	29	R5
Kokenau	83	(2)E3
Kokkola	29	M5
Kokomo	103	D1
Kokpekty	71	Q8
Kokshetau	31	N4
Kokstad	67	D6
Kolaka	83	(2)B3
Kolar	75	C6
Kolari	29	M3
Kolašin	47	G7
Kolda	63	B2
Kolding	29	E9
Kole	65	C4
Kolhapur	75	B5
Kolin	33	E7
Kollam	75	C7
Köln	35	B6
Kolno	33	L4
Koło	33	H5
Kołobrzeg	33	E3
Kologriv	31	H3
Kolomna	31	G3
Kolomyya	47	N1
Kolonedale	83	(2)B3
Kolosovka	31	P3
Kolpashevo	71	Q6
Kolpos Agiou Orous	49	F4
Kolpos Kassandras	49	F4
Kolpos Murampelou	49	H9
Kolskijzaliv	29	S2
Kolskiy Poluostrov	31	G1
Kolumadulu Atoll	75	B8
Koluton	31	N4
Kolva	31	L2
Kolwezi	67	D2
Kolyma	73	R4
Kolymskaya Nizmennost'	73	S3
Kolymskaye	73	T3
Komandorskiye Ostrova	73	V5
Komárno	47	F2
Komárom	47	F2
Komatsu	81	J5
Komi	31	K2
Komló	47	F3
Kom Ombo	61	F3
Komotini	49	H3
Komsa	71	R5
Komsomol'skiy	31	J5
Komsomol'sk-na-Amure	73	P6
Konārka	75	E5
Konda	31	N3
Kondagaon	75	D5
Kondinskoye	31	N3
Kondoa	65	F4
Kondopoga	31	F2
Kondrat'yeva	71	V5
Kondūz	53	J2
Kong Frederik VI Kyst	93	Y4
Kongi	71	R9
Kongola	67	C3
Kongolo	65	D5
Kongsberg	29	E7
Kongur Shan	71	N10
Königsberg = Kaliningrad	33	K3
Königswinter	35	C6
Königs-Wusterhausen	35	J4
Konin	33	H5
Konispol	49	C5
Konitsa	49	C4
Köniz	43	C4
Konjic	47	E6
Konosha	31	H2
Konotop	31	F4
Konstanz	43	E3
Konstinbrod	47	L7
Kontagora	63	F2
Kon Tum	77	D4
Konya	51	E5
Konz	35	B7
Kootenai	97	C1
Kootenay Lake	95	C2
Kópasker	29	(1)E1
Kópavogur	29	(1)C2
Koper	43	J5
Kopeysk	31	M3
Köping	29	J7
Koplik	47	G7
Koprivnica	47	D3
Korba, *India*	75	D4
Korba, *Tunisia*	45	E12
Korbach	35	D5
Korçë	49	C4
Korčula	47	D7
Korea Bay	81	B4
Korea Strait	81	E6
Korhogo	63	C3
Korinthiakos Kolpos	49	E6
Korinthos	49	E7
Kōriyama	81	L5
Korkino	31	M4
Korkuteli	51	D5
Korla	71	R9
Korliki	73	C4
Körmend	47	D2
Kornat	47	C6
Koroba	83	(2)F4
Köroğlu Dağları	49	Q4
Köroğlu Tepesi	49	P4
Korogwe	65	F5
Koronowo	33	G4
Koror	85	D5
Korosten'	31	E4
Korsakov	73	Q7
Korsør	35	G1
Kortrijk	27	F4
Korumburra	87	J7
Koryakskiy Khrebet	73	V4
Koryazhma	31	H5
Kos	49	K8
Kos	49	K8
Kosa	31	L3
Ko Samui	77	C5
Kościerzyna	33	H3
Kosciusko	103	D3
Kosh Agach	71	R8
Koshoba	53	F1
Košice	33	L9
Koslan	31	J2
Kosŏng	81	E4
Kosovo	49	C2
Kosovska Mitrovica	49	C2
Kosrae	85	G5
Kostajnica	43	M5
Kostenets	49	F2
Kosti	61	F5
Kostino	73	D3
Kostomuksha	29	R4
Kostroma	31	H3
Kostrzyn	33	D5
Kos'yu	31	L1
Koszalin	33	F3
Kőszeg	47	D2
Kota	75	C3
Kotaagung	83	(1)C4
Kotabaru	83	(1)F3
Kota Belud	83	(1)F1
Kota Bharu	83	(1)C1
Kotabumi	83	(1)C3
Kota Kinabalu	83	(1)F1
Kotamubagu	83	(2)B2
Kotapinang	83	(1)B2
Kotel'nich	31	J3
Kotel'nikovo	31	H5
Köthen	35	G5
Kotido	65	E3
Kotka	29	P6
Kotlas	31	J2
Kotlik	101	(1)E3
Kotor Varoš	47	E5
Kotov'sk	31	E5
Kottagudem	75	D5
Kotte	75	D7
Kotto	65	C2
Kotuy	73	G3
Kotzebue	101	(1)E2
Kotzebue Sound	101	(1)D2
Kouango	63	H3
Koudougou	63	D2
Koufey	63	G2
Koulamoutou	63	G5
Koum	63	G3
Koumra	63	H3
Koundâra	63	B2
Koupéla	59	C6
Kourou	109	G2
Koutiala	63	C2
Kouvola	31	E2
Kovdor	29	R3
Kovel'	31	D4
Kovin	47	H5
Kovrov	31	H3
Kowanyama	87	H3
Köyceğiz	49	L8
Koygorodok	31	K2
Koykuk	101	(1)E3
Koynas	31	J2
Koyukuk	101	(1)F2
Kozan	51	F5
Kozani	49	D4
Kozheynikovo	71	W3
Kozhikode	75	C6
Kozienice	33	L6
Kozloduy	47	L6
Kōzu-shima	81	K6
Kpalimé	63	E3
Kraai	67	D6
Krabi	77	B5
Kradeljevo	45	M5
Kragujevac	47	H5
Kraków	33	J7
Kraljeviča	43	K5
Kraljevo	47	H6
Kralovice	33	C8
Kramators'k	31	G5
Kramfors	29	J5
Kranj	47	B3
Krapina	45	K2
Krapinske Toplice	43	L4
Krasino	71	J3
Krāslava	29	P9
Kraśnik	33	M7
Krasnoarmeysk	31	N4
Krasnoborsk	31	J2
Krasnodar	31	G5
Krasnohrad	31	G5
Krasnokamensk	73	K6
Krasnosel'kup	73	C3
Krasnotur'insk	31	M3
Krasnoufimsk	31	L3
Krasnovishersk	31	L2
Krasnoyarsk	73	E5
Krasnoyarskoye Vodokhranilishche	71	S6

Name		Page	Grid
Krasnoznamensk	●	33	M3
Krasnystaw	●	33	N7
Krasnyy Chikoy	●	73	H6
Krasnyy Kut	●	31	J4
Krasnyy Yar	●	31	J5
Kratovo	●	49	E2
Kraynovka	●	51	M2
Krefeld	●	27	J3
Kremenchuk	●	31	F5
Kremmling	●	97	E2
Krems	●	43	L2
Kremsmünster	●	43	K2
Krestovka	●	31	K1
Krestyakh	●	73	K4
Kretinga	●	33	L2
Kribi	●	63	F4
Krichim	●	49	G2
Krishna	⊘	75	C5
Krishnagiri	●	75	C6
Kristiansand	●	29	E7
Kristianstad	●	29	H8
Kristiansund	●	29	D5
Kristinehamn	●	29	H7
Kristinestad	●	29	L5
Kriti	⊞	49	H10
Kriva Palanka	●	49	E2
Križevci	●	47	D3
Krk	●	43	K5
Krk	⊞	43	K5
Kroměříž	●	33	G8
Kronach	●	35	G6
Krŏng Kaôh Kŏng	●	77	C4
Kronotskiy Zaliv	⊵	73	U6
Kroonstadt	●	67	D5
Kroper	●	45	H3
Kropotkin	●	31	H5
Krosno	●	33	L8
Krško	●	43	L5
Krugë	●	49	B3
Krui	●	83	(1)C4
Krumbach	●	43	F2
Krung Thep	■	77	C4
Kruså	●	35	E2
Kruševac	●	47	J6
Krychaw	●	31	F4
Krym'	⊘	51	E1
Krymsk	●	51	H1
Krynica	●	33	L8
Krytiko Pelagos	⊟	49	G9
Kryve Ozero	●	47	T2
Kryvyy Rih	●	31	F5
Krzna	⊘	33	N5
Ksar el Boukhari	●	41	N9
Ksen'yevka	●	73	K6
Ksour Essaf	●	51	H1
Kuala Kerai	●	83	(1)C1
Kuala Lipis	●	83	(1)C2
Kuala Lumpur	■	83	(1)C2
Kuala Terengganu	●	83	(1)C1
Kuandian	●	81	C3
Kuantan	●	83	(1)C2
Kuçadasi	●	49	K7
Kučevo	●	47	J5
Kuching	●	83	(1)E2
Kucovë	●	49	B4
Kudat	●	83	(1)F1
Kudus	●	83	(1)E4
Kudymkar	●	31	K3
Kufstein	●	43	H3
Kugmallit Bay	⊵	93	E2
Kühbonān	●	55	G1
Kühdasht	●	51	M7
Küh-e Alījuq	▲	55	D1
Küh-e Bābā	▲	53	J3
Küh-e Būl	▲	55	E1
Küh-e Dīnār	▲	55	D1
Küh-e Fürgun	▲	55	G3
Küh-e Hazārān	▲	55	G2
Küh-e Hormoz	▲	55	F3
Küh-e Kalat	▲	53	G3
Küh-e Kührān	▲	55	G1
Küh-e Lāleh Zār	▲	55	G2
Küh-e Masāhūn	▲	55	F1
Küh-e Safīdār	▲	55	E2
Kuh-e Sahand	▲	51	M5
Kühestak	▲	55	G3
Küh-e Taftān	▲	53	H4

Name		Page	Grid
Kūhhā-ye Bashākerd	⊡	55	G3
Kūhhā-ye Zāgros	⊡	55	D1
Kuhmo	●	29	Q4
Kūhpāyeh	▲	55	G1
Kuito	●	67	B2
Kuji	●	81	L3
Kukës	●	47	H7
Kukhtuy	⊘	73	Q4
Kukinaga	●	81	F8
Kula	●	47	K6
Kulagino	●	31	K5
Kulandy	●	71	K8
Kuldīga	●	29	L8
Kulgera	●	87	F5
Kulmbach	●	35	G6
Külob	●	53	J2
Kul'sary	●	31	K5
Kultsjön	⊘	29	H4
Kulu	●	51	E4
Kulunda	●	71	P7
Kulynigol	⊘	73	C4
Kuma	⊘	31	N3
Kumamoto	●	81	F7
Kumanovo	●	47	J7
Kumara, New Zealand	●	89	C6
Kumara, Russia	●	73	M6
Kumasi	●	63	D3
Kumba	●	63	F4
Kumbakonam	●	75	C6
Kumeny	●	31	K3
Kumertau	●	31	L4
Kumla	●	29	H7
Kumluca	●	49	N8
Kummerower See	⊘	35	H3
Kumo	●	63	G3
Kumta	●	75	B6
Kumukh	●	51	M2
Kunene	⊘	67	A3
Kungrad	●	71	K9
Kungu	●	65	B3
Kungur	●	31	L3
Kunhing	●	77	B2
Kunlun Shan	⊡	75	D1
Kunming	●	79	C6
Kunsan	●	81	D6
Kunszetmarton	●	33	K11
Künzelsau	●	35	E7
Kuolayarvi	●	29	Q3
Kuopio	●	31	E2
Kupang	●	87	B2
Kupino	●	71	P7
Kupreanof Point	⊠	101	(1)F4
Kup''yans'k	●	31	G5
Kuqa	●	71	Q9
Kür	⊘	51	M3
Kura	⊘	53	E2
Kuragino	●	73	E6
Kurashiki	●	81	G6
Kurasia	●	75	D4
Kurchum	●	71	Q8
Kürdämir	●	51	N3
Kurduvadi	●	75	C5
Kürdzhali	●	49	H3
Kure	●	81	G6
Kure Island	⊞	85	J3
Kuressaare	●	29	M7
Kureyka	●	73	D3
Kureyka	⊘	73	E3
Kurgal'dzhinskiy	●	71	N7
Kurgan	●	31	N3
Kurikka	●	29	M5
Kuril Islands = Kuril'skiye Ostrova	⊞	73	S7
Kuril'skiye Ostrova	⊞	73	S7
Kuril Trench	⊘	69	V5
Kuripapango	●	89	F4
Kurmuk	●	61	F5
Kurnool	●	75	C5
Kuroiso	●	81	K5
Kurow	●	89	C7
Kuršènai	●	33	M1
Kursk	●	31	G4
Kuršumlija	●	47	J6
Kurşunlu	●	51	E3
Kuruman	●	67	C5
Kurume	●	81	F7
Kurumkan	●	73	J6

Name		Page	Grid
Kushikino	●	81	F8
Kushimoto	●	81	H7
Kushir	●	73	H6
Kushiro	●	81	N2
Kushmurun	●	31	M4
Kushum	⊘	31	K4
Kuskokwim Bay	⊵	101	(1)E4
Kuskokwim Mountains	⊡	101	(1)F3
Kussharo-ko	⊘	81	N2
Kustanay	●	31	M4
Kütahya	●	51	C4
K'ut'aisi	●	51	K2
Kutan	●	51	M1
Kutchan	●	81	L2
Kutina	●	47	D4
Kutno	●	33	J5
Kutu	●	63	H5
Kutum	●	61	D5
Kuujjua	⊘	93	J2
Kuujjuaq	●	93	T5
Kuujjuarapik	●	93	R5
Kuusamo	●	31	E1
Kuvango	●	67	B2
Kuwait	▲	55	B2
Kuwait = Al Kuwayt	■	55	C2
Kuya	●	31	H1
Kuybyshev	●	71	P6
Kuygan	●	71	N8
Kuytun	●	71	R9
Kuyumba	●	73	F4
Kuznetsk	●	31	J4
Kuzomen'	●	31	G1
Kvaløya, Norway	⊞	29	M1
Kvaløya, Norway	⊞	29	J2
Kvalynsk	●	71	H7
Kwale	●	65	F4
Kwangju	●	81	D6
Kwango	⊘	65	B5
Kwazulu Natal	▣	67	E5
Kwekwe	●	67	D3
Kwidzyn	●	29	K10
Kwilu	⊘	63	H5
Kyakhta	●	73	H6
Kyancutta	●	87	G6
Kyaukse	●	75	G4
Kyeburn	●	89	C7
Kyeintali	●	75	F5
Kyjov	●	43	N2
Kyklades	⊞	49	G7
Kyle of Lochalsh	●	37	G4
Kyll	⊘	27	J4
Kyllini	●	49	D7
Kymi	●	49	G6
Kyŏngju	●	81	E6
Kyōto	●	81	H6
Kyparissia	●	49	D7
Kyperissiakos Kolpos	⊵	49	C7
Kyra Panagia	⊞	49	G5
Kyren	●	73	G6
Kyrgyzstan	▲	71	N9
Kyritz	●	35	H4
Kyrta	●	31	L2
Kyshtovka	●	71	P6
Kystatyam	●	73	L3
Kytalyktakh	●	73	N3
Kythira	●	49	E8
Kythira	⊞	49	F8
Kythnos	⊞	49	G7
Kyūshū	⊞	81	F7
Kyūshū-sanchi	⊡	81	F7
Kyustendil	●	49	E2
Kyusyur	●	73	M2
Kyyiv	■	31	F4
Kyzyl	⊡	71	S7
Kzyl-Dzhar	●	31	N5
Kzyl-Orda	●	31	N6
Kzyltu	●	71	N7

L

Name		Page	Grid
Laascaanood	●	65	H2
Laatzen	●	35	E4
Laba	●	63	F2
La Banda	●	111	J4
La Bañeza	●	41	E2
La Baule	●	39	C6

Name		Page	Grid
Labbezenga	●	59	F5
Labe	⊘	33	E7
Labé	●	63	B2
Labin	●	43	K5
Labinsk	●	51	J1
Laboulaye	●	111	J5
Labrador	▣	93	U6
Labrador City	●	93	T6
Labrador Sea	⊟	93	V4
Lábrea	●	109	E5
Labrieville	●	99	G1
Labuha	●	83	(2)C3
Labuhanbajo	●	83	(2)A4
Labytnangi	●	71	M4
Laç	●	47	G8
Lac à l'Eau Claire	⊘	93	R5
Lacanau	●	39	D8
La Carolina	●	41	G6
Lac Bienville	⊘	93	S5
Lac Brochet	⊘	93	L5
Laccadive Islands	⊞	75	B6
Lac d'Annecy	⊘	43	B5
Lac de Bizerte	⊘	45	D11
Lac Débo	⊘	59	E5
Lac de Kossou	⊘	63	C3
Lac de Lagdo	⊘	63	G3
Lac de Manantali	⊘	63	C2
Lac de Mbakaou	⊘	63	G3
Lac de Neuchâtel	⊘	43	B4
Lac de Retenue de la Lufira	⊘	65	D6
Lac de St-Croix	⊘	43	B7
Lac des Bois	⊘	93	G3
Lac de Sélingue	⊘	63	C2
Lac Do	⊘	59	E5
Lac du Bourget	⊘	43	A5
Lacedónia	●	45	K7
Lacepede Bay	⊵	87	G7
Lac Evans	⊘	93	R6
Lac Faguibine	⊘	59	E5
Lac Fitri	⊘	61	C5
La Charité-sur-Loire	●	39	J6
La Chaux-de-Fonds	●	43	B3
La Chorrera	●	109	C4
Lac Ichkeul	⊘	45	D11
La Ciotat	●	39	L10
Lac La Biche	●	93	J6
Lac La Martre	⊘	93	H4
Lac Léman = Lake Geneva	⊘	43	B4
Lac Mai-Ndombe	⊘	65	B4
Lac-Mégantic	●	99	F1
Lac Minto	⊘	93	R5
Lac Nzilo	⊘	65	D6
Lac Onangué	⊘	63	F5
Láconi	●	45	D9
Laconia	●	99	F2
Lac Payne	⊘	93	S5
La Crosse	●	99	B2
La Cruz	●	95	E7
Lac St-Jean	⊘	99	F1
Lac St. Joseph	⊘	93	N6
Lac Seul	⊘	93	N6
Lac Tumba	⊘	65	B4
Lacul Brateş	⊘	47	Q4
Lacul Razim	⊘	47	R5
Lacul Sinoie	⊘	47	R5
Lac Upemba	⊘	65	D5
La Dorada	●	109	C2
Ladozhskoye Ozero	⊘	31	F2
Ladysmith, South Africa	●	67	D5
Ladysmith, United States	●	99	B1
Ladyzhenka	●	31	N4
La Esmeralda	●	109	D3
Læsø	⊞	29	F8
Lafayette, Ind., United States	●	99	C2
Lafayette, La., United States	●	103	C3
Lafia	●	63	F3
Lafiagi	●	63	F3
La Flèche	●	39	E6
Lafnitz	⊘	43	M3
Laft	●	55	F3
Lagan	⊘	29	G8
Lagan'	●	31	J5
Lage	●	27	L3
Lågen	●	29	E6
Lage's	●	97	D2
Laghouat	●	59	F2

Name	Page	Grid
Lagkadas	49	F4
Lagoa dos Patos	111	L5
Lagoa Mirim	111	L5
Lago Argentino	111	G9
Lago de Cahora Bassa	67	E3
Lago del Coghinas	45	C8
Lago del Flumendosa	45	D9
Lago de Maracaibo	109	C2
Lago de Nicaragua	105	G6
Lago de Poopó	109	D7
Lago di Caine	43	D5
Lago di Como	43	E4
Lago di Garda	43	F5
Lago di Lecco	43	E5
Lago di Lugano	43	E5
Lago d'Iseo	43	E5
Lago di Verano	45	K7
Lago Maggiore	43	D5
Lago Omodeo	45	C8
Lago Rogaguado	109	D6
Lagos, *Nigeria*	63	E3
Lagos, *Portugal*	41	B7
Lago Titicaca	109	D7
Lago Trasimeno	45	G5
La Goulette	45	E12
La Grand-Combe	39	K9
La Grande	97	C1
La Grange	103	E3
La Gran Sabana	109	E2
Laguna	111	M4
Laguna de Caratasca	105	H5
Laguna Madre	103	B4
Laguna Mar Chiquita	107	E7
Lagunillas	109	E7
La Habana	105	H4
Lahad Datu	77	F5
Lahat	83	(1)C3
La Haye-du-Puits	27	A5
Lāhījān	53	F2
Lahn	27	L4
Lahnstein	27	K4
Laholmsbukten	33	B1
Lahore	75	B2
Lahr	43	C2
Lahti	29	N6
Laï	65	B2
Laiagam	83	(2)F4
Lai Chau	77	C2
L'Aigle	27	C6
Laihia	29	M5
Laingsburg	67	C6
Laiwu	79	F3
Laiyuan	79	E3
Lajanurpekhi	51	K2
Lajes	111	L4
Lajosmizse	33	J10
La Junta	97	F3
Lake Abbe	65	G1
Lake Abitibi	99	E1
Lake Albert, *Democratic Republic of Congo/Uganda*	65	D3
Lake Albert, *United States*	97	B2
Lake Almanor	97	B2
Lake Amadeus	87	F4
Lake Andes	97	G2
Lake Argyle	87	E3
Lake Argyle Tourist Village	87	E3
Lake Athabasca	93	K5
Lake Austin	87	C5
Lake Balkhash = Ozero Balkhash	69	L5
Lake Bangweulu	67	E2
Lake Barlee	87	C5
Lake Benmore	89	C7
Lake Blanche	87	H5
Lake Buchanan	101	G2
Lake Callabonna	87	H5
Lake Carey	87	D5
Lake Carnegie	87	D5
Lake Chad	61	B5
Lake Charles	103	C3
Lake Chelan	97	B1
Lake Chilwa	67	F3
Lake City	103	E3
Lake Claire	93	J5
Lake Coleridge	89	C6
Lake Constance	43	E3
Lake Crowley	97	C3
Lake C. W. McConaughy	97	F2
Lake Diefenbaker	93	K6
Lake Disappointment	87	D4
Lake District	37	J7
Lake Dojran	49	E3
Lake Dora	87	D4
Lake Dundas	87	B6
Lake Edward	65	D4
Lake Elwall	97	D1
Lake Erie	99	D2
Lake Eyasi	65	E4
Lake Eyre	85	D8
Lake Eyre Basin	87	G5
Lake Eyre North	87	G5
Lake Eyre South	87	G5
Lake Francis Case	97	G2
Lake Frome	87	H6
Lake Gairdner	87	G6
Lake Geneva	43	B4
Lake Gordon	87	H8
Lake Grace	87	C6
Lake Harbour	93	T4
Lake Hauroko	89	A7
Lake Havasu	101	C2
Lake Havasu City	101	D2
Lake Hopkins	87	E4
Lake Hudson	103	B2
Lake Huron	99	D1
Lake Jackson	103	B4
Lake Kariba	67	D3
Lake Kemp	103	B2
Lake Kerkinitis	47	L8
Lake Kivu	65	D4
Lake Kyoga	65	E3
Lake Ladoga = Ladozhskoye Ozero	31	F2
Lakeland	103	E4
Lake Lefroy	87	D6
Lake Louis	93	H6
Lake Macdonald	87	E4
Lake Mackay	87	E4
Lake Macleod	87	B4
Lake Manapouri	89	A7
Lake Manitoba	93	M6
Lake Manyara	65	F4
Lake Maurice	87	F5
Lake McDonald	97	D1
Lake McMillan	101	F2
Lake Mead	97	D3
Lake Melville	93	U6
Lake Michigan	99	C2
Lake Moore	87	C5
Lake Murray	83	(2)F4
Lake Mweru	65	D5
Lake Mweru Wantipa	65	E5
Lake Nash	87	G4
Lake Nasser	61	F3
Lake Natron	65	F4
Lake Neale	87	E4
Lake Nipigon	93	P6/7
Lake Nipissing	99	E1
Lake Nyasa	67	E2
Lake Oahe	97	F2
Lake of the Woods	99	B1
Lake Ohau	89	B7
Lake Ohrid	49	C4
Lake Okeechobee	103	E4
Lake Onega = Onezhskoye Ozero	25	H1
Lake Ontario	99	E2
Lake O' The Cherokees	99	B3
Lake O' The Pines	103	C3
Lake Paringa	89	B6
Lake Peipus	29	P7
Lake Placid	103	E4
Lakeport	97	B3
Lake Poteriteri	89	A8
Lake Powell	97	D3
Lake Prespa	49	D4
Lake Providence	103	C3
Lake Pskov	29	P7
Lake Pukaki	89	C7
Lake Rotorua	89	F4
Lake Rukwa	65	E5
Lake St. Lucia	67	E5
Lake Sakakawea	97	F1
Lake Scutari	47	G7
Lake Simcoe	99	E2
Lake Superior	99	C1
Lake Tahoe	97	B3
Lake Tanganyika	65	D5
Lake Taupo	89	E4
Lake Te Anau	89	A7
Lake Tekapo	89	C6
Lake Tekapo	89	C6
Lake Texoma	103	B3
Lake Torrens	87	G6
Lake Travis	101	G2
Lake Tschida	97	F1
Lake Turkana	65	F3
Lake Victoria	65	E4
Lakeview	97	B2
Lake Volta	63	D3
Lake Waikare	89	E3
Lake Waikaremoana	89	F4
Lake Wakatipu	89	B7
Lake Wanaka	89	B7
Lake White	87	E4
Lake Wills	87	E4
Lake Winnipeg	93	M6
Lake Winnipegosis	93	L6
Lakewood	97	E3
Lake Woods	87	F3
Lake Xau	67	C4
Lake Yamma Yamma	87	H5
Lakhdaria	41	P8
Lakhimpur	75	D3
Lakhpat	75	A4
Lakin	103	A2
Lakki	75	B2
Lakota	97	G1
Lalín	41	B2
La Línea	41	E8
Lalitpur	75	C4
Lal-Lo	77	G3
La Loche	93	K5
La Louvière	27	G4
La Maddalena	45	D7
Lamar, *Colo., United States*	101	F1
Lamar, *Mo., United States*	103	C2
Lamard	55	E3
La Marsa	45	E12
Lambaréné	63	G5
Lambay Island	37	G8
Lam Chi	77	C3
Lamesa	101	F2
Lamia	49	E6
Lamone	43	G6
Lampang	77	B3
Lampasas	101	G2
Lampedusa	59	H1
Lamu	65	G4
Lanai	101	(2)D3
Lanai City	101	(2)E3
Lancang	77	B2
Lancaster, *United Kingdom*	37	K7
Lancaster, *Mo., United States*	99	B2
Lancaster, *N.H., United States*	99	F2
Lancaster, *Oh., United States*	99	D3
Lancaster, *Pa., United States*	99	E2
Lancaster, *S.C., United States*	103	E3
Lancaster Sound	93	Q2
Lanciano	45	J6
Landau, *Germany*	27	L5
Landau, *Germany*	43	H2
Landeck	43	F3
Lander	97	E2
Landerneau	39	A5
Landor	87	C5
Landsberg	43	F2
Land's End	37	F11
Landshut	43	H2
Landskrona	33	C3
Landstuhl	27	K5
Land Wursten	35	D3
La'nga Co	75	D2
Langarüd	51	N5
Langdon	97	F1
Langeland	35	F2
Langen	27	L5
Langenau	43	F2
Langenhagen	35	E4
Langeoog	35	C3
Langfang	79	F3
Langjökull	29	(1)C2
Langkawi	77	B5
Langkon	77	F5
Langon	39	E9
Langøya	29	H2
Langreo	41	E1
Langres	43	A3
Langsa	77	B6
Langtry	101	F3
Langvatnet	29	G3
Länkäran	51	N4
Lannion	39	B5
L'Anse	99	C1
Lansing	99	D2
Lanxi	79	H1
Lanya	65	E2
Lanzarote	59	C3
Lanzhou	79	C3
Laoag	77	G3
Lao Cai	77	C2
Laohekou	79	E4
Laon	27	F5
La Oroya	109	B6
Laos	77	C3
Laotougou	81	E2
Lapa	111	M4
La Palma	59	B3
La Palma	105	J7
La Paragua	109	E2
La Paz, *Argentina*	111	K5
La Paz, *Bolivia*	109	D7
La Paz, *Mexico*	105	B4
La Pedrera	109	D4
La Perla	101	F3
La Pérouse Strait	79	L1
La Pesca	103	B5
La Pine	97	B2
Lapithos	54	A1
La Plant	97	F1
La Plata	111	K5
Lappajärvi	29	M5
Lappeenranta	29	Q6
Lappland	29	M2
Laptev Sea = More Laptevykh	73	L1
Lapua	29	M5
Łapy	33	M5
La Quiaca	111	H3
L'Aquila	45	H6
Lār	55	F3
Larache	59	D1
Laramie	97	E2
Laramie Range	97	E2
Larantuka	83	(2)B4
Larat	83	(2)D4
Larba	41	P8
Laredo, *Spain*	41	G1
Laredo, *United States*	101	G3
Largo	103	E4
L'Ariana	45	E12
La Rioja	111	H4
Larisa	49	E5
Larkana	53	J4
Larnaka	54	A2
Larne	37	G7
La Rochelle	39	D7
La Roche-sur-Yon	39	D7
La Roda	41	H5
La Romana	105	L5
La Ronge	93	K5
Lar'yak	71	Q5
La Sarre	99	E1
Las Cabezas de San Juan	41	E7
Las Cruces	101	E2
La Serena	111	G4
La Seu d'Urgell	41	M2
La Seyne-sur-Mer	39	L10
Lashio	77	B2
Lashkar Gāh	53	H3
Łask	33	J6
Las Lomitas	111	J3
La Solana	41	G6
Las Palmas	59	B3
La Spézia	43	E6
Las Plumas	111	H7
Last Chance	97	F3
Lastoursville	63	G5
Lastovo	47	D7

Name	Page	Grid
Las Varas	95	E7
Las Varillas	111	J5
Las Vegas, *Nev., United States*	97	C3
Las Vegas, *N.Mex., United States*	101	E1
La Teste	39	D9
Latina	45	G7
Latisana	43	J5
La Toma	111	H5
La Tuque	99	F1
Latur	75	C5
Latvia	29	M8
Lauchhammer	35	J5
Lauenburg	35	F3
Lauf	35	G7
Lau Group	85	J7
Launceston, *Australia*	87	J8
Launceston, *United Kingdom*	37	H11
La Union	41	K7
Laupheim	43	E2
Laura	87	H3
Laurel	103	D3
Lauria	45	K8
Laurinburg	103	F3
Lausanne	43	B4
Laut, *Indonesia*	83	(1)F3
Laut, *Malaysia*	83	(1)D2
Lauter	27	K5
Lauterbach	35	E6
Lava	33	L3
Laval, *Canada*	99	F1
Laval, *France*	39	E5
La Vall d'Uixo	41	K5
Lavant	43	K4
La Vega	105	K5
Laviana	41	E1
La Vila Joiosa	41	K6
Lavras	111	N3
Lavrentiya	73	Z3
Lavrio	49	G7
Lawdar	61	J5
Lawra	63	D2
Lawrence, *New Zealand*	89	B7
Lawrence, *Kans., United States*	99	A3
Lawrence, *Mass., United States*	99	F2
Lawrenceville	103	D2
Lawton	103	B3
Laya	31	L1
Laylä	61	J3
Laysan Island	85	J3
Layton	97	D2
Lazarev	73	Q6
Lázaro Cárdenas	105	D5
Lazdijai	33	N3
Lazo	73	P3
Leadville	97	E3
Leamington	99	D2
Leavenworth, *Kans., United States*	99	A3
Leavenworth, *Wash., United States*	97	B1
Lebach	27	J5
Lebanon	54	C3
Lebanon, *Mo., United States*	99	B3
Lebanon, *N.H., United States*	99	F2
Lebanon, *Pa., United States*	99	E2
Lebanon, *Tenn., United States*	99	C3
Lebel-sur-Quévillon	99	E1
Lębork	33	G3
Lebrija	41	D8
Lebu	111	G6
Lecce	45	N8
Lecco	43	E5
Lech	43	F3
Leck	35	D2
Le Creusot	39	K7
Łęczna	33	M6
Łęczyca	33	J5
Ledmozero	29	R4
Lee	37	D10
Leech Lake	99	B1
Leeds	37	L8
Leek	27	A1
Leer	27	K1
Leesburg	103	E4
Leeston	89	D6
Leesville	103	C3
Leeuwarden	27	H1
Leeward Islands	105	M5
Lefkada	49	C6
Lefkada	49	C6
Lefkimmi	49	C5
Lefkonikon	54	A1
Lefkosia	49	R9
Legaspi	77	G4
Legionowo	33	K5
Legnago	43	G5
Legnica	33	F6
Leh	75	C2
Le Havre	27	C5
Lehrte	35	F4
Leiah	75	B2
Leibnitz	43	L4
Leicester	27	A2
Leiden	27	G2
Leie	27	F4
Leigh Creek	87	G6
Leighton Buzzard	27	B3
Leine	35	E4
Leinster	87	D5
Leipzig	35	H5
Leiria	41	B5
Leitrim	37	D8
Leiyang	79	E5
Lek	27	G3
Lelystad	27	H2
Le Mans	39	F6
Le Mars	99	A2
Lemberg	35	D8
Lemesos	49	Q10
Lemgo	27	L2
Lemieux Islands	93	U4
Lemmer	27	H2
Lemmon	97	F1
Le Muret	39	E9
Lena	41	E1
Lena	73	L4
Lendinare	43	G5
Lengerich	27	K2
Lengshuijiang	79	E5
Lengshuitan	79	E5
Leninsk-Kuznetskiy	71	R7
Leninskoye	31	J3
Lenmalu	83	(2)D3
Lenne	27	K3
Lennestadt	27	L3
Lens	27	E4
Lensk	73	K4
Lenti	43	M4
Lentini	45	J11
Léo	63	D2
Leoben	43	L3
León, *Mexico*	105	D4
León, *Nicaragua*	105	G6
León, *Spain*	41	E2
Leonberg	43	E2
Leonforte	45	J11
Leonidi	49	E7
Leonora	87	D5
Le Perthus	39	H11
Lepsy	71	P8
Le Puy	39	J8
Léré	63	G3
Lérici	43	E6
Lerik	51	N4
Lerma	41	G2
Leros	49	J7
Lerwick	37	L1
Lešak	47	H6
Les Andelys	27	D5
Lesatima	65	F4
Lesbos = Lesvos	49	H5
Les Escaldes	39	G11
Les Escoumins	93	T7
Leshan	79	C5
Les Herbiers	39	D7
Leshukonskoye	31	J2
Leskovac	47	J7
Lesosibirsk	71	S6
Lesotho	67	D5
Lesozavodsk	81	G1
Les Sables-d'Olonne	39	D7
Les Sept Îles	39	B5
Lesser Antilles	105	L6
Lesser Slave Lake	93	J5
Lesvos	49	H5
Leszno	33	F6
Letaba	67	E4
Letchworth	27	B3
Letenye	43	M4
Lethbridge	97	D1
Lethem	109	F3
Leticia	109	D4
Letpadan	77	B3
Le Tréport	27	D4
Letterkenny	37	E7
Leutkirch	43	F3
Leuven	27	G4
Leuze	27	F4
Levadeia	49	E6
Lévanzo	45	G10
Levashi	51	M2
Levaya Khetta	31	P2
Leverkusen	27	J3
Levice	33	H9
Levico Terme	43	G4
Levin	89	E5
Lévis	99	F1
Levitha	49	J7
Levoča	33	K9
Levski	47	N6
Lewes	27	C4
Lewis	37	F3
Lewis and Clark Lake	97	G2
Lewis Range	93	J7
Lewiston, *Id., United States*	97	C1
Lewiston, *Me., United States*	99	F2
Lewistown, *Mont., United States*	97	E1
Lewistown, *Pa., United States*	99	E2
Lexington, *Ky., United States*	99	D3
Lexington, *Nebr., United States*	97	G2
Lexington, *Va., United States*	99	E3
Lexington Park	103	F2
Leyte	77	G4
Lezhë	47	G8
Lhari	75	F2
Lhasa	75	F3
Lhazà	75	E3
Lhokseumawe	77	B5
Lian Xian	77	E2
Lianyuan	77	E1
Lianyungang	79	F4
Liaocheng	79	F3
Liao He	81	B3
Liaoyang	81	B3
Liaoyuan	81	C2
Liard	93	F5
Liard River	93	F5
Libby	97	C1
Libenge	65	B3
Liberal	103	A2
Liberec	33	E7
Liberia	63	B3
Liberia	105	G6
Liberty	103	C1
Libjo	77	H4
Libourne	39	E9
Libreville	63	F4
Libya	61	C2
Libyan Desert	61	D2
Libyan Plateau	61	E1
Licata	45	H11
Lich	35	D6
Lichinga	67	F2
Lichtenfels	35	G6
Lida	29	N10
Lidköping	29	G7
Lido di Óstia	45	G7
Lidzbark Warmiński	33	K3
Liebenwalde	35	J4
Liechtenstein	43	E3
Liège	27	H4
Lieksa	29	R5
Lienz	43	H4
Liepāja	33	L1
Lier	27	G3
Liezen	43	K3
Lifford	37	E7
Lignières	39	H7
Ligueil	39	F6
Ligurian Sea	43	D7
Lihue	101	B2
Lijiang	77	C1
Likasi	65	D6
Lilienfeld	43	L2
Lille	27	F4
Lillebonne	27	C5
Lillehammer	29	F6
Lillerto	43	G3
Lilongwe	67	E2
Liloy	77	G5
Lima, *Peru*	109	B6
Lima, *Mont., United States*	97	D2
Lima, *Oh., United States*	99	D2
Limanowa	33	K8
Limassol = Lemesos	49	Q10
Limbaži	29	N8
Limburg	27	L4
Limeira	111	M3
Limerick	37	D9
Limingen	29	G4
Limni Kastorias	49	C4
Limni Kerkinitis	49	E3
Limni Koronia	49	F4
Limni Trichonida	49	D6
Limni Vegoritis	49	D4
Limni Volvi	49	F4
Limnos	49	H5
Limoges	39	G8
Limon	97	F3
Limón	105	H7
Limoux	39	H10
Limpopo	67	D4
Linares, *Chile*	111	G6
Linares, *Mexico*	101	G4
Linares, *Spain*	41	G6
Lincang	77	C2
Linchuan	79	F5
Lincoln, *United Kingdom*	27	B1
Lincoln, *Ill., United States*	99	C2
Lincoln, *Me., United States*	99	G1
Lincoln, *Nebr., United States*	97	G2
Lincoln, *N.H., United States*	99	F2
Lindenow Fjord	93	Y4
Lindesnes	29	D8
Lindi	65	D3
Lindi	65	F6
Lindos	49	L8
Line Islands	85	L5
Linfen	79	E3
Lingen	27	K2
Lingga	83	(1)C3
Lingshui	77	D3
Linguère	63	A1
Lingyuan	79	F2
Linhal	79	G5
Linhares	109	J7
Linhe	79	D2
Linjiang	81	D3
Linköping	29	H7
Linkou	81	F1
Linosa	45	G13
Lins	111	M3
Linton	97	F1
Linxia	79	C3
Lin Xian	79	E3
Linyi	79	F3
Linz	43	K2
Liobomil'	33	P6
Lipari	45	J10
Lipari	45	J10
Lipcani	47	P1
Lipetsk	31	G4
Lipin Bor	31	G2
Lipno	33	J5
Lipova	47	H3
Lippe	27	L3
Lippstadt	27	L3
Lipsoi	49	J7
Liptovský-Mikuláš	33	J8
Lipu	77	E2
Liqeni i Fierzës	47	H7
Liqeni Komanit	47	G7
Lira	65	E3
Liri	45	H7
Lisala	65	C3
Lisboa	41	A6
Lisbon = Lisboa	41	A6

Name	Page	Grid
Lisburn	37	G7
Liscannor Bay	37	C9
Lishi	79	E3
Lishui	79	F5
Lisieux	27	C5
Liski	31	G4
L'Isle-sur-la-Sorgue	39	L10
Lisse	27	G2
Lištica	45	M5
Listowel	37	C9
Listvyanka	73	H6
Litang	79	C5
Litani	109	G3
Litava	33	F8
Litchfield, Ill., United States	99	C3
Litchfield, Minn., United States	99	B1
Lithgow	87	K6
Lithuania	29	L9
Litke	73	Q6
Litomerice	35	K6
Litomyši	33	F8
Litovel	33	G8
Litovko	73	P7
Little Abaco	103	F4
Little Andaman	75	F6
Little Barrier Island	89	E3
Little Current	99	D1
Little Desert	87	H7
Little Falls	99	B1
Littlefield	101	F2
Little Inagua	105	K4
Little Karoo	67	C6
Little Minch	37	E4
Little Nicobar	75	F7
Little Ouse	27	C2
Little Rock	103	C3
Littleton	97	E3
Litvinov	35	J6
Liupanshui	79	C5
Liuzhou	79	D6
Live Oak	103	E3
Liverpool	37	K8
Liverpool Bay	93	F2
Livingston, United Kingdom	37	J6
Livingston, United States	97	D1
Livingstone	67	D3
Livingstonia	67	E2
Livno	47	E6
Livny	31	G4
Livonia	99	D2
Livorno	43	F7
Liwale	65	F5
Lizard Point	37	G12
Ljubljana	43	K4
Ljugarn	29	K8
Ljungan	29	J5
Ljungby	29	G8
Ljusdal	29	J6
Ljusnan	31	C2
Llandovery	37	J9
Llandudno	37	J8
Llanelli	37	H10
Llanes	41	F1
Llanos	109	C2
Lleida	41	L3
Lli	71	P9
Lloret de Mar	41	N3
Llucmajor	41	N5
Loano	43	D6
Lobatse	67	D5
Löbau	35	K5
Łobez	33	E4
Lobito	67	A2
Locarno	43	D4
Lochboisdale	37	E4
Lochinver	37	G3
Loch Linnhe	37	G5
Loch Lomond	37	H5
Lochmaddy	37	E4
Loch Ness	37	H4
Lockhart	103	B4
Lock Haven	99	E2
Lockport	99	E2
Locri	45	L10
Lodève	39	J10
Lodeynoye	31	F2
Lodge Grass	97	E1
Lodi, Italy	43	E5
Lodi, United States	97	B3
Lodja	65	C4
Lodwar	65	F3
Łódź	33	J6
Loei	77	C3
Lofoten	29	G3
Logan, Ia., United States	99	A2
Logan, N.Mex., United States	101	F1
Logan, Ut., United States	97	D2
Logansport	99	C2
Logatec	43	K5
Logroño	41	H2
Lohiniva	29	N3
Lohr	35	E7
Loikaw	77	B3
Loir	39	F6
Loire	39	D6
Loja, Ecuador	109	B4
Loja, Spain	41	F7
Lokan tekojärvi	29	P3
Lokeren	27	F3
Lokichar	65	F3
Lokichokio	65	E3
Lokoja	63	F3
Lokosovo	31	P2
Loks Land	93	U4
Lolland	35	G2
Lollondo	65	F4
Lolo	97	D1
Lom	47	L6
Lomami	65	C4
Lomas	109	C7
Lomas de Zamora	111	K5
Lombadina	87	D3
Lomblen	83	(2)B4
Lombok	83	(1)F4
Lomé	63	E3
Lomela	65	C4
Lomela	65	C4
Lommel	27	H3
Lomonosovka	31	N4
Lompoc	101	B2
Łomża	33	M4
London, Canada	99	D2
London, United Kingdom	27	B3
London, United States	103	E2
Londonderry	37	E6
Londrina	111	L3
Longarone	43	H4
Long Bay	105	J2
Long Beach	101	C2
Long Branch	99	F2
Long Eaton	27	A2
Longford	37	E8
Long Island, Canada	93	Q5
Long Island, United States	99	F2
Longlac	93	P7
Long Lake	97	F1
Longmont	97	E2
Long Prairie	99	B1
Long Range Mountains	93	V6
Longueuil	99	F1
Longview, Tex., United States	103	C3
Longview, Wash., United States	97	B1
Longwy	27	H5
Long Xuyên	77	D4
Longyan	77	F1
Löningen	27	K2
Lönsdalen	29	H3
Lons-le-Saunier	43	A4
Lookout Pass	97	C1
Loop Head	37	B9
Lopez	77	G4
Lop Nur	71	S9
Lopphavet	29	L1
Loptyuga	31	J2
Lora del Rio	41	E7
Lorain	99	D2
Loralai	75	A2
Lorca	41	J7
Lordegän	55	D1
Lord Howe Island	87	L6
Lordsburg	101	E2
Loreto	105	B3
Lorient	39	B6
Lörrach	43	C3
Lorraine	87	G3
Los Alamos	101	E1
Los Angeles, Chile	111	G6
Los Angeles, United States	101	C2
Los Banos	97	B3
Los Blancos	111	J3
Losheim	27	J5
Lošinj	43	K6
Los Mochis	105	C3
Lospalos	83	(2)C4
Los Telares	111	J4
Los Teques	109	D1
Lost Trail Pass	97	D1
Los'va	31	M2
Los Vientos	111	H3
Lotta	29	Q2
Lotte	27	K2
Louang Namtha	77	C2
Louangphrabang	77	C3
Loubomo	63	G5
Loudéac	39	C5
Louga	63	A1
Loughborough	27	A2
Lough Conn	37	C7
Lough Corrib	37	C8
Lough Derg	37	D8
Lough Foyle	37	E6
Lough Leane	37	C9
Lough Mask	37	C8
Lough Neagh	37	F7
Lough Ree	37	E8
Louhans	39	L7
Louisa	99	D3
Louisiade Archipelago	87	K2
Louisiana	103	C3
Louis Trichardt	67	D4
Louisville, Ga., United States	103	E3
Louisville, Ky., United States	103	D2
Louisville, Miss., United States	103	D3
Loukhi	29	S3
Loulé	41	C7
Louny	35	J6
Loup	97	G2
Lourdes	39	E10
Louth, Australia	87	J6
Louth, United Kingdom	27	C1
Loutra Aidipsou	49	F6
Louviers	27	D5
Lovech	47	M6
Lovell	97	E2
Lovelock	97	C2
Lovosice	35	K6
Lovran	43	K5
Lôvua	67	C2
Lowa	65	D4
Lowell	99	F2
Lower Hutt	89	E5
Lower Lake	97	B2
Lower Lough Erne	37	E7
Lower Post	93	F5
Lowestoft	27	D2
Lowville	99	F2
Loxstedt	35	D3
Loyalty Islands	85	G8
Loyno	31	K3
Loznica	47	G5
L-Travemünde	35	F3
Luama	65	D4
Luampa	67	C3
Lu'an	79	F4
Luanda	65	A5
Luangwa	67	E2
Luangwa	67	E3
Luanping	79	F2
Luanshya	67	D2
Luarca	41	D1
Luau	67	C2
Lubaczów	33	N7
Lubań	33	E6
Lubango	67	A2
Lubāns	29	P8
Lubao	65	D5
Lubartów	33	M6
Lübbecke	27	L2
Lübben	35	J5
Lübbenau	35	J5
Lubbock	101	F2
Lübeck	35	F3
Lubefu	65	C4
Lubero	65	D4
Lubilash	65	C5
Lubin	33	F6
Lublin	33	M6
Lubliniec	33	H7
Lubny	31	F4
Luboń	33	F5
Lubsko	33	D6
Lubudi	65	D5
Lubuklinggau	83	(1)C3
Lubumbashi	65	D6
Lubutu	65	D4
Lucala	65	B5
Lucca	43	F7
Luce Bay	37	H7
Lucedale	103	D3
Lucena, Philippines	77	G4
Lucena, Spain	41	F7
Lučenec	33	J9
Lucera	45	K7
Lucero	101	E2
Lucira	67	A2
Luckenwalde	35	J4
Lucknow	75	D3
Luçon	39	D7
Lucusse	67	C2
Ludden	97	G1
Lüdenscheid	27	K3
Lüderitz	67	B5
Ludhiana	75	C2
Ludington	99	C2
Ludlow	101	C2
Ludogori	47	P6
Luduş	47	M3
Ludvika	29	H6
Ludwigsburg	43	E2
Ludwigsfelde	35	J4
Ludwigshafen	27	L5
Ludwigslust	35	G3
Ludza	29	P8
Luebo	65	C5
Luena	67	B2
Lufeng	77	F2
Lufira	65	D6
Lufkin	103	C3
Luga	29	Q7
Luga	31	E3
Lugano	43	D4
Lugela	67	F3
Lugenda	67	F2
Luggate	89	B7
Lugo	43	G6
Lugoj	47	J4
Lugovoy	71	N9
Lugu	75	D2
Luhans'k	31	G5
Luhuo	79	C4
Lui	77	E2
Luilaka	65	B4
Luino	43	D4
Luis Moya	101	F4
Luiza	65	C5
Lukavac	47	F5
Lukovit	47	M6
Łuków	33	M6
Lukulu	67	C2
Lukuni	65	B5
Luleå	29	M4
Lüleburgaz	49	K3
Lulua	65	D5
Lumbala Kaquengue	67	C2
Lumberton	103	F3
Lumbrales	41	D4
Lumimba	67	E2
Lumsden	89	B7
Lund	33	C2
Lundazi	67	E2
Lundy	37	H10
Lüneburg	35	F3
Lüneburger Heide	35	F4
Lunel	39	K10
Lünen	27	K3
Lunéville	43	B2
Lungau	43	J3

Name	Page	Ref
Luntai	71	Q9
Luohe	79	E4
Luoyang	79	E4
Luozi	65	A4
Lupeni	47	L4
Lūrä Shīrīn	51	L5
Lure	43	B3
Luremo	65	B5
Lurgan	37	F7
Lurio	67	F2
Lusaka	67	D3
Lusambo	65	C5
Lushnjë	49	B4
Lushui	79	B5
Lüshun	79	G3
Lusk	97	F2
Lutembo	67	C2
Lutherstadt Wittenberg	35	H5
Luton	27	B3
Luts'k	31	E4
Lutto	29	P2
Lützow-Holmbukta	112	(2)J3
Luverne	99	A2
Luvua	65	D5
Luwuk	83	(2)B3
Luxembourg [A]	27	H5
Luxembourg	27	J5
Luxeuil-les-Bains	43	B3
Luxor	61	F2
Luza	31	J2
Luza	31	J2
Luzern	43	D3
Luzhou	79	D5
Luzilândia	109	D4
Luznice	43	K1
Luzon	77	G3
Luzon Strait	77	G2
Luzy	39	J7
L'viv	33	N8
Lyady	29	Q7
Lyapin	31	M2
Lycksele	31	C2
Lydenburg	67	E5
Lyme Bay	37	K11
Lymington	27	A4
Lynchburg	99	E3
Lynn	99	F2
Lynn Lake	93	L5
Lynx Lake	93	K4
Lyon	39	K8
Lys	27	E4
Lys'va	31	L3
Lysychans'k	31	G5
Lyttelton	89	D6

M

Name	Page	Ref
Maalosmadulu Atoll	75	B7
Ma'än	54	C6
Maardu	29	N7
Ma'arrat an Nu'män	51	G6
Maas	27	J3
Maasin	77	G4
Maastricht	27	H4
Mabalane	67	E4
Mabanza-Ngungu	63	G6
Mabein	77	B2
Mablethorpe	27	C1
Macapá	109	G3
Macas	109	B4
Macassar Strait	85	B6
Macau	77	E2
Macau	77	E2
Macau	109	K5
Macaúba	109	G6
Macclesfield	37	K8
Macdonnell Ranges	87	F4
Macedonia [A]	49	C3
Maceió	109	K5
Macerata	43	J7
Machakos	65	F4
Machala	109	B4
Macheng	79	F4
Machilipatnam	75	D5
Machiques	109	C1
Macia	67	E4

Name	Page	Ref
Măcin	47	R4
Mack	101	E1
Mackay	87	J4
Mackay Lake	93	J4
Mackenzie	93	G4
Mackenzie Bay	93	D3
Mackenzie Mountains	93	E3
Mackinaw City	99	D1
Macmillan	93	E4
Macmillan Pass	93	F4
Macomb	99	B2
Macomer	45	C8
Macon, Ga., United States	103	E3
Macon, Mo., United States	103	C2
Mâcon	39	K7
Macuje	109	C3
Mādabā	54	C5
Madagascar [A]	67	H3
Madan	47	M8
Madaoua	63	F2
Madeira	59	B2
Madeira	109	E5
Maden	51	H4
Madera	101	E3
Madikeri	75	C6
Madison	99	C2
Madison, Ind., United States	99	C3
Madison, Minn., United States	99	A1
Madison, S.D., United States	97	G2
Madisonville	99	C3
Madiun	83	(1)E4
Mado Gashi	65	F3
Madoi	79	B4
Madona	29	P8
Madras = Chennai, India	75	D6
Madras, United States	97	B2
Madre de Dios	109	C6
Madrid, Philippines	77	H5
Madrid, Spain	41	G4
Madridejos	41	G5
Madura	83	(1)E4
Madurai	75	C6
Maebashi	81	K5
Mae Hong Son	77	B3
Mae Nam Mun	77	C3
Mae Sariang	77	B3
Maevatanana	67	H3
Mafeteng	67	D5
Maffighofen	43	J2
Mafia Island	65	G5
Mafra	111	M4
Mafraq	54	D4
Magadan	73	S5
Magadi	65	F4
Magdagachi	73	M6
Magdalena	109	C2
Magdalena, Bolivia	109	E6
Magdalena, Mexico	101	D2
Magdalena, United States	101	E2
Magdeburg	35	G4
Magdelaine Cays	87	K3
Magelang	83	(1)E4
Magenta	43	D5
Magerøya	29	N1
Maglaj	47	F5
Máglie	45	N8
Magnitogorsk	31	L4
Magnolia	103	C3
Mago	73	P6
Magog	99	F1
Magu	65	E4
Magwe	77	A2
Mahābād	51	L5
Mahagi	65	E3
Mahajamba	67	H3
Mahajanga	67	H3
Mahalapye	67	D4
Mahän	55	G1
Mahanadi	75	D4
Mahanoro	67	H3
Mahasamund	75	D4
Mahavavy	67	H3
Mahbubnagar	75	D5
Mahé Island	67	(2)C1
Mahenge	65	F5
Mahesäna	75	B4

Name	Page	Ref
Mahia Peninsula	89	F4
Mahilyow	31	F4
Mahnomen	99	A1
Mahón	41	Q5
Mahuva	53	K5
Maicao	109	C1
Maidenhead	27	B3
Maidstone	27	C3
Maiduguri	63	G2
Mai Gudo	65	F2
Maímédy	35	B6
Main	35	E7
Mainburg	43	G2
Main-Donau-Kanal	35	G7
Maine	99	G1
Mainé Soroa	63	G2
Maingkwan	77	B1
Mainland, Orkney Is., United Kingdom	37	J2
Mainland, Shetland Is., United Kingdom	37	L1
Maintirano	67	G3
Mainz	35	D6
Maio	63	(1)B1
Majene	83	(2)A3
Majicana	111	H4
Majuro	85	H5
Makale	83	(2)A3
Makamba	65	D4
Makanza	65	B3
Makarora	89	B7
Makarov	73	Q7
Makarska	47	E6
Makar'yev	31	H3
Makat	31	K5
Makeni	63	B3
Makgadikgadi	67	C4
Makhachkala	51	M2
Makhorovka	71	M7
Makindu	65	F4
Makinsk	31	P4
Makiyivka	31	G5
Makkah	61	G3
Makó	47	H3
Makokou	63	G4
Makongolosi	65	E5
Makorako	89	F4
Makoua	63	H4
Maków Mazowiecka	33	L5
Makran	53	G4
Makronisi	49	G7
Mākū	51	L4
Makumbako	65	E5
Makurazaki	81	F8
Makurdi	63	F3
Makūyeh	55	E2
Makuyuni	65	F4
Malabar Coast	75	B6
Malabo	63	F4
Malack	33	F9
Malacky	43	M2
Malad City	97	D2
Maladzyechna	31	E4
Málaga	41	F8
Malaimbandy	67	H4
Malaita	85	G6
Malakal	65	E2
Malakula	85	G7
Malamala	83	(2)B3
Malang	83	(1)E4
Malanje	65	B5
Malanville	63	E2
Malaryta	33	P6
Malatya	51	H4
Malaut	75	C2
Malawi [A]	67	E2
Malaya Baranikha	73	V3
Malaya Vishera	31	F3
Malaybalay	77	H5
Malay Peninsula	77	C6
Malay Reef	87	J3
Malaysia [A]	83	(1)C2
Malbork	33	J3
Malchin, Germany	35	H3
Malchin, Mongolia	71	S8

Name	Page	Ref
Malden Island	85	L6
Maldives [A]	75	B8
Maldonado	111	L5
Malé	43	F4
Male	75	B8
Male Atoll	75	B8
Malegaon	75	B4
Malé Karpaty	43	N2
Malesherbes	39	H5
Maleta	73	H6
Malheur	97	C2
Malheur Lake	97	C2
Mali [A]	59	E5
Malindi	65	G4
Malin Head	37	E6
Malkara	49	J4
Malko Tŭrnovo	47	Q8
Mallaig	37	G4
Mallawi	61	F2
Mallorca	41	P5
Mallow	37	D9
Malmédy	27	J4
Malmesbury	67	B6
Malmö	33	C2
Malmyzh	31	K3
Malone	99	F2
Måløy	29	C6
Malozemel'skaya Tundra	31	K1
Mälselv	29	K2
Malta [A]	45	J13
Malta	97	E1
Malta Channel	45	J12
Maltahöhe	67	B4
Malvern	99	B4
Malý Dunaj	43	N2
Malyy Uzen'	31	J4
Mama	73	J5
Mamadysh	31	K3
Mambasa	65	D3
Mamburao	77	G4
Mamelodi	67	D5
Mammoth Hot Springs	97	D2
Mamonovo	33	J3
Mamoré	109	D6
Mamou	63	B2
Mamoudzou	67	H2
Mamuju	83	(2)A3
Ma'mūl	53	G6
Mamuno	67	C4
Man	63	C3
Mana	101	(2)A1
Manacapuru	109	E4
Manacor	41	P5
Manado	83	(2)B2
Managua	105	G6
Manakara	67	H4
Manali	75	C2
Mananara	67	H4
Mananara Avaratra	67	H3
Mananjary	67	H4
Manantenina	67	H4
Manassas	99	E3
Manaus	109	E4
Manavgat	49	P8
Manbij	51	G5
Manchester, United Kingdom	37	K8
Manchester, Ia., United States	99	B2
Manchester, Ky., United States	99	D3
Manchester, Tenn., United States	99	C3
Manchester, Vt., United States	99	F2
Mand	53	H4
Mandabe	67	G4
Mandal	29	D7
Mandalay	77	B2
Mandalgovĭ	79	D1
Mandan	97	F1
Mandera	65	G3
Mandi	75	C2
Mandi Burewala	75	B2
Mandimba	67	F2
Manding	59	D6
Mandla	75	D4
Mandø	35	D1
Mandsaur	75	C4
Mandurah	87	C6
Mandúria	45	M8

Name	Page	Grid
Mandvi	75	A4
Mandya	75	C6
Manfredonia	45	K7
Manga	63	G2
Manga	109	J6
Mangaia	85	K8
Mangalia	47	R6
Mangalore	75	B6
Mangareva	85	N8
Mangatupopo	89	E4
Mangaweka	89	F4
Manggar	83	(1)D3
Mangit	53	H1
Mangnai	71	S10
Mango	63	E2
Mangoky	67	G4
Mangole	83	(2)C3
Mangonui	89	D2
Mangrove Cay	103	F5
Manhad	75	B5
Manhattan	103	B2
Manhuaçu	109	J8
Mania	67	H3
Maniamba	67	F2
Manicoré	109	E5
Manicouagan	93	T6
Manihiki	85	K7
Maniitsoq	93	W3
Manila	77	G4
Manisa	49	K6
Manistee	99	C2
Manistique	99	C1
Manitoba	93	M6
Manitou	97	G1
Manitoulin Island	99	D1
Manitouwadge	99	C1
Manitowoc	99	C2
Maniwaki	99	E1
Manizales	109	B2
Manja	67	G4
Manjimup	87	C6
Mankato	99	B2
Manley Hot Springs	93	A4
Manlleu	41	N3
Manna	83	(1)C3
Mannheim	27	L5
Manning, Canada	93	H5
Manning, United States	103	E3
Manokwari	83	(2)D3
Manono	65	D5
Manosque	39	L10
Manouane	99	F1
Manouane Lake	93	S6
Manp'o	81	D3
Manra	85	J6
Manresa	41	M3
Mansa	67	D2
Mansel Island	93	Q4
Mansfield, United Kingdom	27	A1
Mansfield, La., United States	103	C3
Mansfield, Oh., United States	99	D2
Manta	109	A4
Manteo	103	F2
Mantes-la-Jolie	27	D5
Mántova	43	F5
Manturovo	31	H3
Manú	109	C6
Manuelzinho	109	G5
Manūjān	55	G3
Manukan	77	G5
Manukau	89	E3
Manukau Harbour	89	E3
Manyberries	97	D1
Manyinga	67	C2
Manyoni	65	E5
Manzanares	41	G5
Manzanillo	105	J4
Manzhouli	73	K7
Manzini	67	E5
Mao	61	C5
Maoming	77	F5
Mapam Yumco	75	D2
Mapi	83	(2)E4
Mapinhane	67	F4
Maple Creek	95	E2
Mapuera	109	E4
Maputo	67	E5
Maqueda	41	F4
Maquela do Zombo	65	B5
Maquinchao	111	H7
Maquoketa	99	B2
Maraba	109	H5
Maracaibo	109	C1
Maracay	109	D1
Marādah	61	C2
Maradi	63	F2
Marāgheh	51	M5
Maralal	65	F3
Marand	51	L4
Maranhão	109	H5
Marañón	109	B4
Mărăşeşti	47	Q4
Marathon, Canada	99	C1
Marathon, United States	101	F2
Marbella	41	F8
Marburg	27	L4
Marcal	43	N3
Marcali	43	N4
March	27	C2
Marche	27	H4
Marchena	41	E7
Mardan	75	B2
Mar del Plata	111	K6
Mardin	51	J5
Maré	85	G8
Mareeba	87	J3
Marettimo	45	F11
Marfa	101	F2
Margate	27	D3
Margherita di Savoia	45	L7
Marghita	47	K2
Margilan	53	K1
Marguerite Bay	112	(2)KK3
María Elena	111	H3
Marianas Trench	85	E4
Marianna	103	D3
Mariánská Lázně	35	H7
Mariazell	43	L3
Mar'ib	61	J4
Maribo	35	G2
Maribor	43	L4
Maridi	65	D3
Marie Byrd Land	112	(2)FF2
Marie Galante	105	M5
Mariehamn	29	K6
Marienberg	35	J6
Mariental	67	B4
Marietta	103	E2
Marietta, Oh., United States	99	D3
Marietta, Okla., United States	103	B3
Mariinsk	71	R6
Marijampolė	33	N3
Marília	111	M3
Marín	41	B2
Marinette	99	C1
Maringá	111	L3
Marino	45	G7
Marion, Ill., United States	99	C3
Marion, Ind., United States	99	C2
Marion, Oh., United States	99	D2
Maripa	109	D2
Mariscal Estigarribia	111	J3
Maritime Alps	43	C6
Marittimo	43	F7
Mariupol'	31	G5
Marīvān	51	M6
Mariy El	31	J3
Marjayoûn	54	C3
Marka	65	G3
Markam	79	B5
Markaryd	33	C1
Marked Tree	103	C2
Marken	27	H2
Markermeer	27	H2
Market Harborough	27	B2
Markham	99	E2
Marki	33	L5
Markit	71	P10
Markkleeberg	35	H5
Markovo	73	W4
Marktoberdorf	43	F3
Marktredwitz	35	H7
Marla	87	F5
Marle	27	F5
Marmande	39	F9
Marmara Adası	49	K4
Marmara Denizi	49	L4
Marmaris	49	L8
Marmolada	43	G4
Marne	27	F5
Maroansetra	67	H3
Marolambo	67	H4
Maroni	109	G3
Marotiri	85	M8
Maroua	63	G2
Marquesas Islands	85	M6
Marquette	99	C1
Marradi	43	G6
Marra Plateau	61	D5
Marree	87	G5
Marrakech	59	D2
Marrupa	67	F2
Marsa Alam	61	F2
Marsabit	65	F3
Marsala	45	G11
Marsberg	27	L3
Marsden	87	J6
Marseille	39	L10
Marseille-en-Beauvaisis	27	D5
Marshall, Ill., United States	103	D2
Marshall, Tex., United States	103	C3
Marshall Islands	85	G4
Marshalltown	99	B2
Marsh Harbour	103	F4
Marsh Island	103	C4
Martapura, Indonesia	83	(1)C3
Martapura, Indonesia	83	(1)E3
Martigny	43	C4
Martigues	39	L10
Martin, Slovakia	33	H8
Martin, United States	97	F2
Martina Franca	45	M8
Martinborough	89	E5
Martinique	105	M6
Martinsburg	99	E3
Martinsville, Ind., United States	99	C3
Martinsville, Va., United States	99	E3
Marton	89	E5
Maruchak	53	H2
Mårvatn	29	E6
Mary	53	H2
Maryborough	87	K5
Maryland	99	E3
Marysville, Canada	99	G1
Marysville, Calif., United States	101	B1
Marysville, Kans., United States	103	B2
Maryville	99	B2
Masai Steppe	65	F4
Masaka	65	E4
Masalembu Besar	83	(1)E4
Masallı	51	N4
Masamba	83	(2)B3
Masan	81	E6
Masasi	65	F6
Masbate	77	G4
Masbate	77	G4
Mascara	59	F1
Maseru	67	D5
Mashhad	53	G2
Masi-Manimba	65	B4
Masindi	65	E3
Maşīrah	53	G5
Masjed Soleymān	53	E3
Maskanah	54	H5
Mason	103	B3
Mason Bay	89	A8
Mason City	99	B2
Masqaṭ	55	H5
Massa	43	F6
Massachusetts	99	F2
Massachusetts Bay	99	G2
Massafra	45	M8
Massa Marittima	45	E5
Massawa	61	G4
Massena	99	F2
Masset	93	E6
Massif Central	39	H8
Massif de Guéra	61	C5
Massif de l'Aïr	59	G5
Massif des Écrins	43	B5
Massif du Chaillu	63	G5
Massif du Tsaratanana	67	H2
Massif Ennedi	61	D4
Massillon	99	D2
Massinga	67	F4
Masteksay	31	K5
Masterton	89	E5
Mastung	53	J4
Masty	29	N10
Masuda	81	F6
Masuguru	67	F2
Masvingo	67	E4
Maşyāf	54	D1
Matadi	65	A5
Matagami	99	E1
Matagorda Island	103	B4
Matakana Island	89	F3
Matakawau	89	E3
Matale	75	D7
Matam	63	B1
Matamoros, Mexico	101	F3
Matamoros, Mexico	101	G3
Matane	99	G1
Matanzas	95	K7
Matara	75	D7
Mataram	83	(1)F4
Mataranka	87	F3
Mataró	41	N3
Mataura	89	B8
Matawai	89	F4
Matehuala	101	F4
Matera	45	L8
Mátészalka	47	K2
Mateur	45	D11
Matheson	99	D1
Mathraki	49	B5
Mathura	75	C3
Mati	77	H5
Matlock	27	A1
Matmata	59	G2
Mato Grosso	109	F6
Mato Grosso	109	F6
Mato Grosso do Sul	109	F7
Matosinhos	41	B3
Maṭraḥ	55	H5
Matrei	43	H4
Matrûḥ	61	E1
Matsiatra	67	H4
Matsu	79	G5
Matsue	81	G6
Matsumae	81	L3
Matsumoto	81	J5
Matsusaka	81	J6
Matsuyama	81	G7
Mattawa	99	E1
Matterhorn	43	C5
Matthews Ridge	109	E2
Mattighofen	35	J8
Mattoon	99	C3
Maturín	109	E2
Maubeuge	27	F4
Maui	101	(2)F3
Maullín	111	G7
Maun	43	K6
Maun	67	C3
Mauna Kea	101	(2)F4
Mauna Loa	101	(2)F4
Mauritania	59	C5
Mauritius	67	(1)B2
Mauron	39	C5
Mauthen	43	H4
Mavinga	67	C3
Mawlaik	77	A2
Max	97	F1
Maya	73	P5
Maya	83	(1)D3
Mayaguana	105	K4
Mayagüez	105	L5
Mayamba	65	B4
Maych'ew	61	G5
Maydh	65	H1
Mayenne	39	E5
Mayenne	39	E5
Mayer	101	D2
Maykamys	71	P8
Maykop	51	J1
Mayly-Say	53	K1

Name	Page	Ref
Maymecha	73	G3
Mayn	73	W4
Mayo	93	D4
Mayor Island	89	F3
Mayotte	67	H2
Mayrhofen	43	G3
Mayskiy	73	M6
Mayumba	63	G5
Mayya	73	N4
Mazagão	109	G4
Mazagran	39	K4
Mazama	97	B1
Mazamet	39	H10
Mazar	71	P10
Mazara del Vallo	45	G11
Mazār-e Sharīf	53	J2
Mazatlán	105	C4
Mažeikiai	33	M1
Mazocahui	101	D3
Mazomora	65	F5
Mazra	54	C5
Mazyr	31	E4
Mazzarino	45	J11
Mbabane	67	E5
Mbala	65	E5
Mbale	65	E3
Mbalmayo	63	G4
Mbamba Bay	67	E2
Mbandaka	65	B3
Mbanga	63	F4
M'banza Congo	65	A5
Mbarara	65	E4
Mbeya	65	E5
Mbomou	65	C3
Mbour	63	A2
Mbuji-Mayi	65	C5
Mbuyuni	65	F5
McAlester	103	B3
McBride	93	G6
McCamey	101	F2
McCammon	97	D2
McClintock	93	N5
McClintock Channel	93	L2
McComb	103	C3
McCook	97	F2
McDermitt	97	C2
McGehee	103	C3
McGrath	101	(1)F3
McKinlay	87	H4
McKinney	103	B3
McLaughlin	97	F1
McLennan	93	H5
McMinnville	99	C3
McPherson	103	B2
McRae	103	E3
Meadow Lake	93	K6
Meadville	99	D2
Meander River	93	H5
Meaux	27	E6
Mecca = Makkah	61	G3
Mechelen	27	G3
Mechernich	27	J4
Mecidiye	49	J4
Mecklenburger Bucht	35	G2
Mecula	67	F2
Meda	41	C4
Medak	75	C5
Medan	83	(1)B2
Médéa	41	N8
Medellín	109	B2
Medenine	59	H2
Medford	97	B2
Medgidia	47	R5
Mediaş	47	M3
Medicine Bow	97	E2
Medicine Hat	93	J7
Medicine Lodge	103	B2
Medina = Al Madīnah	61	G3
Medinaceli	41	H3
Medina de Campo	41	F3
Medina Sidonia	41	E8
Mediterranean Sea	25	E4
Mednogorsk	31	L4
Medveditsa	31	H4
Medvezh'yegorsk	31	F2
Meeker	97	E2
Meerane	35	H6
Meerut	75	C3
Mega	83	(2)D3
Megalopoli	49	E7
Meganisi	49	C6
Megara	49	F6
Megisti	49	M8
Mehrān	51	M7
Mehriz	53	F3
Meiktila	77	B2
Meiningen	35	F6
Meißen	35	J5
Meizhou	77	F2
Mejez El Bab	45	D12
Mékambo	63	G4
Mek'elē	61	G5
Meknès	59	D2
Mekong	77	D4
Melaka	83	(1)C2
Melanesia	85	F5
Melbourne, Australia	87	H7
Melbourne, United States	103	E4
Melchor de Mencos	105	G5
Meldrum Bay	99	D1
Meleuz	31	L4
Mélfi	61	C5
Melfi	45	K8
Melfort	93	L6
Melide	41	B2
Melilla	41	H9
Melita	97	F1
Melitopol'	31	G5
Melk	43	L2
Melkosopochnik	71	N8
Mělník	35	K6
Melo	111	L5
Melton Mowbray	27	B2
Melun	39	H5
Melut	61	F5
Melvern Lake	103	B2
Melville	93	L6
Melville Island, Australia	87	F2
Melville Island, Canada	91	N2
Melville Peninsula	93	P3
Memberamo	83	(2)E3
Memboro	83	(2)A4
Memmert	27	J1
Memmingen	43	F3
Mempawah	83	(1)D2
Memphis, Mo., United States	99	B2
Memphis, Tenn., United States	99	C3
Mena	103	C3
Menai Strait	37	H8
Ménaka	59	F5
Mendawai	83	(1)E3
Mende	39	J9
Menden	27	K3
Mendī	65	F2
Mendoza	111	H5
Menemen	49	K6
Menen	27	F4
Menfi	45	G11
Menggala	83	(1)D3
Meniet	59	F4
Menkere	73	L3
Menominee	99	C1
Menomonee Falls	99	C2
Menongue	67	B2
Menorca	41	Q4
Mentok	83	(1)D3
Menyuan	79	C3
Menzel Bourguiba	45	D11
Menzel Bouzelfa	45	E12
Menzel Temime	45	E12
Menzies	87	D5
Meppel	27	J2
Meppen	27	K2
Meran Merano	43	G4
Merauke	83	(2)F4
Mercato Saraceno	43	H7
Merced	97	B3
Mercedes, Argentina	111	H5
Mercedes, Argentina	111	K4
Mercedes, United States	103	B4
Mercedes, Uruguay	111	K5
Mercury Islands	89	E3
Mergenevo	31	K5
Mergui	77	B4
Mergui Archipelago	77	B4
Mérida, Mexico	105	G4
Mérida, Spain	41	D6
Mérida, Venezuela	105	K7
Meridian	103	D3
Merinha Grande	41	B5
Meriruma	109	G3
Merke	71	N9
Merkys	29	N9
Merowe	61	F4
Merredin	87	C6
Merrill	99	C1
Merriman	97	F2
Merritt	93	G6
Merseburg	35	H5
Mersey	37	J8
Mersin = İcel	49	S8
Mērsrags	29	M8
Merthyr Tydfil	37	J10
Méru	27	E5
Meru	65	F3
Merzifon	51	F3
Merzig	27	J5
Mesa	101	D2
Mesa de Yambi	109	C3
Mesagne	45	M8
Meschede	27	L3
Mesöaria Plain	54	A1
Mesolongi	49	D6
Mesopotamia	51	K6
Messaad	59	F2
Messina, Italy	45	K10
Messina, South Africa	67	D4
Messini	49	E7
Messiniakos Kolpos	49	D8
Mestre	43	H5
Meta	109	C2
Metairie	103	C4
Metaline Falls	97	C1
Metán	111	J4
Metangula	67	E2
Metema	61	G5
Meteor Depth	107	J9
Metković	47	N6
Metlika	43	L5
Metsovo	49	D5
Mettet	27	G4
Mettlach	27	J5
Metz	27	J5
Metzingen	43	E2
Meulaboh	77	B6
Meuse	27	G4
Mexia	103	B3
Mexicali	101	C2
Mexican Hat	101	E1
Mexico	99	B3
Mexico	105	D4
Meymaneh	53	H2
Mezdra	47	L6
Mezen'	31	H1
Mezenskaya Guba	31	H1
Mezhdurechensk	71	R7
Mezöberény	47	J3
Mezökövesd	47	H2
Mezötúr	47	H2
Mfuwe	67	E2
Miajadas	41	E5
Miami, Fla., United States	103	E4
Miami, Okla., United States	103	C3
Miandowāb	51	M5
Miandrivazo	67	H3
Mīāneh	51	M5
Miangyang	79	E4
Mianning	79	C5
Mianwali	75	B2
Mianyang	79	C4
Miaodao Qundao	79	G3
Miao'ergou	71	Q8
Miass	31	M4
Miastko	33	G3
Michalovce	33	L9
Michigan	99	C1
Michipicoten Island	99	C1
Michurinsk	31	H4
Micronesia	85	F4
Mid-Atlantic Ridge	107	G1
Middelburg, Netherlands	27	F3
Middelburg, South Africa	67	D6
Middelfart	35	E1
Middelkerke	27	E3
Middle America Trench	91	L8
Middle Andaman	77	A4
Middlebury	99	F2
Middle Lake	97	C2
Middlesboro	99	D3
Middlesbrough	37	L7
Middletown, N.Y., United States	99	F2
Middletown, Oh., United States	99	D3
Midland, Canada	99	E2
Midland, Mich., United States	99	D2
Midland, Tex., United States	101	F2
Midway Islands	85	J3
Midwest City	103	B2
Midzor	47	K6
Miechów	33	K7
Mielan	39	F10
Mielec	33	L7
Miembwe	65	F5
Mien	33	D1
Miercurea-Ciuc	47	N3
Mieres	41	E1
Miesbach	43	G3
Mī'ēso	65	G2
Miging	75	F3
Miguel Auza	101	F4
Mikhaylovka	31	H4
Mikhaylovskiy	71	P7
Mikino	73	U4
Mikkeli	29	P6
Mikulov	43	M2
Mikun'	31	K2
Mikuni-sammyaku	81	K5
Mikura-jima	81	K7
Mila	59	G1
Milaca	99	B1
Miladhunmadulu Atoll	75	B7
Milan = Milano, Italy	43	E5
Milan, United States	103	D2
Milano	43	E5
Milas	49	K7
Milazzo	45	K10
Miles	87	K5
Miles City	97	E1
Milford, Del., United States	99	E3
Milford, Ut., United States	97	D3
Milford Haven	37	G10
Milford Sound	89	A7
Miliana	41	N8
Milicz	33	G6
Milk	93	J7
Mil'kovo	73	T6
Millau	39	J9
Millbank	97	G1
Milledgeville	103	E3
Miller	97	G2
Millerovo	31	H5
Millington	99	C3
Millinocket	99	G1
Miloro	65	E5
Milos	49	G8
Milton, New Zealand	89	B8
Milton, United States	103	D3
Milton Keynes	27	B2
Miluo	79	E5
Milwaukee	99	C2
Mily	71	L8
Mimizan-Plage	39	D9
Mīnāb	55	G3
Mina Jebel Ali	55	F4
Minas	111	K5
Mīnā' Sa'ūd	55	C2
Minas Gerais	109	H7
Minas Novas	109	J7
Minatitlán	105	F5
Minbu	77	A2
Minchinmávida	111	G7
Mincivan	51	M4
Mindanao	77	G5
Mindelheim	43	F2
Mindelo	63	(1)B1
Minden	27	L2
Mindoro	77	G4
Mindoro Strait	77	G4

Name	Page	Grid
Minehead	37	J10
Mineola	103	B3
Mineral'nyye Vody	51	K1
Minerva Reefs	85	J8
Minfeng	71	Q10
Minga	65	D6
Mingäçevir	51	M3
Mingäçevir Su Anbarı	51	M3
Mingulay	37	D5
Minicoy	75	B7
Minilya Roadhouse	87	B4
Minna	63	F3
Minneapolis	99	B2
Minnesota	99	A1
Minnesota	99	A2
Miño	41	C2
Minot	97	F1
Minsk	31	E4
Minturn	97	E3
Minusinsk	71	S7
Min Xian	79	C4
Min'yar	31	L3
Miquelon	99	E1
Miraflores	109	C3
Miramas	39	K10
Mirambeau	39	E8
Miranda	109	F8
Miranda de Ebro	41	H2
Miranda do Douro	41	D3
Mirandela	41	C3
Mirbāt	53	F6
Mīrjāveh	53	H4
Mirnyy	73	J4
Mirow	35	H3
Mirpur Khas	75	A3
Mirtoö Pelagos	49	F7
Mirzapur	75	D3
Miskolc	47	H1
Misoöl	83	(2)D3
Mişrātah	61	C1
Missinaibi	93	Q6
Missinipe	93	L5
Mission	97	F2
Mississippi	103	C3
Mississippi	103	D2
Mississippi River Delta	103	D4
Missoula	97	D1
Missouri	97	F1
Missouri	99	B3
Missouri City	103	B4
Mistassibi	93	S7
Mistelbach	43	M2
Mitchell	97	G2
Mithankot	53	K4
Mithaylov	31	G4
Mithymna	49	J5
Mito	81	L5
Mits'iwa	53	C6
Mittellandkanal	27	K2
Mittersill	43	H3
Mittweida	35	H6
Mitú	109	C3
Mitzic	63	G4
Miyake-jima	81	K6
Miyako	81	L4
Miyakonojō	81	F8
Miyazaki	81	F8
Miyoshi	81	G6
Mīzan Teferī	65	F2
Mizdah	59	H2
Mizen Head	37	B10
Mizhhir''ya	47	L1
Mizil	47	P4
Mizpe Ramon	54	B6
Mjölby	29	H7
Mjøsa	29	F6
Mkuze	67	E5
Mladá Boleslav	33	D7
Mladenovac	47	H5
Mława	33	K4
Mljet	47	F6
Mmabatho	67	D5
Moa	87	H2
Moanda	63	G5
Moapa	97	D3
Moba	65	D5
Mobaye	65	C3
Mobayi-Mbongo	65	C3
Moberly	99	B3
Mobile	103	D3
Moçambique	67	G3
Môc Châu	77	C2
Mochudi	67	D4
Mocímboa da Praia	67	G2
Mocuba	67	F3
Modane	43	B5
Módena	43	F6
Modesto	97	B3
Módica	45	J12
Mödling	43	M2
Modowi	83	(2)D3
Modriča	47	F5
Moenkopi	101	D1
Moers	27	J3
Moffat	37	J6
Moffat Peak	89	B7
Mogadishu = Muqdisho	65	H3
Mogilno	33	G5
Mogocha	73	K6
Mogochin	71	Q6
Mogok	77	B2
Mohács	47	F4
Mohammadia	41	L9
Mohe	73	L6
Mohembo	67	C3
Mohoro	65	F5
Mohyliv-Podil's'kyy	47	Q1
Moi	29	D7
Moincêr	75	D2
Moineşti	47	P3
Mo i Rana	29	H3
Moissac	39	G9
Mojave	101	C1
Mojave Desert	101	C2
Mokau	89	E4
Mokohinau Island	89	E2
Mokolo	63	G2
Mokoreta	89	B8
Mokp'o	81	D6
Mola di Bari	45	M7
Molat	43	K6
Mol	27	H3
Molde	29	D5
Moldova	47	P2
Moldova	47	R2
Moldova Nouă	47	J5
Molepolole	67	C4
Molfetta	45	L7
Molina de Aragón	41	J4
Molina de Segura	41	J6
Moline	99	B2
Möll	43	J4
Mollendo	109	C7
Molokai	101	(2)D2
Molopo	67	C5
Molsheim	43	C2
Molucca Sea	83	(2)C2
Moma	67	F3
Mombasa	65	G4
Momchilgrad	47	N8
Møn	35	H2
Monach Islands	37	E4
Monaco	43	C7
Monaco	43	C7
Monahans	101	F2
Mona Passage	105	L5
Monbetsu, Japan	81	M1
Monbetsu, Japan	81	M2
Moncalieri	43	C5
Monchegorsk	29	S3
Mönchengladbach	27	J3
Monclova	101	F3
Moncton	93	U7
Mondovi	43	C6
Mondragone	45	H7
Mondy	73	G6
Monfalcone	43	J5
Monforte	41	C5
Monforte de Lemos	41	C2
Monfredónia	45	K7
Monga	65	C3
Mongkung	77	B2
Mongo	61	C5
Mongolia	79	B2
Mongonu	63	G2
Mongora	75	B2
Mongu	67	C3
Mong Yai	77	B2
Mong Yu	77	B2
Monkoto	65	C4
Monmouth	99	B2
Mono	63	E3
Mono Lake	97	C3
Monopoli	45	M8
Monor	33	J10
Monowai	89	A7
Monreal del Campo	41	J4
Monreale	45	H10
Monroe, La., United States	103	C3
Monroe, Mich., United States	99	D2
Monroe, N.C., United States	103	E3
Monroe, Wash., United States	97	B1
Monroe City	103	C2
Monrovia	63	B3
Mons	27	F4
Monschau	27	J4
Monsélice	43	G5
Montabaur	27	K4
Montague Island	107	J9
Montalbán	41	K4
Montana	47	L6
Montana	97	E1
Montargis	39	H6
Montauban	39	G10
Montauk	99	F2
Mont aux Sources	67	D5
Montbard	39	K6
Montbéliard	43	B3
Montblanc	41	M3
Mont Blanc	43	B5
Montbrison	39	K8
Mont Cameroun	63	F4
Montceau-les-Mines	39	K7
Mont-de-Marsan	39	E10
Montdidier	27	E5
Monte Alegre	109	G4
Monte Azul	109	J7
Montebello	99	F1
Monte Bello Islands	87	B4
Montebelluna	43	H5
Monte Calvo	45	K7
Monte Cinto	45	C6
Montecristo	45	E6
Monte Etna	45	J11
Montefiascone	45	G6
Montego Bay	105	J5
Montélimar	39	K9
Monte Limbara	45	D8
Monte Lindo	111	K4
Montemorelos	103	B4
Monte Namuli	67	F3
Montenegro = Crna Gora	47	F7
Monte Perdino	41	L2
Monte Pollino	45	L9
Montepuez	67	F2
Montepulciano	45	F5
Monte Quemado	111	J4
Montereau-faut-Yonne	39	H5
Monterey	99	E3
Monterey Bay	97	B3
Montería	109	B2
Montero	109	E7
Monte Rosa	43	C5
Monterotondo	45	G6
Monterrey	101	F3
Monte Sant'Angelo	45	K7
Montes Claros	109	J7
Montesilvano Marina	45	J6
Montevarchi	43	G7
Montevideo, United States	99	A1
Montevideo, Uruguay	111	K5
Monte Viso	43	C6
Monte Vista	101	E1
Montgomery	103	D3
Monthey	43	B4
Monticello	97	E3
Montijo	41	D6
Montilla	41	F7
Mont Joli	99	G1
Mont-Laurier	99	E1
Montluçon	39	H7
Montmagny	99	F1
Montmedy	27	H5
Mont Mézenc	39	K9
Montone	43	G6
Montoro	41	F6
Mont Pelat	39	M9
Montpelier, Id., United States	97	D2
Montpelier, Vt., United States	99	F2
Montpellier	39	J10
Montréal	99	F1
Montreul	27	D4
Montreux	43	B4
Montrose, United Kingdom	37	K5
Montrose, United States	97	E3
Monts Bagzane	59	G5
Mont Serkout	59	G4
Montserrat	105	M5
Monts Nimba	63	C3
Monts Otish	93	S6
Mont Tahat	59	G4
Monywa	77	A2
Monza	43	E5
Monzón	41	L3
Moonie	87	K5
Moorcroft	97	F2
Moorhead	99	A1
Moosburg	43	G1
Moose Jaw	93	K6
Moose Lake	93	M6
Moosomin	93	L6
Moosonee	93	Q6
Mopti	59	E6
Moqor	53	J3
Mór	47	F2
Mora	29	H6
Móra	41	B6
Moradabad	75	C3
Morafenobe	67	G3
Morag	33	J4
Moramanga	67	H3
Moran	97	D2
Morane	85	N8
Moratuwa	75	D7
Morava	33	G8
Moravské Budějovice	43	L1
Morawhanna	109	F2
Moray Firth	37	J4
Morbach	27	K5
Morbi	75	B4
Mordoviya	31	H4
Moreau	97	F1
Morecambe	37	K7
Moree	87	J5
Morehead	99	D3
More Laptevykh	73	L1
Morelia	105	D5
Morella	41	K4
Moresby Island	101	(1)L5
Moreton Island	87	K5
Morez	39	M7
Morgan	87	G6
Morgan City	103	C4
Morgantown	99	D3
Morges	43	B4
Mori	81	L2
Morioka	81	L4
Morkoka	73	J4
Morlaix	39	B5
Mornington Island	87	G3
Morocco	57	C2
Morogoro	65	F5
Moro Gulf	77	G5
Morombe	67	G4
Mörön	73	G7
Morondava	67	G4
Morón de la Frontera	41	E7
Moroni	67	G2
Moron Us He	75	F2
Morotai	83	(2)C2
Moroto	65	E3
Morpeth	37	L6
Morris	97	G1
Morristown	103	E2
Mors	29	E8
Morshansk	31	H4
Mortain	27	B6
Morteros	111	J5

Name	Page	Grid
Morvern	37	G5
Morwell	87	J7
Mosbach	35	E7
Mosby	97	D1
Moscow = Moskva	31	G3
Mosel	27	K4
Moselle	27	G6
Moses Lake	97	C1
Mosgiel	89	C7
Moshi	65	F4
Mosjøen	29	G4
Moskenesøy	29	F3
Moskva	31	G3
Mosonmagyaróvár	43	N3
Mosquero	101	F1
Moss	29	F7
Mossburn	89	B7
Mosselbaai	67	C6
Mossoró	109	K5
Most	35	J6
Mostaganem	41	L9
Mostar	47	E6
Mostoles	41	G4
Møsvatn	29	E7
Mot'a	61	G5
Motala	29	H7
Motherwell	37	J6
Motihari	75	D3
Motilla del Palancar	41	J5
Motiti Island	89	F3
Motril	41	G8
Motru	47	K5
Motu One	85	L7
Motygino	71	S6
Mouchard	43	A4
Moudjéria	59	C5
Moudros	49	H5
Mouila	63	G5
Moulins	39	J7
Moulmein	77	B3
Moultrie	103	E3
Moundou	61	C6
Mount Adam	111	J9
Mount Adams	97	B1
Mountain Grove	99	B3
Mountain Home	99	B3
Mountain Nile = Bahr el Jebel	65	E2
Mount Alba	89	B7
Mount Aloysius	87	E5
Mount Anglem	89	A8
Mount Apo	77	H5
Mount Ararat	51	L4
Mount Arrowsmith	89	C6
Mount Aspiring	89	B7
Mount Assiniboine	93	H6
Mount Augustus	87	C4
Mount Baco	77	G3
Mount Baker	97	B1
Mount Bartle Frere	87	J3
Mount Bogong	87	J7
Mount Brewster	89	B7
Mount Bruce	87	C4
Mount Cameroun	57	D5
Mount Carmel	97	D3
Mount Columbia	93	H6
Mount Cook	89	C6
Mount Cook	89	C6
Mount Donald	89	A7
Mount Douglas	87	J4
Mount Egmont	89	E4
Mount Elbert	97	E3
Mount Elgon	65	E3
Mount Essendon	87	D4
Mount Evelyn	87	F2
Mount Everest	75	D4
Mount Fairweather	93	D5
Mount Gambier	87	H7
Mount Garnet	87	J3
Mount Hermon	54	C3
Mount Hood	97	B1
Mount Hutt	89	C6
Mount Huxley	89	B7
Mount Isa	87	G4
Mount Jackson	112	(2)MM2
Mount Karisimbi	65	D4
Mount Kendall	89	D5
Mount Kenya = Kirinyaga	65	F4
Mount Kilimanjaro	65	F4
Mount Kirkpatrick	112	(2)AA1
Mount Kosciuszko	87	J7
Mount Liebig	87	F4
Mount Lloyd George	93	G5
Mount Logan	93	C4
Mount Magnet	87	C5
Mount Maunganui	89	F3
Mount McKinley	101	(1)G3
Mount Meharry	87	C4
Mount Menzies	112	(2)L2
Mount Minto	112	(2)Y2
Mount Mulanje	67	F3
Mount Murchison	89	C6
Mount Nyiru	65	F3
Mount Olympus	97	B1
Mount Ord	87	E3
Mount Ossa	87	J8
Mount Owen	89	D5
Mount Paget	111	P9
Mount Pleasant, Ia., United States	99	B2
Mount Pleasant, Mich., United States	99	D2
Mount Pleasant, S.C., United States	103	F3
Mount Pleasant, Tex., United States	103	B3
Mount Pleasant, Ut., United States	97	D3
Mount Pulog	77	G3
Mount Rainier	97	B1
Mount Ratz	93	E5
Mount Richmond	89	D5
Mount Roberts	87	K5
Mount Robson	93	H6
Mount Roosevelt	93	F5
Mount Roraima	109	E2
Mount Ross	89	E5
Mount Shasta	97	B2
Mount Somers	89	C6
Mount Stanley	65	D3
Mount Tahat	57	D3
Mount Travers	89	D6
Mount Tuun	81	D3
Mount Usborne	111	K9
Mount Vernon, Al., United States	103	D3
Mount Vernon, Ill., United States	99	C3
Mount Vernon, Oh., United States	99	D2
Mount Vernon, Wash., United States	97	B1
Mount Victoria, Myanmar	77	A2
Mount Victoria, Papua New Guinea	85	E6
Mount Waddington	93	F6
Mount Washington	93	S8
Mount Whitney	97	C3
Mount Wilson	97	E3
Mount Woodroffe	87	F5
Mount Ziel	87	F4
Moura	41	C6
Mousa	37	L2
Moussoro	61	C5
Moutamba	63	G5
Mouth of the Shannon	37	B9
Mouths of the Amazon	107	G3
Mouths of the Danube	47	S4
Mouths of the Ganges	75	E4
Mouths of the Indus	53	J5
Mouths of the Irrawaddy	77	A3
Mouths of the Krishna	75	D5
Mouths of the Mekong	77	D5
Mouths of the Niger	63	F4
Moûtiers	43	B5
Moutong	83	(2)B2
Moyale	65	F3
Moyen Atlas	59	D2
Moyenvic	27	J6
Moyeroo	71	U4
Moyynty	71	N8
Mozambique	67	E3
Mozambique Channel	67	F4
Mozdok	51	L2
Mozhga	31	K3
Mozirje	43	K4
Mpanda	65	E5
Mpika	67	E2
Mporokoso	65	E5
Mpumalanga	67	D5
Mrągowo	33	L4
Mrkonjić-Grad	43	N6
M'Sila	59	F1
Mtsensk	31	G4
Mtwara	65	G6
Muang Khammouan	77	C3
Muang Không	77	D4
Muang Khôngxédôn	77	D3
Muang Khoua	77	C2
Muang Pakxan	77	C3
Muang Phin	77	D3
Muang Sing	77	C2
Muang Xai	77	C2
Muar	83	(1)C2
Muarabungo	83	(1)C3
Muarawahau	83	(1)F2
Mubarek	71	M10
Mubende	65	E3
Mubrani	83	(2)D3
Muck	37	F5
Muckadilla	87	J5
Muconda	65	C6
Mucur	49	S5
Mudanjiang	81	E1
Mudanya	49	L4
Muddy Gap	97	E2
Mudurnu	49	P4
Mufulira	67	D2
Mughshin	53	F6
Muğla	49	L7
Mugodzhary	31	L5
Mühldorf	43	H2
Mühlhausen	35	F5
Muhos	29	N4
Muhu	29	M7
Muhulu	65	D4
Mukacheve	33	M9
Mukdahan	77	C3
Mukry	53	J2
Mukuku	67	D2
Mulaku Atoll	75	B8
Mulde	35	H5
Muleshoe	101	F2
Mulgrave Island	87	H2
Mulhacén	41	G7
Mülheim	27	J3
Mulhouse	43	C3
Muling	81	G1
Mull	37	G5
Mullaittivu	75	D7
Mullewa	87	C5
Müllheim	43	C3
Mullingar	37	E8
Mulobezi	67	D3
Multan	53	K3
Mumbai	75	B5
Mumbwa	67	D2
Muna	83	(2)B4
Münchberg	35	G6
München	43	G2
Münden	35	E5
Mundo Novo	109	J6
Mungbere	65	D3
Munger	75	E3
Munich = München	43	G2
Münster, Germany	27	K3
Munster, France	43	C2
Munster, Germany	35	F4
Munte	83	(2)A2
Muojärvi	29	Q4
Muonio	29	M3
Muqdisho	65	H3
Mur	43	L4
Muradiye	51	K4
Murang'a	65	F4
Murashi	31	J3
Murat	51	K4
Muratlı	49	K3
Murchison	89	D5
Murcia	41	J7
Murdo	97	F2
Mureş	47	J3
Muret	39	G10
Murfreesboro, N.C., United States	103	F2
Murfreesboro, Tenn., United States	103	D2
Murghob	53	K2
Muriaé	109	J8
Müritz	35	H3
Muriwai	89	F4
Murmansk	29	S2
Murnau	43	G3
Murom	31	H3
Muroran	81	L2
Muros	41	A2
Muroto	81	H7
Murphy	103	E2
Murray	87	H6
Murray	99	C3
Murray Bridge	87	G7
Murray River Basin	87	H6
Murska Sobota	43	M4
Murter	43	L7
Murtosa	41	B4
Murud	75	B5
Murupara	89	F4
Mururoa	85	M8
Murwara	75	D4
Murzuq	59	H3
Mürzzuschlag	43	L3
Muş	51	J4
Müsa	33	N1
Musala	49	F2
Musandam Peninsula	55	G3
Musay'id	55	D4
Muscat = Masqat	55	H5
Musgrave Ranges	87	E5
Mushin	63	E3
Muskegon	99	C2
Muskogee	103	B2
Musoma	65	E4
Mustafakemalpaşa	49	L4
Mut, Egypt	61	E2
Mut, Turkey	49	R8
Mutare	67	E3
Mutarnee	87	J3
Mutnyy Materik	31	L1
Mutoray	71	U5
Mutsamudu	67	G2
Mutsu	81	L3
Mutsu-wan	81	L3
Muttaburra	87	H4
Muyezerskiy	29	R5
Muyinga	65	E4
Muynak	71	K9
Muzaffarnagar	75	C3
Muzaffarpur	75	E3
Muzillac	39	C6
Múzquiz	101	F3
Muztagata	71	N10
Mwali	67	G2
Mwanza	65	E4
Mweka	65	C4
Mwenda	65	D6
Mwene-Ditu	65	C5
Mwenezi	67	E4
Mwenezi	67	E4
Mwinilunga	67	C2
Myanmar	77	B2
Myingyan	77	B2
Myitkyina	77	B1
Myjava	43	N2
Myjava	43	N2
Mykolayiv	33	N8
Mykonos	49	H7
Mymensingh	75	F4
Mynbulak	71	L9
Myndagayy	73	N4
Myōjin	79	K4
Myonggan	81	E3
Myrdalsjökull	29	(1)D3
Myrina	49	H5
Myrtle Beach	103	F3
Mys Alevina	73	S5
Mys Aniva	79	L1
Mys Buorkhaya	73	N2
Mys Dezhneva	73	Z3
Mys Elizavety	73	Q6

Name	Page	Ref
Mys Enkan	73	P5
Mys Govena	73	V5
Mys Kanin Nos	31	H1
Mys Kekurskij	29	S2
Mys Kril'on	79	L1
Myślenice	33	J8
Myślibórz	33	D5
Mys Lopatka, *Russia*	73	T6
Mys Lopatka, *Russia*	73	S2
Mys Navarin	73	X4
Mys Olyutorskiy	73	W5
Mysore	75	C6
Mys Peschanyy	71	J9
Mys Povorotnyy	81	G2
Mys Prubiynyy	31	F5
Mys Shelagskiy	73	V2
Mys Sivuchiy	73	U5
Mys Terpeniya	73	Q7
Mys Tolstoy	73	T5
Mys Yuzhnyy	73	T5
Mys Zhelaniya	71	M2
Myszksw	33	J7
My Tho	77	D4
Mytilini	49	J5
Mývatn	29	(1)E2
Mže	35	H7
Mzimba	67	E2
Mzuzu	67	E2

N

Name	Page	Ref
Naalehu	101	(2)F4
Naas	37	F8
Nabas	77	G4
Naberezhnyye Chelny	31	K3
Nabeul	45	E12
Nabīd	55	G2
Nabire	83	(2)E3
Nablus	54	C4
Nacala	67	G2
Náchod	33	F7
Nacogdoches	103	C3
Nadiad	75	B4
Nador	59	E2
Nadvirna	47	M1
Nadym	31	P1
Nadym	31	P2
Næstved	35	G1
Nafpaktos	49	D6
Nafplio	49	E7
Nagano	81	K5
Nagaoka	81	K5
Nagaon	75	F3
Nagarzê	75	F3
Nagasaki	81	E7
Nagaur	75	B3
Nagercoil	75	C7
Nago	79	H5
Nagold	35	D8
Nagorsk	31	K3
Nagoya	81	J6
Nagpur	75	C4
Nagqu	75	F2
Nagyatád	43	N4
Nagykállš	47	J2
Nagykanizsa	43	N4
Nagykáta	33	J10
Nagykörös	47	G2
Naha	79	H5
Nahanni	93	G4
Nahanni Butte	93	G4
Nahr en Nile = Nile	61	F2
Naiman Qi	79	G2
Nain	93	U5
Nairn	37	J4
Nairobi	65	F4
Naivasha	65	F4
Naizishan	81	D2
Najafābād	53	F3
Nájera	41	H2
Najibabad	75	C3
Najin	81	F2
Najrān	61	H4
Nakamura	81	G7
Nakatsu	81	F7
Nakhl	54	A7
Nakhodka, *Russia*	71	P4
Nakhodka, *Russia*	81	G2
Nakhon Ratchasima	77	C3
Nakhon Sawan	77	B3
Nakhon Si Thammarat	77	B5
Nakina	93	P6
Naknek	101	(1)F4
Nakonde	65	E5
Nakskov	35	G2
Nakten	29	H5
Nakuru	65	F4
Nal'chik	51	K2
Nallihan	49	P4
Nālūt	59	H2
Namagan	71	N9
Namakzar-e Shadad	55	G1
Namanga	65	F4
Namapa	67	F2
Namasagali	65	E3
Nam Can	77	C5
Nam Co	75	F2
Namdalen	29	G4
Nam Dinh	77	D2
Namib Desert	67	A4
Namibe	67	A3
Namibia	67	B4
Namlea	83	(2)C3
Namo	83	(2)A3
Nampa	97	C2
Nam Ping	77	B3
Namp'o	81	C4
Nampula	67	F3
Namsos	29	F4
Namtsy	73	M4
Namur	27	G4
Namwala	67	D3
Namwŏn	81	D6
Nan	77	C3
Nanaimo	97	B1
Nanao	81	J5
Nanchang	79	F5
Nanchong	79	D4
Nancy	43	B2
Nanda Devi	75	C2
Nänded	75	C5
Nandurbar	75	B4
Nangalala	87	G2
Nangapinoh	83	(1)E3
Nangatayap	83	(1)E3
Nangis	39	J5
Nangong	79	F3
Nang Xian	75	F3
Nanjing	79	F4
Nankoku	81	G7
Nannine	87	C5
Nanning	77	D2
Nanortalik	93	X4
Nanpan	77	D2
Nanping	79	F5
Nansei-shotō	79	H5
Nantes	39	D6
Nanton	95	D1
Nantong	79	G4
Nanumea	85	H6
Nanuque	109	J7
Nanyang	79	E4
Napa	97	B3
Napalkovo	71	N3
Napamute	101	(1)F3
Napas	73	C4
Napasoq	93	W3
Napier	89	F4
Naples = Napoli	45	J8
Naples	103	E4
Napo	109	C4
Napoli	45	J8
Naqb Ashtar	54	C6
Nara, *Japan*	81	H6
Nara, *Mali*	59	D5
Narathiwat	77	C5
Narbonne	39	H10
Nardò	45	N8
Nares Strait	91	J2
Narev	33	N5
Narew	33	L5
Narmada	75	C4
Narnaul	75	C3
Narni	45	G6
Narok	65	F4
Närpes	29	L5
Narrabi	87	J6
Narrandera	87	J6
Narsimhapur	75	C4
Nart	79	F2
Narva	29	P7
Narva	29	Q7
Narva Bay	29	P7
Narvik	29	J2
Nar'yan Mar	31	K1
Naryn	73	F6
Năsăud	47	M2
Nashua	99	F2
Nashville	103	D2
Našice	47	F4
Nasik	75	B4
Nasir	65	E2
Nassarawa	63	F3
Nassau	103	F4
Nässjö	29	H8
Nastapoka Islands	93	R5
Nasugbu	77	G4
Naswá	55	G5
Nata	67	D4
Natal	109	K5
Natara	73	L3
Natashquan	93	U6
Natchez	103	C3
Natchitoches	103	C3
National Park	89	E4
Natitingou	63	E2
Natuna Besar	83	(1)D2
Naujoji Akmenė	33	M1
Naumburg	35	G5
Na'ūr	54	C5
Nauru	85	G6
Nauta	109	C4
Nautonwa	75	D3
Navahermosa	41	F5
Navahrudak	29	N10
Navajo Reservoir	97	E3
Navalmoral de la Mata	41	E5
Navalvillar de Pela	41	E5
Navapolatsk	31	E3
Navlya	31	F4
Navoi	71	M9
Navojoa	95	E6
Navrongo	63	D2
Navsari	75	B4
Nawabshah	53	J4
Nāwah	53	J3
Naxçıvan	51	L4
Naxos	49	H7
Naxos	49	H7
Nayakhan	73	T4
Nãy Band, *Iran*	53	G3
Nãy Band, *Iran*	55	E3
Nayoro	81	M1
Nazaré	41	A5
Nazareth	54	C4
Nazarovo	71	S6
Nazca	109	C6
Nazca Ridge	111	E3
Naze	79	H5
Nazilli	49	L7
Nazino	71	P6
Nazran'	51	L2
Nazrēt	65	F2
Nazwá	53	G5
Nazyvayevsk	31	P3
Ndélé	65	C2
Ndjamena	61	B5
Ndjolé	63	G5
Ndola	67	E2
Neale Junction	87	E5
Neapoli	49	F8
Nea Zichni	49	F3
Nebbi	65	E3
Nebitdag	53	F2
Nebo	87	J4
Nebraska	97	G2
Neckar	35	D7
Neckar	35	D8
Neckarsulm	35	E7
Necker Island	85	K3
Necochea	111	K6
Nédély	61	C4
Needles	101	D2
Nefedovo	31	P3
Nefta	59	G2
Neftçala	51	N4
Neftekamsk	31	K3
Neftekumsk	51	L1
Nefteyugansk	31	P2
Nefza	45	D12
Negage	65	B5
Negăr	55	G2
Negēlē	65	F2
Negele	65	F2
Negev	54	B6
Negomane	67	F2
Negombo	75	C7
Negotin	47	K5
Negotino	49	E3
Négrine	59	G2
Negro, *Argentina*	111	J7
Negro, *Brazil*	109	E4
Negros	77	G5
Negru Vodă	47	R6
Nehbandān	53	G3
Nehe	73	M7
Nehoiu	47	P4
Neijiang	79	C5
Nei Monggol	79	E2
Neiva	109	B3
Neixiang	79	E4
Nejanilini Lake	93	M5
Nek'emtē	65	F2
Nelidovo	31	F3
Neligh	97	G2
Nellore	75	C6
Nel'ma	73	P7
Nelson	93	N5
Nelson, *Canada*	97	C1
Nelson, *New Zealand*	89	D5
Nelspruit	67	E5
Nêma	59	D5
Nëman	29	N10
Neman	33	M2
Nemours	39	H5
Nemperola	83	(2)B5
Nemunas	33	P3
Nemuro	81	N2
Nen	73	L7
Nenagh	37	D9
Nenana	101	(1)H3
Nene	27	B2
Nenjiang	73	M7
Neosho	99	B3
Nepa	73	H5
Nepal	75	D3
Nepalganj	75	D3
Nepean	99	E1
Nepomuk	35	J7
Ner	33	H5
Nera	45	G6
Neratovice	35	K6
Neris	33	P2
Nerja	41	G8
Neryungri	73	L5
Nesebŭr	47	Q7
Ness City	103	B2
Netanya	54	B4
Netherlands	27	H2
Netherlands Antilles	105	L6
Nettilling Lake	93	S3
Neubrandenburg	35	J3
Neuburg	35	G8
Neuchâtel	43	B3
Neuenhagen	35	J4
Neufchâteau, *Belgium*	27	H5
Neufchâteau, *France*	39	L5
Neufchâtel-en-Bray	27	D5
Neuhof	35	E6
Neumarkt	35	G7
Neumünster	35	F2
Neunkirchen, *Austria*	43	M3
Neunkirchen, *Germany*	35	C7
Neuquén	111	H6
Neuruppin	35	H4
Neusiedler	33	F10
Neusiedler See	43	M3

Name	Page	Ref.
Neuss	27	J3
Neustadt, *Germany*	27	L5
Neustadt, *Germany*	35	F2
Neustadt, *Germany*	35	F7
Neustadt, *Germany*	35	G6
Neustadt, *Germany*	35	G8
Neustadt, *Germany*	35	H7
Neustrelitz	35	J3
Neu-Ulm	35	F8
Neuwerk	35	D3
Neuwied	27	K4
Nevada	97	C3
Nevada	99	B3
Nevado Auzangate	109	C6
Nevado de Colima	105	D5
Nevado de Cumbal	109	B3
Nevado de Huascaran	109	B5
Nevado de Illampu	109	D7
Nevado Sajama	109	D7
Nevados de Cachi	111	H4
Never	73	L6
Nevers	39	J7
Nevesinje	47	F6
Nevėžis	29	M9
Nevinnomyssk	51	J1
Nevşehir	49	S6
Newala	65	F6
New Albany, *Ind., United States*	99	C3
New Albany, *Miss., United States*	103	D3
New Amsterdam	109	F2
Newark, *N.J., United States*	99	F2
Newark, *Oh., United States*	99	D3
Newark-on-Trent	27	B1
New Bedford	99	F2
Newberg	97	B1
New Bern	103	F2
Newberry	103	E3
New Braunfels	103	B4
New Britain	85	F6
New Brunswick	93	T7
Newburgh	99	F2
Newbury	27	A3
New Bussa	63	E3
Newcastle, *Australia*	87	K6
Newcastle, *United States*	97	F2
Newcastle-under-Lyme	37	K8
Newcastle-upon-Tyne	37	L6
Newcastle Waters	87	F3
New Delhi	75	C3
New England	97	F1
Newe Zohars	54	C5
Newfoundland	93	V5
Newfoundland	93	V7
New Georgia Island	85	F6
New Glasgow	93	U7
New Guinea	69	S10
New Hampshire	99	F2
New Hampton	99	B2
New Hanover	85	F6
Newhaven	27	C4
New Haven	99	F2
New Iberia	103	C3
New Ireland	85	F6
New Jersey	99	F2
New Liskeard	99	E1
New London	99	F2
Newman	87	C4
Newmarket	27	C2
New Meadows	97	C2
New Mexico	101	E2
Newnan	103	E3
New Orleans	103	D4
New Plymouth	89	E4
Newport, *Eng., United Kingdom*	27	A4
Newport, *Wales, United Kingdom*	37	K10
Newport, *Ark., United States*	103	C2
Newport, *Oreg., United States*	97	B2
Newport, *R.I., United States*	99	F2
Newport, *Vt., United States*	99	F2
Newport, *Wash., United States*	97	C1
New Providence	103	F5
Newquay	37	G11
Newry	37	F7
New Siberia Islands = Novosibirskiye Ostrova	73	P1
New Smyrna Beach	103	E4
New South Wales	87	H6
Newton, *Ia., United States*	99	B2
Newton, *Kans., United States*	103	B2
Newtownards	37	G7
New Ulm	99	B2
New York	99	E2
New York	99	F2
New Zealand	89	B5
Neya	31	H3
Neyrīz	55	F2
Neyshābūr	53	G2
Ngabang	83	(1)D2
Ngalu	83	(2)B5
Ngaoundéré	63	G3
Ngara	65	E4
Ngawihi	89	E5
Ngo	63	H5
Ngoura	61	C5
Ngozi	65	D4
Nguigmi	63	G2
Nguru	63	G2
Nha Trang	77	D4
Nhulunbuy	87	G2
Niafounké	59	E5
Niagara Falls	99	E2
Niamey	63	E2
Niangara	65	D3
Nia-Nia	65	D3
Nias	83	(1)B2
Nicaragua	105	G6
Nicastro	45	L10
Nice	43	C7
Nicholls Town	103	F4
Nicobar Islands	77	A5
Nicosia = Lefkosia	49	R9
Nida	33	K7
Nidym	73	F4
Nidzica	33	K4
Niebüll	35	D2
Niedere Tauern	43	J3
Niefang	63	G4
Nienburg	35	E4
Niesky	35	K5
Nieuw Amsterdam	109	F2
Nieuw Nickerie	109	F2
Nieuwpoort	27	E3
Niğde	49	S7
Niger	59	G5
Niger	63	E2
Nigeria	63	F2
Nigoring Hu	79	B3
Niigata	81	K5
Nii-jima	81	K6
Nijar	41	H8
Nijmegen	27	H3
Nikolayevsk-na-Amure	73	Q6
Nikol'sk	31	J3
Nikopol'	31	F5
Nik Pey	51	N5
Nikšić	47	F7
Nilande Atoll	75	B8
Nile	61	F3
Niles	99	C2
Nimach	75	B4
Nîmes	39	K10
Nimule	65	E3
Nin	43	L6
Nine Degree Channel	75	B7
9 de Julio	111	J6
Ning'an	81	E1
Ningbo	79	G5
Ningde	79	F5
Ninghai	79	G5
Ninh Hoa	77	D4
Ninohe	81	L3
Niobrara	97	F2
Niobrara	97	G2
Nioro	59	D5
Nioro du Sahel	63	C1
Niort	39	E7
Nipigon	99	C1
Niquelândia	109	H6
Nirmal	75	C5
Niš	47	J6
Nisa	41	C5
Niscemi	45	J11
Nishinoomote	81	F8
Nisyros	49	K8
Niterói	111	N3
Nitra	33	H9
Nitra	33	H9
Nitsa	31	M3
Niue	85	K7
Nivelles	27	G4
Nizamabad	75	C5
Nizhnekamsk	31	K3
Nizhnekamskoye Vodokhranilishche	31	K3
Nizhneudinsk	73	F5
Nizhnevartovsk	31	Q2
Nizhneyansk	73	P2
Nizhniy Lomov	31	H4
Nizhniy Novgorod	31	H3
Nizhniy Tagil	31	M3
Nizhnyaya Tunguska	73	H4
Nizhyn	31	F4
Nizip	51	G5
Nizza Monferrato	43	D6
Njazidja	67	G2
Njombe	65	E5
Njombe	65	E5
Nkambe	63	G3
Nkhotakota	67	E2
Nkongsamba	63	F4
Noatak	101	(1)F2
Nobeoka	81	F7
Noci	45	M8
Nogales, *Mexico*	101	D2
Nogales, *United States*	101	D2
Nogat	33	J3
Nogent-le-Rotrou	39	F5
Noginsk	31	G3
Noginskiy	71	S5
Nogliki	73	Q6
Noheji	81	L3
Noia	41	B2
Noire	77	C2
Nojima-zaki	81	K6
Nok Kundi	53	H4
Nola, *Central African Republic*	65	B3
Nola, *Italy*	45	J8
Nolinsk	31	J3
Noma-misaki	81	F8
Nome	101	(1)D3
Nomoi Islands	85	F5
Nomo-saki	81	E7
Nong'an	81	C1
Nong Khai	77	C3
Noord-Beveland	27	F3
Noord-Oost-Polder	27	H2
Noordwijk aan Zee	27	G2
Norak	53	J2
Noranda	99	E1
Nordaustlandet	112	(1)L1
Norden	35	C3
Nordenham	35	D3
Norderney	35	C3
Norderstedt	35	F3
Nordfriesische Inseln	35	D2
Nordhausen	35	F5
Nordhorn	27	K2
Nordkapp	29	N1
Nordkinn	29	P1
Nordkinnhalvøya	29	P1
Nordkvaløya	29	J1
Nordli	29	G4
Nördlingen	35	F8
Nord-Ostsee-Kanal	35	E2
Nordstrand	35	D2
Nordvik	71	W3
Nore	37	E9
Norfolk, *Nebr., United States*	97	G2
Norfolk, *Va., United States*	99	E3
Norfolk Island	85	G8
Noril'sk	71	R4
Norman	103	B2
Normanton	87	H3
Norman Wells	93	F3
Nørre Åby	35	E1
Nørre Alslev	35	G2
Norristown	99	E2
Norrköping	29	J7
Norrtälje	29	K7
Norseman	87	D6
Norsk	73	N6
Northallerton	37	L7
Northam	87	C6
North America	85	P2
Northampton	27	B2
North Andaman	77	A4
North Battleford	93	K6
North Bay	99	E1
North Cape	89	D2
North Carolina	103	F2
North Channel	37	G6
North Charleston	103	F3
North Dakota	97	F1
Northeast Providence Channel	103	F4
Northeim	35	F5
Northern Cape	67	C5
Northern Ireland	37	E7
Northern Mariana Islands	85	E4
Northern Province	67	D4
Northern Territory	87	F4
North Foreland	27	D3
North Horr	65	F3
North Iberia	105	F2
North Island	89	D3
North Korea	81	C4
North Little Rock	103	C3
North Platte	95	F3
North Platte	97	F2
North Ronaldsay	37	K2
North Sea	37	N4
North Stradbroke Island	87	K5
North Taranaki Bight	89	D4
North Uist	37	E4
Northumberland Strait	93	U7
North Vancouver	97	B1
North West	67	C5
North West Basin	87	C4
North West Cape	87	B4
North West Christmas Island Ridge	85	K4
North West Highlands	37	G4
Northwest Territories	93	G4
Norton	103	B2
Norton Sound	101	(1)E3
Norway	29	F5
Norwegian Sea	29	B4
Norwich, *United Kingdom*	27	D2
Norwich, *United States*	99	F2
Nos	31	H1
Nos Emine	47	Q7
Nosevaya	31	K1
Noshiro	81	K3
Nos Kaliakra	47	R6
Noşrātābād	53	G4
Nosy Barren	67	G3
Nosy Bé	67	H2
Nosy Boraha	67	J3
Nosy Mitsio	67	H2
Nosy Radama	67	H2
Nosy-Varika	67	H4
Notec	33	G4
Notia Pindos	49	D5
Notios Evvoïkos Kolpos	49	F6
Notre Dame Bay	93	V7
Notsé	63	E3
Nottingham	27	A2
Nottingham Island	93	R4
Nouâdhibou	59	B4
Nouakchott	59	B5
Nouméa	85	G8
Nouvelle Calédonie	85	G8
Nova Gorica	43	J5
Nova Gradiška	43	E4
Nova Iguaçu	111	N3
Nova Mambone	67	F4
Nova Pazova	47	H5
Novara	43	D5
Nova Scotia	93	T8
Novaya Igirma	73	G5
Novaya Karymkary	31	N2
Novaya Kasanka	31	J5
Novaya Lyalya	31	M3
Novaya Zemlya	71	J3
Nova Zagora	47	P7
Novelda	41	K6

Name	Page	Ref
Nové Město	33	F8
Nové Mesto	33	G9
Nové Zámky	33	H10
Novgorod	31	F3
Novi Bečej	47	H4
Novi Iskŭr	47	L7
Novi Ligure	43	D6
Novi Marof	43	M4
Novi Pazar, *Bulgaria*	47	Q6
Novi Pazar, *Yugoslavia*	47	H6
Novi Sad	47	G4
Novi Vinodolski	43	K5
Novoaleksandrovsk	31	H5
Novoalekseyevka	31	L4
Novoanninsky	31	H4
Novocheboksarsk	31	J3
Novocherkassk	31	H5
Novodvinsk	31	H2
Novo Hamburgo	111	L4
Novohrad-Volyns'kyy	31	E4
Novokazalinsk	31	M5
Novokutznetsk	71	R7
Novokuybyshevsk	31	J4
Novo Mesto	43	L5
Novomikhaylovskiy	51	H1
Novomoskovsk	31	G4
Novonazimovo	73	E5
Novorossiysk	51	G1
Novorybnoye	73	H2
Novoselivka	47	S2
Novosergiyevka	31	K4
Novosibirsk	71	Q6
Novosibirskiye Ostrova	73	P1
Novosil'	31	G4
Novotroitsk	31	L4
Novouzensk	31	J4
Novozybkov	31	F4
Nový Bor	35	K6
Nóvý Jičín	33	H8
Novyy Port	71	N4
Novyy Uoyan	73	J5
Novyy Urengoy	71	P4
Novyy Uzen'	71	J9
Nowa Ruda	33	F7
Nowata	103	B2
Nowogard	33	E4
Nowo Warpno	35	K3
Nowra	87	K6
Now Shahr	53	F2
Nowy Dwór Mazowiecki	33	K5
Nowy Sącz	33	K8
Nowy Targ	33	K8
Nowy Tomyśl	33	F5
Noyabr'sk	71	P5
Noyon	27	E5
Nsombo	67	D2
Ntem	63	G4
Ntwetwe Pan	67	C4
Nu	75	G2
Nuasjärvi	29	Q4
Nubian Desert	61	F3
Nudo Coropuna	109	C7
Nueltin Lake	93	M4
Nueva Rosita	101	F3
Nueva San Salvador	105	G6
Nuevo Casas Grandes	101	E2
Nuevo Laredo	101	G3
Nugget Point	89	B8
Nuhaka	89	F4
Nuku'alofa	85	J8
Nuku Hiva	85	M6
Nukumanu Islands	85	F6
Nukunonu	85	J6
Nukus	71	K9
Nullarbor Plain	87	E6
Numan	63	G3
Numazu	81	K6
Numbulwar	87	G2
Numfor	83	(2)E3
Numto	31	P2
Nunarsuit	93	X4
Nunavut	93	M3
Nuneaton	27	A2
Nunivak Island	101	(1)D3
Nunligram	73	Y3
Núoro	45	D8
Nuquí	109	B2
Nura	31	P4
Nurābād	55	D1
Nurata	53	J1
Nurmes	29	Q5
Nürnberg	35	G7
Nürtingen	43	E2
Nurzec	33	M5
Nushki	53	J4
Nutak	93	U5
Nuuk	93	W4
Nuussuaq	93	W2
Nyagan'	31	N2
Nyahururu	65	F3
Nyala	61	D5
Nyalam	75	E3
Nyamlell	65	D2
Nyamtumbo	65	F6
Nyandoma	31	H2
Nyantakara	65	E4
Nyborg	35	F1
Nybro	29	H8
Nyda	71	N4
Nyima	75	E2
Nyingchi	75	F3
Nyírbátor	47	K2
Nyíregyháza	33	L10
Nykarleby	29	M5
Nykøbing	35	G2
Nyköping	29	J7
Nylstroom	67	D4
Nymburk	33	E7
Nynäshamn	29	J7
Nyngan	87	J6
Nyon	43	B4
Nysa	33	D6
Nysa	33	G7
Nyukhcha	31	J2
Nyunzu	65	D5
Nyurba	73	K4
Nyuya	73	K4
Nzega	65	E4
Nzérékoré	63	C3
N'zeto	65	A5
Nzwami	67	G2

O

Name	Page	Ref
Oaho	101	(2)D2
Oahu	85	L3
Oakdale	103	C3
Oakham	27	B2
Oak Lake	97	F1
Oakland	97	B3
Oak Lawn	99	C2
Oakley	103	A2
Oak Ridge	99	D3
Oamaru	89	C7
Oaxaca	105	E5
Ob'	31	N2
Obama	81	H6
Oban	37	G5
O Barco	41	D2
Oberdrauburg	43	H4
Oberhausen	27	J3
Oberkirch	35	D8
Oberlin	103	A2
Oberndorf	43	H3
Oberstdorf	43	F3
Oberursel	35	D6
Obervellach	33	C11
Oberwart	43	M3
Obi	83	(2)C3
Obidos	109	F4
Obigarm	53	K2
Obihiro	81	M2
Obluch'ye	73	N7
Obninsk	31	G3
Obo, *Central African Republic*	65	D2
Obo, *China*	79	C3
Oborniki	33	F5
Obouya	63	H5
Oboyan'	31	G4
Obskaya Guba	71	N4
Obuasi	63	D3
Ob'yachevo	31	J2
Ocala	103	E4
Ocaña, *Colombia*	109	C2
Ocaña, *Spain*	41	G5
Ocean City	99	E3
Ocean Falls	93	F6
Oceanside	101	C2
Och'amch'ire	51	J2
Ochsenfurt	35	E7
Oconto	99	C2
Oda	63	D3
Ōda	81	G6
Ōdate	81	L3
Odda	29	D6
Odemira	41	B7
Ödemiş	49	L6
Odense	35	F1
Oder = Odra	33	F6
Oderzo	43	H5
Odesa	31	F5
Odessa = Odesa, *Ukraine*	31	F5
Odessa, *United States*	101	F2
Odienné	63	C3
Odorheiu Secuiesc	47	N3
Odra	33	F6
Odžaci	47	G4
Oeiras	109	J5
Oelrichs	97	F2
Oelsnitz	35	H6
Oeno	85	N8
Oestev	111	H7
Ofaqim	54	B5
Offenbach	35	D6
Offenburg	43	C2
Ōgaki	81	J6
Ogasawara-shotō	69	T7
Ogbomosho	63	E3
Ogden	97	D2
Ogdensburg	93	R8
Ogilvie Mountains	93	C4
Oglio	43	E5
Ogosta	47	L6
Ogre	29	N8
Ogre	29	N8
O Grove	41	B2
Ogulin	43	L5
Ohai	89	A7
Ohio	99	C3
Ohio	99	D2
Ohre	35	J6
Ohrid	49	C3
Ohura	89	E4
Oiapoque	109	G3
Oil City	99	E2
Oise	27	E5
Ōita	81	F7
Ojinaga	101	F3
Ojos del Salado	111	H4
Oka	73	G6
Okaba	83	(2)E4
Okahandja	67	B4
Okanagan Lake	95	C2
Okano	63	G4
Okanogan	97	C1
Okara	75	B2
Okarem	53	F2
Okaya	81	K5
Okayama	81	G6
Okene	63	F3
Oker	35	F4
Okha, *India*	53	J5
Okha, *Russia*	73	Q6
Okhansk	31	L3
Okhotsk	73	Q5
Okhtyrka	31	F4
Okinawa	79	H5
Okinawa	79	H5
Oki-shotō	81	G5
Okitipupa	63	E3
Oklahoma	103	B2
Oklahoma City	103	B2
Okoppe	81	M1
Okoyo	63	H5
Okranger	29	E5
Oksino	31	K1
Oktinden	29	H4
Oktyabr'sk	31	L5
Oktyabr'skiy	31	K4
Okurchan	73	S5
Okushiri-tō	81	K2
Olancha	97	C3
Öland	29	J8
Olanga	29	Q3
Olathe	103	C2
Olava	35	J7
Olavarría	111	H6
Oława	33	G7
Ólbia	45	D8
Olching	43	G2
Old Crow	101	(1)K2
Oldenburg, *Germany*	35	D3
Oldenburg, *Germany*	35	F2
Oldenzaal	27	J2
Oldham	37	L8
Old Head of Kinsale	37	D10
Olean	99	E2
Olekma	73	L5
Olekminsk	73	L4
Oleksandriya	31	F5
Olenegorsk	29	S2
Olenek	73	J3
Olenëk	73	L2
Olenëkskiy Zaliv	73	L2
Olhão	41	C7
Olib	43	K6
Olinda	109	L5
Oliva	41	K6
Olivet	97	G2
Olivia	99	B2
Olmos	109	B5
Olney	103	B3
Olochi	73	K6
Olonets	31	F2
Olongapo	77	G4
Oloron-Ste-Marie	39	E10
Olot	41	N2
Olovyannaya	73	K6
Olpe	27	K3
Olsztyn	33	K4
Olt	47	M4
Olten	43	C3
Olteniţa	47	P5
Oltu	51	K3
Oluan-pi	77	G2
Olvera	41	E8
Olympia	97	B1
Olympos	49	E4
Olympus	49	Q10
Olyutorskiy	73	W4
Olyutorskiy Zaliv	73	V4
Om'	71	N6
Oma	75	D2
Omae-saki	81	K6
Omagh	37	E7
Omaha	97	G2
Omak	97	C1
Omakau	89	B7
Oman	53	G5
Omapere	89	D2
Omarama	89	B7
Omaruru	67	B4
Omba	75	F6
Ombrone	45	F6
Omdurman = Umm Durman	61	F4
Omegna	43	D5
Omeo	87	J7
Om Hajer	61	G5
Omīdeyeh	55	C1
Omis	43	M7
Ommen	27	J2
Omolon	73	T3
Omoloy	73	N3
Omo Wenz	63	F2
Omsk	71	N6
Omsukchan	73	S4
Ōmū	81	M1
Omulew	33	L4
Omuta	81	F7
Onda	41	K5
Ondangwa	67	B3
Ondjiva	67	B3
Ondo	63	E3
Ondörhaan	79	E1
One and a Half Degree Channel	75	B8

Name	Page	Grid
Onega	31	G2
O'Neill	97	G2
Oneonta	99	F2
Oneşti	47	P3
Onezhskoye Ozero	31	F2
Ongjin	81	C5
Ongole	75	D5
Onguday	71	R7
Oni	51	K2
Onilahy	67	G4
Onitsha	63	F3
Ono	81	J6
Onon	73	J7
Onon	73	J7
Onslow Bay	105	J2
Onsong	81	E2
Ontario	93	N6
Ontinyent	41	K6
Ontonagon	99	C1
Onyx	101	C1
Oodnadatta	87	G5
Oologah Lake	103	B2
Oostburg	27	F3
Oostelijk-Flevoland	27	H2
Oostende	27	E3
Oosterhout	27	G3
Oosterschelde	27	F3
Ootsa Lake	93	F6
Opala	65	C4
Oparino	31	J3
Opava	33	G8
Opelika	103	D3
Opelousas	103	C3
Opheim	97	E1
Opochka	31	E3
Opoczno	33	K6
Opole	33	G7
Opornyy	71	J8
Opotiki	89	F4
Opp	103	D3
Opunake	89	D4
Opuwo	67	A3
Oradea	47	J2
Orahovac	47	H7
Orai	75	C3
Oran	41	K9
Orán	111	J3
Orange	67	C5
Orange, Australia	87	J6
Orange, France	39	K9
Orange, United States	103	C3
Orangeburg	103	E3
Orangeville	99	D2
Orango	63	A2
Oranienburg	35	J4
Orapa	67	D4
Orăştie	47	L4
Oraviţa	47	J4
Orbetello	45	F6
Orco	43	C5
Ordes	41	B1
Ordes Santa Comba	41	B1
Ordu	51	G3
Ordway	97	F3
Öreälven	29	K4
Örebro	29	H7
Oregon	97	B2
Oregon	99	A3
Orekhovo-Zuyevo	31	G3
Orel	31	G4
Orem	97	D2
Orenburg	31	L4
Orestiada	49	J3
Orford Ness	27	D2
Orhei	47	R2
Orihuela	41	K6
Orillia	99	E2
Orinoco	109	D2
Orinoco Delta = Delta del Orinoco	109	E2
Orissaare	29	M7
Oristano	45	C9
Orivesi	29	Q5
Orkla	29	F5
Orkney Islands	37	K3
Orlando	103	E4
Orléans	39	G6
Orlik	73	F6
Orly	27	E6
Ormara	53	H4
Ormoc	77	G4
Ormos Almyrou	49	G9
Ormos Mesara	49	G9
Ornans	39	M6
Örnö	29	K7
Örnsköldsvik	29	K5
Orocué	109	C3
Orofino	97	C1
Oromocto	99	G1
Orona	85	J6
Oronoque	109	F3
Oroqen Zizhiqi	73	L6
Orosei	45	D8
Orosháza	47	H3
Oroszlany	33	H10
Orotukan	73	S4
Oroville	97	B3
Orroroo	87	G6
Orsay	39	H5
Orsha	31	F4
Orsk	31	L4
Orşova	47	K5
Ørsta	29	D5
Ortaklar	49	K7
Orthez	39	E10
Ortigueira	41	C1
Ortisei	43	G4
Ortles	43	F4
Ortona	45	J6
Ortonville	99	A1
Orümīyeh	51	L5
Oruro	109	D7
Orvieto	45	G6
Orville	39	L6
Ōsaka	81	H6
Osäm	47	M6
Osceola	99	B2
Oschatz	35	J5
Oschersleben	35	G4
Osh	71	N9
Oshamambe	81	L2
Oshawa	99	E2
Oshkosh, Nebr., United States	97	F2
Oshkosh, Wis., United States	99	C2
Oshogbo	63	E3
Osijek	47	F4
Ósimo	43	J7
Oskaloosa	99	B2
Oskarshamn	29	J8
Oslo	29	F7
Oslofjorden	29	F7
Osmancık	51	F3
Osmaniye	51	G5
Osnabrück	27	L2
Osor	43	K6
Osorno	111	G7
Osprey Reef	87	J2
Oss	27	H3
Osseo	99	B2
Ossora	73	U5
Ostashkov	31	F3
Oste	35	E3
Osterburg	35	G4
Østerdalen	29	F6
Osterholz-Scharmbeck	35	D3
Osterode	35	F5
Östersund	29	H5
Ostfriesische Inseln	35	C3
Ostiglia	43	G5
Ostrava	33	H8
Ostróda	33	K4
Ostrołęka	33	L4
Ostrov, Czech Republic	35	H6
Ostrov, Russia	31	E3
Ostrova Medvezh'I	73	T2
Ostrov Atlasova	73	S6
Ostrova Vrangelya	91	V4
Ostrov Ayon	73	V2
Ostrov Belyy	71	N3
Ostrov Beringa	73	V6
Ostrov Bol'shevik	71	V2
Ostrov Bol'shoy Begichev	73	J2
Ostrov Bol'shoy Lyakhovskiy	73	Q2
Ostrov Bol'shoy Shantar	73	P6
Ostrov Chechen'	51	M2
Ostrov Iturup	81	P1
Ostrov Kil'din	29	T2
Ostrov Kolguyev	71	H4
Ostrov Komsomolets	71	T1
Ostrov Kotel'nyy	73	P1
Ostrov Kunashir	81	P1
Ostrov Mednyy	73	V6
Ostrov Mezhdusharskiy	71	H3
Ostrov Novaya Sibir'	73	S2
Ostrov Ogurchinskiy	53	F2
Ostrov Oktyabr'skoy	71	S2
Ostrov Onekotan	73	S7
Ostrov Paramushir	73	T6
Ostrov Rasshua	73	S7
Ostrov Shiashkotan	73	S7
Ostrov Shumshu	73	T6
Ostrov Simushir	73	S7
Ostrov Urup	73	S7
Ostrov Ushakova	71	Q1
Ostrov Vaygach	71	K3
Ostrov Vise	71	P2
Ostrov Vosrozhdeniya	71	K9
Ostrov Vrangelya	73	W2
Ostrowiec Świętokrzyski	33	L7
Ostrów Mazowiecka	33	L5
Ostrów Wielkopolski	33	G6
Ostuni	45	M8
Osum	49	C4
Ōsumi-shotō	81	F8
Osuna	41	E7
Oswego	99	E2
Oświęcim	33	J7
Otago Peninsula	89	C7
Otaki	89	E5
Otaru	81	L2
Oţelu Roşu	47	K4
Othonoi	49	B5
Oti	63	E3
Otjiwarongo	67	B4
Otočac	43	L6
Otog Qi	79	D3
Otoineppu	81	M1
Otorohanga	89	E4
Ótranto	45	N8
Otrøy	29	D5
Ōtsu	81	H6
Otta	29	E6
Ottawa	99	E1
Ottawa, Canada	99	E1
Ottawa, Ill., United States	99	C2
Ottawa, Kans., United States	103	B2
Ottawa Islands	93	Q5
Otterøy	29	F4
Ottobrunn	43	G2
Ottumwa	99	B2
Otukpo	63	F3
Ouachita Mountains	103	C3
Ouadâne	59	C4
Ouadda	65	C2
Ouagadougou	63	D2
Oualàta	59	D5
Ouargla	59	G2
Ouarzazate	59	D2
Oudenaarde	27	F4
Oudenbosch	27	G3
Oudtshoorn	67	C6
Oued Medjerda	45	D12
Oued Meliane	45	D12
Oued Tiélat	41	K9
Oued Zem	59	D2
Ouésso	63	H4
Ouezzane	59	D2
Oujda	59	E2
Oulainen	29	N4
Oulu	29	N4
Oulujärvi	29	P4
Oulujoki	29	P4
Oulx	43	B5
Oum-Chalouba	61	D4
Oum-Hadjer	61	C5
Our	27	J4
Ouray	97	E3
Ourense	41	C2
Ouricurí	109	J5
Ourthe	27	H4
Oustreham	27	B5
Outer Hebrides	37	D4
Outjo	67	B4
Outokumpu	29	Q5
Out Skerries	37	M1
Ouyen	87	H7
Ovacık	49	R8
Ovada	43	D6
Ovalle	111	G5
Ovareli	51	L3
Overflakkee	27	G3
Overlander Roadhouse	87	B5
Overland Park	103	C2
Overton	97	D3
Övertorneå	29	M3
Ovidiopol'	47	T3
Oviedo	41	E1
Owaka	89	B8
Owando	63	H5
Owase	81	J6
Owatonna	99	B2
Owensboro	99	C3
Owens Lake	97	C3
Owen Sound	99	D2
Owerri	63	F3
Owo	63	F3
Owosso	99	D2
Owyhee	97	C2
Owyhee	97	C2
Oxford, New Zealand	89	D6
Oxford, United Kingdom	27	A3
Oxnard	101	C2
Oyama	81	K5
Oyapock	109	G3
Oyem	63	G4
Oyen	95	D1
Oyonnax	43	A4
Ózd	33	K9
Ozernovskiy	73	T6
Ozero Alakol'	71	Q8
Ozero Aralsor	31	J5
Ozero Aydarkul'	71	M9
Ozero Balkhash	71	N8
Ozero Baykal	73	H6
Ozero Beloye	31	G2
Ozero Chany	71	P7
Ozero Chernoye	31	N3
Ozero Il'men'	31	F3
Ozero-Imandra	29	R2
Ozero Inder	71	J8
Ozero Janis'jarvi	29	R5
Ozero Kamennoje	29	R4
Ozero Kanozero	29	T3
Ozero Karaginskiy	73	U5
Ozero Khanka	81	G1
Ozero Kolvitskoye	29	S3
Ozero Kovdozero	29	S3
Ozero Kulundinskoye	71	P7
Ozero Kushmurun	31	N4
Ozero Lama	73	D2
Ozero Leksozero	29	R5
Ozero Lovozero	29	T2
Ozero Morzhovets	31	H1
Ozero Njuk	29	R4
Ozero Ozhogino	73	R3
Ozero Pirenga	29	R3
Ozero Pyaozero	29	R3
Ozero Saltaim	31	P3
Ozero Sarpa	31	J5
Ozero Segozeroskoye	31	F2
Ozero Seletyteniz	71	N7
Ozero Sredneye Kuyto	29	R4
Ozero Taymyr	71	U3
Ozero Teletskoye	71	R7
Ozero Tengiz	31	N4
Ozero Topozero	29	R4
Ozero Umbozero	29	T3
Ozero Vygozero	31	G2
Ozero Yalpug	47	R4
Ozero Zaysan	71	Q8
Ozero Zhaltyr	31	K5
Ozero Zhamanakkol'	31	M5
Ozersk	33	M3
Ozhogina	73	R3
Ozhogino	73	R3
Ozieri	45	C8
Ozinki	31	J4

Name	Page	Grid
Ozona	101	F2
Ozurget'i	51	J3

P

Name	Page	Grid
Paamiut	93	X4
Paar	35	G8
Paarl	67	B6
Pabbay	37	E4
Pabianice	33	J6
Pabna	75	E4
Pacasmayo	109	B5
Pachino	45	K12
Pachuca	105	E4
Pacific Ocean	85	M3
Pacitan	83	(1)E4
Packwood	97	B1
Padalere	83	(2)B3
Padang	83	(1)C3
Padangpanjang	83	(1)C3
Padangsidempuan	83	(1)B2
Paderborn	35	D5
Pádova	43	G5
Padre Island	103	B4
Padrón	41	B2
Paducah, Ky., United States	99	C3
Paducah, Tex., United States	101	F2
Padum	75	C2
Paekdu San	81	D3
Paeroa	89	E3
Pafos	49	Q10
Pag	43	K6
Pag	43	L6
Pagadian	77	G5
Pagai Selatan	83	(1)B3
Pagai Utara	83	(1)B3
Pagalu = Annobón	63	F5
Pagan	85	E4
Pagatan	83	(1)F3
Page, Ariz., United States	101	D1
Page, Okla., United States	103	C3
Pagosa Springs	97	E3
Pagri	75	E3
Pahiatua	89	E5
Paia	101	(2)E3
Paide	29	N7
Päijänne	29	N6
Painan	83	(1)C3
Painesville	99	D2
Paisley	37	H6
Paita	109	A5
Pakaraima Mountains	109	E2
Pakch'ŏn	81	C4
Paki	63	F2
Pakistan	53	J4
Pakokku	77	A2
Pakotai	89	D2
Pakrac	43	N5
Paks	47	F3
Pakxé	77	D3
Pala	61	B6
Palafrugell	41	P3
Palagónia	45	J11
Palagruža	45	L6
Palamós	41	P3
Palana	73	U5
Palanga	33	L2
Palangkaraya	83	(1)E3
Palanpur	75	B4
Palantak	53	H4
Palatka, Russia	73	S4
Palatka, United States	103	E4
Palau	45	D7
Palau	85	D5
Palau	85	D5
Palawan	77	F5
Palazzolo Arcéide	45	J11
Palembang	83	(1)C3
Palencia	41	F2
Paleokastritsa	49	B5
Palermo	45	H10
Palestine	103	B3
Palestrina	45	G7
Paletwa	77	A2
Palghat	75	C6
Pali	75	B3
Palikir	85	F5
Palimbang	77	G5
Palk Strait	75	C7
Palma	41	N5
Palma del Rio	41	E7
Palma di Montechiaro	45	H11
Palmanova	43	J5
Palmares	109	K5
Palmarola	45	G8
Palmas	109	H6
Palmas	111	L4
Palm Bay	103	E4
Palmdale	101	C2
Palmerston	89	C7
Palmerston Island	85	K7
Palmerston North	89	E5
Palm Harbor	103	E4
Palmi	45	K10
Palmira	109	B3
Palmyra Island	85	K5
Palojärvi	29	M2
Palopo	83	(2)B3
Palu, Indonesia	83	(2)A3
Palu, Turkey	51	J4
Paluostrov Taymyr	71	R3
Palyavaam	73	W3
Pama	63	E2
Pamhagen	43	M3
Pamiers	39	G10
Pamlico Sound	103	F2
Pampa	101	F1
Pampas	111	J6
Pamplona, Colombia	105	K7
Pamplona, Spain	41	J2
Panagyurishte	47	M7
Panaji	75	B5
Panama	105	H7
Panamá	109	B2
Panama Canal = Canal de Panamá	105	J7
Panama City	103	D3
Panara	43	G6
Panaria	45	K10
Panarik	83	(1)D2
Panay	77	G4
Pančevo	47	H5
Panciu	47	Q4
Pandharpur	75	C5
Panevėžys	33	P2
Pangin	75	F3
Pangkajene	83	(2)A3
Pangkalpinang	83	(1)D3
Pangnirtung	93	T3
Panguitch	97	D3
Pangutaran Group	77	G5
Panhandle	101	F1
Panipat	75	C3
Panjāb	53	J3
Panjgur	53	H4
Pankshin	63	F3
Pantanal	109	F7
Pantar	83	(2)B4
Pantelleria	59	H1
Páola	45	L9
Paoua	65	B2
Pápa	47	E2
Papa	101	(2)F4
Papakura	89	E3
Papantla	105	E4
Paparoa	89	E3
Papa Stour	37	L1
Papa Westray	37	K2
Papenburg	35	C3
Papey	29	(1)F2
Papua New Guinea	85	E6
Papun	77	B3
Pará	109	G5
Para	109	H4
Parabel'	71	Q6
Paracatu	109	J7
Paracel Islands	77	E3
Paracín	47	J6
Pará de Minas	109	J7
Paragould	103	C2
Paragua, Bolivia	109	E6
Paragua, Venezuela	109	E2
Paraguay	107	F6
Paraguay	111	J3
Paraíba	109	K5
Parakou	63	E3
Paralimni	54	A1
Paramaribo	109	F2
Paraná	109	H6
Paraná	109	H6
Paraná	111	J5
Paraná	111	K4
Paraná	111	L3
Paranaguá	111	M4
Paranaíba	109	G7
Paranaíba	109	G7
Paranavaí	111	L3
Paranestio	49	G3
Paraparaumu	89	E5
Parbhani	75	C5
Parchim	35	G3
Pardo	109	J7
Pardubice	33	E7
Pareh	51	L4
Parepare	83	(2)A3
Parga	49	C5
Parigi	83	(2)B3
Parika	109	F2
Parintins	109	F4
Paris, France	39	H5
Paris, Tenn., United States	103	D2
Paris, Tex., United States	103	B3
Parkersburg	99	D3
Park Rapids	99	A1
Parla	41	G4
Parma	43	F6
Parma, Italy	43	F6
Parma, United States	99	D2
Parnaíba	109	J4
Parnassus	89	D6
Pärnu	29	N7
Pärnu	29	N7
Paros	49	H7
Paros	49	H7
Parry Bay	93	Q3
Parry Islands	93	L1
Parry Sound	99	D2
Parsons	103	B2
Parthenay	39	E7
Partinico	45	H10
Partizansk	81	G2
Paru	109	G4
Parvatipuram	75	D5
Paryang	75	D2
Pasadena, Calif., United States	101	C2
Pasadena, Tex., United States	103	B4
Paşalimani Adası	49	K4
Pasawng	77	B3
Paşcani	47	P2
Pasco	97	C1
Pasewalk	35	K3
Pasig	77	G4
Pasinler	51	J3
Pasłęk	33	J3
Pasłęk	33	J3
Pasleka	29	L9
Pašman	43	L7
Pasni	53	H4
Paso de Hachado	111	G6
Paso de Indios	111	H7
Paso de la Cumbre	111	H5
Paso de San Francisco	111	H4
Paso Río Mayo	111	G8
Paso Robles	101	B1
Passau	35	J8
Passo Fundo	111	L4
Passos	109	H8
Pastavy	29	P9
Pasto	109	B3
Pastos Bons	109	J5
Pásztó	47	G2
Patagonia	111	G8
Patan, India	75	B4
Patan, Nepal	75	E3
Patea	89	E4
Pate Island	65	G4
Paterna	41	K5
Paterno	45	J11
Paterson	99	F2
Pathankot	75	C2
Pathein	77	A3
Pathfinder Reservoir	97	E2
Patia	109	B3
Patiala	75	C2
Patmos	49	J7
Patna	75	E3
Patnos	51	K4
Patos de Minas	109	H7
Patra	49	D6
Patraikis Kolpos	49	D6
Patreksfjörður	29	(1)B2
Pattani	77	C5
Pattaya	77	C4
Patti	45	J10
Paturau River	89	D5
Pau	41	K1
Pauini	109	D5
Pauini	109	D5
Paulatuk	101	(1)N2
Paulo Afonso	109	K5
Paul's Valley	103	B3
Päveh	51	M6
Pavia	43	E5
Pãvilosta	29	L8
Pavlikeni	47	N6
Pavlodar	71	P7
Pavlohrad	31	G5
Pavlovsk	31	H4
Pavlovskaya	31	G5
Pavullo nel Frignano	43	F6
Paxoi	49	C5
Paxson	101	(1)H3
Payerne	43	B4
Payette	97	C2
Payne's Find	87	C5
Paysandu	111	K5
Payson	101	D2
Payturma	71	S3
Pazar	51	J3
Pazardzhik	47	M7
Pazin	43	J5
Peace	93	H5
Peace River	93	H5
Peach Springs	101	D1
Pearsall	103	B4
Pebane	67	F3
Pebas	109	C5
Peć	47	H7
Pecan Island	103	C4
Pechora	31	K1
Pechora	31	L1
Pechorskoye More	71	J4
Pechory	29	P8
Pecos	101	F2
Pecos	101	F2
Pécs	47	F3
Pedja	29	P7
Pedra Azul	109	J7
Pedra Lume	63	(1)B1
Pedreiras	109	J4
Pedro Afonso	109	H5
Pedro Juan Caballero	111	K3
Pedro Luro	111	J6
Peel Sound	93	M2
Peene	35	J3
Peenemünde	35	J2
Pegasus Bay	89	D6
Pegnitz	35	G7
Pegu	77	B3
Pegunungan Barisan	83	(1)B2
Pegunungan Iban	83	(1)F2
Pegunungan Meratus	83	(1)F3
Pegunungan Schwaner	83	(1)E3
Pegunungan Van Rees	83	(2)E3
Pehuajó	111	J6
Peine	35	F4
Peißenberg	43	G3
Peixe	109	H6
Pekalongan	83	(1)D4
Pekanbaru	83	(1)C2
Peking = Beijing	79	F3
Peleduy	73	J5
Peleng	83	(2)B3
Pelhřimov	33	E8

Name	Page	Grid
Pelješac	45	M6
Pello	29	N3
Pellworm	35	D2
Pelly Bay	93	P3
Peloponnisos	49	D7
Pelotas	111	L5
Pelym	31	M2
Pemangkat	83	(1)D2
Pematangsiantar	83	(1)B2
Pemba	67	G2
Pemba Island	65	F5
Pembina	97	G1
Pembine	99	C1
Pembroke, Canada	99	E1
Pembroke, United Kingdom	37	H10
Pembroke, United States	103	E3
Peñafiel	41	F3
Peñaranda de Bracamonte	41	E4
Peñarroya-Pueblonuevo	41	E6
Pendleton	97	C1
Pendolo	83	(1)G3
Pend Oreille Lake	97	C1
Pen Hills	99	E2
Peniche	41	A5
Península de Azuero	105	H7
Península de Guajira	105	K6
Península Valdés	111	J7
Péninsule de Gaspé	93	T7
Péninsule d'Ungava	93	R4
Penmarch	39	A6
Penne	45	H6
Pennines	37	K7
Pennsylvania	99	E2
Penrith	37	K7
Pensacola	105	G2
Penticton	97	C1
Penza	31	J4
Penzance	37	G11
Penzhina	73	V4
Penzhinskaya Guba	73	U4
Penzhinskiy Khrebet	73	V4
Peoria, Ariz., United States	101	D2
Peoria, Ill., United States	99	C2
Percival Lakes	87	D4
Peregrebnoye	31	N2
Pereira	109	B3
Pergamino	111	J5
Périgueux	39	F8
Peristera	49	G5
Perito Moreno	111	G8
Perleberg	35	G3
Perm'	31	L3
Përmet	49	C4
Pernambuco	109	K5
Pernik	47	L7
Péronne	27	E5
Perpignan	39	H11
Perrine	103	E4
Perry, Fla., United States	103	E3
Perry, Ga., United States	103	E3
Persepolis	55	E2
Persian Gulf	55	C2
Perth, Australia	87	C6
Perth, United Kingdom	37	J5
Pertuis Breton	39	D7
Peru	99	C2
Peru	109	C6
Peru-Chile Trench	107	D5
Perúgia	45	G5
Pervomays'k	31	F5
Pervoural'sk	31	L3
Pésaro	43	H7
Pescara	45	J6
Pescia	43	F7
Peshawar	75	B2
Peshkopi	49	C3
Peshtera	49	G2
Peski Karakumy	53	G2
Peski Kzylkum	71	L9
Peski Priaral'skiye Karakumy	71	L8
Pesnica	43	L4
Pessac	39	E9
Petah Tiqwa	54	B4
Petalioi	49	G7
Petaluma	97	B3
Pétange	27	H5
Petare	105	L6
Petauke	67	E2
Peterborough, Canada	99	E2
Peterborough, United Kingdom	37	M9
Peterhead	37	L4
Peter I Øy	112	(2)JJ3
Petersburg	99	E3
Petersfield	27	B3
Petershagen	35	D4
Petilia	45	L9
Peto	105	G4
Petre Bay	89	(1)B1
Petrich	49	F3
Petrila	47	L4
Petrinja	43	M5
Petrolina	109	J5
Petropavlovka	73	H6
Petropavlovsk	31	N4
Petropavlovsk-Kamchatskiy	73	T6
Petrópolis	111	N3
Petroşani	47	L4
Petrovac	47	J5
Petrovsk-Zabaykal'skiy	73	H6
Petrozavodsk	31	F2
Petrun	31	M1
Petukhovo	31	N3
Pevek	73	W3
Pezinok	33	G9
Pfaffenhofen	35	G8
Pfarrkirchen	35	H8
Pflach	43	F3
Pforzheim	35	D8
Pfunds	43	F4
Pfungstadt	35	D7
Phalaborwa	67	E4
Phalodi	75	B3
Phan Rang	77	D4
Phan Thiêt	77	D4
Phatthalung	77	C5
Phet Buri	77	B4
Phichit	77	C3
Philadelphia, Miss., United States	103	D3
Philadelphia, Pa., United States	103	E3
Philippeville	27	G4
Philippines	77	G5
Philippine Trench	69	R8
Philips	93	K7
Phillipsburg	97	G3
Phitsanulok	77	C3
Phnum Penh	77	C4
Phoenix	101	D2
Phoenix Islands	85	J6
Phôngsali	77	C2
Phuket	77	B5
Piacenza	43	E5
Piádena	43	F5
Pianosa	45	E6
Piatra-Neamţ	47	P3
Piauí	109	J5
Piazza Armerina	45	J11
Pibor Post	65	E2
Picacho del Centinela	101	F3
Picayune	103	D3
Pichilemu	111	G5
Pico	59	(1)B2
Pico Almanzor	41	E4
Pico Cristóbal Colón	105	K6
Pico da Bandeira	111	N3
Pico da Neblina	109	D3
Pico de Itambé	111	N2
Pico de Teide	59	B3
Pico Duarte	105	K5
Picos	109	J5
Picton, New Zealand	89	D5
Picton, United States	99	E2
Pic Tousside	61	C3
Piedras Negras	101	F3
Pieksämäki	29	P5
Pielinen	29	Q5
Pierre	97	F2
Pierrelatte	39	K9
Piers do Rio	109	H7
Piešťany	33	G9
Pietermaritzburg	67	E5
Pietersburg	67	D4
Pietrasanta	43	F6
Piet Retief	67	E5
Pieve di Cadore	43	H4
Pihlájavesi	29	P6
Pik Aborigen	73	R4
Piketberg	67	B6
Pik Kommunizma	53	K2
Pik Pobedy	71	P9
Piła	33	F4
Pilaya	111	H3
Pilcomayo	109	E8
Pilibhit	75	C3
Pilica	33	J7
Pimba	87	G6
Pimenta Bueno	109	E6
Pinamalayan	77	G4
Pinamar	111	K6
Pinang	77	B5
Pınarbaşı	51	G4
Pinar del Río	105	H4
Pinarhisar	49	K3
Pińczów	33	K7
Pindaré Mirim	109	H4
Pine Bluff	99	B4
Pine Bluffs	97	F2
Pine City	99	B1
Pine Creek	87	F2
Pine Creek Reservoir	99	A4
Pinega	31	H2
Pineios	49	E5
Pine Island Bay	112	(2)GG3
Pineland	103	C3
Pinerolo	43	C6
Pineville, Ky., United States	99	D3
Pineville, La., United States	103	C3
Pingdingshan	79	E4
Pingguo	77	D2
Pingle	77	E2
Pingliang	79	D3
Pingxiang, China	77	D2
Pingxiang, China	77	E1
Pinhel	41	C4
Pini	83	(1)B2
Pinka	43	M3
Pink Mountain	93	G5
Pinneberg	35	E3
Pinsk	31	E4
Pioche	97	D3
Piombino	45	E6
Pioneer	101	D2
Pioneer Mountains	97	D1
Pionerskii	33	K3
Pionerskiy	31	M2
Piotrków Trybunalski	33	J6
Piove di Sacco	43	H5
Piperi	49	G5
Pipestone	99	A2
Pipiriki	89	E4
Piqua	99	D2
Piracicaba	111	M3
Pireas	49	F7
Pirin	49	F3
Piripiri	109	J4
Pirmasens	35	C7
Pirna	35	J6
Pirot	47	K6
Piru	83	(2)C3
Pisa	33	L4
Pisa	43	F7
Pisco	109	B6
Písek	33	D8
Pishīn	53	H4
Pishin	53	J3
Piska	33	L4
Pisticci	45	L8
Pistóia	43	F7
Pisz	33	L4
Pitcairn Islands	85	P8
Piteå	29	L4
Piteälven	31	C1
Piteşti	47	M5
Pithara	87	C6
Pithiviers	39	H5
Pitkyaranta	31	F2
Pitlochry	37	J5
Pitlyar	31	N1
Pitt Island	89	(1)B2
Pittsburg	103	C2
Pittsburgh	99	D2
Pitt Strait	89	(1)B2
Piura	109	A5
Pivka	43	K5
Placer	77	G4
Placerville	101	B1
Plaiamonas	49	E5
Plains	101	F2
Plainview	101	F2
Planalto Central	109	H6
Planalto da Borborema	109	K5
Planalto do Mato Grosso	109	G6
Plankinton	97	G2
Plano	103	B3
Plasencia	41	D5
Plast	31	M4
Plateau Batéké	63	G5
Plateau du Djado	59	H4
Plateau du Limousin	39	F8
Plateau du Tademaït	59	F3
Plateau of Tibet = Xizang Gaoyuan	75	D2
Plateaux Batéké	65	A4
Platinum	101	(1)E4
Plato	105	K7
Plato Ustyurt	71	J9
Platte	103	B1
Platteville	99	B2
Plattling	35	H8
Plattsburgh	99	F2
Plattsmouth	103	B1
Plau	35	H3
Plauen	35	H6
Plavnik	43	K6
Plavsk	31	G4
Playas	109	A4
Plây Cu	77	D4
Pleasanton	101	G5
Pleiße	35	H5
Plentywood	97	F1
Plesetsk	31	H2
Pleven	47	M6
Pljevlja	47	G6
Płock	33	J5
Pločno	47	E6
Ploieşti	47	P5
Plomari	49	J6
Plön	35	F2
Płońsk	33	L5
Plovdiv	47	M7
Plumtree	67	D4
Plungė	33	L2
Plymouth, United Kingdom	37	H11
Plymouth, United States	99	C2
Plyussa	29	Q7
Plyussa	31	E3
Plzeň	33	C8
Po	43	E5
Pocahontas	105	F1
Pocatello	97	D2
Pochet	73	F5
Pochinok	31	F4
Pocking	43	J2
Pocomoke City	99	E3
Podgorica	47	G7
Podkamennaya Tunguska	73	F4
Podol'sk	31	G3
Podravska Slatina	47	E4
Poel	35	G2
Pofadder	67	B5
Poggibonsi	43	G7
Pogradec	49	C4
P'ohang	81	E5
Pohnpei	85	F5
Pohokura	89	F4
Pohořelice	43	M2
Point Arena	95	B4
Point Barrow	101	(1)F1
Point Conception	101	B3
Point Culver	87	D6
Point d'Entrecasteaux	87	B6
Pointe-Noire	63	G5
Point Hope	101	(1)D2
Point Hope	101	(1)D2
Point Pedro	75	D7
Point Sur	97	B3

Name	Page	Grid
Poitiers	39	F7
Pokaran	75	B3
Pokhara	75	D3
Poko	65	D3
Pokrovsk	73	M4
Pola de Siero	41	E1
Poland	33	G6
Polar Bluff	105	F1
Polatlı	49	Q5
Polatsk	31	E3
Police	35	K3
Polichnitos	49	J5
Poligny	39	L7
Poligus	71	S5
Polillo Islands	77	G4
Polis	49	Q9
Polistena	45	L10
Pollachi	75	C6
Pollença	41	P5
Polohy	31	G5
Polomoloc	77	H5
Polonnaruwa	75	D7
Poltava	31	F5
Poltavka	81	F1
Põltsana	29	N7
Poluostrov Shmidta	73	Q6
Poluostrov Yamal	71	M3
Poluy	71	M4
Põlva	29	P7
Polyaigos	49	G8
Polyarnye Zori	29	S3
Polyarnyy	73	X3
Polykastro	49	E4
Polynesia	85	J6
Pombal	41	B5
Pomeranian Bay	33	D3
Pomeroy	97	C1
Pomorie	47	Q7
Pompano Beach	103	E4
Pompei	45	J8
Ponca City	103	B2
Ponce	105	L5
Pondicherry	75	C6
Pond Inlet	93	R2
Ponferrada	41	D2
Poniatowa	33	M6
Ponoy	31	H1
Pons	39	E8
Ponta Delgada	59	(1)B2
Ponta do Podrão	63	G6
Ponta do Sol	63	(1)B1
Ponta Grossa	111	L4
Ponta Khehuene	67	E5
Pont-à-Mousson	39	M5
Ponta Porã	111	K3
Pontarlier	39	M7
Pontassieve	43	G7
Ponta Zavora	67	F4
Pont-d'Alin	39	L7
Ponteareas	41	B2
Ponte da Barca	41	B3
Pontedera	43	F7
Ponte de Sor	41	C5
Pontevedra	41	B2
Pontiac	99	C2
Pontianak	83	(1)D3
Pontivy	39	C5
Pontoise	27	E5
Pontorson	39	D5
Pontrémoli	43	E6
Ponza	45	G8
Poogau	43	J3
Poole	37	L11
Poole Bay	37	L11
Pooncarie	87	H6
Poopó	109	D7
Poopó Challapata	111	H2
Popayán	105	J8
Poperinge	27	E4
Popigay	71	W3
Poplar Bluff	99	B3
Poplarville	103	D3
Popocatépetl	105	E5
Popokabaka	63	H6
Popovača	43	M5
Popovo	47	P6
Poprad	33	K8
Poprad	33	K8
Porangatu	109	H6
Porbandar	53	J5
Porcupine	101	(1)K2
Pordenone	43	H5
Poreč	43	J5
Poret	45	H3
Pori	29	L6
Porirua	89	E5
Porlamar	105	M6
Poronaysk	73	Q7
Poros	49	F7
Porosozero	31	F2
Porozina	43	K5
Porpoise Bay	112	(2)T3
Porriño	41	B2
Porsangen	29	N1
Porsgrunn	29	E7
Portadown	37	F7
Portage	99	C2
Portage la Prairie	97	G1
Port Alberni	97	B1
Port Albert	87	J7
Portalegre	41	C5
Portales	101	F2
Port Arthur, Australia	87	J8
Port Arthur, United States	103	C4
Port Augusta	87	G6
Port-au-Prince	105	K5
Port Austin	99	D2
Port Burwell	93	U4
Port Charlotte	103	E4
Port Douglas	87	J3
Portel, Brazil	109	G4
Portel, Portugal	41	C6
Port Elizabeth	67	D6
Port Ellen	37	F6
Porterville	101	C1
Port Fitzroy	89	E3
Port-Gentil	63	F5
Port Harcourt	63	F4
Port Hardy	93	F6
Port Hawkesbury	93	U7
Port Hedland	87	C4
Port Hope Simpson	93	V6
Port Huron	99	D2
Pórtici	45	J8
Portimão	41	B7
Port Jefferson	99	F2
Portland, Australia	87	H7
Portland, Ind., United States	99	D2
Portland, Me., United States	99	F2
Portland, Oreg., United States	97	B1
Portland Island	89	F4
Port Laoise	37	E8
Port Lavaca	103	B4
Port Lincoln	87	G6
Port Loko	63	B3
Port Louis	67	(1)B2
Port Macquarie	87	K6
Port-Menier	93	U7
Port Moresby	87	J1
Port Nolloth	67	B5
Porto, Corsica	45	C6
Porto, Portugal	41	B3
Porto Alegre	111	L5
Porto Amboim	67	A2
Portocheli	49	F7
Porto do Son	41	A2
Porto Esperidião	109	F5
Portoferraio	45	E6
Pôrto Franco	109	H5
Port of Spain	109	E1
Pôrto Grande	109	G3
Portogruaro	43	H5
Porto Inglês	63	(1)B1
Portomaggiore	43	G6
Pôrto Murtinho	111	K3
Pôrto Nacional	109	H6
Porto-Novo	63	E3
Port Orford	97	B2
Porto San Giórgio	45	H5
Pôrto Santana	109	G3
Porto Santo	59	B2
Pôrto Seguro	109	K7
Porto Tolle	43	H6
Porto Tórres	45	C8
Porto-Vecchio	45	D7
Pôrto Velho	109	E5
Portoviejo	109	A4
Port Pire	87	G6
Portree	37	F4
Port Renfrew	97	B1
Port Said = Bûr Sa'îd	61	F1
Port St. Johns	67	D6
Port Shepstone	67	E6
Portsmouth, United Kingdom	27	A4
Portsmouth, N.H., United States	99	F2
Portsmouth, Oh., United States	99	D3
Portsmouth, Va., United States	99	E3
Port Sudan = Bur Sudan	61	G4
Port Sulphur	103	D4
Port Talbot	37	J10
Portugal	41	B5
Portugalete	41	G1
Port-Vendres	39	J11
Port-Vila	85	G7
Port Warrender	87	E2
Posadas	111	K4
Poschiavo	43	F4
Poshekhon'ye	31	G3
Poso	83	(2)B3
Posõng	81	D6
Posse	109	H6
Pößneck	35	G6
Post	101	F2
Postmasburg	67	C5
Postojna	43	K5
Posušje	47	E6
Potapovo	71	R4
Poteau	103	C2
Potenza	45	K8
P'ot'i	51	J2
Potiskum	63	G2
Potlatch	97	C1
Potosi	109	D7
Potsdam, Germany	35	J4
Potsdam, United States	99	F2
Pottuvil	75	D7
Poughkeepsie	99	F2
Pourerere	89	F5
Pouto	89	E3
Póvoa de Varzim	41	B3
Povorino	31	H4
Powder	97	E1
Powder River	97	E2
Poweli River	93	G7
Poyang Hu	79	F5
Požarevac	47	J5
Poza Rica	105	E4
Požega	47	H6
Poznań	33	F5
Pozoblanco	41	F6
Prabumulih	83	(1)C3
Prachatice	33	D8
Prachuap Khiri Khan	77	B4
Prado	109	K7
Præstø	35	H1
Prague = Praha	33	D7
Praha	33	D7
Praia	63	(1)B2
Prainha	109	G4
Prairie du Chien	99	B2
Prapat	83	(1)B2
Praslin Island	67	(2)B1
Pratas = Dongsha Qundao	79	F2
Prato	43	G7
Pratt	97	G3
Prattville	103	D3
Praya	83	(1)F4
Preetz	35	F2
Preili	29	P8
Premnitz	35	H4
Premuda	43	K6
Prentice	99	B1
Prenzlau	33	C4
Preobrazhenka	73	H4
Preparis Island	77	A4
Preparis North Channel	77	A3
Preparis South Channel	77	A4
Přerov	33	G8
Presa de la Boquilla	101	E3
Presa de las Adjuntas	101	G4
Presa Obregón	101	E3
Prescott	97	D4
Preševo	47	J7
Presho	97	G2
Presidencia Roque Sáenz Peña	111	J4
Presidente Prudente	111	L3
Presidio	101	F3
Preslav	47	P6
Presnogorkovka	31	N4
Prešov	33	L9
Presque Isle	99	G1
Přeštice	35	J7
Preston, United Kingdom	37	K8
Preston, Minn., United States	99	B2
Preston, Mo., United States	99	B3
Pretoria	67	D5
Preveza	49	C6
Priargunsk	73	K6
Pribilof Islands	101	(1)D4
Priboj	47	G6
Příbram	33	D8
Price	97	D3
Prichard	103	D3
Priego de Córdoba	41	F7
Priekule	29	L8
Prienai	33	N3
Prieska	67	C5
Priest Lake	97	C1
Prievidza	33	H9
Prijedor	47	D5
Prijepolje	47	G6
Prikaspiyskaya Nizmennost'	31	K5
Prilep	49	D3
Primorsk	29	Q6
Primorsko Akhtarsk	31	G5
Prince Albert	93	K6
Prince Albert Peninsula	93	H2
Prince Albert Sound	93	H2
Prince Charles Island	93	R3
Prince Edward Island	57	G10
Prince Edward Island	93	U7
Prince George	93	G6
Prince of Wales Island, Australia	87	H2
Prince of Wales Island, Canada	93	L2
Prince of Wales Island, United States	93	E5
Prince of Wales Strait	93	H2
Prince Patrick Island	91	Q2
Prince Regent Inlet	93	N2
Prince Rupert	93	E6
Princess Charlotte Bay	87	H2
Princeton, Canada	97	B1
Princeton, Ill., United States	99	C2
Princeton, Ky., United States	99	C3
Princeton, Mo., United States	99	B2
Prince William Sound	93	B4
Príncipe	63	F4
Prineville	97	B2
Priozersk	29	R6
Priština	47	J7
Pritzwalk	35	H3
Privas	39	K9
Privolzhskaya Vozvyshennost	31	H4
Prizren	47	H7
Probolinggo	83	(1)E4
Proddatur	75	C6
Progreso	105	G4
Prokhladnyy	51	L2
Prokop'yevsk	71	R7
Prokuplje	47	J6
Proletarsk	31	H5
Proliv Longa	73	X2
Proliv Vil'kitskogo	71	U3
Prophet	93	G5
Propriano	45	C7
Prorer Wiek	35	J2
Proserpine	87	J4
Prosna	33	G6
Prosperidad	77	H5
Prostojov	33	G8
Proti	49	D7
Provadiya	47	Q6
Prøven = Kangersuatsiaq	93	W2
Providence	99	F2
Providence Island	67	(2)B2
Provideniya	73	Z4

Name	Page	Grid
Provincetown	99	F2
Provins	39	J5
Provo	97	D2
Provost	93	J6
Prudhoe Bay	101	(1)H1
Prudnik	33	G7
Prüm	27	J4
Pruszków	33	K5
Prut	47	R4
Pružany	33	P5
Prvić	43	K6
Pryluky	31	F4
Prypyats'	25	G2
Przasnysz	33	K4
Przemyśl	33	M8
Przeworsk	33	M7
Psara	49	H6
Psebay	51	J1
Pskov	31	E3
Ptolemaïda	49	D4
Ptuj	43	L4
Pucallpa	109	C5
Pucheng	79	F5
Puch'ŏn	81	D5
Púchov	33	H8
Pucioasa	47	N4
Puck	33	H3
Pudasjärvi	29	P4
Pudozh	31	G2
Puebla	105	E5
Pueblo	97	F3
Puelches	111	H6
Puelén	111	H6
Puente-Genil	41	F7
Puerto Acosta	109	D7
Puerto Aisén	111	G8
Puerto Alegre	109	E6
Puerto Angel	105	E5
Puerto Ayacucho	105	L7
Puerto Barrios	105	G5
Puerto Berrío	109	C2
Puerto Cabezas	105	H6
Puerto Carreño	105	L7
Puerto del Rosario	59	C3
Puerto de Navacerrada	41	G4
Puerto Guarini	109	F8
Puerto Heath	109	D6
Puerto Inírida	109	D3
Puerto Leguizamo	109	C4
Puerto Libertad	101	D2
Puerto Limón	109	B3
Puertollano	41	F6
Puerto Maldonado	109	D6
Puerto Montt	111	G7
Puerto Nuevo	105	K7
Puerto Peñasco	101	D2
Puerto Princesa	77	F5
Puerto Real	41	D8
Puerto Rico	105	L5
Puerto Rico	109	D6
Puerto Rico Trench	107	E1
Puerto Santa Cruz	111	H9
Puerto Suárez	109	F7
Pukapuka	85	N7
Pukatawagen	93	L5
Pukch'ŏng	81	E3
Pukë	47	G7
Pula	43	J6
Pulaski	99	E2
Puławy	33	M6
Pullman	97	C1
Pułtusk	29	L10
Pulu	71	Q10
Pülümür	51	H4
Puncak Jaya	83	(2)E3
Puncak Mandala	83	(2)F3
Pune	75	B5
Punia	65	D4
Puno	109	C7
Punta Albina	67	A3
Punta Alice	45	M9
Punta Angamos	111	G3
Punta Arena	97	B3
Punta Arenas	111	G9
Punta Ballena	111	G4
Punta Dungeness	111	H9
Punta Eugenia	105	A3
Punta Galera	111	G6
Punta Gallinas	105	K6
Punta Gorda	103	E4
Punta La Marmora	45	D8
Punta Lavapié	111	G6
Punta Lengua de Vaca	111	G5
Punta Mala	109	B2
Punta Mariato	105	H7
Punta Medanosa	111	H8
Punta Negra	109	A5
Punta Norte, *Argentina*	111	J7
Punta Norte, *Argentina*	111	K6
Punta Pariñas	109	A5
Punta Rasa	111	J7
Puntarenas	105	H6
Punta San Gabriel	101	D3
Punta San Telmo	105	D5
Punta Sarga	59	B4
Puponga	89	D5
Puqi	79	E5
Puri	75	E5
Purmerend	27	G2
Purpe	73	B4
Purukcahu	83	(1)E3
Purus	109	E5
Puruvesi	29	Q6
Pusan	81	E6
Pushkin	31	F3
Püspökladany	33	L10
Putao	77	B1
Putaruru	89	E3
Putian	79	F5
Putna	47	P4
Puttalami	75	C7
Putten	27	G3
Puttgarden	35	G2
Putumayo	109	C4
Puuwai	101	(2)A2
Puy de Dôme	39	H8
Puy de Sancy	39	H8
Puysegur Point	89	A8
Pweto	65	D5
Pwllheli	37	H9
Pyal'ma	31	G2
Pyatigorsk	51	K1
Pyè	77	B3
Pyhäjärvi	29	M6
Pylos	49	D8
Pyŏktong	81	C3
P'yŏnggang	81	D4
P'yŏngyang	81	C4
Pyramid Island	89	(1)B2
Pyramid Lake	97	C2/3
Pyrenees	39	E11
Pyrgos	49	D7
Pyrzyce	33	D4
Pyshchug	31	J3
Pytalovo	29	P8

Q

Name	Page	Grid
Qadīmah	53	C5
Qādub	53	F7
Qagan Nur	79	F2
Qal'aikhum	53	K2
Qalamat Nadqān	55	D5
Qalāt	53	J3
Qal'at Bīshah	53	D5
Qal'eh-ye Now	53	H3
Qamdo	79	B4
Qamīnīs	61	C1
Qaraaoun	51	F7
Qardho	65	H2
Qartaba	54	C2
Qasr Farafra	61	E2
Qatanā	54	D3
Qatar	55	D4
Qatrāna	54	D5
Qattâra Depression	61	E2
Qāyen	53	G3
Qazangöldag	51	M4
Qazax	51	L3
Qazımämmäd	51	N3
Qazvīn	53	E2
Qena	61	F2
Qeqertarsuatsiaat	93	W4
Qeqertarsuatsiaq	93	V2
Qeqertarsuup Tunua	93	V3
Qeshm	55	F3
Qeshm	55	G3
Qeys	55	G3
Qezel Owzan	51	N5
Qezi'ot	54	B6
Qianshanlaoba	71	Q8
Qiaowan	79	B2
Qidukou	75	G2
Qiemo	71	R10
Qijiang	79	D5
Qijiaojing	71	S9
Qila Saifullah	53	J3
Qilian	79	C3
Qingdao	79	G3
Qinghai Hu	79	B3
Qinghai Nanshan	79	B3
Qingjiang	79	F4
Qingshuihe	79	E3
Qingyang	79	D3
Qingyuan, *China*	79	E6
Qingyuan, *China*	79	G2
Qinhuangdao	79	F3
Qinzhou	77	D2
Qionghai	77	E3
Qiqian	73	L6
Qiqihar	73	L7
Qīr	55	L2
Qira	71	Q10
Qiryat Ata	54	C4
Qiryat Motzkin	54	C4
Qiryat Shemona	54	C3
Qishn	53	F6
Qolleh-ye Damāvand	53	F2
Qom	53	F3
Qomishēh	53	F3
Qornet es Saouda	54	D2
Qorveh	51	M6
Qotūr	51	L4
Quang Ngai'	77	D3
Quangolodougou	63	C3
Quang Tri	77	D3
Quanzhou	77	F2
Quaqtaq	93	T4
Quarto Sant'Elena	45	D9
Quba	51	N3
Quchan	53	G2
Québec	99	F1
Quedlinburg	35	G5
Queen Charlotte	93	E6
Queen Charlotte Islands	93	E6
Queen Charlotte Sound	93	E6
Queen Charlotte Strait	93	F6
Queen Elizabeth Islands	91	M2
Queen Maud Gulf	93	L3
Queensland	87	G4
Queenstown, *Australia*	87	J8
Queenstown, *New Zealand*	89	B7
Queenstown, *South Africa*	67	D6
Queets	97	B1
Quelimane	67	F3
Quemado	101	E2
Querétaro	105	D4
Quesnel	93	G6
Quetta	53	J3
Quezaltenango	105	F6
Quezon	77	F5
Quezon City	77	G4
Qufu	79	F3
Quibala	67	A2
Quibdó	105	J7
Quijotoa	101	D2
Quilmes	111	K5
Quilpie	87	H5
Quimbele	65	B5
Quimilí	111	J4
Quimper	39	A5
Quimperlé	39	B6
Quincy	99	B3
Qui Nhon	77	D4
Quionga	65	G6
Quirindi	87	K6
Quito	109	B4
Qujing	77	C1
Qumar He	75	F1
Qumaryan	75	F1
Qurayyāt	53	G5
Qurghonteppa	53	J2
Qurlurtuuq	93	H3
Qus	61	F2
Quseir	61	F2
Quzhou	79	F5

R

Name	Page	Grid
Raab	43	L3
Raahe	29	N4
Raalte	27	J2
Raasay	43	G4
Raas Caseyr	65	J1
Raas Xaafuun	65	J1
Rab	43	K6
Rab	43	K6
Rába	47	E2
Raba	83	(2)A4
Rabak	61	F5
Rabat	45	J13
Rabat	59	D2
Rabca	43	N3
Rābigh	53	C5
Rabka	33	K8
Rach Gia	77	D5
Racine	99	C2
Ráckeve	47	F2
Rădăuți	47	N2
Radbuza	35	H7
Radeberg	35	J5
Radebeul	35	J5
Radhanpur	75	B4
Radnevo	47	N7
Radom	33	L6
Radomir	47	K7
Radomsko	33	J6
Radoviš	49	E3
Radstadt	33	C10
Raduzhnny	71	P5
Radviliškis	33	N2
Rae-Edzo	93	H4
Raetihi	89	E4
Raevavae	85	M8
Rafaela	111	J4
Rafah	54	B5
Rafaï	65	C3
Rafhā	53	D4
Rafsanjān	55	G1
Raglan	89	E3
Ragusa	45	J12
Raha	83	(2)B3
Rahad el Berdi	61	D5
Rahimyar Khan	53	K4
Raichur	75	C5
Raiganj	75	E3
Raigarh	75	D4
Rainach	43	L4
Rainbow Lake	93	H5
Rainier	97	B1
Rainy Lake	99	B1
Rainy River	99	B1
Raipur	75	D4
Rai Valley	89	D5
Rajahmundry	75	D5
Raja-Jooseppi	29	Q2
Rajapalaiyam	75	C7
Rajgarh	75	C3
Rajkot	53	K5
Raj Nangaon	75	D4
Rajshahi	75	E4
Rakhiv	47	M1
Rakovica	43	L6
Rakovník	33	C7
Rakovski	47	M7
Rakvere	29	P7
Raleigh	103	F2
Ralik Chain	85	G5
Ram	54	C7
Rama	105	H6
Ramallah	54	C5
Rambouillet	39	G5
Rameswaram	75	C7
Rämhormoz	55	C1
Ramla	54	B5

Name	Page	Ref
Ramlat Rabyānah	61	C3
Râmnicu Sărat	47	Q4
Râmnicu Vâlcea	47	M4
Rampur, *India*	75	C2
Rampur, *India*	75	C3
Ramree Island	77	A3
Ramsgate	37	P10
Ramtha	54	D4
Ranau	83	(1)F1
Rancagua	111	G5
Ranchi	75	E4
Randazzo	45	J11
Randers	29	F8
Randijaure	29	K3
Randolph	97	G2
Rânes	27	B6
Rangamati	75	F4
Rangiora	89	D6
Rangoon = Yangon	77	B3
Rankin	101	F2
Rankin Inlet	93	N4
Ranong	77	B5
Ransiki	83	(2)D3
Ŗānya	51	L5
Rapa	85	M8
Rapalla	45	D4
Rapallo	43	E6
Rapar	53	K5
Raperswil	43	D3
Rapid City	97	F2
Rapid River	99	C1
Rapla	29	N7
Rapur	53	J5
Raroia	85	N7
Rarotonga	85	K6
Râs Abu Shagara	61	G3
Ra's al Ḥadd	53	G5
Ra's al Ḥazrah	55	D4
Ra's al Hilāl	61	D1
Ra's al Khajī	55	C2
Ra's al Khaymah	55	F4
Ra's al Kūh	55	G4
Ra's al Muraysah	61	E1
Ra's al 'Udayd	55	D4
Ra's az Zawr	55	C3
Râs Banâs	61	G3
Ras Beddouza	59	C1
Ras Bir	61	H5
Ras Dashen Terara	61	G5
Ra's-e Barkan	55	C2
Raseiniai	29	M9
Râs el Nafas	54	B7
Ra's Fartak	53	F6
Râs Ghârib	61	F2
Rasht	51	N5
Rāsk	53	H4
Raška	47	H6
Ras Kasar	61	G4
Ra's Madrakah	53	G6
Râs Nouâdhibou	59	B4
Rason Lake	87	D5
Rass Jebel	45	E11
Rass Mostefa	45	F12
Rassokha	73	H2
Rast	47	L6
Ras Tannūrah	55	D3
Rastatt	27	L6
Rastede	35	D3
Ratak Chain	85	H4
Ratangarh	75	K4
Rat Buri	77	B4
Rath	75	C3
Rathenow	35	H4
Rathlin Island	37	F6
Ratlam	75	C4
Ratnagiri	53	K6
Raton	97	F3
Ratta	73	C4
Ratten	43	D4
Ratzeburg	35	F3
Raudhatain	55	B5
Raukumara Range	89	F4
Rauma	29	L6
Rausu	81	N1
Rǎut	47	R2
Ravalli	97	D1
Ravānsar	51	M6
Rāvar	55	G1
Ravenna	43	H6
Ravensburg	43	E3
Ravensthorpe	87	D6
Ravnina	53	H2
Rāwah	51	J6
Rawaki	85	J6
Rawalpindi	53	K3
Rawa Mazowiecka	33	K6
Rawāndiz	51	L5
Rawicz	33	F6
Rawlinna	87	E6
Rawlins	97	E2
Rawson	111	J7
Rawu	75	G3
Raychikhinsk	73	M7
Raymond	97	B1
Raymondville	101	G3
Rayong	77	C4
Razdol'noye	81	F2
Razgrad	47	P6
Razlog	47	L8
Reading, *United Kingdom*	37	M10
Reading, *United States*	99	E2
Realicó	111	J6
Rebbenesøya	29	J1
Rebun-tō	79	L1
Rechytsa	31	F4
Recife	109	L5
Recklinghausen	27	K3
Recknitz	35	H3
Reconquista	111	K4
Recreo	111	H4
Red, *Canada/United States*	97	G1
Red, *United States*	103	B3
Reda	33	H3
Red Bluff	101	B1
Red Cloud	103	B1
Red Deer	93	J6
Redding	97	B2
Redditch	27	A2
Redfield	97	G2
Red Lake	93	N6
Red Lakes	95	H2
Red Lodge	97	E1
Red Oak	99	A2
Redon	39	C6
Redondela	41	B2
Red River = Song Hông	77	C2
Red Sea	61	G3
Redwater	93	J6
Red Wing	99	B2
Redwood City	97	B3
Redwood Falls	99	A2
Reed City	99	C2
Reedsport	97	B2
Reefton	89	C6
Rega	33	E4
Regen	35	H7
Regen	35	J8
Regensburg	35	H7
Regenstauf	35	H7
Reggane	59	F2
Réggio di Calabria	45	K10
Réggio nell'Emilia	43	F6
Reghin	47	M3
Regina	95	F1
Rehau	35	H6
Rehoboth	67	B4
Rehovot	54	B5
Reichenbach	35	H6
Reigate	37	M10
Reims	27	G5
Reinach Bad	43	C3
Reindeer Lake	93	L5
Reinosa	41	F1
Reisi	45	J11
Reliance	93	K4
Relizane	59	F1
Remada	59	H2
Remagen	27	K4
Rembang	83	(1)E4
Remeshk	55	H3
Remiremont	39	M6
Remscheid	27	K3
Rena	29	F6
Rendína	49	F4
Rendsburg	35	E2
Rengat	83	(1)C3
Reni	47	R4
Renmark	87	H6
Rennes	39	D5
Reno	43	G6
Reno	97	C3
Rentería	41	J1
Renton	97	B1
Renukut	75	D4
Reo	83	(2)B4
Replot	29	L5
Reprêsa de Balbina	109	F4
Represa de Samuel	109	E5
Represa de Sao Simao	109	G7
Represa Ilha Solteíra	109	G7
Represa Tucuruí	109	H4
Republic	97	C1
Republic of Ireland	37	D8
Repulse Bay	87	J4
Requena	109	C5
Reşadiye	51	G3
Resen	47	J8
Réservoir Cabonga	99	E1
Réservoir Caniapiscau	93	T6
Réservoir de La Grande 2	93	R6
Réservoir de La Grande 3	93	R6
Réservoir de La Grande 4	93	S6
Réservoir Gouin	99	F1
Réservoir Manicouagan	93	T6
Réservoir Opinaca	93	R6
Réservoir Pipmuacan	99	G1
Reshteh-ye Kühhā-ye Alborz	53	C2
Resistencia	111	K4
Reşiţa	47	J4
Resolute	93	N2
Resolution Island, *Canada*	93	U4
Resolution Island, *New Zealand*	89	A7
Resovo	49	K3
Rethel	27	G5
Rethymno	49	G9
Réunion	67	(1)B2
Reus	41	M3
Reutlingen	35	E8
Revda	31	L3
Revillagigedo Island	101	(1)L4
Revin	27	C5
Revivim	54	B5
Revúca	33	K9
Rewa	75	D4
Rexburg	97	D2
Reykjanes	29	(1)B3
Reykjavík	29	(1)C2
Reynosa	103	B4
Rezat	35	F7
Rezé	39	D6
Rēzekne	29	P8
Rezina	47	R2
Rezovo	47	R8
Rheda-Wiedenbrück	35	D5
Rhein = Rhine	43	C2
Rheinbach	27	K4
Rheine	27	K2
Rheinfelden	43	C3
Rhin = Rhine	43	C2
Rhine	43	C2
Rhinelander	99	C1
Rho	43	E5
Rhode Island	99	F2
Rhodes = Rodos	49	L8
Rhondda	37	J10
Rhône	39	K9
Rhyl	37	J8
Ribadeo	41	C1
Ribas do Rio Pardo	111	L3
Ribe	29	E9
Ribeauville	39	N5
Ribeirão Prêto	111	M3
Ribeiria = Santa Eugenia	41	A2
Ribera	45	H11
Riberalta	109	D6
Ribnica	45	J3
Rìbnița	47	S2
Ribnitz-Damgarten	35	H2
Říčany	35	K6
Riccione	43	H7
Richardson Mountains	101	(1)K2
Richfield	97	D3
Richland	97	C1
Richlands	99	D3
Richmond, *Australia*	87	H4
Richmond, *New Zealand*	89	D5
Richmond, *Ky., United States*	99	D3
Richmond, *Va., United States*	99	E3
Ridgecrest	101	C1
Ridgway	99	E2
Ried	43	J2
Riesa	35	J5
Rieti	45	G6
Rifle	97	E3
Rīga	29	N8
Riggins	97	C1
Rigolet	93	V6
Rijeka	43	K5
Riley	97	C2
Rimava	33	J9
Rimavská Sobota	33	K9
Rímini	43	H6
Rimouski	99	G1
Rineia	49	H7
Ringe	35	F1
Ringkøbing	29	E8
Ringkøbing Fjord	29	D9
Ringsted	35	G1
Ringvassøya	29	J1
Rinteln	35	E4
Rio Branco	109	D5
Río Colorado	111	J6
Río Cuarto	111	J5
Rio de Janeiro	111	N3
Rio de Janeiro	111	N3
Río de la Plata	111	K6
Río Gallegos	111	H9
Rio Grande	101	E2
Río Grande, *Argentina*	111	H9
Río Grande, *Mexico*	101	F4
Rio Grande	111	L5
Rio Grande City	103	B4
Rio Grande do Norte	109	K5
Rio Grande do Sul	111	L4
Ríohacha	105	K6
Río Largartos	105	G4
Riom	39	J8
Río Mulatos	109	D7
Rionero	45	K8
Rionero in Vulture	47	C9
Río Tigre	109	B4
Rio Verde	109	G7
Rio Verde de Mato Grosso	109	G7
Ripley, *Oh., United States*	99	D3
Ripley, *Tenn., United States*	99	C3
Ripley, *W.Va., United States*	99	D3
Ripoll	41	N2
Ripon	37	L7
Rishiri-tō	73	Q7
Rishon le Ziyyon	54	B5
Ritchie's Archipelago	77	A4
Ritzville	97	C1
Rivadavia	111	G4
Riva del Garda	43	F5
Rivarolo	43	C5
Rivas	105	G6
Rivera, *Argentina*	111	J6
Rivera, *Uruguay*	111	K5
Riversdale	67	C6
Riversdale Beach	89	E5
Riverton, *Canada*	93	M6
Riverton, *New Zealand*	89	A8
Rivesaltes	39	H11
Rivière-du-Loup	99	G1
Rivne	31	E4
Rivoli	43	C5
Riwoqê	75	G2
Riyadh = Ar Riyāḑ	55	B4
Rize	51	J3
Rizhao	79	F3
Roanne	39	K7
Roanoke	99	D3
Roanoke Rapids	103	F2

Name	Page	Grid
Robe	87	G7
Robertsfors	29	L4
Robertval	99	F1
Roboré	109	F7
Robstown	103	B4
Roccastrada	45	F6
Rochefort, *Belgium*	27	H4
Rochefort, *France*	39	E8
Rochelle	99	C2
Rocher River	93	J4
Rochester, *United Kingdom*	27	C3
Rochester, *Minn., United States*	99	B2
Rochester, *N.H., United States*	99	F2
Rochester, *N.Y., United States*	99	E2
Rockall	25	C2
Rockefeller Plateau	112	(2)EE2
Rockford	99	C2
Rockhampton	87	K4
Rock Hill	99	D4
Rock Island	99	B2
Rocklake	97	G1
Rockport	97	B1
Rock Rapids	99	A2
Rock Springs	97	E2
Rocksprings	101	F3
Rocky Mount	99	E3
Rocky Mountains	93	F5
Rødby Havn	35	G2
Roddickton	93	V6
Rodez	39	H9
Rodi Gargánico	45	K7
Roding	35	H7
Rodney	99	D2
Rodopi Planina	47	M7
Rodos	49	L8
Rodos	49	L8
Roebourne	87	C4
Roermond	27	J3
Roeselare	27	F4
Roes Welcome Sound	93	P4
Rogers City	99	D1
Rogerson	97	D2
Rogliano	45	D6
Rogue	97	B2
Rohrbach	43	K2
Rohtak	75	C3
Roi Et	77	C3
Roja	29	M8
Rokiškis	29	N9
Rokycany	33	C8
Rolla	99	B3
Rolleston	89	D6
Rolvsøya	29	M1
Roma	83	(2)C4
Roma, *Australia*	87	J5
Roma, *Italy*	45	G7
Roman	47	P3
Romania	47	L4
Romans-sur-Isère	39	L8
Rombas	27	J5
Rome = Roma	45	G7
Rome, *Ga., United States*	103	D3
Rome, *N.Y., United States*	99	E2
Romney	99	E3
Romny	31	F4
Rømø	35	D1
Romorantin-Lanthenay	39	G6
Rona	37	G2
Ronan	95	D2
Roncesvalles	41	J2
Ronda	41	E8
Rondônia	109	E6
Rondônia	109	E6
Rondonópolis	109	G7
Rondu	53	L2
Rongcheng	79	G3
Rønne	33	D2
Ronneby	29	H8
Ronne Entrance	112	(2)JJ3
Ronne Ice Shelf	112	(2)MM2
Ronse	27	F4
Roosendaal	27	G3
Roper Bar	87	F2
Roraima	109	E3
Røros	29	F5
Rosário	109	J4
Rosario, *Argentina*	111	J5
Rosario, *Mexico*	95	D6
Rosario, *Mexico*	95	E7
Rosario, *Paraguay*	111	K3
Rosário Oeste	109	F6
Rosarito	95	C6
Rosarno	45	K10
Roscommon	37	D8
Roseau	105	M5
Roseburg	97	B2
Roseires Reservoir	61	F5
Rose Island	85	K7
Rosenburg	101	G3
Rosenheim	43	H3
Roses	41	P2
Rosetown	93	K6
Rosica	47	N6
Rosignano Solvay	43	F7
Roșiori de Vede	47	N5
Roskilde	29	G9
Roslavl'	31	F4
Rossano	45	L9
Ross Ice Shelf	112	(2)Z1
Ross Lake	97	B1
Roßlau	35	H5
Rosso	59	B5
Rossosh'	31	G4
Ross River	93	E4
Ross Sea	112	(2)AA2
Røssvatnet	29	G4
Røst	29	G3
Rostāq	55	E3
Rosthern	93	K6
Rostock	35	H2
Rostov	31	G3
Rostov-na-Donu	31	G5
Rostrenen	39	B5
Roswell	101	F2
Rota	85	E4
Rotarua	89	F4
Rote	83	(2)B5
Rotenburg, *Germany*	35	E3
Rotenburg, *Germany*	35	E5
Roth	35	G7
Rothenburg	35	F7
Roto	87	J6
Rott	43	H2
Rotterdam	39	K2
Rottnen	33	E1
Rottumeroog	27	J1
Rottumerplaat	27	J1
Rottweil	43	D2
Rotuma	85	H7
Roubaix	27	F4
Rouen	27	D5
Rouiba	41	P8
Round Mountain	87	K6
Round Rock	103	B3
Roundup	97	E1
Rousay	37	J2
Rouyn	99	E1
Rovaniemi	29	N3
Rovereto	43	G5
Rovigo	43	G5
Rovinj	43	J5
Rovuma	65	F6
Rowley Island	93	R3
Rowley Shoals	87	C3
Roxas	77	G4
Roxburgh	89	B7
Royal Leamington Spa	27	A2
Royal Tunbridge Wells	27	C3
Royan	39	D8
Roye	27	E5
Royston	27	C2
Rozdil'na	47	T3
Rožňava	33	K9
Rrëshen	49	B3
Rtishchevo	31	H4
Ruacana	67	A3
Ruahine Range	89	E5
Ruapehu	89	E4
Ruapuke Island	89	B8
Ruarkela	75	D4
Ruatahuna	89	F4
Ruatoria	89	G3
Ruawai	89	D3
Rub' al Khālī	53	E6
Rubi	65	C3
Rubtsovsk	71	Q7
Ruby	101	(1)F3
Rudan	55	G3
Ruda Śląska	33	H7
Rudbar	53	H3
Rüdersdorf	35	J4
Rüdkøbing	35	F2
Rudnaya Pristan'	81	H2
Rudnyy	31	M4
Rudolstadt	35	G6
Rüdsar	51	P5
Rue	27	D4
Ruffec	39	F7
Rufiji	65	F5
Rugby, *United Kingdom*	27	A2
Rugby, *United States*	95	G2
Rügen	33	C3
Ruhnu	29	M8
Ruhr	27	L3
Rum	37	F5
Ruma	47	G4
Rumāh	55	B4
Rumaylah	55	B4
Rumbek	65	D2
Rum Cay	105	K4
Rumigny	27	G5
Rumoi	81	L2
Runanaga	89	C6
Rundu	67	B3
Ruoqiang	71	R10
Ruo Shui	79	C2
Rupa	43	K5
Rupat	83	(1)C2
Rupert	93	R6
Rupert	97	D2
Rurutu	85	L8
Ruse	47	N6
Rushon	75	G3
Rushville, *Ill., United States*	99	B2
Rushville, *Ind., United States*	99	C3
Rushville, *Nebr., United States*	97	F2
Russell	97	G3
Russellville, *Ark., United States*	103	C2
Russellville, *Ky., United States*	103	D2
Rüsselsheim	35	D7
Russia	29	L9
Russia	69	M3
Rust'avi	51	L3
Ruston	103	C3
Rutana	65	D4
Rute	41	F7
Ruteng	83	(2)B4
Rutland	99	F2
Rutog	75	C2
Ruvo di Puglia	45	L7
Ruvuma	65	F6
Ruzayevka	31	H4
Ružomberok	33	J8
Rwanda	65	D4
R-Warnemünde	35	H2
Ryazan'	31	G4
Ryazhsk	31	H4
Rybinsk	31	G3
Rybinskoye Vodokhranilishche	31	G3
Rybnik	33	H7
Rychnov	33	F7
Ryde	27	A4
Rye Patch Reservoir	97	C2
Ryki	33	L6
Ryl'sk	31	F4
Ryn-Peski	31	J5
Ryōtsu	81	K4
Rypin	33	J4
Ryukyu Islands = Nansei-shotō	79	H5
Rzeszów	33	M7
Rzhev	31	F3

S

Name	Page	Grid
Sa'ādatābād, *Iran*	55	E1
Sa'ādatābād, *Iran*	55	F2
Saale	35	G6
Saalfeld	35	G6
Saalfelden	43	H3
Saanen	43	B2
Saar	27	J5
Saarbrücken	27	J5
Saarburg	27	J5
Saaremaa	29	L7
Saarlouis	27	J5
Saatli	51	N4
Saatly	53	E2
Saba	105	M5
Sab' Ābār	54	E3
Šabac	47	G5
Sabadell	41	N3
Sabah	83	(1)F1
Sabang	77	B5
Sabhā	59	H3
Sabiñánigo	41	K2
Sabinas	101	F3
Sabinas Hidalgo	101	F3
Sabine	103	B3
Sabine Lake	103	C3
Sabinov	33	L8
Sabkhet el Bardawîl	54	A5
Sable Island	93	V8
Sablé-sur-Sarthe	39	E6
Sabôr	41	D3
Sabun	71	Q5
Sabzevār	53	G2
Săcele	47	N4
Sachanga	67	B2
Sachs Harbour	93	G2
Säckingen	43	C3
Sacramento	97	B3
Sacramento	97	B3
Şad'ah	53	D6
Sadiqabad	53	K4
Sadiya	75	G2
Sado	41	B6
Sadoga-shima	81	K4
Sadon	51	K2
Sado-shima	79	K3
Sa Dragonera	41	N5
Säffle	29	G7
Safford	101	E2
Safi, *Jordan*	54	C5
Safi, *Morocco*	59	D2
Safonovo, *Russia*	31	F3
Safonovo, *Russia*	31	J1
Safranbolu	49	Q3
Saga, *China*	75	E3
Saga, *Japan*	81	F7
Sagami-nada	81	K6
Sagar	75	C4
Sagastyr	71	Z3
Sage	97	D2
Saginaw	99	D2
Sagiz	31	K5
Sagiz	31	K5
Saguache	97	E3
Sagua la Grande	105	H4
Sagunt	41	K5
Sahāb	54	D5
Sahagún	41	E2
Sahara	57	C3
Saharah el Gharbîya	61	E2
Saharanpur	75	C3
Saharsa	75	E3
Şahbuz	51	L4
Sahel	57	C4
Sahiwal	53	K3
Sahuaripa	101	E3
Šahy	47	F1
Saïda, *Algeria*	59	F2
Saïda, *Lebanon*	54	C3
Sa'idābād	55	F2
Saidpur	75	E3
Saigo	81	G5
Saigon = Hô Chi Minh	77	D4
Saiha	75	F4
Saihan Toroi	79	C2
Saiki	81	F7
Saimaa	29	P6
Saimbeyli	51	G4
Sä'in	55	F1
Saindak	53	H4
St. Albans	27	B3
St-Amand-Montrond	39	H7
St. Andrä	43	K4
St. Andrews	37	K5

Name	Page	Ref.
St. Anthony	93	V6
St. Arnaud	89	D5
St. Augustin	27	K4
St. Augustine	103	E4
St. Austell	37	H11
St-Avold	27	J5
St. Barthélémy	105	M5
St-Brieuc	39	C5
St. Catharines	95	L3
St-Chamond	39	K8
St-Claude	39	L7
St. Cloud	99	B1
St. David's	37	G10
St-Denis, France	27	E6
St-Denis, Réunion	67	(1)B2
St-Dié	43	B2
St-Dizier	39	K5
Ste-Anne-de-Beaupré	99	F1
Ste-Menehould	27	G5
Saintes	39	E8
Stes-Maries-de-la-Mer	39	K10
St-Étienne	39	K8
St-Étienne-du-Rouvray	27	D5
St-Félicien	99	F1
St-Florentin	39	J5
St-Flour	39	J8
St. Francis	97	F3
St. Gallen	43	E3
St-Gaudens	39	F10
St. George, Australia	87	J5
St. George, United States	97	D3
St. Georgen	43	D2
St. Georges	99	F1
St. George's	105	M6
St. George's Channel	37	F10
St-Germain-en-Laye	27	E6
St-Girons	39	G11
St. Helena	57	C7
St. Helena Bay	57	B6
St. Helens, United Kingdom	37	K8
St. Helens, United States	97	B1
St. Helier	39	C4
St-Hubert	27	H4
St. Ignace	99	D1
St. Ives	37	G11
St-Jean-d'Angely	39	E8
St-Jean-de-Luz	39	D10
St-Jean-de-Maurienne	43	B5
St-Jean-sur-Richelieu	99	F1
St. John	93	T7
St. John's	93	W7
St. Johnsbury	99	F2
St. Joseph	99	B3
St-Jovité	99	F1
St. Kilda	37	D4
St. Kitts-Nevis	105	M5
St. Laurent	109	G2
St-Laurent-en-Grandvaux	43	A4
St. Lawrence	99	G1
St. Lawrence Island	101	(1)C3
St-Léonard	99	G1
St-Lô	27	A5
St. Louis, Senegal	59	B5
St. Louis, United States	99	B3
St. Lucia	105	M6
St. Maarten	105	M5
St-Malo	39	D5
St. Marys	99	D2
St. Matthew Island	101	(1)C3
St-Mihiel	27	H6
St. Moritz	43	E4
St-Nazaire	39	C6
St-Nicolas-de-Port	43	B2
St. Niklaas	27	G3
St-Omer	27	E4
St-Palais	39	D10
St-Pamphile	99	G1
St-Paul	43	B6
St. Paul	97	G2
St. Paul	99	B2
St. Peter	99	B2
St. Peter Ording	35	D2
St. Peter-Port	39	C4
St. Petersburg = Sankt-Peterburg	31	F3
St. Petersburg	103	E4
St-Pierre-et-Miquelon	93	V7
St. Pierre Island	67	(2)A2
St-Pol-de-Léon	39	A5
St-Pol-sur-Ternoise	27	E4
St-Pölten	43	L2
St-Quentin	27	F5
St-Raphaël	43	B7
St. Siméon	99	G1
St. Stephen	99	G1
St. Thomas	99	D2
St-Tropez	43	B7
St. Truiden	27	H4
St-Valéry-sur-Somme	27	D4
St. Veit	43	K4
St. Veit an der Glan	47	K4
St. Vincent and the Grenadines	105	M6
St-Vincent-les-Forts	43	B6
St-Vith	27	J4
Saipan	85	E4
Sajószentpéter	33	K9
Sākākah	53	D4
Sakaraha	67	G4
Sakarya	49	N4
Sakarya	49	N4
Sakata	81	K4
Sakchu	81	C3
Sakha	73	N3
Sakhalin	73	Q6
Sakhalinskiy Zaliv	73	Q6
Sakhon Nakhon	77	C3
Şaki	51	M3
Sakishima-shotō	79	H6
Sakskøbing	35	G2
Sal	31	H5
Sal	63	(1)B1
Sala	29	J7
Šal'a	33	G9
Salacgrīva	29	N8
Sala Consilina	45	K8
Saladillo	111	K6
Salado	111	J4
Salālah	53	F6
Salamanca, Mexico	105	D4
Salamanca, Spain	41	E4
Salamanca, United States	99	E2
Salamina	49	F7
Salamīyah	54	E1
Salar de Uyuni	111	H3
Salawati	83	(2)D3
Salayar	83	(2)B4
Salbris	39	H6
Saldus	29	M8
Sale	87	J7
Salekhard	71	M4
Salem	97	B2
Salem, India	75	C6
Salem, United States	99	C3
Salerno	45	J8
Salgótarján	33	J9
Salida	97	E3
Salihli	49	L6
Salihorsk	31	E4
Salima	67	E2
Salina	45	J10
Salina, Kans., United States	97	G3
Salina, Ut., United States	97	D3
Salinas, Brazil	109	J7
Salinas, Ecuador	109	A4
Salinas, Mexico	101	F4
Salinas, United States	101	B1
Salinas Grandes	111	J4
Salinópolis	109	H4
Salisbury, United Kingdom	27	A3
Salisbury, Md., United States	99	E3
Salisbury, N.C., United States	99	D3
Salisbury Island	93	R4
Şalkhad	54	D4
Salla	29	Q3
Salluit	93	R4
Salmās	51	L4
Salmon	97	C1/D1
Salmon	97	D1
Salmon Arm	93	H6
Salmon River Mountains	97	C1
Salo	29	M6
Salon-de-Provence	39	L10
Salonta	47	J3
Sal'sk	31	H5
Salsomaggiore Terme	43	E6
Salt	54	C4
Salta	111	H3
Saltee Islands	37	F9
Saltillo	101	F3
Salt Lake City	97	D2
Salto	111	K5
Salton Sea	101	C2
Saluda	103	E3
Salûm	61	E1
Saluzzo	43	C6
Salvador	109	K6
Salvadore	107	H5
Salween	77	B2
Salyan	51	N4
Salyersville	99	D3
Salym	31	P3
Salzach	43	H2
Salzburg	43	J3
Salzgitter	35	F4
Salzwedel	35	G4
Samaipata	109	E7
Samar	77	H4
Samara	31	K4
Samarinda	83	(1)F3
Samarkand	53	J2
Sāmarrā'	51	K6
Şamaxı	51	N3
Sambalpur	75	D4
Sambas	83	(1)D2
Sambava	67	J2
Sambhal	75	C3
Sambir	33	N8
Sambre	27	F4
Same	65	F4
Sami	49	C6
Sämkir	51	M3
Samoa	85	J7
Samobor	43	L5
Samoded	31	H2
Samokov	47	L7
Šamorín	33	G9
Samos	49	J7
Samos	49	J7
Samothraki	49	H4
Samothraki	49	H4
Sam Rayburn Reservoir	103	C3
Samsang	75	D2
Samsø	29	F9
Samsun	51	G3
Samtredia	51	K2
Samut Songkhram	77	B4
San	33	L7
San	63	D2
Şan'ā	61	H4
Sanaga	63	G4
San Ambrosio	111	F4
Sanana	83	(2)C3
Sanana	83	(2)C3
Sanandaj	51	M6
San Angelo	101	F2
San Antonia Abad	41	M6
San Antonio, Chile	111	G5
San Antonio, United States	105	E3
San Antonio de los Cobres	111	H3
San Antonio-Oeste	111	H7
Sanāw	53	F6
San Benedetto del Tronto	45	H6
San Bernardino	101	C2
San Bernardo	111	H5
San Borja	109	D6
San Carlos, Chile	111	G6
San Carlos, Philippines	77	G3
San Carlos, Venezuela	109	D3
San Carlos de Bolívar	111	J6
San Carlos del Zulia	109	C2
San Carlos Lake	101	D2
San Cataldo	45	H11
Sanchahe	81	C1
Sanchakou	75	P10
Sanchor	75	B4
Sanchursk	31	J3
San Clemente Island	101	C2
San Cristóbal	85	G7
San Cristóbal, Argentina	111	J5
San Cristóbal, Venezuela	109	C2
San Cristóbal de las Casas	105	F5
Sancti Spíritus	105	J4
Sandakan	83	(1)F1
Sandane	29	D6
Sandanski	49	F3
Sanday	37	K2
Sandefjord	29	F7
Sanders	101	E1
Sanderson	101	F2
Sandfire Flat Roadhouse	87	D3
San Diego	101	C2
Sandıklı	49	N6
Sandnes	29	C7
Sandnessjøen	29	G4
Sandoa	65	C5
Sandomierz	33	L7
San Donà di Piave	43	H5
Sandoway	75	F5
Sandpoint	97	C1
Sandray	37	E5
Sandviken	29	J6
Sandy	97	D2
Sandy Cape	87	K4
Sandy Island	87	D2
Sandy Lake	93	N6
Sandy Lake	93	N6
Sandy Springs	103	E3
San Felipe	95	D5
San Félix	111	E4
San Fernando, Chile	111	G5
San Fernando, Mexico	103	B5
San Fernando, Philippines	77	G3
San Fernando, Spain	41	D8
San Fernando de Apure	109	D2
Sanford, Fla., United States	103	E4
Sanford, N.C., United States	103	F2
San Francis	103	A2
San Francisco, Argentina	111	J5
San Francisco, United States	97	B3
Sangamner	75	B5
Sangān	53	H3
Sangar	73	M4
Sangāreddi	75	C5
Sângeorz-Bāi	47	M2
Sangerhausen	35	G5
Sangha	63	H4
Sanghar	53	J4
San Gimignano	43	G7
San Giovanni in Fiore	45	L9
San Giovanni Valdarno	43	G7
Sangkha Buri	77	B3
Sangkulirang	83	(1)F2
Sangli	75	B5
Sangmélima	63	G4
Sangre de Cristo Range	101	E1
Sangsang	75	E3
Sangue	109	F6
Sangüesa	41	J2
Sanjō	81	K5
San Joaquin Valley	97	B3
San Jose	97	B3
San José	105	H7
San Jose de Buenavista	77	G4
San José de Chiquitos	109	E7
San Jose de Jáchal	111	H5
San José del Cabo	105	C4
San José de Ocuné	109	C3
San Juan	105	H4
San Juan, Argentina	111	H5
San Juan, Costa Rica	105	H6
San Juan, Puerto Rico	105	L5
San Juan, United States	101	E1
San Juan Bautista	111	K4
San Juan de los Cayos	109	D1
San Juan de los Morros	109	D2
San Juan Mountains	97	E3
San Julián	111	H8
Sankt-Peterburg	31	F3
Sankuru	65	C4
Sanliurfa	51	H5
San Lorenzo	101	D3
Sanlúcar de Barrameda	41	D8
San Lucas	105	C4
San Luis	111	H5
San Luis Obispo	101	B1
San Luis Potosí	105	D4
San Luis Rio Colorado	101	D2

Name	Page	Grid
San Marcos	103	B4
San Marino	43	H7
San Marino	43	H7
San Martín	109	E6
Sanmenxia	79	E4
San Miguel	105	G6
San Miguel	109	E7
San Miguel de Tucumán	111	H4
San Miguel Island	101	B2
San Miniato	43	F7
San Nicolas de los Arroyos	111	J5
San Nicolás de los Garzas	103	A4
San Nicolas Island	101	C2
Sânnicolau Mare	47	H3
Sanok	33	M8
San Pedro, Philippines	77	G4
San-Pédro	63	C4
San Pablo	77	G4
San Pedro, Argentina	111	J3
San Pedro, Bolivia	109	E7
San Pedro de las Colonias	101	F3
San Pedro Sula	105	G5
San Pellegrino Terme	43	E5
San Pietro	45	C9
Sanqaçal	51	N3
San Rafael	111	H5
San Remo	43	C7
San Roque	41	E8
San Salvador	103	G5
San Salvador	105	G6
San Salvador de Jujuy	111	H3
Sansar	75	C4
San Sebastián = Donostia	41	J1
San Sebastian de los Reyes	41	G4
Sansepolcro	43	H7
San Sévero	45	K7
Sanski Most	43	M6
San Stéfano	45	H8
Santa Ana, Bolivia	109	D7
Santa Ana, El Salvador	105	G6
Santa Ana, Mexico	101	D2
Santa Ana, United States	101	C2
Santa Bárbara	95	E6
Santa Barbara	101	C2
Santa Barbara Island	101	C2
Santa Catalina	111	H4
Santa Catalina Island	101	C2
Santa Catarina	111	L4
Santa Clara, Columbia	109	D4
Santa Clara, Cuba	95	K7
Santa Clarita	101	C2
Santa Comba Dão	41	B4
Santa Cruz	111	G9
Santa Cruz, Bolivia	109	E7
Santa Cruz, United States	101	B1
Santa Cruz de Tenerife	59	B3
Santa Cruz Island	101	B2
Santa Cruz Islands	85	G7
Santa Eugenia	41	A2
Santa Fe	97	E3
Santa Fé	111	J5
Sant'Agata di Militello	45	J10
Santa Isabel	85	F6
Santa Isabel	111	H6
Santa la Grande	95	K7
Santa Margarita	95	D7
Santa Maria	59	(1)B2
Santa Maria, Brazil	111	L4
Santa Maria, United States	101	B2
Santa Maria das Barreiras	109	H5
Santa Marta	105	K6
Santana do Livramento	111	K5
Santander	41	G1
Sant'Antíoco	45	C9
Santa Pola	41	K6
Santarém, Brazil	109	G4
Santarém, Spain	41	B5
Santa Rosa, Argentina	111	J6
Santa Rosa, Acre, Brazil	109	C5
Santa Rosa, R.G.S., Brazil	111	L4
Santa Rosa, Calif., United States	97	B3
Santa Rosa, N.Mex., United States	101	F2
Santa Rosa Island	101	B2
Santa Vitória do Palmar	111	L5
Sant Boi	41	N3
Sant Carlos de la Ràpita	41	L4
Sant Celoni	41	N3
Sant Feliu de Guixols	41	P3
Santiago	111	G5
Santiago, Brazil	111	L4
Santiago, Dominican Republic	105	K5
Santiago, Philippines	77	G3
Santiago, Spain	41	B2
Santiago de Cuba	105	J5
Santiago del Estero	111	J4
Santo André	111	M3
Santo Antão	63	(1)A1
Santo Antônio de Jesus	109	K6
Santo Antônio do Içá	109	D4
Santo Domingo	105	L5
Santo Domingo de los Colorados	109	B4
Santoña	41	G1
Santos	111	M3
San Vicente	77	G3
San Vincenzo	45	E5
Sanya	77	D3
Sao Bernardo do Campo	109	E4
São Borja	111	K4
São Carlos	111	M3
São Félix, M.G., Brazil	109	G6
São Félix, Pará, Brazil	109	G5
São Filipe	63	(1)B2
São Francisco	109	J6
São João de Madeira	41	B4
São Jorge	59	(1)B2
São José do Rio Prêto	111	L3
São Luís	109	J4
São Miguel	59	(1)B2
Saône	39	K7
São Nicolau	63	(1)B1
São Paulo	111	L3
São Paulo	111	M3
São Paulo de Olivença	109	D4
São Raimundo Nonato	109	J5
São Tiago	63	(1)B1
São Tomé	63	F4
São Tomé	63	F4
São Tomé and Príncipe	63	F4
São Vicente	63	(1)A1
São Vicente	111	M3
Saparua	83	(2)C3
Sapele	63	F3
Sapes	49	H4
Sapientza	49	D8
Sa Pobla	41	P5
Sapporo	81	L2
Sapri	45	K8
Sapudi	83	(1)E4
Sapulpa	103	B2
Saqqez	51	M5
Sarāb	51	M5
Sara Buri	77	C4
Sarajevo	47	F6
Sarakhs	53	H2
Saraktash	31	L4
Saramati	75	G3
Saran	71	N8
Saranac Lake	99	F2
Sarandë	49	C5
Sarangani Islands	83	(2)C1
Saranpul	31	M2
Saransk	31	J4
Sarapul	31	K3
Sarapul'skoye	73	P7
Sarasota	103	E4
Sarata	47	S3
Saratoga	97	E2
Saratoga Springs	99	F2
Saratov	31	J4
Saravan	53	H4
Sarawak	83	(1)E2
Saray	49	K3
Saraykoy	49	L7
Sarayönü	49	Q6
Sarbāz	53	H4
Sarbīsheh	53	G3
Sárbogárd	47	F3
Sar Dasht	51	L5
Sardegna	45	E8
Sardinia = Sardegna	45	E8
Sardis Lake	103	B3
Sar-e Pol	53	J2
Sargodha	53	K3
Sarh	63	H3
Sārī	53	F2
Saria	49	K9
Sarıkamış	51	K3
Sarıkaya	51	F4
Sarikei	83	(1)E2
Sarina	87	J4
Sariñena	41	K3
Sarīr Tibesti	61	C3
Sariwŏn	81	C4
Sark	39	C4
Sarkad	47	J3
Sarkand	71	P8
Sarikaraağaç	49	P6
Şarkışla	51	G4
Şarköy	49	K4
Sarmi	83	(2)E3
Särna	29	G6
Sarnia	99	D2
Sarny	31	E4
Sarolangun	83	(1)C3
Saronno	43	E5
Saros Körfezi	49	J4
Sárospatak	33	L9
Sarre	39	M5
Sarrebourg	39	N5
Sarreguemines	39	N4
Sarria	41	C2
Sartène	45	C7
Sartyn'ya	31	M2
Saruhanli	49	K6
Sārur	51	L4
Sárvár	43	M3
Sarvestän	55	E2
Sarviz	47	F2
Sarykamyshkoye Ozero	71	K9
Saryozek	71	P9
Saryshagan	71	N8
Sarysu	71	M8
Sary-Tash	53	K2
Sarzana	43	E6
Sasaram	75	D4
Sasebo	81	E7
Saskatchewan	93	K6
Saskatchewan	93	L6
Saskatoon	93	K6
Saskylakh	71	W3
Sassandra	63	C4
Sassari	45	C8
Sassnitz	35	J2
Sassuolo	43	F6
Satadougou	63	B2
Satara	75	B5
Satna	75	D4
Sátoraljaújhely	33	L9
Satti	75	C2
Satu Mare	47	K2
Satun	83	(1)B1
Sauce	111	K5
Saudi Arabia	53	D4
Sauk Center	99	B1
Saulgau	43	E2
Saulieu	39	K6
Sault Ste. Marie, Canada	99	D1
Sault Ste. Marie, United States	99	D1
Saumlakki	83	(2)D4
Saumur	39	E6
Saunders Island	107	J9
Saurimo	65	C5
Sauđárkrókur	29	(1)D2
Sava	43	L5
Savaii	85	J7
Savalou	63	E3
Savannah	91	K6
Savannah, Ga., United States	103	E3
Savannah, Tenn., United States	103	D2
Savannakhet	77	C3
Savaştepe	49	K5
Savè	63	E3
Save	67	E4
Sāveh	53	F2
Saverne	35	C8
Savigliano	43	C6
Savona	43	D6
Savonlinna	29	Q6
Savu	83	(2)B5
Sawahlunto	83	(1)C3
Sawai Madhopur	75	C3
Sawqirah	53	G6
Sawu Sea	83	(2)B4
Sayanogorsk	71	S7
Sayansk	73	G6
Sayhūt	53	F6
Säylac	61	H5
Saynshand	79	E2
Sayram Hu	71	Q9
Say'ün	53	E6
Say-Utes	71	J9
Sazan	49	B4
Sazin	53	K2
Scafell Pike	37	J7
Scalea	45	K9
Scarborough	37	M7
Scarp	37	E3
Schaalsee	35	F3
Schaffhausen	43	D3
Schagen	27	G2
Scharbeutz	35	F2
Schärding	43	J2
Scharhörn	35	D3
Scheeßel	35	E3
Schefferville	93	T6
Scheibbs	43	L3
Schelde	27	F3
Schenectady	99	F2
Scheveningen	27	G2
Schiedam	27	G3
Schiermonnikoog	27	H1
Schio	43	G5
Schiza	49	D8
Schkeuditz	35	H5
Schlei	35	E2
Schleiden	27	J4
Schleswig	35	E2
Schlieben	35	J5
Schlüchtern	35	E6
Schneeberg	35	G6
Schneeberg	35	H6
Schönebeck	35	G4
Schongau	43	F5
Schöningen	35	F4
Schouwen	27	F3
Schramberg	43	D2
Schreiber	99	C1
Schrems	43	L2
Schull	37	C10
Schwabach	35	G7
Schwäbische Alb	43	E2
Schwäbisch-Gmünd	43	E2
Schwäbisch-Hall	35	E7
Schwalmstadt	35	E6
Schwandorf	35	H7
Schwarzenbek	35	F3
Schwarzenberg	35	H6
Schwarzwald	43	D3
Schwaz	43	D3
Schwechat	33	F9
Schwedt	33	D4
Schweich	27	J5
Schweinfurt	35	F6
Schwenningen	43	D2
Schwerin	35	G3
Schweriner See	35	G3
Schwetzingen	35	D7
Schwyz	43	D3
Sciacca	45	H11
Scicli	45	J12
Scobey	97	E1
Scotia Ridge	111	K9
Scotia Sea	112	(2)A4
Scotland	37	H5
Scott City	97	F3
Scott Inlet	93	T2
Scott Island	112	(2)Z3
Scott Reef	87	D2
Scottsbluff	97	F2
Scottsboro	99	C4
Scotty's Junction	101	C1
Scranton	99	E2
Scunthorpe	37	M8
Seal	93	M5
Sea of Azov	31	G5

Name	Page	Grid
Sea of Galilee	54	C4
Sea of Japan	81	G3
Sea of Marmara = Marmara Denizi	49	L4
Sea of Okhotsk	73	Q5
Sea of the Hebrides	37	E4
Searchlight	101	D1
Searcy	99	B3
Seaside	97	B1
Seattle	97	B1
Sebeş	47	L4
Sebkha Azzel Matti	59	F3
Sebkha de Timimoun	59	E3
Sebkha de Tindouf	59	D3
Sebkha Mekerrhane	59	F3
Sebkha Oum el Drouss Telli	59	C4
Sebkhet de Chemchâm	59	C4
Sebnitz	35	K6
Sebring	103	E4
Secchia	43	F6
Sechura	109	A5
Secretary Island	89	A7
Secunderabad	75	C5
Sécure	109	D7
Sedalia	99	B3
Sedan	27	G5
Sedano	41	G2
Seddonville	89	C5
Sede Boqer	54	B6
Sedeh	53	G3
Sederot	54	B5
Sédico	43	H4
Sedom	54	C5
Seeheim	67	B5
Seelow	35	K4
Seesen	35	F5
Seevetal	35	E3
Séez	43	B5
Seferihisar	49	J6
Segamat	83	(1)C2
Segezha	31	F2
Seghnān	53	K2
Ségou	63	C2
Segovia	41	F4
Segré	39	E6
Séguédine	59	H4
Seguin	103	B4
Segura	41	H6
Sehithwa	67	C4
Sehnde	35	E4
Seiland	29	M1
Seiling	103	B2
Seinäjoki	29	M5
Seine	39	F4
Sekondi	63	D3
Selassi	83	(2)D3
Selat Bangka	83	(1)D3
Selat Berhala	83	(1)C3
Selat Dampir	83	(2)D3
Selat Karimata	83	(1)D3
Selat Makassar	83	(1)F3
Selat Mentawai	83	(1)B3
Selat Sunda	83	(1)D4
Selawik	101	(1)F2
Selb	35	H6
Selby	97	G1
Selçuk	49	K7
Selebi-Phikwe	67	D4
Sélestat	43	C2
Selfoss	29	(1)C3
Seligman	101	D1
Seljord	29	E7
Selkirk	95	G1
Selkirk Mountains	95	C1
Sells	101	D2
Selm	27	K3
Selmer	99	C3
Selpele	83	(2)D3
Selvas	109	C5
Selwyn Lake	93	L5
Selwyn Mountains	101	(1)L3
Semanit	49	B4
Semarang	83	(1)E4
Sematan	83	(1)D2
Sembé	63	G4
Seminoe Reservoir	97	E2
Seminole, Okla., United States	97	G3
Seminole, Tex., United States	101	F2
Semiozernoye	71	L7
Semipalatinsk	71	Q7
Semiyarka	71	P7
Semois	27	H5
Semporna	83	(1)F2
Sena Madureira	109	D5
Senanga	67	C3
Senatobia	103	D3
Sendai	81	L4
Senec	43	N2
Seneca	103	E3
Senegal	63	A2
Senégal	63	B1
Senftenberg	35	J5
Senhor do Bonfim	109	J6
Senica	33	G9
Senigallia	43	J7
Senj	43	K6
Senja	29	J2
Senlis	27	E5
Sennar	53	B7
Senneterre	99	E1
Sens	39	J5
Senta	47	H4
Seoni	75	C4
Seoul = Sŏul	81	D5
Separation Point	89	D5
Sept-Îles	93	T6
Seraing	27	H4
Serakhs	53	H2
Seram	83	(2)D3
Seram Sea	83	(2)C3
Serbia = Srbija	47	H6
Serdobsk	31	H4
Serebryansk	71	Q8
Sered'	47	E1
Şereflikoçhisar	49	R6
Seregno	43	E5
Serein	39	J6
Seremban	83	(1)C2
Serenje	67	E2
Sergelen	79	E1
Sergeyevka	31	N4
Sergipe	109	K6
Sergiyev Posad	31	G3
Seria	83	(1)E2
Serifos	49	G7
Serik	49	P8
Seringapatam Reef	87	D2
Sermata	83	(2)C4
Seronga	67	C3
Serov	31	M3
Serowe	67	D4
Serpa	41	C7
Serpukhov	31	G4
Serra Acari	109	F3
Serra Curupira	109	E3
Serra da Chela	67	A3
Serra da Espinhaço	109	J7
Serra da Ibiapaba	109	J4
Serra da Mantiqueira	111	M3
Serra de Maracaju	111	K3
Serra do Cachimbo	109	F5
Serra do Caiapó	109	G7
Serra do Roncador	109	G6
Serra dos Carajás	109	G5
Serra dos Dois Irmãos	109	J5
Serra dos Parecis	109	E6
Serra do Tiracambu	109	H4
Serra Estrondo	109	H5
Serra Formosa	109	F6
Serra Geral de Goiás	109	H6
Serra Geral do Paraná	109	H7
Serra Lombarda	109	G3
Serra Pacaraima	109	E3
Serra Parima	109	E3
Serra Tumucumaque	109	F3
Serra da Estrela	41	C4
Serres, France	39	L9
Serres, Greece	49	F3
Serrinha	109	K6
Sertã	41	B5
Serui	83	(2)E3
Servia	49	D4
Sêrxü	79	B4
Sese Islands	65	E4
Sesfontein	67	A3
Sesheke	67	C3
Sessa Aurunca	45	H7
Sestri Levante	43	E6
Sestroretsk	29	Q6
Sestrunj	43	K6
Sesvete	43	M5
Setana	81	K2
Sète	39	J10
Sete Lagoas	109	J7
Setesdal	29	D7
Sétif	59	G1
Settat	59	D2
Setúbal	41	B6
Sŏul	85	C2
Seurre	39	L7
Sevana Lich	51	L3
Sevastopol'	51	E1
Seven Lakes	101	E1
Sevenoaks	27	C3
Severn, Canada	93	P5
Severn, United Kingdom	37	K10
Severnaya Dvina	31	H2
Severnaya Osetiya	51	L2
Severnaya Zemlya	71	U1
Severn Estuary	37	J10
Severnoye	31	K4
Severnyy	71	L4
Severobaykal'sk	73	H5
Severodvinsk	31	G2
Severomorsk	29	S2
Severoural'sk	31	M2
Severo-Yeniseyskiy	71	S5
Sevier Lake	97	D3
Sevilla	41	E7
Sevlievo	47	N7
Seward Peninsula	101	(1)E2
Seyakha	71	N3
Seychelles	67	(2)B2
Seychelles Islands	57	J6
Seydişehir	49	P7
Seydisfjöður	29	(1)G2
Seyhan	51	F5
Seymchan	73	S4
Seymour, Australia	87	J7
Seymour, Ind., United States	103	D2
Seymour, Tex., United States	103	B3
Sézanne	39	J5
Sezze	45	H7
Sfakia	49	G9
Sfântu Gheorghe	47	N4
Sfax	59	H2
's-Gravenhage	27	G2
Sha'am	55	G3
Shabunda	65	D4
Shabwah	53	E6
Shache	71	P10
Shādegān	55	C1
Shadehill Reservoir	97	F1
Shagamu	63	E3
Shagonar	71	S7
Shag Rocks	111	N9
Shahbā'	54	D4
Shahdāb	55	G1
Shahdol	75	D4
Shah Fuladi	53	J3
Shahjahanpur	75	C3
Shahrak	53	H3
Shahr-e Bābāk	55	F1
Shahrtuz	53	J2
Shakhrisabz	53	J2
Shakhtërsk	73	Q7
Shakhty	31	H5
Shakhun'ya	31	J3
Shaki	63	E3
Shakotan-misaki	81	L2
Shama	65	E5
Shamattawa	93	N5
Shamrock	101	F1
Shand	53	H3
Shandong Bandao	79	G3
Shangani	67	D3
Shangdu	79	E2
Shanghai	79	G4
Shangqui	79	F4
Shangrao	79	F5
Shangzhi	79	H1
Shangzhou	79	D4
Shantarskiye Ostrova	73	P5
Shantou	79	F6
Shanwei	77	F2
Shanyin	79	E3
Shaoguan	79	E6
Shaoxing	79	G5
Shaoyang	79	E5
Shapkina	31	K1
Shaqrā'	55	A4
Sharga	71	T8
Sharjah = Ash Shāriqah	55	F4
Shark Bay	85	B8
Shark Reef	87	J2
Sharm el Sheikh	61	F2
Sharūrah	53	E6
Shashe	67	D4
Shashi	79	E4
Shasta Lake	97	B2
Shatsk	31	H4
Shats'k	33	N6
Shaubak	54	C6
Shawano	99	C2
Shcherbakove	73	U3
Shchigry	31	G4
Shchuch'ye	71	L6
Shchuchyn	29	N10
Sheberghān	53	J2
Sheboygan	99	C2
Sheffield, New Zealand	89	D6
Sheffield, United Kingdom	37	L8
Sheffield, Al., United States	99	C4
Sheffield, Tex., United States	101	F2
Shegmas	31	J2
Shelburne	93	T8
Shelby	97	D1
Shelbyville	99	C3
Shelikof Strait	101	(1)F4
Shenandoah	99	A2
Shendam	63	F3
Shendi	61	F4
Shenkursk	31	H2
Shenyang	81	B3
Shenzhen	79	E6
Shepetivka	31	E4
Shepparton	87	J7
Sherbro Island	63	B3
Sherbrooke	99	F1
Sheridan	97	E2
Sherkaly	31	N2
Sherlovaya Gora	73	K6
Sherman	103	B3
's-Hertogenbosch	27	H3
Shetland Islands	37	M1
Shetpe	71	J9
Sheyenne	97	G1
Sheykh Sho'eyb	55	E3
Shiant Islands	37	F4
Shibata	81	K5
Shibetsu, Japan	81	M1
Shibetsu, Japan	81	N2
Shibotsu-jima	81	P2
Shiderty	71	N7
Shihezi	71	R9
Shijiazhuang	79	E3
Shikarpur	53	J4
Shikoku	81	G7
Shikoku-sanchi	81	G7
Shikotan-tō	81	P2
Shikotsu-ko	81	L2
Shiliguri	75	E3
Shilka	73	K6
Shilka	73	K6
Shillong	75	F3
Shilovo	31	H4
Shimabara	81	F7
Shimla	75	C2
Shimoda	81	K6
Shimoga	75	C6
Shimo-Koshiki-jima	81	E8
Shimoni	65	F4
Shimonoseki	81	F7
Shināş	55	G4
Shīndan	53	H3
Shingū	81	H7
Shinjō	81	L4

Place	Page	Ref
Shinyanga	65	E4
Shiono-misaki	81	H7
Shiprock	97	E3
Shiquan	79	D4
Shirakawa	81	L5
Shīrāz	55	E2
Shire	67	E3
Shiretoko-misaki	81	N1
Shiriya-zaki	81	L3
Shīr Kūh	53	F3
Shivpuri	75	C3
Shiyan	79	E4
Shizuishan	79	D3
Shizuoka	81	K6
Shkodër	47	G7
Shomishko	71	K8
Shorap	53	J4
Shoreham	27	B4
Shoshone, Calif., United States	97	C3
Shoshone, Id., United States	97	D2
Shoshoni	97	E2
Shostka	31	F4
Show Low	101	E2
Shoyna	31	H1
Shreveport	103	C3
Shrewsbury	37	K9
Shuangliao	81	B2
Shuangyashan	73	N7
Shubarkuduk	71	K8
Shulan	81	D1
Shumagin Islands	101	(1)E5
Shumen	47	P6
Shumikha	31	M3
Shuqrah	53	E7
Shurchi	53	J2
Shūr Gaz	55	H2
Shurinda	73	J5
Shuryshkary	31	N1
Shuya	31	H3
Shuyang	79	F4
Shwebo	77	B2
Shymkent	71	M9
Sialkot	53	K3
Siatista	49	D4
Šiauliai	33	N2
Sibay	31	L4
Šibenik	47	C6
Siberia = Sibir	69	N3
Siberut	83	(1)B3
Sibi	53	J4
Sibigo	83	(1)B2
Sibir	69	N3
Sibiu	47	M4
Sibolga	83	(1)B2
Sibu	83	(1)E2
Sibuco	77	G5
Sibut	65	B2
Sicilia	45	G11
Sicilian Channel	45	F11
Sicily = Sicilia	45	G11
Šid	47	G4
Siddipet	75	C5
Siderno	45	L10
Sidi Barrani	61	E1
Sidi Bel Abbès	59	E1
Sidi Kacem	59	D2
Sidirokastro	49	F3
Sidney	97	F2
Sidoan	83	(2)B2
Sidorovsk	71	Q4
Sieburg	27	K4
Siedlce	33	M5
Sieg	27	K4
Siegen	27	L4
Siemiatycze	33	M5
Siĕmréab	77	C4
Siena	43	G7
Sierpc	33	J5
Sierra Blanca	101	E2
Sierra Colorada	111	H7
Sierra de Calalasteo	111	H4
Sierra de Córdoba	111	H5
Sierra de Gata	41	D4
Sierra de Gúdar	41	K4
Sierra del Nevado	111	H6
Sierra de Perija	105	K7
Sierra Grande	111	H7
Sierra Leone	63	B3
Sierra Madre	105	F5
Sierra Madre del Sur	105	E5
Sierra Madre Occidental	95	E6
Sierra Madre Oriental	101	F3
Sierra Morena	41	E6
Sierra Nevada, Spain	41	G7
Sierra Nevada, United States	101	B1
Sierra Vizcaino	95	D6
Sierre	43	C4
Sifnos	49	G8
Sig	41	K9
Sigean	39	H10
Sighetu Marmației	47	L2
Sighișoara	47	M3
Siglufjörður	29	(1)D1
Sigmaringen	43	E2
Signal Mountain	99	C3
Siguiri	63	C2
Sihanoukville	77	C4
Siilinjärvi	29	P5
Siirt	51	J5
Sikar	75	C3
Sikasso	63	C2
Sikea	49	F4
Sikeston	99	C3
Sikhote Alin	81	H1
Sikinos	49	G8
Siklós	47	F4
Siktyakh	73	L3
Sil	41	C2
Šilalė	33	M2
Silandro	43	F4
Silba	43	K6
Silchar	75	F4
Şile	49	M3
Silhouette Island	67	(2)B1
Siliana	45	D12
Silifke	51	E5
Siling Co	75	E2
Silistra	47	Q5
Silivri	49	L3
Siljan	29	H6
Sillamäe	29	P7
Silsbee	103	C3
Siluas	83	(1)D2
Šilutė	33	L2
Silvan	51	J4
Silver Bay	99	B1
Silver City	101	E2
Silver Lake	97	B2
Silver Plains	87	H2
Simanggang	83	(1)E2
Simao	79	C6
Simav	51	C4
Simcoe	99	D2
Simeonovgrad	47	N7
Simeria	33	N12
Simeuluë	83	(1)A2
Simferopol'	51	F1
Şimleu Silvaniei	47	K2
Simmerath	27	J4
Simojärvi	29	P3
Simpang	83	(1)C3
Simpson Desert	87	G4
Sinabang	83	(1)B2
Sinai	61	F2
Sinaia	47	N4
Sinalunga	45	F5
Sinanju	81	C4
Sincelejo	109	B2
Sinclair's Bay	37	J3
Sindangbarang	83	(1)D4
Sindelfingen	35	E8
Sines	41	B7
Singa	61	F5
Singapore	83	(1)C2
Singapore	83	(1)C2
Singaraja	83	(1)E4
Singen	43	D3
Sîngerei	47	R2
Singida	65	E4
Singkawang	83	(1)D2
Singkep	83	(1)C3
Singkilbaru	83	(1)B2
Singleton	87	K6
Siniscóla	45	D8
Sinj	47	D6
Sinjär	51	J5
Sinkat	61	G4
Sinni	45	L8
Sinop	51	F2
Sinsheim	35	D7
Sinton	103	B4
Sinŭiju	81	C3
Sinyaya	73	L4
Sió	47	F3
Siófok	47	F3
Sion	43	C4
Sioux City	99	A2
Sioux Falls	99	A2
Sioux Lookout	95	H2
Siping	81	C2
Sipiwesk	93	M5
Sipura	83	(1)B3
Sira	29	D7
Siracusa	45	K11
Sir Banī 'Yās	55	E4
Sir Edward Pellew Group	87	G3
Siret	47	P2
Siret	47	Q4
Sīrgān	53	H4
Şiria	33	L11
Siri Kit Dam	77	B3
Sirk	55	G3
Sirohi	75	B4
Sirsa	75	C3
Sirsi	75	B6
Sisak	47	D4
Sisian	51	L4
Sisimiut	93	W3
Sisŏphŏn	77	C4
Sisseton	97	G1
Sistema Central	41	E4
Sistema Iberico	41	H3
Sisteron	43	A6
Sitapur	75	D3
Sitasjaure	29	J3
Siteia	49	J9
Sitges	41	M3
Sithonia	49	F4
Sitka	93	D5
Sittard	27	H4
Sittwe	75	F4
Sivand	55	E1
Sivas	51	G4
Siverek	51	H5
Sivrihisar	49	P5
Siwa	61	E1
Siyäzän	51	N3
Sjælland	29	F9
Sjenica	47	H6
Sjenica Jezero	47	G6
Sjöbo	33	C2
Skädlderviken	33	B1
Skaerbaek	35	D1
Skagen	29	F8
Skagerrak	29	D8
Skantzoura	49	G5
Skardu	53	L2
Skaulo	29	L3
Skawina	33	J8
Skegness	27	C1
Skellefteå	29	L4
Ski	29	F7
Skiathos	49	F5
Skidal'	33	P4
Skien	29	E7
Skikda	59	G1
Skipton	37	L8
Skjern	29	E9
Škofja Loka	43	K4
Skopelos	49	F5
Skopje	47	J7
Skövde	29	G7
Skovorodino	73	L6
Skowhegan	99	G2
Skuodas	29	L8
Skye	37	F4
Skyros	49	G6
Skyros	49	G6
Slagelse	35	G1
Slaney	37	F9
Slano	47	E7
Slantsy	29	Q7
Slaný	35	K6
Slatina	47	M5
Slave	91	N3
Slave Lake	93	J5
Slavonska Požega	47	E4
Slavonski Brod	47	F4
Slavyanka	81	F2
Slavyansk-na-Kubani	51	H1
Sławno	33	F3
Sleaford	27	B1
Sleeper Islands	93	Q5
Slidell	103	D3
Sligo	37	D7
Sligo Bay	37	D7
Sliven	47	P7
Slobozia, Moldova	47	S3
Slobozia, Romania	47	Q5
Slonim	29	N10
Slough	27	B3
Slovakia	33	H9
Slovenia	43	K4
Slovenj Gradec	43	L4
Slovenska Bistrica	43	L4
Slov''yans'k	31	G5
Słubice	33	D5
Slunj	43	L5
Słupca	33	G5
Słupsk	33	G3
Slutsk	31	E4
Slyudyanka	73	G6
Smålandsfarvandet	35	G1
Smallwood Reservoir	93	U6
Smargon'	29	P9
Smederevo	47	H5
Smila	31	F5
Smirnykh	73	Q7
Smiths Falls	99	E2
Smokey Hills	103	B2
Smoky	93	H6
Smøla	29	D5
Smolensk	31	F4
Smolyan	49	G3
Smooth Rock Falls	99	D1
Smyrna	103	E3
Snæfell	29	(1)F2
Snake	97	C1
Snake River Plain	97	D2
Snåsavatnet	29	F4
Sneek	27	H1
Snezhnogorsk	71	R4
Snežnik	43	K5
Snina	33	M9
Snøhetta	29	E5
Snøtinden	29	G3
Snowdon	37	H8
Snowdrift	93	J4
Snowville	97	D2
Snyder	101	F2
Soalala	67	H3
Soanierana-Ivongo	67	H3
Soa-Siu	83	(2)C2
Sobral	109	J4
Sochaczew	33	K5
Sochaux	43	B3
Sochi	51	H2
Socorro	101	E2
Socotra = Suquţrā	53	F7
Socuéllamos	41	H5
Sodankylä	29	P3
Söderhamn	29	J6
Södertälje	29	J7
Sodo	65	F2
Soe	83	(2)B4
Soest	27	L3
Sofia = Sofiya	47	L7
Sofiya	47	L7
Sofiysk, Russia	73	N6
Sofiysk, Russia	73	P6
Sofporog	29	R4
Sōfu-gan	79	L5
Sogamoso	109	C2
Sognefjorden	29	C6
Sogod	77	G4
Sog Xian	75	F2
Sohâg	61	F2

Name	Page	Grid
Soignies	27	G4
Soissons	27	F5
Sokch'o	81	E4
Söke	49	K7
Sokhumi	51	J2
Sokode	63	E3
Sokol	31	H3
Sokółka	29	M10
Sokolo	63	C2
Sokolov	35	H6
Sokołów Podlaski	33	M5
Sokoto	63	F2
Sokoto	63	F2
Sokyryany	47	Q1
Solander Island	89	A8
Solapur	75	C5
Sölden	43	F4
Solenzara	45	D7
Solikamsk	31	L3
Sol'-Iletsk	31	L4
Soliman	45	E12
Solingen	27	K3
Sollefteå	29	J5
Soller	41	N5
Solna	29	J7
Solomon Islands	85	F6
Solothurn	43	C3
Solov'yevsk	73	K6
Šolta	47	D6
Soltau	35	E4
Sol'tsy	31	F3
Solway Firth	37	J7
Solwezi	67	D2
Soma	49	K5
Sōma	81	L5
Somalia	65	H2
Sombor	47	G4
Sombrerete	101	F4
Somerset, Australia	87	H2
Somerset, Ky., United States	99	C3
Somerset, Pa., United States	99	E2
Somerset Island	93	N2
Someş	47	K2
Somme	27	E4
Sommen	29	H8
Sömmerda	35	G5
Sømna	29	F4
Sondags	67	D6
Sønderborg Ærø	35	E2
Sondershausen	35	F5
Sóndrio	43	E4
Songavatn	29	D7
Songea	65	F6
Song Hông	77	C2
Songhua	79	H1
Songhua Hu	81	D2
Songhua Jiang	81	D1
Songkan	79	D5
Songkhla	77	C5
Songnam	81	D5
Songnim	81	C4
Songo	67	E3
Songololo	63	G6
Songpan	79	C4
Sonid Yuoqi	79	E2
Sonid Zuoqi	79	E2
Son La	77	C2
Sonneberg	35	G6
Sono	109	H6
Sonora	101	B1
Sonora	101	D3
Sonoyta	101	D2
Sonsorol Islands	83	(2)D1
Sonthofen	43	F3
Sopot	29	K9
Sopron	43	M3
Sora	45	H7
Soracaba	111	M3
Sorel	99	F1
Sorgun	51	F4
Soria	41	H3
Sorø	35	G1
Soroca	47	R1
Sorochinsk	31	K4
Sorong	83	(2)D3
Soroti	65	E3
Sørøya	29	L1
Sorrentó	45	J8
Sorsele	29	J4
Sorso	45	C8
Sort	41	M2
Sortavala	29	R6
Sørvagen	29	G3
Sosnogorsk	71	J5
Sosnovo	29	R6
Sosnowiec	33	J7
Sos'va	31	M3
Sos'vinskaya	31	M2
Soto la Marina	101	G4
Soubré	63	C3
Soufli	49	J3
Souilly	27	H5
Souk Ahras	45	B12
Sŏul	81	D5
Soulac-sur-Mer	39	D8
Soumussalmi	29	Q4
Soûr	54	C3
Soure	41	B5
Sour el Ghozlane	41	P8
Souris	95	F2
Souris	95	G2
Sousa	109	K5
Sousse	59	H1
South Africa	67	C6
South America	91	J9
Southampton, Canada	99	D2
Southampton, United Kingdom	27	A4
Southampton Island	93	Q4
South Andaman	75	F6
South Atlantic Ocean	111	P6
South Australia	87	F5
South Baymouth	99	D1
South Bend	99	C2
South Boston	99	E3
South Carolina	103	E3
South Charleston	103	E2
South China Sea	77	E4
South Dakota	97	F2
South Downs	27	B4
South East Cape	87	J8
South East Point	87	J7
Southend-on-Sea	27	C3
Southern Alps	89	B6
Southern Cross	87	C6
Southern Indian Lake	93	M5
South Georgia	111	P9
South Harris	37	F4
South Haven	99	C2
South Hill	99	E3
South Island	89	B6
South Korea	81	D5
South Lake Tahoe	97	B3
South Orkney Islands	112	(2)A3
South Pacific Ocean	111	P6
South Platte	97	F2
Southport	37	J8
South Ronaldsay	37	K3
South Sandwich Islands	112	(2)C4
South Sandwich Trench	107	H9
South Saskatchewan	95	D1
South Shetland Islands	112	(2)MM4
South Shields	37	L7
South Taranaki Bight	89	D4
South Uist	37	E4
South West Cape, Auckland Island	89	(2)A1
South West Cape, Australia	87	H8
Southwest Cape	89	A8
South West Pacific Basin	85	L9
Southwold	27	D2
Sovata	47	N3
Sovetsk, Russia	29	L9
Sovetsk, Russia	31	J3
Soweto	67	D5
Sōya-misaki	81	L1
Sozopol	47	Q7
Spa	27	H4
Spain	41	F5
Spalding	27	B2
Sparks	101	C1
Spartanburg	103	E3
Sparti	49	E7
Sparwood	97	D1
Spassk-Dal'niy	81	G1
Spearfish	97	F2
Spencer	99	A2
Spencer Gulf	87	G6
Spetses	49	F7
Spey	37	J4
Speyer	27	L5
Spiekeroog	35	C3
Spiez	43	C4
Spišska Nová Ves	33	K9
Spitsbergen	112	(1)P2
Spittal	43	J4
Split	47	D6
Spokane	97	C1
Spoleto	45	G6
Spooner	99	B1
Sprague	97	C1
Spratly Islands	77	E4
Spray	97	C2
Spree	35	K4
Spremberg	35	K5
Spring	103	B3
Springbok	67	B5
Springe	35	E4
Springer	101	F1
Springerville	101	E2
Springfield, Colo., United States	101	F1
Springfield, Ill., United States	99	C3
Springfield, Mass., United States	99	F2
Springfield, Mo., United States	99	B3
Springfield, Oh., United States	99	D3
Springfield, Oreg., United States	97	B2
Springfield, Vt., United States	99	F2
Spring Hill	103	E4
Springs	67	D5
Springs Junction	89	D6
Springsure	87	J4
Springville, Al., United States	103	D3
Springville, N.Y., United States	99	E2
Squamish	97	B1
Squinzano	45	N8
Srbija	47	H6
Srbobran	47	G4
Sredenekolymsk	73	S3
Sredinnyy Khrebet	73	T6
Srednesibirskoye Ploskogor'ye	73	F3
Srednogorie	49	G2
Śrem	33	G5
Sretensk	73	K6
Srikakulam	75	D5
Sri Lanka	75	D7
Srinagar	75	B2
Stack Skerry	37	H2
Stade	29	E10
Stadlandet	29	C5
Stadskanaal	27	J2
Stadtallendorf	35	E6
Stadthagen	35	E4
Staffa	37	F5
Staffelstien	35	F6
Stafford	37	K9
Staines	27	B3
Stainz	43	L4
Stakhanov	31	G5
Stalowa Wola	33	M7
Stambolijski	49	G2
Stamford, United Kingdom	27	B2
Stamford, United States	99	F2
Standish	99	D2
Stanford	99	D3
Stanke Dimitrov	49	F2
Stanley, Australia	87	J8
Stanley, Falkland Islands	111	K9
Stanley, United States	97	F1
Stanovaya	73	T3
Stanovoye Nagor'ye	73	J5
Stanovoy Khrebet	73	L5
Staphorst	27	J2
Stapleton	97	F2
Starachowice	33	L6
Stara L'ubovňa	33	K8
Stara Pazova	47	H5
Stara Planina	49	F1
Staraya Russa	31	F3
Stara Zagora	47	N7
Starbuck Island	85	L6
Stargard Szczeciński	29	H10
Starkville	103	D3
Starnberg	43	G2
Starnberger See	43	G3
Start Point	39	B3
Staryy Oskol	31	G4
Staszów	33	L7
Statesboro	103	E3
Statesville	103	E2
Staunton	103	F2
Stavanger	29	C7
Stavoron	27	H2
Stavropol'	51	J1
Stavropol'skaya Vovyshennost'	31	H5
Steamboat Springs	97	E2
Steens Mountains	97	C2
Stefansson Island	93	L2
Stege	35	H1
Ştei	47	K3
Stein	35	G7
Steinach	43	G3
Steinfurt	27	K2
Steinjker	29	F4
Stenay	27	H5
Stendal	35	G4
Steno Antikythiro	49	F9
Stephenville	103	B3
Sterling	97	F2
Sterling City	101	F2
Sterling Heights	99	D2
Sterlitamak	31	L4
Sternberk	33	G8
Stettiner Haff	29	G10
Stevenage	27	B3
Stevens Point	99	C2
Stevens Village	101	(1)H2
Stewart	93	K5
Stewart	101	(1)K3
Stewart Island	89	A8
Steyr	43	K2
Stillwater	103	B2
Stinnett	101	F1
Štip	49	E3
Stirling	37	J5
Stjørdal	29	F5
Stockach	43	E3
Stockerau	43	M2
Stockholm	29	K7
Stockport	37	K8
Stockton, Calif., United States	101	B1
Stockton, Kans., United States	101	G1
Stockton-on-Tees	37	L7
Stœng Trêng	77	D4
Stoke-on-Trent	37	K8
Stokksnes	29	(1)F2
Stolac	47	F6
Stolberg	27	J4
Stolin	31	L4
Stollberg	35	H6
Stonehaven	37	K5
Stony Rapids	93	K5
Stör	35	E2
Stora Lulevatten	29	K3
Stord	29	C7
Store Bælt	35	F1
Støren	29	F5
Store Sotra	29	B6
Storlien	29	G5
Storm Bay	87	J8
Storm Lake	99	A2
Stornoway	37	F3
Storozhevsk	31	K2
Storozhynets'	47	N1
Storsjøen	29	F6
Storsjön, Sweden	29	G5
Storsjön, Sweden	29	J6
Storuman	29	J4
Storuman	29	J4
Stour	27	C2
Stowmarket	27	D2
Strabane	37	E7
Stradella	43	E5
Strait of Belle Isle	93	V6
Strait of Bonifacio	45	D7
Strait of Dover	27	D4
Strait of Georgia	97	B1

Name	Page	Grid
Strait of Gibraltar	41	E9
Strait of Hormuz	55	G3
Strait of Juan de Fuca	97	B1
Strait of Malacca	83	(1)C2
Straits of Florida	103	E5
Strakonice	35	J7
Stralsund	29	G9
Strand	67	B6
Stranda	29	D5
Strandavatn	29	D6
Stranraer	37	H7
Strasbourg	43	C2
Strasburg	101	F1
Strǎşeni	47	R2
Stratford, *Canada*	99	D2
Stratford, *United States*	97	F3
Stratford-upon-Avon	27	A2
Strathroy	99	D2
Stratoni	49	F4
Stratton	99	F1
Straubing	43	H2
Straumnes	29	(1)B1
Strausberg	35	J4
Streaky Bay	87	F6
Streator	99	C2
Strehaia	47	L5
Strelka, *Russia*	73	E5
Strelka, *Russia*	73	S4
Strezhevoy	31	Q2
Strimonas	49	F4
Strofades	49	C7
Strómboli	45	K10
Strömsund	29	H5
Stronsay	37	K2
Stroud	37	K10
Struga	49	C3
Strugi-Krasnyye	29	Q7
Strumica	49	E3
Stryjama	47	M7
Stryy	33	N8
Stryy	33	N8
Strzegom	33	F7
Strzelce Opolskie	33	H7
Strzelin	33	G7
Sturgeon Bay	99	C2
Sturgeon Falls	99	E1
Sturgis, *Ky., United States*	99	C3
Sturgis, *S.D., United States*	97	F2
Sturkö	33	E1
Štúrova	33	H10
Sturt Stony Desert	87	G5
Stuttgart, *Germany*	43	E2
Stuttgart, *United States*	103	C3
Stykkishólmur	29	(1)B2
Suai	83	(2)C4
Suakin	61	G4
Subcule	61	H5
Subi Besar	83	(1)D2
Sublette	101	F1
Subotica	47	G3
Suceava	47	P2
Suck	37	D8
Sucre	109	D7
Sudak	51	F1
Sudan	61	E5
Sudan	63	D2
Suday	31	H3
Sudbury, *Canada*	99	D1
Sudbury, *United Kingdom*	27	C2
Sudd	65	E2
Sudová Vyshnya	33	N8
Suez = El Suweis	61	F2
Suez Canal	61	F1
Suffolk	103	F2
Sugun	53	L2
Suḩār	55	G4
Suhl	35	F6
Suide	79	E3
Suifenhe	81	F1
Suihua	73	M7
Suippes	27	G5
Suir	37	E9
Suixi	79	E6
Suizhong	79	G2
Suizhou	79	E4
Sukabumi	83	(1)D4
Sukadana	83	(1)D3
Sukhinichi	31	G4
Sukhona	31	H3
Sukkertoppen = Maniitsoq	93	W3
Sukkur	53	J4
Sula	31	K1
Sula	31	K1
Sula Sgeir	37	F2
Sulawesi	83	(2)A3
Sulejówek	33	L5
Sule Skerry	37	H2
Sulgachi	73	N4
Sulina	47	S4
Sulingen	27	L2
Sullana	109	A4
Sullivan	103	C2
Sulmona	45	H6
Sulphur Springs	103	B3
Sultanhanı	49	R6
Sultanpur	75	D3
Sulu Archipelago	77	G5
Sulu Sea	77	F5
Sulzbach	27	K5
Sulzbach-Rosenberg	35	G7
Sulzberger Bay	112	(2)CC2
Sumatera	83	(1)C2
Sumatra = Sumatera	83	(1)C2
Sumba	83	(2)A5
Sumbawa	83	(2)A4
Sumbawabesar	83	(2)A4
Sumbawanga	65	E5
Sumbe	67	A2
Šumen	51	B2
Sumenep	83	(1)E4
Sumisu-jima	81	L8
Sumkino	31	N3
Summer Lake	97	B2
Summerville	103	E3
Summit	93	B4
Šumperk	33	G8
Sumqayıt	51	N3
Sumter	103	E3
Sumy	31	F4
Sunbury	99	E2
Sunch'ŏn	81	D6
Sun City	67	D5
Sundance	97	F2
Sundarbans	75	E4
Sunday Strait	87	D3
Sunderland	37	L7
Sundridge	99	E1
Sundsvall	29	J5
Sundsvallsbukten	29	J5
Sungaipenuh	83	(1)C3
Sungei Petani	77	C5
Sunnyvale	97	B3
Sun Prairie	99	C2
Suntar	73	K4
Suntsar	53	H4
Sunwu	73	M7
Sunyani	63	D3
Suomussalmi	31	E2
Suŏ-nada	81	F7
Suonenjoki	29	P5
Suordakh	73	P3
Suoyarvi	31	F2
Superior	95	H2
Supetar	47	D6
Süphan Daği	51	K4
Sūqash Shuyūkh	55	B1
Suqian	79	F4
Suquṭrā	53	F7
Sūr	53	G5
Sura	31	J4
Surab	53	J4
Surabaya	83	(1)E4
Sūrak	55	H4
Surakarta	83	(1)E4
Šurany	47	F1
Surat	75	B4
Surat Thani	77	B5
Surdulica	47	K7
Sûre	27	H5
Surfers Paradise	87	K5
Surgut	71	N5
Surgutikha	71	R5
Surigao	77	H5
Surin	77	C4
Surinam	109	F3
Surkhet	75	D3
Sürmaq	55	E1
Surovikino	31	H5
Surskoye	31	J4
Surt	59	J2
Surtsey	29	(1)C3
Susa	43	C5
Şuşa	51	M4
Sušac	47	D7
Susak	43	K6
Susanville	97	B2
Suşehri	51	H3
Sušice	35	J7
Susitma	101	(1)G3
Susuman	73	R4
Susurluk	49	L5
Sutherland	67	C6
Sutlej	75	B3
Suusamyr	71	N9
Suva	85	H7
Suvorov Island	85	K7
Suwałki	33	M3
Suwannaphum	77	C3
Suweilih	54	C4
Suweima	54	C5
Suwŏn	81	D5
Suzak	31	N6
Suzhou, *China*	79	F4
Suzhou, *China*	79	G4
Suzuka	81	J6
Suzu-misaki	81	J5
Svalbard	112	(1)Q2
Svalyaya	47	L1
Svartenhuk Halvø	93	V2
Svatove	31	G5
Sveg	29	H5
Svendborg	29	F9
Šventoji	29	N9
Sverdrup Islands	112	(1)DD2
Svetac	47	C6
Sveti Nikole	49	D3
Svetlaya	73	P7
Svetlogorsk	33	K3
Svetlograd	51	K1
Svetlyy, *Russia*	33	K3
Svetlyy, *Russia*	71	L7
Svidník	33	L8
Svilengrad	49	J3
Svishtov	47	N6
Svitava	33	F8
Svitovy	33	F8
Svobodnyy	73	M6
Svratka	33	F8
Svyetlahorsk	31	E4
Swain Reefs	87	K4
Swains Island	85	J7
Swakopmund	67	A4
Swale	37	K7
Swan	107	C2
Swan Hill	87	H7
Swan Islands	105	H5
Swan River	93	L6
Swansea, *Australia*	87	J8
Swansea, *United Kingdom*	37	J10
Swaziland	67	E5
Sweden	29	H6
Sweetwater	101	F2
Swider	33	L5
Swidnica	33	F7
Świdnik	33	M6
Świdwin	33	E4
Świebodzin	33	E5
Swift Current	95	E1
Swindon	27	A3
Świnoujście	29	H10
Switzerland	43	C4
Syalakh	73	L3
Syamzha	31	H2
Sydney, *Australia*	87	K6
Sydney, *Canada*	93	U7
Syke	27	L2
Syktyvkar	31	K2
Sylacauga	103	D3
Sylhet	75	F4
Sylt	29	E9
Sylvania	99	D2
Sym	71	R5
Sym	71	R5
Symi	49	K8
Synya	31	L1
Syracuse, *Kans., United States*	101	F1
Syracuse, *N.Y., United States*	99	E2
Syrdar'ya	53	J1
Syrdar'ya	71	L8
Syria	53	C3
Syrian Desert = Bādiyat ash Shām	54	D4
Syrna	49	J8
Syros	49	G7
Sytomino	31	P2
Syzran'	31	J4
Szamos	47	K1
Szamotuły	33	F5
Szarvas	33	K11
Szczecin	33	D4
Szczecinek	33	F4
Szczytno	33	K4
Szeged	47	H3
Szeghalom	47	J2
Székesfehérvár	47	F2
Szekszárd	47	F3
Szentendre	47	G2
Szentes	47	H3
Szerencs	33	L9
Szigetvár	47	E3
Szolnok	47	H2
Szombathely	47	D2
Szprotawa	33	E6

T

Name	Page	Grid
Tab	47	F3
Tabarka	45	C12
Tabas	53	G3
Taber	97	D1
Table Cape	89	G4
Tabong	75	G3
Tábor	33	D8
Tabor	73	R2
Tabora	65	E5
Tabou	63	C4
Tabrīz	51	M4
Tabuaeran	85	K5
Tabūk	53	C4
Tacheng	71	Q8
Tachov	35	H7
Tacloban	77	H4
Tacna	109	C7
Tacoma	95	B2
Tacuarembó	111	K5
Tacurong	83	(2)B1
Tadjoura	61	H5
Tadmur	51	H6
Tadoussac	99	G1
Taech'ŏn	81	D5
Taegu	81	E6
Taejŏn	79	H3
Tafahi	85	J7
Tafalla	41	J2
Tafila	54	C6
Tafi Viejo	111	H4
Taganrog	31	G5
Taganrogskiy Zaliv	31	G5
Tagul	73	F6
Tagum	77	H5
Tagus	41	B5
Taharoa	89	E4
Tahiti	85	M7
Tahoe Lake	93	K2
Tahoka	101	F2
Tahoua	63	F2
Tahrūd	55	G2
Tai'an	79	F3
T'ai-chung	79	G6
Taihape	89	E4
Taihe	79	E5
Taikeng	79	E4
Tailem Bend	87	G7
Tain	37	H4
T'ai-nan	79	G6
T'ai-Pei	79	G6
Taiping	83	(1)C1

Name	Page	Grid
Taipingchuan	81	B1
T'ai-tung	77	G2
Taivalkoski	29	Q4
Taiwan	77	G2
Taiwan Strait	77	F2
Taiyuan	79	E3
Taizhou	79	F4
Ta'izz	53	D7
Tajikistan	53	J2
Tajima	81	K5
Tajo	25	D3
Tak	77	B3
Takaka	89	D5
Takamatsu	81	H6
Takaoka	81	J5
Takapuna	89	E3
Takasaki	81	K5
Takayama	81	J5
Takefui	81	J6
Takengon	83	(1)B2
Takestän	53	E2
Takht	73	P6
Takhta-Bazar	53	H2
Takhtabrod	71	M7
Takhtakupyr	71	L9
Takijuq Lake	93	J3
Takikawa	81	L2
Takoradi	63	D4
Taksimo	73	J5
Takua Pa	77	B5
Takum	63	G3
Talak	59	F5
Talara	109	A4
Talas	71	N9
Tal'at Müsá	51	G6
Talavera de la Reina	41	F5
Talaya	73	S4
Talbotton	103	E3
Talca	111	G6
Talcahuano	111	G6
Taldykorgan	71	P9
Tälesh	53	E2
Taliabu	83	(2)B3
Talibon	77	G4
Talitsa	31	M3
Tall 'Afar	51	K5
Tallahassee	103	E3
Tallaimannar	75	C7
Tall al Laḥm	55	B1
Tallinn	29	N7
Tall Kalakh	54	D2
Tallulah	95	H5
Tall 'Uwaynät	51	K5
Tälmaciu	47	M4
Tal'menka	71	Q7
Talon	73	R5
Tāloqān	71	N10
Taloyoak	93	N3
Talsi	29	M8
Taltal	111	G4
Tama	99	B2
Tamale	63	D3
Tamanrasset	59	G4
Tamanthi	75	G3
Tamási	47	F3
Tamazunchale	95	G7
Tambacounda	63	B2
Tambey	71	N3
Tambo	87	J4
Tambov	31	H4
Tambu	83	(2)A3
Tambura	65	D2
Tampa	103	E4
Tampere	29	M6
Tampico	105	E4
Tamsagbulag	79	F1
Tamsweg	43	J3
Tamworth, Australia	87	K6
Tamworth, United Kingdom	27	A2
Tana, Kenya	65	G4
Tana, Norway	29	P2
Tanabe	81	H7
Tanacross	101	(1)J3
Tanafjorden	29	Q1
Tanaga Island	101	(3)C1
T'ana Häyk'	61	G5
Tanahgrogot	83	(1)F3
Tanahjampea	83	(2)A4
Tanahmerah	83	(2)F4
Tanami	87	E4
Tanami Desert	87	F3
Tánaro	43	C6
Tandag	77	H5
Tăndărei	47	Q5
Tandil	111	K6
Tanega-shima	81	F8
Tanew	33	M7
Tanezrouft	59	E4
Tanga, Russia	73	J6
Tanga, Tanzania	65	F5
Tanger	59	D1
Tangermünde	35	G4
Tanggu	79	F3
Tangmai	75	G2
Tangra Yumco	75	E2
Tangshan	79	F3
Tanimbar	85	D6
Tanjona Ankaboa	67	G4
Tanjona Bobaomby	67	H2
Tanjona Masoala	67	J3
Tanjona Vilanandro	67	G3
Tanjona Vohimena	67	H5
Tanjung	83	(1)F3
Tanjungbalai	83	(1)B2
Tanjung Cangkuang	83	(1)C4
Tanjung Datu	83	(1)D2
Tanjung d'Urville	83	(2)E3
Tanjungkarang Telukbetung	83	(1)D4
Tanjung Libobo	83	(2)C3
Tanjung Mengkalihat	83	(1)F2
Tanjungpandan	83	(1)D3
Tanjung Puting	83	(1)E3
Tanjungredeb	83	(1)F2
Tanjung Selatan	83	(1)E3
Tanjungselor	83	(1)F2
Tanjung Vals	83	(2)E4
Tankovo	71	R5
Tankse	75	C2
Tanlovo	31	P1
Tanney	27	G5
Tanout	63	F2
Tanta	61	F1
Tan-Tan	59	C3
Tanzania	65	E5
Tao'an	79	G1
Taomasina	67	H3
Taongi	85	J4
Taormina	45	K11
Taos	101	E1
Taoudenni	59	E5
Taourirt	59	E2
T'ao-yuan	77	G2
Tapa	29	N7
Tapachula	105	F6
Tapajós	109	F4
Tapauá	109	E5
Tapolca	47	E3
Tappahannock	103	F2
Tapsuy	31	M2
Tapuaenuku	89	D6
Taquarí	109	F7
Tara	31	Q3
Tara	71	N6
Tarābulus	59	H2
Taracua	109	D3
Tarāghin	59	H3
Tarakan	77	F6
Taran	71	N3
Taranaki = Mount Egmont	89	E4
Tarancón	41	H5
Taranto	45	M8
Tarapoto	109	B5
Tarare	39	K8
Tarascon	39	K10
Tarauacá	109	C5
Tarauacá	109	C5
Tarawa	85	H5
Tarawera Lake	89	F4
Tarazona	41	J3
Tarbes	39	F10
Tarbet	37	F4
Tarcoola	87	F6
Taree	87	K6
Tarfaya	59	C3
Târgoviște	47	N5
Târgu Frumos	47	Q2
Târgu Jiu	47	L4
Târgu Lăpuş	47	L2
Târgu Mureş	47	M3
Târgu-Neamţ	47	P2
Târgu Ocna	47	P3
Târgu Secuiesc	47	P3
Tarhunah	59	H2
Tarif	55	E4
Tarifa	41	E8
Tarija	111	J3
Tarīm	53	E6
Tarim	71	Q9
Tarim Pendi	71	Q10
Tarīn Kowt	53	J3
Tariskay Shan	71	Q9
Taritatu	83	(2)E3
Tarkio	103	B1
Tarko Sale	71	P5
Tarlac	77	G3
Tarn	39	H10
Tarna	33	K10
Tärnaby	29	H4
Târnăveni	47	M3
Tarnogskiy Gorodok	31	H2
Târnovo	49	K2
Tarnów	33	K7
Tarnowskie Góry	33	H7
Taro	43	E6
Taroom	87	J5
Taroudannt	59	D2
Tarquínia	45	F6
Tarragona	41	M3
Tarras	89	B7
Tàrrega	41	M3
Tarso Emissi	61	C3
Tarsus	51	F5
Tartagal	111	J3
Tartu	29	P7
Ţarţūs	54	C2
Tarutyne	47	S3
Tarvisio	43	J4
Tasbuget	31	N6
Tashigang	75	F3
Tashir	51	L3
Tashkent	71	M9
Tash-Kömür	71	N9
Tashtagol	71	R7
Tasiilaq	93	Z3
Tasikmalaya	83	(1)D4
Taskesken	71	Q8
Tasman Bay	89	D5
Tasmania	85	E10
Tasmania	87	H8
Tasman Mountains	89	D5
Tasman Sea	89	B3
Tăşnad	47	K2
Taşova	51	G3
Tassili du Hoggar	59	F4
Tassili-n'-Ajjer	59	G3
Tasty	71	M9
Tata, Hungary	47	F2
Tata, Morocco	59	D3
Tatabánya	47	F2
Tatarbunary	47	S4
Tatariya	31	J3
Tatarsk	71	P6
Tatarskiy Proliv	73	P7
Tateyama	81	K6
Tathlina Lake	93	H4
Tatta	53	J5
Tatvan	51	K4
Tauá	109	J5
Tauberbischofsheim	35	E7
Tauern	43	J4
Taumarunui	89	E4
Taung-gyi	75	G4
Taungup	75	F5
Taunsa	75	B2
Taunton, United Kingdom	37	J10
Taunton, United States	99	F2
Taunus	27	L4
Taunusstein	27	L4
Taupo	89	F4
Tauragė	33	M2
Tauranga	89	F3
Tauroa Point	89	D2
Tavda	31	N3
Tavda	31	N3
Tavira	41	C7
Tavoy	77	B4
Tavşanli	51	C4
Taw	37	J11
Tawas City	99	D2
Tawau	83	(1)F2
Tawitawi	83	(1)F1
Taxkorgan	71	P10
Tay	37	J5
Tayga	71	R6
Taylorville	103	D2
Taym	53	C4
Taymā'	61	G2
Taymura	73	F4
Taymylyr	73	L2
Tay Ninh	77	D4
Tayshet	73	F5
Tayuan	73	L6
Tayyebäd	53	H3
Taza	59	E2
Tazeh Kand	51	M4
Tazenakht	59	D2
Tăzirbū	61	D2
Tazovskiy	71	P4
Tazovskiy Poluostrov	71	N4
Tazungdam	77	B1
T'bilisi	51	L3
Tchamba	63	G3
Tchibanga	63	G5
Tchin Tabaradene	59	G5
Tczew	33	H3
Te Anau	89	A7
Te Araroa	89	G3
Te Aroha	89	E3
Te Awamutu	89	E4
Teberda	51	J2
Tébessa	59	G1
Tebingtinggi	83	(1)B2
Téboursouk	45	D12
Techa	31	M3
Techiman	63	D3
Tecuala	101	D4
Tecuci	47	Q4
Tedzhen	53	H2
Tees	37	L7
Tegal	83	(1)D4
Tegernsee	43	G3
Tegina	63	F2
Tegucigalpa	105	G6
Tegul'det	71	R6
Te Hapua	89	D2
Te Haroto	89	F4
Tehek Lake	93	M3
Teheran = Tehrän	53	F2
Tehrän	53	F2
Teignmouth	37	J11
Tejo = Tagus	41	B5
Te Kaha	89	F3
Tekirda	49	K4
Tekirdağ	51	B3
Teknaf	75	F4
Teku	83	(2)B3
Te Kuiti	89	E4
T'elavi	51	L3
Tel Aviv-Yafo	54	B4
Telegraph Creek	101	(1)L4
Telén	111	H6
Teles Pires	109	F5
Telford	37	K9
Telfs	43	G3
Teller	101	(1)D2
Telsen	111	H7
Telšiai	33	M2
Teltow	35	J4
Teluk Berau	83	(2)D3
Teluk Bone	83	(2)B3
Teluk Cenderawasih	83	(2)E3
Telukdalem	83	(1)B2
Teluk Kumai	83	(1)E3
Teluk Sampit	83	(1)E3
Teluk Sukadana	83	(1)D3
Teluk Tomini	83	(2)B2
Tema	63	D3

Name	Page	Ref
Tembenchi	71	T4
Temerin	47	G4
Temerloh	77	C6
Teminabuan	83	(2)D3
Temochic	101	E3
Tempe	101	D2
Témpio Pausária	45	D8
Temple	101	G2
Temryuk	51	G1
Temuco	111	G6
Tenali	75	D5
Tendaho	61	H5
Ten Degree Channel	75	F7
Tendrara	59	E2
Ténéré	59	G5
Ténéré du Tafassasset	59	G4
Tenerife	59	B3
Ténès	59	F1
Tenggarong	83	(1)F3
Tenke	67	D2
Tenkodogo	63	D2
Tennant Creek	87	F3
Tennessee	91	K6
Tennessee	95	J4
Tenojoki	29	P2
Tenteno	83	(2)B3
Tenterfield	87	K5
Teo	41	B2
Teófilo Otoni	109	J7
Tepehuanes	95	E6
Tepic	95	F7
Teplice	33	C7
Ter	41	N2
Terceira	59	(1)B2
Terek	51	L2
Teresina	109	J5
Tergnier	27	F5
Termez	53	J2
Términi Imerese	45	H11
Termirtau	71	N7
Térmoli	47	C8
Ternate	83	(2)C2
Terneuzen	27	F3
Terni	45	G6
Ternitz	43	M3
Ternopil'	31	E5
Ternuka	89	C7
Terracina	45	H7
Terrassa	41	N3
Terre Haute	103	D2
Terry	97	E1
Tersa	31	H4
Terschelling	27	H1
Teruel	41	J4
Tervel	51	B2
Tervola	29	N3
Teseney	61	G4
Teshekpuk Lake	101	(1)F1
Teshio	81	L1
Teslin	101	(1)L3
Teslin	101	(1)L3
Tessalit	59	F4
Têt	39	H11
Tete	67	E3
Teterow	35	H3
Teteven	49	G2
Tétouan	59	D1
Tetovo	47	H8
Teuco	111	J3
Teulada	45	C10
Tevere	45	G6
Teverya	54	C4
Tevriz	31	P3
Te Waewae Bay	89	A8
Texarkana	103	C3
Texas	95	F5
Texel	27	G1
Teya	71	S5
Teykovo	31	H3
Thaba Putsoa	67	D5
Thabazimbi	67	D4
Thailand	77	C4
Thai Nguyên	77	D2
Thal	75	B2
Thale Luang	77	C5
Thamarīt	53	F6
Thames	37	L10
Thamūd	53	E6
Thane	75	B5
Thanh Hoa	77	D3
Thanjavur	75	C6
Thann	43	C3
Tharad	75	B4
Thar Desert	75	B3
Thargomindah	87	H5
Tharwāniyyah	55	E5
Thasos	49	G4
Thasos	49	G4
Thaton	77	B3
Thaya	33	E9
The Bahamas	103	F4
The Bluff	103	F4
The Dalles	97	B1
Thedford	97	F2
The Fens	27	B2
The Gambia	63	A2
The Granites	87	E4
Thelon	93	L4
The Minch	37	F3
The Naze	27	D3
Thenia	41	P8
Theniet el Had	41	N9
Theodore Roosevelt	109	E5
Theodore Roosevelt Lake	101	D2
The Pas	93	L6
Thermaikos Kolpos	49	E4
Thermopolis	97	E2
The Sisters	89	(1)B1
The Solent	27	A4
Thessalon	99	D1
Thessaloniki	49	E4
Thetford	37	N9
Thetford Mines	99	F1
The Twins	89	D5
The Wash	37	N9
The Weald	27	B3
The Whitsundays	87	J4
Thief River Falls	99	A1
Thiers	39	J8
Thiès	63	A2
Thika	65	F4
Thimphu	75	E3
Þingvallavatn	29	(1)C2
Thionville	27	J5
Thira	49	H8
Thira	49	H8
Thirasia	49	H8
Thiruvananthapuram	75	C7
Thisted	29	E8
Þistilfjöður	29	(1)F1
Thiva	49	F6
Thiviers	39	F8
Þjórsá	29	(1)D2
Tholen	27	G3
Thomasville	103	E3
Thompson	93	H6
Thompson	93	M5
Thompson Falls	97	C1
Thomson	103	E3
Thonon-les-Bains	43	B4
Þórisvatn	29	(1)D2
Þorlákshöfn	29	(1)C3
Þorshöfn	29	(1)F1
Thouars	39	E7
Thrakiko Pelagos	49	H4
Three Kings Island	89	C2
Three Rivers	99	C2
Throckmorton	103	B3
Thuin	27	G4
Thun	43	C4
Thunder Bay	99	C1
Thuner See	43	C4
Thung Song	77	B5
Thüringer Wald	35	F6
Thurso	37	J3
Tīāb	55	G3
Tianjin	79	F3
Tianmen	79	E4
Tianqiaoling	81	E2
Tianshifu	81	C3
Tianshui	79	D4
Tianshuihai	53	L2
Tiaret	59	F1
Tibati	63	G3
Tibboburra	87	H5
Tibesti	61	C3
Tibet = Xizang	75	E2
Tiburón	105	B3
Tîchît	59	D5
Tichla	59	C4
Ticino	43	D4
Ticul	105	G4
Tidjikdja	59	C5
Tieling	81	B2
Tielongtan	75	C1
Tielt	27	F3
Tienen	27	G4
Tien Shan	71	Q9
Tien Yen	77	D2
Tierra Amarilla	97	E3
Tiétar	41	E4
Tiflis = T'bilisi	57	H1
Tifton	103	E3
Tifu	83	(2)C3
Tighina	47	S3
Tignère	63	G3
Tigre	109	B4
Tigris	51	K6
Tijuana	95	C5
Tikanlik	71	R9
Tikhoretsk	31	H5
Tikhvin	31	F3
Tikrīt	51	K6
Tiksi	73	M2
Tilburg	27	H3
Tilichiki	73	V4
Tillabéri	63	E2
Tillamook	97	B1
Tilos	49	K8
Timanskiy Kryazh	31	K2
Timaru	89	C7
Timashevsk	31	G5
Timber Creek	87	F3
Timerloh	83	(1)C2
Timimoun	59	F3
Timişoara	47	J4
Timmins	99	D1
Timon	109	J5
Timor	83	(2)C4
Timor Sea	87	E2
Tinaca Point	85	C5
Tindivanam	75	C6
Tindouf	59	D3
Tineo	41	D1
Tinglev	35	E2
Tingo Maria	109	B5
Tingri	75	E3
Tingsryd	33	E1
Tiniroto	89	F4
Tinnsjø	29	E7
Tinogasta	111	H4
Tinos	49	H7
Tinos	49	H7
Tinsukia	75	G3
T'i'o	61	H5
Tipperary	37	D9
Tirana = Tiranë	49	B3
Tiranë	49	B3
Tirari Desert	87	G5
Tiraspol	47	S3
Tire	49	K6
Tiree	37	F5
Tirschenreuth	35	H7
Tirso	45	C9
Tiruchchirāppalli	75	C6
Tirunelveli	75	C7
Tirupati	75	C6
Tiruppur	75	C6
Tiruvannamalai	75	C6
Tisa	47	H4
Tišnov	33	F8
Tisza	33	M9
Tiszaföldvár	47	H3
Tiszafüred	47	H2
Tiszaújváros	33	L10
Tit-Ary	71	Z3
Titel	47	H4
Titova Korenica	43	L6
Titovo Velenje	45	K2
Titu	47	N5
Titusville	103	E4
Tivaouane	59	B6
Tiverton	37	J11
Tívoli	45	G7
Tiyās	54	E2
Tizi Ouzou	59	F1
Tiznit	59	D3
Tjeldøya	29	H2
Tjørkolm	29	D7
Tlemcen	59	E2
Tmassah	61	C2
Toad River	93	F5
Tobago	105	M6
Tobelo	83	(2)C2
Tobermorey	87	G4
Tobermory, *United Kingdom*	37	F5
Tobermory, *United States*	99	D1
Tobi	83	(2)D2
Toblach	43	H4
Toboali	83	(1)D3
Tobol	31	M4
Tobol	31	M4
Tobol'sk	31	N3
Tobseda	31	K1
Tocantins	109	H5
Tocantins	109	H5
Tocee	43	D4
Tocopilla	111	G3
Todi	45	G6
Tofino	97	A1
Togo	63	E3
Toimin	45	H2
Toi-misaki	81	F8
Tōjō	81	G6
Tok	101	(1)J3
Tokar	61	G4
Tokat, *Sudan*	53	C6
Tokat, *Turkey*	53	C1
Tokelau	85	J6
Tokmak	71	P9
Tokoroa	89	E4
Toksun	71	R9
Tok-tō	79	J3
Toktogul	71	N9
Tokushima	81	H6
Tokuyama	81	F6
Tōkyō	81	K6
Tolaga Bay	89	G4
Tōlañaro	67	H4
Tolbo	71	S8
Toledo, *Brazil*	111	L3
Toledo, *Spain*	41	F5
Toledo, *United States*	99	D2
Toliara	67	G4
Tolitoli	83	(2)B2
Tol'ka	71	Q5
Tol'ka	71	Q5
Tollense	35	J3
Tolmezzo	43	J4
Tolmin	43	J4
Tolna	47	F3
Tolosa	41	H1
Tol'yatti	31	J4
Tolybay	71	L7
Tom'	71	R6
Tomah	99	B2
Tomakomai	81	L2
Tomar	41	B5
Tomaszów Lubelski	33	N7
Tomaszów Mazowiecki	33	K6
Tombouctou	59	E5
Tombua	67	A3
Tomé	111	G6
Tomelloso	41	H5
Tomini	83	(2)B2
Tommot	73	M5
Tomo	109	D2
Tompo	73	P4
Tom Price	87	C4
Tomra	75	E2
Tomsk	71	Q6
Tomtor	73	Q4
Tomu	83	(2)D3
Tonalá	105	F5
Tondano	83	(2)B2
Tønder	35	D2

Name	Page	Ref
Tonga	65	E2
Tonga	85	J7
Tonga Islands	85	J8
Tongareva	85	K6
Tonga Trench	85	J8
Tongbai	79	E4
Tongchuan	79	D4
Tongduch'ŏn	81	D5
Tongeren	27	H4
Tonghae	81	E5
Tonghua	81	C3
Tongliao	79	G2
Tongling	79	F4
Tongshi	77	D3
Tongue	97	E1
Tongyu	79	G2
Tónichi	95	E6
Tonj	65	D2
Tonk	75	C3
Tonkābon	53	F2
Tônlé Sab	77	C4
Tonnay-Charente	39	E8
Tönning	35	D2
Tonopah	97	C3
Tooele	97	D2
Toora-Khem	71	T7
Toowoomba	87	K5
Topeka	95	G4
Topki	71	R6
Topliţa	47	N3
Topock	101	D2
Topol'čany	33	H9
Topolobampo	95	E6
Torbali	49	K6
Torbat-e Heydarīyeh	53	G2
Torbat-e Jām	53	H2
Tordesillas	41	F3
Torells	41	N2
Torgau	35	H5
Torgelow	33	C4
Torhout	27	F3
Torino	43	C5
Tori-shima	81	L8
Torneälven	29	L3
Torneträsk	29	K2
Tornio	29	N4
Toro	41	E3
Toronto	99	E2
Tororo	65	E3
Toros Dağları	51	E5
Torquay	37	J11
Torrance	101	C2
Torreblanca	41	L4
Torre de Moncorvo	41	C3
Torrejón de Ardoz	41	G4
Torrelavega	41	F1
Torremolinos	41	F8
Torrent	41	K5
Torreón	101	F3
Torres Strait	87	H2
Torres Vedras	41	A5
Torrevieja	41	K6
Torrington	97	F2
Tortolì	45	D9
Tortona	43	D6
Tortosa	41	L4
Tortum	51	J3
Torūd	53	G2
Toruń	33	H4
Tory Island	37	D6
Torzhok	31	G3
Tosa-wan	81	G7
Tostedt	35	E3
Tosya	49	S3
Totaranui	89	D5
Tôtes	27	D5
Tot'ma	31	H3
Totora	109	D7
Tottori	81	H6
Touba, *Ivory Coast*	63	C3
Touba, *Senegal*	63	A2
Tougan	63	D2
Touggourt	59	G2
Toul	39	L5
Toulépleu	63	C3
Toulon	39	L10
Toulouse	39	G10
Toummo	59	H4
Toungoo	77	B3
Tourcoing	27	F4
Tournai	27	F4
Tours	39	F6
Touws River	67	C6
Towanda	99	E2
Towari	83	(2)B3
Towcester	27	B2
Towner	97	F1
Townsend	97	D1
Townshend Island	87	K4
Townsville	87	J3
Toxkan	71	P9
Toyama	81	J5
Toyohashi	81	J6
Toyooka	81	H6
Toyota	81	J6
Tozeur	59	G2
Trâblous	54	C2
Trabzon	51	H3
Tracy	99	A2
Trail	97	C1
Traiskirchen	43	M2
Trakai	29	N9
Tralee	37	C9
Tralee Bay	37	B9
Tramán Tepuí	109	E2
Tranås	29	H7
Trancoso	41	C4
Trang	77	B5
Trangan	83	(2)D4
Transantarctic Mountains	112	(2)B1
Trapani	45	G11
Trappes	27	E6
Traun	43	K2
Traunreut	43	H3
Traunsee	43	J3
Traversay Islands	107	H9
Traverse City	99	C2
Travnik	47	E5
Trbovlje	43	L4
Trébbia	43	E6
Třebíč	33	E8
Trebinje	47	F7
Trebišov	47	J1
Trebnje	43	L5
Trebon	43	K1
Tregosse Islets	87	K3
Trelew	111	H7
Trelleborg	29	G9
Tremonton	97	D2
Tremp	41	L2
Trenčín	33	H9
Trent	37	M8
Trento	43	G4
Trenton, *Canada*	99	E2
Trenton, *United States*	99	F2
Trepassey	93	W7
Tres Arroyos	111	J6
Três Corações	109	H8
Tres Esquinas	109	B3
Tres Lagos	111	G8
Trespaderne	41	G2
Treuchtlingen	43	F2
Treviglio	43	E5
Treviso	43	H5
Triangle	67	H4
Tricase	45	N9
Trichur	75	C6
Trier	27	J5
Trieste	43	J5
Triglav	43	H4
Trikala	49	D5
Trikomon	54	A1
Trilj	43	M7
Trincomalee	75	D7
Trinidad	109	E1
Trinidad, *Bolivia*	109	E6
Trinidad, *United States*	101	F1
Trinidad, *Uruguay*	111	K5
Trinidad and Tobago	109	E1
Trinity Islands	101	(1)G4
Trino	43	D5
Trion	103	D3
Tripoli, *Greece*	49	E7
Tripoli = Trâblous, *Lebanon*	54	C2
Tripoli = Tarābulus, *Libya*	59	H2
Trischen	35	D2
Tristan da Cunha	57	B9
Trivandrum = Thiruvananthapuram	75	C7
Trjavna	51	A2
Trnava	47	E1
Trogir	47	D6
Troina	45	J11
Troisdorf	35	C6
Trois Rivières	99	F1
Troitsk	31	M4
Troitsko-Pechorsk	31	L2
Trojan	49	G2
Trollhättan	29	G7
Trombetas	109	F4
Tromsø	29	K2
Trona	97	C3
Trondheim	29	F5
Trondheimsfjørden	29	E5
Troodos	51	E6
Trotuş	47	P3
Trout Lake, *N.W.T., Canada*	93	G4
Trout Lake, *Ont., Canada*	93	N6
Troy, *Al., United States*	103	D3
Troy, *N.Y., United States*	99	F2
Troyan	47	M7
Troyes	39	K5
Trstenik	47	J6
Trudovoye	81	G2
Trujillo, *Peru*	109	B5
Trujillo, *Spain*	41	E5
Truro, *Canada*	93	U7
Truro, *United Kingdom*	37	G11
Trusovo	71	J4
Truth or Consequences	101	E2
Trutnov	33	E7
Tryavna	49	H2
Trzcianka	33	F4
Trzebnica	33	G6
Tsetserleg	73	G7
Tshabong	67	C5
Tshane	67	C4
Tshikapa	65	C5
Tshuapa	65	C4
Tsiafajavona	67	H3
Tsimlyanskoy Vodokhranilishche	31	H5
Tsiroanomandidy	67	H3
Ts'khinvali	51	K2
Tsuchiura	81	L5
Tsugaru-kaikyō	81	L3
Tsumeb	67	B3
Tsumkwe	67	C3
Tsuruga	81	J6
Tsuruoka	81	K4
Tsushima	81	E6
Tsuyama	81	H6
Tua	41	C3
Tual	83	(2)D4
Tuân Giao	77	C2
Tuapse	51	H1
Tubarão	111	M4
Tübingen	43	E2
Tubize	27	G4
Tubruq	61	D1
Tubuai	85	M8
Tubuai Islands	85	L8
Tucano	109	K6
Tuchola	33	G4
Tucson	101	D2
Tucumcari	101	F1
Tucupita	109	E2
Tucuruí	109	H4
Tudela	41	J2
Tuguegarao	77	G3
Tugur	73	P6
Tui	41	B2
Tuktoyaktuk	101	(1)L2
Tula, *Mexico*	101	G4
Tula, *Russia*	31	G4
Tulare	97	C3
Tulcea	47	R4
Tulkarm	54	B4
Tullamore	37	E8
Tulle	39	G8
Tulln	43	M2
Tuloma	29	S2
Tulsa	95	G4
Tulsequah	101	(1)L4
Tulun	73	G6
Tulung La	75	F3
Tulu Weiel	65	E2
Tumaco	109	B3
Tumän	53	H2
Tumen	81	E2
Tumereng	109	E2
Tumkur	75	C6
Tumut	87	J7
Tunca	49	J3
Tunceli	51	H4
Tunduru	67	F2
Tundzha	47	P8
Tungir	73	L5
Tungku	83	(1)F1
Tungsten	101	(1)M3
Tungusk	71	S5
Tunis	59	H1
Tunisia	59	E2
Tunja	109	C2
Tupelo	103	D3
Tupik	73	L6
Tupiza	111	H3
Tupper Lake	99	F2
Tuquan	79	G1
Tura, *India*	75	F3
Tura, *Russia*	73	G4
Turan	71	S7
Turangi	89	E4
Turayf	61	G1
Turbat	53	H4
Turbo	109	B2
Turda	47	L3
Turek	33	H5
Turgay	71	L8
Turgay	71	L8
Turgayskaya Stolovaya Strana	71	L7
Türgovishte	47	P6
Turgutlu	49	K6
Turhal	51	G3
Turin = Torino	43	C5
Turinsk	31	M3
Turiy Rog	81	F1
Turka	73	H6
Türkeli Adası	49	K4
Turkestan	71	M9
Turkey	51	F1
Turkmenbashi	53	F1
Turkmenistan	53	G2
Turks and Caicos Islands	105	K4
Turks Islands	105	K4
Turku	29	M6
Turma	73	N6
Turnhout	27	G3
Turnov	33	E7
Turnu Măgurele	47	C3
Turpan	71	R9
Turpan Pendi	71	S9
Turquino	107	D2
Turtas	31	N3
Turtkul'	53	H7
Turtle Island	87	K3
Turu	71	U5
Turugart Pass	71	P9
Turukhan	73	C3
Turukhansk	71	R4
Turukta	73	K4
Tuscaloosa	103	D3
Tuscola	103	D2
Tuticorin	75	C7
Tutonchany	73	E4
Tutrakan	47	P5
Tuttle Creek Reservoir	103	B2
Tuttlingen	43	D3
Tutuila	85	K7
Tuvalu	85	H6
Tuxpan, *Mexico*	95	G4
Tuxpan, *Mexico*	95	G7
Tuxtla Gutiérrez	105	F5
Tuyên Quang	77	D2
Tuy Hoa	77	D4
Tuymazy	31	K4
Tuz Gölü	51	E4
Tuz Khurmātū	51	L6

Name	Page	Grid
Tuzla	47	F5
Tver'	31	G3
Tweed	37	K6
Twentynine Palms	101	C2
Twilight Cove	87	E6
Twin Buttes Reservoir	101	F2
Twin Falls	97	D2
Twizel	89	C7
Two Harbors	99	B1
Tyachiv	47	L1
Tygda	73	M6
Tyler	95	G5
Tylkhoy	73	U4
Tym	71	Q6
Tynda	73	L5
Tyne	37	K6
Tynemouth	37	L6
Tynset	29	F5
Tyra	71	S7
Tyrifjorden	29	F6
Tyrnavos	49	E5
Tyrrhenian Sea	45	F8
Tyry	73	P4
Tysa	33	N9
Tyukyan	73	K4
Tyumen'	71	M6
Tyung	73	K3
Tyva	73	F6

U

Name	Page	Grid
Uaupés	109	D3
Ubá	109	J8
Ubaitaba	109	K6
Ubangi	65	B3
Ube	81	F7
Úbeda	41	G6
Uberaba	109	H7
Uberlândia	109	H7
Überlingen	43	E3
Ubon Ratchathani	77	C3
Ubrique	41	E8
Ucayali	109	B5
Uchami	71	T5
Ucharal	71	Q8
Uchiura-wan	81	L2
Uchkuduk	71	L9
Uckermark	35	J3
Ucluelet	97	A1
Uda, Russia	73	F5
Uda, Russia	73	N6
Udachnyy	73	J3
Udagamandalam	75	C6
Udaipur	75	B4
Uddevalla	29	F7
Uddjaure	31	C1
Uddjaure Storavan	29	K4
Udine	43	J4
Udmurtiya	31	K3
Udon Thani	77	C3
Udupi	75	B6
Uecker	35	J3
Ueckermünde	35	J3
Ueda	81	K5
Uele	65	C3
Uelen	73	AA3
Uel'kal	73	Y3
Uelzen	35	F4
Ufa	31	L3
Ufa	31	L4
Uganda	65	E3
Ugep	63	F3
Ugine	43	B5
Uglegorsk	73	Q7
Uglich	31	G3
Ugljan	43	L6
Ugol'nyye Kopi	73	X4
Ugulan	73	S4
Uh	47	K1
Uherské Hradiště	33	G8
Uherský Brod	33	G8
Uiju	81	C3
Uil	31	K5
Uil	31	K5
Uinta Mountains	97	D2
Uitenhage	67	D6

Name	Page	Grid
Újfehértó	47	J2
Ujiji	65	D4
Ujjain	75	C4
Ujung Pandang	83	(2)A4
Ukerewe Island	65	E4
Ukhta	71	J5
Ukiah	97	B3
Ukkusissat	93	W2
Ukmergė	33	P2
Ukraine	25	G3
Ulaanbaatar	73	H7
Ulaangom	71	S8
Ulan	79	B3
Ulan Bator = Ulaanbaatar	79	D1
Ulan-Ude	73	H6
Ulchin	81	E5
Uldz	73	J7
Ulety	73	J6
Ulhasnagar	75	B5
Uliastay	71	T8
Ulindi	65	D4
Ullapool	37	G4
Ullŭng do	81	F5
Ulm	43	F2
Ulog	47	F6
Ulongue	67	E2
Ulsan	81	E6
Ulu	73	M4
Ulubat Gölü	49	L4
Uluqqat	53	K2
Ulukışla	51	F5
Ulungur Hu	71	R8
Ulunkhan	73	J5
Uluru	87	F5
Ulu-Yul	73	D5
Ulva	37	F5
Ulverston	37	J7
Ulya	73	Q5
Ul'yanovsk	31	J4
Ulytau	71	M8
Uman'	31	F5
Umarkot	53	J4
Umba	31	F1
Umeå	29	L5
Umeälven	29	J4
Umfolozi	67	E5
Ummal Arānib	59	H3
Umm al Jamājim	55	A3
Umm Durman	61	F4
Umm Keddada	61	E5
Umm Lajj	61	G3
Umm Qaşr	55	B1
Umm Ruwaba	61	F5
Umnak Island	101	(1)E5
Umtata	67	D6
Umuarama	111	L3
Unalakleet	101	(1)E3
Unalaska Island	101	(1)E5
Underberg	67	D5
Ungava Bay	93	T5
Ungheni	47	Q2
Ungwana Bay	65	G4
União da Vitória	111	L4
Unije	43	K6
Unimak Island	101	(1)D5
Unim Bāb	55	D4
Unini	109	E4
Union	99	B3
Union City	105	G1
Union Springs	103	D3
United Arab Emirates	53	F5
United Kingdom	37	G6
United States	91	M5
Unna	27	K3
Unraven	101	E1
Unst	37	M1
Unstrut	35	G5
Unzha	31	H3
Upernavik	93	W2
Upernavik Kujalleq	93	V2
Upington	67	C5
Upolu	85	J7
Upper Hutt	89	E5
Upper Klamath Lake	97	B2
Upper Lake	97	C2
Upper Lough Erne	37	E7

Name	Page	Grid
Upper Sandusky	99	D2
Uppsala	29	J7
Upsala	99	B1
'Uqlat al 'Udhaybah	55	B2
Urad Houqi	79	D2
Urakawa	81	M2
Ural	31	K5
Ural Mountains = Ural'skiy Khrebet	25	L1
Ural'sk	31	K4
Ural'skiy Khrebet	25	L1
Urambo	65	E5
Uranium City	93	K5
Uraricoera	109	E3
Uray	31	M2
Urbana, Ill., United States	99	C2
Urbana, Oh., United States	99	D2
Urbania	43	H7
Urbino	43	H7
Urdzhar	71	Q8
Uren'	31	J3
Urengoy	71	P4
Urgench	53	H1
Urho	71	R8
Uritskiy	31	N4
Urla	49	J6
Urlaţi	47	P5
Uroševac	47	J7
Uro-teppa	53	J2
Urt	79	C2
Uruaçu	109	H6
Uruapan	105	D5
Urucurituba	109	F4
Uruguaiana	111	K4
Uruguay	111	K5
Uruguay	111	K5
Ürümqi	71	R9
Urus Martan	51	L2
Uryupino	73	L6
Uryupinsk	31	H4
Urzhum	31	K3
Urziceni	47	P5
Usa	71	L4
Uşak	51	C4
Usedom	35	J3
Useless Loop	87	B5
Usfān	53	C5
Ushtobe	71	P8
Usingen	35	D6
Usk	37	J10
Usman'	31	G4
Usol'ye Sibirskoye	73	G6
Ussel	39	H8
Ussuri	81	G1
Ussuriysk	79	J2
Usta	31	J3
Ust'-Alekseyevo	31	J2
Ust'-Barguzin	73	H6
Ust' Chaun	73	W3
Ústí	33	F8
Ústica	45	H10
Ust'-Ilimsk	73	G5
Ústí nad Labem	33	D7
Ust'-Ishim	71	N6
Ustka	33	F3
Ust'-Kamchatsk	73	U5
Ust'-Kamenogorsk	71	Q8
Ust'-Kamo	71	T5
Ust'-Karenga	73	K6
Ust'-Khayryuzovo	73	T5
Ust'-Kulom	31	K2
Ust'-Kut	73	G5
Ust'-Kuyga	73	P3
Ust'-Labinsk	51	H1
Ust'-Maya	73	N4
Ust'-Mukduyka	71	R4
Ust'-Muya	73	K5
Ust' Nem	31	K2
Ust'-Nera	73	Q4
Ust'-Nyukzha	73	L5
Ust'-Olenek	73	K2
Ust'-Omchug	73	R4
Ust' Ozernoye	73	D5
Ust' Penzhino	73	V4
Ust'-Pit	73	E5
Ustrem	31	N2
Ust'-Sopochnoye	73	T5

Name	Page	Grid
Ust' Tapsuy	31	M2
Ust'-Tarka	71	P6
Ust'-Tatta	73	N4
Ust'-Tsil'ma	71	J4
Ust' Un'ya	31	L2
Ust'-Urkima	73	L5
Ust' Usa	31	L1
Ust'-Uyskoye	71	L7
Usu	71	Q9
Usuki	81	F7
Utah	95	D4
Utah Lake	97	D2
Utata	73	G6
Utena	29	N9
Uthal	53	J4
Utica	99	E2
Utiel	41	J5
Utrecht	27	H2
Utrera	41	E7
Utsjoki	29	P2
Utsunomiya	81	K5
Uttaradit	77	C3
Uummannaq	31	K4
Uummannaq Fjord	93	V2
Uummannarsuaq	93	Y5
Uusikaupunki	29	L6
Uvalde	105	E3
Uvargin	73	X3
Uvat	31	N3
Uvinza	65	E5
Uvira	65	D4
Uvs Nuur	71	S7
Uwajima	81	G7
Uy	31	M4
Uyar	71	S6
Uyuk	71	N9
Uyuni	111	H3
Uzbekistan	71	L9
Uzhhorod	47	K1
Užice	47	G6
Uzunköprü	47	P8

V

Name	Page	Grid
Vaal	67	D5
Vaasa	29	L5
Vác	47	G2
Vacaria	111	M4
Vachi	53	E1
Vadodara	75	B4
Vado Ligure	43	D6
Vadsø	29	Q1
Vaduz	43	E3
Værøy	29	G3
Vaganski Vhr	43	L6
Vagay	31	N3
Váh	33	H8
Vakh	31	Q2
Valbonnais	43	A6
Valcheta	111	H7
Valdagno	43	G5
Valday	31	F3
Val-de-Meuse	43	A2
Valdemoro	41	G4
Valdepeñas	41	G6
Valdez	93	B4
Valdivia	111	G6
Val-d'Or	99	E1
Valdosta	95	K5
Valdres	29	E6
Valea lui Mihai	47	K2
Valence	39	K9
Valencia, Spain	41	G5
Valencia, Venezuela	109	D1
Valencia de Alcántara	41	C5
Valenciennes	27	F4
Vălenii de Munte	47	P4
Valentia Island	37	B10
Valentine	97	F2
Valenza	43	D5
Valera	109	C2
Valga	31	E3
Val Horn	95	F5
Valjevo	47	G5
Valka	29	N8
Val'karay	73	X3

171

Name	Page	Grid
Valkeakoski	29	N6
Valkenswaard	27	H3
Valladolid, *Mexico*	105	G4
Valladolid, *Spain*	41	F3
Valledupar	109	C1
Vallée de Azaouagh	59	F5
Vallée du Tîlemsi	59	F5
Vallée-Jonction	99	F1
Vallejo	97	B3
Vallentuna	29	K7
Valletta	45	J13
Valley City	97	G1
Valley Falls	97	B2
Valley of the Kings	61	F2
Valli di Comacchio	43	H6
Vallorbe	43	B4
Valls	41	M3
Valmiera	29	N8
Valognes	27	A5
Val-Paradis	99	E1
Valparai	75	C6
Valparaíso, *Chile*	111	G5
Valparaíso, *Mexico*	101	F4
Valsad	75	B4
Val'tevo	31	H2
Valuyki	31	G4
Valverde del Camino	41	D7
Vammala	29	M6
Van	51	K4
Vanadzor	51	L3
Vanavara	73	G4
Van Buren	99	G1
Vancouver, *Canada*	97	B1
Vancouver, *United States*	97	B1
Vancouver Island	93	F7
Vandalia	103	D2
Vanderbijlpark	67	D5
Vanderhoof	93	G6
Van Diemen Gulf	87	F2
Vänern	29	G7
Vangaindrano	67	H4
Van Gölü	51	K4
Van Horn	101	F2
Vanimo	83	(2)F3
Vanino	73	Q7
Vankarem	73	Y3
Vanna	29	K1
Vännäs	29	K5
Vannes	39	C6
Vanrhynsdorp	67	B6
Vantaa	29	N6
Vanua Levu	85	H7
Vanuatu	85	G7
Van Wert	99	D2
Vanzevat	31	N2
Vanzhil'kynak	73	C4
Varāmīn	53	F2
Varanasi	75	D3
Varangerfjorden	29	R2
Varaždin	47	D3
Varazze	43	D6
Varberg	29	G8
Vardar	49	E3
Varde	29	E9
Vardenis	51	L3
Vardø	29	R1
Varel	35	D3
Varéna	33	P3
Varese	43	D5
Vârful Moldoveanu	47	M4
Vârfurile	47	K3
Varginha	111	M3
Varkaus	29	P5
Varna	51	B2
Värnamo	29	H8
Varnsdorf	35	K6
Várpalota	47	F2
Varto	51	J4
Varzi	43	E6
Varzy	39	J6
Vásárosnamény	47	K1
Vasilikos	54	A2
Vaslui	47	Q3
Västerås	29	J7
Västervik	29	J8
Vasto	45	J6
Vasvár	43	M3
Vatan	39	G6
Vathia	49	E8
Vatican City	45	F7
Vatnajökull	29	(1)E2
Vatomandry	67	H3
Vatra Dornei	47	N2
Vättern	29	H7
Vaughn	101	E2
Vawkavysk	33	P4
Växjö	29	H8
Vayuniya	75	D7
Vazhgort	31	J2
Vecht	27	J2
Vechta	27	L2
Vecsés	47	G2
Vedaranniyam	75	C6
Vedea	47	N6
Veendam	27	J1
Veenendaal	27	H2
Vega	29	F4
Vega	101	F1
Vegreville	93	J6
Vejen	35	E1
Vejer de la Frontera	41	E8
Vejle	29	E9
Vel'	71	G5
Vela Luka	47	D7
Velenje	43	L4
Veles	49	D3
Vélez-Málaga	41	F8
Velika Gorica	43	M5
Velika Plana	47	J5
Velikaya	73	W4
Velikiye Luki	31	F3
Velikiy Ustyug	31	J2
Veliko Tŭrnovo	47	N6
Vélingara	63	B2
Velingrad	47	L7
Velita Kladuša	43	L5
Velké Meziříčí	33	F8
Velký Krtíš	33	J9
Velletri	45	G7
Vellinge	33	C2
Vellore	75	C6
Velopoula	49	F8
Vel'sk	31	H2
Velten	35	J4
Velva	97	F1
Venaria	43	C5
Vence	43	C7
Venda Nova	41	C3
Vendôme	39	G6
Venev	31	G4
Venézia	43	H5
Venezuela	109	D2
Vengurla	75	B5
Veniaminof Volcano	101	(1)F4
Venice = Venézia	43	H5
Venice	103	D4
Venlo	27	J3
Venray	27	H3
Venta	31	D3
Ventimiglia	43	C7
Ventotene	45	H8
Ventspils	29	L8
Vera, *Argentina*	111	J4
Vera, *Spain*	41	J7
Veracruz	105	E5
Veraval	75	B4
Verbania	43	D5
Vercelli	43	D5
Verdalsøra	29	F5
Verde	109	G8
Verden	35	E4
Verdun	27	H5
Vereeniging	67	D5
Vereshchagino	73	D4
Verín	41	C3
Verkhneimbatsk	73	D4
Verkhnetulomskoye Vodokhranilishche	29	R2
Verkhneural'sk	31	L4
Verkhniy Baskunchak	31	J5
Verkhnyaya Amga	73	M5
Verkhnyaya Toyma	31	J2
Verkhnyaya Tura	31	L3
Verkhovyna	47	M1
Verkhoyansk	73	N3
Verkhoyanskiy Khrebet	73	M3
Vermillion	97	G2
Vermont	95	M3
Vernal	97	E2
Verneuil	27	C6
Vernon, *France*	27	D5
Vernon, *United States*	103	B3
Vero Beach	103	E4
Veroia	49	E4
Verona	43	F5
Versailles	27	E6
Verviers	27	H4
Veselí	43	N2
Vesijarvi	29	N6
Vesoul	35	B9
Vesterålen	29	G2
Vestfjorden	29	G3
Vestmannaeyjar	29	(1)C3
Vestvagøy	29	G2
Vesuvio	45	J8
Veszprém	47	E2
Vet	67	D5
Vetluga	31	J3
Vetluga	31	J3
Veurne	27	E3
Vevey	43	B4
Vezirköprü	51	F3
Viana do Castelo	41	B3
Vianden	27	J5
Viangchan	77	C3
Viaréggio	43	F7
Viaréggio	45	E5
Viborg	29	E8
Vibraye	39	F5
Vic	41	N3
Vicenza	43	G5
Vichuga	31	H3
Vichy	39	J7
Vicksburg	103	C3
Victor Harbor	87	G7
Victoria	87	H7
Victoria, *Argentina*	111	J5
Victoria, *Canada*	97	B1
Victoria, *Chile*	111	G6
Victoria, *Malta*	45	J12
Victoria, *Romania*	47	M4
Victoria, *Seychelles*	67	(2)C1
Victoria, *United States*	103	B4
Victoria de las Tunas	105	J4
Victoria Falls	67	D3
Victoria Island	93	J2
Victoria Land	112	(2)W2
Victoria Strait	93	M3
Victoria West	67	C6
Victoriaville	99	F1
Vidalia	95	K5
Vidamlja	33	N5
Videle	47	N5
Vidin	47	K6
Viedma	111	J7
Vienna = Wien	43	M2
Vienna	99	C3
Vienne	39	F7
Vienne	39	K8
Vientiane = Viangchan	77	C3
Vierzon	39	H6
Vieste	45	L7
Vietnam	77	D3
Viêt Tri	77	D2
Vigan	77	G3
Vigévano	43	D5
Vigia	109	H4
Vigo	41	B2
Viho Valentia	45	L10
Vijayawada	75	D5
Vik	29	(1)D3
Vikna	29	E4
Vila de Conde	41	B3
Vilafranca del Penedès	41	M3
Vila Franca de Xira	41	A6
Vila Nova de Gaia	41	B3
Vilanova y la Geltrú	41	M3
Vila Real	41	C3
Vila-real	41	K5
Vilhelmina	29	J4
Vilhena	109	E6
Vilija	29	N9
Viljandi	29	N7
Vilkaviškis	33	N3
Villa Ahumada	105	C2
Villablino	41	D2
Villacarrillo	41	G6
Villach	43	J4
Villacidro	45	C9
Villa Constitución	95	D7
Villa de Cos	105	D4
Villafranca	43	F5
Villafranca de los Barros	41	D6
Villagarcia	41	B2
Villagrán	101	G4
Villahermosa	105	F5
Villa Huidobro	111	J5
Villalba	41	C1
Villaldama	101	F3
Villalpando	41	E3
Villamartín	41	E8
Villa Montes	111	J3
Villanueva	101	F4
Villanueva de Cordoba	41	F6
Villa Ocampo	101	E3
Villaputzu	45	D9
Villarrobledo	41	H5
Villa San Giovanni	45	K10
Villavelayo	41	H2
Villavicencio	109	C3
Villaviciosa	41	E1
Villedieu-les-Poêles	27	A6
Villefranche-de-Rouergue	39	H9
Villefranche-sur-Saône	39	K8
Villena	41	K6
Villeneuve-sur-Lot	39	F9
Villers-Bocage	27	B5
Villers-Cotterêts	27	F5
Villerupt	27	H5
Villeurbanne	39	K8
Villingen	43	D2
Vilnius	29	N9
Vilsbiburg	43	H2
Vilshofen	43	J2
Vilvoorde	27	G4
Vilyuy	73	L4
Vilyuysk	73	L4
Vilyuyskoye Vodokhranilishche	73	J4
Vimoutiers	27	C6
Vimperk	43	J1
Viña del Mar	111	G5
Vinaròs	41	L4
Vincennes	103	D2
Vineland	99	F3
Vinh	77	D3
Vinkovci	47	F4
Vinnytsya	31	E5
Vinson Massif	112	(2)JJ2
Vinstri	29	E6
Vinzili	31	N3
Vioolsdrift	67	B5
Vipava	43	J5
Vipiteno	43	G4
Vir	43	L6
Virac	77	G4
Viranşehir	51	H5
Virawah	75	B4
Virden	97	F1
Vire	27	B6
Virginia	95	L4
Virginia	99	B1
Virginia Beach	99	E3
Virgin Islands, *United Kingdom*	107	E2
Virgin Islands, *United States*	107	E2
Virihaure	29	J3
Virôchey	77	D4
Virovitica	47	E4
Virton	27	H5
Virtsu	29	M7
Virudunagar	75	C7
Vis	47	D6
Visalia	97	C3
Visby	29	K8
Viscount Melville Sound	93	J2
Viseu, *Brazil*	109	H4
Viseu, *Portugal*	41	C4
Vişeu de Sus	47	M2
Vishakhapatnam	75	D5

Name	Page	Grid
Vishera	71	K5
Vishnevka	71	N7
Visoko	47	F6
Visp	43	C4
Visselhövede	35	E4
Vistula = Wisła	25	F2
Viterbo	45	G6
Viti Levu	85	H7
Vitim	73	J5
Vitolište	49	D3
Vitória	111	N3
Vitória da Conquista	109	J6
Vitoria-Gasteiz	41	H2
Vitré	39	D5
Vitry-le-François	27	G6
Vitsyebsk	31	F3
Vitteaux	39	K6
Vittel	43	A2
Vittória	45	J12
Vittório Véneto	43	H5
Viveiro	41	C1
Vivi	71	T4
Vize	49	K3
Vizhas	31	J1
Vizianagaram	75	D5
Vizinga	71	H5
Vizzini	45	J11
Vjosë	49	C4
Vladikavkaz	51	L2
Vladimir	31	H3
Vladivostok	81	F2
Vlasotince	47	K7
Vlasovo	73	N2
Vlieland	27	G1
Vlissingen	27	F3
Vlorë	49	B4
Vltava	33	D8
Vöcklabruck	43	J2
Vodice	43	L7
Vodnjan	43	J6
Vogelsberg	35	E6
Voghera	43	D6
Vohipeno	67	H4
Vöhringen	43	F2
Voi	65	F4
Voinjama	63	C3
Voiron	39	L8
Voitsberg	43	L3
Vojens	35	E1
Vojmsjön	29	J4
Vojvodina	47	G4
Volary	35	J8
Volcán Antofalla	111	H4
Volcán Barú	105	H7
Volcán Cayambe	109	B3
Volcán Citlaltépetl	91	L7
Volcán Corcovado	111	G7
Volcán Cotopaxi	109	B4
Volcán Domuyo	111	G6
Volcán Lanin	111	G6
Volcán Llullaillaco	111	H3
Volcán San Pedro	111	H3
Volcán Tajumulco	105	F5
Volga	31	J5
Volgodonsk	31	H5
Volgograd	31	H5
Völkermarkt	43	K4
Volkhov	31	F3
Völklingen	27	J5
Volksrust	67	D5
Volochanka	71	S3
Volodarskoye	31	N4
Vologda	31	H3
Volonga	31	J1
Volos	49	E5
Volosovo	29	Q7
Volta Redonda	109	J8
Volterra	43	F7
Volti	43	D6
Volzhskiy	31	H5
Voorne	27	F3
Voranava	29	N9
Vorderrhein	43	E4
Vordingborg	35	G1
Voreios Evvoïkos Kolpos	49	E6
Voreria Pindos	49	C4
Vorkuta	31	M1

Name	Page	Grid
Vormsi	29	M7
Vorona	31	H4
Voronezh	31	G4
Vorstershoop	67	C5
Võru	29	P8
Vosges	43	C2
Voss	29	D6
Vostochno-Sibirskoye More	73	U2
Vostochnyy Sayan	71	T7
Vostok Island	85	L6
Votkinsk	71	J6
Vozhgora	31	J2
Vranje	47	J7
Vranov	33	L9
Vranov nad Toplau	47	J1
Vratsa	47	L6
Vrbas	47	E5
Vrbas	47	G4
Vrbovsko	43	J6
Vrendenburg	67	B6
Vršac	47	J4
Vryburg	67	C5
Vryheid	67	E5
Vsetín	33	G8
Vućitrn	47	J7
Vukovar	47	G4
Vuktyl'	31	L2
Vulcănești	47	R4
Vulcano	45	J10
Vung Tau	77	D4
Vuollerim	29	L3
Vuotso	29	P2
Vyatka	31	K3
Vyazemskiy	73	N7
Vyaz'ma	31	F3
Vyborg	29	Q6
Vychegda	31	K2
Vyksa	31	H3
Vylkove	47	S4
Vynohradiv	33	N9
Vyshniy Volochek	31	F3
Vyškov	33	G8
Vytegra	31	G2

W

Name	Page	Grid
Wa	63	D3
Waal	27	H3
Waalwijk	27	H3
Wabē Shebelē Wenz	65	G2
Waco	103	B3
Wad Banda	61	E5
Waddān	61	C2
Waddeneilanden	27	G1
Waddenzee	27	H1
Wadena	99	A1
Wādī al Fārigh	61	C1
Wādī al Hamīm	61	D1
Wadi Halfa	61	F3
Wādī Mūsā	54	C6
Wad Medani	61	F5
Wadsworth	101	C1
Wafangdian	79	D3
Wafangdian	81	A4
Wagga Wagga	87	J7
Wahai	83	(2)C3
Wahiawa	101	(2)C2
Wahpeton	97	G1
Waiau	89	D6
Waiblingen	43	E2
Waidhofen	43	K3
Waidhofen an der Ybbs	47	B2
Waigeo	83	(2)D3
Waiheke Island	89	E3
Waihi	89	E3
Waikabubak	83	(2)A4
Waikaia	89	B7
Waikaremoana	89	F4
Waikato	89	E4
Waikawa	89	B8
Wailuku	101	(2)E3
Waimate	89	C7
Waingapu	87	B1
Wainwright	101	(1)F1
Waiouru	89	E4
Waipara	89	D4

Name	Page	Grid
Waipawa	89	F4
Waipiro	89	G4
Waipukurau	89	F5
Wairoa	89	F4
Waitakaruru	89	E3
Waitaki	89	C7
Waitangi	89	(1)B1
Waitara	89	E4
Waiuku	89	E3
Wajima	81	J5
Wajir	65	G3
Wakasa-wan	81	H6
Wakayama	81	H6
Wakeeney	101	G1
Wakefield	37	L8
Wake Island	85	G4
Wakkanai	81	L1
Waku-Kungo	67	B2
Wałbrzych	33	F7
Walcheren	27	F3
Wałcz	33	F4
Waldmünchen	35	H7
Waldshut-Tiengen	43	D3
Walen See	43	E3
Wales	37	J9
Wales Island	93	P3
Walgett	87	J6
Walker Lake	101	C1
Walkerville	87	J7
Wall	97	F2
Wallaceburg	99	D2
Walla Walla	97	C1
Wallis et Futuna	85	J7
Walpole	87	C6
Walsall	37	L9
Walsenburg	97	F3
Walsrode	35	E4
Waltershausen	35	F6
Walvis Bay	67	A4
Wamba	65	D3
Wana	53	J3
Wanaaring	87	H5
Wanaka	89	B7
Wandel Sea	91	A1
Wandingzhen	77	B2
Wanganui	89	E4
Wanganui	89	E4
Wangen	43	E3
Wangerooge	35	D3
Wangiwangi	83	(2)B4
Wan Hsa-la	77	B2
Wanxian	79	D4
Wanyuan	79	D4
Warangal	75	C5
Warburg	35	D5
Ward	89	E5
Wardha	75	C4
Waregem	27	F4
Waremme	27	H4
Waren	35	H3
Warendorf	27	K3
Warka	33	L6
Warmandi	83	(2)D3
Warminster	37	K10
Warm Springs	97	C3
Warren, Mich., United States	99	D2
Warren, Oh., United States	99	D2
Warren, Pa., United States	99	E2
Warrensburg	99	B3
Warrenton	67	C5
Warri	63	F3
Warrington, United Kingdom	37	K8
Warrington, United States	103	D3
Warrnambool	87	H7
Warsaw = Warszawa	33	K5
Warstein	35	D5
Warszawa	33	K5
Warta	33	F5
Warwick	37	L9
Wasatch Range	101	D1
Wasco	101	C1
Washap	53	H4
Washburn Lake	93	K2
Washington	97	B1
Washington, N.C., United States	99	E3

Name	Page	Grid
Washington, Pa., United States	99	D2
Washington, Ut., United States	97	D3
Washington D.C.	91	J6
Wassenaar	27	G2
Wasserburg	43	H2
Watampone	83	(2)B3
Waterbury	99	F2
Waterford	37	E9
Waterloo	99	B2
Watersmeet	99	C1
Watertown, N.Y., United States	99	E2
Watertown, S.D., United States	97	G1
Watertown, Wis., United States	99	C2
Waterville	99	G2
Watford	27	B3
Watford City	97	F1
Watmuri	83	(2)D4
Watrous	93	K6
Watsa	65	D3
Watseka	103	D1
Watson Lake	101	(1)M3
Wau	65	D2
Waubay Lake	97	G1
Waukegan	99	C2
Waukesha	99	C2
Waurika	103	B3
Wausau	95	J3
Waverly	99	C3
Wavre	27	G4
Wawa	99	D1
Wāw al Kabīr	61	C2
Waxxari	71	R10
Waycross	103	E3
Waynesboro, Ga., United States	103	E3
Waynesboro, Miss., United States	103	D3
Waynesville	99	D3
Weaverville	97	B2
Weber	89	F5
Webi Shaabeelle	65	G3
Webster	97	G1
Weddell Island	111	J9
Weddell Sea	112	(2)A2
Wedel	35	E3
Weed	97	B2
Weert	27	H3
Wei	79	D4
Weichang	79	F2
Weida	35	H6
Weiden	35	H7
Weifang	79	F3
Weihai	79	G3
Weilburg	35	D6
Weilheim	43	G3
Weimar	35	G6
Weinan	79	D4
Weinheim	35	D7
Weining	79	C5
Weipa	87	H2
Weiser	97	C2
Weißenburg	35	F7
Weißenfels	35	G5
Weißwasser	35	K5
Weixi	77	B1
Wejherowo	33	H3
Welkom	67	D5
Welland	27	B2
Wellesley Islands	87	G3
Wellingborough	39	E1
Wellington, New Zealand	89	E5
Wellington, Colo., United States	97	F2
Wellington, Kans., United States	103	B2
Wells	97	C2
Wellsboro	99	E2
Wellsford	89	E3
Wellton	101	D2
Wels	43	K2
Welwyn Garden City	27	B3
Wenatchee	97	B1
Wenchang	77	D2
Wenga	65	B3
Wenman	109	(1)A1
Wentworth	87	H6
Wen Xian	79	C4
Wenzhou	79	G5
Werder	35	H4
Werdēr	65	H2

Name	Page	Grid
Werl	27	K3
Werneck	35	F7
Wernigerode	35	F5
Werra	35	F6
Wertheim	35	E7
Wesel	27	J3
Wesel Dorsten	35	B5
Weser	35	E4
Wessel Islands	87	G2
West Antarctica	112	(2)GG2
West Bank	54	C4
West Branch	99	D2
West Cape	85	G10
West End	103	F4
Western Australia	87	D5
Western Cape	67	B6
Western Ghats	75	B5
Western Reef	89	(1)B1
Western Sahara	59	C4
Wester Ross	37	G4
Westerschelde	27	F3
Westerstede	27	K1
Westerwald	27	K4
West Falkland	111	J9
West Frankfort	103	D2
West Glacier	97	D1
West Lunga	67	C2
West Memphis	103	C2
Weston	99	D3
Weston-super-Mare	37	K10
West Palm Beach	103	E4
West Plains	99	B3
Westport, New Zealand	89	C5
Westport, Republic of Ireland	37	C8
Westray	37	J2
West Siberian Plain = Zapadno-Sibirskaya Ravnina	69	L3
West Virginia	99	D3
West Wendover	97	D2
West Yellowstone	97	D2
Wetar	83	(2)C4
Wetaskiwin	93	J6
Wete	65	F5
Wetumpka	103	D3
Wetzlar	35	D6
Wewak	83	(2)F3
Wexford	37	F9
Wexford Harbour	37	F9
Weyburn	95	F2
Weymouth	37	K11
Whakatane	89	F3
Whale Cove	93	N4
Whalsay	37	M1
Whangarei	89	E2
Wharfe	37	L7
Wheeler Peak	101	E1
Wheeler Ridge	101	C2
Wheeling	103	E1
Whitby	37	M7
White, Nev., United States	97	C3
White, S.D., United States	93	L8
White Bay	93	V6
White Cliffs	87	H6
Whitecourt	93	H6
Whitefish Point	99	C1
Whitehaven	37	J7
Whitehorse	101	(1)L3
White Island	89	F3
Whitemark	87	J8
White Mountain Peak	97	C3
White Mountains	93	S8
Whitemouth	97	G1
White Nile = Bahr el Abiad	61	F5
White River, Canada	99	C1
White River, United States	97	F2
White Sea = Beloye More	31	G1
White Sulphur Springs	97	D1
Whiteville	103	F3
White Volta	63	D3
Whitney	99	E1
Whyalla	87	G6
Wichita	103	B2
Wichita Falls	103	B3
Wick	37	J3
Wickenburg	101	D2
Wicklow Mountains	37	F8
Widawka	33	J6
Wieluń	33	H6
Wien	43	M2
Wiener Neustadt	43	M3
Wieringermeer Polder	27	G2
Wiesbaden	35	D6
Wiesloch	35	D7
Wiesmoor	35	C3
Wigan	37	K8
Wiggins	97	F2
Wil	43	E3
Wilbur	97	C1
Wilcannia	87	H6
Wildeshausen	35	D4
Wilhelmshaven	35	D3
Wilkes-Barre	99	E2
Wilkes Land	112	(2)U2
Willapa Bay	97	B1
Willemstad	109	D1
Williams, Australia	87	C6
Williams, Ariz., United States	97	D3
Williams, Calif., United States	97	B3
Williamsburg	99	E3
Williams Lake	93	G6
Williamson	103	E2
Williamsport	99	E2
Willis Group	87	K3
Williston, Fla., United States	103	E4
Williston, N.D., United States	97	F1
Williston Lake	93	G5
Willmar	99	A1
Willow	101	(1)H3
Willowmore	67	C6
Willow River	99	B1
Willow Springs	99	B3
Wilmington, Del., United States	99	E3
Wilmington, N.C., United States	103	F3
Wilson	99	E3
Wilson Reservoir	103	B2
Wilson's Promontory	87	J7
Wiluna	87	D5
Winamac	99	C2
Winchester, United Kingdom	37	L10
Winchester, Ky., United States	99	D3
Winchester, Va., United States	99	E3
Windhoek	67	B4
Windischgarsten	43	K3
Windom	99	A2
Windorah	87	H5
Windsor, Canada	99	D2
Windsor, United Kingdom	27	B3
Windsor, United States	103	F2
Windward Islands	105	N6
Windward Passage	107	D2
Winfield, Al., United States	103	D3
Winfield, Kans., United States	101	G1
Wingate Mountains	87	E2
Winisk	93	P5
Winisk	93	P6
Winisk Lake	93	P6
Winnemucca	97	C2
Winner	97	G2
Winnfield	95	H5
Winnipeg	93	M7
Winona, Minn., United States	99	B2
Winona, Miss., United States	103	D3
Winschoten	27	K1
Winsen	35	F3
Winslow	101	D1
Winston-Salem	99	D3
Winterberg	35	D5
Winter Harbour	93	J2
Winterswijk	27	J3
Winterthur	43	D3
Winton, Australia	87	H4
Winton, New Zealand	89	B8
Wisbech	37	C2
Wisconsin	95	H2
Wisconsin	99	B2
Wisconsin Dells	99	C2
Wisconsin Rapids	99	C2
Wisła	33	H4
Wisła	33	H8
Wisłoka	33	L8
Wismar	35	G3
Wissembourg	35	C7
Witney	27	A3
Witten	27	K3
Wittenberge	35	G3
Wittenoom	87	C4
Wittingen	35	F4
Wittlich	27	J5
Wittmund	35	C3
Wittstock	35	H3
Witzenhausen	35	E5
W. J. van Blommesteinmeer	109	G2
Wkra	33	K5
Władysławowo	33	H3
Włocławek	33	J5
Włodawa	33	N6
Wodzisław Śląski	33	H7
Wohlen	43	D3
Wokam	83	(2)D4
Woking	37	M10
Wolf Creek	97	D1
Wolfen	35	H5
Wolfenbüttel	35	F4
Wolf Point	97	E1
Wolfratshausen	43	G3
Wolfsberg	43	K4
Wolfsburg	35	F4
Wolgast	35	J2
Wollaston Lake	93	K5
Wollaston Peninsula	93	H3
Wollongong	87	K6
Wołomin	33	L5
Wolsztyn	33	F5
Wolverhampton	37	K9
Wŏnju	81	D5
Wŏnsan	81	D4
Woodbridge	27	D2
Woodburn	97	B1
Woodland	97	B3
Woodstock, Canada	99	G1
Woodstock, United Kingdom	27	A3
Woodstock, United States	99	C2
Woodville, New Zealand	89	E5
Woodville, Miss., United States	103	C3
Woodville, Tex., United States	103	C3
Woodward	97	G3
Woody Head	89	E3
Woonsocket, R.I., United States	99	F2
Woonsocket, S.D., United States	97	G2
Worcester, South Africa	67	B6
Worcester, United Kingdom	37	K9
Worcester, United States	95	M3
Wörgl	43	H3
Workington	37	J7
Worksop	27	A1
Worland	97	E2
Worms	35	D7
Wörth	35	D7
Worthing	37	M11
Worthington	95	G3
Wosu	83	(2)B3
Wotu	83	(2)B3
Wowoni	83	(2)B3
Wrangell	93	E5
Wrangell Mountains	93	C4
Wray	95	F3
Wrexham	37	K8
Wrigley	93	G4
Wrocław	33	G6
Września	33	G5
Wu	79	D5
Wubin	87	C6
Wubu	79	E3
Wuchang	79	H2
Wuchuan	79	E2
Wuday'ah	53	E6
Wudu	79	C4
Wuhai	79	D3
Wuhan	79	E4
Wuhu	79	F4
Wüjang	75	C2
Wukari	63	F3
Wuli	75	F2
Wunsiedel	35	G6
Wunstorf	35	E4
Wuppertal	35	C5
Würzburg	35	E7
Wurzen	35	H5
Wushi	77	P9
Wusuli	79	J1
Wutach	43	D3
Wuwei	79	C3
Wuxi	79	G4
Wuxu	77	D2
Wuyuan	79	D2
Wuzhong	79	D3
Wuzhou	77	E2
Wye	37	J9
Wyndham	87	E3
Wynniatt Bay	93	J2
Wyoming	95	E3
Wyszków	33	L5
Wytheville	103	E2

X

Name	Page	Grid
Xaafuun	65	J1
Xàbia	41	L6
Xaçmaz	51	N3
Xaidulla	71	P10
Xainza	75	E2
Xai-Xai	67	E4
Xam Nua	77	C2
Xankändi	51	M4
Xanten	27	J3
Xanthi	49	G3
Xapuri	109	D6
Xar Moron	73	K8
Xàtiva	41	K6
Xiahe	79	C3
Xiamen	77	F2
Xi'an	79	D4
Xiangcheng	79	E4
Xiangfan	79	E4
Xianghoang	77	C3
Xianghuang Qi	79	E2
Xiangtan	79	E5
Xianning	79	E5
Xianyang	79	D4
Xiaogan	79	E4
Xiao Hinggan Ling	73	M7
Xiaonanchuan	75	F1
Xichang	77	C1
Xigazê	75	E3
Xi Jiang	79	E6
Xilinhot	79	F2
Xincai	79	E4
Xingcheng	79	G2
Xinghua	79	F4
Xingtai	79	F3
Xingu	109	G5
Xingyi	77	C1
Xinhe	71	Q9
Xining	79	C3
Xinjin	79	G3
Xinmin	81	B2
Xintai	79	E3
Xinxiang	79	E3
Xinyang	79	E4
Xinyu	79	F5
Xinyuan	71	Q9
Xinzhou	79	E3
Xinzo de Limia	41	C2
Xique Xique	109	J6
Xi Ujimqin Qi	79	F2
Xiushui	79	E5
Xiwu	75	G2
Xixia	79	E4
Xi Xiang	79	D4
Xizang	75	C2
Xizang Gaoyuan	75	D2
Xuanhua	79	E2
Xuchang	79	E4
Xuddur	65	G3
Xuwen	77	E2
Xuzhou	79	F4

Y

Name	Page	Grid
Ya'an	79	D3
Yabassi	63	F4
Yabēlo	65	F3
Yablonovyy Khrebet	73	J6
Yabrūd	54	D3
Yabuli	81	E1
Yacuma	109	D6

Name	Page	Grid
Yadgir	75	D5
Yagodnyy	31	N3
Yahk	93	H7
Yakima	97	B1
Yako	63	D2
Yakoma	65	C3
Yaksha	31	L2
Yakumo	81	L2
Yaku-shima	81	F8
Yakutat	101	(1)K4
Yakutsk	73	M4
Yala	77	C5
Yalova	49	M4
Yalta	51	F1
Yalu	81	D3
Yalutorovsk	31	N3
Yamagata	81	L4
Yamaguchi	81	F6
Yamarovka	73	J6
Yambio	65	D3
Yambol	47	P7
Yamburg	71	P4
Yamdena	83	(2)D4
Yamoussoukro	63	C3
Yampa	97	E2
Yampil'	47	R1
Yamsk	73	S5
Yan'an	79	D3
Yanbu'al Baḩr	53	C5
Yancheng	79	G4
Yandun	79	A2
Yangambi	65	C3
Yangbajain	75	F2
Yangdok	81	D4
Yangi Kand	51	N5
Yangjiang	77	E2
Yangon	77	B3
Yangquan	79	E3
Yangshuo	77	E2
Yangtze = Chang Jiang	79	D4
Yangzhou	79	F4
Yanhuqu	75	D2
Yani-Kurgan	71	M9
Yanji	81	E2
Yankton	97	G2
Yano-Indigirskaya Nizmennost'	73	N2
Yanqi	71	R9
Yanqing	79	F2
Yanshan	77	C2
Yanskiy Zaliv	73	N2
Yantai	79	G3
Yaoundé	63	G4
Yap	85	D5
Yapen	83	(2)E3
Yaqui	95	E6
Yaransk	31	J3
Yardımcı Burnu	49	E8
Yare	27	D2
Yaren	85	G6
Yarensk	31	J2
Yari	109	C3
Yarkant	53	L2
Yarkovo	31	N3
Yarlung Zangbo	75	F3
Yarmouth	93	T8
Yaroslavl'	31	G3
Yar Sale	31	P1
Yartsevo	31	F3
Yashkul'	31	J5
Yasnyy	31	L4
Yāsūj	55	D1
Yatağan	49	L7
Yathkyed Lake	93	M4
Yatsushiro	81	F7
Yavari	109	C5
Yawatongguzlangar	71	Q10
Yaya	71	R6
Yayladağı	51	F6
Yazd	53	F3
Yazdān	53	H3
Yazd-e Khvāst	55	E1
Yazoo City	103	C3
Ydra	49	F7
Ye	77	B3
Yea	87	J7
Yecheng	53	L2
Yecla	41	J6
Yefremov	31	G4
Yegendybulak	71	P8
Yei	65	E3
Yekaterinburg	31	M3
Yelets	31	G4
Yell	37	L1
Yellowknife	93	J4
Yellow River = Huang He	79	C3
Yellow Sea	79	G3
Yellowstone	97	E1
Yellowstone Lake	97	D2
Yeloten	53	H2
Yelva	71	J5
Yelwa	63	E2
Yemen	53	D7
Yemetsk	31	H2
Yenakiyeve	31	G5
Yengisar	53	L2
Yenihisar	49	K7
Yenisey	71	S6
Yeniseysk	71	S6
Yeniseyskiy Kryazh	71	S5
Yeo Lake	87	D5
Yeovil	37	K11
Yeppoon	87	K4
Yeraliyev	71	J9
Yerbogachen	73	H4
Yerevan	51	L3
Yerington	97	C3
Yerkov	49	S5
Yerkoy	51	F4
Yermak	71	P7
Yermitsa	31	K1
Yernva	71	J5
Yershov	31	J4
Yerupaja	109	B6
Yerushalayim	54	C5
Yesil'	31	N4
Yeşilhisar	51	F4
Yeşilköy	49	L4
Yessey	71	U4
Yevlax	51	M3
Yevpatoriya	31	F5
Yeyik	71	Q10
Yeysk	31	G5
Yibin	79	C5
Yichang	79	E4
Yichun, China	79	E5
Yichun, China	79	H1
Yilan	79	H1
Yıldız Dağları	49	K2
Yıldızeli	51	G4
Yinchuan	79	D3
Yingcheng	79	E4
Yingkou	79	G2
Yining	71	Q9
Yirga Alem	65	F2
Yitomio	29	M3
Yitulihe	73	L6
Yiyang	79	E5
Yli-Kitka	29	Q3
Ylivieska	29	N4
Ylöjärvi	29	M6
Yoakum	103	B4
Yoboki	61	H5
Yogyakarta	83	(1)E4
Yokadouma	63	G4
Yoko	63	G3
Yokohama, Japan	81	K6
Yokohama, Japan	81	L3
Yokosuka	81	K6
Yokote	81	L4
Yola	63	G3
Yonago	81	G6
Yonezawa	81	L5
Yong'an	77	F1
Yongdeng	79	C3
Yŏnghŭng	81	D4
Yongren	77	C1
Yongxiu	79	F5
Yonkers	99	F2
York, United Kingdom	37	L8
York, Nebr., United States	97	G2
York, Pa., United States	99	E3
Yorkton	93	L6
Yoshkar Ola	31	J3
Yōsu	81	D6
Yotvata	54	C7
You	77	D2
Youghal	37	E10
Youghal Bay	37	E10
Youngstown	99	D2
Yozgat	51	F4
Yreka	97	B2
Ystad	33	C2
Ysyk-Köl	71	P9
Ytre Sula	29	B6
Ytyk-Kyuyel'	73	N4
Yu	77	D2
Yuan	77	C2
Yuanjiang	77	C2
Yuanmou	77	C1
Yuanping	79	E3
Yucatán	105	F5
Yucatan Channel	105	G4
Yuci	79	E3
Yudoma	73	Q4
Yueyang	79	E5
Yugorenok	73	P5
Yugoslavia	47	H6
Yugo-Tala	73	S3
Yukagirskoye Ploskogor'ye	73	S3
Yukon	101	(1)E3
Yukon Territory	101	(1)K2
Yukorskiy Poluostrov	71	L4
Yüksekova	51	L5
Yukta	73	H4
Yuli	71	R9
Yulin, China	77	E2
Yulin, China	79	D3
Yuma	101	C2
Yumen	79	B3
Yumin	71	Q8
Yuncheng	79	E3
Yun Xian	77	C2
Yuogi Feng	71	R8
Yurga	71	Q6
Yurimaguas	109	B5
Yurla	31	K3
Yuroma	31	J1
Yur'yevets	31	H3
Yu Shan	77	G2
Yushkozero	29	S4
Yushu, China	79	B4
Yushu, China	79	H2
Yusufeli	51	J3
Yutian	71	Q10
Yuyao	79	G4
Yuzhno Kuril'sk	81	N1
Yuzhno-Sakhalinsk	73	Q7
Yuzhno-Sukhokumsk	51	L1
Yuzhnoural'sk	31	M4
Yverdon-les-Bains	43	B4
Yvetot	27	C5

Z

Name	Page	Grid
Zaanstad	27	G2
Ząbkowice Śląskie	33	F7
Zabok	43	L4
Zābol	53	H3
Zabrze	33	H7
Zacatecas	101	F4
Zadar	43	L6
Zadonsk	31	G4
Zafora	49	J8
Zafra	41	D6
Zāgheh-ye-Bālā	51	M6
Zagora	59	D2
Zagreb	43	L5
Zagyva	33	K10
Zāhedān	53	H4
Zahirabad	75	C5
Zahlé	54	C3
Zahrān	53	D6
Zaječar	47	K6
Zakamensk	73	G6
Zākhō	51	K5
Zakopane	33	J8
Zakynthos	49	C7
Zakynthos	49	C7
Zala	43	M4
Zalaegerszeg	43	M4
Zalari	73	G6
Zalaszentgrót	43	N4
Zalău	47	L2
Zalim	53	D5
Zaliv Aniva	73	Q7
Zaliv Kara-Bogaz Gol	53	F1
Zaliv Kresta	73	Y3
Zaliv Paskevicha	31	L5
Zaliv Shelikhova	73	T5
Zaliv Terpeniya	73	Q7
Zamakh	53	E6
Zambezi	67	C2
Zambezi	67	E3
Zambia	67	D2
Zamboanga	77	G5
Zamora	41	E3
Zamość	33	N7
Zanda	75	C2
Zandvoort	27	G2
Zanesville	103	E2
Zangguy	53	L2
Zanjān	51	N5
Zannone	45	H8
Zanzibar	65	F5
Zanzibar Island	65	F5
Zaozernyy	71	S6
Zapadnaya Dvina	31	E3
Zapadno-Sibirskaya Ravnina	71	L5
Zapadnyy Sayan	71	S7
Zapata	101	G3
Zaporizhzhya	31	G5
Zaprešić	43	L5
Zaqatala	51	M3
Zara	51	G4
Zarafshan	71	L9
Zaragoza	41	K3
Zarand	55	G1
Zaranj	53	H3
Zarasai	29	P9
Zaraza	109	D2
Zarechensk	29	R3
Zaria	63	F2
Zărneşti	47	N4
Zarqā'	54	D4
Zarqān	55	E2
Żary	33	E6
Zarzadilla de Totana	41	J7
Žatec	33	C7
Zavetnoye	31	H5
Zavidovići	47	F5
Zavitinsk	73	M6
Zayarsk	71	U6
Zaysan	71	Q8
Zayü	77	B1
Zbraslav	33	D8
Zēbāk	53	K2
Zēbār	51	L5
Zeebrugge	27	F3
Zefat	54	C4
Zeilona Góra	33	E6
Zeist	27	H2
Zeitz	35	H5
Zelenoborskiy	29	S3
Zelenograd	31	G3
Zelenogradsk	33	K3
Zelenokumsk	51	K1
Zella-Mehlis	35	F6
Zell am See	43	H3
Zémio	65	D2
Zemlya Alexsandry	71	G1
Zemlya Frantsa-Iosifa	71	J2
Zemlya Vil'cheka	71	L1
Zempoalteptl	105	E5
Zenica	47	E5
Zerbst	35	H5
Zermatt	43	C4
Zeta Lake	93	K2
Zeulenroda	35	G6
Zeven	35	E3
Zevenaar	27	J3
Zeya	73	M6
Zeya	73	M6
Zeydābād	55	F2
Zeyskoye Vodokhranilishche	73	M5
Zgharta	54	C2

Zgierz	● 33	J6
Zgorzelec	● 33	E6
Zhailma	● 31	M4
Zhaksy	● 31	N4
Zhaksykon	◪ 31	N5
Zhaltyr	● 31	N4
Zhambyl	● 71	N9
Zhanatas	● 71	M9
Zhangbei	● 79	E2
Zhangguangcai Ling	▲ 79	H2
Zhangjiakou	● 79	E2
Zhangling	● 73	L6
Zhangwu	● 79	G2
Zhangye	● 79	B3
Zhangzhou	● 77	F2
Zhanjiang	● 77	E2
Zhaodong	● 73	M7
Zhaoqing	● 77	E2
Zhaosu	● 71	Q9
Zhaoyuan	● 79	H1
Zharkamys	● 71	K8
Zharkent	● 71	P9
Zharma	● 71	Q8
Zharyk	● 71	N8
Zhaxigang	● 75	C2
Zheleznogorsk	● 31	G4
Zhengzhou	● 79	E4
Zhenjiang	● 79	F4
Zherdevka	● 31	H4
Zhetybay	● 71	J9
Zhezkazgan	● 71	M8
Zhigalovo	● 73	H5
Zhigansk	● 73	L3
Zhilinda	● 73	J2
Zhob	● 53	J3
Zholymbet	● 71	N7
Zhongba	● 75	D3
Zhongdian	● 79	B5
Zhongning	● 79	D3
Zhongshan	● 77	E2
Zhongze	● 79	G5
Zhoukou	● 79	E4
Zhuanghe	● 79	G3
Zhucheng	● 79	F3
Zhumadian	● 79	E4
Zhuo Xian	● 79	F3
Zhytomyr	● 31	E4
Žiar	● 33	H9
Zibo	● 79	F3
Zichang	● 79	D3
Zieriksee	● 27	F3
Ziesar	● 35	H4
Zigong	● 79	C5
Ziguinchor	● 59	B6
Zikhron Ya'aqov	● 54	B4
Žilina	● 33	H8
Zillah	● 61	C2
Zima	● 73	G6
Zimbabwe	Ⓐ 67	D3
Zimmi	● 63	B3
Zimnicea	● 47	N6
Zinder	● 63	F2
Zinjibār	● 61	J5
Zirc	● 33	G10
Žirje	▨ 45	K5
Zistersdorf	● 43	M2
Zitava	◪ 33	H9
Zittau	● 35	K6
Ziway Hāyk'	◪ 65	F2
Zixing	● 77	E1
Zlaté Moravce	● 33	H9
Zlatoust	● 31	L3
Zlín	● 33	G8
Zlīţan	● 59	H2
Złotów	● 33	G4
Zmeinogorsk	● 71	Q7
Znamenskoye	● 71	N6
Žnin	● 33	G5
Znojmo	● 43	M2
Zoigê	● 79	C4
Zomba	● 67	F3
Zongo	● 65	B3
Zonguldak	● 49	P3
Zouar	● 61	C3
Zouérat	● 59	C4
Žovka	● 33	N7
Zrenjanin	● 47	H4
Zschopau	● 35	J6
Zug	● 43	D3
Zugdidi	● 51	J2
Zuger See	◪ 43	D3
Zugspitze	▲ 35	F9
Zuid-Beveland	⊘ 27	F3
Zuni	● 101	E1
Zunyi	● 79	D5
Županja	● 47	F4
Zürich	● 43	D3
Zuru	● 63	F2
Žut	▨ 45	K5
Zutphen	● 27	J2
Zuwārah	● 61	B1
Zuyevka	● 71	J6
Zvishavane	● 67	E4
Zvolen	● 33	J9
Zvornik	● 47	G5
Zwedru	● 63	C3
Zweibrücken	● 27	K5
Zwettl	● 43	L2
Zwickau	● 35	H6
Zwiesel	● 35	J7
Zwolle	● 27	J2
Zyryanka	● 73	S3
Zyryanovsk	● 71	Q8
Żywiec	● 33	J8

World Political

Equatorial Scale 1 : 78 000 000

ARCTIC OCEAN

Ellesmere Island

GREENLAND
(Denmark)

Greenland
Sea

Baffin Bay

Victoria
Island

Baffin Island

Beaufort Sea

Arctic Circle

ALASKA
(U.S.)

Yukon

Anchorage

Mackenzie

Nuuk
(Godthåb)

ICELAND

Reykjavik

Norwegian
Sea

Bering
Sea

Gulf of
Alaska

CANADA

Hudson
Bay

REPUBLIC OF
IRELAND

UNITED
KINGDOM

NETHER-
LANDS

Dublin

London

BEL

Edmonton

Calgary

Winnipeg

Lake Superior

Paris

FRANCE

Vancouver

ROCKY MOUNTAINS

Missouri

Lake
Huron

Lake
Michigan

Chicago

St. Lawrence

Québec

Ottawa

Montréal

Toronto

Detroit

New York

ANDORRA

MONACO

Seattle

Denver

UNITED STATES

Philadelphia

Washington D.C.

PORTUGAL

Acores
(Portugal)

SPAIN

San Francisco

Kansas City

Madrid

Alger

Los Angeles

San Diego

Phoenix

Dallas

Atlanta

Bermuda
(U.K.)

ATLANTIC
OCEAN

Madeira
(Portugal)

Rabat

Casablanca

MOROCCO

Houston

Mississippi

New Orleans

Islas Canarias
(Spain)

WESTERN
SAHARA
(Morocco)

ALGERIA

SAHAR

Tropic of Cancer

HAWAII
(U.S.)

Rio Grande

Monterrey

MEXICO

Gulf of
Mexico

THE
BAHAMAS

CAPE
VERDE

Nouakchott

MAURITANIA

MALI

Guadalajara

Ciudad
de México

La Habana

CUBA

DOMINICAN REP

Santo
Domingo

PUERTO RICO (U.S.)

Dakar

SEN.

Banjul

Niger

GUATE-
MALA

BELIZE

HAITI

ST KITTS-NEVIS

ANTIGUA & BARBUDA

THE GAMBIA

GUINEA-BISSAU

Bamako

Niame

BURKINA

Guatemala

HONDURAS

JAMAICA

Caribbean Sea

DOMINICA

ST LUCIA

Bissau

Conakry

GUINEA

N

EL SALVADOR

NICARAGUA

ST VINCENT &
THE GRENADINES

BARBADOS

Freetown

SIERRA LEONE

IVORY
COAST

GHANA

Porto-
Novo

Managua

Costa

RICA

San José

Caracas

GRENADA

TRINIDAD & TOBAGO

Monrovia

LIBERIA

Yamous

soukro

Accra

PANAMA

Panama

VENEZUELA

Georgetown

FRENCH
GUIANA (Fr.)

EQUAT. GUIN

COLOMBIA

Bogotá

GUYANA

SURINAM

SÃO TOMÉ
& PRÍNCIPE

Islas Galápagos
(Ecuador)

Quito

ECUADOR

Amazon

Belém

Fortaleza

Equator

PACIFIC
OCEAN

Iquitos

Manaus

Recife

KIRIBATI

PERU

Lima

BRAZIL

Salvador

French
Polynesia

Arequipa

La Paz

BOLIVIA

Sucre

Brasília

Belo Horizonte

Tropic of Capricorn

Pitcairn Is.
(U.K.)

PARAGUAY

Río de Janeiro

São Paulo

Curitiba

Asunción

Porto Alegre

CHILE

Córdoba

URUGUAY

Santiago

ARGENTINA

Buenos
Aires

Montevideo

Punta
Arenas

Falkland
Islands
(U.K.)

South Georgia
(U.K.)

Antarctic Circle

South Sandwich
Islands
(U.K.)

Bellinghausen
Sea

Weddell Sea

Ross Sea